BECOMING PARTAKERS of the DIVINE NATURE

RICHARD C. CHEWNING

Becoming Partakers of the Divine Nature

Copyright © 2013 Richard C. Chewning

Published by Great Rock Publishing
625 Robert Fulton Highway
Quarryville, PA 17566

Printed in the United States of America

All rights reserved.
ISBN-10: 978-0615826875
ISBN-13: 0615826873

No part of this publication may be reproduced, stored in a retrieval system, or transmitted in any form or by any means—for example, electronic, photocopy, recording—without prior written permission of the publisher. The only exception is brief quotations in printed reviews.

Unless otherwise indicated, Scripture quotations are from the Holy Bible, New American Standard, Copyright © 1977, 2000 by The Lockman Foundation.

Cover Design: Scott Cole, Churchill Strategies

DEDICATED

— to —

The One who inspired the Apostle Paul to write…
"And what do [I] have that [I] did not receive?"
1 Corinthians 4:7

God the Father,
God the Only Begotten Son,
God the Holy Spirit

Table of Contents

TABLE OF CONTENTS I
FOREWORD I
ACKNOWLEDGMENTS III
PREFACE V
THE BACKDROP XI
CHAPTER 1 1
    THE MIND OF CHRIST

PART 1 19
    WHAT IS THE DIVINE NATURE?

CHAPTER 2 21
    GOD: THE SELF-REVEALING/TRANSCENDENT ONE

CHAPTER 3 41
    THE TRINITY: OUR MODEL AND MENTOR

CHAPTER 4 59
    GOD IS SPIRIT: THE REALITY NECESSITATING FAITH

CHAPTER 5 73
    GOD IS HOLY: HE WANTS US TO BE HOLY

CHAPTER 6 85
    GOD IS IMMUTABLE: WE REST IN HIS RELIABILITY

CHAPTER 7 97
    GOD IS OMNIPRESENT: OUR ETERNAL HELPER

CHAPTER 8 111
    GOD IS WISE: HIS WISDOM IS OURS UPON REQUEST

CHAPTER 9 123
    GOD IS GOOD: AN IMPORTANT REASON TO DESIRE, LOVE, AND SERVE HIM

CHAPTER 10 141
    GOD IS OMNIPOTENT: HOW ARE WE TO MIRROR HIS POWER?

CHAPTER 11 155
    GOD IS SOVEREIGN: EVEN OVER ALL FORMS OF SUFFERING

CHAPTER 12 169
    GOD IS LOVE: WHAT DOES THIS REALLY MEAN?

PART 2 181
    HOW DO PEOPLE BECOME PARTAKERS OF THE DIVINE NATURE?

CHAPTER 13 183

HUMAN NATURE: THE WORLD'S DESCRIPTION/GOD'S DESCRIPTION

CHAPTER 14 .... **199**
BEING CREATED IN THE IMAGE OF GOD: WHAT DOES THIS REALLY MEAN?

CHAPTER 15 .... **209**
THE BIBLICAL CONCEPT OF THE HEART: A COMPRESSED DEPICTION

CHAPTER 16 .... **219**
THE HEART: THE LOCATION OF OUR MIND

CHAPTER 17 .... **233**
THE HEART: THE LOCATION OF OUR PASSIONS

CHAPTER 18 .... **251**
THE HEART: THE LOCATION OF OUR VOLITION

CHAPTER 19 .... **261**
THE HEART: LOVE IS THE MOTIVATOR

CHAPTER 20 .... **271**
GOD IMPARTS ASPECTS OF HIS DIVINE NATURE TO RENOVATED HEARTS

PART 3 .... **297**
MANIFESTING CHRIST'S DIVINE NATURE

CHAPTER 21 .... **299**
CHRIST'S DIVINE NATURE MANIFESTED IN DATING RELATIONSHIPS

CHAPTER 22 .... **313**
CHRIST'S DIVINE NATURE MANIFESTED IN MARRIAGE

CHAPTER 23 .... **331**
CHRIST'S DIVINE NATURE MANIFESTED IN THE FAMILY

CHAPTER 24 .... **345**
CHRIST'S DIVINE NATURE MANIFESTED IN SINGLENESS

CHAPTER 25 .... **359**
CHRIST'S DIVINE NATURE MANIFESTED IN BUSINESS

CHAPTER 26 .... **375**
CHRIST'S DIVINE NATURE MANIFESTED IN GOVERNMENT

CHAPTER 27 .... **387**
CHRIST'S DIVINE NATURE MANIFESTED BEFORE THE WATCHING WORLD

CHAPTER 28 .... **393**
CONCLUSION

THE EPILOGUE **403**
TO GOD BE THE GLORY

SCRIPTURE INDEX **409**

Foreword

I remember sitting in the Williamsburg Room of the Quarryville Presbyterian Retirement Community in 2005 asking Dick Chewning about bringing about change in an individual. Dick quietly drew a triangle depicting man's heart. He showed the balance between our mind, passions and will - all components of the heart. I was drawn into his discussion of the three aspects and asked for more. Over the next several years, Dick sent me chapters of the book which he had been working on for over 30 years. Little did I know how that afternoon discussion would lead to being part of the publishing of *Becoming Partakers of the Divine Nature*.

I believe that there are really three books in this work: Part 1, a book discussing the attributes of God based on Scripture and Stephen Charnock's *The Existence and Attributes of God*. Part 2, a book discussing our hearts and the relationship between the mind, passion and will—all attributes of the heart. And Part 3, a book that combines the attributes of God with the attributes of our heart helping us become more Christlike in our relationships in seven areas of life. Each could stand on its own but together give a complete picture of how God restores to us the divine nature that we lost at the fall of man.

Dick writes in the tradition of a Puritan. Many components and side roads will help build your understanding of his ideas like the unpeeling of the layers of an onion. Dick uses a unique approach to show how God, through the Holy Spirit, grows us in the sanctification process. The merging of the divine nature of God's attributes with us as unique image-bearers of God through the mind, passions, and will of our hearts leads us to a fresh understanding of God at work in us.

This is a book that will require you to consider the attributes of God, your heart and each of seven different relationship areas more than once or twice. You will benefit from letting his words marinate in your mind and heart as the Holy Spirit works to restore true knowledge, righteousness and holiness to you for His Glory.

I pray that you would see and love Jesus more fully as a result of your engagement of this work.

Long before that afternoon when I asked Dick about how people change, I had read several of the books that Dick had written about business. Specifically, *Business Through the Eyes of Faith*, and the four volume work *Christian in the Marketplace Series*. These works have been invaluable to those desiring to work and live with ethics grounded in the Word of God. From *Business through the Eyes of Faith* to "God's glory, through eyes of faith"

Robert B. Hayward, Jr.
President and CEO, Quarryville Presbyterian Retirement Community

Acknowledgments

The dedication acknowledges the One deserving recognition for the truth and value contained in this work. Any untruth is my responsibility. Regarding the human endeavors, Shirley, my faithful wife since 1955, is first in line for thanks. For over fifty-five years she has typed, edited my work, and encouraged me.

Dr. Richard Scott invited me to Baylor University in 1985 to fill the Harry and Hazel Chavanne Chair of Christian Ethics in Business. I had been blessed to work under the leadership of other good men but Dean Scott was the best. This work was conceived and begun under his guardianship.

Following my retirement from Baylor in 2000, I was invited to John Brown University (JBU) to be a guest Scholar in Residence. During my six and a half years there, President Balzer retired, Dr. Charles "Chip" Pollard became the president, and Dr. Ed Erickson became the Vice President of Academics Affairs. These leaders made me feel at home and a part of the JBU community. But the individual who assisted me the most at JBU was Sue Daugherty, a secretary. I am technologically illiterate and Sue rescued me repeatedly from the computer diagram swamp and repeatedly brought me logistical support. A special thanks is due Sue. And Dr. Delia Haak, a JBU colleague, read most of the manuscript as it was being created and provided me much encouragement and moral support.

In God's providence, though, it was Robert B. Hayward, Jr., President and CEO of the Quarryville Presbyterian Retirement Community (QPRC), who became the catalyst that has led to the publishing of this volume. Robert is a vociferous reader and he read much of this book as it was being written. He asked the QPRC Board of Directors for permission to publish the book. The Board gave him permission to move forward.

So the polishing of the manuscript began. Kathy Sutherland, Robert Hayward's Executive Assistant, and Robert Delancy, a retired editor living at QPRC, took the book in hand. I am much indebted to them both for their helpful and faithful work.

In the Lord's providence, Bob Delancy had spent his life editing—working often with the New American Standard Bible, the translation in which I had spent my life working. And Bob, a seminary graduate, knows and loves Greek. He corrected my Greek work where it was needed, and his technical work on the footnotes and annotations was a Godsend. He also had a kind way of telling me when he believed something could be improved. The entire work is vastly improved because of Bob Delancy's talents and gifts.

Finally, but far from last, Robert A. Peterson, PhD, Professor of Systematic Theology at Covenant Theological Seminary took the manuscript in hand and made it much easier to read by tightening the text, and employing the gifts the Lord has given him to say what I had said in clearer and simpler language. Robert is a "wordsmith."

Thank you one and all!

Preface

The Purpose

I write to promote a serious examination of the attributes of God and of his desire to impart specific aspects of his character into the renovated hearts of his adopted children through the work of the Holy Spirit (2 Peter 1:4)—so that their new lives would shine before men in such a way that others might see their good works and glorify their Father who is in heaven (Matt. 5:16). We are not only saved by God's grace, we are also sanctified by his grace.

A human cannot change another human's heart. God alone is in the business of renovating hearts. And to his glory, God imparts aspects of his divine nature to his redeemed image-bearers (2 Peter 1:4; Heb. 12:10-11; Eph. 4:13, 24). He is the genesis of authentic Christlike character and behavior. Apparent righteousness born otherwise is either evidence of common grace or is counterfeit. One implication is that reading this book will not make the reader more moral or Christlike. It can be read profitably, however, if it serves as a stimulus to seek a deeper relationship with the Triune God who alone rebuilds us in the likeness of Christ.

This is not a traditional scholarly work. It does not reference many authors; it simply makes use of God's disclosure of himself in Scripture and his expressed will for those who bear his image.

Besides the Spirit's use of Scripture in my life, the three works that have most impacted me and this work were *The Existence and Attributes of God* by Stephen Charnock, *The Trinity* by Edward Bickersteth, and *The God Who Is There* by Francis Schaeffer.[1] The Bible alone, though, has my allegiance. It is the only written work superintended and guarded by the Holy Spirit.

The Conception, Birth and Development

Some time ago my wife asked me if I would please write my obituary. She did not want to face that challenge at the time of my death, should she survive me. I agreed and did so. That caused me to reflect on my seventy-nine years, and many memories surfaced.

I had a dissertation proposal rejected in early 1963 that was designed to examine the diminishing impact of the Protestant ethic in the 20th century-marketplace. Max Weber had argued that the Protestant ethic had been instrumental in the rise of capitalism. Because of this rejection I did a dissertation

---

[1] Stephen Charnock, *Discourses upon the Existence and Attributes of God*, 2 vols. (Grand Rapids, MI: Baker, 1979; orig., pub. posthumously in 1682); Edward Bickersteth *The Trinity* (Grand Rapids: Kregel, 1957); Francis A. Schaeffer, *The God Who Is There* (Downers Grove, IL: InterVarsity, 1968).

in the field of finance rather than in that of my deeper interest, business and its environment.

But by the end of the 1970's the national accrediting association of business schools mandated the teaching of business ethics. The faculty where I had been teaching twenty years asked me if I would take on the task. They were unaware that for seventeen years I had been studying the Bible as a text book asking the Lord what his Word had to say to those who worked in the marketplace. He had shown me a great deal so I jumped at the chance to switch from finance to applied ethics.

Five years later some of my publications had attracted the attention of a few people at Baylor University where I was subsequently invited to become the Harry and Hazel Chavanne Professor of Christian Ethics in Business.

In 1985, while at Baylor, for no particular reason that I was conscious of I became almost obsessed with the question, what does the Bible mean when it refers to the *heart*? The word heart, in both Hebrew and Greek, appears in the Bible over 900 times. But what does it really refer to? All my life I had thought that the word heart did not include my mind. It seemed to refer to feelings of compassion and empathy and other such emotions, but the mind was not associated with the meaning of the word heart. So I looked up the word heart in *Baker's Dictionary of Theology*. It stated that Paul had used the word fifty-two times: fifteen times to denote personality; thirteen times to speak of the seat of emotional states of consciousness; eleven times to refer to the intellect; and thirteen times to speak of human volition.[2] The Bible's use of the word heart suddenly grew exponentially in my mind. The idea embodied in the word heart does incorporate our mind as well as our passions and will. I was excited. And as I later discovered, at least 600 of the 900 uses of the word heart in Scripture refer to the mind. The following fifteen years of study gave rise to the framework, focus, and core of what has become Part 2 of this volume.

Preceding what was just described was another parallel line of study that was not united with the above mentioned interest until the late 1990's. The other line of interest was awakened in me in 1961 when my earthly spiritual daddy told me that he had never encountered anyone who professed faith in Christ who seemed to be so devoid of any real understanding of God's true nature. He kindly added quickly though that he was sure I was smart enough to read and digest the book mentioned above that had been written by Stephen Charnock in the late 1680's. (I had professed faith in Christ as my Savior in 1944 when I was eleven years old, but Christ did not truly become my Lord and Savior until 1961 when I was twenty-eight.)

The Existence and Attributes of God was like cool springs of water given to a thirsty soul. Charnock insightfully explores the biblical revelation regarding

---

[2] Everett F. Harrison, ed., *Bakers Dictionary of Theology* (Grand Rapids, MI: Baker, 1960), 262.

God's transcendent nature. But if his transcendent nature can be allegorically likened to a twenty rung ladder and the biblical revelation permits us to climb to rung twelve, then why had I been standing on the ground? And then it dawned on me. I had never heard anyone preach on the attributes of God until my earthly spiritual daddy did. And I might ask readers: When did you last hear a sermon that focused on God's attributes? Furthermore, I had never heard Christ's miracles tied directly to a specific attribute of God in a sermon. God had never been presented to me as the high, exalted, and awesome God revealed in Scripture. I had been taught that Christ had died for my sins, and that God loved me, but I was suffering from an acute case of spiritual malnutrition. The gracious gift of being able to understand so much about God's awesome transcendent nature became the stimulus behind the writing of Part 1 of this book.

God's attributes are rarely the focus of a sermon or discussion, because he is transcendent and his attributes are hard to describe in evidential ways unless we are taught to do this by connecting God's acts in history with specific occurrences in the Scripture. Part 1 examines the conceptual and theological words typically used to describe God's attributes. I have endeavored to make them meaningful and acceptable by relating them to a wide array of Scriptures and to everyday life. By acceptable I mean that many Christians in the church are being taught a modified neo-orthodox understanding of certain attributes such as God's immutability and omniscience. In doing so, God is being made into the image of humankind, thus diminishing his stature, nature, and glory. He is thereby represented as a smaller God than he has revealed himself to be in Scripture.

What brought the first two parts of this book together was my providential reading of 2 Peter 1:4: "For by *these* [v. 2 "true knowledge"; v. 3 "divine power"] he has granted to us his precious and magnificent promises, in order that by them you might become partakers of the divine nature." This sealed the matter in my mind. God desires to form aspects of his divine nature (Part 1) into the hearts of his children (Part 2) in order that they may become Christlike and live a life that reflects God's own nature (Part 3). The third part contains practical illustrations of what relational living looks like when Christians display the fruit being borne in their renovated hearts that mirror the character of their Creator/Redeemer.

Presuppositional Anchors

Underlying everyone's thought processes are presuppositions—things that are conceived to be true beforehand and serve as the foundation on which our thoughts unconsciously rely. Our presuppositions are our underlying beliefs and assumptions that are unstated but serve as the basis for our thoughts and actions.

Nine presuppositions undergird this volume. They appear below without elaboration. Everything else rests on these foundational beliefs. The entire book stands or falls on their veracity. It is only fair for readers to see them at the beginning.

Presupposition 1: Our presuppositions predetermine how we will order, interpret, and integrate the data we encounter in life and integrate into our perceptions of reality. Beliefs precede and shape both reason and presumed knowledge when we are engaged in the contemplation of virtues, values, morals, spiritual reality, and all other qualitative aspects of life.

Presupposition 2: God created humans, and only humans, in his image. And we have the capacity, in our post-fall condition, to be regenerated and have our image renovated so we can: (a) possess true knowledge, as God possesses true knowledge (Col. 3:10; John 14:16-18, 21, 23); (b) be righteous as God is righteous; not only with an imputed righteousness, as important as that reality is, but also we can grow in manifested righteousness (Eph. 4:23-24); and (c) be holy as God is holy. We can grow in true holiness by being separated from evil (Eph. 4:23-24), a process that will only be completed when we are glorified.

Presupposition 3: God lives in his redeemed children (Col. 1:26-27) and subsequently: (a) forms Christ in them (Gal. 4:19); and (b) develops the mind of Christ in them (1 Cor. 2:11-16).

Presupposition 4: The Holy Spirit effectively and sufficiently (not exhaustively) forms Christ's mind in God's children through the use of Scripture that has the power, in the Spirit's hands, to transform human hearts (Eph. 5:26; Titus 3:5; Heb. 4:12).

Presupposition 5: All spiritual and material reality in the created order was called into being and shaped by God with meaning and purpose. These realities can, therefore, be reassociated with God and his purposes. To do this correctly requires his help and his special revelation (Scripture). Correctly reassociating God's creation with him is true evidence of a godly world/life-view.

Presupposition 6: God gives saving faith to his adopted children, and it is only through this faith that the possibilities outlined in presuppositions 3, 4 and 5, above, can be appropriated so as to become a reality in our lives (Rom. 12:3; Heb. 11:1; Eph. 2:8-9).

Presupposition 7: The Word of God—Scripture—is infallible and completely trustworthy. It is the account of God's purposes and redemptive love for his people. The Bible is sufficient as a guide for faith and practice; it is necessary for the formation of the mind of Christ in believers' hearts; it is authoritative regarding salvation and eternal life; and it is clear and understandable when it is permitted to testify to God's full, intended meaning through the use of its whole message (Acts 5:20; 20:27).

Presupposition 8: The true nature of God can be encountered, engaged, and truly comprehended (not exhaustively) through the reading of Scripture in the anointing power of the Holy Spirit so that believers can be both illumined and partake of the character of God (2 Peter 1:4; Eph. 4:13, 24; Heb. 12:10). This book, then, is only useful in the final analysis as God uses it to draw readers to himself through the Word.

Presupposition 9: I write also on the assumption that Christ must reveal to the individual reader the truth regarding his or her true nature so that the heart may be humbled and thereby grow in its desire to be drawn closer to the Trinity.

Notes to readers:

1) When "Lexical #" appears, the references are to *Strong's Exhaustive Concordance.*

2) Italics in Scripture references indicate emphasis added by the author.

The Backdrop

We are to prepare to resist in the evil day. (Eph. 6:13)

The first chapter sets forth a presupposition that undergirds the rest of the book: An individual can have an accurate world/life-view only when he or she possesses the *mind of Christ*. The Bible tells us that Christ is being formed in God's children (Gal. 4:19). In addition, Scripture tells us that the person in whom this formation is taking place is being given the mind of Christ as it is revealed in Scripture (1 Cor. 2:16). These two facts are critical to the book's integrity because it is built on the belief (presupposition) that the Holy Spirit is transforming the lives of those who surrender their lives to Christ by imparting aspects of God's divine attributes to them (2 Peter 1:4). And the mind of Christ—a component of his divine nature—is an aspect of what is being imparted. It then follows that when the Holy Spirit writes the Word of God on the mind of his people they come to possess a corresponding number of God's thoughts about himself, them, and life. Those so blessed have partaken of an aspect of God's divine nature: his thoughts; his knowledge.

We are born into a world that is under the absolute sovereign rule of the LORD God Almighty, but God has given his archenemy, Satan, permission to rule over much that transpires in the world (John 12:31; 14:30; 16:11; 2 Cor. 4:4; Eph. 2:2). Christians, however, know "our struggle is not against flesh and blood, but against the rulers, against the powers, against the world forces of this darkness, against the spiritual forces of wickedness in the heavenly places" (Eph. 6:12). The life of Christians is spent in spiritual warfare, unless they are hiding their light under a basket. The North American Christian community finds itself at this time in history in a hostile intellectual environment, one that approves and supports much that is ungodly. And tragically, much of what is ungodly is flaunted publicly.

People's beliefs precede and determine what they profess to know in the spiritual, ethical, and moral areas of reality—spheres of truth which do not pertain directly to the physical universe. There are many, however, who believe that knowledge precedes beliefs in these intangible areas; and multitudes contend that there is no sure way of knowing any spiritual or moral truth whatsoever! While these latter two premises are popular in our culture, they stand in contradiction to biblical evidence and the argument here. The presupposition upon which this book rests is that our foundational beliefs regarding our origin, nature, and moral character guide our thinking and subsequent knowledge about values and morals. How do you know that what you think you know about right and wrong is really knowable?

1

The Mind of Christ: The Essential Component of a Christian's World/Life-View

For who among men knows the thoughts of a man except the spirit of the man which is in him? Even so the thoughts of God no one knows except the Spirit of God. Now we have received, not the spirit of the world, but the Spirit who is from God, so that we may know the things freely given to us by God, which things we also speak, not in words taught by human wisdom, but in those taught by the Spirit. . . .. But a natural man does not accept the things of the spirit of God, for they are foolishness to him; and he cannot understand them, because they are spiritually appraised. But he who is spiritual appraises all things, yet he himself is appraised by no man. For who has known the mind of the Lord, that he will instruct Him? But we have the mind of Christ. (1 Cor. 2:11-16)

What is a world/life-view? What did Paul mean when he wrote, "We have the mind of Christ" (1 Cor. 2:16)? What is the main difference between a Christian and a non-Christian world/life-view? In what areas of the heart is a Christian's world/life-view altered when the mind of Christ becomes real in him or her? Is there such a Thing as *the* Christian World/Life-View? Are all Christians expected to have the same world/life-view? Can a Christian have a bifurcated (split) world/life-view? What is the relationship between our presuppositions, hermeneutics, and world/life-view? These questions are answered below. Addressing them will help us understand what it means to say that we have the mind of Christ. Having the mind of Christ is the key to the formation of a Christian world/life-view.

What Is a World/Life-View?

Our world/life-view is how we see and interpret reality. It is our picture of what is true—both encountered and imagined. It embodies our deepest beliefs. It is the integration of what we have experienced and incorporated into a personally accepted and understood perception of the world and of life around us. One's world/life-view is his concept of the genesis, meaning, purpose, and end of what exists. It is the arrangement of our human nature and personal experiences into a pattern of reality that makes sense to us. It is what our heart sees, interprets, and acts upon. It is our depiction of reality into which a person integrates and assimilates all his subsequent experiences.

A real complication we face when attempting to provide a clear understanding of our world/life-view to others is that our world/life-view is never holistically present in our consciousness at a point in time. What is present is always an excerpted and segmented portion of a much larger world/life-view.

Only God has all of the past, present, future, and possible outcomes completely in his consciousness at all times.³ Humans think about reality in circumstantial segments. Only as an experience unfolds can we interpret the event in the context of our larger world/life-view.

The implications of this are very significant. This is what allows us to have internal contradictions inside our world/life-view. In fact, many divide their world/life-view into separate and seemingly unrelated areas in their minds. What they might conceive of as being reality in the sphere of politics may never be associated with what they think about and do in their family. They treat them as if they exist in two entirely different worlds.

Our world/life-view is also very stimuli-sensitive. And because the segment of it that is consciously before our mind's eye at any point in time is so small and incomplete, it is easily overshadowed, diverted, or even driven from our mind by distractions. Scripture acknowledges this challenge when it says, "Let us also lay aside every encumbrance and the sin which so easily entangles us, and let us run with endurance the race that is set before us, fixing our eyes on Jesus, the author and perfecter of faith" (Heb. 12:1-2). The idea of fixing our eyes on Jesus is an admonition to keep him at the center of our world/life-view while acknowledging that we are easily distracted and thereby prevented from doing so.

Our world/life-view is not put together consciously or deliberately. It is generated degree by degree through the intermixing of our *a priori* sense of good and evil, which is inherently a part of our heart from our conception, and the *a posterior* information gleaned from post-conception experiences.⁴ World/life-views are constructed one experience at a time. Each new experience is either consciously or unconsciously related to prior experiences that are perceived to have some relationship to the newest experience. The span and complexity of the various experiences quickly grow larger.

The complexities of life move people to unconsciously begin to categorize their experiences into bundles of similarity—whether they are truly similar or not. This allows for faster and less complex analysis. It creates stereotypes. It provides pigeonholes into which we can file and catalogue certain events and people in an effort to absorb and digest the seemingly never-ending stream of stimuli that bombards us. For example, we have mental file-folders for rednecks, chauvinists, feminists, liberals, conservatives, evangelicals, Democrats, Republicans, and a host of other stereotypical groupings.

A simple way to describe a world/life-view is by analogy. Think of the human mind as a giant picture puzzle. Assume it is currently made up of 25

---

³ Charnock, *Discourses Upon the Existence and Attributes of God*. For God's infinite knowledge and understanding, see vol. I, chapter 8, 406-497.
⁴ The *a priori* position holds that humans from conception onward possess a moral sensibility that is described in Gen. 2:17, Rom. 1:18-31, and other passages. This is the grounds for speaking of humans' accountability before God after the fall of Adam and Eve. Modern day secular philosophers scoff at such a belief. They maintain the *a posteriori* position that posits the human spirit is a "blank slate" at conception and that all knowledge is acquired after birth.

million individual pieces, and that it is expandable to 1 billion pieces. Further assume that no human can put together and bring into focus more than 5,000 pieces of the puzzle at any one time. In fact, 1,000 pieces is the average number put together (unconsciously or consciously) when reflecting on people and things. When people think or communicate, they are relating to and/or offering other people segments of their 25 million piece puzzle, 1,000 pieces at a time. But their complete world/life-view is never consciously before them, or their listener, at any one point in time.

People do, however, learn to bundle a number of smaller picture segments of their world/life-view under the umbrella of a single piece of the puzzle that comes to represent for them a larger but unarticulated segment of the big picture. For example, words like cosmology, existentialism, salvation, forgiveness, science, transportation, regeneration, vacation, hunting, dancing, and movies come to represent a packet of pictures for those who frequently use such terms. The word *heart* is a good illustration of such a word. Unpacking this word is one of my five pervasive objectives for writing.[5] The word "heart," and all it embodies, has been at the core of my professional endeavors for over twenty years. Words can and do carry ideas larger than themselves.

Similar world/life-views generally have related foundational presuppositions. When people's secondary presuppositions are also similar, their collective world/life-views will be more alike. They will find more agreement on what they individually believe is right or wrong, , moral or immoral. The more uniform the basics, the greater similarity between the expected and agreed-upon outcomes. World/life-views have profound impacts on the ways we live. This reality is behind the proverb, "For as he thinks within himself, so he is" (Prov. 23:7). We live in accordance with what we truly believe.

Our world/life-view is our current and developing comprehension of the big picture of reality. Typically, we are comfortable with other people who have world/life-views similar to our own. Those with dissimilar world/life-views either tend intentionally to avoid one another or to seek common ground in special activities or narrowly focused agendas. The familiar expression, "Birds of a feather flock together," reflects this sentiment.

---

[5] The other four objectives are: (1) that those who know about God might, by his grace and the Holy Spirit's power, come truly to know God; (2) that those who truly know God would grow in their desire to partake of the divine nature; (3) that those who are partaking of the divine nature would ask for the grace to grow in their manifestation of practical holiness; and (4) that God would give us an abiding and deep passion to glorify him.

The World/Life-View diagram that appears below depicts a human eye, the entrance point for the stimulus that bombards our physical sensory perceptions that are in turn integrated into our already existing world/life-view. The people, place, things, etc. to the left of the eye, represent the stimulus input. Right behind the eye we see life experience and human nature lines representing filters through which the external stimulus passes and is examined and organized in the heart as the new input is correlated with the foundational and secondary presuppositions already in place. This generally takes place in an instant and is sorted in a way that makes a psychologically satisfying picture. These filters could be likened to Venetian blinds that can be adjusted degree by degree by either life's temporal/psychological experiences or the work of the Holy Spirit. But the filters cannot be adjusted (reprogrammed, altered, or eradicated) by the mere will of the person within whom they exist. They are a part of the individual's total persona. All of this stimulus or data is absorbed in the heart, which contains the presuppositions that guide our thinking. The heart component of the diagram is the substantive focus of chapters 13–20.

The Eye, the Heart, and World/Life-Views

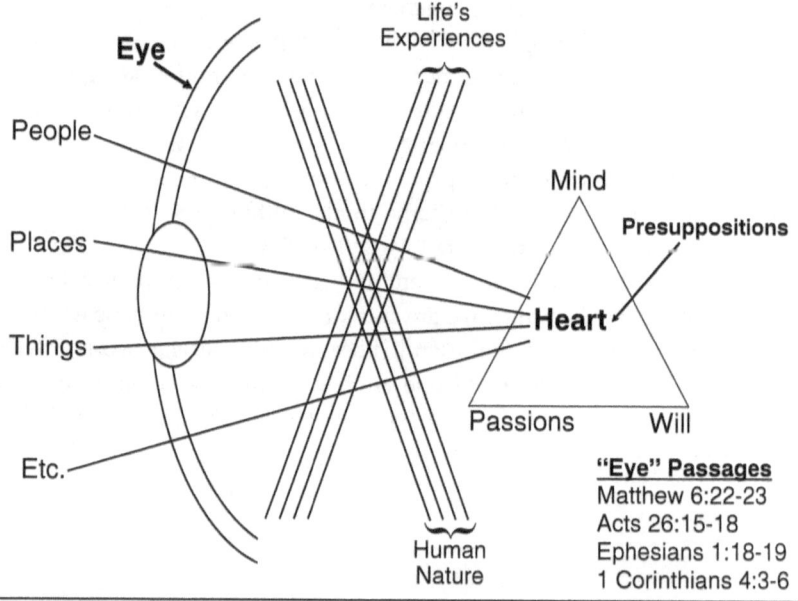

Figure 1 *World/Life-View Diagram*

"The eye is the lamp of the body; so then if your eye is clear, your whole body will be full of light. But if your eye is bad, your whole body will be full of darkness. If then the light that is in you is darkness, how great is the darkness!" Matthew 6:22-23

I am indebted to Reginald F. McLelland, PhD, a professor of philosophy at Covenant College, who presented, in the early 1990's, what is ostensibly the left-hand side of the World/Life-View diagram. See Figure 1. He drew the eye on a chalkboard while making the point that people are constantly being bombarded with information that they must sort and file as they continually pack new information into their existing world/life-view.[6] Combining this insight with the biblical model of the "heart" is my contribution to the larger picture.

Matthew 6:22-23, the first biblical listing in the lower right corner of the diagram, tells us that the eye is the lamp of the body. The three additional passages listed there all either mention the eyes of the heart or unmistakably point to the concept of the heart seeing. These are concepts that expand one's spiritual understanding that accompanies the realization that God is not only real, but dwells in his children. And furthermore, he enlightens their perception regarding true knowledge—that we can truly know reality in both the spiritual and temporal realms, in a way that corresponds to God's true knowledge (Col. 3:10).

So what is a world/life-view? It is our comprehension (analysis) of reality as we have encountered it both outside and inside ourselves. The diagram depicts how we look out on the world and filter what we see and experience through a series of screens that are made up of our inherent human nature and life's experiences. And what we see is organized and integrated with the presuppositions that reside in our heart—a unity of the mind (intellect), passions (desires, affections, identity needs), and will (volition).

Chapters 15–20 explore how the Holy Spirit renovates and permanently imparts aspects of the divine nature into the hearts of God's children. The Spirit performs the miracle of rebirth in us; the miracle of renovating and transforming us; the miracle of having Christ formed in us (Gal. 4:19); the miracle of having the mind of Christ imparted to us (1 Cor. 2:16); and the miracle of our partaking of his divine nature (2 Peter 1:4).

Chapters 21–27 discuss how all of this leads to a mature new life in Christ that manifests practical holiness.

What Did the Apostle Paul Mean When He Wrote, "We Have the Mind of Christ"?

Was the "we" Paul employed in this statement used in reference to himself—sometimes referred to as the royal we? (I am an apostle; we have the mind of Christ.) Or was it a collective we? (I and the Christians in Corinth all have the mind of Christ.) It was a collective we. The thought being developed by Paul in his first letter to the Corinthians is not unlike God's statement through Moses to the Israelites in the wilderness: "He humbled you and let you be hungry, and fed you with manna which you did not know . . . that He might make you understand that man does not live by bread alone, but man lives by

---

[6] Reginald F. McLelland began developing his world/life-view model in his dissertation. He published an essay on it in the John Sanderson Festschrift: Nicholas Barker and Reginald F. McLelland, eds., *Where Is the Salt? Essays and Studies in Honor of John W. Sanderson, Jr.* (Covenant College, 1997), "Philosophy and the Prophet," 1-11.

everything that proceeds out of the mouth of the LORD" (Deut. 8:3[7]). Likewise, Christ's statement to his disciples: "for all things that I have heard from My Father I have made known to you," conveys the same idea (John 15:15). To have the Word of God in our hearts is to have the mind of Christ in our hearts.

It is extremely important to rightly understand the relationship between the Word of God and the mind of Christ. Deuteronomy 8:3 and John 15:15 closely tie the two together. The Holy Spirit uses the Word of God to renew and renovate Christians' minds (Rom. 12:2; Titus 3:5; Eph. 5:26). 1 Corinthians 2:11-13 tells us plainly that: "the thoughts of God no one knows except the Spirit of God. [But] we have received, not the spirit of the world, but the Spirit who is from God, so that we may know the things freely given to us by God . . . not in words taught by human wisdom, but in those taught by the Spirit." We can conclude, then, that what God wants us to know regarding his thoughts he has made available to us in the Bible, in the form of written statements. The Bible reveals to us the mind of God.

Paul's statement, "We have the mind of Christ," needs only several common-sense clarifications to make it a dependable, meaningful, and workable addition to our world/life-view. First, this reality is limited to Christians because they are the ones in whom the Holy Spirit dwells (Rom. 8:9; 1 Cor. 6:19; Eph. 2:19-22). Non-Christians do not have the mind of Christ. They may have thoughts and ideas that are compatible with the mind of Christ in many physical areas and in some moral areas that are revealed through natural law, but the truth they hold is theirs by common grace, not saving grace.

Second, the statement has a wide range of potentiality. A person may have a great deal of the mind of Christ in his heart; or he may have a very limited amount of the revealed mind of Christ there. The degree depends upon the amount of Scripture—and its applicable principles—that the Holy Spirit has written and incorporated into one's heart (Jer. 31:33; Ezek. 11:19-20; 36:26-27). In other words, Christians have the opportunity to have the mind of Christ, but they do not unless they are correctly employing God's Word to the subject under consideration. A particular Christian's world/life perspective on an issue does not automatically reflect the mind of Christ. The perspective must pass the test of Scripture: Does the expressed view concur with God's revealed Word? We can say, for example, that sexual unions between humans and animals, between people of the same sex, and between a married person and someone other than his or her spouse are all perversions of God's expressed will. They are not reflective of the mind of Christ. But to love one's neighbor, as Scripture defines love, *is* reflective of the mind of Christ.

The most significant thing, when thinking about what it means to have the mind of Christ, is that those born from above begin to realize that the Holy Spirit

---

[7] Christ quotes this passage to the Tempter in the wilderness following forty days and nights of fasting (Matt. 4:1-4).

is transforming their mind. He begins the process by renovating them "to a *true knowledge* according to the image of the One who created him" (Col. 3:10). The mind that becomes Christ-centered, a mind that conceives of Christ as being at the heart of all reality, begins to relate the temporal things that are observed with the spiritual reality that rests behind them. This creates a vastly expanded understanding of reality.

This association of things temporal with things spiritual begins to take root in the minds of those adopted into God's family as soon as they are regenerated. God becomes real to them in a new way. Christ's incarnation becomes important. We can (and should) spend our life chewing on the implications of this truth. Getting to know the Holy Spirit who comes and resides in the believer's heart is an ever-growing enlightenment. This whole process embodies the restoration of true knowledge. Our ability to reconnect the temporal and spiritual facets of reality is an indicator that we have been given the mind of Christ. This is a restored ability found only in those who have been born from above. It is gift from God.

Finally, having the mind of Christ is never to be thought of as having Christ's mind *exhaustively*. Christians are given Christ's mind sufficiently but never exhaustively. We are given Christ's mind to accomplish God's purposes in our lives. The thief on the cross probably had very little of Christ's mind, but he had it sufficiently to be qualified by God for heaven (Col. 1:12; Luke 23:39-43). It is critical to understand the distinction between having something sufficiently and having it exhaustively. Finite humans cannot have any exhaustive knowledge. God does, however, give us a sufficient supply of the knowledge we need to carry out his will. To want exhaustive knowledge is to want to be God.

What Is the Main Difference between a Christian and a Non-Christian World/Life-View?

Non-Christians do not have the Spirit of God abiding in them (Rom. 8:9; John 14:17; 1 Cor. 2:14). And without the abiding presence of the Spirit of God, the mind of Christ is not present in them. And without the mind of Christ being developed in them, their world/life-view is devoid of many qualities of discernment that are present or waiting to be formed in the world/life-view of a Christian. The non-Christian would not think, for example, that all of history has been under the sovereign rule of the Lord God Almighty and that even every hot spot in the world today is under God's sovereign watch. Nor would the non-Christian see a tree and pause to reflect upon the awesome creative ability of the God who created and sustains the process that gives the earth and its inhabitants the pleasure and benefits of so many varieties of trees. But Christian can see with the eye of the heart a spiritual and moral quality associated with a tree that a non-Christian cannot see. The Christian sees a tree that a purposeful God planned for human use and enjoyment, and for his own glory. The Christian and the tree have the same Creator; the tree therefore had a *Spirit*-genesis. But "a natural man does not accept the things of the Spirit of God, for they are foolishness to him; and he cannot understand them, because they are spiritually appraised" (1 Cor. 2:14). And God declared on the third day of creation that trees were good, a moral declaration connoting that a stewardship responsibility is associated with its care and use. The tree has much more associated with it from the Christian's perspective than his or her non-Christian friend can comprehend. The non-Christian does not mentally connect things in the temporal sphere of reality with the spiritual realm of reality.

The Christians' world/life-view is informed, in countless ways, by the mind of Christ when the Holy Spirit begins to form Christ's mind into their mental picture of reality. The old, unseeing mind is regenerated and becomes a new, "seeing" mind. The Holy Spirit accomplishes this transformational work through the use of the truth of Scripture. This truth is written in the heart of the believer as he or she receives it by faith under the tutelage of the Holy Spirit. It is, for example, by faith that the Christian comes to know that God called the universe into being out of that which was not visible, by the power of his expressed will (Genesis 1; Heb. 11:3; 2 Peter 3:5). It is by faith that the Christian comes to know that Christ is God incarnate, the Son of God. It is by faith that the Christian knows that Christ came to atone for our sins. The believer trusts in the Bible's historic record regarding Christ's life, death, and resurrection. This type of revealed truth becomes the substance that gives birth to new presuppositions about life, its purpose and its meaning. This revelation provides true knowledge to the heart of believers. It now becomes possible for relationships, with both God and other humans, to be formed and sustained on a totally different plane. The spiritual reality just described becomes the doorway to God's forgiveness, and is the ground for the elimination of guilt that so affects the lives of non-Christians. A Christian's world/life-view varies dramatically from a non-Christian's world/life-view.

The world/life-view of Christians incorporates more and more of the essential components contained in Christ's world/life-view as the mind of Christ is expanded, and integrated into the Christian's perception of reality. Physical and spiritual realities are connected, and a number of physical truths take on new meaning or are even reshaped. A transformation process takes place as one's imperfect old knowledge is related to the Author of all reality. One's old knowledge becomes modified and assumes the character of true knowledge.

In What Areas of the Heart Is a Person's World/Life-View Altered When the Mind of Christ Becomes a Reality in Him or Her?

Like leaven in bread, every facet of our heart is eventually renovated by the inclusion of Christ's mind. The heart is the seat of our: (a) mind (innate knowledge of good and evil; beliefs about our genesis; general knowledge); (b) passions (desires, affections, the identity needs[8]); and (c) will (volition: the ability

---

[8] William T. Kirwan integrated the idea of identity needs into his *Biblical Concepts for Christian Counseling: A Case for Integrating Psychology and Theology* (Grand Rapids, MI: Baker, 1984).

to determine, choose, and respond to external and/or internal stimuli that affect our mind and/or passions).

What is important to understand here is that God is gradually performing a heart transplant—removing our heart's attachment to the things of the world and reattaching it to him. The heart becomes sensitive to the spiritual dimensions of reality. It becomes aware of the personal and active presence of God within and all around. The mind of Christ is being formed in the heart through the Holy Spirit's direct and indirect application of the Word.[9] Such spiritual sensitivity is nonexistent in an unspiritual, unregenerate person, for "a natural man does not accept the things of the Spirit of God, for they are foolishness to him; and he cannot understand them, because they are [must be] spiritually appraised" (1 Cor. 2:14). We will briefly examine the areas of the heart that are impacted when the mind of Christ is formed in it (Gal. 4:19):[10]

1. Mind: beliefs about our genesis

2. Passions: the need to be successful and avoid failure

3. Will: when our passions override our mind

A brief statement about each of the three points is in order.

Mind: beliefs about our genesis. Unregenerate persons do not accept the things that God's Spirit makes plain to Christians. When a natural person is regenerated by the Holy Spirit and comprehends that Jesus is his Savior (Eph. 1:18; Acts 26:18; 2 Cor. 4:6), such a change in basic beliefs offers evidence that the perceiver has become a new person who now possesses, to a degree, the mind of Christ. The thief on the cross probably understood no more than that (Luke 23:32, 39-43). Believing and living in the light of the fact that Jesus Christ is God the Son, who clothed himself in flesh to come and take away the sins of the world, is strong evidence of true spirituality.

Before regeneration and conversion, however, the typical belief of Westerners concerning their genesis is that their existence is accounted for by some unknown cosmic chance occurrence. Without an almighty, purposeful, creating, and loving God, people must rely upon their concocted god to explain their existence and seek life's meaning out of their misperceived reality. God's loving nature is the foundational transforming truth regarding his purposeful creation that sets the tone for our new belief regarding our origin.

It is not an impersonal god that created the universe and humanity. It is a loving God who created all that was ever created for his own glory (Isa. 42:8; 43:7; 44:23).[11] We are the beneficiaries of his grace and mercy, extended to us

---

[9] *Direct* application of the Word is reading or hearing it expounded with immediate application grasped in the heart. *Indirect* application of the Word is making a connection between an aspect of a providential event and a recalled truth in the Word.

[10] The mind, passions, and will constitute the components of the heart, and they are inseparable aspects of the heart, though we speak about them as if they were separable.

[11] In the beginning God created *ex nihilo*—out of nothing that preexisted (Heb. 11:3).

through the finished work of God the Son, the Lord Jesus Christ. This new knowledge implanted in the heart (mind) regarding one's genesis becomes a foundational building block in a renovated world/life-view. And having such knowledge informs us that the possessor has some of the mind of Christ.

Passions: the need to succeed and desire to avoid failure. Persons with the mind of Christ soon realize that they are not alone, but are being renovated, empowered, and guided by the Holy Spirit who lives in them.[12] The Spirit brings to the Christian a new understanding of success. The world has its definitions of success—being promoted; becoming wealthy; receiving special recognitions—and in a temporal sense, these things do symbolize success. But in God's eyes, success is measured in the development of the fruit of the Spirit in his people (Gal. 5:22-26; Matt. 7:15-20), in their obedience to God's will (Matt. 7:21-23; John 14:21, 23); in their sharing in his holiness, with its fruit of righteousness (Heb. 12:10-11); and in their use of the gifts of the Spirit that are given to every member of the body of Christ for its edification (Rom. 12:6-8; Eph. 4:11-13).

Although failure, from the world's perspective, is not achieving some worldly objective, in God's eyes failure is rejecting Christ and forfeiting the purposes God has for humans before they turned their back to him (Luke 7:30).

Will: when our passions override our mind, we act (will) to gratify the passions. Those not in God's family have little reason to struggle with the conflict that arises frequently between their knowledge and their desires. And indeed, when conflict arises, a process of rationalization begins to promote the desire as it searches for ways to set aside what the mind may be weakly saying. Desires tend to override, even dominate, the mind of the unregenerate unless the consequences of ignoring the mind are severe enough to cause real pain.

Christians, on the other hand, also struggle with the old nature that still resides within them. Most temptations fall somewhere on the continuum of interaction between what Christ has done by transforming our mind and the besetting desire(s) that happen to be the individual's thorn in their psyche. But Christians have some defenses and help: they can flee; they can receive inner strength from the Holy Spirit upon request; or they can employ the self-control that is being developed in them by the Holy Spirit.[13] And at times our passion may override our knowing what is righteous, whereupon the Spirit convicts us so that confession and repentance are made real and our Lord mercifully grants forgiveness. But the will is an inseparable part of the heart and needs Christ's renovation as much as the mind and the passions do.

Is There Such a Thing as the Christian World/Life-View?

Yes! Christ has *the* perfect, inerrant world/life-view. God alone possesses the full and flawless perspective on all reality—past, present, future. This then raises another question: Can a Christian have *the* Christian world/life-view? No!

---

[12] Renovated: Col. 3:10; Eph. 4:22-24; empowered: John 14:12; 15:4-5; and guided: John 14:26; 16:13.
[13] Prov. 16:32; 25:28.

Why not? Because, as Scripture teaches, Christians "see through a mirror in a riddle" and "know in part."[14] Our residual sin nature and finitude prevent us from seeing and knowing as Christ sees and knows. But that there is a world/life-view that embodies true knowledge, and that can be accurate regarding temporal/spiritual matters, is profoundly important for three reasons.

First, Christ's (God's) world/life-view is the only accurate one in the universe. This presents us immediately with several corollary truths:

(1) The mind of Christ—his world/life perspective—is the most important source of truth. We have been told to seek his face continually (Pss. 105:4; 27:8). Do we do this, or do we spend more time seeking other pleasures? We would do well to seek Christ's personal help through prayer and fellowship with him as he unfolds the truths imbedded in the Scripture when we read it in faith.

(2) The Holy Spirit, who indwells Christ's people, teaches them God's truth in propositional form in the Scriptures (John 14:26; 16:13). The implications of this are plain. Christians need to spend lots of time in the Bible, prayerfully dependent upon the Holy Spirit's willingness to teach them. That is the role he has in God's economy. We might ask ourselves: Am I doing my part? Am I coming to Christ and seeking his mind? Or am I being lazy and presumptuous—assuming he will give me his mind when I need it?

(3) Christ's world/life-view is imparted to his people over time, to a degree sufficient for their salvation and sufficient to accomplish the tasks to which he has called them. God's grace remains as much a key to the development of Christians' world/life-view as it is in their calling, regeneration, conversion, justification, adoption, sanctification, and glorification.[15] Christ's mind, with its transforming world/life-view, is given to his people. It is not acquired, earned, or self-developed. We should, however, ask for it. He will give us himself.

Second, we are to seek the mind of Christ, not the mind of Augustine, Thomas Aquinas, Martin Luther, John Calvin, Jacob Arminius, John Wesley, or any other famous theologian. All of these people embodied the mind of Christ partially and imperfectly. We are not to call people to Augustine or Calvin or Wesley. We are to call people to Jesus Christ. I say this not to criticize God's chosen servants. The follower of another human, however, has put that person between himself and Christ. This means Christ will be filtered and interpreted second-hand. It is good to listen to other people who call us to Christ, but we must be careful that it is *Christ* whom we are seeking and not the other person. This has huge implications for our hermeneutics.[16]

Third, all Christians must acknowledge they bring much to the study of Scripture that impedes their spiritual understanding. We bring the residual errors from our old nature; we bring the interpretations of Scripture, including

---

[14] While 1 Cor. 13:12 is generally translated either "we see in a mirror dimly" or "we see through a glass darkly," the translation above is from the original Greek.
[15] This list of terms is called theologically the *ordo salutis*—the order of salvation.
[16] Hermeneutics is the science of biblical interpretation.

errors that we learned from our spiritual mentors; and we introduce what brings comfort and makes sense to us personally. Familiarity, comfort, and security are often more important to us psychologically than truth, which may be unfamiliar, uncomfortable, and may expose our false security.

True hermeneutics is impossible without the work of the Holy Spirit in the hearts of humble believers. What can persons do then not to resist the Holy Spirit and to interpret the Bible correctly? Hermeneutics is an art and a science and we must ask Christ to help us with both. A basic rule of biblical hermeneutics has been expressed as follows:

> The infallible rule of interpretation of Scripture is the Scripture itself; and therefore, when there is a question about the true and full sense of any [portion of] Scripture (which is not manifold, but one), it must be searched and known by other places that speak more clearly.[17] (See 2 Peter 1:20-21; Acts 15:13-18.)

The hermeneutics is a humanly-developed means to help us understand Scripture. And while it is commendable to employ its tools, its imperfections are a mirror of the imperfections of the process itself, and of those who employ it. The Holy Spirit is the only true interpreter of Scripture.

Are All Christians Expected to Have the Same World/Life-View?

"Now I know in part, but then I shall know fully just as I also have been fully known" (1 Cor. 13:12). This is a humbling truth. We can only know in part now, in our fallen, albeit redeemed state. But truth that humbles us is good, for we need to walk with Christ in humility. We will only gain full knowledge at our glorification. All of us have to live with the imperfections and misunderstandings that accompany us now, even as believers. No two Christians, therefore, can have exactly the same world/life-view.

The more that people's world/life-views resemble each other's, however, the more likely they are to join together in fellowship. The more their views diverge, the more likely they are to separate and seek those with more compatible views. While acknowledging these differences, however, there is a broad consensus on the essentials of the Christian faith—and those who profess these essentials receive one another as brothers and sisters in Christ. They agree to disagree on a number of issues. But these differences sometimes make it such that those who differ are simply not psychologically comfortable functioning in the same fellowship. This is sad, and it presents a confusing testimony to the watching world. This can also reflect spiritual pride, poor hermeneutics, and other defects. This harms the unity in the body of Christ sought by the Holy Spirit (Eph. 4:15-16; John 17:23). God's mercy in tolerating our diverse world/life-views—that leads to Christians separating from one another—is amazing! He endures us for Christ's sake (Rom. 15:30; 1 John 2:12; Isa. 48:9, 11). "Oh, the depth

---

[17] *The Westminster Confession of Faith* (Edinburgh: William Blackwood & Sons, Ltd., 1969), chapter 1, paragraph 9. See also: 2 Tim. 3:16; Rom. 15:4.

of the riches both of the wisdom and knowledge of God! How unsearchable are His judgments and unfathomable His ways!" (Rom. 11:33).

Can a Christian Have a Bifurcated (Split) World/Life-View?

Yes, world/life-views can be bifurcated, trifurcated, or even multifurcated—because they are so segmented at any given time that it is easy for them to exhibit internal inconsistencies and contradictions. This insight rests on the presupposition that there is a standard world/life-view that serves as a benchmark for our individual world/life-views. The mind of Christ, revealed in Scripture, is our reference point for determining God's mind on a matter. The question we should then ask is: Is my perspective in conformity with Scripture? Of course, most people do not accept this evangelical presupposition, and even those who do are still inconsistent at times. There are, in fact, a number of situations in which different world/life-views are to be expected—for no one knows God's Word exhaustively or can interpret it perfectly.

To illustrate, here is an innocent bifurcation. A person may believe and practice, to the best of his understanding, the Scriptural teaching that God is not a respecter of persons—he does not show favoritism toward specific racial, ethnic, or gender groups, nor economic or social classes. (This biblical principle is revealed in James 2:1-13; Rom. 2:11; Acts 10:34; Deut. 1:17.) Yet this same person, while striving to live this out in his interpersonal relationships, may reveal that, in his opinion, the criminal courts should be lenient in the administration of justice to poor persons when they are apprehended for stealing the basic necessities of life. Your friend may believe the poor constitute a special case in the eyes of God. In proposing a standard with a special consideration provision for the poor he may be unaware of the contradiction between what he professes concerning God and what he suggests concerning public policy.

Please note that the majority of the biblical references given in the above paragraph, which support the principle that God is no respecter of persons, are from the New Testament; all of the biblical references supporting the tough love consequences being set forth in the next paragraph are from the Old Testament. This observation is significant to what follows next.

Has Christ revealed his mind (position) to us on matters concerning the poor? Are the poor to be treated as a special class of persons under the civil and criminal laws? God's Word says, "You shall do no injustice in judgment; you shall not be partial to the poor nor defer to the great, but you are to judge your neighbor fairly" (Lev. 19:15). We are not to be partial to a poor man in his dispute (Ex. 23:3). Indeed, the stiffest restitution for a theft found in all of Scripture is laid on *the poor*. He must repay sevenfold; he must give all the substance of his house [if it is necessary to pay the debt] (Prov. 6:30-31). Biblically, the thief may even be sold for his theft (Ex. 22:3). Why are the poor subject to such harsh consequences for the sin of stealing in the Old Testament? The answer to this question may be *inferred* from two plain teachings about God that, when related to the issue before us, provide a just and loving answer.[18]

First, God, through his sovereignly administered providence, establishes (permissibly or actively) who is to be rich and who is to be poor in this life (1 Sam. 2:7; Prov. 30:7-9; Deut. 8:17-18). Second, pride is an abomination in God's sight (Isa. 13:11; 2:10-11; Prov. 8:13; 16:18) and he will purge it from his children (Heb. 12:5-11; Prov. 3:11-12). These two additional facts pertain to the case under consideration. God, to be sure, loves the poor, and wants his empowered people to defend the rights of the non-empowered—the poor, the mute, the weak, orphans and widows (Prov. 29:7; 31:8-9; Pss. 41:1; 82:3-4). The poor are always in our midst, however, as a test for all people's hearts (Deut. 15:7-11; 1 John 3:17-19; Matt. 26:11). If the poor, though, bitterly complain against their lot in life and refuse to seek God's face and his ordained remedy for poverty, or exhibit so much pride that they refuse to ask their neighbors for help and resort to stealing, God's purposes and clear instructions are thereby either consciously or unconsciously rejected.[19] It may be inferred that the commanded sevenfold repayment is to cleanse the poor thief of his false pride—an act of God's tough love—(see Heb. 12:4-13).

But what is the mind of Christ concerning the treatment of a poor thief? Should the Old Testament law guide us in our thinking? Or should New Testament Christology guide us—what we believe Christ would do though he did not address this issue? Would Christ recommend something different from the Old Testament? Does the Old Testament contain the mind of Christ or does only the New Testament contain his mind? How do the two Testaments fit together?

What Is the Relationship between Our Presuppositions, Hermeneutics and World/Life-View?

The Holy Spirit generates and builds in God's adoptees a saving faith in the saving work of Christ that gives birth to our most fundamental presuppositions: God is the Author of spiritual and physical reality; God is the Creator; God is all-powerful; God is life; God is eternal; and most importantly, God is love, for he died to redeem the ungodly. But many other understandings regarding God's attributes come from our hermeneutics—how we interpret his infallible Word. Our hermeneutics has a profound impact on our world/life-view. Inappropriate hermeneutics will supply much misinformation that will pervert our beliefs about both God and humanity. A misguided person will naturally believe his

---

[18] Inferred truth is an important part of God's "whole counsel" (Acts 5:20; 20:20, 27) given to his children. The doctrine of the Trinity, for example, is a truth that is inferred (developed from, not explicitly stated) throughout the Old and New Testaments about the nature of God. Inferred truth is that which is absolutely compatible with the explicit revelation of Scripture and in no way contradicts it or casts a shadow over other explicitly revealed truth.

[19] Because we are moral creatures created in the image of God we know that stealing is wrong, and God has told us that we should not steal (Exod. 20:15 [the 8th commandment]; 21:16; Lev. 19:11, 13; Matt. 19:18; Rom. 13:9).

resulting world/life-view is in conformity with the mind of Christ while, in fact, he will be misrepresenting that mind.

Recognized classifications identify major hermeneutic groupings in the church. For example, there are sharp differences between the interpretations of Scripture propagated by Jacob Arminius and John Calvin. And there are those who consider themselves to be covenantal, or Anabaptist, or dispensational, or Reformed. There are hundreds of thousands of people in each of these groups, and they all believe they are hermeneutically correct. But they cannot all be correct and they do not all have the mind of Christ to the same extent. They may all have the mind of Christ to a degree, but their very differences are over the mind of Christ—and he is not divided. The thing to be amazed by is not that such groups exist, or that our world/life-view can be so different as a result of our participation in a particular hermeneutic fellowship, but that the mercy of God is so broad and deep. Isn't it wonderful that we are not required to be theologically perfect? We are saved by grace!

What causes such diverse interpretations of Scripture? There are at least four things that complicate and muddy the hermeneutic waters. (1) We become Christians with pre-taught views of reality. Many of these old ideas die easily, others die hard. (2) In many Christian fellowships there is an absence of what the Bible refers to as the whole purpose and the whole counsel of God (Acts 5:20; 20:20, 27). This results in an unbalanced biblical diet. (3) The hermeneutical sphere in which we experienced our spiritual rebirth has a great impact on our thinking. We almost feel guilty if we begin to deviate from the hermeneutics of our spiritual parents. This is tragic for it raises the question: Are we united with Christ or with a particular hermeneutic describing the mind of Christ? And (4) our delight in our own thinking can fool us into the practice of reading into Scripture our own preferences in order to have a God with whom we are comfortable. We see and believe what we desire to see and believe.

We need to remember that the heart is more deceitful than all else and is desperately sick; who can understand it? (Jer. 17:9).

The question of determining the just treatment for the poor thief, raised above, plainly illustrates the conundrum. It is a good illustration of how our hermeneutics can shape and determine our world/life-view.

Perhaps it is best at this point to start with a new question: If the civil authorities, not the church, are responsible for dealing with thieves, should a Christian sitting on a jury come to the trial believing the jurors are there to offer the mercy of Christ to unbelievers, or to uphold the law of the state governing the unrighteous—hoping that the guilty persons might become aware of their ungodliness and subsequently turn to Christ?

If one believes that God's Word portrays a gradual unfolding of his mind as we progress through the Scripture from Genesis to Revelation, then the Old Testament revelation is believed to be compatible with that of the New Testament. The New Testament does not set aside the Old Testament. It expands and clarifies the truth already revealed there. But if one believes the New

Testament supersedes the Old Testament, then in that case the Old Testament is more likely to be set aside or ignored.

And this is important because much of God's specific teaching regarding his own character is revealed in the Old Testament. Is the God of the Old Testament the same as the God of the New Testament? This question was debated during the first two centuries after Christ's resurrection. Church councils concluded that there is only one God revealed in the Scriptures of both Testaments. The early church declared that there was no contradiction regarding God's attributes as they were revealed in the two Testaments.

The Old Testament contains God's mind as it concerns criminal law, civil law, ceremonial law (foreshadowing Christ's sacrifice), personal moral law, and the gospel of God's foreshadowed acts of redemption. These laws were all given to the nation of Israel. The church, and not a nation, is now God's instrument for taking his gospel to every corner of the world.

This means the criminal and civil laws are to be understood now as the responsibility of the nation states, not the body of Christ, the church. The Law was given to be light, revealing God's perfect character and will. It was given to the nation Israel so that those who sought God's will would know how much they needed his grace, for they knew they could not perfectly keep the Law. They looked forward to the coming Messiah. We look back on the coming of Jesus Christ, the only one who ever perfectly kept the Law's requirements. The church now lives by a new law, the law of faith in Christ. "By what kind of law? Of works? No, but by a law of faith. For we maintain that a man is justified by faith apart from works of the Law" (Rom. 3:27-28).

So, how should a present-day Christian relate to issues in the states' civil and criminal courts? Should we consider both Old and New Testament perspectives in such courts, or only a New Testament one? Which hermeneutic should we use when carrying out our civic duties? Or should we only ask, "What does state law mandate?" and ignore the biblical standards? All viewpoints cannot be correct! Should the poor thief be shown mercy? Should he be excused his debt? Or should he be required to only pay for what he stole, dollar for dollar? Or should he pay double? Or should he pay the sevenfold amount as set forth in Proverbs 6:30-31? Or should he be imprisoned? Christians hold all of these positions. This is how our hermeneutic impacts our perceptions of what we should do. What is the mind of Christ regarding this whole matter?

It should be evident why many avoid hermeneutics. It divides the church. But hermeneutics, how we interpret the Bible, is unavoidable. The human mind, by its nature, must engage in hermeneutics. Too often, though, hermeneutics is an illusory scapegoat, used to cover up presuppositions *we desire* rather than true hermeneutic issues. For example, there are those that say husbands and wives should share equally the headship position in their family because, as Christians, they are redeemed and therefore ought to view themselves as a couple in an innocent, pre-fall relationship. This differs from the historic biblical position that says Christ is the head of the husband and the husband is the head of his wife (1

Cor. 11:3; Eph. 5:23-24; Gen. 3:16). The proponents of this new understanding may claim that any differences are hermeneutic in nature. But this is not so! It is a difference in presuppositions, not hermeneutics. The new presupposition is that fallen but redeemed people should return to a pre-fall state of relationships—assuming that male headship was established after the fall (Gen. 3:16). Or they presuppose that the pre-fall state is the normative state, and so we should strive for it now. But this headship question is addressed in both the Testaments and they agree. In short, there is a hierarchal trinity in marriage—namely Christ, the husband, and the wife.

Another example of advocates interjecting a new presupposition into a discussion and calling the differences hermeneutic is the current argument that women should assume the leadership roles of pastor/priest and ruling elder. Some defend this on the grounds that there was an ever-increasing elevation of women's worth and dignity—equaling that of men—in the progressive unfolding of Scripture from Genesis through Revelation. And this is true! But does it validate the idea that women should assume roles in life that would be identical with those of men? Dignity and roles are lumped together, and some conclude that the elevation of women was intended to continue in this new way after the close of the biblical canon.

The issue in this particular case is one of presupposing that the canon of Scripture is not closed, and the movement of the revelation that stopped at the close of the New Testament continues on its course in the direction that it was presumed to be going at the time of its closure. This is a presupposition without biblical warrant. The real issue is, by whose authority is this new revelation or continuance of revelation to be verified? The new argument is not about the authority of Scripture, it is about continuing what God began. This is not a hermeneutic issue; it is an issue regarding presuppositions. Where does our authority lie—in our minds that generate such presuppositions or in God's Word?

The point is: We need to be careful when we have differences in our world/life-views over things that we believe are differences in biblical interpretation to make sure the differences are really not presuppositional. In either case, we need understanding, patience, and humility. The focus of our discussion is very different when we deal with presuppositions than when the differences are truly hermeneutic in nature.

There are a number of places, in fact, where Christians cause those in the world who do not accept the Lordship of Christ to scoff at us as a confused and ignorant people. We disagree in public over capital punishment. We disagree in public on free-market and government-regulated economic forces.

Environmental issues openly divide us. These all have presuppositional roots that are exposed through our hermeneutics. To the world, Christians present a very divided and confusing front. This hurts the testimony of all who profess Christ before the watching world.

And then there are the internal squabbles that arise between theologians over free will, predestination, and other issues that flow from their respective hermeneutics. And need one mention the various millennial positions that have divided the church for a century?

So what impact do our presuppositions and hermeneutics have on our world/life-view? A profound impact! And this should drive all Christians to prayerful supplication for Christ to grant us grace in forming his mind in us through the Holy Spirit's use of the Word. We all certainly need to walk humbly before God, knowing that the mind of Christ is being formed in us degree by degree—but being careful to recognize that for now we see through a mirror in a riddle (1 Cor. 13:12). There is a profound shaping interaction between our presuppositions and our hermeneutics. But rather than be discouraged, we should all strive to be Bereans:

> The brethren immediately sent Paul and Silas away by night [from Thessalonica] to Berea, and when they arrived, they went into the synagogue of the Jews. Now these were more noble-minded than those in Thessalonica, for they received the word with great eagerness, examining the Scriptures daily to see whether these things were so. Therefore many of them believed, along with a number of prominent Greek women and men. (Acts 17:10-12)

Conclusion

The mind of Christ is the essential component that must be present and integrated into the heart—mind, passions, and will—of anyone who wants to have a Christian world/life-view. Remember, the thief on the cross had very little of the mind of Christ, but it was enough for his salvation. A regenerate heart with the mind of Christ in it will begin placing Christ, the Father, and the Holy Spirit at the center of one's world/life-view. It is the mind of Christ that brings the light of truth to our perceptions; and that mind begins the conscious and unconscious association of all that we believe, perceive, and know into conformity with the almighty Creator-Redeemer God. The mind of Christ is the distinctive leaven shaping a Christian's world/life-view. A growing relationship with God, and the resulting true knowledge of him, will begin to reshape our world/life-view so that we will increasingly understand reality as Christ wants us to interpret it. For after all, "It is God who is at work in [us], both to will and to work for His good pleasure" (Phil. 2:13). Furthermore, Christians should never forget that "apart from [Christ] you can do nothing" (John 15:5).

Part 1

What Is the Divine Nature?

We can "become partakers of the divine nature." (2 Peter 1:4)

The following chapters embody a sevenfold message: (1) God is the Wellspring of all creation and therefore is the only *true reference point* to which all of creation should be related in our mind, passions, and will. (2) We have been created to truly know God, as he is pleased to reveal himself to us. (3) God's true nature has been revealed to us through creation, his self-revelation in Christ, and the biblical record of his acts in history. And the Holy Spirit brings it to life in believers' hearts. (4) Every attribute of God has a profound implication for our understanding of God, and as a result our understanding of ourselves. (5) God wants us to truly know him. To just know *about* him is not sufficient. (6) God intends for his adopted children to partake of significant aspects of his divine nature: "His divine power has granted to us everything pertaining to life and godliness, through the *true knowledge* of Him. . . . For by these He has granted to us His precious and magnificent promises, so that by them *you may become partakers of the divine nature*" (2 Peter 1:3-4; also see Heb. 12:10 and Eph. 4:13). And (7) God wants us to grow in our relationship with him so that we grow in our love for him and our neighbors. These seven truths have deep implications for the human heart, and how we manifest practical holiness—the focus of the two sections that follow our study of God's attributes.

2

God: The Self-Revealing/Transcendent One

I AM WHO I AM. (Ex. 3:14)

What an awesome privilege we have! We can, by God's grace, truly know our Redeemer God. He is a self-revealing God. For example, he spoke directly to Adam and Eve before their fall (Gen. 1:28-30; 2:16-17). And he spoke to them again after their fall (Gen. 3:9-13, 16-19). In addition, God revealed himself to Abraham just before the destruction of Sodom and Gomorrah (Gen. 18:16-33; we know this was Christ revealing himself to Abraham: John 8:56-58). Indeed, Christ was present with his people throughout the Old Testament, revealing God's will to them.

Many theologians agree that the expression "the angel of the LORD," found repeatedly in the Old Testament, refers to the pre-incarnate Christ. He appeared to his people in the form of a *theophany*—a visible manifestation of God, who is spirit (John 4:24). After Christ's subsequent incarnation, life, death, and resurrection, there is no longer a need, however, for the children of God to see him in a physical form. The incarnate Christ is the perfect manifestation of God. He is God incarnate (Col. 2:9). After Christ ascended into heaven in bodily form, he and the Father sent the Holy Spirit to dwell in his children, and to care for them. And his people come to truly know him for he lives in them and reveals God to them (John 14:16-17).

The Bible, however, records a few of God's chosen servants being granted the exceptional privilege of seeing either a particular attribute of God or of seeing the pre-incarnate Christ in a manner that overwhelmed them. Isaiah saw aspects of God's *holiness*, and when he did, he was undone—"Woe is me, for I am ruined!" (Isa. 6:1-7). Job was given the privilege of discerning aspects of God's *glory*, and declared, "My eye sees You; therefore I retract, and I repent in dust and ashes" (Job 42:5-6). Daniel had a series of visions of God and his intentions that distressed Daniel's spirit and alarmed him greatly (Dan. 7:9-15). In one vision, after the Son of Man (a theophany of Christ) spoke to him, Daniel was exhausted and sick for days (Dan. 8:15-27). John saw the Alpha and the Omega on the isle of Patmos and fell at his feet as a dead man (Rev. 1:8-20). He saw something of Christ's eternal *majesty*.

God is so majestic that everyone who has ever glimpsed him has been terrified, awestruck, and wondered why he was not consumed by God's very presence. There are no words to describe adequately the inexpressible wonder of God's personage. Isaiah's, Job's, Daniel's, and John's responses to seeing aspects of God's character reveal to us the benumbing consequences of encountering the

True and Living God. God is like a refiner's fire (Mal. 3:2). Few of his children have been blessed with a direct exposure to his attributes. The wonder of his nature generally rises in our hearts degree by degree, over many years. His grandeur grows in our consciousness as he dwells with us and we come to know him more intimately.

It is important to realize that before he created anything God decided how much he wanted to reveal of himself to his image-bearers. He says, "The secret things belong to the LORD our God, but the things revealed belong to us and to our sons forever" (Deut. 29:29). God is both knowable and transcends knowing. The Bible contains the full record of what he has chosen to reveal of himself. And it is the Holy Spirit who makes this revelation alive for those whom God draws near to himself (Pss. 65:4; 73:28; Prov. 3:32). What is not revealed about God in the Bible remains his *secret*. He is beyond finding out apart from his self-revelation.

God has revealed to us a multitude of his attributes. There are times in our lives, however, when a particular attribute of God may become more important to us than the other attributes. This has been true for me; perhaps it has also been true for you. What characteristic of God is most important to you now? And why is that so? I was twenty-eight years old when Christ became my Lord. His *holiness* stood out to me as most significant then. And perhaps it *is* his most important attribute! It is the only attribute that is used in Scripture to qualify some of his other attributes—his *holy arm* (power; omnipotence), for example (Isa. 52:10).

Later, however, when I struggled with the whole concept of living by faith, having learned early on not to trust people, I needed more than the realization that God was perfectly holy. God delivered me from my mental anguish regarding trust and faith by immersing me in the truth that he is, by nature, a spirit (John 4:23). I realized that this necessitated my relating to him on a spirit-to-spirit basis—he, as a spirit, related with me; and I, as an incarnate spirit, was to relate with him. This truth, added to my other understandings of God, proved to be the key that freed me from anxiety of living by faith rather than by sight. My experience is not normative, but God's being a spirit was foremost in my thinking and my delight in him for a time.

Then in 1988, when my youngest son broke his neck and became a quadriplegic, God's sovereignty completely dominated my thinking and appreciation of him. I could depend on him! He was in charge of my son's life; he was in charge of my life. He had a good (wise) reason for allowing this tragedy to occur. The tragedy would be transformed into a blessing. God would use it to transform my son more and more into the likeness of Christ (Rom. 8:28-29).

Later, the goodness of God became the focus of my love for him. How awesome are the many benefits that have come to me and those I love, both by way of the Lord's created order and by the grace of his act of redemption—the kindness of God poured out on me and my family through his gracious and infinitely wise providence!

Currently it is God's omnipresence that is foremost in my thinking as he and I relate to each another. His presence is my strength and my hope. His nearness is my joy and my rest.

Which attribute of God I will next be paying most attention to—and enjoying the most—as I continue to grow in my relationship with him, I do not know. Which attribute of God will be needed to bring comfort and/or strength to me, or which attribute will simply delight me tomorrow, only God knows today. And the same is true in your life.

When God commands us to love him with all of our heart, we are to love him for who he is as well as for what he does. Contemplating the Trinity is vital because of the dynamic relationship that exists between the persons of the Godhead. This intimate relationship is revealed to us in order to teach us about how we ought to relate to one another. The Trinity models key aspects of interpersonal relationships that are important both to our relationship with the Almighty and to our everyday relationships with other people. Contemplating the Trinity can help us understand a number of life's most perplexing interpersonal paradoxes.

My attempt to faithfully set forth many aspects of God's personality is complicated by: (a) the necessity of accurately describing the clear revelation of Scripture; (b) ferreting out and faithfully describing the important inferences associated with the clear revelation; and (c) the need to stop short of making statements that are merely speculative and not knowable, lest I cross over the line into the unrevealed mysteries of God.

Theologians have never claimed to have identified all of God's attributes. Neither do any two theologians seem to select the same list of attributes to describe, for God's nature is complex beyond our comprehension. God's nature is both knowable and held by him in secret. He is knowable to the degree that he has pleased to reveal himself. Yet he is beyond our ability to know—he is transcendent. There are, however, a number of God's characteristics that the majority of theologians agree we can know. Sometimes God's attributes are broken down into two categories: his *natural* attributes, associated with his being; and his *moral* attributes, associated with his behavior. I follow this schema, but not because it is theologically better, for God is holistic and indivisible. In truth, he cannot be compartmentalized or segmented. But this separation provides a way for us, as finite humans, to grapple with aspects of our Creator-Redeemer God in a way that is faithful to his self-revelation—the I AM WHO I AM! (Ex. 3:14).

God's Natural Attributes

1. Spirituality (ch. 4)
2. Immutability (ch. 6)
3. Omnipresence (ch. 7)
4. Omnipotence (ch. 10)
5. **Aseity**
6. **Eternity**
7. **Infinitude**
8. **Omniscience**
9. Invisibility
10. Life

God's Moral Attributes

11. Holiness (ch. 5)	15. Sovereignty (ch. 11)	19. Justice
12. Wisdom (ch. 8)	16. **Patience**	20. Wrath
13. Goodness (ch. 9)	17. Righteousness	
14. Love (ch. 12)	18. Mercy	

Each of the attributes listed above will be touched on, to some degree, in chapters 2–12. Before we begin reflecting on the five attributes to be discussed in this chapter, it will be profitable to reflect on the transcendent, unknowable aspects of God's nature before we discuss the revealed dimensions of his attributes. There is a special blessing associated with the discernment of God's transcendent character, for such insight brings us face-to-face with mystery that points to the awesome glory of God.

The Mystery Associated with God's Transcendent Characteristics

God's infinite and eternal character is such that the contemplation of any of his attributes will soon bring us to the outer limits of our capacity to know. This leaves us with a mystery that inhabits our curiosity. And human nature is such that we often try to solve the unsolvable. But there are many mysteries God does not intend us to solve. Mystery belongs to him! He has said as much: "The secret things belong to the LORD our God, but the things revealed belong to us and to our sons forever" (Deut. 29:29). The problem we face, though, is determining where we are on the continuum between the revealed and the secret. We are foolish to cross over the line which separates the one from the other. The issue is an important one because mystery (God's secret) is extremely important to the spiritual health and peace of his children. If we claim to have an answer to what really remains God's secret, we diminish our view of God's grandeur; we make him over into our own image; and we replace the mystery with a false presupposition that creates false knowledge. And false knowledge is a poor substitute for the protection and humility that mystery provides us.

Mystery is good for us. It protects us. This is a good reason to delight in it. There are things we are better off not knowing. For example, who really wants to know today the day and hour when he will die? Or would we want to know that in ten years we will begin a seven-year battle with cancer? Mystery is our friend in these matters. God has perfect foreknowledge, but he protects us by keeping many things out of sight until the time is right, according to his wisdom. There are many mysteries associated with God's omniscience, but his foreknowledge must reside in the corner of our mind reserved for mystery.

Mystery also humbles us. This is another good reason to enjoy it. To know that some things are beyond our finite capacity to understand fosters adoration, reverence, honor, and trust toward the One so great that he is confronted by no mysteries. Christians trust and worship a transcendent God. To truly know God is to be awed by his grandeur. To know that what is a mystery for us is not a mystery for him only increases his glory. Believing we have solved unsolvable mysteries, and teaching others our imaginary answers, only diminishes the spiritual health of everyone involved.

The problem of creating answers often arises when we begin with a biblical truth and then push it too far, either by extending the truth beyond its legitimate bounds through logic or by manipulating the truth to make it fit our way of interpreting Scripture. I can illustrate this by relating the theology and mystery associated with God's sovereign rule over all and his granting to humans the freedom to make choices with eternal consequences. The mystery and tension that accompany attempts to reconcile these indisputable facts are enormous. I mention the topics of divine sovereignty and human freedom merely to illustrate the appropriateness of mystery. Readers probably already have a staked-out position regarding the two competing subjects. We are not trying to reconcile the positions. Scripture asks us to acknowledge the tension, and the mystery accompanying them.

Part of the tension between these two ideas comes from the fact that God's sovereignty is revealed to us through special revelation while human freedom (also described in Scripture) is revealed to us repeatedly through natural revelation—experiential as well as observed. Which kind of revelation, special or natural, should be the governing revelation? The reader probably already has a presupposition in place that is guiding his or her answer to this question!

The Bible says much about God's election and about humans' moral accountability for their actions. Is it possible for God to have absolute rule over who is saved (election) while humans simultaneously have freedom to make choices? Scripture attests to both of these truths. We can either believe that both are true and admit that we cannot comprehend how it can be so—it is an unfathomable mystery. Or we can invent answers that bring us a pseudo-psychological peace. We will look at two answers offered by those trying to solve the mystery.

Some who want human choice to prevail when explaining the biblical text regarding election, say things such as, "Those who are not saved refused to adequately exercise their free will to choose God." But Scripture is clear. Humans either have an old nature (unregenerated) or a new nature (regenerated). There is no third-type of human nature in the Bible. We must, then, conclude: Humans are only free to exercise their will in a manner consistent with their nature. We are either slaves of sin or slaves of righteousness (Rom. 6:19-22). The biblical evidence points to a mystery, including the following three points:

First, "But as many as received Him, to them He gave the right to become children of God . . . who were born not of blood, nor of the will of the flesh nor of the will of man but of God" (John 1:12-13).[20] Scripture always attributes rebirth (regeneration) to the work of the Holy Spirit, never to an act of human will.

Second, "No one can come to Me unless the Father who sent Me draws him

---

[20] See also John 3:1-12; 1 Peter 1:1-2.

. . . . For this reason I have said to you that no one can come to Me unless it has been granted him from the Father" (John 6:44, 65). It is true that everyone freely exercises his or her will. But a person's will is always exercised in keeping with his or her existing nature—an old, dead-to-God, unregenerate nature, or a new, alive-to-God, regenerate nature.[21]

Third, "He chose us in Him before the foundation of the world, that we would be holy and blameless before Him. In love He predestined us to adoption as sons through Jesus Christ to Himself, according to the kind intention of His will . . . . In Him also we have obtained an inheritance, having been predestined according to His purpose who works all things after the counsel of His will" (Eph. 1:4-5, 10-11). Scripture does not teach a high view of human ability to choose God prior to his regenerative work. Rather, regeneration always precedes our conversion experience. When regenerated by the Spirit, people will choose Christ and trust him as Savior.

The doctrine of God's sovereign election appears frequently in both the Old and New Testaments. But this doctrine appears, to those who emphasize our freedom to choose, to be irreconcilable with the doctrine that God is love (1 John 4:8, 17). Is God's love reconcilable with the teaching of election? Would a loving God elect some people and by-pass others?

Even those, however, who love the biblical doctrine of election can have problems with the mystery of Christ's love for those who eternally reject his love. Some say things like, "God loves only the elect." This may ease their minds, but it overlooks much biblical evidence that appears to contradict that conclusion. That evidence includes the following:

First, "This is good and acceptable in the sight of God our Savior, who desires all men to be saved and to come to the knowledge of the truth" (1 Tim. 2:3-4). The context of this passage does not involve the elect but the making of entreaties and prayers . . . on behalf of all men, for kings and all who are in authority (vv. 1-2). Does God desire all people to be saved and come to the knowledge of the truth regarding salvation? Scripture certainly indicates here that he does. A person challenging this passage will be adding to the Scripture if he says this plain language applies only to the elect. (Deut. 4:2; 12:32; Prov. 30:6; and Rev. 22:18 warn us not to add to God's Word.)

Second, the rich young ruler came to Jesus and asked him what he needed to do to inherit eternal life. Scripture records the following: "Looking at him, Jesus felt a love for him and said to him . . ." (Mark 10:21). Following Jesus's response we are told, "But at these words he was saddened, and he went away grieved" (Mark 10:22). The words and context both tell us that Christ loved the rich young ruler and let him go. How could that be?

---

[21] Being dead to God does not imply a lack of unawareness that there is a righteous and loving God (Rom. 1:18-32); it simply means that unregenerate persons cannot, because of their ungodly nature, choose a godly direction (9:19-24).

Third, and what of Christ's lament: "Jerusalem, Jerusalem, who kills the prophets and stones those who are sent to her! How often I wanted to gather your children together, the way a hen gathers her chicks under her wings, and you were unwilling" (Matt. 23:37)? Did Jesus not really want to gather the people to himself? Christ really wanted them to be saved, not merely desired in some passive manner. People who override these passages, and others like them—John 3:16 for example—can only do so by using hermeneutic gymnastics.

To our minds, we have a paradox. The elect are saved and God is love are two clearly revealed teachings of Scripture. But our logic and Scriptures that we have trouble fitting with our logic trouble us as we attempt to reconcile the two attributes of God—he is *sovereign*; he is *love*.

As we move forward it will become clear that every attribute of God has its knowable and unknowable aspects. And the latter aspects must be consigned to the category of *mystery* if we are to hold God in the elevated position he deserves. To falsely "resolve" a true mystery is to bring God down to our level and rob him of the glory due him. The human's desire to resolve mysteries is understandable. Mystery creates discomfort. It calls into question our intellectual abilities. By nature, we like to solve mysteries. But the true mysteries that are associated with God's transcendent qualities are healthy for us. Mystery elevates God. If we will stop at the end of God's revealed knowledge and let the awesomeness of his transcendent glory have its rightful impact on our hearts, we will *grow* in the wonder of his eternal and infinite character. The God who has revealed himself sufficiently for us to know and love him is to be *feared* with a fear that ranges all the way from terror to absolute awe. A healthy fear of God that emanates from an intimate relationship with him is the beginning of wisdom (Prov. 9:10).

God's Aseity

What in the world is *aseity*? Few people have even heard of it. Then it follows that not many have had the joy of contemplating its wonder. Just what is God's aseity? Aseity is a Latin word indicating God's absolute independence from all that is external to him. There is comfort and delight in comprehending God's absolute independence. God has never had a need. Throughout eternity he has been sufficient in himself. And he will never experience a need. God had no need to create and no need for what he has created. God is complete in himself; he is whole, lacking nothing. He stands uniquely in his eternal, Trinitarian totality!

This truth about God starkly contrasts the human condition. We have been created as totally dependent creatures. We depend upon God for every breath we draw. We are needy in every respect. The contrast could not be greater! God is absolutely without a need. Many, when first introduced to this notion, do not like it, for they presuppose this must lead to a cold, dispassionate, and loveless God. Their own need to be loved (a universal need) creates a strong resistance to acknowledge such a basic attribute. After all, what kind of God is he who does not need to be loved? Does he not command us to love him with our whole heart? Does this not imply that he needs to be loved too?

Scripture portrays God as much more awesome than One who needs to be loved. It does tell us that God is love (1 John 4:8), but the agape love that is God's love is not rooted in mere feelings. Our love is often emotionally based. But God's agape love is anchored in his will. He sets his mind upon loving us. God's love is an immutable commitment of his will to give us to his Son and to redeem us. God's love is more than an emotion; it is his will to do what is best for us. Love anchored in his immutable will is a source of great comfort for Christians. God's benevolent behavior toward us is immutably fixed in who he is.

If we stopped to ask, "Do I really want a God who has a need in his life?" we would conclude that such a God would lack something important in his character. Obviously, he would be lacking what he needed. To illustrate, he would not be unchanging. He would be subject to vacillations between unmet and met needs. He might be moody, even grouchy, when his needs were unattended. The truth is, when we conceive of God as having needs, we are creating a God in our own likeness.

Scripture speaks of a beginning of the created order (Gen. 1.1; Ps. 102:25; Isa. 40:21; John 1:1–2; Heb. 1:10). In contrast, God had no beginning. He is eternal. The very doctrine of God's ex nihilo[22] creation bears unambiguous and secure testimony to his aseity (Heb. 11:3). He stood independent of his creation for an eternity prior to his calling it into existence. Not only is that true, he was also as immutable (unchanging) then as he is now. Therefore, it cannot be reasonably argued that he called the created order into being out of need. God lived for an eternity past without a need for the created order we now enjoy.

Scripture bears another kind of witness to God's *aseity*. Consider, for example:

> A voice says, "Call out." Then he answered, "What shall I call out?" All flesh is grass, and all its loveliness is like the flower of the field. The grass withers, the flower fades, when the breath of the LORD blows upon it; surely the people are grass. . . . Behold, the Lord GOD will come with might, with His arm ruling for Him. Behold, His reward is with Him, and His recompense before Him. . . . . Behold, the nations are like a drop from a bucket, and are regarded as a speck of dust on the scales; behold, He lifts up the islands like fine dust. . . . All the nations are as nothing before Him, they are regarded by Him as less than nothing and meaningless. (Isa. 40:6-7, 10, 15, 17)[23]

What does God's infallible Word say about our meaning to him? We are regarded by him as less than nothing and meaningless. Is this biblical hyperbole? We need to examine the Scriptures to see if what has been said is a repeated theme or an isolated expression.

---

[22] Latin, meaning from or out of nothing.

[23] Whenever the words LORD or GOD appear in an English language Old Testament (rather than Lord or God), it indicates that the word is *Yahweh* (יהוה), the most revered Hebrew name for God.

> If you are righteous, what do you give to Him? Or what does He receive from your hand? (Job 35:7). Can a vigorous man be of use to God .... Is there any pleasure to the Almighty if you are righteous, or profit if you make your ways perfect? (Job 22:2-3)

Thoughtful persons might ask themselves, "Did God destroy all of humanity, except Noah and his immediate family, because God needed or desired his fallen image-bearers?" (Genesis 6–7, especially 6:5-7). Or, "Has God had a cause to be more pleased with humanity since the days of Noah than he was during Noah's days?" Certainly not, for he said to Isaiah,

> For the sake of My name I delay My wrath, and for My praise I restrain it for you, in order not to cut you off .... For My own sake, for My own sake, I will act; for how can My name be profaned? And My glory I will not give to another. (Isa. 48:9, 11)

Paul said of every (unsaved) human being:

> There is none righteous, not even one; ... there is none who seeks for God .... they have become useless; there is none who does good, there is not even one .... Their throat is an open grave .... (Rom. 3:10-13)

Scripture presents God in an eternal, unchanging, perfected glory. Scripture presents human beings, however, in three historic conditions: (1) Adam and Eve were created without sin (Gen. 1:31). Even in this state of perfection, however, we could not say they warranted God's love, but they did receive and enjoy it. (2) Adam and Eve fell and all of their posterity with them (Ps. 51:5; Rom. 5:12-21). And those who *remain* enslaved to their fallen sin nature will die in that nature (Rom. 6:23; 8:6, 13; Gal. 6:8), to be forever removed from the presence of the Creator (Matt. 7:21-23; 25:41; Luke 16:19-31; Rev. 20:11-15). Surely in such a godless state, no one deserves love. (3) And those who are regenerated and believe in Christ's atoning sacrifice for forgiveness will inherit eternal life (John 10:28; 17:2; Rom. 5:21; 6:23; 8:38-39) as transformed, glorified image-bearers (Rom. 8:17, 30; 9:23; John 17:22). The Father imputes Christ's perfections to believers, and they are the eternal recipients of God's love. Those who remain unregenerate are described in the four negative biblical texts quoted above.

Christians who conceive of a high view of mankind (God created us because he needed people to love and people to love him) unintentionally produce a low view of God. We need a biblically accurate view of both God and humanity. The Bible's high view portrays God as independent of his creation—he has no emotional, psychological, or spiritual needs. In his Trinitarian state God is complete!

God's children are the beneficiaries of his eternal attribute of love, but God has no need to love us. His love nature has, from all eternity, been wholly satisfied between God the Father, God the Son, and God the Holy Spirit. Nor is there any externally compelling condition that requires God to reveal his love to anyone outside the Godhead. *Indeed, we are loved, but for Christ's sake* (Eph. 4:23; 1 John 2:12). We are not loved because we are lovable or ought to be loved. God's independence from all of his creation can only be reconciled with the many biblical affirmations that declare: God's children are precious to him; they are loved; and they are honored (Isa. 43:1-5, 7, for example), by grasping the overarching reality. *The Father has an immutable, infinite, and eternal love for his Son that is rooted in the nature of the Father and the nature of the Son. This is the key to our finding joy in God's aseity. All that God says and does for us is for Christ's sake. We were created for Christ* (Col. 1:16). The extension of God's love toward us is an act of pure, undeserved grace—no one can say they deserve God's love.

How then are we to engage the question, "Why did God create; and why did he create image-bearers to love him when he derives no personal benefit from doing so?" God addresses this question in a conversation he had with Isaiah.

> Do not fear, for I have redeemed you; I have called you by name; you are Mine! When you pass through the waters, I will be with you; and through the rivers, they will not overflow you. When you walk through the fire, you will not be scorched, nor will the flame burn you. For I am the LORD your God, the Holy One of Israel, your Savior . . . . Since you are precious in My sight, since you are honored and I love you, I will give other men in your place and other peoples in exchange for your life. Do not fear, for I am with you; I will bring your offspring from the east, and gather you from the west . . . . Bring My sons from afar, and My daughters from the ends of the earth, everyone who is called by My name, and whom I have created for My glory. (Isa. 43:1-7)

In God's infinite wisdom it pleased him to manifest his glory to a body of created angels and created image-bearers. Why? Because he knew it would be an infinite and perfect good for there to be others, outside of the Trinity, to contemplate, engage, and enjoy his glory—the awesome, heavy, majestic wonder of his complete personality. We were created to have the joy of knowing and worshiping him. We are the beneficiaries of this act of pure *grace*.

God knows himself perfectly. And God loves himself perfectly. But God's self-love is not to be compared with human perverted, egocentric self-love. God does not seek his creature's love and adoration *for his own sake*. God is restoring us, his redeemed children, to a new state in which we can fully enjoy his awesome nature and his manifold benefits. As recipients of such blessings we grow in our love for him, and in so doing we worship him from our heart. We do not add to or take away from God by our love and worship of him; but we do glorify God in this way by showing forth the fulfillment of his eternal plan to have a people who would come to see his awesome glory and reflect it back to him. God manifests his glory to us *for our sake*.

Readers may still object to such interpretations by asking, "Do we not grieve God? Do we not impact him emotionally?" (Ps. 78:40; Isa. 63:10; Eph. 4:30). God has been eternally grieved by our foreknown sins. His omniscient foreknowledge of every sin, united with his holy character, is manifested in his perfect and eternal grief.[24] This is why Jesus Christ was crucified—in the mind of God—before the foundations of the world were ever laid.[25] God has also had the attribute of wrath throughout eternity. The consequences of sin will be dealt with, one way or another—by redemption or hell. When we grieve God, it is a current event for us, but it is the actualization of an eternally foreknown event for God. He has been eternally grieved by our particular sins. We realize that we do indeed grieve him in the present time by our sins. Let us then, by God's grace, seek to "lay aside every encumbrance and the sin which so easily entangles us" (Heb. 12:1-3; 1 Peter 2:1-3).

The aseity of God is awesome and mind-boggling to contemplate. His absolute independence of all that is external to him is so unlike us. All that is external to him is dependent upon him. All created beings are needy by nature. We were created so we might acknowledge our Creator as the provider of every good and perfect gift that he bestows on us to satisfy our needs (James 1:17).

Our deepest need is to truly know God—the Father, Son, and Holy Spirit. To know him is to have eternal life (John 17:3). The contemplation of God's *aseity* is a broad highway to humility and gratitude for us—two attitudes that should grace God's adoptees (Mic. 6:8; Isa. 57:15; 66:2; Col. 2:6-7; 1 Tim. 4:4; Heb. 12:28; Rom. 14:6). It is humbling to realize that every breath we take depends on God's goodness. Every law of the universe stays its course because all things hold together through Christ (Col. 1:17; Heb. 1:3). The heavens and the earth will roll up like a scroll and disintegrate when he ceases to sustain them (Isa. 34:4; Rev. 6:14; 2 Peter 3:10).

It is humbling to realize that God has no obligation toward his creation, except those he has freely taken upon himself *for Christ's sake*—his promises made to us. The *heart* that grasps the truth regarding God's unsearchable goodness to his dependent creatures cannot but overflow with gratitude and praise. O Lord, help us see your absolute *aseity!*—for in it rests the fact that your love is free, fixed, and not subject to fits of passion and anger as is ours. May we love the realization that you, O Father, give us everything out of your heart of love for Christ's sake!—this includes your gift of us to him as "his inheritance"! (Eph. 2:18).

God's Eternal Nature

A friend of mine chastised me one day for having spoken at length about God's eternal nature. He said it was a waste of everybody's time to discuss a matter we would eventually have to acknowledge was beyond our understanding. I responded with a question, "If God deemed his eternal nature important enough to reveal it to us, should we not grasp as much understanding of it as we can and *then* admit its incomprehensible quality?" He insisted that we

---

[24] Those who struggle with God's knowing everything before it happens, because they presume that such requires a fatalistic structure to reality, should contemplate Ps. 139:15-16 while being assured that Scripture nowhere countenances fatalism or determinism. God's perfect foreknowledge is simply inscrutable (Isa. 40:28).
[25] See Rev. 13:8.

would be better off studying only those things that we could get our minds around. I reminded him that every attribute of God eventually leads us to the transcendent realm, because his every attribute is both eternal and infinite.

It is exceedingly rewarding to be filled with true knowledge of God's eternal nature. We become aware of ourselves in the midst of an ongoing time continuum. God created the time continuum but exists beyond its limitations. He is eternal, outside of time. But I was born in 1933. I have never known anything but a time continuum. Because we enter life in the midst of the continuum we have less trouble conceiving of a never-ending future than we do with the notion of a past with no beginning. It is easier to think of not having an ending than it is of not having a beginning. We have not experienced a life that had no beginning. But God is unlike us. He has always existed. He had no beginning! "Before the mountains were born or You gave birth to the earth and the world, even from everlasting to everlasting, You are God" (Ps. 90:2).[26]

We struggle when we think about *eternity* because we attach time to its meaning. We presuppose that eternity cannot be understood apart from some construct of time, for we are time-bound creatures. We, therefore, make more progress in our thinking if we identify eternity with God, not time. God is eternal. He has an eternal duration. His eternal nature is one of his attributes. He alone is eternal. Time is not eternal. Time is associated with sequencing within the confines of a spatial construct. God existed before there was any spatial construct; there is no sequencing in God's nature. In fact, being eternal connotes a negative attribute—it denies God a measure of time! When we say he is eternal, we are declaring that God is timeless.

Stephen Charnock (1628–1680) wrote *Discourses upon the Existence and Attributes of God* (posthumously published in 1682), in which he said:

> Time began with the foundation of the world; but God being before time, could have no beginning in time. Before the beginning of the creation, and the beginning of time, there could be nothing but eternity. . . . To be in time is to have a beginning; to be before all time is never to have a beginning, but always to be. . . . It is as easily deduced that he that was before all creatures is eternal, as he that made all creatures is God. If he had a beginning, he must have it from another, or from himself; if from another, that from whom he received his being would be better than he, so more a God than he. He cannot be God that is not supreme; he cannot be supreme that owes his being to the power of another. He would not be said only to have immortality as he is (1 Tim. vi. 16), if he had it dependent upon another; nor could he have a beginning from himself; if he had given beginning to himself, then he was once nothing; there was a time when he was not; if he was not, how could he be the Cause of himself? . . . He that is not, cannot be the cause that he is; if, therefore, God doth exist, and hath not his being from another, he must

---

[26] Also see: Gen. 21:33; Pss. 9:7; 41:13; 93:2; 102:27; Jer. 10:10; Hab. 1:12; 1 Tim. 6:16; 2 Tim.1:9; Heb. 1:10-12; Rev. 4:9-11.

exist from eternity. Therefore, when we say God is from and of himself, we mean not that God gave being to himself; but it is negatively to be understood that he hath no cause of existence without himself. Whatsoever number of millions of millions of years we can imagine before the creation of the world, yet God was infinitely before those.[27]

The concept of time involves *sequencing*—a thing or event following after a prior thing or event. God existed eternally before he created the sequencing phenomenon. There was no time sequencing prior to creation. God's existence and essence are eternal and unrelated in any way to sequencing. No aspect of God's personality stands in relationship to any other dimension of God's personality in a sequential order. God's holiness was not sequentially developed. God's knowledge was not sequentially gleaned and stored. God's mercy did not suddenly appear at an opportune moment when needed. God has not sequentially developed his power to a point where it can now be called infinite. God has for all eternity been absolutely holy, omniscient, merciful, and omnipotent. God has eternally been perfect. He did not grow up to be God. He has always been completely God. If there was sequencing within God's personality, then God would not be immutable (eternally unchanging), which he is (Heb. 13:8; Mal. 3:6; Ps. 102:26-27).

God's eternal character means that his existence has been and will be forever. It also underlines his eternal perfection with regard to every aspect of his nature. Every aspect of every attribute is eternal. God is the I AM of eternity (Ex. 3:13-14). God is the only One who is eternal life; he is Life (John 1:4; 5:26; 11:25-26; 14:6). None besides God has life as a self-possessed attribute. All others who possess life have it as a gift from God (John 1:4; 5:26; 11:25-26; 14:6). God's children inherit eternal life, when we inherit Christ who is Eternal Life (1 John 1:2). God gives his children everlasting life—a life that will never end—and that eternal life is Christ.

Numerous comforts for us flow from contemplating God's eternal nature. For example, our parents will forsake us in their death (Ps. 27:10), but God has promised that he will never forsake us (Heb. 13:5). Only the eternal One can make such a promise. That only God possesses an eternal nature is a reliable affirmation of the truth that Christ is God—he was before times eternal (Col. 1:16-17; John 8:8; 17:5; Isa. 9:6; Mic. 5:2). All knowledge—past, present, future, and suppositional—is always, without interruption, wholly present in God's consciousness. We can rest assured that our God knows what he is doing. He knows what he allows to happen. He has promised to use it all for our good (Rom. 8:28-29). God also knows the sequences of time and all that occurs in them, but he does not personally come to know things sequentially. He knows the tomorrows perfectly, today. Recognizing God's eternal nature is a humbling experience. How can we dare doubt or question the counsels and actions of such an awesome One? But we

---

[27] Charnock, Stephen, *Discourses Upon the Existence and Attributes of God*, vol. 1, 281-282.

do question him, and we shouldn't! His eternal perfection is the everlasting assurance of his children's eternal well-being.

God's Infinite Nature

Everything created is *finite*. Everything related to God's personhood is *infinite* (Ps. 147:5; Isa. 40:28; Rom. 11:33; Job 11:7-8). God's being and attributes are without bounds; they are innumerable and infinite. Because they are infinite, they are inscrutable. How marvelous it is to know that God is beyond understanding. One so large in every dimension of his nature quickly exhausts our finite limits of comprehension. How terrible it would be to have a God who could be reduced to our limits of understanding. That the finite could grasp the infinite would speak poorly for the infinite. Paul could never have written, "Oh, the depth of the riches both of the wisdom and knowledge of God! How unsearchable are His judgments and unfathomable His ways!" (Rom. 11:33). If the infinite were comprehendible by the finite, the very idea of being innumerable (beyond counting), inscrutable (beyond understanding), or unsearchable (beyond finding out) would be meaningless. The finite would be as the infinite.

As eternity is outside of the bounds of time, infinity is outside of the parameters of measurement. Infinity is the unity of continuous continuity (it just keeps going) that describes the boundless nature and character of God. God, and God alone, is infinite. Every aspect of God is infinite. Every attribute of God is infinite in its perfection and dimension. If any quality or quantity of God were not infinite, God would be an incomplete and imperfect God.

God is spirit, and as such he is an eternal and infinite spirit. His spirit has always been and is everywhere. King David confessed: "Where can I go from Your Spirit? Or where can I flee from Your presence? If I ascend to heaven, You are there; if I make my bed in Sheol, behold, You are there" (Ps. 139:7-8). God's omnipresence is a manifestation of his infinity. He is everywhere. God is omnipotent, too—all-powerful. How powerful is God? He is infinitely powerful (Heb. 11:3; Ps. 62:11; Rev. 4:11; 19:1). God is infinitely holy. His holiness is infinitely pure and perfect. God is infinitely good and infinitely wise. To be infinite is to be God.

These first three attributes of God are not attributes that we mortals partake of in our redeemed nature. We are never going to have the quality of aseity. We will never be infinite. And we can never claim to have been eternal. We will, by God's grace, have everlasting life but never as it refers to eternity past. But we can grow in our gratitude, humility, security, peace, joy, trust, and love as we contemplate these majestic qualities found only in God. He possesses these attributes; we are the beneficiaries of them.

God's Omniscient Nature

God's knowing everything seems innocent enough on the surface. But when the teaching is pondered, and we see that it not only includes all past and current knowledge but also all future knowledge, along with all possible outcomes, this attribute of God can be disturbing. Why? Because to believe that God is all-knowing—and he is (Ps. 147:5; Isa. 40:28; 11:2)[28] —implies, to those troubled by the doctrine, that God's perfect foreknowledge of everything requires that everything is fatalistically predetermined. This corollary belief, that everything must be fatalistically predetermined if God has perfect foreknowledge, is incompatible with God's revelation of himself. It also would reduce him to a God who resembles us. The awe-inspiring revelation is that humans do freely exercise their will in keeping with their nature, but that God has from all eternity foreknown what our free choices and their consequences would be because of his infinite knowledge of our nature. This seems to our finite minds to be impossible. It is, of course, impossible for mere mortals to have such knowledge. But it is not at all impossible for God. This truth simply presents us with another inscrutable mystery. But to reject the Bible's clear teaching regarding God's omniscient character is to reduce his character to the level of our own capacity for knowledge!

God's knowledge is infinite. There is nothing beyond his knowing. God's knowledge is eternal. He has known everything—past, present, future and possible—throughout eternity. Knowledge is inherent to God's independent eternal and infinite nature. God never obtained knowledge. He is knowledge; and humans grow in knowledge. God is the wellspring of all knowledge. God knows all things distinctly—absolutely and fully (1 Cor. 13:12). We know nothing fully. God knows all things infallibly (Isa. 14:24; 46:10). We know sufficiently, but never perfectly or exhaustively. God knows all things immutably (Ps. 139:1-6, 16; Isa. 46:9-10). Our knowledge is ever changing. God knows all things perpetually. He is always in the act of knowing all things, for all things are present eternally before him. Nothing is ever out of his focused consciousness. And God did not come upon his knowledge sequentially. All knowledge has been, for eternity, a part of God. His omniscient nature is an attribute of his personality.

The things just said are hard even to retain in the conscious level of our minds for they bespeak of a reality that transcends us. They are nevertheless true, for God has told us so.

As previously stated, the affirmation that God knows all things past, present, future and possible causes consternation for some Christians. God's foreknowledge and suppositional knowledge are the two that transcend our comprehension, while we maintain the integrity of free human choice. Here is a prime illustration of where a misconstrued presupposition—believing that God has perfect foreknowledge must lead us to believe in fatalism or determinism—can mislead us. To reject God's infinite and eternal foreknowledge is to reject a foundational truth regarding his nature. Can Scripture put to rest such reservations?

---

[28] The word understanding is used in each of these biblical passages to connote that God's knowledge is always related to his meaning and purpose for a particular thing's existence. God's knowledge is not disconnected or composed of irrelevant trivia. All things are relevant to him.

Scripture tells us God possesses infinite and eternal knowledge. This includes foreknowledge, even the foreknowledge of every person's nature—unregenerate and regenerate—so that what people freely do has been eternally foreknown by God. Four biblical illustrations highlight this truth:

> Your eyes have seen my unformed substance; and in Your book were written all the days that were ordained for me, when as yet there was not one of them. (Ps. 139:16)

> Since his [our] days are determined, the number of his [our] months is with You, and his [our] limits You have set so he [we] cannot pass. (Job 14:5)

> They divide my garments among them, and for my clothing they cast lots. (Ps. 22:18—a detailed prophecy made centuries before it occurred.)

> I am God, and there is no one like Me, declaring the end from the beginning, and from ancient times things which have not been done. (Isa. 46:9-10)

Can there really be any doubt about God having infinite and eternal foreknowledge? Have God's prophecies—revelations of his foreknowledge—ever failed to become reality? To doubt God's foreknowledge is either to renounce the authority of Scripture—make God out to be what he cannot be, a liar—or in our minds to make him into someone like us.

And God's suppositional knowledge is simply unheard of or ignored by most Christians. It also seems to offer less of a psychological threat to people than does his foreknowledge. What is *suppositional* knowledge? It knows the possible outcomes of alternative courses of action that will never actually take place, but could if other choices were made. Here are three biblical accounts that highlight this type of divine knowledge.

> Woe to you, Chorazin! Woe to you, Bethsaida! For if the miracles had occurred in Tyre and Sidon which occurred in you, they would have repented long ago in sackcloth and ashes. (Matt. 11:21)

> Then David said, "O LORD God of Israel, Your servant has heard for certain that Saul is seeking to come to Keilah to destroy the city on my account. Will the men of Keilah surrender me into his hand? Will Saul come down just as Your servant has heard? O LORD God of Israel, I pray, tell Your servant." And the LORD said, "He will come down." Then David said, "Will the men of Keilah surrender me and my men into the hand of Saul?" And the LORD said, "They will surrender you." Then David and his men, about six hundred, arose and departed from Keilah, and they went wherever they could go. When it was told Saul that David had escaped from Keilah, he gave up the pursuit. (1 Sam. 23:10-13)

> But the Pharisees and the lawyers rejected God's purpose for themselves, not having been baptized by John. (Luke 7:30)

God knows infinitely and eternally all of the other possible outcomes that would occur if we took alternative courses of action. Such knowledge is inscrutable.

God is truly omniscient. This is a dimension of his character that can offer us enormous solace. We can be certain that God is never surprised, caught off guard, or needs to stop and figure out "Where do we go from here?" There are no hills or curves in life that obscure God's knowledge of what is ahead for us. We can be certain that God knows what he is doing. He is Lord over all. And more than that, we can have confidence that he will lead us both by his Word and his merciful providence in paths of righteousness for his name's sake (Ps. 23:3).

What of us? Do we possess past, present, future, and suppositional knowledge? All people have some knowledge of the past. Non-Christians living in this era of relativism question the accuracy of anybody's knowledge of the past, but Christians who know the Scripture truly know those things recorded in its historic accounts. The Holy Spirit superintended their recording. And we know much that is associated with our personal history. The same is true for our knowledge regarding our present experiences that are tomorrow's history. People possess some past and present knowledge, as incomplete and imperfect as it may be. We do partake, in a limited degree, of this aspect of God's character—we possess some past and present knowledge.

But do we have access to any future and suppositional knowledge? Yes, but very limited amounts. The promises of God that are still waiting to be fulfilled are certain to occur at their appointed time in the future, and we can know now that they will occur. That Christ is coming again is an example of foreknowledge. God has given us this foreknowledge. Other kinds of future knowledge, though not as certain as God's promises, are also part of our God-given ability to know. Future plans constitute a form of foreknowledge. James might refer to this as "If-the-Lord-wills" knowledge—our plans will work out if they are in keeping with God's will (James 4:15). We all make plans for many things in life—vacations, buying homes, going grocery shopping. Many of these plans work out as planned, while some do not. Humans are futuristic in their orientation as well as historic and contemporary.

We even make stabs at suppositional thinking. Looking down the road sometimes causes us to change our minds about projected behavior—it has an unhealthy-looking outcome. Competitive strategies are often built around a survey of possible actions, and many are eliminated before a final decision is made because of probability of failure. Examining probable consequences before specific actions are undertaken is a means of attempting to presuppose potential outcomes. And there is wisdom in undertaking such contemplations.

God has told us of his willingness to impart to us aspects of his ability to truly know the past (biblical history); the present (spiritual discernment); the future (his promises); and suppositional knowledge (his applied wisdom, and the consequences of ignoring it). Our knowledge, however, is nothing compared with his; but he does want to impart more knowledge than most seem eager to receive.

God's Patient Nature

Christians sometimes quip, "Don't ask God for patience or he may hear your prayer and put you in an extremely trying situation that requires a lot of 'patience practice.'" Such quipping acknowledges that the speaker knows just how hard patience is to come by in his or her own character. If you have children, you have many memories of having your patience stretched to its limits. Or if you have a friend who is always late, you know what it is to grow impatient. We have to learn patience. God has no such need; he is by his nature patient. But we are never intentionally to try his patience. God's patience is surely tested enough by the residual consequences of our fallen nature as he patiently forms Christ in us.

Scripture assures us, however, that the LORD is slow to anger (Nah. 1:3). Throughout Scripture God's patience is closely associated with his longsuffering with his people, and with restraining his wrath. Humans are faced with the need for two kinds of patience: one related to longsuffering as we live with other humans; the other related to contending with the need to endure. God's patience is only manifested, however, in its relationship to his longsuffering with his image-bearers. Stephen Charnock stated in his discourse on God's patience:

> Slowness to anger, or admirable patience, is the property of the divine nature. As patience signifies suffering, so it is not in God. The divine nature is impassible; incapable of any impair, it cannot be touched by the violences of men, nor the essential glory of it be diminished by the injuries of men; but as it signifies a willingness to defer, and an unwillingness to pour forth his wrath upon sinful creatures, he moderates his provoked justice, and forbears to revenge the injuries he daily meets with in the world. He suffers no grief by men's wronging him, but he restrains his arm from punishing them according to their merits; and thus there is patience. . . . This attribute is so great a one, that it is signally called by the name of "Perfection" (Matt. v. 45, 48). He had been speaking of divine goodness, and patience to evil men, and he concludes, "Be you perfect," &c., implying it to be an amazing perfection of the divine nature, and worthy of imitation.[29]

If there were no divine patience, there would be no time for divine mercy. If there were no time for divine mercy, there would be no time for repentance, forgiveness, and salvation. Without God's perfect patience, Adam and Eve would have been destroyed immediately following their fall, and with them their posterity—us. God's attributes of grace, mercy, patience, kindness, and goodness are all prerequisites for our salvation (Ps. 145:8-9). We are to regard the patience of our Lord to be salvation (2 Peter 3:15). And why does God manifest his patience toward us? "For the sake of My name I delay My wrath, and for My praise I restrain it for you, in order not to cut you off" (Isa. 48:9). We were created for God's glory (Isa. 43:7); God's glory is manifested in his patience.

Patience in God's children is referred to as a fruit of the Spirit (Gal. 5:22). It is clearly an attribute God wants to impart to his children. It is imparted, but not by infusion. Rather, it is built, by one test after another. By overcoming the urge to be

---

[29] Charnock, *Discourses Upon the Existence and Attributes of God*, vol. 2, 477-478.

impatient we build patience. Spirit-built patience also relies upon self-control in many cases, another fruit of the Spirit.

Summary

Contemplating God's *aseity* (absolute independence from the created order) should cause us to echo John the Baptist's statement regarding Christ: "He must increase, but I must decrease" (John 3:30). It leads to an elevated view of God, and a sobering view of mankind. God does not need anything, including us, but he loves us.

God's *eternal* nature is outside of time. He is eternal; time is a created phenomenon involving sequencing. God's attributes have been eternally existent and eternally perfect. God did not grow into being God. He did not mature. He is the eternal I AM.

God is *infinite*—beyond measurement—having absolute perfection in every dimension of his personality. He is qualitatively and quantitatively infinite.

God is *omniscient*—knowing everything in the past, present, future, and all possible outcomes. God does not learn, nor is he ever surprised by any event. God is knowledge; God is eternal and infinite knowledge.

God is *patient*—he restrains his wrath and provides time for his mercy to bear in us the fruits of repentance and forgiveness that accompany salvation, which is given us for the sake of Christ: "For by Him all things were created, both in the heavens and on earth, visible and invisible, whether thrones or dominions or rulers or authorities—all things have been created through Him and for Him" (Col. 1:16).

Conclusion

The Christian's world/life-view can be enlarged and enriched by meditating on both the knowable and the transcendent (inscrutable) aspects of God's attributes. Christians ought to reflect on all revealed aspects of God's character and peer into the expanse of his unfathomable character to be simultaneously awed and humbled by his grandeur. The tendency of our fallen nature is either to have a self-focused interest in God because of what he can do for us, or to create a God in our own likeness. Such a God is, at best, distorted. At worst, the created God is no Divinity at all. In either case, we miss the greater blessing—the blessing of truly knowing the God who is behind the gracious provisions we enjoy. May God bless us with a yearning to truly know him, the One who is Trinitarian.

3

The Trinity: Our Model and Mentor

*I will give them a heart to know Me, for I am the Lord;
and they will be My people . . . . (Jer. 24:7)*

What a promise! But I am in my seventies and do not yet even know *myself* fully. Indeed, there is the old me that struggles and fights against the new me. It is a blessing that the old me does not have dominion over the new me, but there is conflict within of which I cannot completely rid myself (Rom. 6:11-19; 7:15-25). Can I truly know myself then? And if so, what path must I tread to come to know myself?

The biblical answer is revealed in Christ's paradoxical statement: "He who does not take his cross and follow after Me is not worthy of Me. He who has found his life will lose it, and he who has lost his life for My sake will find it" (Matt. 10: 38-39). To be focused on self is the path of death. Taking up our cross means dying to oneself, as we follow Christ. And as we follow Christ we come to *know* him; and as we come to know him we come to know the Father and the Holy Spirit. To know the Father and the Son is to have eternal life (John 17:3)! And what has God promised, but that he will give us a heart to know him?

It is important for Christians to contemplate the mystery of the Trinity. No one can fully comprehend there being one God in three Persons: Father, Son, and Holy Spirit. We cannot fathom how the three members of the Godhead are one. The incredible fact that the three are one, in perfect unity while assuming diverse roles in their mutual relations, is justification enough to examine the Godhead. But more importantly, God who has revealed himself to us as one-in-three gave us this clear yet incomprehensible revelation of himself so we would know something of his relational roles within the Godhead. Is it not in our own relational roles that we encounter the worst and best qualities in ourselves? Is not our very nature revealed in our relationships? Knowing God in his relational dynamics can only increase our comprehension and heighten our desire to become more like him in our own relationships with him and one another.

The church traditionally discusses the Trinity in the context of each member's role in our redemption. We learn from Scripture that the Father sent his Son, Jesus Christ, to become a man to live a sinless life. Why? So that he could offer himself as an atoning sacrifice to redeem us from eternal death. Christ reconciles us with the Father by his death and resurrection (Rom. 5:10). The Holy Spirit brings us to Christ, our Savior. Those in Christ are set free to enjoy fellowship with the persons of the Trinity. This traditional teaching is important, but I will focus on what we can learn from the personal relationships between the persons of the Trinity that is *transferable* into our own relationships.

There is one God in three persons—God the Father, God the Son, and God the Holy Spirit—united in the eternal Godhead. The Son has been eternally begotten from the Father, not created (John 1:14, 18), and the Holy Spirit has eternally proceeded from the Father and the Son (John 15:26; Gal. 4:6). The unity within the Godhead is so perfect that Scripture tells us that if one member of the Trinity is with us, the other members are also present (John 14:7-11, 16-18, 23). Yet the persons of the Godhead are simultaneously three distinct Persons, each with an assumed role. The three are one; the one is three. And this is where our minds can go no further; It transcends our finite ability to comprehend.

Even though the doctrine of the Trinity exceeds our comprehension, God wants us to learn much about his intentions for us—how we should relate to one another—by observing how the members of the Trinity do so. He wants us to see their relationship in Scripture so we can understand his desires for us regarding our earthly relationships.

From the beginning God, in his infinite wisdom, ordained a number of positive coworking tensions that, when in proximity to one another in the fallen order, create what appear to be conflicting tensions. A physical law example of positive coworking tensions is centrifugal force and gravity, which pull in opposite directions and so hold the earth in its designated relationship to the sun. Another example of a positive coworking tension (though often experienced in a negative form) is our desire to be free of personal constraints while recognizing our need for self-control. Who among us has not experienced *that* tension? We will examine five perceived tensions that exist in our interpersonal relationships which are modeled perfectly in the relationships between the persons of the Godhead. We can glean much of the wisdom embodied in God's directives regarding how we should live together by examining God's personal relationships in the Godhead.

There are created realities that often seem to be opposed to one another. For example, we often view equality and inequality in that light. Someone might ask, "What is the conceptual framework in which we should view these seemingly competing dimensions of reality? Are they concepts that are generally found reflecting unity or should they be viewed as irreconcilable? And if the conflicts we believe ought to be in harmony are found in disharmony—how do we reconcile them?"

The Trinity serves as a reconciling model. Harmony and perfect unity exist between the members of the Godhead. Every aspect of their relationship is perfect and is a model to be emulated! The thesis is simple: God has revealed the interpersonal relationships that exist between the persons of the Godhead so we can observe a model in the Scriptures, understand it in our hearts, and emulate it with the help of the Holy Spirit.

The following is an outline of five positive tensions we will examine. They point us to perfections revealed in the Trinity and call to mind the tensions *we* encounter in the same areas.

TRINITY	**HUMANITY**
Equality/Inequality	Equality/Inequality
Authority/Submission	Authority/Submission
Individual/Community	Individual/Community
Rights/Responsibilities	Rights/Responsibilities
Freedom/Control	Freedom/Control

Equality/Inequality

Equality in the Godhead: There is absolute equality between the three members of the Godhead: God the Father, God the Son, and God the Holy Spirit (Matt. 28:19).[30] Each member is truly God. Every attribute of God ascribed to a particular member of the Godhead is ascribed to the other two persons as well.[31] In their equality they are to be equally honored, adored, feared, and devotedly served. There is neither distinction in their worth nor the possibility of their being of different minds (John 5:19, 30; 6:38; 8:28-29). The three are truly one God, united in their eternal perfection and sharing a perpetual equality as God.

Inequality in the Godhead: Equality between the members of the Godhead pertains to their essence, their inherent nature. But there is also a discernible inequality between them as it pertains to their actions, their assumed roles. There is a true difference in the roles each has assumed. These functional differences are referred to in theology as the economy of the Godhead. God the Father, for example, has from all eternity been the Head of the Godhead (John 1:14; 6:37; 17:1-6; 14:26; 15:26). The Father is the author of all things—"from whom are all thing" (1 Cor. 8:6). But God the Son is the Creator of all things—"by whom are all things, and we exist through Him" (1 Cor. 8:6; Col. 1:16; John 1:3). And the Holy Spirit brought form to the unstructured earth (Gen. 1:2) and renews the face of the ground (Ps. 104:30).

The Head of the Godhead—God the Father—reveals himself as Father. God is called Father over 110 times in the Gospel of John alone.[32] We are adopted into his family (Rom. 8:12-17). The second person of the Trinity—God the Son—is the only member of the Godhead who took on flesh and came in the likeness of man (Phil. 2:5-8). The Son of God obeys the Father, not vice versa (John 5:26; 6:57; 8:16-18; 14:28). Yet the Father gave his Son a people and a kingdom, before times eternal (Matt. 11:27; Luke 22:29; John 6:37; Titus 1:1-2 and 2 Tim. 1:9).

The Holy Spirit is presented as the Helper, Comforter (*paracletos*; John 14:16). He is the guide, teacher, comforter and the one who convicts God's

---

[30] See also Matt. 3:16,17; 22:41-46; Mark 1:10-11; John 1:1, 2, 14, 18; 16:7-15; 17:5.
[31] Edward Bickersteth (1825–1906), while engaged in addressing the heresies of Unitarianism in his day, wrote *The Trinity* (Grand Rapids, MI: Kregel, 1959).
[32] See also Ps. 89:26; Isa. 63:16; 64:8; Jer. 3:19; 2 Sam. 7:14.

children (John 16:7-15). The Holy Spirit represents himself always as subservient to the Father and the Son (John 14:26; 15:26; 16:13-14).

In sum: Each member of the Trinity assumes a different role as he associates with the created order, while remaining equal with the other persons of the Godhead. God has modeled a perfect illustration of the unity and harmony which can exist between *equality* and *inequality* (diverse and unequal roles). Each member of the Godhead accepts his role without resentment or jealousy regarding the other members' roles. Our fallen psyche, however, has considerable difficulty holding these two realities in equilibrium. We delight in equality in some situations and find it offensive in others. The same is true in our reflections about human inequality. We give lip service to its appropriateness in one situation and chafe about it in another. Pride and arrogance seem to foster perspectives on equality and inequality that differ from those generated in a humble and self-effacing heart. And who among us has not discovered that both arrogance and humility inhabit our heart?

Human Equality

Absolute equality exists between: males and females; people of all races and nationalities; the bright and the dumb; the rich and the poor; the sick and the healthy; and the old and the young. The sanctity and worth of individuals' lives are neither enhanced nor diminished by such diversities. We all possess the same worth regardless of our life's experiences. Scripture affirms this truth in three ways. First, all humanity has been created in the image of God (Gen. 1:27; 5:1-2; 9:6). Second, we all have one natural father, Adam, in whom we all fell (Rom. 5:12-21). Adam is our common head from whom we all acquired our sin nature after the fall. And third, God is no respecter of persons (James 2:1-7, Eph. 6:9; Gal. 2:6; 3.28).[33] He calls his children from every nation, tribe, and tongue (Dan. 3:4; 5:19; Rev. 5:9; 7:9).

The implications of this are profound. All human beings are authentic persons. They belong to God, not to us, a corporation, or a government. All people deserve the respect God affords them. Another's personhood is as valuable as our own, regardless of our stations in life. We should not demean or undermine anyone's personal worth or dignity. "There are no little people and no big people in the true spiritual sense."[34] But the disrespect of one individual for another prevails too often. If we really believed in equality in our hearts we would exhibit more of the fruit of the Spirit (Gal. 5:22-23) in our conversations about, and relationships with others. We often do not treat friends and enemies the same; but God does (Matt. 5:44-48; Luke 6:27-38).

---

[33] See also Rom. 2:11; Acts 10:34; 2 Chron. 19:7; Deut. 1:17; 10:17.
[34] Francis A Schaeffer, *No Little People* (Downers Grove: InterVarsity Press, 1974), 17.

Human Inequality

A bugaboo for fallen humanity is just how to cope with apparent natural inequalities. The human community, for example, struggles with many issues related to distributive justice. How should scarce resources be distributed? Should *fairness principles* be followed in making distributions: i.e., give equal shares, or at least amounts that are based on needs? Or should *due principles* be followed in distributions: reward people's efforts, merits, or contributions? Egalitarians, socialists, progressives, and communists answer the question, "Use the 'fairness principles'!" They generally desire a form of government redistribution of wealth to equalize the natural inequalities that arise for many reasons. Libertarians and utilitarians answer, "Use the 'due principles'!" They tend to believe that people should not be required by those in authority to relinquish the fruit of their labor or good fortune. They claim that the relinquishment of one's wealth should be voluntary and not compulsive.

Should individuals who are stronger, more intelligent, or better positioned by birth, be allowed to enjoy the benefits derived from their advantages—inequalities—or are such advantages undeserved, and therefore their benefits should be taken away? People's world/life-views diverge exceedingly on these matters. And Christians frequently do not agree with one another. If Christians cannot agree on such matters while having the Scripture to guide them, what chance is there for a peaceful resolution regarding such matters anywhere in the world?

God's Word also teaches our obligation to honor people who from God's perspective are due respect. For example, our parents, regardless of our age or theirs, are to be honored (Matt. 15:3-9). Those who rule over us are to be respected (Rom. 13:7). And those who are charged by God with our spiritual oversight are to be considered worthy of double honor (1 Tim. 5:17). The concept of honoring is attached to the worth of the position (differentiated role), not merely to meritorious performance by the person in the position. To illustrate, true widows are to be honored (1 Tim. 5:3), and husbands are to honor their wives (1 Peter 3:7). All positions ordained by God are honorable. They are to be assumed in service to him and not with a spirit of jealousy regarding others' position or rewards, but in a sincere commitment to Christ.

Here is the crux of the issue: How does contemplating the unity and role diversity modeled by the Trinity help Christians deal with tensions when encountering the world's perversions of God's ordained *inequalities* in abilities and roles? And further, what of the ungodly emotions we encounter in ourselves when our personal perception of what is fair and just regarding role diversities or exceptional abilities is violated? How are we to deal with these emotions? The first question is the easier to answer. We are to apply God's truth wherever it is needed, and thereby to seek justice in every arena of life. Both role and ability differentiation are God-ordained and are, then, to be recognized, honored, and rewarded. Moreover, we need to remember that God has declared, "From everyone who has been given much, much will be required; and to whom they entrusted much, of him they will ask all the more" (Luke 12:48).

The second question goes to the heart of the issue. The Spirit of God is at work in his people to create godly attitudes and a spirit of contentment. Attitudes of covetousness, greed, jealously, resentment, and selfishness rule people's lives far too frequently. Such attitudes foster discontentment. Scripture speaks of the attitude of the righteous (Luke 1:17) and urges us to have the self-emptying attitude of Christ (Phil. 2:5-17). A true knowledge of God and his sovereign purposes can foster the creation of a godly attitude in us that can in turn lead to a *learned contentment* (Phil. 4:11-13; Luke 12:15-34; Heb. 13:5-6; 1 Tim. 6:6-11). This heart-transforming work, however, is under the sole authority of the Holy Spirit. No one else can affect it.

Authority/Submission

Authority in the Godhead: Jesus Christ is the eternally-begotten Son of the Father (John 3:16, 18; Ps. 2:7). The Father alone has authority over the Son (John 10:29; 14:28). This authority was exercised when he sent his Son to become the incarnate, savior God (John 17:3, 8). Furthermore, the works the Father wanted the Son to do (in his humanity) were assigned to him by the Father (John 17:4; 4:34) and first taught to him by the Father.[35] He also had the authority to give his Son an inheritance—those who were to be saved (John 6:37, 44-45, 65; 17:6, 9). The Father had the authority to give his Son all authority over mankind (John 17:2). The Father also gave everything in creation to his Son (John 3:35; Luke 10:22). The Father had full authority to do these things as they were first his, and he had the right to give them to his Son.[36]

God the Father also exercises his authority regarding the work of God the Holy Spirit. It is the Father (along with the Son) who sends the Holy Spirit to dwell in and with his children (John 14:16, 26; 15:26). The Holy Spirit could, but does not, speak to God's children on his own initiative (John 16:13); he speaks, teaches, and guides, according to what he hears from the Father and the Son. He is subservient to them (John 14:16).

God the Father is the first person of the Trinity. God the Son is the second person of the Trinity. God the Holy Spirit is the third person of the Trinity. This concept of a ranking in the Trinity is an ancient formulation reflecting the economy within the Godhead. It represents a positional hierarchy that has existed throughout eternity.[37]

If the Father, Son and Holy Spirit live and work in the context of a positional hierarchy, it is logical to believe that the persons of the Trinity would want us to live in unity and harmony in the context of some type of hierarchical

---

[35] There is an insoluble mystery in the perfect unity in Christ of two complete natures—the divine and the human.
[36] The Son was eternally begotten of the Father. The Father was not begotten of the Son.
[37] Both 2 Tim. 1:9 and Titus 1:2 conclude with the Greek phrase "before times eternal," so we can infer that the positional hierarchy has always existed.

structure. And God *has* revealed his mind regarding a family structure and a church structure. It is amazing, however, how many want to alter God's declared structure and set up a different one in the name of modern thinking. Hermeneutical debates rage over the interpretation of God's Word in these two foundational areas.

Submission in the Godhead: God the Son voluntarily, with delight, submitted to the will of the Father (John 5:30, 36; 6:38). Christ came to do his Father's will, not his own. Yet in his humanity Christ acknowledged that the will of the Father was difficult to rejoice in during specific trials (Matt. 26:39, 42; Mark 14:34-36; Luke 22:42-44). And the Father on more than one occasion sent a ministering angel to strengthen Jesus in his agony (Mark 1:13; Luke 22:43). But Christ perfectly submitted to the Father's will always. Indeed, Christ said, "My food is to do the will of Him who sent Me and to accomplish His work" (John 4:34). The implication is that Jesus derived inner, spiritual strength from doing the Father's will.

The Father asks us to emulate Christ and to do his will. Christ even asks, "Why do you call Me, 'Lord, Lord,' and do not do what I say?" (Luke 6:46). And he warns, "Not everyone who says to Me, 'Lord, Lord,' will enter the kingdom of heaven, but he who does the will of My Father who is in heaven will enter" (Matt. 7:21). God has revealed the submission that exists between the persons of the Godhead as an example for us. We too are to learn how to live submitted to the will of others above us. I am afraid that we too often pick and choose whom we will submit to, rather than learning and following God's prescription.

God the Holy Spirit also lives in submission. He, upon the determination of the Father and the request of the Son, goes to reside in the lives of the individual children the Father has given the Son (Luke 11:13; John 14:16; 15:26). The Spirit's work is to glorify Christ and not himself (John 16:14; 7:39). He is the one who superintended the writing of Scripture (2 Peter 1:20-21; 2 Sam. 23:2; Acts 1:16). It is he who takes the Word of God and uses it to cleanse us (Titus 3:5; Eph. 5:26). It is he who brings us to Christ. It is through faith in the finished work of Christ that we are saved. We are not saved through faith in the Spirit's work, although we do believe that the Spirit both dwells in us and works in us. He is subservient to Christ and the Father (John 14:16).

A life lived in godly submission is not the life of a sub-standard person. Our culture and our old nature both tell us that a submissive role is a demeaning role. Does the Holy Spirit have a demeaning role? The question demands a loud negative answer. The Holy Spirit is truly God and shares an eternal and infinite equality with the other persons of the Godhead. His submissive role only adds to his glory. His work does not draw as much attention as that of Christ or the Father. But his work in our lives is every bit as significant as the work of the other persons of the Trinity. The Holy Spirit is our tutor, trainer, and comforter. He is God with us. He is Christ in us. Oh, how eternally grateful all Christians will be for his longsuffering, kindly work with us, for it is with *difficulty* that the righteous is saved. (1 Peter 4:18) The Holy Spirit works hard to save us!

Human Authority

Words such as "authority," "leader," "boss," and "head" all serve as synonyms at different times. They connote the right of a person or group to make decisions, give directions, and order others to do their will. People's use of authority probably discloses as much about their core personality as anything does. The sin nature that permeates the heart pulls people to use their authority in self-serving ways.

Godly people may be transformed attitudinally and behaviorally to see those under them as authentic people whose worth is to be respected. But generally those in authority conceive of subordinates as means to an end, even while rewarding them well as employees. God does not judge by what the eye sees or the ear hears (as we must) but he looks on the heart of those in authority. He knows what the true motives are (Isa. 11:3; Jer. 17:10).

> No matter how we may dress up the language of leadership, Christ said: You know that the rulers of the Gentiles lord it over them, and their great men exercise authority over them. It is not this way among you, but whoever wishes to become great among you shall be your servant, and whoever wishes to be first among you shall be your slave; just as the Son of Man did not come to be served, but to serve, and to give His life a ransom for many. (Matt. 20:25-28)

Christ recognizes our propensity to promote self-inflated grandiosity and warns us about self-serving attitudes (Matt. 23:11; Mark 9:35; Phil. 2:5-16). Christ's authority and godly human authority are rooted in *love* and *service*. To root authority elsewhere is to pervert it.

Years ago when the language of servant leadership began to become popular, and I was Chairman of the Board at a Christian college, I suggested to board members that we avoid servant leadership language. I noted that our old nature would gradually gravitate to the leadership aspect and *forget* the servant aspect! Instead, I suggested that we emphasize the biblical call to be servants and have a curriculum that focused on calling the students to be servants. The suggestion died quickly. The response was, "Who would pay good money to have their children educated to be servants? Leaders, yes, but servants, no!" There was a bit of laughter, and the matter died a quiet death.

Human Submission

The word "submission" typically carries a negative connotation. It is generally thought to be a compulsively based, dehumanizing placement of one person under another. Culturally, the notion of necessary submission is accepted at the intellectual level *for others*—for those in the military, for example. But the general idea of submission is psychologically repugnant to fallen minds. We tend to think of oppression when the idea comes up. We want to be politically correct, so we speak of sanitary engineers rather than of janitors, or of sales associates rather than of salespersons. This is done to remove the stigma of being in a lowly (subordinate) position. If elements of gender or race enter a discussion of submission, the temperature of those discussing it is even more likely to rise.

Biblically, the concept of submission is a positive one when the parties involved are seeking God-ordained relationships. For example:

Employer/employee relationships
(Eph. 6:5-9; Col. 3:22-25; 1 Tim. 6:1-5; Titus 2:9-10)

Husband/wife relationships
(1 Peter 3:1-6; Col. 3:18; Eph. 5:15-24; Gen. 3:16)

Parent/child relationships
(Eph. 6:1-4; Col. 3:20-21; Prov. 6:20; Ex. 20:12)

Citizen/governor relationships
(Rom. 13:1-7; Titus 3:1-2; 1 Peter 2:13-17)

God calls us to submission, in the name of, and for the sake of Christ (Eph. 6:5-7, 9; Col. 3:22-24; 1 Tim. 6:1-3).[38]

God calls us to roles of submission because these roles reveal the optimal structure for relationships he has designed. We can ignore God's design but cannot expect him to bless our design as he would his own. God also wants us to assume roles voluntarily. The designs are for our benefit, not God's. The voluntary submission of our will to Christ's is a mark of our love for him. A clear expression of God's desire for us to submit voluntarily to Christ is when Paul identifies himself as a *doulos*—a *voluntary* bond-slave whose will is consumed in following his master's will (Rom. 1:1; Phil. 1:1; and Titus 1:1). Indeed, gladly to accept a submissive role designed by God is a mark of his special grace at work. The person in submission is not in the role because he has less value than the person he submits to, but he has been trained by the Holy Spirit to understand that God's blessings and love accompany his design.

Individual/Community
God—the Three Persons

Scripture clearly teaches that there is but one God, in three persons, of one substance[39] (Deut. 6:4; 1 Cor. 8:4, 6; Matt. 28:19; 2 Cor. 13:14). Each of these divine persons is distinct. Each has a personal identity. They are each identified in Scripture by the use of personal pronouns. And each bears his individual name(s).

God the Father is called Father by Christ over 110 times in the Gospel of John alone (John 2:16; 4:23; 5:17, 20-23 are a few examples). The Father has revealed himself as the Head of the Godhead (Deut. 4:15-16; John 4:24; Luke 24:39), and he has chosen to reveal himself as the Father, in spite that he is without a sex gender. Christ repeatedly refers to God the Father as "he," "him," "himself," indicating his individuality (Matt. 12:27; John 5:38; 6:27, 29, 38, 39). The Father also clearly identifies himself as an individual. For example, at Christ's baptism the Father said, "This is My beloved Son, in whom I am well-pleased" (Matt. 3:17;

---

[38] Also read: Titus 2:10; Col. 3:18; 3:23-24; Eph. 5:22; 6:1; 1 Peter 2:13, 15-16.
[39] Substance, in this instance, is not referring to materiality but a quality of spirit that is indefinable, for God is spirit.

also see Ps. 2:7 and Isa. 42:1). This same declaration was made at the time of Christ's transfiguration (Matt. 17:5). God the Father has revealed himself as a divine person.

God the Son is distinct from the Father and the Holy Spirit. He, too, is a person.[40] Christ affirms his individuality in numerous ways. For example, he said, "I have come down from heaven, not to do My own will, but the will of Him who sent Me" (John 6:38). Hebrews joins the chorus of Scripture by quoting Prophets and the Psalms that witness to the unique person of Christ and his unique role of Sonship. Christ is declared to be the one worthy of angelic worship, the righteous one, the eternal King, the Creator, and the eternal, sovereign ruler of all (Heb. 1:5-14). Again, Scripture uses numerous personal pronouns to refer to Christ (Rev. 1:8, 17-18; John 1:1-4). Christ the Son is a person.

God the Holy Spirit is a person, also.[41] He has properties and actions that can only be ascribed to an independent and wholly intelligent personality.[42] The Spirit has intelligence (2 Cor. 2:10-11), affections (Rom. 15:30; 5:5), and a will (1 Cor. 12:11; John 3:8; Acts 16:6-7). In addition, he performs many actions that can only be performed by persons. For example, he convicts the world of sin, righteousness, and judgment (John 16:8). He performs miracles (Ezek. 3:12; 8:3; Acts 2:4; 8:39; Rom. 15:19). He inspired the sacred writers (2 Peter 1:21). He speaks expressly of events in the latter times (1Tim. 4:1). He appoints ministers in the church (Acts 20:28). He commands and forbids (Acts 8:29; 11:12; 13:2; 16:6-7). He intercedes for us in prayer (Rom. 8:26). And he teaches, comforts, and guides us into all truth (John 16:26).

God—the Trinity as Community

The agreement and unity between the three persons of the Godhead is so absolute, infinite and eternal that they are to be contemplated as one God. There is but one God, in three Persons. This unity is so great that Christ could say in response to Philip's request that he show the disciples the Father:

> Have I been so long with you, and yet you have not come to know Me, Philip? He who has seen Me has seen the Father; how can you say, 'Show us the Father'? Do you not believe that I am in the Father, and the Father is in Me? The words that I say to you I do not speak on My own initiative, but the Father abiding in Me does His works. Believe Me that I am in the Father, and the Father in Me; otherwise believe because of the works themselves. (John 14:9-11)

"Hear, O Israel! The LORD is our God; the LORD is one! And you shall love the LORD your God with all your heart and with all your soul and with all your might" (Deut. 6:4-5). The declaration is clear: The LORD our God is one. The New Testament has the same clarity: "There is no God but one, and . . . there is but one

---

[40] Bickersteth, *The Trinity*, 24-38.
[41] Edward Bickersteth, *The Holy Spirit: His Person and Work* (Grand Rapids: Kregel, 1959).
[42] Ibid., 40.

God" (1 Cor. 8:4, 6). Both Testaments consistently declare that there is only one God and he alone is to be worshiped.

The mystery of personality and unity of the Trinitarian persons is once again before us. We cannot fully comprehend it, but *we are attracted to it*. I am attracted to it as it regards my life with God. I too want to be one with the Trinity—collectively and individually. And I am attracted to it as it regards my relationship with my wife. We are two individuals with Christ as the Head of our union, but our growing in oneness over the decades of our marriage is real and wonderful. The mystery of individuality and unity grows sweeter, if not more explainable, as our relationships with God and our best friends continue to mature.

Human Individuality

There are different traditions in the Western church regarding God's call. The Reformed tradition emphasizes the call of the individual. This has resulted in a cultural pull, over the centuries, toward radical individualism.[43] Those in the Mennonite tradition have a different sense of God's calling, a communalized one. They are called to die to self and make a commitment to serve the community of believers.[44]

The tensions between our being simultaneously an individual and a member of a community are as old as the fall. We are individuals who are accountable to Christ for our every thought, word, and action (Rom. 14:12; 1 Peter 4:5; 1 Cor. 4:5; Prov. 16:2). We will each give an account for our sins. Fathers are not accountable for their children's sins; and children are not accountable for their father's sins (Jer. 31:29-30; Ezek. 18:20). God has known each of us as individuals before times eternal and gave us to Christ as an inheritance before we existed (Titus 1:1-2). Furthermore, Christ made it clear that "of all that He [the Father] has given Me I lose nothing, but [will] raise it up on the last day" (John 6:39). Scripture highlights our individuality by revealing that God has waiting in heaven a special name for every heir of eternal life (Rev. 2:17).

The Holy Spirit distributes spiritual gifts to each individual just as he wills for the building up of the body of Christ (1 Cor. 12:11). Every member of God's family is given a spiritual gift. We are individually saved (1 Cor. 12:11), individually sanctified (2 Thess. 2:13), and will be individually glorified (Rom. 8:17, 30).

Human Community

There are three primary communities in which God involves his children. The Holy Spirit, therefore, gives instructions for the building up of each of these communities—the family, the church, and the world.

The godly family begins as a reflective microcosm of the Trinity—Christ is the Head; the husband is the second person; and the wife is the third person in the

---

[43] Calvin Redekop, Stephen Ainlay, and Robert Siemens make this point in *Mennonite Entrepreneurs* (Baltimore: The Johns Hopkins University Press, 1995).
[44] Ibid.

bonds of marriage—an earthly trinity. Christ is the true head of both the husband and the wife (1 Cor. 11:3; Eph. 1:22; 5:23). God created Eve from the pre-created substance of Adam (Gen. 2:21-23). They shared a common substance. She was created and brought to Adam because Adam was in need of a helper *corresponding* to him (Gen. 2:18; 1 Cor. 11:9). They—husband and wife—are joined together and they are one in the sight of God—one substance reunited as one flesh in marriage, according to God's purpose (Matt. 19:5-6).

Humans are at all times simultaneously individuals and connective beings. The human genesis (post-Adam) is derived from a connective union (1 Cor. 11:11-12). Our life is sustained through Christ's constant connective relationship with us—a preserving work (Col. 1:17; Heb. 1:3). And we are given talents and spiritual gifts for the purpose of serving others (Rom. 15:2; 1 Cor. 12:7). Being connective is integral to our overarching purpose.

Scripture teaches that the (invisible) church is the body of Christ and that we members are to be united in peace and harmony for the common good (1 Cor. 12; Rom. 12:4-13; Eph. 4:1-16). This is clearly the intended purpose of God and is only possible under the Holy Spirit's superintending work. We are one body in Christ (1 Corinthians 12:12-27).

As for the rest of the world, with its myriad of institutions and organizations, Christ wants his children to be light and healing salt in its midst (Matt. 5:13-16). We are called to live at peace with all people, insofar as it depends upon us to do so, while remaining faithful to Christ (Rom. 12:18).

Rights/Responsibilities
God's Rights

Any discussion of God's rights must be primarily developed from biblical *inferences*, though there are some forthright statements which make it very clear that God does what he chooses to do. For example, when Paul addresses the church in Rome he made the following point:

> You will say to me then, "Why does He still find fault? For who resists His will?" On the contrary, who are you, O man, who answers back to God? The thing molded will not say to the molder, "Why did you make me like this," will it? Or does not the potter have a right over the clay, to make from the same lump one vessel for honorable use and another for common use? (Rom. 9:19-21)

The Philippians were told, "It is God who is at work in you, both to will and to work for His good pleasure" (Phil. 2:13). The Bible simply presents God as God. It does not argue for his authority or rights. It simply presents God in all his glory, and reveals his acts toward us. His awesome character simply carries with it his right to do whatever he chooses.

His character, however, circumscribes his rights. There are people who object to the idea that God can be said to have any limitations, but his rights are embodied in his nature. It is in this sense and this sense only that God can be said to be limited. He cannot not be God. He cannot become mutable when he is eternally and infinitely immutable. He cannot become unholy. God cannot, by his very nature, be or do anything that would violate his divine nature.

God is purposeful and "works all things after the counsel of His will" (Eph. 1:11). He is absolutely sovereign. He does what he will, and his will reflects perfectly his character. *God has an eternal, infinite, and inherent right to do whatever he chooses to do.* Every other so-called right thought of by humanity must be analyzed in the light of God's self-possessed rights. All rights external to God are *derived* rights, rights that God establishes. As we shall discuss shortly, all human rights that are genuine rights are rights God has granted us.

God's Responsibilities

Being the only autonomous and sovereign I AM WHO I AM, God is only responsible to himself. There is no external accountability associated with God. It is said of him, "He has mercy on whom He desires, and He hardens whom He desires" (Rom. 9:18).[45] He does what he will without being answerable to anybody.

The concept of responsibility is associated with God only in the sense that he has voluntarily willed to place himself under certain commitments. These commitments might be said to be God's obligations (responsibilities). For example, God has made certain promises to his image-bearers, both the unregenerate and regenerate, and we may infer that God therefore has a responsibility to keep his word. Such responsibilities are to be understood as self-imposed. God undertook them out of no necessity or obligation to the created order. They were undertaken as a manifestation of his personage.

God's covenants with his people are examples of his assuming certain self-accepted obligations. For after all, God cannot lie or break his word (Num. 23:19; Titus 1:2; Heb. 6:18). God initiated the covenants with mankind. God set the terms of the covenants; there was no negotiating. We see God making a covenant with Abraham in Genesis 15, and still another covenant with him in Genesis 17. The Old Testament records a number of God's covenants with his children. There is, in fact, only one covenant made by God that includes more than his image-bearers in it. It is God's covenant with Noah, after the flood, in which he included "every living creature that is with you, the birds, the cattle, and every beast of the earth with you; of all that comes out of the ark, even every beast of the earth" (Gen. 9:8-11). And centuries later, Christ declared his own blood to be the blood of the covenant (Matt. 26:28; Heb. 9:20).

What a blessing it is to know that God has accepted the responsibility to keep his covenants. Even the requirements God places on us in the covenants are fulfilled by us through the Holy Spirit's work. To illustrate: We are *commanded* to

---

[45] This difficult passage is to be understood as follows: Subsequent to the fall, everyone is born with a heart that is ungodly and that will, by its nature, become hard in the presence of God. God does not take regenerated hearts (hearts of flesh) and harden them, but his very presence hardens the clay heart (unregenerate heart) to yet harder stone.

"love the LORD your God with all you heart and with all your soul and with all your might" (Deut. 6:5). But who can obey such a commandment? Can we will ourselves to do what our nature does not allow us to do? God himself answers: "Moreover the LORD your God will circumcise your heart and the heart of your descendants, to love the LORD your God with all you heart and with all your soul, so that you may live" (Deut. 30:6). God commands and he enables us to fulfill his commandments.

The demand of the new covenant made in Christ's blood, is that we truly *believe* that he died to pay the price for our sins and that we are forgiven and are thereby reconciled to the Trinity through his finished work. Who can create saving *faith* in the heart of a person? What is the *genesis* of saving faith? Faith that leads to salvation is a free gift of God, placed in our heart by the Holy Spirit (Rom. 12:3; Eph. 2:8; 4:7). Faith is the beginning evidence of the Holy Spirit's work of circumcision. He and he alone circumcises hearts.

Human Rights

Human rights are only definable (and defensible) in the light of God's special revelation. Such rights manifest God's grace to us. True rights are a gift from God (James 1:17) and are not merited. Many have defined what they call rights, but their so-called rights are indefensible without a transcendent basis.[46] The founding fathers of our nation understood this when they spoke of inalienable rights[47] and produced the Bill of Rights.[48] John Warwick Montgomery, in *Human Rights and Human Dignity*, speaks of three generations of human rights.[49] But mankind has begun playing god and assigns rights to more and more categories of human wants and non-human things in the environment—animals, bodies of water, trees. Such rights are mere human preferences and lose their warrant when unsupported by God's Word.

God's intended rights for his image-bearers can be garnered from his Word. For example, humans have the right to worship God (Ex. 20: 3-6; Deut. 6:1-5, 13-15); a right to one day of rest in seven (Ex. 20:8-11; Lev. 26:2); a right to life (Ex. 20:13; Matt. 5:21-26); and a right to seek private property (Ex. 20:15, 17; Lev. 19:11, 13). And we are commanded by God to protect the rights of the mute, the afflicted, the needy, orphans, widows, and the poor (Prov. 29:7; 31:8-9). God hates oppression (Isa. 3:14-15; Eccl. 4:1-2) and loves true godly freedom (Rom. 6:17-23). Whenever we speak of human rights we ought to ask ourselves, has God assigned them to us? If not, they are not inalienable.

---

[46] John Warwick Montgomery unfolds this reality in *Human Rights and Human Dignity* (Grand Rapids: Zondervan, 1986).
[47] The Declaration of Independence (paragraph 2) says ". . . all men. . . are endowed by their Creator with certain inalienable Rights."
[48] The first ten amendments to the Constitution of the United States are called the Bill of Rights.
[49] Montgomery, *Human Rights and Human Dignity*, 26-29.

Human Responsibilities

Scripture has a great deal more to say about human responsibilities than human rights. This is a manifestation of our fallen nature to be concerned about our rights, but it is contrary to that nature to be oriented toward our God-defined responsibilities. God's Word has a lot to say to us about these. For example, God finds fault with employers for driving their workers hard (Isa. 58:1-7, esp. v. 3). And God requires us "to do justice, to love kindness, and to walk humbly with your God" (Mic. 6:6-8)

God's Old Testament precepts lay out a litany of our responsibilities both toward God and toward our neighbors. This law is good for the Christian to meditate on for it reveals the perfect will of God. But the law must be used lawfully (1Tim. 1:8). It must not become our measure for our righteousness, for Christ alone is our righteousness (1 Cor. 1:30). A study of the law reveals our imperfections and provides us an opportunity to be grateful for God's mercy in not giving us what we deserve—but to appreciate his grace for giving us what we do not deserve. The sin that the law reveals also affords the opportunity to ask God to continue the work of sanctification in us he has already begun.

The standards set before us in the New Testament are as high as those placed before us in the Old Testament, but with a more intense focus. The New Testament focuses more on our *heart*, our *attitudes*, and our *responses* to God and our neighbors, and not just our conduct. While these matters are clearly present in the Old Testament, they do not have the primary focus that they do in the New Testament. Nevertheless, both Testaments clearly set forth our responsibilities before God.

Freedom/Control

God's Freedom

God is absolutely free to be God. God is not free to violate his nature. It is, in fact, God's very nature that determines true freedom. What is outside of God's nature is license. Therefore, freedom (from the human perspective) is always to be conceived of as a *qualified* possibility or state. There is no such thing as absolute, unqualified freedom. Rather, God is free *to* . . . ; God is free *from* . . . ; God is free *for*. God is not simply free in some abstract sense. Each member of the Godhead enjoys absolute freedom within the immutable antecedent of his nature.

Philosophers and theologians have been interested for centuries in the subject of freedom as it relates to free will. In light of the above paragraph, does God have free will? God is free to exercise his will within the constraints of his infinite and eternal nature. God is not free to exercise his will in any manner that would contradict his nature. This reality is very important, for it has important implications for discussion about human will.

Insofar as there can be true freedom, it must be seen in the light of God's freedom. There are no constraints, *external to God*, to mar his possessing absolute freedom. His omniscience, omnipotence, wisdom, and holiness afford him perfect freedom to do as he wills. He alone embodies true freedom as a self-possessed reality, and thus does whatever he pleases (Pss. 135:6; 115:3; Dan. 4:35).

God's Self-control

God the Father, God the Son, and God the Holy Spirit perfectly manifest what we call self-control. God's *patience* with his image-bearers is a manifestation of his self-control. God has no need for self-control in the relationships that exist within the Trinity. God's desire to be patient with us manifests his mercy and grace. He exercises self-control (patience) for the sake of his own name (Isa. 48:9). It is impossible for God ever to be out of control. Yet it *is* possible for God to cease *showing forth* his self-control—for his patience can come to an end regarding a particular individual or group (Num. 16:1-35; Gen. 18:16-33; 19:1-29; Acts 5:1-11).

God has no inner conflicts in his personality to trigger the need for one aspect of his nature to overrule another aspect. The unity, perfection, and wholeness of his personality eliminate the possibility of God's ever *needing* to control himself. God's self-control has no genesis in a need. Its genesis is in his love, for God is love (1 John 4:8, 16).

If there were no divine patience, there would be no time for divine mercy. And if that were the case, there would be no time for repentance, forgiveness, and salvation. Without God's perfect patience, Adam and Eve and all their posterity, including us, would have been destroyed immediately following the fall.

Human Freedom

Unregenerate humans are slaves to their fallen nature (John 8:34; Rom. 6:16-23; 2 Peter 2:19). They are only free to sin—to pervert God's expressed will and to seek their own will. They are "dead" to God (Eph. 2:1-10; Gen. 2:17). Even their best righteousness is like a filthy garment before him (Isa. 64:6). Even "a good act" performed by an unregenerate person—one that helps others—is regarded by God as unclean because the thoughts and motives behind the act were not covered by the righteousness of Christ (1 Cor. 4:5; Prov. 16:2; 1 Sam. 16:7). The unregenerate freely exercise their will, but it is a will that leads them to the second death (Prov. 14:12; Rev. 2:11; 20:14-15).

Regenerate Christians are mildly schizophrenic. We struggle at different times, and to varying degrees, with our old nature. We are to count our old nature as dead (Rom. 6:1-14; 7:14–8:17). But the children of God, thankfully, have a new nature (2 Cor. 5:17; Eph. 4:24; Col. 3:10). We are a new creation (Gal. 6:15). We are in our new regenerate state, free from our former slavery to sin, and are given the freedom and power to pursue righteousness (1 Tim. 6:11; 2 Tim. 2:22; John 1:12). The Spirit of God, using the Word, trains God's children to live within the righteous parameters established by God. Without the guidance and help of the Holy Spirit all humans will stray into licentiousness—a disregard for the bounds of godliness (Rom. 3:10-18; Pss. 14:1-3; 5:9; Isa. 59:7-8). As children of God, we will be chastened by God daily as the Spirit shows us our deviations from God's revealed character (Job 7:17-18). For example, while we are driving to work an external stimulus may bring to our mind ungodly thoughts that are immediately followed by a conviction of conscience—which leads to prompt confession and request for forgiveness. We confess and plead with God to continue his sanctifying work in us so that we may become more like Christ both inwardly and outwardly (Luke 11:37-41).

Christ came to free us from sin—the consequences of our past, present and future sins, and the enslavement to our old nature (Rom. 8:2; 2 Cor. 3:17; 1 Peter 2:16). Jesus said:

> "If you continue in My word, then you are truly disciples of Mine; and you will know the truth, and the truth will make you free." They answered Him, We are Abraham's descendants and have never yet been enslaved to anyone; how is it that You say, 'You will become free'? Jesus answered them, "Truly, truly, I say to you, everyone who commits sin is the slave of sin. And the slave does not remain in the house forever; the son does remain forever. So if the Son makes you free, you will be free indeed." (John 8:31-36)

Human Self-control

Self-control, like freedom, is vastly different for human beings than for God. People are mutable and fallen; God is immutable and holy. Christians even have a divided nature—an old nature to be counted as dead, and a new nature being empowered to put off the old and to put on the new (Eph. 4:22-24; Col. 3:8-10). To put on the new is to put on Christ (Gal. 3:27). To put on Christ is to become like him, degree by degree. To do this is to grow in self-control, a fruit of the Holy Spirit (Gal. 5:22-23).

Scripture says, "He who rules his spirit [is better] than he who captures a city" (Prov. 16:32). Impatience, one of the primary ways we exhibit our faltering self-control, is manifested in many forms. My wife has helped me to become conscious of my muttering when other drivers do not drive as I want them to. To date, though, there has been no road rage. God is gracious! But the Lord, my wife, and I know that I struggle with impatience. Delays in air travel can try our patience. Slow service in a restaurant can try our patience. In fact there is no area in life where patience cannot be tested if other people or events do not meet our expectations. This may embarrass us, but God knows it is true. We might as well confess it. But having our patience tried while not losing our self-control is good. Peter tells us that self-control produces perseverance, and perseverance leads to godliness, and godliness leads us to brotherly kindness—love (2 Peter 1:6-7). This is what Proverbs 16:32, quoted above, commends: "He who rules his spirit [is better] than he who captures a city."

Conclusion

God the Father, God the Son, and God the Holy Spirit are one God. The living and dynamic relationship between the three divine persons is a *model* for God's children. God alone can impart to us the wisdom we need to desire and seek his very nature (Heb. 12:10; 2 Cor. 3:18; 2 Peter 1:4) whereby we may harmonize the positive co-working tensions that often confound us.

The tensions just discussed—(1) equality/inequality (role diversity); (2) authority/submission; (3) individual/community; (4) rights/responsibilities; (5) freedom/control—are irreconcilable and unfathomable in the context of fallen human nature. They are often seen as contradictions rather than as complements that glorify one another. They generate philosophical differences between well-meaning people. Only God's nature and behavior make sense out of them and bring conceptual harmony to their coexistence. Only the Holy Spirit can harmonize them in our lives. The Trinity is truly our *mentor* as well as our *model* in these matters. May Christ continue to renovate us into his likeness so we may show the world that these perceived tensions are really sources of blessings in God's economy.

4

God Is Spirit: The Reality Necessitating Faith

God is spirit. (John 4:24)

Few Christians reflect on the significance that God is spirit. Typically this fact is either taken for granted or overlooked. My wife, upon reading an early draft of this chapter, said, "I never gave much thought to 'God is spirit.' I learned as a nine-year old in catechism class that the answer to the question, 'What is God?' was 'God is spirit, and has not a body like men.' I simply accepted the fact without reflection on it." She accepted a truth without comprehension.

Ah, the faith of a child! I was not taught anything about God's nature as a youngster. Furthermore, as a young boy I had learned to distrust people, and this distrust made the topic of living by faith in someone whom I could not see disquieting. How was I to trust someone whom I had not seen if I could not trust those whom I had seen? The Holy Spirit eventually came to my rescue.

Faith, for most people, embraces the simple notion of believing: "I believe this or that." That is why polls reveal that a large percentage of people consider themselves Christians even though their lives do not reflect the tenets of the Christian faith. Belief, to such people, simply means giving intellectual assent to an idea. It does not require them to live in accordance with their religious profession. Biblically, this is hypocrisy!

The Holy Spirit, on the other hand, elevates beliefs in the lives of committed Christians to a level where they truly trust God and live a life consistent with their beliefs. Belief and willingness to live it out become synonymous. My personal spiritual development was emotionally painful because of my *lack* of trust. Because I could not trust various visible individuals, how could I trust an invisible God? The Holy Spirit, however, used the truth that God is spirit to help me through the trust crisis I faced.

If the Spirit of Christ does not dwell in people, they will rarely think about anything spiritual. Their reality typically revolves around things material, rational, and emotional. The death of a loved one may stimulate brief reflections on ideas related to life after death—but even these passing thoughts are typically limited to physical images of the departed and not to spiritual matters. Christians, too, generate physical images when thinking about a departed loved one, but they have thoughts about their loved one's spirit departing the body and entering God's presence (Luke 23:43; Acts 7:59; Eccl. 12:7). We hear statements like "Dad is now with Christ," or "Mom is in heaven," which mean their spirit is now with Christ in heaven.

Those in Christ, while perhaps not having spent a great deal of time contemplating the quality of things spiritual, will nevertheless have an interest in things spiritual not generally present in non-Christians. We believe in the spiritual, that it is important and discernible, and we believe that *God is spirit* (John 4:24; 14:17; Rom. 8:16; Heb. 2:4).

That God is spirit and that we his image-bearers were created as incarnate spirits means that any true communication between God and us has to be spirit-to-spirit (Gen. 2:7). This reality can only be talked about meaningfully by acknowledging that it is permanently rooted in one's faith-based presuppositions regarding the nature of God and our nature. Such presuppositions are only provable or demonstrable by God, not by humans.[50] We will explore seven important presuppositions associated with the belief that God is spirit.

Presupposition # 1

Our mental conception of spirit is best understood as an aggregation of beliefs about a form of non-corporeal life, beliefs inductively arrived at through a process of *logical negation* applied to special revelation. It is much easier to state what a spirit is *not* (negation) than to say what a spirit *is* (affirmation). This reality is necessitated by our finitude, with its accompanying limited empirical sense-perceiving modes (taste, touch, smell, sight, and hearing) that cannot engage a spirit. Our finite characteristics prevent us from comprehending God's infinite aspects except through the process of logical negation. God's special revelation leaves us with this task. For example, Scripture tells us that God is *infinite* (2 Chron. 2:6; Job 11:7-8; Rom. 11:33) but in defining what this means we are forced to resort to negations, such as "God has no bounds" or "God is without limitations." We cannot affirm what is beyond our comprehension apart from God's special revelation that he is infinite. This reality forces us to state what infinity is by stating what it is not. Likewise, what God is not strengthens and affirms what God is.

Presupposition # 2

God, as spirit, has no bodily form. We know this from Christ's conversation with his disciples following his resurrection and from logical negation. He appeared to his disciples and they thought they were seeing a spirit. He said: "See My hands and My feet, that it is I Myself; touch Me and see, for a spirit does not have flesh and bones as you see that I have" (Luke 24:37-39, note the *logical negation*).

Readers may object, however, when we say that God as spirit has no *form*—even while accepting Christ's statements that God is spirit and a spirit lacks flesh and bones. That God is spirit and has neither flesh nor bones fully agrees with the statement that God has no corporeal or material qualities associated with his essential being. We use the word "God" to speak of God essentially and not

---

[50] The reality of spirit is not provable by the scientific method.

personally, as words like "Father," "Son," or "Comforter" denote him. So we might say that God as Christ took on the *form* of a man, and the Holy Spirit appeared in the *form* of a dove (Matt. 3:16; Mark 1:10; Luke 3:22; John 1:32) and as tongues of fire (Acts 2:3).

Even so, God has no *form*. This is one reason why we are commanded by God to make no representation of him:

> So watch yourselves carefully, since *you did not see any form* on the day the LORD spoke to you at Horeb from the midst of the fire, so that you do not act corruptly and make a graven image for yourselves in the *form* of any figure ... (Deut. 4:15-16. Also see: Ex. 20:4; Lev. 19:4; 26:1; Deut. 27:15).

Having no form, he may also be said to have no figure, no thickness, or length of body. Any of these descriptions, if expressed as affirmations, would violate God's infinite characteristic. Humans think of persons as having shape, size, and height. We have our feet on the ground and our heads in the air. But God has no such localization of his attributes. God is omnipresent—everywhere—and all of God's attributes are present everywhere. His mind is not in one part of the universe and his "arms" or "hands" (anthropomorphic terms used to describe his power) in another part.

Presupposition # 3

God is *invisible*. Paul wrote to Timothy, "Now to the King eternal, immortal, invisible, the only God, be honor and glory forever and ever. Amen" (1 Tim. 1:17). And Paul taught God's invisibility when he taught that Christ was "the image of the invisible God" (Col. 1:15). Further reinforcing this reality is the revelation that "the Father dwells in unapproachable light; whom no man has seen or can see" (1 Tim. 6:16). Indeed, no human "has seen God at any time" (John 1:18). God is not simply unobservable in the sense of being out of sight; he is unseen because he cannot be seen. His essence is undetectable by any of the corporeal senses.

Presupposition # 4

God is of a *spiritual essence* that is infinitely above any gross and corporeal matter. Corporeal matter has connective elements (cells, electrons, protons) that constitute its substance. God is spirit and has no connective elements in his being. This also means he has no *spiritual* connective elements in his being. God is not an infinitely-connected-together series of spiritual elements. He is a simple, pure, uncompounded being.[51] He is the I AM WHO I AM.

Presupposition # 5

If God were not a simple, pure, uncompounded being he could not be described as *immutable*. Compounded and connected things are sequenced—which means they arrived at their current state in some order of arrangement

---

[51] Charnock, *Discourses Upon the Existence and Attributes of God*, vol. 1, 182-183.

which necessitated change that is allowed by an original state of mutability. If mutability were a character of a spirit's beginning, it could revert to a previous state later. Immutability could not be an inherent condition of any compounded being.

Presupposition # 6

If God were not a simple, pure, uncompounded being he could not be described as *infinite*. Why is this so? Because sequencing is required for compounding, and infinity demands there be a unity of one, not a multitude of numbers. Infinity is independent of any form of measurement. God is a simple infinite unity, and his purity as a spirit rests in his simple unity.

> All multitude begins in, and is reduced to unity. As above multitude there is an absolute unity, so above mixed creatures there is an absolute simplicity. You cannot conceive number without conceiving the beginning of it in that which was not number, viz. a unit. You cannot conceive any mixture, but must conceive some simple thing to be the original and basis of it.[52]

> If God were not a pure spirit, he could not be one. If God had a body ... he would be made up of distinct parts, and those of a distinct nature, as the members of a human body are. Where there is the greatest unity, there must be the greatest simplicity; but God is one. As he is free from any change, so he is void of any multitude (Deut. vi. 4): The Lord our God is one Lord.[53]

God's other attributes, such as his aseity (absolute independence) and his omnipresence are also dependent upon his being a simple, pure, uncompounded spirit. He would be dependent upon his own parts was he not pure spirit.

Presupposition # 7

God is the Father of created spirits (Heb. 12:9), but as a spirit he must be conceived of as being infinitely above any idea associated with his human or angelic created spirits. The human spirit is likened to the breath of God (Gen. 2:7; 6:17; 7:22; Isa. 2:22; 42:5) symbolizing a non-corporeal *created essence*—not the uncreated essence of God. Otherwise we would view ourselves as *modes* of God in the pantheistic sense. Christians reject pantheism, for Scripture teaches us that we are a distinct creation, not made from God's essences. The air, which is invisible, has physical, gaseous qualities that are sensorial in character; and, likewise, created spirits are finite entities even while not being sensorially measurable. Our spirits occupy limited space.

The essence of God's spirit is as different from our created spirit as wool and a synthetic fiber differ. The difference is infinite. The same is true regarding angelic spirits. Even Satan, believed to be God's most powerful created spirit, is not to be compared with God in any manner whatsoever, as some people do. For

---

[52] Ibid., 183.
[53] Ibid., 184.

example, Rabbi Harold Kushner in, *When Bad Things Happen to Good People*, says, "I recognize his [God's] limitations. He is limited in what he can do ... [yet] I can worship a God who hates suffering but cannot eliminate it."[54] He later asks, "Are you capable of forgiving and loving God even when you have found out that he is not perfect? ... Can you learn to love and forgive him despite His limitations?"[55] Kushner implies that evil—and he believes in an angelic person named Satan—is as powerful as God. Scripture repudiates such a notion. It tells us that "the lawless one will be revealed whom the Lord will slay with the breath of His mouth" (2 Thess. 2:8). And it promises that "the devil who deceived them [will be] thrown into the lake of fire and brimstone, where the beast and the false prophet are also; and they will be tormented day and night forever and ever" (Rev. 20:10). Created spirits are as nothing when compared with God the eternal spirit.

God's essential nature—spirit—is incomparable to any created spirit. He is as infinitely above them in his essence as he is infinitely above them in his attributes. God is the most simple, pure, uncompounded, spiritual spirit that exists. Gold and aluminum are metal. Are they to be compared to one another? Superficially, perhaps, but their differences are profound. So it is when comparing God as spirit with one of his created spirits.

To summarize: God as a spirit has no bodily form. He is invisible and not discernible to our physical senses. He, in his *essence*, has no corporeal matter or connective elements, spiritual or otherwise, associated with his spirit. He is a simple, pure, and uncompounded being. And neither is the quality of his spirit to be likened to the quality of those spirits he has created. His spirit quality is reflective of his infinite and eternal nature, without beginning and boundless.

The Significance that God Is Spirit

God has told us that among all of his creatures only humans have been made in his image (Gen. 1:26-27; 5:1; Eph. 4:24; Col. 3:10). We are first going to discuss what it does not mean (negation) to be created in the image of God. Then we will have a quick look at what it does mean without any significant elaboration.

For over twenty years I asked students, in nearly one hundred classes devoted to Christian ethics, how many of them believe they are created in the image of God. The response has been close to a unanimous affirmation that they do believe this. But when I have asked the follow-up question, What does it *mean* when we say that we have been created in the image of God?, only one student, in all those years, was ever able to answer the question biblically. The initial answer—we are created in the image of God—was correct. But the content or meaning of that answer was misleading, for it was not grounded in Scripture.

---

[54] Harold S. Kushner, *When Bad Things Happen to Good People* (New York: Avon Books, 1981), 134.
[55] Ibid., 148.

Created in God's Image: Five Negations, One Affirmation

What follows are five commonly held beliefs about what it means to be made in the image of God, all of which are false. They do not reflect what the Bible says. Also included is one affirmation about what being made in the image of God means according to Scripture.

Negation # 1

Some people associate our being made in the image of God with the false concept that God has a material body with features similar to those of a human or some other imaginable creature. This idea was repudiated earlier in Presupposition # 2. God has no body, parts, or compounds associated with his being spirit. It is amazing, though, how many think of God as actually sitting on a throne in a physical body.

Negation # 2

Students frequently will start by pointing out the obvious—God is a Creator; no one with a Christian world/life-view will argue that point. And that humans too have the ability to build and create things is certainly true. These two facts lead them to deduce that this is one specific facet of what it means to be made in the image of God. This is good logic, but being built on a false premise it generates a false conclusion which plays right into the hands of humanistic philosophers and their distorted world/life-views.

How can two such truths generate a false conclusion? It is because they are built on a false premise. Nowhere does God equate his and our creativity with our being in his image. God had something totally different in mind when he declared that he would make mankind, male and female, in his image.

Furthermore, many other created creatures are endowed with creative abilities; but God has not described *them* as bearing his image. Birds build nests. They are creative; but they are not bearers of God's image. Beavers build dams in ponds and small rivers. They are creative, but they do not bear the image of God. Bees build hives and honeycombs. They are creative. But they too are not image-bearers of God. So it is false to equate creativity with being created in the image of God.

Christians who equate creativity with bearing God's image feed the extremists in the animal rights movement by tacitly implying that humans are merely more sophisticated animals—further evolved than lesser species. The only way for Christians to separate themselves from such humanistic presuppositions is to adhere to God's definition of what it means for us to have been made in his image. God alone has the authority to state his intentions. Being creative is not an aspect of God's definition of what it means for humans to be divine image-bearers. Creativity is an endowment from God, to be sure, but it is not one of the three biblical distinctives that are associated with humans alone.

Negation # 3

Many believe that it is humanity's ability to communicate complex thoughts and ideas that qualifies them as bearers of God's image. It is certainly true that humans do have the capability to express their thoughts through diverse forms of communication—body language, intonations, words, pictures, and sounds. However, animals and birds also have forms of communication that are interpreted by both their own kind and by perceptive humans. For example, before a very young child has learned to speak, he or she has already learned to communicate his or her thoughts by means of gurgling, whining and crying. A parent can distinguish between a cry of pain, a cry of hunger, and a cry of a thwarted will. But in the same way, a dog's master can grasp the significance of his pet's growling, whimpering, and barking, each of which has its own range of meanings. To illustrate: a dog may have a pretend growl when engaged in a tug-of-war with his master to gain control of an old towel that both are pulling on; this differs from a growl of warning when confronted with a stranger's unfamiliar actions. Animals definitely communicate, and their communication is interpretable by other animals as well as humans.

Even so, the greater sophistication of the human's communication does not properly qualify us for the belief that we are created in God's image. To claim our status on this ground seems logical enough, but once again it does not meet God's test—his definition of what it means to be created in his image. The Christian's use of such an unbiblical argument only plays, once again, into the hands of those who repudiate the Christian world/life-view. It does so by aligning the human with other created species—even if we are placed at the top of the list! We simply become another form of animal—a higher one perhaps, but another animal nonetheless.

Negation # 4

Still others believe that it is humans' ability to make intelligent choices that distinguishes them from the other animals as made in God's image. Once again, while this is an important human characteristic, it is not what distinguishes us from the other creatures, from God's perspective, the only one that matters. He did the creating, and he established the unique, distinguishing characteristics that place us above all of his other created creatures.

Even cows make rather sophisticated choices. It is from our observation of cows that we humans have coined the expression "The grass is always greener on the other side of the fence." Cows graze selectively. They carefully choose among clover, grass, and other foliage as they graze back and forth across a pasture. They have preferences and choose their favorites first. If their favorite clover or grass happens to be in short supply within the bounds of their field, they will stick their head through the fence and seek to get what they want on the other side. They are not dumb when it comes to their taste for their favorite food.

Choice-making is at its zenith with humans. But all living creatures make choices, and it is not a sophistication of choice distinction that sets humans apart as God's image-bearers. We can rightly claim it, for God has told us it is so. But we must be able to articulate it so as to distinguish ourselves from the rest of his creatures. We are not just further up the evolutionary scale for we have been discretely created.

Negation # 5

The final negation to be examined here is the belief held by many Christians that it is humans' higher intellectual capacity to think abstractly that sets us apart from all other creatures. They contend that this is the most important characteristic in our being God's image-bearers.

This notion has at least three flaws. First, one hundred percent of the human race can think, and does think, in concrete terms, but only about twenty percent of the population engages in abstract thinking as a matter of course. Second, this would imply that those who engage in abstract thinking are higher beings than their less-abstract-thinking counterparts. Third, the biggest flaw, however, rests with the fact that God does not list abstract thinking as one of the three distinguishing characteristics that uniquely describe us as bearing his image.

Most perplexing, however, is why Christians—people who bear God's image and profess to believe in such an important aspect of their personal identity—exhibit so little interest in learning what God says in Scripture concerning their being his image-bearers. Compounding the problem of ignorance is that many Christians have been authoritatively taught that our being in the image of God involves one or more of the notions that have been negated above.

An Affirmation

Here is a bare outline of the biblical teaching on the image of God. The Bible provides three windows into the mind of God regarding what it means for the humans alone to have been created in God's image. The first window is found in Colossians 3:10: "Put on the new self who is being renovated to a *true knowledge* according to the image of the One who created him." Simply put, this means that humans can truly know reality, as does their Creator God. But to believe as the postmodernists do, that the human cannot truly know anything, opens the door to a myriad of perversions that completely undercut the dignity and sanctity of the human—who was made just a little lower than *Elohim*, God himself (Ps. 8:5).

The second window is found in Ephesians 4:24: "Put on the new self, which in the likeness of God has been created in *righteousness*." Humans alone are innately endowed with the capacity to be righteous. We are moral beings. Dogs are not. Dogs are not immoral when they bite us.

The third window is a continuation of the second one: "Put on the new self, which in the likeness of God has been created in righteousness and *holiness* of the truth" (Eph. 4:24). Humans can be holy—a characteristic reserved for God's image-bearers. (There are no holy cows!)

Humans can have *true knowledge* (including knowing God) as God does, can be *righteous*, and can be *holy*. These three inherent capacities are the only things that uniquely distinguish the human from all other created creatures. The human's creative capacity, communication skills, the ability to make choices and think abstractly are more fully developed and sophisticated than in any other life form, but the possession of those latter capabilities is not what distinguishes humans from God's other creatures.

The Application that God Is Spirit

Two great necessities emerge from this discussion. First, all genuine communication between God and his image-bearers must be carried out on a *spirit-to-spirit* basis. And second, the reality that God is spirit means that we must *live by faith* if we are to have an intimate relationship with him. These two facts profoundly impact our daily lives.

The Necessity for Spirit-to-spirit Communication

Our big faith premise is that *God is spirit*. It was asserted, "His image-bearers were created as incarnate spirits. . . ." This assertion is another biblically-grounded presupposition. The biblical statement, "Then the LORD God formed man of dust from the ground, and breathed into his nostrils the breath of life; and man became a living being," [soul, Gen. 2:7 margin] implies that humans are embodied spirits. Scripture has much evidence of this. For instance, Christ's statement to the thief on the cross: "Truly I say to you, today you shall be with Me in Paradise" implies that the man's *spirit* would leave his body at death and go to Paradise (Luke 23:43). And Christ's last statement on the cross, as he breathed his last, "Father, into Your hands I commit My spirit" (Luke 23:46), means that Jesus understood that his spirit would leave his body for a period of time. My point is not to argue that humans are embodied spirits but to assert that this is what Christians have *believed*—held as a presupposition—from the time the faith began.

The human spirit is understood to house the human's *heart*—mind, passions (desires, affections, identity needs), and volition (will). The spirit, biblically, encompasses the life and activity principles associated with the human heart. And the Bible teaches that the spirit never dies (John 11:25-26). The Westminster Confession of Faith affirms that the human spirit is a distinct essence that was created to reside in the body, but can be separated from it:

> The bodies of men, after death, return to dust, and see corruption: but their souls [spirits], which neither die nor sleep, having an immortal subsistence, immediately return to God who gave them. The souls [spirits] of the righteous, being then made perfect in holiness, are received into the highest heavens, where they behold the face of God, in light and glory, waiting for the full redemption of their bodies. And the souls [spirits] of the wicked are cast into hell, where they remain in torments and utter darkness, reserved to the judgment of the great day. Besides these two places, for souls [spirits] separated from their bodies, the Scripture acknowledgeth none. [There is no Purgatory.]
>
> At the last day . . . all the dead shall be raised up, with the selfsame bodies, and none other (although with different qualities), which shall

be united again to their souls [spirits] forever. (chapter XXXII, paragraphs I & II)

The strongest biblical testimony, however, for the necessity for spirit-to-spirit communication is in Romans: "The Spirit himself testifies with our spirit that we are children of God" (Rom. 8:16). This great truth involves what Scripture declares to be the greatest mystery of the ages—*Christ in you* (Col. 1:26-27). Yes, Christians are the temple of the Holy Spirit (1 Cor. 3:16; 6:19). Three Scriptural truths unite these thoughts: (a) people *reborn* by the Holy Spirit, in response to God's will (John 3:3-8), (b) are given the Holy Spirit to indwell them (John 14:16-17), and (c) he subsequently persuades them that they truly are God's adopted children (Rom. 8:14-17).

Scripture reinforces the importance of spirit-to-spirit communion: "the true worshipers will worship the Father in spirit and truth; for such people the Father seeks to be His worshipers" (John 4:23). Here God distinguishes between the true and the false worshipers. True worshipers have a spirit-to-spirit relationship with him. Unregenerate people do not have such a relationship with God for they are alienated from God—dead to him (Gen. 2:17; Eph. 2:4-5). They cannot discern the mind of Christ revealed in Scripture (1 Cor. 2:14). Some may partially discern it, but they reject the truth because they are estranged from God. They are without excuse, however, for they do know God *sufficiently* to be held accountable for rejecting him (Rom. 1:18-21).

God communes spirit-to-spirit with his children through the application of Scripture to their hearts and his personal involvement in their lives. He gives them Christ's peace, convicts them of sin, and leads them to repentance. The Holy Spirit impresses the Word on believers' minds where it may be meditated on (Ps. 1:2). The written Word is used by the Spirit to teach, lead, and correct Christians. And the Holy Spirit brings the Word of God to their minds when they are called upon to share the Word as counsel or to evangelize (John 14:26; 2:22).

Christians respond to God's entering into an intimate relationship with them by pouring out their hearts to him in prayer. They express their adoration of him; they confess their sins to him; they offer him praise and thanksgiving; and they make known to him their hearts' desires. Before there is a word on our tongues, however, God knows it (Ps. 139:4; Heb. 4:13). He knows what we need and want *before* we ask him (Matt. 6:8). One might ask then, why pray if God knows everything before we even ask? We clearly do not pray to *inform* God of anything. But a heart made alive by God and aligned with him will pray. It is its new nature to do so. It cannot help but pray, for it is like an uninhibited spring of water that derives its source from the circulating depths of the ocean. The heart must turn to God and mirror what it has received. It does so through prayer, an act of spirit-to-spirit communication.

We Must Live by Faith—There Is No Alternative

As we said, peoples' *beliefs* underlie what they *know* in the qualitative areas of life—spiritual matters, morals, and values. Their presuppositions establish how they order the data they encounter—life's experiences, observations, information. This very truth makes the typical non-Christians psychologically uncomfortable because their identity is anchored in the world—and the notion of faith premises leaves them feeling insecure. They may relegate these categories to pie-in-the-sky religion, for from the humanist's perspective they have little to do with daily life. God, at best, belongs in a small corner of his or her life. And Jesus certainly has nothing to do with important daily family, business, or political concerns. So these people place their faith in the natural order, in themselves, or in a god that has been created in their own likeness.

Self-deception is a primary mark of humankind's fall. Our first father, Adam, manifested this perverted attempt at self-protection when he told God right after his fall, "The woman whom *You gave* to be with me, *she gave me* from the tree, and I ate" (Gen. 3:12). Adam tried to shift the blame for his actions onto both God and Eve. Adam's effort failed, but the tendency for people to attempt to escape from their moral culpability is nearly universal—until they are regenerated. Our failure to recognize that our world/life-view is always rooted in faith-based presuppositions is another example of self-deception. It is a frightening business to face one's shaky underpinnings, so most non-Christians scoff and laugh at the idea of living by faith.

This may be why so few intellectually honest people are found among the intelligentsia. Intellectual honesty requires acknowledging our own presuppositions. So a diversion is often created, and faith is ridiculed. Faith is called funny names. It is called "blind faith" or "a leap-of-faith." Sometimes faith is conceived of as the power of positive thinking. Only Christians can think of faith as an objectively grounded dimension of reality. The non-Christian (and the unorthodox Christian) can only conceive of faith in amorphous and subjective terms.

There Are Three Faith Constructs Discernible in Our Culture

Each has its subscribers. They are: (a) blind faith; (b) a leap-of-faith; and (c) substantive/evidential faith—the biblical one. Let us briefly look at each of these.

Blind Faith

Non-Christians, who do not discern the things of the Spirit of God, generally believe that Christians are people who live by blind faith. That is reasonable from their perspective. Since they do not see what Christians see, they have little choice but to believe that Christians do *not* see what they profess to see (1 Cor. 2:14; Eph. 1:18-19; Job 42:5-6). They therefore conclude that Christians walk by blind faith.

And well-meaning but errant pastors sometimes promote this same kind of thinking, even among Christians, when they say, "Oh, you just have to believe"—as if faith is something to be self-manufactured from within without intelligent content. This also fosters the culturally accepted notion that faith and the ability to reason are separated from each another.

Christ, on the other hand, called those who rejected his teaching "blind guides of the blind." He said, "If a blind man guides a blind man, both will fall into a pit" (Matt. 15:14). But he prefaced this statement with the phrase "Let them alone," referring to the blind guides. Why? Because it does no good to attempt to persuade people who are spiritually dead and unmoved by God's truth that they are spiritually blind. They are in need of the *gospel* and regeneration, not persuasive arguments grounded in what totally turns them off: God and his truth. They are dead to God—want no part of him. We are to bear witness to God's revealed truth, but regeneration does not come by argumentation, except as the Holy Spirit may make God's Word logical and effective to the listener in breaking down a barrier of misperception.

What is the result of such spiritual blindness? Those who reject Christ are those who consign themselves to the darkness that they call light, and deceive themselves by substituting their self-devised truth for God's revealed truth. They thereby place *themselves* in the position of having to navigate life by blind faith— faith that is grounded and nurtured in mere temporal concepts; faith that is not based on God's acts in human history; and faith that is not guided by the Holy Spirit. They make fun of Christians' faith but they are actually ensnared in the very kind of faith they ridicule—*blind faith*.

Leap-of-faith

This common condition of dependence is rooted in one's personal experiences. It is a form of *knowledge* obtained via *relationships* with people or things, often in a moment of time, through intuition or feelings. The leap dimension of this is people's willingness to venture their most basic world/life-view presuppositions on risky feelings or intuitive experiences. The person grabs hold of his or her personal feeling experiences for the validation of his or her basic, governing knowledge. For example, a young person may have a rich emotional experience at a church camp. This can be the beginning of a genuine relationship with Christ or the beginning of a personal leap-of-faith. If he is attracted to Christ and truly places his faith in Christ *alone*, it is probably the beginning of the development of evidential faith in his life. But if he is attracted to the emotional experience and that emotional experience becomes the *proof* underlying his beliefs, he may well be on the leap-of-faith path of life.

If our faith rests on our emotional experiences or our independent thoughts (intuition), we psychologically place *ourselves* at the epicenter of reality. We assume the responsibility for determining reality and truth. Our view of reality will become tied eventually to the content of our existential experience—the feeling or intuition we associate with our leap-of-faith that connects us to the presumed foundations of reality. I trust my "xyz" existential experience because I *feel* it is the right thing to do. Or, I trust my *intuition* because there is nothing else to trust. This is a dark path to walk. Our emotions become our guide, and they are subject to our external circumstances. Or we place our trust in our intuitive thoughts—which are just as shaky.

Evidential Faith

The faith that God gives his children is rooted in objective reality, not a subjective experience or wish. God-given faith is a faith rooted in historical/legal events. What is a historical/legal faith and what makes it objective in character? A two-part explanation will answer the question.

First, faith in Christ, and the God whom Christ manifests to his people through his life, death and resurrection, is a gift from God (Rom. 12:3, 6; Acts 3:16; Eph. 4:7).[56] It is faith that is imparted to individuals by the loving work of the Holy Spirit. It is a particular faith: it is faith in the God of Christ. It is not generic faith—that is, faith in what the human mind conjures up as being relevant.

Second, biblical faith is substantive/evidential faith that is rooted in the historical and legal dimensions of reality. Hebrews 11:1 says: "Now faith is the assurance of things hoped for, the conviction of things not seen". The Greek word for "assurance" (*hypostasis*) may also be translated as "substance." And the biblical idea of the word "hope" is not something to be wished for. It is a hope tied to a historical reality that gives rise to a future expectation. And the Greek word for "conviction" (*elenchos*) can be translated as "evidence" or "proof." So when we think of biblical faith being grounded in assurance, substance, evidence or proof, it is easy to understand why such faith is to be thought of as objective.

And God has acted in the time/space reality of history. Our faith is to be based upon the historical evidence of God's acts in history. He has created; he has spoken to us in a propositional, written form—the Bible; he has acted on our behalf in ways that only an eternal, infinite, gracious, and merciful God could have. And he has sent his Son in the likeness of human flesh to redeem us. The acts of God that are recorded in Scripture constitute the *historical* aspect of what is sometimes referred to as the historic/legal proof of the truth that undergirds the Christian faith. Our faith is not rooted in philosophy, abstract ideas, or in nice wishes. It is rooted in the God who has acted in the historical time/space dimensions of the created order.

The *legal* aspect of this historical/legal proof rests on the reality that God's acts were not carried out privately. There were many witnesses to his acts, over many generations. Most of God's acts were done in public in view of numerous witnesses. Paul appeals to the legal aspect of this reality when he tells the people in Corinth of Christ's resurrection:

> For I delivered to you as of first importance what I also received, that Christ died for our sins according to the Scriptures, and that He was buried, and that He was raised on the third day according to the Scriptures, and that He appeared to Cephas, then to the twelve. After that *He appeared to more than five hundred brethren at one time*, most of whom remain until now, but some have fallen asleep; then He appeared

---

[56] See: Rom. 10:17; 1 Peter 1:5; Eph. 2:8; Luke 17:5-10; Gal. 3:23-25; Heb. 12:2; James 2:5.

to James, then to all the apostles; and last of all, as to one untimely born, He appeared to me also. (1 Cor. 15:3-8)

God gives his people evidential faith that is rooted in the time, space, historical/legal activities of the invisible spirit who is God.

Conclusion

How might our understanding that we can only communicate with God in a spirit-to-spirit relationship and in the context of our possession of substantive/evidential faith influence our daily life?

Early in my walk with Christ I had been very uneasy with the realization that God wanted me to *trust* him. I was negatively influenced by experiences in my formative years, and as my budding relationship with Christ grew, I equated trust with faith. Real faith required genuine trust. I wanted a tangible God, one who would not require so much faith. I wanted a visible God. I wanted a personal God who would belong to me and who would protect me from suffering. It was a long journey for me from wanting such a God to loving and trusting the God who would be with me when I was in pain or anguish. There were so many important aspects of God's nature missing in my understanding that if my early longings had mirrored reality, the God I thought I wanted would have been inadequate to meet my real needs.

The Holy Spirit began renovating me by allowing my disturbed spirit to seek for God. I had no idea how to enter into a deep personal relationship with God. For years I could not satisfy my longing. Christ forcefully, but mercifully, convicted me later on with the words of John, "You search the Scriptures because you think that in them you have eternal life . . . and you are unwilling to come to Me" (John 5:39-40). This truth pierced my spirit. The Spirit of Christ then gently began transforming me from *knowing about God* to the secure haven of *truly knowing God*. The Holy Spirit continued graciously to write the Word of God in my heart (Jer. 31:31-34; John 14:26; Ps. 40:8) but the Word was no longer a substitute for Christ. It became his personal message to me—about himself and his whole counsel (Acts 5:20; 20:20, 27).

"God is spirit" was one of the personal messages given me that established deep roots in my heart (John 4:24). Pondering this truth over a period of time created in me the faith (strong persuasion) that the truth that God is spirit made it reasonable for me to rest in the reality that I could only relate to the Father, Son and Holy Spirit on a spirit-to-spirit basis. In addition, God's words, "Cease striving [let go, relax] and know that I am God" (Ps. 46:10) also became connected in my mind with the reality that God is spirit. My spiritual panic attacks subsided and finally disappeared. *God* was in charge of my spiritual growth and development, not me. I could relax and trust God in the relationship he had established between himself and me. I had grown to *truly know him* as a spirit whose very *nature* made him completely trustworthy.

5

God Is Holy: He Wants Us to Be Holy

*As obedient children, do not be conformed to the former lusts which were
yours in your ignorance, but like the Holy One who called you,
be holy yourselves also in all your behavior; because it is written,
You shall be holy, for I am holy. (1 Peter 1:14-16)*

God is holy (Lev. 19:2; Isa. 6:3; Rev. 4:8). This is a simple declaration of reality revealed in the Bible. But an *effectual discernment* of the reality of God's holiness depends upon God's *grace*.

There is nothing a human can do to create an *experiential* awareness of God's absolute purity and moral perfection. Such soul-filling discernment has undone everyone who has ever perceived a substantial degree of it. So we must recognize a distinction between these two realities: God is holy, and the effectual *discernment* of that fact. For the effectual discernment of God's holiness—occasioned by God's grace—is an integral part of the transformation of one's heart into the likeness of Christ. A mere intellectual recognition is not adequate.

Christians need, degree by degree, to discern God's holiness. This discernment is transformational! It creates a meek and humble spirit. It leads to such a poverty of spirit that we mourn and long for the righteousness of Christ! This is at the heart of his teaching concerning the blessings that are potentially ours, in the beatitudes in his Sermon on the Mount (Matt. 5:3-6).

The following will not, indeed *cannot*, create the experiential grasping of God's holiness. Neither can it create a hungering on readers' part to be holy. That requires the work of the Holy Spirit. It is, nevertheless, essential to consider: (a) God's holiness; (b) the reality of evil; (c) the reconciliation of God's holiness with that reality; and (d) his insistence that his children be holy.

God Is Holy

God is called the holy One of Israel (Isa. 1:4). He is the holy God (Josh. 24:19; 1 Sam. 6:20; Ps. 71:22). And Isaiah is filled with references to the Holy One whose very name is Holy (Isa. 57:15). What does it mean to be holy? Holiness is a quality of the very *essence* of God, an innate aspect of his nature. Only he is inherently holy. God can endow his regenerated people with a degree of his holy nature, but their possession of such a nature is always a gift from God, wrought in them by the Holy Spirit's renovating work. Only those saints who have died in Christ and are subsequently glorified are restored to a full state of holiness.

Holiness is not a natural condition enjoyed by any fallen person, for when our father Adam discarded his original holiness, we, his posterity, lost it as well. Nor is holiness a self-obtained or self-possessed attribute of any created being.

The vocabulary by which we attempt to describe the reality of holiness is limited. We take a stab at it by using words like *purity* or *moral perfection*. Even words like these, however, send us scurrying outside of ourselves for meaningful examples, because we are not personally pure or morally perfect. We are, in fact, their very antithesis.

Some may object to being called the antithesis of purity and moral perfection. Are there not *degrees* of impurity and imperfection? Yes, but such thinking misses the point. Measuring ourselves by ourselves may be psychologically comforting to us—but that comfort only makes it more difficult for us to discern our true depravity. The problem is that we are comparing one impurity with another. The very best person simply has no conception of just how ungodly he really is in his own self-righteousness. This is because he has no true conception of the *infinite holiness* of God. How terrified morally pure people would be if the holiness of God were suddenly revealed to them as it was to Isaiah and to John (Isa. 6:3-5; Rev. 1:17).

Holiness is, however, very hard to apprehend for two good reasons. First, when we contemplate the total amount of human conduct, there is very little that can be called holy. But the second, and most important, inhibitor to the discovery of holiness is that in order to see holiness we must see it through the eye of the heart (Eph. 1:18-19; Acts 26:15-18; 2 Cor. 4:3-6). To illustrate: Job, the most righteous man of his day, was finally brought to the point where he said: "I have heard of Thee by the hearing of the ear; but now my eye sees Thee; therefore I retract, and I repent in dust and ashes" (Job 42:5-6). He said this to God at the conclusion of much suffering and personal loss. What caused Job to now acknowledge that though he had *heard* the truths of God—yes, he believed and lived out the truths in his life—only now could he *see*? What caused him to retract the complaints he uttered while suffering and to repent of his anger? In the chapters (38–41) preceding Job's life-transforming enlightenment, the Almighty confronted Job with a series of questions that the Holy Spirit used to bring Job to a true understanding of God's majestic glory—his perfect power, wisdom, and sovereign plan.

Peter had an experience similar to Job's. After he had fished all night, without success, and Jesus asked him to cast his nets out one more time, he saw, through the eye of his heart, Jesus very differently. When the nets encompassed so many fish that they began to break, "he fell down at Jesus's feet, saying, 'Go away from me Lord, for *I am a sinful man*, O Lord!'" (Luke 5:8). The Holy Spirit had enlightened the eye of Peter's heart so he saw Jesus in an entirely new light: Jesus was the holy Lord of the universe; and Peter, by contrast, was a wretched sinner.

Jesus is the archetype of what it means for us to be holy. He was absolutely holy (Acts 2:27; 3:14) and was without sin (2 Cor. 5:21; 1 Peter 2:22). There was no impurity to be found in him. He never had a bad attitude, never had an intemperate or impure thought. His motives were never self-centered and he never acted in an ungodly way. He exhibited a moral perfection that emanated from a pure heart. What would a holy person look like? He or she would manifest the spirit of Jesus.

But we need to address a subsequent question. What does Scripture convey when it states: "He Himself [Jesus] was *tempted* in that which He has suffered" (Heb. 2:18). Or that "we do not have a high priest who cannot sympathize with our weaknesses, but one who has been *tempted* in all things as we are, yet without sin" (Heb. 4:15). The Greek word for tempted basically means tested.[57] God uses tests or temptations to expose persons' hearts—either to themselves or their neighbors; God already knows the heart. So temptations can be described in Scripture in either a positive or negative way. Jesus, it must be remembered, was never enticed—tempted in the negative way. He never faced testing based on an unholy nature.

An illustration helps. When we read, "Jesus was led up by the Holy Spirit into the wilderness to be tempted by the devil" (Matt. 4:1), we see both the negative and positive connotations of temptation. Clearly, the devil was testing Jesus to bring about evil. The devil wanted the second Adam to fall as the original Adam had. The Holy Spirit, however, could not have had that intent when he led Jesus into the wilderness—he is the *Holy* Spirit. His intent was that Jesus might be tried (tested, proven) by the events, and by withstanding the devil's evil intention it be made manifest that he is truly the Son of God. Yes, Jesus faced and withstood, in a godly way, every trial, test, and temptation that all other mortals have encountered, yet without sin. His tests were means to teach him obedience (Heb. 5:8). Jesus's trials have proven that he is holy and worthy of worship along with the Father and the Holy Spirit.

It can be inferred from Scripture also that God's holiness is his *most important* attribute. Minimally, his holiness seems to be the attribute which, above all his other attributes, he wants believers to apprehend. This is inferred by the facts that: (a) it is God's most often referred-to attribute; (b) the word "holy" is used in conjunction with a number of his other attributes—more so than any other conjoining of his attributes; (c) his holiness is the only attribute that is expressed in Scripture in the form of a trilogy; and (d) God's Spirit is called the Holy Spirit.

Holiness: God's Most Often Referred-to Attribute

Suppose a world leader was asked to write his autobiography and to convey what he regarded as the most significant, guiding element of his personality. No one would choose the quality of holiness. Courage, decisiveness, compassion, prudence, sincerity, integrity or some other characteristic would, mostly likely, be chosen to reveal one's idea of his or her central core.

---

[57] Lexical # 3985: *peirazo*.

Nowhere in Scripture does God say "Holiness is My most important attribute"; but holiness is the mark of God's personality most often noted. This is significant. God is the author of Scripture, and authors will highlight things they deem important. It appears that this is what God has done regarding his holiness. He wants us to be thoroughly informed of this reality regarding himself. His holiness is his glory and his beauty (Pss. 27:4; 29:1-2; 110:3).

This awesome truth about God—he is holy—is intended to be both a *warning* and a *calling* to the unholy. Those who are not holy instinctively know that they cannot have fellowship with a God who is holy. Their own corrupt nature warns them to flee from him lest they be consumed by his purity. All are excluded from living in the presence of a holy God while in their fallen, sinful state (Ps. 76:7; Nah. 1:6; Mal. 3:2; Luke 21:36; Rev. 6:17). The lost have, knowingly or not, a great fear of the holy God. But God's holiness is also a clear light calling the unholy to Jesus, the Savior.[58] Holiness is attractive. It provides great peace when we are wrapped in it. Jesus is the perfect manifestation of God's holiness in human form. And Christ invites everyone to come to him and receive his grace (John 7:37. Also see 4:10, 14; 6:35, 51).

Holiness: Conjoined with Other Attributes

No attribute is used as often as an adjective to modify other attributes as God's holiness. For example, in Psalm 98:1 we read, "O sing to the LORD a new song, for He has done wonderful things, His right hand and His *holy arm* have gained the victory for Him." The word "arm," as used here and elsewhere in Scripture, signifies God's power—so his omnipotence is holy. God's holiness is the most beautiful and glorious of all his attributes: his truth is holy truth (Rev. 6:10). His name, which signifies all his attributes, is holy (Ps. 103:1).[59] The words that God speaks are holy (Ps. 105:42). His justice is a holy justice (Acts 3:14). His wisdom is a holy wisdom; we receive his holy wisdom as the Holy Spirit conveyed it to us (Acts 6:3). As Charnock wrote: "Without it [God's holiness], his patience would be an indulgence to sin, his mercy a fondness, his wrath a madness, his power a tyranny, his wisdom an unworthy subtlety."[60]

Holiness: The Only Attribute Expressed in the Form of a Trilogy

No other attribute appears in Scripture in a succession such as "Holy, Holy, Holy, is the LORD of hosts, the whole earth is full of His glory" (Isa. 6:3). Or as, "Holy, Holy, Holy, is the LORD God, the Almighty, who was and who is and who is to come" (Rev. 4:8). Holiness is God's most exalted attribute. No other one is so held up for praise and adoration. It is the attribute of greatest value

---

[58] Jesus's substitutionary death—he suffered the death we deserve—is at the heart of the good news that God the Father has provided a sure way back into fellowship with him through the gift of his Son. God the Father looked upon the anguish of the soul of his Son and was satisfied that the full price of redemption had been paid (Isa. 53:11). The holy God is both *just* (all sin must be punished to the fullest) and the *justifier* (able to find a just way to declare his chosen people not guilty)—Rom. 3:26.

[59] See also Lev. 20:3; 22:2, 32; 1 Chron. 16:35; 29:16; Ps. 33:21; 105:3; 106:47; 145:21.

[60] Charnock, *Discourses Upon the Existence and Attributes of God*, vol. 2, 113-114.

among all the attributes of infinite perfection. It is the controlling attribute. It sets the tone and determines the quality of all else about God.

The Holy Spirit Is the Primary Name Given God's Spirit

The Spirit of God, the third person of the Trinity, is repeatedly presented in Scripture as the *Holy Spirit*. He is not referred to as the All-wise Spirit or the Powerful Spirit on a recurring basis. No attribute is so frequently associated with the Spirit of God. The coupling of the attribute "holy" with a personal reference to the Spirit occurs over ninety times in the New Testament. God clearly desires us to know that the Spirit is holy. The Spirit of God is never to be confused or associated with anything that is not holy. His nature is holy; holiness is his passion.

We can conclude that God's purity, moral perfection, or holy nature is his most defining and significant attribute. It is the attribute that pervades and glorifies his whole being. The awesome I AM WHO I AM is first and foremost *holy*. We conclude this because holiness is: (a) the most often referred-to attribute, (b) the most frequently coupled attribute with God's other attributes, (c) the only attribute used as a trilogy, and (d) the name given to God's Spirit.

Evil: Its Existence in a Universe Created and Ruled by a Holy God

No inquiry is more bewildering than reconciling the reality of evil in the world (with its resulting injustices and suffering) with the fact that a *holy, loving, good,* and *wise* God sovereignly rules over all. Since God's holiness is coupled with many of his other attributes, here we focus on the existence of evil in a universe made by a holy God. We will not relate evil to God's goodness and love, for whatever applies to evil as it relates to God's holiness also applies to evil as it relates to his other attributes. We will examine the genesis, character, and types of evil.

The Genesis of Evil

Evil did not exist in eternity past—the period before God created time and all that is contained therein. Evil had its beginning in history. That beginning is external to both God and his image-bearers. And God is neither the Creator nor the cause of evil. He foreknew evil before times eternal, but had nothing to do with its origination apart from his permitting it to arise within a perfect but mutable angelic creature.

Readers are forewarned that the genesis of evil is an *inscrutable mystery*. The question "How did Satan corrupt himself?" is logical, but its answer remains unsolvable. God said through Moses: "The secret things belong to the LORD our God, but the things revealed belong to us and to our sons forever" (Deut. 29:29). To force an answer to the "how question" reveals the mind of the person supposing, but does not accord with the mind of God. It is his will that we live with a level of mystery.

Evil was not inherent in anything when God created the universe. He declared the entire creation to be very good (Gen. 1:31). Evil was nowhere to be found! Furthermore, the Holy God, the Creator, cannot be tempted by evil, nor can he tempt anyone to do evil (James 1:13). Where did evil originate, then, if God is not its author, and there is no other God beside him? (See Deut. 4:35, 39; 32:39; Isa. 43:10-11; 44:6-8; 45:5-6; Mark 12:32).

Scripture does not give us a complete theology of angels, but it furnishes a few bits of information concerning them. Though some theologians disagree, most agree that Ezekiel 28:11-19 and Isaiah 14:4-21 provide insights into the genesis of evil. Ezekiel addresses the King of Tyre, but also reveals much about the one whom the King of Tyre emulated—Lucifer or Satan. Isaiah likewise addresses the pagan King of Babylon, understood to be a follower of Satan throughout much of Scripture. These two passages have two applications: First, they apply to the two kings, and second they also apply to Satan, the spiritual progenitor of the two kings.

Ezekiel's text is the key to understanding the genesis of evil.

> Thus says the Lord GOD, You had the seal of perfection, full of wisdom and perfect in beauty. You were in Eden, the garden of God; every precious stone was your covering: [an enumeration of the stones follows]. On the day that you were created they were prepared. You were the anointed cherub who covers, and I placed you there. You were on the holy mountain of God.... You were blameless in your ways from the day you were created until unrighteousness was found in you.... Your heart was lifted up because of your beauty; *you corrupted your wisdom by reason of your splendor.* (vv. 12-17)

Here we discover that the evil one was given the seal (or stamp) of perfection from the beginning (v. 12). No evil was in him. He was created by God before Adam and Eve and placed in the Garden of Eden (vv. 13-14). This created one was blameless until unrighteousness appeared (v. 15). And how did his sin emerge out of blamelessness? Apparently he became enamored with himself (v. 17). He fell in love with himself, was filled with pride, and *corrupted* himself (v. 17). He perverted wisdom—the knowledge and understanding that should lead to godly ends (v. 17).

Isaiah picks up on the same theme.

> How you have fallen from heaven, O star of the morning, son of the dawn! ... you who have weakened the nations! But you said in your heart, I will ascend to heaven; I will raise my throne above the stars of God, and I will sit on the mount of assembly in the recesses of the north. I will ascend above the heights of the clouds; I will make myself like the Most High. (vv. 12-14)

Pride emerges from the *heart* of the evil one. He desires to make himself equal to, if not better than God (v. 14). He intends to put himself on a throne (v. 13) rather than remain in his appointed place in the Garden of Eden (described in Ezekiel). He wants to be God.

The Bible leads us to conclude that Satan was created in perfection but *corrupted himself* with self-generated pride. Pride was formed in his heart and emerged when he focused on his own God-endowed beauty and wisdom.

The Character of Evil

As we saw, God saw all that he had made, and it was very good (Gen. 1:31). Therefore evil is not a quality to be associated with the created substance of any material or spiritual entity. Rather, evil is the *perversion* of God's intended purpose and the *misuse* of both his created order and the people he placed in it. The fall changed the original conditions of human perception. The human world/life-view was radically altered. Mankind could no longer perceive the reality of God or his creation correctly. This resulted in sin, or missing the mark, manifesting what is wicked. Sin is anything that is not in conformity with God's design, purposes and will. Sin takes the form of impure and twisted motives, thoughts, and actions.

The Types of Evil

Theologians discuss two types of evil, but do not agree on whether there are really one or two types. Clearly, there is *moral* evil. Those who possess the knowledge of good and evil are deemed to be moral beings by God. They are accountable to him. Humans acquired the knowledge of good and evil through eating the forbidden fruit in the Garden of Eden (Gen. 2:15-17; 3:1-7). Adam and Eve had the latent potential for the knowledge of good and evil prior to their fall, but its activation was only realized after each ate from the tree of the knowledge of good and evil. They were and we are morally accountable to God, for we do know what is right and wrong. This kind of knowledge is inherent (Rom. 1:18-21; Eph. 5:3-6).

We do not know how Satan (and the rebel angels that followed him) came to possess moral knowledge. But we know that they too are accountable to God, and that the angels who rebelled face eternal damnation as a consequence of their moral choice (Rev. 19:20; 20:13-14).

The second type of evil is sometimes called the evil of natural suffering. When Adam and Eve sinned and fell the rest of the physical order fell with them (Gen. 3:17-19; Rom. 8:19-22). God cursed the ground (Gen. 3:17). We do not know very much of what the fall of the physical order entails, but we do know that it occurred and has evident consequences. For example, is cancer a consequence of the fall? Yes! The entire genetic breakdown (deterioration) that was ushered in with the fall[61] is a precursor to cancer and other debilitating diseases and birth defects. And the tree of life was denied to Adam and Eve (Gen. 3:22-24). This was done as an act of *grace*—so they would not eat of the tree of life and live

---

[61] In Genesis 5 we learn that humans routinely lived to what would be called extraordinary ages today. In 6:3 we learn that God established the intended age to be 120 years. Yet by the time that Psalms was put together we read: "As for the days of our life, they contain seventy years, or if due to strength, eighty years" (Ps. 90:10). Genetic deterioration becomes apparent over the centuries.

eternally in their fallen state. But if they had not fallen they could have eaten from the tree of life—and death would have been impossible! Earthquakes, floods, fires, and other natural disasters would have been no threat to them, assuming such things would have existed without the fall of the created order. (I believe they would *not* have existed.) Now such natural disasters are a threat to the lives of all people.

The Bible is clear that God is the sovereign ruler over his creation, including the natural acts of violence the physical order brings us. Christ calmed the sea (Matt. 8:23-27; Mark 4:35-41). God used a strong wind to bring the meat (quail) to his children in the wilderness (Num. 11:31). An eruption of the earth destroyed Sodom and Gomorrah in fire and brimstone, according to God's will (Gen. 19:23-25). The Lord's intended use of such natural forces is for a variety of *godly* purposes: to reveal his Lordship; to demonstrate his loving care; to bring about godly justice as a warning to those in subsequent generations (2 Peter 2:6). It is because God sometimes uses physical, natural calamities to effect his active will that many theologians do not consider such disasters in terms of the evil of natural suffering. God has no active part in bringing about evil. He always has a holy intent for everything.

But Satan is allowed at times to use the same natural forces of the fallen physical order to tempt people to blaspheme God, to find fault with his rule, or to cause suffering. Job endured this reality (Job 1:13-19). Satan stirred up evil men to steal Job's donkeys and oxen (v. 15). His sheep were consumed by fire (v. 16). Three bands of Chaldeans stole his camels (v. 17). And his ten children died when a strong wind destroyed the eldest's home (v. 19). The adverse natural forces and evil human behavior were all under the influence of Satan, and collectively could well be called the evil of natural suffering. The sovereign rule and permissive will of God were in effect, however, when Satan set out to destroy Job. By God's grace, Job stood strong and Satan failed.

My opinion is that it is better simply to speak of all natural suffering as just that, natural suffering—and avoid the label the evil of natural suffering. This avoids the possibility of ascribing evil to God. Humans do not know, when a form of natural suffering befalls them, if it emanates from the natural consequences of the fall (under God's permissive will), from the active will of Satan (under the same will), or from the active will of God who occasionally acts directly upon his created order. Our comfort comes by faith in the sovereign, holy God who is able to take every event and use it to shape his children to Christ's image (Rom. 8:28-29).

God's Holiness Is Not Diminished by Evil's Existence

Why did God allow evil to exist as a part of his created order? Why would a wise and holy God tolerate evil between the fall and Christ's final judgment? Evil will not exist for eternity. Does evil have a purpose? These are tough questions. Charnock commends Camero for not being "too busy and rash in inquiries and conclusions about the reason of God's providence in the matter of sin."[62] But then Charnock continues for thirty-one pages to explain that God's holiness is not blemished by the existence of evil.[63]

Let's begin with the question: Does evil have a *purpose*? Yes, it does. Its purpose is to glorify God—to declare his awesome, severe, wondrous, majestic, honored nature. The angelic hosts who did not follow Satan but who in the heavens declare continuously that God is "Holy, Holy, Holy" do not find God's glory and holiness diminished by his permitting evil to emerge from a perfect angel.

God created Adam and Eve, and us, for his glory (Isa. 43:7; 44:23). But our first parents fell. Did the fall glorify God? The *act* that brought about the fall did not glorify God, but God's *wisdom* in allowing the fall proclaims his awesome glory! How is this so? His glory is shown because, if there had been no fall, much we known about him would never have been revealed to Adam and Eve, or their posterity. God would not have manifested his infinite love in the incarnation, life, death, and resurrection of Jesus the Christ, the Son of God, our Savior. There would have been no need of a Savior. The greatness of God's love is profoundly manifested in sending his Son to suffer for the sins of those who fell and rejected their own Creator. The magnitude of God's *love* would have remained hidden for eternity.

In addition, God's *power over death* would have remained forever unknown. Death brings us face-to-face with mortality. It forces us to ask many questions about life's meaning that would have remained unasked without the fall. God's patience and longsuffering would have been hidden from us. There would have been no need to manifest them without the fall.

His *mercy* would have gone undetected. There was no need for it without the fall, but as a consequence of it he bestows compassion upon those deserving his wrath. As a result, we are beneficiaries of his gracious care. His *justice* would have been superfluous and unknown to his image-bearers. In the midst of Adam and Eve's perfect innocence there was no need for justice. Without the fall, there would be no violations of God's holy demands and no need for retribution.

God's *holiness* would also have been taken for granted. There would have been nothing with which to contrast it. God's capacity for wrath would have been forever unknown. And his *goodness* would have paled in comparison to what we known of it today. His goodness—expressed in our having temporal physical benefits—is poured out upon and enjoyed by the just, and the unjust. That kind goodness would have never been revealed without the fall.

Furthermore, we would not enjoy numerous special *benefits* in this life and the next due to God's redemption, had there been no fall. We would still lack the knowledge of good and evil. God, in wisdom, allowed us to acquire that knowledge through the fall. Why did God allow this to happen through the fall

---

[62] Charnock, *Discourses Upon the Existence and Attributes of God*, vol. 2, 140.
[63] Ibid., 140-171.

rather than simply create us with the knowledge of good and evil? The answer to this question resides in God's infinite wisdom and has not been revealed to us. We can speculate about an answer, but that only results in our assuming the role of God. We do know that God is glorified through *all* of his creation. And he sovereignly rules it (permissively and actively) in a way that is completely keeping with his absolute holiness and perfect wisdom.

God's *wisdom* would appear radically different than it is if there were there no sin. In fact, God's allowing sin to emerge in Satan, and then allowing him to lead our first parents into rebellion are manifestations of God's infinite wisdom. Before time, God determined that allowing the fall to occur was the wisest thing to permit. He allowed it; he has worked with it. Submitting to God's wisdom is the ultimate answer to the question: "Why did God allow evil to become a part of reality?" We must simply bear witness to the *wisdom* of God.

God Decrees That His Children Are to Be Holy

It is an amazing thing to contemplate God's word to his children, "You shall be holy, for I am holy" (1 Peter 1.16; Lev. 11:44-45; 19:2; 20:7). Holiness is analogous to absolute *purity* and *moral perfection*. Neither of these categories is a remote possibility even for believers prior to their glorification after death (Heb. 11:40; 12:23b; Rev. 6:9-11). Only God possesses these characteristics. Then what is it God requires of those who live under this command?

Holiness, in addition to involving purity and moral perfection, also includes being *separated* from evil and being *set apart* to God (Luke 7:30). He talks about these latter two dimensions of holiness when he tells his people to be holy as he is holy. We are to be unattached to evil. We are to stop being profane in both mind and with mouth (James 3:8-12). We are to cut ties with pornography—our eyes are not to search for another's nakedness (Lev. 18:6-18). We are to stop gossiping (Prov. 20:19; 2 Cor. 12:20) and telling lies, even little *white* ones (1 John 2:21). We are to love righteousness (Matt. 5:6) and the law of God.[64] His law tells us what is *unholy* when it is says: "you shall not." And it tells us what is *holy* when it says "you shall."

Christians are not to be *antinomian*—saying that the law of God does not benefit them (Matt. 5:17-19). It is true that Christians are not to fear being judged by the law. Those who have faith in Christ will not be judged according to the law. And neither are Christians to think they can curry special favor with God by more closely keeping the law. We can never earn God's love. The law tells us what God is like and mirrors his holiness. When Christians look into the light of the law it illumines and exposes their deformed character and behavior.

But God does not leave us in a state of stagnant deformity. Upon regenerating a human spirit God begins a work of renovation to bring his children into increasing conformity to the likeness of Christ. God the potter begins

---

[64] We refer here to God's moral law, not to his civil or ceremonial law. While the latter two types of law have their important place in Scripture, the discussion here is limited to God's moral law.

reshaping the old lump of clay into a new vessel. This godly work is called progressive *sanctification*. The Holy Spirit's work of sanctification is his transforming the unholy into the holy. This is God's work alone. And how does he do it? The Spirit takes God's law, testimonies, ways, precepts, statutes, commandments, judgments, ordinances and words—all synonyms for God's Scripture (see Ps. 119:1-24)—and uses it to *cleanse* and *transform* his children's minds, passions, and wills (their hearts) into Christ's likeness (Eph. 5:26; Rom. 12:1-2). This godly work of sanctification is life-long.

Biblically sanctification describes people being *set apart* for God's purposes and being *separated* from what is polluted. Sanctification is the ongoing process of creating holiness. Sanctification and holiness are very closely related in the Scripture. For example, we read, "Pursue . . . *sanctification* without which no one will see the Lord" (Heb. 12:14). This can also be translated, "Pursue . . . *holiness* without which no one will see the Lord." Biblically, being sanctified is God's setting us apart from the unholy unto the holy. Those who were unholy—far removed from purity and moral perfection—are being renovated into God's holy people.

Christ's declaration, "You are to be *perfect*, as your heavenly Father is *perfect*" (Matt. 5:48), is another example of this same kind of directional declarative. Christians are being called to grow up to full maturity. They are not being called to literal perfection.[65] They are being called to acknowledge their total dependence upon the Holy Spirit's active work of *sanctification* to grow in Christ. God repeatedly shows his children their true needs, not so they will try to rid themselves of their deficiencies, but so they may learn their total dependence upon Christ's Spirit for their growth—sanctification.

Christians are encouraged to practice holiness—to do all in their power to follow Christ in every circumstance in life. For instance, to make an effort to avoid polluting our minds by guarding what we put into them. Or we might plan to call on someone shut-in once a week. Or we might plead with Christ for the inner strength to break an ungodly habit. These alterations in life are manifestations of Christlikeness—godly behavior motivated by a love for Christ. This is living *like* Christ *for* Christ. By this we indicate that we are partakers of God's divine nature and share Christ's holiness (Heb. 12:10; 2 Peter 1:4; Eph. 4:24).

---

[65] The Greek word used for perfect here is *teleios* and it conveys the idea of completion. We are being called to grow up, to be mature. The word does not convey a demand for moral perfection.

6

God Is Immutable: We Rest in His Reliability

*Of old You founded the earth; and the heavens are the work of Your hands.
Even they will perish, but You endure; and all of them will wear out
like a garment; like clothing You will change them and
they will be changed. But You are the same, and Your years
will not come to an end. (Ps. 102:25-27)*

Those who question God's perfect foreknowledge (treated with his omniscience in chapter 2) will probably have trouble accepting that he is *immutable*—unchanging in any way, at any time. This will be so because if God does not have foreknowledge of what will happen in the future, then he will be perpetually learning about yesterday's future which is today's happenings. Underlying this supposition is the idea that God's knowledge is constantly changing. Such a God would be very different from the God of Scripture and whom the church has always accepted.

Much depends on our accurately comprehending God's revealed nature. Our confidence in his promises is tied to what we think about his immutability. The strength of our assurance of salvation is related to our conviction that God is immutable. The very stability of God himself is related to his immutability! If God is not immutable, then every one of his attributes is subject to change. I have heard people say, God is immutable in the "essentials" but not in the "nonessentials." When I ask them to define these two terms, there has only been silence.

Another notion that often guides our unconscious thinking but is foreign to God's character is the presupposition that God exhibits only *one* aspect of his personality at a time—as we mortals do. For example, we assume that if he is angry, then he is not peaceful at the same time. We assume such because that is our experience! We are not angry and peaceful at the same time. We typically manifest our personality one aspect at a time. But this is not the case with God. The omnipresent God is not required to manifest himself in the same way at any given moment in time to persons in different geographical locations. He is free and able to manifest different aspects of his nature simultaneously to millions of people in numberless locations. God can manifest all of his attributes at all times in all places, *simultaneously*! He and we are obviously not alike in this regard.

God can bring to bear one particular attribute on his children or his enemies at any particular time—even while he exposes other attributes to other people! For example, I may be subject to God's chastisement while you are simultaneously experiencing his comfort. God also can manifest all that he is at all times *perpetually*! He perpetually manifests his holiness and also his love. And simultaneously he hates all that violates his love—but he controls his just wrath until the proper time to display it.

God is all that he is at *all* times. But we can only be aware of one of his qualities at any given time. To illustrate: God is right now revealing to someone a particular aspect of his character that is completely different from what he is revealing to someone else. He can expose any attribute to as many individuals, in as many locations, as he chooses—at one point in time.

Scripture testifies to God's immutability throughout (Mal. 3:6; Ps. 102:25-27; Heb. 13:8). He has been, is, and will be forever unalterable in his attributes and personality. There is no variability whatsoever in God (James 1:17). Immutability carries with it not only the idea that God *does not* change but also that he *cannot* change. This profound truth about God is mind-boggling for us mortals who are ever changing. We are never the same from one minute to the next! Yet God has revealed himself as the eternal, never-changing I AM WHO I AM (Ex. 3:13-15). The very name, I AM WHO I AM, implies the property of immutability.

Contemplating God's immutability immediately raises a number of questions, or to some, *problems*. These questions or problems require seeking the whole counsel of God's Word to be resolved. We need the whole counsel to prevent some from concluding that internal contradictions exist in the Bible. Much is at stake in rightly thinking about God's immutability. Deep thinking on this point reinforces an exalted view of God. Shallow thinking, on the other hand, ill-treats the transcendent grandeur of God. Such reasoning lowers our understanding of God and creates an unwarranted, elevated view of humanity!

Here are three important questions regarding God. First, has God ever learned anything? Second, does God ever forget anything? Third, does God ever change his mind? For example, does prayer change God's mind? God obviously has a will, but does he ever modify it? And do God's emotions, such as his jealousy and wrath fluctuate with circumstances? Because God is immutable the answer all of these questions is No! Readers, however, may protest, "We can quote Scriptures that provide a 'yes' answer to several of these questions." On the surface, the protest appears warranted. But this is why consulting the whole counsel of God's Word is so important in addressing multifaceted questions regarding his nature.

The Whole Counsel of God

The preceding two paragraphs used the phrase "the whole counsel of God" without explanation. What interpretative principle is intended by this expression? The concept is simple but its working out is not so simple. The whole message (Acts 5:20), the whole purpose (20:27), and everything profitable in God's Word (20:20) must be taught. Every question should be examined in the light of *all* that Scripture says. This ought to be done because the simple, apparent message of any text may be *incomplete*, and therefore open to wrong interpretation. For example, Jesus, when teaching the crowd on the mountain, said, "For if you forgive others for their transgressions, your heavenly Father will also forgive you. But if you do not forgive others, then your Father will not forgive your transgressions" (Matt. 6:14-15). What does this mean?

This statement could be construed to mean humans must first forgive their neighbors before God will forgive them. Some interpret Jesus's words just that way—we must forgive first; God will subsequently forgive. Ongoing questions about this text's interpretation indicate there is confusion in the light of other teachings about forgiveness. This passage must be seen in the context of the whole counsel of Scripture—*all* that the Bible says about forgiveness.

The Word of God teaches that if a person *willfully refuses* to forgive a neighbor's sin, the refuser will not be (and has not been) forgiven his sins (Matt. 18:35; Mark 11:25-26). The controlling principles associated with forgiveness, however, are two: (a) our sins have been forgiven us for Christ's sake (Pss. 25:11; 79:9; Isa. 48:9-11; 1 John 2:12); and (b) we are to forgive others even as God has forgiven us (Eph. 4:32; Matt. 18:21-35).

The first principle, forgiveness for Christ's sake, tells of the true motivation governing God's forgiveness. First and foremost, God the Father's love of his Son, Jesus Christ, has motivated the Father to forgive our sins—they are forgiven for *Christ's* sake (John 17:22-26). And second, the Father's desire to give his Son a people as an inheritance from creation has motivated the Father to provide a way that people could be justly forgiven (Eph. 1:4-14).

The second principle—because we have been forgiven we are to forgive *others*—is best exemplified in Jesus's parable, where a slave forgiven a great debt refuses to forgive a fellow-slave a very small debt (in Matt. 18:21-35). The forgiving lord comes back and demands full payment from the previously forgiven slave. The parable does *not* teach that God withdraws previously granted forgiveness. It teaches that those who, upon being convicted of their sin nature and specific acts of sin have truly apprehended God's forgiveness will willingly forgive those who have sinned against them. They know the debt they owed God far exceeds any debt a human could ever owe them.

Christ's statement "He who is forgiven little, loves little" (Luke 7:47)[66] conveys the same truth. Those who rightly perceive God's holiness and their own depravity but have tasted the deep joy of God's forgiveness, that cost the death of Christ, will count any trespasses against them negligible when compared with the debt God has forgiven them. Thus he who refuses to forgive his neighbor is one who does not value any forgiveness he supposedly received from God. Real forgiveness is remembered, cherished, and reciprocated! Only those who have known true forgiveness are empowered by the love of Christ to truly forgive others from the heart (Matt. 18:35). This is the teaching of the whole counsel of Scripture.

---

[66] To be forgiven little shows an attitude of ingratitude. Even a small sin infinitely offends a holy God.

Immutability in the Light of Substantive Questions

Has God ever learned anything? Has God ever forgotten anything? The third question—Has God ever changed his mind about anything?—is the one that causes the greatest theological controversy. Partial biblical evidence can be gathered and arranged to answer this question so as to lead to two possible misperceptions. One might erroneously conclude that the Bible itself presents conflicting information. Or one might conclude that the Bible does not communicate clearly and is therefore terribly difficult to interpret. We hear beliefs of this type all too often!

The first question challenging God's immutable nature—"Has God ever learned anything?"—is the easiest of the three to answer, but the answer also has its detractors. The following words appeared in chapter 2 in the section entitled *God's Omniscient Nature*:

> God's knowledge is infinite . . . God's knowledge is eternal. He has known everything—past, present, future and suppositional – *throughout eternity*. Knowledge is *inherent* to God's independent (*aseity*), eternal and infinite nature. God never obtained knowledge. God *is* knowledge . . . . God knows all things distinctly—absolutely and fully (1 Corinthians 13:12) . . . . God knows all things infallibly (Isaiah 14:24; 46:10) . . . . God knows all things immutably (Psalm 139:1-6, 16; Isaiah 46:9-10) . . . God knows all things perpetually.

We cannot comprehend how the infinite and eternal God could *be*, in his very being—I AM WHO I AM—the sum total of all past, present, future, and possible knowledge. This is especially true when we consider that God permits his image-bearers to freely exercise their will according to their nature. We do not know how God has prior knowledge of our future thoughts, motives, and actions. We are simply told that such knowledge is inscrutable (Isa. 40:28),[67] and that God possesses all knowledge eternally! No, God has never learned anything. No evidence is offered biblically and no evidence can be offered from human history to contradict the biblical teaching that God is omniscient—all-knowing throughout eternity.

The learning process that is such an integral part of human experience (and a testimony to our mutability) is totally absent in God's own experience. God is *not* a learner. Human reasoning thus reinforces the truth of God's immutability.

The second question to challenge God's immutable character is "Has God ever forgotten anything?" Some make this inquiry because they recall passages that seem to imply that God chooses to forget the past sins of his children. Isaiah, for example, quotes God: "I, even I, am the one who wipes out your transgressions for My own sake, and I will not remember your sins" (Isa. 43:25).[68] Jeremiah likewise reports God's declaration, "I will forgive their iniquity, and their sin I will remember no more" (Jer. 31:34). Similarly, Hebrews records the

---

[67] Isaiah 40 speaks powerfully of God's incomprehensible greatness.
[68] Also consider the same idea in Ps. 103:12; Isa. 38:17; and Mic. 7:19.

same thought: "For I will be merciful to their iniquities, and I will remember their sins no more" (Heb. 8:12), and later: "Their sins and their lawless deeds I will remember no more" (Heb. 10:17). How are we to understand these renunciations of memory? Has God indeed forgotten our sins?

To take literally that God could expunge from his memory an act or thought attacks the veracity of Scripture by declaring null and void two of God's revealed attributes. The biblical declaration that God is the same yesterday, today, and forever (immutable) would be a lie. He would be different today than he was at some time in the past when he presumably still remembered certain sins. Furthermore, the loss of memory, intentional or otherwise, would undermine the revelation that God is all-knowing (omniscient). He would presumably not know some things today that had occurred in the past. Neither of these conditions can stand the test of the whole message of Scripture.

It is God's not remembering sins that presses the question regarding the extent of his memory, which in turn contests his immutability.[69] But Scripture is plain. After God has looked upon "the anguish of His [Christ's] soul, He [the Father] will see it and be satisfied .... He [Christ] will bear their iniquities" (Isa. 53:11). The debt that the sinner owes God is *forgotten*—the debt has been paid; God has no reason to demand restitution. It is not that God does not remember what the sins were, or that a debt was due. It is that he will no longer bring the sins up for payment, for a debt is no longer due. Christ has paid the debt for the elect! God has neither a loss of memory nor diminished ability to remember when he says, "I will remember no more." It is the sinner's nature that God has changed—he or she has been regenerated by the Holy Spirit (John 3:3-8; 2 Cor. 5:17; 1 Peter 1:3, 23). The sinner is a new person who by faith has received Christ's full payment for the debt. The sinner has changed; and God has applied Christ's payment to the sinner's account payable. God has not changed! His immutability stands firm.

The third question—"Has God ever changed his mind about anything?"—troubles many Christians. It is troublesome because there are a number of *apparent* contradictions in the Scriptures. Reflect for a moment, however, on the conclusion just drawn—the sinner has undergone a change; God did not change. The principle embodied in this conclusion will be employed now to address the third question. What is the principle? God never changes; but he does change the disposition of affairs—the administration, arrangement, and settlement of affairs—for things and people outside himself.

A second principle that will help us analyze these apparent contradictions is that God has ordained that we will be included in the process of accomplishing results ordained by his immutable will. Rom. 10:13-15 illustrates this point:

---

[69] Some people may contend that what is needed is a new, qualified definition of "immutability." But to qualify the classical and historical definition is to become a theological taxidermist—one who stuffs a substitute meaning into an authentic doctrine by ignoring, and thus subverting, the whole counsel of God.

Whoever will call on the name of the Lord will be saved. How then will they call on Him in whom they have not believed? And how will they believe in Him whom they have not heard? And how will they hear without a preacher? How will they preach unless they are sent?

God has planned deeply to involve his children in his work of evangelism and discipleship. This is what biblical preaching is designed to bring about. We share in God's work not because he needs us, but because that is how he has chosen to accomplish his ends. This God-ordained human involvement in the working out of his eternal purposes brings great meaning to the lives of all who are called to labor in the company of their Creator. Human acts are important in accomplishing God's immutable will! This truth also plays a central role in reconciling what appear to be contradictory revelations.

We should remember, however, that our laboring in God's company is not a do-it-yourself proposition. It is Christ living within Christians that makes the work effective! It is the Holy Spirit's motivating and leading his people that results in the desired ends. "For it is God who is at work in you, both to will and to work for His good pleasure" (Phil. 2:13). His children depend upon his enabling power to accomplish anything that is well-pleasing to him.

With these two principles in mind, let us now examine the third question: "Has God ever changed his mind about anything?" The first example of an apparent biblical contradiction that seems to challenge the immutability of God is:

> **Challenge:** So the LORD changed His mind about [repented of, KJV] the harm which He said He would do to His people. (Ex. 32:14)
>
> **Affirmation:** Also the Glory of Israel will not lie or change His mind, for He is not a man that He should change His mind. (1 Sam. 15:29)

To interpret the apparent contradiction to God's immutability—"So the LORD changed his mind"—we need to see the context of the verse. Then the first principle needs to be invoked, "Did God change (or allow change to occur in) the disposition of affairs for things and people outside himself?" The context in Exodus 32 is Aaron's creation of a golden calf for the people to worship when Moses delayed coming down from the mountain where he had gone to be with God. Upon observing the people's worship of the calf, God said to Moses, "I have seen this people, and behold, they are an obstinate people. Now then let Me alone, that My anger may burn against them and that I may destroy them; and I will make of you a great nation" (vv. 9-10).

The second principle must also be applied—God includes us in the process of accomplishing results ordained by his immutable will. Moses is, in this context, a type of Christ. He foreshadows Christ's future and perfect work. "Moses entreated the LORD his God, and said, 'O LORD, why does Your anger burn against Your people…'" (v. 11). He prayed for the people. He reminded God of his promises to Abraham, Isaac and Israel—as if God needed reminding (vv. 12-13). No, it is the readers who need to be reminded of God's promises, for he breaks none of them. He did not break his promises here. It is recorded in verse 14, quoted above, that "God changed His mind." But God had no final intention of breaking his promises, even when he spoke of destroying the people.

Before times eternal God had his perfect intercessor, his Son, Jesus Christ, scheduled to become incarnate later to take away the sins of his people. Moses, here, previews the intercessory work of the Christ to come. Following the worship of the golden calf, God changed the disposition of affairs for the people outside of himself by raising up an intercessor, Moses, a type of Christ, to stand in the gap between God and sinful humanity. Moses foreshadowed the work of Christ (Rom. 8:34) and the Holy Spirit (vv. 26-27) that continues to this day. God had ordained that without intercessory work on behalf of the rebels he would utterly destroy them. But he has raised up an intercessor at every point in history when he desired to reveal his longsuffering, merciful, faithful, and kind intentions toward those who deserve his full wrath!

Remember the second principle—God has ordained to use his children in doing his work of salvation and discipleship. This is what God did with Moses. He did not need Moses; he does not need us. He could have ordained other methods. But he did not do so; he ordained the use of his children. We are to pray for those whom God places in our lives that need such help. Moses was the one ordained to fulfill this function then. Except for Moses' intercession God would have destroyed the people of Israel. But he knew in eternity that he would *not* destroy them because he had prepared Moses to be an intercessor.

Intercessors are an important, ordained link between our holy God and sinful humanity. Moses assumed the role of an intercessor and God used Moses' intercession to reveal to subsequent generations both God's decree regarding intercessory prayer and the impact of that prayer on the disposition of the sinful affairs of Aaron and the people. The affairs between God and his people were materially altered, from God's perspective, by Moses' intercession! God did *not* change! The affairs *external* to God changed!

Some of God's complex thinking is revealed in the above illustration, but God's immutable character stayed intact. Those experiencing the events in Exodus 32:1-14 certainly would have interpreted them as revealing a change in God's intentions to destroy them. And Moses subsequently recorded the event as showing "the LORD changed His mind." But the whole message of God portrays a fuller purpose behind the events that took place at Mount Sinai.

Another similar and challenging example is:

> **Challenge:** And the LORD was sorry [repented, KJV] that He had made man on the earth, and He was grieved in His heart. (Gen. 6:6)
>
> **Affirmations:** For I, the LORD, do not change; therefore you, O sons of Jacob, are not consumed. (Mal. 3:6)
>
> God is not a man, that He should lie, nor a son of man, that He should repent; has He said, and will He not do it? Or has He spoken, and will He not make it good? (Num. 23:19)

The same two principles can be applied to this example to dispel the conflict. This involves: (a) placing the passages above in their larger context; (b) observing how the situation external to God changes over time; and (c) observing God's inclusion of his chosen people in his ordained purposes: Noah and his family were saved from the flood by God's grace (Genesis 6-9).

Some may wonder, "Is God rigid and unfeeling in his character? If he is unchanging, then he must be 'frozen'!" Such thinking stems from a misunderstanding of God's immutability. God is eternally and infinitely filled with *joy*; simultaneously he is eternally and infinitely filled with *wrath*. He is *all* that he has always been! He is infinitely and eternally complete and whole. This is beyond our capacity to comprehend. To his finite and mutable image-bearers he discloses only tiny aspects of his attributes. And he does this in accordance with his perfect understanding of what is best for us at any time in our lives. But no, God is not unfeeling or frozen. He is simply unchanging in his infinite and eternal completeness and wholeness.

The last example of apparent contradiction is the three passages below. They will be studied in the light of the whole biblical counsel to know what God *consistently* communicates.[70]

> **Challenge:** And the prayer offered in faith will restore the one who is sick. . . . The effective prayer of a righteous man can accomplish much. (James 5:15-16)
>
> Whatever you ask in My name, that will I do, so that the Father may be glorified in the Son. If you ask Me anything in My name, I will do it. (John 14:13-14)
>
> **Affirmation:** And this is the confidence which we have before Him, that, if we ask anything according to His will, He hears us. (1 John 5:14)

The two challenging Scriptures relate to prayer. "Does prayer change the mind of God?" Many think so. But if so, is God still immutable? James tells us that prayer will "accomplish much." Elsewhere James says, however, that if we ask amiss we will not receive what we ask for (James 1:5-8; 4:3). John seems to say we can ask for "anything" we want. But 1 John 5:14 places an important limitation—"if we ask anything according to His will"—on what those who pray should expect. What does the whole counsel of God's Word reveal about this? If prayer does not change God, or move him to act, then why pray?

James literally speaks of a "prayer of faith"—a prayer offered from the wellspring of faith. And from where does genuine faith arise? It is a gift from God (Rom. 12:3; Eph. 2:8). Faith is not an attribute of the heart that we can be turn on and off at will. The disciples recognized this when they asked Christ to

---

[70] This book is based on the presupposition that God's truth is not contradictory. The Bible does not contain irreconcilable, contradictory revelation. If it seems so, then God has provided, in the whole Bible, sufficient revelation for us to discern the consistent and larger truth. It is reasonable to hold that any single biblical verse or passage may be unable to either fully or clearly communicate the complete truth on a given matter.

increase their faith (Luke 17:5-10). But God expands our faith only as we exercise the faith already given us (Luke 17:5-10).

James speaks next of the "effective prayer"—one born of genuine faith—of a "righteous man." And who is righteous? Only Christ of all who have ever lived is proclaimed to be righteous in his own works. The people who are accounted righteous are those who trust that Christ died for their sins. So people of faith offer their prayers to God through Christ's efficacy. Indeed, the Holy Spirit himself dwells in them and not only teaches them how to pray according to God's will but also prays for them when they do not know how to pray (Rom. 8:26-27; Eph. 6:18; Jude 20). From this perspective, God's mind is not being changed. Instead, God's children are being taught in a way that slowly brings them into conformity with his will.

The context of John 14:13-14 is one of *doing God's will* while loving and obeying him (see John 13:34-35; 14:15, 21, 23). If we love Christ, we will seek to do his will. It is in loving and obeying him that he invites us to ask for anything we want that agrees with his character and purposes. When we ask with wrong motives we will not be answered (James 4:3). And we ought to be grateful for this limitation—for who wants God to answer a bad prayer or one that would hinder God's great wisdom? A growing child of God wants increasingly to see the perfect will of God done in everything. "Yet not my will, but Thine be done" becomes, over time, an identifying mark of the maturing Christian.

First John 5:14 sums up nicely the whole purpose of God: "And this is the confidence which we have before Him, that, if we ask anything according to His will, He hears us." God is training us to be like Christ, and Christ's "meat" was to do the will of the Father (John 4:34). He never wanted his own will to prevail at the expense of the will of the Father (Matt. 26:39, 42; Mark 14:36; Luke 22:42).

So what shall we conclude? First, that prayer does not change God. He stands forever immutable, with an everlasting, loving commitment to his people. We also conclude that God is at work in his people, training them to pray for the things the Holy Spirit teaches them are in keeping with his will. Furthermore, we delight in the realization that God invites us—yes, has ordained for us—to be *participants in his work* by praying for the very things he desires. It is *God's will* that we petition him! Through prayer we join in the mission of God—with God.

This understanding should not, however, cause God's children to fail to ask for what is on their hearts. An earthly father does not chastise his small child for asking for what is not good for him. He simply says "No," with or without an explanation. This is a part of training our children. Likewise, God our Father sometimes says "No" to our requests. He does this because he *loves* us. He is training our hearts to discern what is in keeping with his perfect will. A "No" answer is as much an answer to prayer as is a "Yes" answer. Would any of us really want to change the mind of our infinitely wise Father?

Reasons to Revere God's Absolute Immutability

We generally take God's attributes for granted. We rarely pause to ponder the awesomeness of his character. The glory of God is unmistakably evident in every one of his characteristics. His glory is further magnified in the *indivisible unity* of his attributes. God would cease to be God if any of his attributes were slightly altered. His immutability is an essential property of his divinity. Without it he would cease to be God! He would suddenly become made in the image of mankind. Human nature would suddenly become the standard for assessing life's eternal verities. Thank God, such a ghoulish thought has no place in reality!

Consider God's holiness: his purity, moral perfection and separation from all that is unholy. This is the crown of his glory—his most defining and important attribute! Now imagine if God were mutable rather than immutable. He could become unholy in his thoughts and deeds. His decrees could become temporary preferences. Unholy justice might be forthcoming: God, for instance, might become an arbitrary respecter of persons—only the poor or rich might be saved. A changing, unholy God could play games with his creatures as it suited his every whim!

If God were mutable rather than immutable, there could be no guarantee that he would remain omnipotent, omniscient, omnipresent, or even infinite and eternal. His power, if mutable, could diminish to the point of ineffectiveness so as to jeopardize his sovereign rule. Satan might emerge as a threat to God's rule, for he could get weary and need some time to recuperate.

God's memory could fail him if he were mutable—there goes his omniscience! He might forget the grand and perfect design he had for the future, so that ad-libbing would become necessary. He might suddenly desire to make up a new future as time marched on. The really sad aspect of this make-believe scenario, however, is that there are people who have this kind of world/life-view concerning God. They make him in their own fallen image.

Scripture frequently uses the metaphor of God being like a *rock*, signifying his immutability (Deut. 32:15, 18, 30; Pss. 18:31, 46; 89.26, 1 Cor. 10:4). The metaphor of the rock is used because there is no other natural, physical element as hard, stable, and unchanging. Scripture uses this metaphor for several other reasons too. First and foremost, it describes a reality of God—he is *unchanging*. Second, God's immutability signifies his absolute *dependability* to us. There is nothing in the created order that is stable; only the eternal God does not change. And finally, God's being the only unchanging reference point makes him a true haven of security for us who recognize our desperate need to be changed into Christ's likeness.

Personal Beliefs and Conduct Derived from God's Immutability

God's immutability cries out to us to become people whose word is their bond. And when we faithfully keep our word, trust becomes its fruit. Trust is an essential component of integrity. And integrity is a prized component of good character. God's word is his bond. When God says he will do something, we know he will do it. We trust him! He cannot lie; he cannot change his mind. We too should be able to be counted on, even if keeping our word works to our own disadvantage (Ps. 15:1, 4b).

Abraham's willingness to sacrifice his son Isaac is a clear example of Abraham's complete confidence in God's integrity—God would keep his word in every detail:

> God tested Abraham. . . . He said, Take now your son, your only son, whom you love, Isaac, and go to the land of Moriah; and offer him there as a burnt offering on one of the mountains of which I will tell you. So Abraham rose early . . . and took two of his young men with him and Isaac his son. . . and went to the place of which God had told him. On the third day Abraham. . . saw the place from a distance. Abraham said to his young men, Stay here. . . and I and the lad [Isaac] will go over there; *and we will worship and return to you.* (Gen. 22:1-5)

The ongoing account reveals: (a) Abraham's willingness to sacrifice his son, and (b) God's intervention to stop the sacrifice at the last moment. But a question demands to be answered: How could Abraham trust God so much as to be willing to sacrifice his son whom he loved so much? God graciously answers:

> By faith Abraham, when he was tested, offered up Isaac; and he who had received the promises was offering up his only begotten son; it was he to whom it was said, "In Isaac your descendants shall be called." He considered that God is able to raise people even from the dead. (Heb. 11:17-19)

Abraham knew God would do what he had said he would do. God had already revealed the immutable character of his promises and his power when Sarah bore Isaac in her extreme old age. Hebrews says that Abraham knew God would bring *descendants* forth from Isaac—he had promised it. By faith, then, Abraham told the young men to wait, for he and *Isaac* would return. Abraham thought they would return after Isaac's resurrection! It was due to this conviction that Abraham was willing to sacrifice Isaac at God's request.

All trust in the relationships of life is grounded in the keeping of one's word. God's word is his bond, his guarantee; our word ought to be the same. We who identify with the name of Christ are never to break our word. To do so is to drag Christ's name through the mud. Such behavior is a rejection of Christ—probably unintended, but nonetheless real.

Psalm 15 asks, "O LORD, who may abide in Your tent? Who may dwell on Your holy hill? He who walks with integrity. . . . He [who] swears to his own hurt and does not change" (Ps. 15:1-2, 4). At the core of integrity is the unfailing routine of keeping one's word even when it means financial loss or disappointment. Swearing to one's own hurt and not changing was lived out dramatically in the 1930's and 1940's. A number of families who had lost their farms in bankruptcy foreclosures continued to pay the banks for decades. They did this although the courts had removed all legal requirements for repayment. Why would they do this? It was their sense of Christian *duty*—their word was tied to their profession of faith in Christ.

There is no biblical justification set forth for breaking one's word. There is, however, a remedy given whereby one may seek to be released from a foolish or damaging commitment:

> My son . . . if you have been snared with the words of your mouth, have been caught with the words of your mouth, do this then, my son, and deliver yourself; since you have come into the hand of your neighbor, go, humble yourself, and importune your neighbor. Give no sleep to your eyes, nor slumber to your eyelids; deliver yourself like a gazelle from the hunter's hand and like a bird from the hand of the fowler. (Prov. 6:1-5)

The admonition is clear: Go, humble yourself, and importune your neighbor. We may plead for a release from an obligation with the person to whom we made the commitment. But the right of release resides with that person. And it is in the response to our request for release that either the merciful or the demanding providence of our Sovereign Lord is revealed!

It is precisely at the point of considering the possibility of encountering demanding providence, that most—even many Christians—take matters into their own hands. This typically begins with rationalization: "I made a verbal commitment. It is not in writing; I will deny it." Or, "I will see if my lawyer can find a loophole in the contract, and I'll avoid the consequences that way." Perhaps the most popular avoidance procedure in business today, however, is to seek protection under the bankruptcy laws—to let our creditors suffer our financial hardships.

Avoidance of demanding providence may be more subtle. People may say something as inconsequential as "Great, I will meet you at the library this afternoon at 4:30" and then *conveniently* forget the commitment when a more attractive opportunity arises. We may even cover the first sin of failure by lying we got distracted and forgot. But the real problem is that we often take what we say so lightly that we do not even consider our commitments to be obligations! God sees it differently. We dare not ignore that we are accountable to Christ for all that proceeds from our mouth—all we say shall be shouted from the housetop (Luke 12:2-3).

We mutable humans are unable to partake of God's quality of immutability, but our marriage vows, contracts, and words of intent should all be guarded carefully and carried out meticulously because we are God's children. He requires the putting off of the "old self" and the putting on of the "new person" in Christ (Eph. 4:22-24; Col. 3:9-10). The importance of the commitment of our will to do God's will should grow as we mature in Christ. The will to avoid evil, and the will to embrace righteousness, should become core commitments in our heart.

The conclusion is obvious. *God is immutable* and consequently wholly trustworthy. His promises and testimonies are unalterable. We who bear his name should plead with him to enable us always to be faithful to our word. By doing so in matters small and large, we witness to the reality that we are Christ's disciples. "O Lord, help us to keep our word and bear Your name with integrity."

7

God Is Omnipresent: Our Eternal Helper

"Can a man hide himself in hiding places so I do not see him?"
declares the LORD. "Do I not fill the heavens and the earth?"
declares the LORD. (Jer. 23:24)

God is *omnipresent*—present everywhere (Ps. 139:7-12; Jer. 23:24; 2 Chron. 2:6). There is nowhere in the eternity of time or the infinity of space where God has not been in the past, is not present now, and will not be present in the future. He is eternally present everywhere with the fullness of his attributes. His every attribute is universally, continuously, infinitely, and eternally part of him in his *repletive* presence—completely filling all places. All of God is everywhere. He is everywhere present in the essential simplicity of his spirit nature.

It can be said that God is so thoroughly everywhere present that . . . "in Him we live and move and exist" (Acts 17:28). He is not excluded from being anywhere even by some other object's possession of a particular area of space. We live *in* him; we move *in* him; and exist *in* him. This is not, however, to be confused with *pantheism*—the view that the divine is all-inclusive, and that man and Nature are not independent of God but are elements of his Being.[71] The created order is not a mode of God, nor is it a part of God. God is independent of his creation (his *aseity*). But having no molecular structure, as a pure spirit he is capable of occupying the same space simultaneously with the molecular or spiritual elements he created, without confusion or necessary union. He simultaneously occupies the same tiniest space the smallest created element does, yet he is independent of that component. He is literally everywhere—and nowhere excluded.

Many presuppositions are attached to one's perception of this reality—God is omnipresent, or he is not omnipresent. First, let us look at two different paradigms regarding God's omnipresence. We will consider the following two questions: (1) How do unregenerate people avoid or rationalize the absence of God? and (2), What practical or helpful benefits do Christians derive from meditating on God's omnipresence? Then, we will proceed to an examination of what Christ meant when he said:

> I will ask the Father, and He will give you another Helper [*paracletos*: one called alongside to help], that He may be with you forever; that is

---

[71] Anthony Flew, *A Dictionary of Philosophy* (Macmillan Press: London, England, 1979), 243.

the Spirit of truth, whom the world cannot receive, because it does not see Him or know Him, but *you know Him* because He abides with you and will be in you. (John 14:16-17)

How can we distinguish between these two seemingly opposing truths: "God is omnipresent" and God the Father "will give you another Helper . . . the Spirit of truth . . . [who] will be in you." These truths will be differentiated by answering yet another question: (3) "How can the Holy Spirit be 'sent' or 'given' when he is already present?" Sending him when he is already present appears to be either a contradiction or a redundancy. But it is neither. This truth warrants differentiating the two realities—he is present; he will be sent.

How Unregenerate People Deny God's Presence

Denial mechanisms take many forms. People can *repress* truth so it is driven from their consciousness and will not surface with ordinary stimuli; a subconscious desire keeps the truth buried. People can also intentionally *suppress* truth; the truth surfaces, but they quickly find a way—rationalization or trivialization—to put it out of their mind.[72] Truth may also be *supplanted* by finding a distraction to focus on as a substitute. Or people may simply *reject* the truth and replace it with a self-satisfying perspective on the topic that they want to avoid.[73]

Adam and Eve believed that they could hide from God's presence. Soon after eating the forbidden fruit "they heard the sound of the LORD God walking in the garden . . . , and the man and his wife hid themselves from the presence of the LORD God among the trees of the garden" (Gen. 3:8). They sought to hide for they were afraid of God (Gen. 3:10). Their fear and desire to hide from God were new and evidences of their alienation from him. All, since the fall, enter the world fallen and alienated from God. We all enter life focused on the importance of *self*.

People try to hide from God in many ways, a foolish endeavor in the light of God's omnipresence. But hide they will try. It is silly-fun to watch a two-year-old put his hands up to cover his eyes and then observe his confidence that you cannot see him because he cannot see you. Otherwise rational adults irrationally mimic this procedure figuratively when they repress, suppress, or reject the fact that God sees every *thought and action* of every human always.

Scripture is replete with examples that people repress, suppress, reject, or ignore the truth that God is omnipresent. For example, the wicked fool "says to himself, 'God has forgotten; He has hidden His face; He will never see it'" (Ps. 10:11). The arrogant and the wicked think, "How does God know? And is there knowledge [of this sin] with the Most High?" (Ps. 73:11). Some even go so far as to

---

[72] See Rom. 1:18-23. Verse 18 speaks of people who suppress the truth in unrighteousness. People who do this are described as being without excuse for doing so (v. 20). Verses 24-32 that follow are progressive, negative illustrations of what occurs as a result of suppressing the awareness of God, and of thereby implicitly rationalizing his absence or nonexistence.

[73] Prov. 14:12 provides an example: "There is a way which seems right to a man, but its end is the way of death." See also Rom. 6:21, where Paul asks, "Therefore what benefit were you then deriving from the things of which you are now ashamed? For the outcome of those things is death."

claim, "The LORD does not see, nor does the God of Jacob pay heed" (Ps. 94:7). These people do not believe that God is right there with them, observing everything. They think and act as if God were blind, deaf, or absent.

Ezekiel recorded these words from the LORD: "Son of man, do you see what the elders of the house of Israel are committing in the dark, each man in the room of his carved images? For they say, 'The LORD does not see us.'" (Ezek. 8:12). And again, "He said to me, 'The iniquity of the house of Israel and Judah is very, very great, and the land is filled with blood and the city is full of perversion; for they say, 'The LORD has forsaken the land, and the LORD does not see!'" (Ezek. 9:9). The idea that God does not see what is going on in the world is a demonstrative problem of many who detest the idea of an omnipresent and omniscient God.[74]

People can be self-deluded and believe that when they think about evading their taxes that God does not know or care about their planned deceit. Or that God is ignorant that they plan to cheat on their calculus exam the next day, or lift a term paper off of the Internet to submit to their professor as their own work. Our psychological ability to believe that we are alone and unnoticed with regard to both our *thoughts* and *actions* is an inherent ability we all possess. We all have an innate predisposition "to hide . . . from the presence of God"—a clear mark of the fall (Gen. 3:8). We remain unconscious that we are hiding from him until we are made conscious of doing so by the regenerating and illumining work of the Holy Spirit.

The biblical record of Elijah's encounter with the prophets of Baal on Mount Carmel is a classic example of not grasping the reality of God's omnipresence (1 Kings 18:1-40). Elijah and the prophets of Baal entered into a contest where those prophets would call upon the name of their god to produce fire from heaven to consume their sacrifice to him. And Elijah was to subsequently call on the name of the LORD to do the same. The two sides agreed beforehand that the God who answered by fire would be declared the true God.

The prophets of Baal went first, and offered their sacrifice and called upon Baal from morning until noon to consume their offering by fire sent from heaven. But there was no answer, and they began to leap about the altar, presumably to get the attention of their god and to encourage him to act. Elijah mocked those prophets and said, "Call out with a loud voice, for he is a god; either he is occupied or gone aside, or is on a journey, or perhaps he is asleep and needs to be awakened" (1 Kings 18:27). And the prophets responded by crying out all the louder to their god, as if Elijah's suggestion was a reasonable explanation for his failure to respond.

The prophets of Baal's perception of their god was pathetic. In their minds he possessed many of the same weaknesses that are common to humans—he could be preoccupied and so pay no attention. Or maybe he was away and was not present to hear them. Or worse yet, perhaps fatigue had overtaken him and

---

[74] See also Ps. 64:1-6 (v. 5 in particular) and Dan. 5:22-23.

he was sleeping. It is clear that the prophets of Baal and their followers did not conceive of God as being omniscient, omnipresent, or omnipotent. Their god was completely without knowledge. He was absent and not with them. He was impotent!

The Practical Benefits Derived from Meditating on God's Omnipresence

God communes with his children on a Spirit-to-spirit basis—the Holy Spirit interacts directly with our spirits. The practical benefits made available to us by reason of his perpetual presence impact our spirits first, and then are subsequently manifested in a godly response. The benefits are at least six: *intimacy, assurance of eternal life, courage, perseverance, peace,* and *joy.* Remembering these magnificent and life-changing gifts that are ours in communion with God moves us to worship him with appreciation.

1. Intimacy

Intimacy connotes an intensely personal and sharing relationship between two parties. God says that "He is intimate with the upright" (Prov. 3:32). The Hebrew word used for intimate in this context is *cowd*. It literally means "couch" or "cushion." The idea is one of God sitting on a couch or cushion with an upright person and sharing his thoughts with him.[75] We are familiar with the expression "a penny for your thoughts." We hear that statement when one friends notices another friend in deep thought and utters those words to offer the friend an opportunity to express what is on his mind. True intimacy is sharing our deepest thoughts with one another. This requires genuine trust if it is to foster a continued intimate relationship.

In today's culture, unregenerate males (and immature Christians) tend to equate intimacy with sexual activity. The Old Testament presents sexual activity in a very different light. Intercourse outside of the context of marriage is always presented in language like Judah *went in to* Tamar (Gen. 38:15-19). The expression "went in to" recognizes the physical reality of sexual union but overlooks God's deeper purposes of a maturing, intimate oneness in spirit, emotion *and* flesh. In the context of marriage, intercourse is—with few exceptions[76]—represented in the language that "the man [Adam] *knew* his wife Eve" (Gen. 4:1). "He knew her" conveys *intimacy*. The couple's union takes place in the context of sharing their whole lives with one another—especially what is on their minds. Such sharing is necessary for true oneness.

The New Testament is even more explicit in its charge to husbands.

> You husbands in the same way, live with your wives in an *understanding* way, as with someone weaker, since she is a woman;

---

[75] An upright person is one who has been accounted as righteous by God in keeping with his just requirements: the person believed God (the Old Testament requirement) or trusts in the substitutionary death of Christ (the New Testament requisite).
[76] See Gen. 29:30, Ruth 4:13, and 2 Sam. 12:24.

and show her honor as a fellow heir of the grace of life, *so that your prayers will not be hindered*. (1 Peter 3:7)

The Greek word for "understanding" here is *gnosis*. It is *"knowledge"* acquired experientially and over time. We are to listen, talk, inquire, and gain understanding of our spouse's innermost being as we live with her or him. The Song of Songs likens the wife to "a garden locked [up]" and "a spring [of water] sealed up" (4:12), to be carefully unlocked and unsealed. Indeed, those who ignore God's will regarding these keys to interpersonal intimacy risk stifling their intimacy with him—"so that your prayers will not be hindered."

How does God share his mind with us? How do we share our mind with him? God shares his mind with us in the direct revelation of Scripture, and through our personal experiences in the context of his eternal decrees and his providence that provide the conditions for our lives. Our focus is on God's direct revelation of Scripture. The Holy Spirit superintended their writing, and in them God reveals his personality, his desires for his creation, and his will for us. Paul expresses this best:

> For who among men knows the thoughts of a man except the spirit of the man which is in him? Even so the thoughts of God no one knows except the Spirit of God. Now we have received, not the spirit of the world, but the Spirit who is from God, so that we may know the things freely given to us by God.... We have the mind of Christ. (1 Cor. 2:11-12, 16)

The Spirit of God who lives in our hearts knows the thoughts of God, and shares these thoughts with his people in the Scriptures. In doing so, he is being intimate with his children. Indeed, his intimacy is so close that we are said to "have the mind of Christ."

God's intimacy with his people spontaneously draws from them expressions of delight and gratitude. Scripture records many such outpourings:

> But as for me, the nearness of God is my good (Ps. 73:28).

> How blessed is the one whom You choose and bring near to You to dwell in Your courts (Ps. 65:4).

> In Your presence is fullness of joy (Ps. 16:11).

> When You said, "Seek My face," my heart said to You, "Your face, O LORD, I shall seek" (Ps. 27:8).

> Seek the LORD and His strength; seek His face continually (Ps. 105:4).

Enjoying God's intimacy is a fruit of abiding in Christ, which in turn is a fruit of grace that follows walking in the paths of Christ. This, in turn, flows out of living "on every word that proceeds out of the mouth of God" (Deut. 8:3; Matt. 4:4)—honoring the mind of Christ, as revealed in God's Word. We enjoy God's deepest intimacy when he writes his Word on our hearts and personally teaches us what is on his heart, just as he has promised:

> This is the covenant which I will make with the house of Israel after those days, declares the LORD: I will put My law within them and on their heart

I will write it; and I will be their God, and they shall be My people. And they will not teach again, each man his neighbor and each man his brother, saying, "Know the LORD," for they will all know Me, from the least of them to the greatest of them, declares the LORD, for I will forgive their iniquity, and their sin I will remember no more. (Jer. 31:33-34)

We, on the other hand, share our thoughts with God in two ways. One way qualifies the sharing and is intimate. The second way *may* also be intimate, but generally disqualifies itself by being non-relational. We will look at these in order.

(a) Praying to God is speaking to him, and his hearing us—he is omnipresent. Prayer is sharing our *heart* with him, if it is sincere and not merely rote. Christ said, "When you are praying, do not use meaningless repetition . . .[or] suppose that [you] will be heard for [your] many words" (Matt. 6:7). Remember, God is intelligent—so intelligent in fact that Christ could say, "Your Father knows what you need before you ask Him" (Matt. 6:8). Prayer, then, is a pouring out of our innermost thoughts to our Father, to our Savior and Brother, and to our Helper and Teacher. It is an intimate act that bonds us together.

Prayer should not to be thought of as the child of God coming to his or her Father to change his mind. Prayer is the expression of our heart's desires to the infinitely wise Creator/Sustainer. We do so in the belief that our desires have been formed in keeping with his perfect will and his desire to renovate us into Christ's image. He will answer our prayers, and reveal the answer through the unfolding circumstances in our lives. "No" may be a wiser answer than "yes." Another answer is: "My solution requires more time and will take a different course than you have thought." But in every case, prayer is an expression of deep intimacy.

(b) Yet it is also true that God knows our every thought whether it is expressed aloud or not.[77] When our thoughts are directed to God in silence, this is silent prayer.[78] These God-directed thoughts are also intimate in character. The reality is that most Christians do not consciously keep their thoughts directed to Christ or the Father most of the time. They are not in an intimate relationship with God when their thoughts are directed elsewhere. But God is no less aware of their thoughts. They are sharing their thoughts with God unintentionally in this case. This is the second way of sharing—which is non-relational.

Non-Christians live a life *continually* without intimacy, for they are alienated from God. This is so even though he knows their every thought. Christians, on the other hand, go *in* and *out* of their times of intimacy with Christ, the Father, and the Comforter. This, I believe, is what Jesus meant when he said,

---

[77] 1 Cor. 4:5 and Ps. 139:4. The psalmist says, "Even before there is a *word* on my tongue, behold, O LORD, You know it all." God knows the whole thought before any of it is spoken: "There is no creature hidden from His sight, but all things are open and laid bare to the eyes of Him with whom we have to do" (Heb. 4:13).

[78] The Christian unintentionally confirms his or her belief that God knows every unspoken thought when one's prayers are offered to him silently.

"I am the door; if anyone enters through Me, he will be saved, and will go *in* and *out* and find pasture" (John 10:9). "Going out" from the time of intimacy, does not imply that Christ no longer abides in us. It merely means our relational focus is, for the time, redirected to living the life Christ has called us to—with family, friends, coworkers, neighbors, and the created order. But *intimacy* with Christ, the Father and the Holy Spirit is an eternal benefit that specifically belongs to believers by virtue of God's grace.

2. Assurance of Salvation

"I do believe; help my unbelief" (Mark 9:24). Waves of doubt, uncertainties, and fears rooted in distrust are not uncommon experiences in the lives of those young in their years of walking with Christ. As babies learn to turn over, then crawl, walk, and finally run, Christians must grow up in Christ. God the Father sends the Holy Spirit to give us new life in Christ, and after that he *remains* with us for the explicit purpose of growing us up into Christ's likeness.[79] But especially during the early stages of one's walk with Christ, doubts about one's salvation— or even about God's existence—can assail immature Christians. Satan does not relinquish any of his children without a fight, and he throws missiles of doubt at young believers (Eph. 6:16; Luke 22:31-32). Martin Luther reportedly said that Satan, like a dog on a leash, cannot advance one step closer to God's children than he allows him to. God is sovereign even over Satan. Indeed, God's allowing Satan to disturb us belongs to his larger purpose to build us up in Christ.

God gradually develops in us strong roots of faith that give rise to genuine assurance of our union with Christ. His intimate and nurturing encouragement facilitates our increased faith—resulting in assurance—by training us to abide by the express will of God. That is why, when the apostles asked Christ to increase their faith, he responded:

> If you had faith like a mustard seed, you would say to this mulberry tree, "Be uprooted and be planted in the sea"; and it would obey you. Which of you, having a slave plowing or tending sheep, will say to him when he has come in from the field, "Come immediately and sit down to eat"? *But* will he not say to him, "Prepare something for me to eat, and properly clothe yourself and serve me while I eat and drink; and afterward you may eat and drink"? (Luke 17:5-8)

The disciples were probably puzzled at Jesus's response to their request that he increase their faith. Faith—Greek: *pistis* (conviction of God's truthfulness)—is a gift of God, but is not an inoculation. It is a natural response to the Holy Spirit's opening new Christians' eyes of the heart wide enough for them to be persuaded that Jesus is God's Son who has atoned for their sins. Through faith, God the Father declares them to be judicially righteous. But the expansion of that initial saving faith occurs through a *walk* of faith in which that

---

[79] New birth: John 3:1-11; 2 Cor. 5:17; 1 Peter 1:3, 23; James 1:18; and John 1:13. Christian growth: John 14:16-17, 26; 15:26; 16:7-14; 1 Thess. 4:2-7.

faith is tested and matures through *practice*. This fact—the thrust of the clause beginning with "but"—is at the heart of Christ's answer to the disciples' request for greater faith.

3. Courage

"Do not fear those who kill the body but are unable to kill the soul; but rather fear Him who is able to destroy both soul and body in hell" (Matt. 10:28). Fear may come from many sources. But the fear of death is certainly near the top of the list of the fears of lost persons. And Christians need Christ's preparatory work in their hearts to equip them to face the last great enemy—death (1 Cor. 15:25-26).[80] But God has promised to be with his people in the midst of all of their trials and tribulations, even death (Heb. 13:5-6; Pss. 27:5; 46:1-3).

God has revealed, through some dramatic events, just how his presence can eliminate fear when his children know he is with them in the midst of great dangers, even certain death.[81] But our interest does not lie in the dramatic. Paul, asked the Father to grant the Ephesians," according to the riches of His glory, *to be strengthened with power through His Spirit in the inner man;* so that Christ may dwell in your hearts through *faith*" (Eph. 3:14-17). The indwelling Spirit of Christ works genuine spiritual courage in believers. This strength is implanted and nurtured in our innermost being or heart. The courage comes through the assurance of God's ceaseless presence. Godly courage is given to us by the omnipresent and intimate eternal Spirit.

What we need most is not the boldness to face physical danger but the courage to face the rejection and ridicule that frequently accompanies obedient lives. For instance, when a Christian refrains from laughing at a vulgar joke, those who laughed are likely to interpret the silence as a rebuke. Suddenly the Christian is no fun to be with or is a prude. Christians are called to be salt and light in the world; but when they are, darkness resists their light and the cauterization of their salt. It takes *courage* to walk in Christ's paths among the ungodly.

4. Perseverance

Christians' confidence that they will persevere to the end is not placed in their own ability. It is a confidence in *Christ's* ability and determination to keep those whom the Father has given him from falling away. The Scriptures abundantly attest to this: "All that the Father gives Me will come to Me.... And this is the will of Him who sent Me, that *of all that He has given Me I lose nothing*" (John 6:37, 39). "And I give eternal life to them, and they will never perish; and *no one will snatch them out of My hand*" (10:28). Peter would testify to this reality.

---

[80] "He must reign until He has put all His enemies under His feet. The last enemy that will be abolished is death."

[81] We see this when Elisha and his attendant are surrounded by the army of the king of Aram (2 Kings 6:8-23), and when Shadrach, Meshach, and Abednego show calm composure when facing certain death by fire (Dan. 3:8-30).

For Christ told Peter before he grievously denied him, "I have prayed for you, that *your faith may not fail*" (Luke 22:32). Paul wrote, "He who began a good work in you will *perfect* it until the day of Christ Jesus" (Phil. 1:6). It is God who perfects his work in his children to enable them to persevere in the faith he graciously gave them. After he empowers them to become his children[82] he continues, *without loss or failure*, his work of grace in their lives.

The Word testifies to God's perseverance. As the Christian experientially encounters Christ's persevering help in his or her life, *confidence* in his full intention to persevere with them grows. It is, then, God's *own* perseverance that becomes the foundation of our conviction that we will persevere through the thick and thin of life (Rom. 8:35-39). It is the ever-present, *omnipresent* Spirit of Christ that makes this all a reality for God's children.

To meditate on God's eternal presence brings comforting memories of God's *intimacy* with us, an ever-deepening *assurance* of our right relationship with him, a godly *courage* that allows us to represent Christ's world/life-view in all circumstances, and the belief that we will *persevere* in our Christian testimony. And two more invaluable benefits are also bestowed on believers who know and love God's *omnipresence*: Christ's *peace* and an abiding *joy*.

5. Peace

There is the peace of the world—very fleeting. There also is unfounded peace—peace that exists when none rightly should. And there is the peace of Christ.

Worldly peace is the absence of conflict or emotional stress that creates anxiety. Innumerable illustrations of worldly peace are frequently around us. For example, our nation is not at war with another sovereign state now. My spouse and I are not bickering. Our child is no longer sick. There have been no gang rumbles in our town lately. My parents have not criticized me lately. The boss is no longer screaming at us anymore. The aftermath of the tornado is behind us and our lives are no longer being tossed and turned by the flow of devastating news.

Mental conflicts and emotional stress are also generated by perceptions of reality that are out of harmony with one's self-serving world/life-view—thereby disrupting personal peace. For example someone else was given the job promotion that should have been mine. Or the teacher's grade was not fair. My heartthrob turned me down when I asked her out. My parents' failure to love me the way they should caused my sense of loneliness. These are peace-robbing anxieties that emerge from blocked expectations or thwarted desires.

The world offers a variety of means to come to grips with the above-mentioned anxieties that destroy personal peace. In the case of the lost promotion, the unfortunate person may become bitter, seek another job, or seek

---

[82] John 1:12-13: "But as many as received Him, to them He gave the right to become children of God . . . who were born not of blood nor of the will of the flesh nor of the will of man, but of God."

to improve his job performance. The world is full of self-help suggestions, many of which are pseudo-helps, and a few of which are legitimate. But generally the world has not the wisdom to distinguish between false and true helps. And worse yet, even the true, God-prescribed aids [83] are only temporary helps unless the deepest need of all is met—a personal relationship with the Author, Redeemer, Counselor God.

Unfounded peace, peace that exists when none rightly should, is another form of worldly peace. Jonah experienced this peace when he fled from God and boarded the ship for Tarshish:

> And [Jonah] went down into [the ship] to go with them to Tarshish from the presence of the LORD. And the LORD hurled a great wind on the sea . . . so that the ship was about to break up. Then the sailors became afraid . . . but Jonah had gone below into the hold of the ship, lain down, and fallen sound asleep. (Jonah 1:3-5)

Jonah believed at the beginning of this journey that he was able to run from God. He had no understanding of God's *omnipresence*. From his perspective God was left behind and he was free to enjoy peace and quiet. The storm intervened, the ship's captain woke Jonah up, and the sailors cast lots to see who was causing their calamity. The lot fell on Jonah, and he subsequently told the sailors to throw him into the sea so the storm would subside (Jonah 1:6-12). His unfounded peace was shattered; God was there castigating him, and he knew he was guilty.

Unfounded peace is a by-product of self-deception, ignorance, or rebellion. A wrong understanding of God is a sure way of making an unintentional appointment with transient peace. Self-deception, a consequence flowing from the fall, is ever-present in the lives of those who reject Christ as the embodiment of all Truth (John 1:14; 14:6). The human who is not in fellowship with Christ by the indwelling Spirit must find peace in the world on his or her own.

The peace of Christ, on the other hand, is his personal *gift* to all who know him. His peace is given at a time of his own determination; he administers his peace according to his infinite wisdom—when it will accomplish his will in his child's life. "Peace I leave with you; My peace I give to you" (John 14:27). The peace Christ gives his people may be a pervasive sense of "all is well with my soul." His peace will also be present when external circumstances scream at us "all is *not* well." His peace is a balm that quiets the *heart*. His peace is shown within us by the power of the *omnipresent* Holy Spirit, the all-wise Comforter.

6. Joy

The following quote captures God's gift to his children of joy in the Lord.
Contrary to paganism, joy is coupled with moral rectitude [righteousness]. Pure joy is joy in God as both its source and object. God is a God of joy (Ps. 104:31); the joy of the Lord is strength (Neh. 8:10); in

---

[83] Proverbs is full of practical wisdom to be followed in dealing with many of life's self-inflicted behavioral and attitudinal problems.

his presence is fullness of joy (Ps. 16:11). The highest expressions of joy in the Old Testament are found in Psalms.

The New Testament regards joy as essentially a divine bestowal: it is the proper response of the soul to the gospel (Luke 2:10); closely related to the work of the Holy Spirit in Acts and the Epistles; listed as one of the fruits of the Spirit (Gal. 5:22); and has an eschatological aspect as a feature of the world to come (e.g., the joy of the Lord in Matt. 25:21, 23, and my joy in John 15:11; 17:13).

As a gift of God, joy is unknown to the world (1 Cor. 2:14), but paradoxically the believer may rejoice in afflictions and sufferings with joy unspeakable and full of glory (Acts 5:41; 2 Cor. 6:10; 1 Peter 1:6, 8; 4:13). Joy is not gaiety without gloom, but victory of faith (D. M. Edwards, ISBE, *in loco*).[84]

The *omnipresent* Holy Spirit bestows divine joy to the hearts of God's children. The world cannot taste this kind of joy apart from God. The idea of rejoicing in afflictions and sufferings with joy unspeakable is ridiculous to those without Christ. But to those *in* Christ it is an experienced reality and a strong, bonding affirmation of the presence of the *omnipresent* God.

How Can the Holy Spirit Be Sent or Given When He Is Already Present?

Scripture tells us that the Holy Spirit is sent and given to God's children (Luke 11:13; John 14:16-17). What does this mean? Is he not *already* omnipresent? Is this a contradiction?

The Holy Spirit is always *everywhere* present. *He must, however, make his presence known* if we are to become aware of it—for he is an invisible spirit. The world has no desire to think about God's nearness; God's children need to feed fully upon the reality of his nearness. On rare occasions when God desired to publicly manifest the sending of his Spirit—like the Spirit descending upon Jesus at his baptism (Matt. 3:13-17; Luke 3:21-22) or the Spirit coming upon the disciples at Pentecost (Acts 2:1-4)—he was manifested as a *theophany*: a visible manifestation of God to provide evidence of his presence.

The Holy Spirit Makes Himself Personally Known Only to God's Children (John 14:17).

We *know him* and he testifies with our spirits that we are children of God (Rom. 8:16). This self-revealing work is essential for the believer's life in Christ. And because Christ has asked the Father to give his Spirit to the newly adopted believers, he comes to be with them *forever* (John 14:16). So while God is *omnipresent*, he makes his presence known only to his children. This can be equated with the omnipresent Holy Spirit's being sent or given to the children of God.

---

[84] *Baker's Dictionary of Theology* (Grand Rapids: Baker, 1960), 299-300. Westlake T. Purkiser wrote this essay.

One last question needs to be answered, however. How do Christians know if they truly know God rather than merely know about him? Indeed, it is interesting to note that Christians are called upon to examine themselves to make certain that Christ really does dwell in them (2 Cor. 13:5; 2 Peter 1:10; 1 Cor. 10:1-12). The answer rests in the work of the Holy Spirit, not in things that Christians are required to do. The Holy Spirit does the following ten (10) things in the life of the child of God that *serve as the believer's evidence* that he or she truly knows Christ:

First, the Spirit bears witness with our spirits that we are God's children (Rom. 8:14-16 KJV). What does this look like? To illustrate, it could be the Holy Spirit's speaking to our hearts through the Word of God so that we are persuaded that this specific Scripture applies to us. For example, one might read, "No one can come to Me [Jesus said] unless the Father who sent Me draws him (John 6:44)," and conclude: "I have been drawn to Christ, and that is the special work of God the Father—so I am really a child of God!"

Second, we are assured of our relationship with Christ if we bear godly fruit—it identifies us (Matt. 7:13-23). Scripture speaks of two kinds of godly fruit: (a) the fruit of the Spirit described in Galatians 5:22-23. We might called this primary fruit. (Also see: Hos. 14:8; 2 Peter 1:2-10.) And (b) there is the fruit of works (described in James 2:14-20 and 1 Cor. 3:10-15).

Third, Jesus said, "If you love Me, you will keep My commandments" (John 14:15; also 14:21, 23; 15:10; 1 John 2:4-6; 5:3; 2 John 6). Loving and obeying Christ is strong evidence of knowing him.

Fourth, God puts his Word in our hearts and teaches us its usefulness (Jer. 31:31-34; Ps. 40:8; John 14:26; 1 John 2:27; 1 Thess. 4:1-12).

Fifth, the Holy Spirit calls the Word to our minds, as we need it (John 14:26; Luke 12:1-2; 21:12-15; Matt. 10:16-20).

Sixth, the Spirit renovates us so we bear witness of Christ and seek to give him all the glory; we cease to glorify self (John 15:26-27; 16:14). The Christian becomes Christ-focused; Christ increases, we decrease (John 3:30).

Seventh, the Holy Spirit convicts us of our sin nature, and of any particular sins that we need to repent of and be cleansed from (John 13:8-10; 15:3; 16:8; Eph. 5:25).

Eighth, the Spirit guides us into all truth (John 16:13; 15:26; 14:17).

Ninth, Christ gives us his peace—not the peace of the world, but his peace: he removes the alienation between us and the Trinity; he eliminates our guilt; and he gives us a sense that all is well with our soul (body/spirit) (John 14:27; 16:33; Phil. 4:6-7; Col. 3:15).

Tenth, love becomes a central part of our new nature (1 John 4:7-8, 11-13). Paul refers to Christ's presence *in* his people as "the mystery which had been hidden from the past ages and generations, but has now been manifested to his saints, to whom God willed to make known what is the riches of the glory of this mystery among the Gentiles, which is *Christ in you*, the hope of glory" (Col. 1:26-

27). The omnipresent God makes his abode with and in us, and we are thereby enabled to truly know him.

Conclusion

Meditating on God's *eternal presence* conveys multiple blessings. His children recall times when Christ manifested his true *intimacy* to them by sharing his *heart* (mind, passions, and will) with them through his Word. What a joy it is to know the intimacy of Christ! And through the Spirit's use of Scripture, we are blessed with the *assurance* of our inclusion in God's family. Many Christians struggle with the assurance of salvation, some for years, but the omnipresent Spirit of Christ, in his good time, assures his people of their place in the family of God. These blessings create within believers a sense of stability that is reflected in a growing *courage* that allows them to stand up for Christ in the world where he is despised. God's children become Christ's ambassadors!

And as God perseveres with his children during the years when they are being transformed into the likeness of Christ, they are thereby enabled to *persevere* in their walk with him. Apart from God's perseverance with his children there would be *no* perseverance on their part. Everyone who walks with Christ is also blessed with his *peace* on those numerous occasions when seemingly unsettling events offer no hope of peace at all. The peace of Christ indeed passes all understanding! It is his special gift.

The most unusual benefit Christians receive from the reality of God's *omnipresence* is the *joy* that they experience in the midst of affliction and suffering. This is a paradox. Joy experienced in the midst of suffering is an impossibility, a pure contradiction from the world's perspective; but it is a true possibility—an experienced *reality*—for the afflicted children of God.

How blessed the children of God are when they live in the very presence of the *omnipresent* God. The longer one abides in Christ, the more memories he or she has of the personal benefits that are so closely associated with the presence of Christ who abides with us *forever* (John 14:16). Christians should stir up their memories in this regard, for by doing so they grow in their appreciation of both who God is and what benefits they derive from his very being—the Being who is the only I AM WHO I AM.

8

God Is Wise: His Wisdom Is Ours Upon Request

Oh, the depth of the riches both of the wisdom and knowledge of God! How unsearchable are His judgments and unfathomable His ways! (Rom. 11:33)

God alone is wise (Rom. 16:27). His wisdom is a property of his eternal, immutable nature. He did not acquire it. He is simply by *nature* infinitely wise. It was "He who established the world by His wisdom, and by His understanding . . . stretched out the heavens" (Jer. 51:15). All that he wills—causes and decrees—manifests his infinite wisdom. *There is nothing that takes place within the created order that is outside of the realm of God's faultless wisdom.*

Are such statements true? Yes! Even the fall and the resulting sin that has entered the world manifest the infinite wisdom of God. It is even said that "the wrath of man shall praise You," and "with a remnant of wrath You will gird Yourself" (Ps. 76:10). Such perplexing truths are beyond our full comprehension. The following reminds us of our finitude as we face the unfathomable depths of God's infinite and perfect attributes: "How unsearchable are His judgments and unfathomable His ways" (Rom. 11:33). How wonderful that God is at once searchable and unsearchable, fathomable and unfathomable, and comprehensible and incomprehensible.[85]

Just what is *wisdom*? In order to answer we will first build a hierarchy of definitions. Their importance is highlighted by Isaiah 11:2. Here we find that the Spirit of the LORD, who was prophesied to come and rest upon Jesus, is "the spirit of knowledge," "the spirit of understanding," and "the spirit of wisdom" (see Prov. 2:6 also.) Knowledge precedes understanding, and understanding precedes wisdom, *in the human's experience, not God's*. We will therefore develop the hierarchy of definitions in the order of knowledge, understanding and wisdom, for our partaking of God's wisdom relies on knowledge and understanding.

Knowledge

Two types of knowledge exist for humans during their waking hours. First, there are observable *static facts*—what surrounds us in our environment—and these facts, being stored in our memory, are ready for recall given an appropriate

---

[85] God can only be described as searchable, fathomable, and comprehensible in the context of his special revelation of himself, delivered in Scripture.

stimulus. Individual facts make up the raw material of our knowledge and may be combined to make up a complex system of knowledge. For example, a person can possess many facts about a car and thus know much about them—an aggregation of thousands of parts assembled. *Static facts*, either as individual components or as aggregated combinations, comprise the raw material of what makes up knowledge.

The second type of knowledge might be called *dynamic facts* –knowledge about systems that are either alive or in motion. I'll use the automobile again as an example. A person can know how the thousands of parts that go into the assembly of an automobile fit together, and can, as a result, understand how they work together to make the car run. Or, to give another example, a person can apprehend how the blood circulates through the human body. These are examples of *dynamic* forms of knowledge.

Living in an information age has led many today to believe that knowledge is power. On the surface, this seems plausible. The sheer volume of information continuously transmitted across a myriad of delivery systems, plus the potential importance of this knowledge, leads people to assume that those with the knowledge have an advantage that gives them competitive power. This *can* be true, but information separated from understanding and wisdom is also the raw material for *bad decisions* and *chaos*. Knowledge is the foundation for both wrong thinking and right thinking! Understanding and wisdom both rest on knowledge, but knowledge without them could be likened to a torpedo without its guidance system—lots of latent power but with little chance of reaching an appropriate objective.

Regarding God's knowledge, however, the distinctions just outlined regarding human knowledge are irrelevant in light of his *infinite* and *eternal* knowledge—absolute knowledge of everything past, present, future, and suppositional. He is omniscient—all-knowing. Without this perfect knowledge God would not be absolutely wise.

Understanding

In the forward-looking sense, understanding is the comprehension of the probable consequences of the cause-and-effect outcomes of specific proposed actions or non-actions. Understanding is the comprehension of the dynamic consequences that accompany the interaction between the specific details that comprise our knowledge base. Understanding embodies the grasping of consequential relationships and the effects of combining specific causes. For example, touching a hot stove with a bare finger will bring about pain. It must be acknowledged, however, that unanticipated countervailing forces may come into play that will skew the anticipated outcomes. But it is the understanding of this very reality which allows people to make mid-course corrections in their ongoing decision-making processes.

It is human understanding that provides the opportunity for the individual or group to have some level of control over the outcome of their decisions. Without understanding, there would be no possible sense of direction associated with any type of decision-making. We need understanding prior to taking an action. Understanding builds upon and follows knowledge—and precedes wisdom. But before moving on to wisdom, we need to think more about understanding.

Understanding also has a backward-looking aspect to it. God understands that we are but frail creatures made of the dust of the earth (Pss. 103:14; 78:39). He understands why every human does everything he or she does—he knows our *past*. And we too learn from or gain understanding from our past experiences. So understanding, like knowledge, may be static or fluid, and it may be backward-looking or forward-looking. With God, of course, all matters—past, present, and future—stand before him perpetually and eternally.

Knowledge and understanding that are associated with the physical, temporal realm, but which are unassociated with the spiritual, eternal realm, are *incomplete* forms of knowledge and understanding. We, God's image-bearers, have the potential to have *the mind of Christ*, and the regenerate children of God actually have that potential *fulfilled* in them to some degree.

To illustrate: the brilliant unregenerate mind, while having a profound grasp of the knowledge and understanding of some significant temporal reality, will nevertheless lack the deeper knowledge and understanding that surrounds that reality unassociated with its Creator. He misses the deeper knowledge and understanding that is associated with God's ultimate purposes that manifest his glory, power, and wisdom. When we read Job 38–41 and contemplate Job's confession in chapter 42,[86] we see a clear shift from incomplete to full knowledge and understanding. The illuminating work of the Holy Spirit in Job's life transformed his former understanding of reality into a humiliating heap of repentance. This occurred as God revealed his majesty to him in God's sovereign rule over the laying of the foundation of the earth (Job 38:4), his ruling of the sea (v. 8), and his ability to cause the dawn to know its place (v. 12) Knowledge and understanding that are appropriately connected to their Creator are profoundly full and deep.

God's understanding, though not usually listed as an attribute, is one of his distinguishing characteristics—a true attribute. The psalmist says, under the Holy Spirit's guidance, "His understanding is infinite" (Ps. 147:5). And the prophet Isaiah writes, "His understanding is inscrutable"—so deep as to be beyond searching out (Isa. 40:28). God understands every effect brought about by every cause; and he understands the *antecedent* to every cause. His understanding is infinite, and his knowledge and understanding undergird his infinite wisdom.

---

[86] "I have declared that which I did not understand, things too wonderful for me, which I did not know. ... I have heard of You by the hearing of the ear, but now my eye sees You; therefore I retract, and I repent in dust and ashes" (Job 42:3, 5).

Wisdom

God's wisdom has three *core* components and two *environmental* components. The core components constitute the heart of wisdom, while the environmental ones provide a broader context in which to contemplate God's infinite wisdom. The first core element is the comprehension of the right end of a matter, *as determined by God*. The second core factor is the right end working itself out through *appropriate means and circumstances*. And the third core component is the right end nurtured by *the right reasons*.

The two environmental components that always underlie God's wisdom are his complete foreknowledge of all second causes and their consequences, and that God's wisdom always takes into account the true freedom he gave his image-bearers. The absence of any of these five elements disqualifies the outcome from being called the wisdom of God.

God's wisdom can also be called his *light* that leads his children along the true, good, and satisfying path of life. His wisdom is declared in his Word, and is made effective in our hearts by the Holy Spirit. God's wisdom is perfectly embodied in *Christ*, who is God's wisdom *incarnate* and sent to his people (1 Cor. 1:24, 30). Indeed, God alone (Father, Son and Holy Spirit) *is* wisdom and its only true wellspring (Rom. 16:27).

Wisdom is part of God's essence. It is not an addition to or something acquired by him. His knowledge and understanding are infinite and perfect, so the complete picture of the right ends and appropriate means and circumstances, in the context of his right reasons, is ever before him. His absolute foreknowledge of the actions and reactions of all second causes[87] is such that God ordains the accomplishment of the right end for all of his creation! Indeed, he has declared the end from the beginning (Isa. 46:10) without denying us the freedom to exercise our own will—a will that manifests the current state of our nature. We now turn too these five aspects.

1. Wisdom Embodies Right Ends, as Determined by God

The right end to anything can only be discerned in the light of God's sovereign purposes, as revealed in the Scripture. Not a sparrow falls to the ground apart from his will. God never misses anything that either will take place or does take place. He infallibly rules over and through everything. Those who fear that this teaching leads to determinism or fatalism are encouraged to stick with this proposition now, for Scripture renounces both determinism and fatalism. But at the same time it unambiguously declares the absolute sovereign rule of God over all.

Consideration of any right end necessitates considering it in a *context*. For example, there are eternal ends, temporal ends, and many intermediate ends— the end of a meal; the end to a court case; the end of a hospital stay. God's

---

[87] Second causes are all movements and actions within the created order—human behavior, storms, laws of physics in action.—that are separate from the movements and actions of God, the First Cause.

children, having access to the mind of Christ, have access to God's wisdom concerning a multitude of ends.

God's revealed wisdom declares that the *eternal end* of those redeemed by God's grace, through faith in Christ, is eternal life (Matt. 25:46; John 3:16; 10:28; 17:2-3; Acts 13:48; Rom. 2:7; 6:23). Christians know that at death they do not face an eternity separated from God. Instead, they will experience a resurrected life of eternal perfection that is lived in joyful and purposeful communion—which resounds to the glory of the Trinity.

Equally true, however, is the revelation of the eternal punishment awaiting those who have suppressed God's truth in unrighteousness. In rejecting Christ as Lord and Savior, they reject eternal life. They rely upon their own self-righteousness to please the self-created gods they serve. And they thus live in accordance with their own self-will, not the creative will of God. Their *eternal end* is their eternal separation from any fellowship with their Creator (Matt. 5:29-30; 8:12; 13:40-42; Mark 9:42-49; Luke 16:22-26; 2 Peter 2:4ff.; Rev. 19:19-20; 20:14-15).

Eternal life with God and eternal separation from him are both infinitely *wise* ends from his perspective. No human knows why God allows some image-bearers to persist in their rejection of his mercy that ends in their choosing eternal hell. Or why God pursues other equally rebellious image-bearers but initiates a Spirit-generated rebirth (John 1:13; 3:3-8; 1 Peter 1:23; 1 John 2:29) within them that results in their choosing Christ and the gift of eternal life. Both ends are, however, infinitely wise even though we cannot comprehend such wisdom.

Intermediate ends, on the other hand, serve as means to greater ends in God's economy. A temporal end might be the completion of a college degree program, or having one's leg amputated to stop the spread of bone cancer. The first example is a joyous conclusion to an extended period of study in anticipation of applying the benefits acquired. And the second example would be a very sobering experience that causes the patient to reflect upon the meaning of life. But *all* intermediate ends are under the sovereign rule of our loving Heavenly Father.

Romans 8:28-29 speaks to this great truth. It reveals that "God causes all things to work together for good to those who love God, to those who are called according to His purpose. For whom He foreknew, He also predestined to become conformed to the image of His Son, so that He would be the firstborn among many brethren." The simple and great events of life are *all* foreordained by God for our good—that we would be conformed to the image of Christ. That is the highest of all intermediate ends. We see it in God's use of temporal realities as he shapes the hearts of his children into Christ's likeness. He does this so that his children will fulfill his purpose for them both in temporal life and in preparation for eternal life (Acts 13:36).

But those who reject God's purpose are left to their own devices and move ever closer to their chosen self-destructive ends where all things do *not* work together for their good (Luke 7:30-35). Here we make a brief excursion to see what the Bible says about those who willfully persist in their separation from

Christ. First, those who reject the truth about Christ are without excuse, for deep within they know the truth (Rom. 1:1-20; Jer. 5:21-31). Since in God's eyes no one is righteous (Ps. 143:2; Isa. 64:6), then God must decide who will receive his mercy (Rom. 9:15-16, 18; Ex. 33:19), since none deserve it. Indeed, we all deserve the wrath of God. But it is important to note that God does not *cause* any human being to reject him. When Scripture declares that God said "I will have mercy on whom I have mercy" (Rom. 9:15), and follows it with "He hardens whom He desires" (v. 18), it is *not* saying that God took a good heart and hardened it. Then just what *is* involved in the idea that God *hardens* hearts?

An analogy helps us understand that "God hardens whom He desires." If we put a ball of wax on a sidewalk on a hot day and let the sun shine on the wax, it will become soft. But if a dish of ready-to-pour concrete were placed next to the ball of wax on the same hot day, the sun would harden the concrete. The difference in the results is due to the nature of the *substance* being placed on the sidewalk, not in the temperature of the sun.

Now let us apply this to our human condition. All humans are conceived and born in sin—have a *sin nature* that is alienated from God. But God has mercy on those whom he chooses to give to his Son as an inheritance (Ps. 33:12; Rom. 9:18). And this mercy is effectively poured out on them as the Holy Spirit effects their new birth—changes their old nature (heart of liquid concrete) to a *new nature* (heart of wax).

But one may ask, "Is it fair for God to do this sort of thing?" Paul asked this question in Rom. 9: "What shall we say then? There is no injustice with God is there? May it never be!" (verse 14). Then he adds: "So then *it does not depend on the man who wills or the man who runs*, but on God who has mercy" (verse 16). If no one deserves God's mercy, then those who are *not* its beneficiaries are not dealt with unjustly when God's mercy is not effectually applied to their hearts, making them new creatures (2 Cor. 5:17; Rom. 6:4; Gal. 6:15).

Today many Christians still quarrel with God over this. But so did many in Paul's day and he met their objections head-on:

> You will say to me then, "Why does He still find fault? For who resists His will?" On the contrary, who are you, O man, who answers back to God? The thing molded will not say to the molder, "Why did you make me like this, will it?" Or does not the potter have a right over the clay, to make from the same lump one vessel for honorable use and another for common use? What if God, although willing to demonstrate His wrath and to make His power known, endured with much patience vessels of wrath prepared for destruction? And *He did so to make known the riches of His glory upon vessels of mercy, which He prepared beforehand for glory*. (Rom. 9:19-23)

Perhaps Peter had a statement like this in mind when he said that some of Paul's letters had in them "are some things hard to understand, which the untaught...distort" (2 Peter 3:16).

The point of our excursion is straightforward: *All would remain eternally alienated from God without the merciful intervention of the Holy Spirit in the lives of those whom the Father gives and draws to Christ, so they may become Christ's eternal inheritance* (John 6:37, 44, 65; Matt. 13:11). Those who are given *new life in Christ* are as *unworthy* of receiving the gift of eternal life as are those who do not receive the gift. Scripture never reveals why God chooses particular individuals to receive eternal life and why others are left to their own devices that culminate in their eternal separation from God. But Scripture does repeatedly set forth the facts regarding God's mercy and grace.

Christians, though, may be certain that God foreknows every event in their lives and intends it for their eventual edification in the likeness of Christ (Rom. 8:28-29)—the greatest *intermediate end*. And becoming *more* like Christ is preparation for the much-anticipated *eternal end*—being like Christ forever! The non-Christians' *inheritance, however, is what they receive in this life* (Job 21:7-19; Pss. 17:14; 73:3-7; Luke 16:25-26).

Christians seeking God's wisdom need to ask if their own hearts are fixed on God's right ends, a key component of wisdom. God reveals many right ends in his Word. We must examine our being-sought-after ends and examine them in the light of God's right ends. Will our intended action glorify God? Will it lead to a constructive end for those who are impacted by it? Is what we are contemplating loving and holy? If we can answer these questions affirmatively, we can know that we are seeking God's wisdom.

2. Wisdom Involves the Right End Waiting for and Working Itself out through Appropriate Means and Circumstances

This dimension of wisdom is more easily grasped and applied in the temporal realm than it is in the interface between the spiritual and temporal facets, involving faith in God's participation. The following example, of a fundamentally temporal right intermediate end seeking an appropriate means and circumstance to bring about the desired end, illustrates the point.

If a person with an abscessed tooth has much swelling but little pain, goes to his dentist, he may deem it best to begin a regimen of antibiotics before pulling the tooth, thus reducing the possible spread of the infection that might occur if the tooth is pulled immediately. This kind of temporal wisdom comes from the dentist's medical training which is based on years of clinical observations and experience. We need this kind of temporal wisdom repeatedly every day. It applies to people in their relationship to the maintenance of things—be they cars, boats, houses, machinery, or whatever.

This second core element of wisdom involves people and their *stewardship* responsibilities before God. For example, people need wisdom when they buy a house. They must decide how big a house; the length of the mortgage; a fixed or a variable rate of interest; in what school district they should buy. Wisdom is needed in buying a car—should we pay cash or buy it on credit; should we buy a new or a used car; what make and model is appropriate. Much of the wisdom that pertains to our personal relationships with temporal objects is obtainable through natural observations and common sense. This level of wisdom is available to all, regardless of the state of their heart before God. But Christians have a deeper and more fundamental responsibility before God than just worldly-wise sensible behavior. Christians have a stewardship responsibility that may find them making choices based on things other than utilitarian criteria. Our love for Christ may lead us to do things that are deemed ultraconservative or ultraliberal from a prudential, utilitarian perspective.

One can argue that non-Christians likewise have such a stewardship responsibility—and this will prove to be true on the day they give account before Christ (Matt. 5:16 and 1 Peter 2:12). Yet as long as they remain alienated from Christ they will suppress God-motivated notions (Rom. 1:18-32). But wisdom for *Christians* regarding decisions about housing, cars, work, and hundreds of other matters, is to be settled before Christ on the basis of their *faith* in his leading.

This deeper form of wisdom, which seeks the right end while waiting for the appropriate means and circumstances, is the wisdom of knowing: (a) when to be quiet and when to speak; (b) when to lend a helping hand and when to stand by and watch; (c) when to encourage and when to correct; (d) when to try again and when to quit—and a host of other countervailing alternatives. Here again we are called upon to act in *faith*. We seek Christ's wisdom in the Scriptures, and we seek his mind regarding the temporal matters before us. We use the best sense he has given us, and we proceed in the belief that we are doing what he would have us do. Only time will prove if the Holy Spirit applied our acts and words—our perceived wisdom—to the situation we believed we were led to address. God alone is Wisdom. We simply seek to be instruments of his wisdom.

3. *Wisdom Is Revealed in the Right End Nurtured by the Right Reasons*

This third and final core component inherent in God's wisdom is the area requiring the greatest work in our lives by the Holy Spirit if we are to manifest God's wisdom.

Right reasons are an eternal and inherent property of God's nature. Every facet of his sovereign rule, manifested through both his creative will and decretive will, manifests his *glory*. Absolutely everything that transpires ultimately redounds to God's glory. Indeed, we were ultimately created *for his glory* (Isa. 43:7).

The key question, then, which anyone should ask when seeking the right reasons that would *nurture* a right end, should be "Will this action *glorify* God?" This, of course, leads to other important questions. Do we long to glorify God? When was the last time a strong desire to glorify God motivated me? By God's grace, the desire to glorify him can yet become the guiding reason in our hearts. This should be the beginning of our quest for a right reason that is sufficient to *nurture* a right end. The right ends God wants us to seek are generally cognitively discerned and volitionally acted upon. The appropriate means and circumstances that we are to relate to the right ends are also, mostly, cognitively discerned and volitionally acted upon. But the right reason component of wisdom is a *motivational* and *attitudinal* matter.

In our fallen world right reasons are generally crowded from our mind by our reasons, with little regard for God's reasons. This should not be so in Christians' lives. God's reasons always redound to his eternal glory, for they are the motivating force guiding the circumstances and means he uses to bring about his desired ends. This reality lay behind Christ's discourse with his disciples when they encountered the blind man and asked, "Rabbi, who sinned, this man or his parents, that he would be born blind?" They associated blindness with a divine punishment for sin. Christ's response provided a new world/life-view, "It was neither that this man sinned, nor his parents; but it was so that the works of God might be displayed in him" (John 9:2-3).

God's absolute rule over horrible circumstances is also evident in his discourse with Moses when he complained about God's telling him to go back to Egypt to confront Pharaoh. Moses said, "I am slow of speech and slow of tongue," to which God responded, "Who has made man's mouth? Or who makes him mute or deaf, or seeing or blind? Is it not I, the LORD?" (Ex. 4:11). Even human defects are part of God's infinitely *wise* decrees realized through providence. What he causes and what he permits are *both* his will, and they redound to his eternal *glory*.

The tragic events that befall us are our homework to train us in godly thoughts, motives, and behavior (1 Cor. 4:5). Right reasons generate the motivation and will to see the circumstances through to the right end. In this way the right reasons *nurture* the right end—encourage its accomplishment. Knowing God's reason—to conform us to the likeness of Christ (Rom. 8:28-29)—is a balm for tough circumstances. Right reasons are the womb of love's power to help us see life's means as God's vehicle to transport us toward our *eternal* end. And in the same manner, all intermediate ends are steppingstones along life's path. Everything has its purpose in God's economy. To live out this world/life-view is to *glorify* our great God.

4. Wisdom Is Shown by God's Complete Foreknowledge of All Second Causes and Their Consequences

Our foreknowledge is extremely limited; God's is infinite. The difference indicates how dependent we are on God's provision of his wisdom for us to have godly wisdom.

Second causes are all activities of humans, animals, mechanics, and nature. All activities set in motion by God's act of creation (God is the first cause) are second causes. For example, a person who walks out of her home, gets into the car, and drives to the post office to mail a letter, performs a number of second cause activities and sets into motion more second causes—the activities of the mail handlers, those of the recipient of the letter, etc. Should a car accident occur on the way to the post office, a more complicated set of second causes are set in motion. A dog barking is a second cause. So is a clock running. A hurricane and a wave are both second causes. All behavior that flows from God's creation—apart from his active participation—is known as a second cause phenomenon.

Now God knows all second causes before any of them occur. In fact, he has known them all perfectly from eternity past. Psalm 139:15-16 and Job 14:5 both make this point:

> My frame was not hidden from You, when I was made in secret, skillfully wrought in the depths of the earth; Your eyes have seen my unformed substance; and in Your book were written all the days that were ordained for me, when as yet there was not one of them.

> Since his days are determined, the number of his months is with You; and his limits You have set so that he cannot pass.

How can this be without some form of determinism or fatalism being at work? We must say with Isaiah, "His understanding is inscrutable" (Isa. 40:28). Indeed, God challenged the people of Isaiah's day to declare what was going to transpire in the future that they might be recognized as gods (Isa. 41:22-23; 44:7-8; 46:9-10). Only God infallibly knows the future, and he asks, "To whom then will you liken Me that I would be his equal?" (Isa. 40:25, 18).

But the point here is that God's infinite wisdom not only encompasses right ends, appropriate means and right reasons, but it rests atop his perfect foreknowledge which gives him the complete picture of outcomes. This complete picture is an essential component of God's perfect wisdom, for without it he would be as much in the dark as his creatures.

We have limited foreknowledge. Ours operates within the confines of God's established physical and moral laws that are observable in what we call natural law. We know when the sun will rise and set. We know the ocean's tides. We grasp the concept of gravity. We know that stealing will get us in trouble. The best source of our foreknowledge, however, is in Scripture. The Holy Spirit teaches God's children that his revelation of moral law is good and perfect, guiding them to bear good fruit. We do not have to experiment with pornography to know that it undermines God's best intentions for us—for it devalues the person posing, it undermines one's respect for the body, and it puts images in the observer's mind that are easily brought back to consciousness. We do not have to practice unnatural sexual relationships to discover their consequences—God has told us they are harmful. Gossiping, coveting, lying, stealing, being unfaithful, and many other ungodly behaviors are to be avoided with the Spirit's help. Our foreknowledge extends this far, but little further. We know that unhealthy consequences will result from certain behavior or thought patterns.

But we do not know if the young person we are considering marrying will prove as attractive to us in ten years as he or she does now. Nor do we know if the risk we are taking in our business will result in a success or failure. We do not know if we will get through next week without a bad accident. Our foreknowledge is extremely limited when compared to God's perfect foreknowledge. Yet our very limitation reminds us of our true dependence upon God's guidance in all of life. It is wonderful that he promised, "If any of you lacks wisdom, let him ask of God, who gives to all generously and without reproach, and it will be given to him" (James 1:5).

5. God's Wisdom Takes into Account the True Freedom He Has Bestowed upon Us

The greatest testimony to the magnitude of God's wisdom is his perfect foreknowledge of our free choices—that he has eternally known and factored into his perfect wisdom. There is no more mind-boggling demonstration of the awesomeness of God's omniscience and wisdom than this: he has known throughout eternity what I would freely choose at every turn and has incorporated this into his eternal purposes, infallibly and unchangeably (Isa. 40:28; 42:9). Wow! What an I AM he is (Ex. 3:14; John 8:24, 28, 58)!

Our personalities and actions are so perfectly known by God that what passes as true freedom for us has been eternally fixed and certain in his mind. It is not fixed and certain in the sense that God has caused what we choose and therefore it must come to pass in a fatalistic sense, but only in the sense that his insight into us is so complete that he knows with certainty what we will freely choose before we make our choices. Our free acts are fixed in his mind and have been real parts of his infinite knowledge from all eternity.

Conclusion

God's wisdom is his perspective on right ends nurtured by right reasons that are worked out through appropriate means, in the context of both his eternal foreknowledge and the freedom he gave us to make choices within the confines of our nature.

Only God is wise (Rom. 16:27). And we have access to portions of his wisdom through: (a) observing the natural laws (physical and moral) in the created order; (b) reading his revealed wisdom in Scripture; and (c) asking God for wisdom in specific circumstances. If prayer is accompanied by genuine faith, he will answer through the unfolding of his gracious providence.

It is *wise* to wear seat belts. They protect our bodies from being thrown around in an accident. It is *wise* to form good work habits. Bad ones will lead to unemployment. It is *wise* to obey those in authority. Disobedience leads to discipline. There are multitudes of situations in which we observe aspects of God's wisdom as we respect his natural laws. God's common grace—his goodness manifested in the lives of both the righteous and the unrighteous—has placed us all in an environment designed to bestow blessings on his entire creation.

The propositional truth in Scripture is available to anyone. These truths are God's wisdom given to any who will read them. Most of the temporal wisdom revealed in the Bible does not require special spiritual discernment to understand it. Even people with little interest in religion commonly accept the last six of the Ten Commandments as valid. Proverbs is full of prudential wisdom that could be called common sense because it so closely reflects the observable in daily life. Scripture is a fountain of God's wisdom.

The wisdom spoken about in the two preceding paragraphs could be called general wisdom—wisdom God provides to all through the natural and moral laws in the created order. It is wisdom available to all who consider what will generate a positive outcome by acting or not acting in specific ways. But there is wisdom which only the Holy Spirit can impart that should be called special-guidance wisdom. It is wisdom related to decisions that are intertwined with the necessity for foreknowledge. "Lord, you know that I have four employment opportunities open to me. Which should I take? Which one moves me along your path?" "O Lord, I need your help. I believe John is about to ask me to marry him and I am unsure. He is a godly man, but I am not certain he is the 'right one' for me. Please give me your discernment."

The opportunities before us in life, and the questions generated by them, seem endless. The first company we work for after graduation is not necessarily the one we should still work for five years later. Where should our children go to college? What neighborhood should we buy a house in? Such decisions are not always clear. And does God care about such trivia? Well, if not a sparrow falls to the ground apart from his decretive will, he has things in mind for us! How do we discern his wisdom? *"Ask, and it will be given to you; seek, and you will find; knock, and it will be opened to you"* (Matt. 7:7). God's wisdom is available when his children sincerely ask. But his answer is not always found in a Scripture verse. His answer may rest in the desires of our heart. Is the desire godly or selfish? The answer to our prayer may come from an accurate assessment of our own motives. The Spirit may lead us by remaining silent and letting our own thoughts lead the way. The Spirit may use anything he chooses to lead us to what God intends to use *to conform us to the image of Christ*. God's *ultimate* wisdom is revealed to us in Christ: "But by His doing you are in Christ Jesus, who became to us wisdom from God, and righteousness and sanctification, and redemption" (1 Cor. 1:30). What we truly know is that we are to *live by faith*, knowing that the Spirit is *with* us; he is leading us, and he will conform us to Christ's likeness through using our choices and by using the consequences that flow from them as well.

9

God Is Good: An Important Reason to Desire, Love, and Serve Him

And Jesus said to him, "Why do you call Me good?
No one is good except God alone." (Luke 18:19)

Why did God create anything or anyone? Why did he create the vast universe, angels, and human beings in his image? What m*otivated* him to become a Creator? Which attribute most moved him to display all his attributes by making a comprehensive creation, and then allowing it to fall? What motivated him to reveal himself to us? The highest end of creation is the revelation of his awesome glory! But what facet of his divine nature moved him to create, and thereby reveal his majesty? He had no need to create; he derives no personal benefit from his creation. Then *why* did he create?

Scripture does not explicitly answer these questions. But it is reasonable to believe that God's being *good* motivated him to create. In its word: God knew it would reveal his *goodness* to create creatures who would bear his image and thereby could truly know him (Gen. 1:27; 5:1; 9:6; Col. 3:10). This fact, coupled with his *agape* love—his intention to seek the highest good for his human creatures—persuades us that his goodness was an attribute that moved him to create.

Indeed, we cannot separate the two attributes—God's *goodness* and *love*—because his goodness displays his love. Love propels God into action, which in turn puts on display his other attributes—and their results reveal his infinite goodness! We, his children, especially appreciate his goodness when we contemplate his acts of creation, redemption, and providence. These three spheres clearly show his goodness to us. It is within these spheres that we encounter his intentions, thoughts and behavior—all of which are only *good*.

Stephen Charnock, in his classic *The Existence and Attributes of God*, said, "As God is great and powerful, he is the object of our understanding; but as good and bountiful, he is the object of our love and desire."[88] He reflected the truth expressed by John, "We love, because He first loved us" (1 John 4:19). Charnock was also expressing the truth that we also love God because he is good and bountiful to us, as Psalm 116:1-2, 12-13 makes abundantly clear:

---

[88] Charnock, *Discourses Upon the Existence and Attributes of God*, vol.2, 219.

> I *love* the LORD, *because* He hears my voice and my supplications. *Because* He has inclined His ear to me, *therefore* I shall call upon Him as long as I live.... What shall I render to the LORD *for all His benefits* toward me? I shall lift up the cup of salvation and call upon the name of the LORD.

The Psalmists constantly rejoice how close and good God has been to them. After God delivered David from the hand of King Saul, David says," I love You, O LORD. . . . In my distress I called upon the LORD, and cried to my God for help; He heard my voice. . . . He sent from on high, He took me; He drew me out of many waters. He delivered me from my strong enemy. . . . He rescued me" (Ps. 18:1, 6, 16-17, 19). David had experienced God's *goodness* in providential rescue from the hands of Saul. He knew that all was under God's sovereign control. And he declared, "I love You," because God had heard and rescued him.

Our recognition of the good which God continually pours out upon us motivates us to *desire, love,* and want to *serve* him. We come to know God's love for us through his demonstrated goodness to us. That is his essential component that enables us to truly desire, love, and serve him. And therefore, it is reasonable to believe that it was God's desire for us to know him through his goodness that led him to create a people who could know that goodness.[89]

God's very *goodness* seems to be behind his acts of creation, redemption, and providence. This view is supported by God's declaration at the end of each creation day that its results were *good* (Gen. 1:4, 10, 12, 18, 21, 31). And at the conclusion of his creative endeavors "God saw all that He had made, and behold, it was *very good*" (v. 31). May Christ fill our hearts with a deeper desire for, love of, and joy in serving him, as we focus on how good God is by contemplating his acts of *creation, redemption,* and *providence*.

God Is Good: As Revealed through Creation

> For since the creation of the world His invisible attributes, His eternal power and divine nature, have been clearly seen, being understood through what has been made, so that they are without excuse. For even though they truly knew [lit.] God, they did not honor Him as God or give thanks; but they became futile in their speculations, and their foolish heart was darkened (Rom. 1:20-21).

Scripture tells us that at least some of God's invisible attributes are clearly seen in his creation. Indeed, several aspects of God's nature are named in the text—his invisible attributes; his eternal power; his divine nature. The Spirit says

---

[89] Such speculation concerning which attribute of God is most fundamental, or at the core of his decision to create, is surreal—for God's attributes are not divisible. He is a holistic, unified, indivisible Spirit. Why then attempt the impossible? Because, while God humbled Isaiah by showing him his holiness (Isa. 6:3-7), and Job by circumcising the eyes of his heart so he could see God's glory (Job 42:1-6), most of God's children are sanctified more slowly through their repeated failures that are tended to by God's applied *goodness* that is *experientially received* by them in its many forms. God's goodness is applied to our lives to heal us and further transform us into the very likeness of Christ (Rom. 8:28-29). Oh what love!

there is no excuse for people not to comprehend through observing the created order that the Creator is *powerful*, and that that fact ought to move us to *honor* him—for his awesome omnipotence.

Furthermore, the Spirit declares that the power exhibited in the created order is *eternal*. Thus God's eternal nature is declared! And logic dictates that God's power *must* be eternal; otherwise he would cease to be the Creator God; he would be a mutable God if his power were not eternal. If God were a developing God he would have been no God at all at some time in eternity past. He could not have come into being from nothing—and if he had to grow up, there would have to have been another GOD who was the Creator of God. The very notion of God demands that he be *eternally* God and as therefore being *eternally* perfect in all his attributes.

The eternal power of God points to a *third* attribute: God must be an eternally *immutable* God. If God's power is eternal and unchanging, then God must be *immutable*. It follows that if I AM WHO I AM (Ex. 3:14) could mutate in *any* of his attributes then he would be mutable in *all* of them. And if he were mutable in every aspect of his nature, he could not be God. He would of necessity be a god that exists by some chance accident in a chance-accident universe.

It also follows that if God's power is so incomprehensible—so awe-invoking as to demand that we honor him, because such a wonder has been revealed through the creation—then a *fourth* attribute of God is revealed: his power is infinite—inscrutable, beyond searching out. No one can measure the power involved in calling the created order into being when there was no existence beside the Trinity. (Heb. 11:3). The very word "infinite" describes just such realities—things that are real, but which exceed the human capacity to calculate.

Creation also reveals a *fifth* attribute of God. The Creator is the possessor and giver of *life* (John 5:26; 6:33; 11:25; 14:6). Life forms are seen throughout creation. Their existence declares their origin to be from One supremely greater than they. All life external to God's own infinite and eternal life is life *given as a gift*. Our life did not originate within ourselves. The created order reveals that in this physical universe all life has a beginning and a conclusion.[90] Indeed, the Life Giver is the only one who possesses life in and of himself. He is *Life*.

These five attributes of God are all clearly discernible through his creation—he is *omnipotent* (all-powerful); *eternal* (outside of time); *immutable* (unchanging); *infinite* (beyond measurement); and the sole self-possessor of *life*. Contemplating these attributes expands our understanding of God, but a *sixth* attribute can open the door of our heart so we can truly *desire*, *love*, and *serve* him. Creation reveals that God is *good*! Yes, very good. In fact, he is *infinitely* good!

---

[90] Through God's revealed plan of redemption and judgment—special revelation—we are made aware that eternal life with God, or eternal life separated from God, are also parts of his eternal plan.

The *goodness* of God poured out upon us through his creative acts surround us. We taste, touch, hear, smell, and see the Creator's *goodness*. It is all around us to be enjoyed.

God's goodness is revealed unmistakably though the creation. For example, the sun and the rain nurture an enormous variety of plant and animal life. The earth's natural resources are vast, and beneficial to all that exists. The variety and abundance of the food supply that the created order places before all creatures is staggering to contemplate—the fruits, nuts, berries, grains, roots, vegetables, and eatables from the sea, air and land. We tend to take all this for granted, but the physical bounty around us and its ability to replenish itself declares God's glory and proclaims his infinite *goodness*.

The air we breathe, the clothes we wear, the shelter we enjoy, the beauty of the earth, the water that refreshes us, the birds that sing, the worms that aerate the ground, the energy that warms us, the colors that please us, the medicines that foster healing, and the beyond-counting other temporal things that benefit us—*all* declare that God is *good*. And his redeemed children desire, love and serve him *because* he is good.

Only God can open our hearts to see the true depth of what is revealed to us through creation. God's conversation with Job in Job 38–41 illustrates this, where God asks him a number of questions regarding his creation. Prior to this conversation with God Job had maintained that he was faultless. Then God confronted him, "Who is this that darkens counsel by words without knowledge? Where were you when I laid the foundation of the earth? Where were you, Job, when I enclosed the sea with doors, when, bursting forth, it went out from the womb . . . and I placed boundaries on it . . . and [said], 'Here shall your proud waves stop'?" (38: 2, 4, 8-11).

The conversation continues. "Have you ever in your life commanded the morning, and caused the dawn to know its place? . . . Have you entered the storehouses of the snow, or have you seen the storehouses of the hail? Can you lead forth a constellation in its season . . . ? Who has put wisdom in the innermost being or given understanding to the mind? Who prepares for the raven its nourishment, when its young cry to God and wander about without food?" (38:12, 16, 22, 32, 36, 41). God's questioning continues on and on, and only befuddles Job all the more.

Job answered the LORD, "Behold, I am insignificant; what can I reply to You? I lay my hand on my mouth" (40:4). Job then declares he will not say anything more. But the LORD answered Job, "Now gird up your loins like a man; I will ask you, and you instruct Me. Will you really annul My judgment? Will you condemn Me that you may be justified?" (vv. 7-8). And the climax comes when Job answered the LORD, "I know that You can do all things, and that no purpose of Yours can be thwarted . . . . I have declared that which I did not understand, things too wonderful for me, which I did not know . . . . I have heard of You by the hearing of the ear; but now my eye sees You; *therefore I retract, and I repent in dust and ashes*" (42:2-6).

God revealed himself to Job by drawing his attention to his personal involvement in every detail of creation and its operations. What might we say if asked to say a few words about a simple maple leaf given to us? Would we speak as a botanist? Or would we say a few words about how the leaf reveals the wonder of God the designer, Creator, and sustainer of the leaf? God has assigned us the task of subduing and ruling his created order (Gen. 1:26, 28; Ps. 8:6-8) but to focus on the creation and to fail to reflect upon the Creator reveals spiritual poverty. For to understand just how *good* God is, and to know that he provided us with the vast *riches* of his creation to enjoy, can, by the power of the Holy Spirit, cause us to ascribe to him the highest possible worth—worth that becomes *worship* that declares his *glory*.

God's acts of creation leave all humanity without excuse for neglecting his worship, and for failing to seek his face. The goodness of God revealed in the created order is not revealed to the same degree or in the same light as his goodness revealed in his work of *redemption*. We turn now to God's acts of redemption and consider how profoundly our redemption reveals the depth of his character, and specifically his *goodness*.

God Is Good: As Revealed through Redemption

We will take a brief side trip to establish how *good* the Trinity is to redeem a people from eternal hell. God never caused anyone to choose a world/life-view that would lead him or her to hell. But God *permitted* Adam and Eve to make a decision that resulted in their immediate spiritual death and their eventual physical death, and *our* subsequent spiritual/physical death. But even more importantly, our first parents' original sin caused them to hide from God, revealing an alienated nature that we all inherited. We can all say with David, "We were brought forth [born] in iniquity, and in sin my mother conceived me [so that I had a 'sin nature' from conception]" (Ps. 51:5, with interpretative additions). We all, following our fallen nature, choose to reject God's Lordship until by his *grace* he effects our rebirth so we are restored to his fellowship.

The theological excursion establishes that God *knew* our first parents would disobey his instructions, be the first to sin, and pass on to their posterity a sin nature. God knew this would be the case *before creation*! We know this because God the Father gave those who were to be redeemed to Christ—to be his inheritance (Eph. 1:18)—*before times eternal*! We know this because Paul writes in Titus 1:1-2, ". . . for the faith of those chosen of God and the knowledge of the truth which is according to godliness, *in the hope of eternal life*, which God, who cannot lie, *promised before times eternal*" (literal Greek).

And to whom did God make promises in eternity? To the persons of the Trinity. For Paul speaks of "God, who has saved us, and called us with a holy calling . . . according to His own purpose and grace *which was granted us in Christ Jesus from all eternity*" [2 Tim. 1:8-9 literally: "before times eternal"]. Scripture even tells us that the redeemed have had their names recorded in "the book of life of the Lamb" from the foundation of the world (Rev. 13:8).

We must understand the full implications that God the Father knew that the creation of image-bearers would require the painful crucifixion of his Son, Jesus Christ, *if* any of his people were to enjoy an eternal relationship with him. God the Son also knew this would be the certain consequence of his creative acts. And God the Holy Spirit knew it would be his task to convict of their sins those whom he would bring to Christ. The Spirit regenerates the spiritually dead so they become alive to God and accept by faith the majestic Triune God's *work of redemption*.

It is profitable for us the redeemed to contemplate the *price* God paid to redeem us, for nothing reveals the *goodness* of God as his work of redemption. Reflect on the perfect unity, harmony, and love between the persons of the Godhead before times eternal. And remember the aseity of God—he had no needs whatsoever in the perfection of his existence. And yet all three persons of the Trinity knowingly created us who would reject and despise them. They would be misunderstood. They would be thought of as being very limited in their knowledge. They would be thought of as being subject to change. And they would find their image-bearers creating them in their own likeness, not understanding just how holy, eternal, infinite, powerful, righteous, wise, just, and sovereign their Creator really is.

Indeed, humans alienated from God do not even think about him unless they make him impotent, manageable, and small. Many years ago a commercial airliner en route to Hawaii from San Francisco, suddenly encountered violent air and the plane plunged out of control for about ten thousand feet. They had not quite reached the halfway point between destinations. Because the pilot knew some passengers had sustained minor injuries he decided to return to San Francisco. This occurred before there was any airport security, and TV reporters asked the passengers questions as they disembarked. A frightened passenger's comment is still in my mind. This man was emotionally shaken. But when asked, "Were you frightened by the turbulence?" he said, "No." When asked, "Were you frightened by the sudden plunge of the plane through space?" again he answered "No." So, "Then what scared you?" The response was clear: "Thoughts of God filled my mind as we were plunging, and this nearly scared me to death. I have not thought about God for years!" And these thoughts still run around in my head.

I often couple this memory with the thought that the fear of the LORD is the beginning of wisdom. The passenger was scared because he thought of God as a God who would judge him for ignoring him. This idea of God as judge was the source of his fear. The distance, however, between the *terror* of the LORD and the *awe* of the LORD is only a redemptive act away. I hope that someone who knew Christ shared the good news of Christ's redemptive love with that man.

Nothing in all creation reveals the depth and breadth of just how *good* God is as does the Trinity's participation in actions to redeem a people for Christ's inheritance. Christ's own behavior best describes his participation when Paul says:

> Have this attitude in yourselves which was also in Christ Jesus, who, although He existed in the form of God, did not regard equality with God a thing to be grasped, but emptied Himself [laid aside His privileges], taking the form of a bond-servant, and being made in the likeness of men. And being found in appearance as a man, He humbled Himself by becoming obedient to the point of death, even death on a cross. (Phil. 2:5-8)

I cannot comprehend Christ's love that caused him to give up his privileges in the Godhead and take on flesh, and to humble himself by dying a criminal's death—suffering the wrath of his Father, which he did not deserve. Can we not hear the echo of Christ's question: "Why do you call Me good? No one is good except God alone?" And can we fail to respond, as did Thomas upon seeing the risen Lord, "My Lord and my God!" Such *goodness* has led God to redeem a people for himself—a people who *know* him, *love* him, and long to *please* him!

We return to the topic of redemption. The word redeem has a number of usage nuances: to restore; to deliver from; to recover; to purchase; to reconcile; or to supply satisfaction for a wrong committed. In Christian theology it is significant that when Scripture speaks of God's redemptive work it incorporates all of these nuances. For example, Christ's redemptive work is to be understood as a past, present, and ongoing event in the individual Christian's life.

Redemption incorporates our *removal from* the kingdom of Satan and our *deliverance into* the kingdom of Christ (Acts 7:34). It includes the *escape* from the snares of the devil (2 Tim. 2:25-26). It connotes Christ's *purchase* of his bride, the church (1 Cor. 6:20). It is God's act that brings about *reconciliation* between him and those who have been deeply alienated from him (Rom. 5:10-11). In its depths, however, redemption means that the very holiness of God that is offended by sin required that God's just nature be *satisfied*. Christ the Son's taking the terrible wrath of God the Father upon himself in our stead wonderfully satisfied God's justice. God has shown himself thereby capable of being both *just* and a *justifier*, a holy *redeemer* (Rom. 3:26). The most beautiful declaration of this wonder occurs in Isaiah 53:3-11:

> He was despised and forsaken of men, a man of sorrows and acquainted with grief; and . . . we did not esteem Him. Surely our griefs He himself bore . . . . But He was pierced through for our transgressions, He was crushed for our iniquities . . . and by His scourging we are healed. All of us like sheep have gone astray . . . but the LORD has caused the iniquity of us all to fall on Him. He was oppressed and He was afflicted, yet He did not open His mouth . . . . But the LORD was pleased to crush Him . . . if He would render Himself as a guilt offering, He will see His offspring. . . . As a result of the anguish of His soul, He will see it and be satisfied; by His knowledge the Righteous One, My Servant, will justify the many, as He will bear their iniquities.

Hallelujah! God provided a way for our redemption. Has there ever been such *goodness* shown as in God the Father's intentional sending of his only begotten Son to, first, live a sinless life and qualify himself to become the perfect sacrificial lamb, and then to freely offer himself up as the substitutionary sacrifice for sinners? No, there is no *goodness* that can be compared or equated with God's gracious and merciful work of redemption!

The Holy Spirit's regenerative work enables the dead-to-Christ person to embrace the truth of Christ's sacrifice, setting in motion a renovative process: the Spirit's work of cleansing our heart through Scripture (Titus 3:5); his sustaining our walk with Christ (Heb. 10:36-39); his setting us apart to follow Christ (Rom. 6:22); his comforting us (2 Cor. 1:3-11); his chastening us (Heb. 12:4-13). All believers need this assistance until the day of their final redemption.

This *renovative* work of the Holy Spirit is like our purchasing an old house that needs thorough renovation. We undertake the necessary work of re-wiring, re-plumbing, re-flooring, re-plastering, and re-roofing in order to turn the house into a home we will enjoy. Similarly, those who become the temples of God (1 Cor. 3:16; 6:19) undergo a renovative procedure for the rest of their lives as the Spirit transforms them more and more into Christ's likeness. This renovative work has an immediate, ongoing, and lasting impact on the believer's world/life-view. To be reborn means they see and hear as they could not before. They no longer want to hide from God. Instead, he becomes One to be worshiped in the wonder of his true identity.

God Is Good: As Revealed through Providence

The ideas regarding God's *providence* challenge many, for three reasons. First, Scripture's teaching regarding providence has been neglected for over a hundred years. For this reason, most Christians are unfamiliar with the reality that *God governs everything great and small* through providence. Providence is a forgotten truth. Second, we North Americans have enjoyed so much freedom to do as we please that the idea of our choices being under the authority of an omnipotent, omniscient, holy God has not entered many minds. And finally, our personal experiences tell us that *we* are in charge of our choices—and we are! Therefore few have ever asked, "If I am in charge of my choices, how can it be that God rules everything?" Can we be responsible for our actions and yet acknowledge that God's *providence* governs all?

God's goodness is clearly seen in his *providence*. Given this assertion, then: (a) What is providence? And, (b) How does it work? The answer to the first question is simple, but is hard for many to digest because it does not fit their perceptions of their own experiences. Providence is, nonetheless, biblically, *God's immutable guidance*. How sweeping is his guidance? Does God just guide in the big things of life, or does he guide the small things too?

For instance, are the words of Matthew 10:29-30 to be taken literally?—"Are not two sparrows sold for a cent? And yet *not one of them will fall to the ground apart from your Father. But the very hairs of your head are all numbered.*" Does this mean that every duck shot by a hunter, and every bird killed by a car, and all birds that die of old age, all live within the framework of God's providence? And has God been tallying my hair count after every shower?

Are children who are born with birth defects, or born dead, or born healthy into a Christian home, all equally under God's guidance? How shall we understand Exodus 4:11: "The LORD said to him [Moses], 'Who has made man's mouth? Or who makes him mute or deaf, or seeing or blind? Is it not I the LORD?'" These words seem harsh at first. What could God mean when he says that he *makes* some people mute, deaf, or blind? Does the word "makes" here imply that God is the *cause* of such defects? No. Then does it mean that God is so in control of everything that *what he allows* in the natural unfolding of life is as much a part of his *will* as those things he actively causes? Yes, Scripture wants us to understand *providence* in this way.

Providence embodies both God's *active will*, what he causes to happen, and his *permissive will*, what he permits to happen. His *permissive will* is sometimes referred to as his *decretive will*—that which God foreknew with certainty would happen if his creatures were allowed to make their own free choices. This is God's will *permitting* things to happen—without *causing* good and bad things to happen. The *certainty* of these freely chosen outcomes is, however, so *fully foreknown* by God that, from his side, they are *decreed*—fixed, certain to occur, though not caused by him.

Returning to Exodus 4:11: When God asks "Or who makes him mute or deaf, or seeing or blind? Is it not I, the LORD?" he does *not say* that he has *caused* people to be mute, deaf, or blind. He says that he is so much in charge of everything, always, that nothing happens apart from either his causing it or his foreknowing and permitting it. Furthermore, he desires that we all comprehend that he is not ashamed to accept this sovereign responsibility for all of reality.

God's *rule* through his active involvement in the affairs of human beings and his permissive allowance of human free choice is very clearly demonstrated in Acts 2:23:

> This Man [Jesus], delivered over by the predetermined plan and foreknowledge of God, you nailed to a cross by the hands of godless men and put Him to death.

Yes, God was in charge of Christ's crucifixion. God actively led Jesus to be crucified. But he allowed godless men to exercise their free will according to their fallen nature—and they crucified the sinless Son of God. This was God's will.

The mystery embodied in the doctrine of *providence* is mind-boggling. We cannot fathom such wisdom or grandeur. The greatness of God's rule is awesome. But his children come to trust and find great comfort in his *providence*. They learn that *God's providence is good* as they experience the reality found in God's promise to them in Rom. 8:28-29:

> And we know that God causes all things to work together for good to those who love God, to those who are called according to His purpose. For those whom He foreknew, He also predestined to become conformed to the image of His Son, so that He would be the firstborn among many brethren.

We answered the first question, "What is providence?"—it is God's absolute oversight and control of everything, either by permission or causation. But the second question, "How does providence work?", requires more explanation. The following answer mirrors a document prepared by theologians, called together by the English Parliament, who worked together from 1643 until 1649.[91] Their work is found in The Westminster Confession of Faith (WCF), including chapter V "Of Providence." The following seven points paraphrase the first three paragraphs of that chapter.

(1) It is God who upholds, arranges, directs, and governs all creatures, actions and things, from the greatest even to the smallest, by his wise and holy *providence*. (Heb. 1:3; Dan. 4:34-35; Ps. 135:6; Acts 17:24-31; Job 38; 39; 40; 41)

(2) Everything that goes on in creation is according to God's infallible foreknowledge, and the free and immutable counsel of his own will. (Isa. 41:23; 44:7-8; 45:21; Prov. 16:9; 20:24; Eph. 1:11b)

(3) Everything that does happen resounds to the praise of his glory, wisdom, power, justice, *goodness*, and mercy. (Isa. 63:14; Eph. 3:10; Rom. 9:17; Gen. 45:7; Ps. 145:7)

(4) God, the first cause, accepts absolute responsibility for *superintending*—causing or allowing—all second causes. Second causes are those things and activities that flow from God's initial creative acts, and all of the fallout that takes place as a result of these subsequent second cause activities. (Ex. 4:10-11; Matt. 11:4-6; Luke 1:20, 64; John 9:1-3)

(5) We know God accepts this responsibility because *all things come to pass immutably and infallibly* in *relation to the foreknowledge and decree of God*. (Acts 2:23; 3:18; 4:28; Matt. 26:34, 75; Isa. 46:5, 10-11)

(6) God has decreed that the overwhelming majority of our providential experiences will be the result of the natural consequences flowing from second causes. (Gen. 8:22; Isa. 10:5-7; Gen. 50:20; Mic. 4:11-12; Acts 2:22-23)

(7) God, in his *providence*, ordinarily makes use of the second causes but is free to work with, against, or without the second causes, as he wishes. (Acts 27:31, 44; Isa. 55:10; Hos. 1:7; Job 34:10; Rom. 4:19-21; 2 Kings 6:6; Dan. 3:27)

We will now unpack these seven points. Reading the Scriptures listed with the seven points will help those unfamiliar with the doctrine of providence.

(1) It is God who upholds, arranges, directs, and governs all creatures, actions and things, from the greatest even to the smallest, by his wise and holy providence. (Heb. 1:3; Dan. 4:34-35; Ps. 135:6; Acts 17:24-31; Job 38; 39; 40; 41)

---

[91] *The Book of Church Order of the Presbyterian Church in America*, Fifth Edition, 1990, Section entitled: The Confession of Faith; subsection: The Origin and Formation of the Confession of Faith, xiv.

God Is Good: An Important Reason to Desire, Love, and Serve Him   133

Job, Scripture's suffering saint, believed that what befell him was under God's control—*providence*. That is clear from his words following the loss of all his wealth and family, except his wife: "The LORD gave and the LORD has taken away. Blessed be the name of the LORD." Through all this Job did not sin nor ascribe unseemliness to God (Job 1:21-22). Even though Job's horrible losses had occurred at the hands of evil men and through the forces of a fallen natural order, he believed that every loss in his life was under God's superintended oversight.

God knew that *Satan* desired to undo Job before any of these horrific events occurred. We know this from Job 1:7-12:

> And the LORD said to Satan, "From where do you come?" Then Satan answered the LORD and said, "From roaming about on the earth and walking around on it." And the LORD said to Satan, "Have you <u>set your heart on</u> My servant Job? For there is no one like him on the earth, a blameless and upright man, fearing God and turning away from evil." Then Satan answered the LORD, "Does Job fear God for nothing? Have You not made a hedge about him and his house and all that he has, on every side? You have blessed the work of his hands, and his possessions have increased in the land. But *put forth Your hand* now and touch all that he has; he will surely curse You to Your face." Then the LORD said to Satan, "Behold, all that he has is in your power, only do not put forth your hand on him." So Satan departed from the presence of the LORD. (The underlined phrase is a literal Hebrew translation.)

It is clear that even Satan, the one fostering evil, is under divine limitations. This same point is reinforced in 2:1-6, when Satan is restricted as to how much he can harm Job. He may undermine Job's health, but he is not allowed to take his life. And similarly, in Luke 22:31-32, Jesus says: "Simon, Simon, behold, Satan has demanded permission to sift you like wheat; but I have prayed for you, that your faith may not fail; and you, when once you have turned again, strengthen your brothers."

King David also held to God's complete rule, "Your eyes have seen my unformed substance; and in Your book were written all the days that were *ordained* for me, when as yet there was not one of them" (Ps. 139:16).

Those who find it hard to believe that God has this degree of control over everything fear such a belief would require assent to determinism and fatalism—which they *rightly reject*, for Scripture teaches neither. This fear is tackled in the WCF chapter "Of Providence":

> (2) Everything that goes on in creation is according to God's infallible foreknowledge, and the free and immutable counsel of his own will. (Isa. 41:23; 44:7-8; 45:21; Prov. 16:9; 20:24; Eph. 1:11b)

God possesses complete foreknowledge of everything that will happen in the future (Ps. 139:16, Job 14:5 and Isa. 49:9-10). In the language of Isaiah 40:28, "God's understanding is inscrutable." It is beyond human comprehension.

The possession of foreknowledge proves that its *only* possessor is God. Isaiah says, "Let them bring forth and declare to us what is going to take place . . . that we may know that you are gods" (41:22-23). And again, "And who is like

Me? . . . Let them declare to them the things that are coming and the events that are going to take place. Do not tremble and do not be afraid; have I not long since announced it [what is coming] to you and declared it? And *you are My witnesses*. Is there any God beside Me, or is there any other Rock? I know of none" (44:7-8). These verses attest to God's perfect foreknowledge. Hundreds of fulfilled prophesies in Scripture also attest to the same.

God not only foreknows perfectly all that will take place, but all that occurs in history also is in harmony with the free and immutable counsel of his will. He is not only aware of everything that will happen, he is also willing to *actively* and *permissively* superintend all that he *ordains* to take place. God knows the natural consequences of all thoughts and actions; and he is free to intervene by acting in the situation or by letting the natural fallout take place without intervening. Every course God chooses reflects his will and perfect wisdom.

Here is the third point in the WCF's chapter "Of Providence":

(3) Everything that does happen resounds to the praise of his glory, wisdom, power, justice, *goodness*, and mercy. (Isa. 63:14; Eph 3:10; Rom. 9:17; Gen. 45:7; Ps. 145:7)

The glory of God's *goodness* is portrayed through his governance by providence. Indeed, the awesome weight of his goodness is displayed in his divine guidance of everything in creation, including the *free* activity of humans. God's providence or divine guidance can only be characterized as being *good* insofar as it relates to his children.

One may object to so encompassing a statement, "*Everything* . . . resounds to the praise of his [attributes]," when considering the suffering of some of God's children. But that confuses comfort with God's goodness shown in transforming us into Christ's likeness. Paul spells this out, "And we know that God causes all things to work together for good" (Rom. 8:28). God can bestow no greater gift upon his children, for to become like Christ embodies the ability to love God whole-heartedly and to love others even as Christ loves us. If God can use life's hardships to produce such an end, they are but instruments of *grace* in his hands. Paul agrees, "For I consider that the sufferings of this present time are not worthy to be compared with the glory that is to be revealed to us" (Rom. 8:18; also 2 Cor. 4:16-17; 1 Peter 4:13).

The fourth and fifth points made in "Of Providence" are:

(4) God, the first cause, accepts absolute responsibility for *superintending*—causing or allowing—all second causes. Second causes are those things or activities that flow from God's initial creative acts, and all of the fallout that takes place as a result of these subsequent second cause activities. (Ex. 4:10-11; Matt. 11:4-6; Luke 1:20, 64; John 9:1-3)

First, God was before all other causes—before people were created and given choices and actions to perform; before the sun, wind, rain and all other natural forces were created.—and he is therefore the first cause.

Second, God's accepting the responsibility for second cause consequences is illustrated in John 9:1-3. Jesus's disciples, upon seeing a man born blind, wondered if his blindness was because of his parents' sin or his own. Many today directly connect a bad experience and their previous inappropriate conduct, thinking, "I am being punished." Others interpret unfortunate circumstances as random, chance events without a connection to any god. But Jesus explained, "It was neither that this man sinned, nor his parents; but it was in order that the works of God might be displayed in him." Jesus clarifies that the man was born blind because God *permitted* it to display his work in the man that would bring glory to him. God has an infinitely wise purpose behind everything he either does or allows.

Furthermore, the truth of this point is reinforced by the fact that:

(5) We know God accepts this responsibility because *all things come to pass immutably and infallibly* in *relation to the foreknowledge and decree of God.* (Acts 2:23; 3:18; 4:28; Matt. 26:34, 75; Isa. 46:5, 10-11)

This means that in God's mind he already knows today all that will take place in every tomorrow, and that what will take place tomorrow is immutably set. And when it occurs it will be realized in every detail as God foreknew it would, as he *decreed*. Wow! But does this not point to determinism or fatalism? No. God's foreknowledge of free human choices does not turn those choices into fatalistic ones. It simply points to God's transcendent, omniscient character that is beyond our ability to comprehend (Isa. 40: 28; Ps. 147:5; Rom. 11:33).

People encountering this revelation regarding God have even done silly things like changing their choices at the last minute to show those who hold such beliefs that they can throw God off the track. They fail to realize that God knows their nature and character so completely that he foreknew they would act in such a way, and this reveals their desire to renounce God's immutable foreknowledge and superintending oversight—an impossibility.

What is entailed in the idea that God "decrees" what takes place? What does it mean that something is decreed? It means the event is necessitated to take place. What is meant by "necessitated to happen"? Its certainty of taking place is assured by God's will —either by his active or permissive will. But regardless, it will happen immutably and infallibly because his active and his permissive wills are *both* to be understood as God's immutable will.

How we view this point concerning *God's providence* greatly determines the size of our God and our degree of comfort. To believe God foreknows and superintends every detail results in our perceiving an awesome and majestic God. To believe that God does not have perfect foreknowledge leaves us with a God who can be caught off guard, and who needs to regain control. This represents a smaller God, who resembles our limited nature. The smaller God could even make a *mistake* in allowing certain things. We could believe that he erred in allowing a certain event to hurt us. There is no comfort in that! Indeed, resentment may result. Those who cling to the larger understanding of God have a basis to trust his wisdom and goodness in the midst of suffering. They know he is *good* and will use all events for *their good* and *his glory*.

The sixth point regarding *providence* is:

(6) God has decreed that the *overwhelming* majority of our providential experiences will be the result of the natural consequences flowing from second causes. (Gen. 8:22; Isa. 10:5-7; Gen. 50:20; Mic. 4:11-12; Acts 2:22-23)

God has determined that our life's experiences should, *for the most part*, flow from what occurs in the realm of second causes—created things that produce consequences independent of God's continuing causative activity. For example, if someone makes *a free choice* to climb a cherry tree and eat some ripe cherries, he experiences the joys, or difficulties, associated with doing so. But if he falls while climbing the tree, and breaks his arm, he has experienced a *cause and effect* consequence of his free choice to climb the tree. Breaking his arm is a *providential experience*—in this case, an experience God foreknew and allowed, but did not cause.

Could God have prevented this accident? Certainly, by intervening—actively becoming involved. But typically God does not actively involve himself in such ongoing daily affairs.

The question just answered leads us to look at the seventh aspect of God's *providence*.

(7) God, in his *providence*, ordinarily makes use of the second causes but is free to work with, against, or without the second causes, as he wishes. (Acts 27:31, 44; Isa. 55:10; Hos. 1:7; Job 34:10; Rom. 4:19-21; 2 Kings 6:6; Dan. 3:27)

This means that God ordinarily allows the fallout from the various second causes to happen, without his intervention, and to produce their consequences in our lives. For example, God is not likely to intervene in our decision to go to a concert where we will contract the flu. And he is not going to tell us whom to marry, apart from the general instruction to marry only in the Lord (1 Cor. 7:39). God has promised to be with us in the midst of life and its many repercussions, but has not promised to keep us from adversity, suffering and sorrows.

At the same time God is free to act against, above, or outside of the forces of nature and to protect an individual from certain death in a flood if he so chooses, for example. God is free to set aside the laws of nature he created. He did this when Christ turned the water into wine at the wedding in Cana (John 2:6-10). God is not constrained to work in and through the normal effects of second causes. But we are not to test him by expecting him to work outside of the second causes, but he is *able* to do so whenever he might choose.

God's direct involvement in our lives is typically limited to regenerating and sanctifying the elect (John 6:37, 39; Phil. 1:6; 2:13; 1 Cor. 12:7-11). God generally does not actively engage in the day-to-day decisions of anyone. He directs his children by altering their world/life-view, which leads them to make new free choices. He alters their desires by renovating their hearts so they grow to desire what he desires. God draws them to himself so they want increasingly to do his will. But this transformation is chiefly a heart transformation that overflows into every area of life. It reveals believers' partaking of his divine nature (2 Peter 1:4).

It is mind-boggling to contemplate that God knows the future infallibly, as Scripture attests. The Old Testament's prophetic words fulfilled in the life, death, and resurrection of Christ testify to this. And Christians believe that this reflects the reality of the Triune God. Indeed, to deny God foreknowledge is to make him in our own limited likeness.

We cannot comprehend how God knows today the free choices we will make tomorrow. But he knows our nature that well! He made us and knows our every like and dislike. He knows us so thoroughly that he knows how we will react to every stimulus. And what we encounter is not only derived from the physical elements that surround us, but also from the spiritual forces at work in the world—both the divine and the demonic. Immediately after the fall God put enmity between the children of God and the children of the devil (Gen. 3:14-15). The struggle between righteousness and unrighteousness is ongoing! Paul points out the reality that we "struggle . . . against the spiritual forces of wickedness in the heavenly places" and not simply against flesh and blood (Eph. 6:12). God's providence is ruling in the midst of all of this.

God's providence with second causes in the mixture of the natural order and human activity is incomprehensible. We cannot fathom it! This leaves us with three alternatives. We can refuse to think about the reality of God's providence; we can deny his providence and worship a small God; or we can let his awesome rule, through providence, elevate our *awe* for him so that we worship a very large God who transcends our ability to comprehend how glorious he is!

The church's historic position is that God rules over and through everything in the created order, through his superintending providence. Every hair is numbered. No sparrow falls to the ground apart from his will. And he uses every event and action that touches believers to conform them more and more into Christ's likeness.

The Westminster Confession says all that I have said about God's *providence*:

> God, the great Creator of all things, doth uphold, direct, dispose, and govern all creatures, actions, and things, from the greatest even to the least, by his most wise and holy providence, according to his infallible foreknowledge, and the free and immutable counsel of his own will, to the praise of the glory of his wisdom, power, justice, goodness, and mercy.
>
> Although in relation to the foreknowledge and decree of God, the first cause, all things come to pass immutably and infallibly; yet by the same providence, he ordereth them to fall out according to the nature of second causes, either necessarily, freely, or contingently.
>
> God in his ordinary providence maketh use of means, yet is free to work without, above, and against them, at his pleasure.

What are we to conclude? Certainly that God's providence is indeed *good*. And our confidence rests in his promise to use all the events of providence to conform us to the likeness of Christ! This is the greatest *good* that God could bestow upon us! We conclude, then, that God's *goodness* is profoundly revealed through *providence*.

Conclusion

Surely we understand better now why Christ told the rich young ruler that *no one* is good except God alone (Luke 18:19). Even if we forget our sin nature, and act in a manner that seems good, could we ever rightfully be thought of as good in the light of *God's* being good?

We should be grateful to God and anyone whom we see emulating his goodness. This is so because a good act either reveals God's common grace at work or the fruit of his maturing work in believers' lives. But in and of ourselves, "there is none righteous, not even one" (Rom. 3:10; Ps. 14:3). Our own righteousness is no righteousness at all compared to God's righteousness. Nevertheless we are to strive to be *good like Christ*. God desires to *impart* his good character to his *children*.

We are to emulate Christ in all that we do while confessing our need for his work *in* us if we are to accomplish anything good. Christ made this clear:

> Abide in Me, and I in you. As the branch cannot bear fruit of itself unless it abides in the vine, so neither can you unless you abide in Me. I am the vine, you are the branches; he who abides in Me and I in him, he bears much fruit, for apart from Me you can do nothing. (John 15:4-5)

We are not good, and cannot be good in and of ourselves; we are accounted as good by God's grace, and can *to a degree* be good in Christ. As Christ's righteousness is imputed to us through our faith in him, so we are being transformed to be good to a greater degree as God works in us. This is similar to God's admonition, "You shall be holy, for I am holy" (1 Peter 1:16; Lev. 11:45). These are *directional* concepts. They point us in the direction God is moving us as we abide in him. God is moving us toward holiness and *goodness*, even though its completion will only take place in our future glorification.

But our *desire* to know God better, to be with him more, to fellowship with him, will only increase as we contemplate God's goodness displayed through *creation, redemption,* and *providence*. The more we experience God's creation and sense the benefits we derive from it, over time we will come to desire the Creator more than his benefits. To be awe-struck by the beauty of any aspect of God's creation is wonderful; but even more wonderful is knowing the One capable of creating the awe-inspiring beauty and us who are awe-inspired. God's creation declares his *goodness*, and his children *desire* him because of the benefits they derive from his beneficence poured out upon them through his creation.

As we grow to become more like him, we begin also to desire that his good creation be used to meet all human beings' needs. His creation takes on a meaning that transcends mere selfish enjoyment of its benefits. Christians discover a developing desire to share the created goodness with *others* too. It is through this process that we emulate God's goodness.

The Spirit's redemptive work in us, however, is an even *stronger* activator, generating a more *powerful* desire to be in fellowship with God, than does the recognition of his goodness in creation. As the Spirit makes known to us how *ungodly* we are and almost simultaneously immerses us in God's mercy in Christ's sacrificial death for us, our *desire* for Christ greatly increases. When we become acutely aware of our fallen nature we want the righteousness of Christ all the more (Matt. 5:6)! Our recognized *need* for him heightens our *desire* for him.

And does not our growing awareness of God's *goodness*, poured out upon us in salvation, move us to share his goodness with the lost? Does this not motivate evangelism in the name of Christ? Can something so sweet to us be kept a secret? Surely not! The precious gift of the good news is freely given and those who receive it want to share it.

Christ's healing of the Gerasene demonic who had lived in the tombs and terrorized all who came near him set in motion events that reveal God's desire for us to share the gospel. "And as He [Jesus] was getting into the boat [to go away], the man who had been demon-possessed was entreating Him that he might accompany Him. And He did not let him, but He said to him, 'Go home to your people and report to them what great things the Lord has done for you, and how He had mercy on you'" (Mark 5:18-19).

Realizing that God governs every aspect of our lives through providence generates a great desire to be *near* him. The awareness of our dependency on him; the understanding that his will is always best; and the trials we undergo stimulate us to desire to be more *like* him.

I think of the son of a good Christian friend who had his right leg amputated just below the knee due to a recent hit and run motorcycle accident. And this young amputee has yet to embrace Christ. How will this providential event affect his understanding of God? Will he resent God for allowing this to happen to him? Or will he reflect on the fact that he was not killed and separated from any further opportunity to embrace Christ as Savior—and thereby become eternally grateful? Will he become grateful that he did not become a quadriplegic, as did my youngest son in a recreational vehicle accident years ago? What will the outcome be? The answer rests in God's hands. Will God, the first cause, act to redeem this young man, or will God allow second causes to play out their consequences apart from his redemptive intervention? Since no one deserves God's grace, whatever the outcome, God is and will be eternally *good*.

God created within us the *capacity* to desire him. And he has given us this capacity to *satisfy* the desires he created, for they are motivational channels he uses to renovate the distorted images of his fallen children *into the likeness of Christ*. God's satisfying of the *God-oriented* desires of his children produces within them a *love* for him. The love of God grows bright when the *desire for God* is great; the love for God grows dim when the desire for God is replaced by a mere desire for *the benefits* he gives. The derived benefits can all too quickly become idols we serve. How sad! We can want the salvation Christ offers but quickly ignore his lordship. We can enjoy life's pleasures, but find ourselves complaining when confronted with life's sufferings.

The God-oriented desire that matures into a genuine *love of God* grows when it is yoked to *humility*. God often calls us to humble ourselves before him. For example, James 4:10 says, "Humble yourselves in the presence of the Lord, and He will exalt you" (see also Matt. 18:4; 1 Peter 5:5-6; 2 Chron. 7:14; 34:27). How do we humble ourselves? By *remembering* our propensity toward self-centeredness and sin; by *remembering* our status before God and the mercy bound up in knowing him; and by *remembering* our constant need for his purifying work.

People who associate the innumerable benefits they derive from the created order with the *Creator*, and who love the Triune God because they know he has redeemed them are *motivated* to *serve* him. And what does it mean to serve God? The standard by which God's children are to assess their service—their response to the *goodness* of God poured out upon them through his *creation, redemption* and *providence*—is the *commitment of their lives* to his *revealed will*. They are to be Christlike in their relationships with family members, employers, employees, neighbors, enemies, strangers, friends, and all who are over them in positions of authority. This is the focus of our concluding seven chapters.

Let us take comfort that we are not left alone to fulfill the exceedingly high calling of Christ. Indeed, the call is beyond our ability to achieve in our own strength. But we are encouraged by God's Word, "He who began a good work in you will perfect it until the day of Christ Jesus," and "for it is God who is at work in you, both to will and to work for His good pleasure" (Phil. 1:6; 2:13). God will enable us to live by faith, and to serve Christ in a manner acceptable to him. We strive; he enables; and all of the glorious results are accredited to his work for us as we enjoy his *goodness* and grow in our ability to emulate him—become partakers of the divine nature (2 Peter 1:4).

10

God Is Omnipotent: How Are We to Mirror His Power?

Ah Lord GOD! Behold, You have made the heavens and the earth by Your great power and by Your outstretched arm! Nothing is too difficult for You. (Jer. 32:17)

Nothing is too difficult for God! These are not just nice words. They are tied to God's demonstrated ability! What an awesome reality to comprehend and trust in!

How has God demonstrated that nothing is too difficult for him? In two spheres: (1) the sphere of creation and (2) the sphere of human experience. Creation is the sphere that serves as the material stage on which we engage reality. This is the foundational sphere where God demonstrates his infinite power at the beginning of time, before any human presence. In the second sphere, that of human experience, God also demonstrates that there is nothing too hard for him. After considering these two spheres, we will ask, "How are we to mirror God's power?"

Jeremiah 32:17 tells that the very existence of the heavens and earth declares that there is nothing too difficult for God. Both declare God's omnipotent character and eternal glory. Christians know this to be true, but other world/life-views hold that the material substances that comprise the physical universe are themselves eternal! These different understandings give rise to much of what Christians object to in science texts today. This materialistic world/life-view is foundational to many whose lives declare that the real values are found in things material.

Can Christians refute the claims of materialists? Yes, for we add to the biblical evidence that acquired through our personal redemptive experience. But to those without Christ, our claim that nothing is too hard for God is meaningless. Paul teaches this when he says that the unregenerate person "does not accept the things of the Spirit of God, for they are foolishness to him; and he cannot understand them" (1 Cor. 2:14). The natural man is dead to God and unable to understand the truths associated with the non-temporal or spiritual sphere of reality.

Scripture rejects the materialists' faith premise that all physical matter is eternal. "By faith we understand that the worlds were prepared by the word of God, so that what is seen was not made out of things which are visible" (Heb. 11:3). Naturally, such an understanding can only be accepted by faith, because no humans were present to observe creation. The statement "what is seen was not made out of things which are visible" is referred to by theologians as creation *ex nihilo*—creation was called into being *out of nothing*. Atheists, however, scoff at the biblical evidence and ask why they should pay attention to a book full of fables—their view of the Bible.

Physicists have had a hard time seeking the physical genesis of the universe. Did all of the matter that comprises the material universe exist in the form of a tiny ball of matter that suddenly exploded—creating a "big bang"? If so, where did the original ball of matter come from? Did God create it and explode it, or was it eternal in nature? Or did a big bang ever occur? These conjectures reflect a variety of world/life-views based on different faith presuppositions.

People who hold a materialistic world/life-view have no evidence to back up their faith premise that matter is eternal. Their belief structure is a non-verifiable view of reality that lacks an eternal hope. Life, from their perspective, is what you can make of it at the present. Life has no lasting meaning or purpose. Rejecting a God for whom there is nothing too difficult, they live by blind faith in their unsubstantiated presuppositions.

Believers, on the other hand, are not stuck with an independent, non-verifiable view of reality regarding the universe's origin. They have a host of evidences from God in the sphere of human experience, plus their personal redemptive experience which reinforces their assurance that nothing is too difficult for God. This second sphere of experience strengthens Christians' belief that God created the universe. In this second sphere God has provided us with an abundance of historical evidence that he can do anything he chooses to do. This time-space evidence verifies that God has acted according to his own will at points in time; that the acts are recorded in history; and that they were observed by witnesses. This is a historic/legal kind of proof. It reminds us the Christian faith is evidential faith, not blind faith or a leap-of-faith.

What are some historical evidences God gives to demonstrate nothing is too difficult for him? They are of two types: miraculous evidences, and those where providence is so strong as to be unmistakably ordered by God's hand. *Miraculous* describes occurrences that deviate from the ordinary laws of nature. *Providential* describes biblically recorded events foretold before they occurred.

God's Almighty Power

We recounted Job's encounter with God where he asked Job many questions about ordinary realities: the ocean remaining within its bounds, the clouds, the snow and the hail, the raven, the dumb ostrich, etc. Job's response? He was deeply humbled by God's majestic power revealed in the ordinary aspects of creation, that he had overlooked. And God has also chosen to do out-of-the-ordinary things occasionally—not to generate faith in his children's hearts but to strengthen their existing faith. Miracles do not create faith; miracles fortify existing faith.

A Miraculous Example of God's Power

The first time the question "Is anything too difficult for the LORD?" occurs is in Genesis 18:14. The LORD appeared to Abraham and told him that his aged wife, Sarah, would have a son within a year (vv. 1, 10). When Sarah heard this she laughed, for she was long past the age of childbearing (vv. 12, 11). But she did have a son, Isaac, within a year, at the age of ninety-one and Abraham was one hundred (17:17; 21:5). Is anything too *difficult* for the LORD?

A Providential Example of God's Power

Abraham did not think that anything was too hard for the LORD after Isaac was born. He subsequently demonstrated his trust in God when God tested him by asking him to offer his son as a sacrifice (Gen. 22:1-8). Abraham obeyed. He took his promised son Isaac and put him on the altar to sacrifice him to the LORD (v. 9). How could Abraham do this? God had promised him a son by Sarah and God had kept his promise. God had also promised to give Abraham descendants through Isaac, as many as the stars in the heavens (Gen. 15:5). He promised that these descendants would come from Isaac's line, not Eliezer's, nor Ishmael's (Gen. 17:19, 21; 15:2-4; 17:18-21). But there was something else in Abraham's mind.

Hundreds of years later the Holy Spirit revealed what was at the center of Abraham's thinking when he prepared to sacrifice Isaac. Hebrews 11:17-19 declares, "He considered that God is able to raise people even from the dead" (v. 19). What faith! Abraham had experienced God's keeping his promises. And God had promised that through Isaac God would fulfill more promises. So Abraham believed God even if it meant he would have to raise Isaac from the dead. Abraham knew God could do this, for "nothing is too difficult for [God]."

A Miraculous Example of God's Power

Miracles were uncommon in the years before the life of Christ, but during the ministries of the prophets Elijah and Elisha a number of miracles forespoke of things later to be associated with Christ's ministry. The widow of Zarephath and her son experienced such a miracle. The LORD told Elijah to go to Zarephath and to stay there with a widow who would provide for him (1 Kings 17:9). Upon entering the city, he saw a woman gathering sticks and asked her for a drink of water (v. 10). As she was going to get the water he asked her for a piece of bread too (v. 11). She responded:

> "As the LORD your God lives, I have no bread, only a handful of flour in the bowl and a little oil in the jar; and behold, I am gathering a few sticks that I may go in and prepare for me and my son, that we may eat it and die." Then Elijah said to her, "Do not fear; go, do as you have said, but make me a little bread cake from it first, and bring it out to me, and afterward you may make one for yourself and for your son. For thus says the LORD God of Israel, 'The bowl of flour shall not be exhausted, nor shall the jar of oil be empty, until the day that the LORD sends rain on the face of the earth.'" (vv. 12-14) [This was at the beginning of a three-year drought.]

The widow did what Elisha asked, and she and her household continued to eat from the bowl and jar throughout the drought. Neither the flour nor the oil was exhausted, as the LORD had spoken.

This multiplication of the original short supply of flour and oil foreshadows the two occasions when Christ multiplied the loaves and the fish (Matt. 14:13-21; 15:32-39). Is anything too difficult for the LORD?

A Providential Example of God's Power

Israel's crossing the Jordan River into the Promised Land was an event combining prophesies with providence (Josh. 3:1-17). After Moses's death the LORD raised up Joshua to lead Israel into the Promised Land. God promised them the land beyond the Jordan years before Moses died. Indeed, Moses had sent spies into the land long before they entered it (Num. 13:17-24). When the time came for Joshua to lead them across the Jordan River, it was at flood stage. But God shared his foreknowledge[92] with Joshua regarding how he was going to help them across the river overflowing its banks.

The priests were to carry the ark of the covenant to the Jordan, and when they got to the river they were to stand still at the edge of the floodwater (Josh. 3:8). The priests were to then enter the river before the people (v. 11). And God said, "And it shall come about when the soles of the feet of the priests who carry the ark of the LORD, the Lord of the earth, shall rest in the waters of the Jordan, the waters of the Jordan shall be cut off, and the waters which are flowing down from above shall stand in one heap" (v. 13). And the prophecy was fulfilled!

> And when those who carried the ark came into the Jordan, and the feet of the priests carrying the ark were dipped in the edge of the water (for the Jordan overflows all its banks all the days of harvest), the waters which were flowing down from above stood and rose up in one heap, a great distance away at Adam, the city that is beside Zarethan; and those which were flowing down toward the sea of the Arabah, the Salt Sea, were completely cut off. So the people crossed opposite Jericho. And the priests who carried the ark of the covenant of the LORD stood firm on dry ground in the middle of the Jordan while all Israel crossed on dry ground, until all the nation had finished crossing the Jordan (vv. 15-17).

The town of Adam was up-river from the point of the crossing. There were high cliffs on both sides of the Jordan there. God foreknew that there would be a caving in of the cliffs that would temporarily dam up the Jordan at the very time that the Israelites would be carrying the ark of the covenant to the edge of the river. The providentially created earthen dam cut off the Jordan long enough for the people to cross the river on dry land.

God incorporated a providential event into his plan for getting the children of Israel into the Promised Land—by the collapsing of cliffs into the Jordan River.

---

[92] Shared foreknowledge becomes prophecy.

The event was so profound that it became an affirmation for the people that the LORD was with Joshua as he had been with Moses before him (v. 7 and 4:14). It also had a demoralizing effect on the people whose land was being invaded (5:1; 6:1-2). Is there anything too difficult for God?

Other Old Testament Examples of God's Power

There are more both miraculous and providential events in the Old testament, like the floating of the axe head lost in the river—a miracle (2 Kings 6:5-7). Or God's using a strong wind to divide the waters of the Red Sea (Ex. 14:21), and to drive quail into the camp (Num. 11:31)—revealing his ability to use natural things to manifest his providence. There was Elijah's raising of the widow's son from the dead (1 Kings 17:17-24); Elijah being taken to heaven bodily (2 Kings 2:1, 11); Elisha's raising the Shunammite woman's son from the dead (4:20, 32-36). All these revealed God's power over his natural order. Nothing is too difficult for God!

New Testament Illustrations of God's Power

Jesus's first miracle, turning water into wine at the wedding in Cana of Galilee, was a public manifestation of his divine glory (John 2:1-11). He walked on water (Matt. 14:25-27). He healed a leper (Luke 5:12-13). He healed a paralytic (5:18-26). He gave sight to a man born blind (John 9:3-7). He raised Lazarus from the dead after he had been in the tomb four days (John 11:17, 38-44). They all declare, "Nothing is too difficult for You" (Jer. 32:17, 27; Zech. 8:6; Matt. 19:26; Luke 1:37; Rom. 4:21). These are a small sample of the recorded miracles Jesus performed, all testifying to his being the eternal God who became man (Phil. 2:7).

The greatest miracle of all, however—the one that testifies that Jesus Christ is God incarnate—was his being raised from the dead, even by his own authority. There are numerous inscrutable realities associated with Christ's person. For example, Scripture testifies to the fact that almighty God became incarnate and so was both God and fully man. And in the absolute unity of the Godhead we encounter the fact that God the Father dissociated himself from God the Son as he hung on the cross and cried, "My God, My God, why have You forsaken Me?" (Matt. 27:46; Mark 15:34). Although the being of the Godhead remained intact, amazingly the eternal fellowship between the Father and Son was broken! Neither can Christ's affirmation be fully understood when he declared that the Father gave him authority to lay down his life and to take it up again (John 10:17-18).[93] How could one who is dead raise his own body (John 2:19-22; 10:17-18)? Surely, because he is the God-man!

There is no clearer demonstration that "Nothing is too difficult for You" than Christ's resurrection. Paul declares that this is "of first importance" (1 Cor. 15:3). Indeed, death is "the last enemy that will be abolished" (15:26). Paul even

---

[93] Scripture attests to the unity of the three persons of the Godhead when it ascribes Jesus's resurrection to the Father (Gal. 1:1), to the Spirit (Rom. 8:11), and to Jesus himself (John 10:17-18).

goes so far as to say, "If the dead are not raised, let us eat and drink, for tomorrow we die" (15:32). The person who trusts in God's promises of his own resurrection can say with confidence, "Death is swallowed up in victory," and then ask, "O death, where is your victory? O death, where is your sting?" (15:54-55).

The miraculous and providential events recounted call attention to God's awesome power that is sometimes referred to as his "mighty arm," "mighty hand," or "mighty power," all indicating God's infinite strength (Ex. 32:11; Deut. 3:24; 4:34; 5:15; 6:21).

God's Gentle Power

But there is a gentle power associated with Almighty God as well. And it is to this that we now turn. The prophet Isaiah said God's chosen Servant would come with such gentle power:

> Behold, My Servant, whom I uphold; My chosen one in whom My soul delights. I have put My Spirit upon Him .... He will not cry out or raise His voice, nor make His voice heard in the street. A bruised reed He will not break, and a dimly burning wick He will not extinguish; He will faithfully bring forth justice [righteousness]. (Isa. 42:1-3)

Christ, God in the flesh, exhibited a righteous zeal when he chased the moneychangers from the temple (John 2:14-16; Matt. 21:12-13). And at times he bluntly confronted the Pharisees, Sadducees, and lawyers to expose their ungodly motives and hatred of him. They resented deeply his open revelation of their ungodliness, but Jesus was a very gentle Servant.

It is the Servant's gentle use of power that is central to our understanding of God's desire for how we should use the limited power he has given us. It is important to note that Christ is still serving his people today. God the Father has promised to give the Holy Spirit to those who ask Him (Luke 11:13). And the Holy Spirit and the Spirit of Christ are one and the same (Rom. 8:9). Those who belong to Christ are, in fact, the temples of his Spirit (1 Cor. 3:16; 6:19). And what has the Holy Spirit, the Spirit of Christ, done in the lives of those the Father gave to Christ?

The Spirit of God has granted them spiritual rebirth (John 3:3, 5-8; 1 Peter 1:23; 2 Cor. 5:17). He leads them to heart-expressed repentance (Acts 20:21; Rom. 2:4). The Spirit forms in each believer faith essential to obtain eternal life (Eph. 2:8). They are justified before God through the imputation of Christ's righteousness, received through faith, resulting in the elimination of the enmity that previously existed between them and God, and the granting of Christ's peace to them (Rom. 5:1, 9). They are adopted into God's family (Rom. 8:14-17, 23). And they are tutored into maturity—sanctified (John 17:17; 1 Thess. 5:23).

We will reflect on each of the six areas in which the Spirit of Christ works with gentle power in the lives of the adopted brothers and sisters of Christ—spiritual rebirth; repentance; faith; justification; adoption; and sanctification.

First, *spiritual rebirth*: "Truly, truly, I say to you, unless one is born again he cannot see the kingdom of God." "Truly, truly, I say to you, unless one is born of water [cleansing] and the Spirit he cannot enter into the kingdom of God." "That which is born of the flesh is flesh, and that which is born of the Spirit is spirit" (John 3:3, 5, 6).

Christ's statements convey a few simple truths. First, someone who has not experienced the rebirth by the Holy Spirit cannot understand the realities associated with the new life. Second, the person who has not been cleansed by the blood of Christ and born again by the Spirit cannot enter God's kingdom. And finally, physical birth is insufficient for a spiritual relationship with God—for we can only relate to him effectively on a spirit-to-Spirit plane which requires a spiritual rebirth (John 4:24).

Do you know the precise time you were spiritually reborn? You may remember when you and your attitudes began to awaken to spiritual truths. You may recall when you found yourself with a new understanding of God and his character. Many changes immediately follow one's spiritual rebirth but these changes are evidence of the rebirth, not the rebirth itself. The rebirth precedes all such changes. The rebirth is solely the Holy Spirit's work, as Christ said: "You must be born again. The wind blows where it wishes . . . [you] do not know where it comes from and where it is going; so is everyone who is born of the Spirit" (John 3:7-8). The Spirit of Christ regenerates the person God chooses.[94] Prior to that he or she is dead to Christ (Eph. 2:1, 5; Col. 2:13). The rebirth is gentle. It is indiscernible in and of itself. But after the rebirth occurs the emerging transformation in new believers' lives ranges from a quiet growth in transformed spirit to a raging torrent of changing perceptions, with doubts and reassurances, elation and depression, and other conflicting adjustments as the new life takes shape. But the Spirit is patient, gentle, kind, reassuring, and an ever-present Helper as the journey takes place.

Second, *repentance*: The Holy Spirit convinces us that certain things we thought about and did in the past were inappropriate in the light of Christ's character, and we realize that we need to be cleansed from guilt. This conviction of sin and the need for cleansing is precious evidence of God's love for us. For God is faithful and righteous to forgive us of our sins if we confess them and ask him to forgive us (1 John 1:8-10). That is the reason Christ is called "the Lamb of God who takes away the sin of the world" (John 1:29).

Repentance is: (a) recognition of a particular sin we have committed; (b) sincere acknowledgment of the sin to Christ, through prayer; (c) request for the Holy Spirit's help to stop the particular offense; (d) accepting by faith the forgiveness granted us in Christ; and (e) thanking Christ for the resultant restored peace in our hearts.

---

[94] Experience leads many to conclude that they chose Christ and that he subsequently chooses them. Scripture attests to another reality: God chooses those to be spiritually reborn; the Holy Spirit performs the spiritual rebirth; and the new person in Christ asks Christ to be his Lord and Savior as a result of his rebirth. God is the first to choose: Ps. 65:4; Isa. 45:4; Matt. 22:14; Mark 13:20; Luke 18:7; John 15:16, 19; Rom. 8:33; 9:11; 11:5, 7; Col. 3:12; 2 Thess. 2:13; 2 Tim. 2:10; Titus 1:1; James 2:5; and 2 Peter 1:10.

The Holy Spirit is with us throughout the process of repenting. He gently encourages and trains those in Christ to seek and accept the grace that is so evident in the gift of forgiveness. The Spirit of Christ's convicting us of sin and leading us to repentance is one of the many ways that we know him personally (John 14:16-18; 16:7-8).

Nevertheless, Christians who resist the Spirit's gentle call to repentance will be disciplined as necessary by God. We see this in 2 Samuel 12:1-14, where the Lord sends the prophet Nathan to confront King David about his adultery with Bathsheba; having her husband Uriah killed; and then acting as if nothing had happened. David was quick to repent, though, when Nathan confronted him (see Psalm 51) and was mercifully told that his sins were forgiven (2 Sam. 12:13). But even the gracious gift of forgiveness did not keep David from experiencing a host of frightful consequences—the child conceived in adultery died; one of his sons challenged his right to be king; and his followers split into two kingdoms.

Third, *faith*: All of God's spiritual blessings are received by faith. This is because our relationship with God is one we experience on a Spirit-to-spirit basis.

We must first recognize that saving faith is a gift from God! As we said, there are various kinds of faith. There is blind faith, with no firm grounding in reality. There is the leap-of-faith, which is attached to a personal emotional experience. But Scriptural faith is rooted in the evidence created by God in the historical reality of his involvement with his people. This kind of faith must be preceded by a spiritual experience that opens the eye of the heart to God and our relationship to him. Everybody has faith; not everybody has faith in Christ and his saving work, however. Saving faith is a gift God gives to his children by the gentle inward working of the Holy Spirit. And it is evidenced by an authentic response to Christ's lordship in all of life.

Paul counsels, "For through the grace given to me I say to everyone among you not to think more highly of himself than he ought to think; but to think so as to have sound judgment, as God has allotted to each a measure of faith" (Rom. 12:3). The controlling and guiding element is the revelation that God gives each of his children a measure of faith. Saving faith is God's gift to us. It is only by Spirit-imparted-and-developed faith that we can think of ourselves as God does—"Do not think too highly of yourself." It is only by God-given faith that we have sound judgment regarding life and its challenges. It is God who gives us genuine, God-honoring faith! This is evidenced by Christ's disciples' request that they be *given* more faith (Luke 17:5-10).

Christ's response is illuminating.

> The apostles said to the Lord, "Increase our faith!" And the Lord said, "If you had faith like a mustard seed, you would say to this mulberry tree, 'Be uprooted and be planted in the sea'; and it would obey you. Which of you, having a slave plowing or tending sheep, will say to him when he has come in from the field, 'Come immediately and sit down to eat'? But will he not say to him, 'Prepare something for me to eat, and properly clothe yourself and serve me while I eat and drink; and afterward you may eat and drink'? He does not thank the slave

because he did the things which were commanded, does he? So you too, when you do all the things which are commanded you, say, 'We are unworthy slaves; we have done only that which we ought to have done.'"

The disciples' question showed that they thought they had sufficient faith for life's normal requirements—but they desired more faith, because they were Christ's apostles. His response is an antidote for pride: The disciples had very little faith, for if they even had faith the size of a mustard seed they could ask the mulberry tree to be planted in the sea, and it would do so.

The rest of Christ's response goes to the core of how faith is developed in God's children's hearts. They, in Christ's illustration, spend their time plowing and tending sheep, and upon coming home to rest and eat dinner they are to serve at the Master's table. It would seem that even as their physical endurance increases through the expansion of the requirements placed on them, so faith is increased by its being stretched. And the expanded faith that emerges is to be anticipated and used, but not gloated over. It is the natural consequence of spiritual exercise—"So you too, when you do all the things which are commanded you, say, 'We are unworthy slaves; we have done only that which we ought to have done'" (v. 10).

Peter understood that his faith had been given to him, as he makes clear when he opens his second letter:

> Simon Peter, a bond-servant and apostle of Jesus Christ, to those who have <u>received</u> [obtained] a faith of the same kind as ours, by the righteousness of our God and Savior, Jesus Christ (2 Peter 1:1).

The Greek word here for "received" is the word "obtained" (*lagchano* means "to receive by divine allotment").[95] Peter indicates that he knows that there are other kinds of faith than saving faith, for he used the phrase "a faith *of the same kind* as ours." The other forms of faith are humanly derived, but the Spirit of Christ gives saving faith to Christians, bit by bit over time.

Paul also noted that faith is a gift from God when he wrote: "For by grace you have been saved through faith; and that not of yourselves, it is the gift of God; not as a result of works, so that no one may boast" (Eph. 2:8-9). But a questions sometimes arises, "To what does the phrase 'and that not of yourselves,' refer?" Many, assuming that the thrust of the sentence is that salvation is not obtained by good works, use it in evangelism to teach that fact. And that usage is fine. However, I and many others see "not of yourselves" as referring particularly to saving faith, which is itself a gift God gives to his children.

Romans 12:3, Luke 17:5-10 and 2 Peter 1:1 assert that faith is a gift from God and it is therefore appropriate to conclude that both salvation and faith are gifts from God.

---

[95] Joseph H. Thayer, *Thayer's Greek-English Lexicon of the New Testament* (Peabody, MA: Hendrickson, fifth printing, January 2002), 367, notation # 2975.

Fourth, *justification*: When people are spiritually reborn, repent of their offenses against God, and believe in their hearts that Christ lived a perfect life and died for them, in order to satisfy God's just demands, he declares them justified. And they are his children. Those justified have had all their sins pardoned and are accepted as righteous before God, for Christ's righteousness has been placed on them like a great robe (Isa. 53:11). The Father now sees them through the shed blood of Christ. Those justified can rest in Christ's finished work.

The doctrine of justification was a hallmark of the sixteenth-century Reformation when those who protested against the teachings of the Roman Catholic Church taught that one is justified by faith alone, and not by faith plus works. While those who have been given saving faith will, out of joy, respond to God's gift of salvation by following his will, those works are a by-product of salvation and not a combined faith plus works basis for salvation. Since the act of justification is God's act alone—human beings play no part except receiving it by faith—it is made real to the believer by the Holy Spirit's gentle application to the heart.

These truths regarding justification can all be found in the following Scriptures: Job 25:4; Isaiah 45:25; Romans 3:21-28; 4:5, 25; 5:1, 8-9, 16-19; 8:30-33; Galatians 2:15-16; 3:24; and Titus 3:5-7. Those who have experienced spiritual rebirth, repented of their sins, and been given saving faith through which they receive justification, are adopted into God's family.

Fifth, *adoption*: Blessed are those who grow up and realize that they were born into a family that truly loved them. None of us asked to be born. We had no choice regarding which family God would providentially place us in. We had no control over the character and conduct of our natural parents at the time of our conception, our birth, and in the early years of our rearing. What a helpless, out-of-our-control reality we experienced! Indeed, many have been greatly blessed by God's providential provision for them in their birth family. But many so blessed have wasted the good beginning and provision they were afforded.

Conversely, many have been badly scarred in their emotions and thinking, and in a few cases have had their bodies harmed by the experiences in their birth families. Some few have even been born into a living nightmare. But even those born into a good family can resist Christ and exhibit evil hearts. For example, Cain murdered his brother Abel (Gen. 4:8-12). And why? "Because his deeds were evil, and his brother's were righteous" (1 John 3:12). This reveals how our fallen nature can pervert God's intentions and drag us away from his gracious purposes.

In reality, families are found to lie on a continuum from blessed to horribly blighted as a result of the fall of Adam and Eve. In his mercy God sends the Holy Spirit to bring spiritual rebirth to people all along the continuum of fallen life—from those born into homes where Christ is Lord, to those born into homes where Christ's love is rejected. Both environments are potential spiritual maternity wards where spiritual rebirths are required before one can be brought into the family of God.

Spiritual rebirth transports us into a much larger family than our temporal one; it ushers us into the family of God, the invisible church. We become God's adopted children, the very children of God. Scripture expresses it thus:

> For all who are being led by the Spirit of God, these are sons of God. For you have not received a spirit of slavery leading to fear again, but you have received a spirit of adoption as sons by which we cry out, 'Abba! Father!' The Spirit Himself testifies with our spirit that we are children of God, and if children, heirs also, heirs of God and fellow heirs with Christ, if indeed we suffer with Him so that we may also be glorified with Him. (Rom. 8:14-17)

It is wonderful to note that this Scripture makes it clear that the Holy Spirit leads us to the point that we can emotionally and intellectually comprehend God as our real Father. For some children of God, their comprehension of God as their loving Father constitutes only a brief journey. But for others it is a long and hard journey because their earthly father was a living contradiction of the character of God the Father. Their journey to truly knowing (Col. 3:10) God as one who holds them to be precious in his sight (Isa. 43:4) can be long and painful.

This text makes it plain that those adopted immediately become heirs of God's infinite benefits—joint heirs with Christ. And what is their inheritance? They will inherit eternal life, the eternal presence of God, and a home in the New Jerusalem where there will be no more pain or tears. And they will be glorified so that the residual of the old nature will be forevermore done away with. They will be perfected even as Christ is perfect. What an inheritance to anticipate! By faith, the reality of this becomes part of the hope chest of the Christian.

Those who have been spiritually reborn; have repented of their sins; been given the gift of saving faith; received their judicial pardon; and been received into God's family through adoption are immediately put under the care of the Holy Spirit who begins to renovate their character through a maturing process referred to as sanctification.

Sixth, *sanctification*: To be sanctified means to be set apart by God from the larger, unregenerate pool of humanity to be transformed into new persons. These individuals grow in their ability to possess true knowledge, as God does (Col. 3:10); become more and more righteous, like Christ (Eph. 4:22-24); and are become holy, as God originally intended (vv. 22-24). Sanctification is the process whereby God imparts his very nature to the hearts of his children, degree by degree (2 Peter 1:4; Heb. 12:10; and 1 John 3:2).

To be sanctified is to be set apart to be conformed to the image of Christ. This requires God's use of all things in his children's lives to conform them to Christ's likeness (Rom. 8:28-29). We examine God's character now because all of the attributes we have studied contain aspects of his nature that he wants to impart to us. For this reason, we will not elaborate on God's sanctification of his children here, but will explain it in detail in the closing two sections.

God's power is so great that we can assert with the prophet Jeremiah that "Nothing is too difficult for [God]" (Jer. 32:17). God's power is awesome and beyond comprehension. But we have also shown that we generally encounter God's power in our lives daily in its gentle display: his bringing about spiritual rebirths; leading the reborn to repentance; building faith in their lives; justifying them so they can rest from attempts of self-righteousness; adopting them so they will inherit all of God's eternal blessings; and he continues his good work of sanctification in them. So now we ask, "How are his children to mirror his power?"

How Are We to Mirror God's Power?

Most children from five to ten years are power possessed! They want to be powerful like Superman. Many adults are also driven by a desire for power. Humanity's fall perverted our understanding of God's intended purpose in granting us a modicum of his power. God told our first parents, before the fall, to "subdue . . . and rule over the fish of the sea and over the birds of the sky and over every living thing that moves on the earth" (Gen. 1:28). And God empowered them to carry out his desires and be stewards of his creation. But humanity's desire for and use of power has too frequently been oriented toward ruling over fellow human beings as if they were included in the God's mandate concerning every living thing that moves on the earth.

The human desires for acceptance, recognition, status, and power are often perverted, and become marks of humanity's fall. This drive for power is a perversion of the God-created desire within all of us to be competent and successful. Underlying these perverted drives are basic motivations which reveal self-centeredness and self-aggrandizement. Christ confronted this malignant predisposition, found even among his disciples. James and John desired to have a favored position with Christ when he would be elevated to future glory. They asked him if they could sit, one on his right and one on his left. The other disciples became indignant when they heard this request. Jesus's response is illuminating.

> You know that those who are recognized as rulers of the Gentiles lord it over them; and their great men exercise authority over them. But it is not this way among you, but whoever wishes to become great among you shall be your servant; and whoever wishes to be first among you shall be slave of all. For even the Son of Man did not come to be served, but to serve, and to give His life a ransom for many. (Mark 10:42-45)

All Christians need to heed Christ's words. He contrasts the Gentiles—those who do not know him as Savior—and believers. "It is not this way among you," Christ told his disciples. Christian greatness is found in dying to our self-orientation and becoming servants to those whom Christ puts into our lives. This is at the core of Jesus's admonition, "If anyone wishes to come after Me, he must deny himself, and take up his cross daily, and follow Me" (Luke 9:23). The ungodly nature is seen in our desire to control our outward environment—our spouse; our employees; our employer; our neighbor; our competitor; our _____ (fill in the blank).

Much confusion regarding power arises from our failure to realize that much of the power that people suppose they have is really power associated with a specific position they hold and is not an inherent power they possess. Much power is entrusted—power associated with the position of being a corporate executive, a member of the city council, a policeman, a teacher, an automobile driver, a parent of young children. When the individual is removed from the position of power, he surrenders the power he had when associated with that position.

Inherent power is very different from entrusted power. And even inherent power has two different dimensions. First, there is the inherent ability to do things that manifest the use of one's physical body—lift a weight; type; participate in athletic events; be persuasive; walk; swim; and thousands of other uses of human energy that can be expended either positively or negatively.

Second, there is the internal, invisible power within associated with the control of the human spirit. It is called self-control. And it is not unfair to suggest that self-control is at the core of God's original intention for our use of the power he gave us. Self-control is one of the fruits of the Spirit (Gal. 5:23). But it has been enormously diminished by the fall. Self-expression, in its worst twisted forms, has replaced self-restraint.

We are told, "He who is slow to anger is better than the mighty, and he who rules his spirit, than he who captures a city" (Prov. 16:32). Isn't that amazing! God says the person who exercises self-control is better than the mighty. That is a perspective not held by the unsaved.

The first murder took place when Cain failed to master his anger and killed his brother Abel. Cain was a tiller of the ground, and he brought God an offering. Cain's younger brother Abel was a herdsman, and he too brought God an offering. God regarded Abel's offering with favor, but not Cain's. So he became very angry (Gen. 4:5). God confronted Cain about his inappropriate attitude, and warned him, "And if you do not do well, sin is crouching at the door [of your heart]; and its desire is for you, but you must master it" (v. 7). Cain did not master his spirit; he did not exercise self-control. He was a child of the evil one and allowed his resentment of his brother's righteous life to anger him so that he chose to kill him (1 John 3:12).

Our most critical power struggles take place at the door of the heart, in our innermost being. Here we wrestle with the ethical and spiritual issues of life—divorce, sexual temptations, how we will treat other people, how we obey those in authority, whether or not we will take up our cross daily. Paul prayed that Christ's people would "be strengthened with power through His Spirit in the *inner man*" (Eph. 3:16). He prayed that Christ might live in their hearts. Paul longed for this, "so that you will walk in a manner worthy of the Lord, to please him in all respects, bearing fruit in every good work and increasing in the knowledge of God; strengthened with all power, according to His glorious might, for the attaining of all steadfastness and patience" (Col. 1:10-11). Paul knew he could "do all things through Him who strengthens me" (Phil. 4:13).

There is a paradoxical relationship between God's almighty power and our power that achieves God's eternal purposes. Christ told Paul, "My . . . power is perfected in weakness," and he came to realize this truth and said he would "rather boast about my weaknesses, that the power of Christ may dwell in me." He added, "I am well content with weaknesses . . . for when I am weak, then I am strong" (2 Cor. 12:9-10). As God employs a Christian in his service, as he brings about a spiritual rebirth, provides the gifts of repentance and faith, makes known his gift of justification to him, persuades him of his adoption into his family, and carries out his work of sanctification in his life—it is here the paradox of power is manifested. God, and only God, will receive the glory for the work of renovation that occurs when we with our old nature are transformed into new persons in the likeness of Christ (Isa. 42:8; 48:11).

We were created to work, and work requires the utilization of various forms of power. And our ancestors learned that there were some animals that had more physical strength than they did, so in their exercise of dominion they harnessed the animals' power and thereby extended their own power. This ability to increase the power available to the human race has been added to extensively through processes of mechanization—steam engines, gasoline engines, electrical engines, jet engines, atomic engines. None of these even come close, however, to equaling the power manifested in a powerful hurricane or volcanic eruption. And these natural powers are not even to be compared with God's infinite and eternal power, a portion of which was manifested in his acts of creation.

Conclusion

Where does this leave us? How are we who love Christ to use the power God has given us? Christians know that God the Father has put all things under the authority of his Son (Eph. 1:22-23; 1 Cor. 15:27-28). This leads us to seek to use God-given power in ways that honor him and his authority over them. They will thus use their power to promote love, joy, and peace; will employ their power patiently, with kindness; aim to produce goodness and faithfulness; apply it with gentleness; show self-control; and properly use the gifts of the Spirit God gave them. Personal power employed to other ends is probably misused power.

Entrusted power—power associated with a position with which we have been entrusted—must meet additional tests beyond those just outlined. Power employed by those in positions of government needs to be examined in the light of its being used equitably on behalf of all who live under their governing authority. There are moral questions that surround the decisions of those in positions of authority in the various institutions in the society in which they live. God's Word provides ample standards to evaluate the consequences of power. We will elaborate on these ideas in chapters 21–27.

So God intends that we use power, in its many and diverse forms, to serve humanity, not in building up one's power base for personal, self-centered advantages. Power was created to help, not harm. It was given to us to build up life-giving benefits for others, not to tear down life. Power is to be employed in a Christlike manner, for Christ-honoring objectives. And the Holy Spirit trains Christ's followers to use the power entrusted to them in Christ-honoring ways.

11

God Is Sovereign:
Even Over All Forms of Suffering

The LORD has established His throne in the heavens;
and His sovereignty rules over all. (Ps. 103:19)

We who live in a free and representative society have no experience of what it means to live under a king. Kings, in today's world, are generally figureheads, without real authority. As a result, we can only imagine what is expected of subjects in a realm ruled by a king. God's kingdom is not of this world (John 18:36), but is real in the hearts of his children, who are growing up to comprehend what it means to live under the rule of the King of kings. God is the Sovereign King over everything that transpires in the universe. His rule is absolute, even though his enemies are left with their freedom to reject his authority until the Day of Judgment.

We previously treated God's comprehensive rule over evil, including the truth that his holiness is not diminished by the existence of evil. Here we deal with God's sovereign rule over *suffering*. This is extremely important because there is no place where our faith is more tested than in the crucible of suffering. And *authentic faith* is never more exhibited than when Christians suffer in full view of a community and bear a testimony that glorifies God.

We naturally avoid suffering. And the reason is simple: suffering is sorrowful (Heb. 12:11). But it is an element of God's economy, and he *ordained* suffering to be a part of the human experience. In his infinite wisdom, God included suffering as one of his holy, just, and gracious means to bring about his perfect ends. Indeed, the Father's only Son, Jesus Christ, came from heaven to earth to suffer on our behalf (1 Peter 3:18). In eternity the persons of the Godhead agreed that the Son would become incarnate, be despised, forsaken, afflicted, rejected, scourged, mocked, and crucified by those who rejected their Creator. It was with the very *suffering of Christ's soul* that the Father was satisfied (Isa. 53:11). He was satisfied with a just payment for sins. The payment, Christ's atonement, satisfied God's own demands for justice. Humanity's sins have been fully paid for, our debt eternally satisfied. Christ's suffering in agony is incomprehensible, but it was sufficient to redeem humanity. Christ came to redeem a people whom the Father chose from among fallen rebels (Eph. 1:4-5, 7, 11, 18; John 6:37, 39, 44). What unfathomable love!

We will touch on two areas of suffering. The first category is called "common sufferings"—that to which everybody is subjected, the *redeemed* and the *unredeemed*. This category has two sub-heads, *physical* and *emotional* suffering, which reflect Christ's words, "He [God] causes His sun to rise on the evil and the good, and sends rain on the righteous and the unrighteous" (Matt. 5:45). Jesus meant that God pours out his good provisions on those who love him and those who do not, and that *suffering* will be a reality for both groups. The second major category of suffering pertains *only* to Christians. It is a suffering instigated by those who reject Christ. This category is "sufferings to which Christians are called."

Before we investigate the two categories of suffering, we examine a paradox known only to those redeemed in Christ.

A Biblical Paradox: Joy in the Midst of Suffering

There is a biblical *paradox* regarding suffering. It helps us to comprehend God's use of suffering in human experience. The paradox is found in places like Acts 5, where some apostles were jailed for preaching Christ's death and resurrection in Jerusalem. They were brought before the high priest and his associates and ordered to cease public teaching about Jesus. Peter and the other apostles told the Council they would obey *God*, who had told them to "speak . . . the whole message of this Life" (v. 20), and not obey mere men. These words were met with deep anger. Gamaliel, a respected Council member, then advised the assembly to leave the apostles alone lest the body be found later to have been fighting against God. The Council accepted Gamaliel's advice, but before releasing the apostles *they had them flogged*. We read, "So they went on their way from the presence of the Council, *rejoicing that they had been considered worthy to suffer shame for His name*" (v. 41). The paradox is evident: *joy along with suffering*!

Gladness of *heart* is a fruit of the Spirit (Gal. 5:22). This can arise when the suffering is united with a proper understanding of what God is accomplishing through it. He *redeems* suffering—"God causes all things to work together for good to those who love God, to those who are called according to His purpose" (Rom. 8:28). This does not mean that joy always *immediately* accompanies suffering; but joy can be coupled with it. The Thessalonians "received the word in much tribulation with the joy of the Holy Spirit" (1 Thess. 1:6). And Jesus "for the joy set before Him endured the cross" (Heb. 12:2). The point is: joy and suffering are not always strangers.

Our *attitude* toward suffering is very important. I pray that the Holy Spirit might help all believers eventually to accept suffering as an instrument of good in their Savior's hands. God is *good*, even in the midst of suffering! We will keep the paradox in view—joy and suffering can be simultaneously experienced!

Here is an outline of the two categories of suffering to be discussed.

Common Sufferings

Physical suffering emanating from:
 1. Natural disasters
     a) Loss of property
     b) Loss of life
 2. Genetic decay resulting from the fall

        a) Limited life span
        b) Birth defects, diseases, and infections
    3. Accidents
        a) Avoidable
        b) Unavoidable
Emotional suffering emanating from:
    1. Worry
        a) About others' physical and spiritual condition
        b) About our own physical and spiritual condition
    2. Psychological suffering
        a) Emanating from broken relationships
        b) Chemically induced
    3. Spiritual suffering
        a) False expectations or perceptions
        b) Guilt

Sufferings to Which Christians Are Called

Physical Suffering Emanating from:

Natural disasters: (a) *Loss of property*: When earthquakes, floods, hurricanes, tornadoes, mud slides, and wildfires, occur in areas where humans live and work, there is usually a great deal of property damage. This is generally called a natural disaster. The destruction of important property is ordinarily accompanied by a sense of loss that often assumes a form of grief—a loss of tangible symbols which kept us tied to past memories; a loss of valuable assets; the temporary loss of life's routine; or the loss of our means of livelihood. Life's routines are disrupted.

Human responses to such losses are diverse. A bitter spirit may be revealed. The question may be asked, "Why me?" The answer, "Why *not* you?" is not very reassuring. Anger or self-pity may surface. A determined resolve to rebuild and start again may come to the fore. Or an idol may have been lost, and depression sets in. However, the Spirit of the Lord may use the disaster as a wake-up call for some to reflect on God's mercy in sparing their lives. And some, like Job, may say, "The LORD gave and the LORD has taken away. Blessed be the name of the LORD" (Job 1:21).

Natural disasters: (b) *Loss of life*: Both those who love God and those who do not know him die in natural disasters. They may have suffered little in their death, or they may have suffered much before dying. Those who suffered and subsequently died were providentially afforded an opportunity to exercise their *faith* in the object of their trust—themselves, the doctors, or Christ—during their time of continued life.

People who lose loved ones in natural disasters are faced with the added trauma of the unexpected loss that accompanies all such deaths. Their initial reactions may vary, but the recovery responses generally follow the pattern of the stages of grieving—(a) shock; (b) anger; (c) guilt; (d) depression; and finally, (e) acceptance. The emotional suffering in such circumstances is handled in the context of where one's *faith* is rooted. Those who grieve *in* Christ over the loss of a loved one who knew Christ do not grieve as do those who have no hope of the glorious resurrection of their loved one. *Faith* can unite sorrow and joy at such times.

Two of Job's many losses were the result of natural disasters—fire from heaven which destroyed the sheep and the servants watching them, and the great wind that took his children's lives. Job did not waiver, though, but declared, "Blessed be the name of the LORD," in the face of his crushing losses (Job 1:21-22).

Genetic decay *resulting from the fall*: (a) *Limited life span*: Adam and Eve were created physically perfect, able to live forever. With their fall, though, death became an expectation. Their original genetic make-up was uncontaminated by the effects of sin. But their physical life expectancy was altered by the fall. Even though life expectancy remained long contrasted with later generations, they still faced physical death. Genesis 5 records the life spans of Adam's immediate descendants. Adam lived 930 years; Seth 920 years; Enosh 905 years; Kenan 910 years; Mahalalel 895 years; Jared 962 years; Methuselah 969 years; Lamech 777 years; and Noah 950 years. And on it went, until the Lord declared that the normal life span would be 120 years (Gen. 6:3). And still later, life expectancy was reduced to its current norm of 70 years (2 Sam. 19:32; Ps. 90:10). This all confirms that everyone faces physical death, suffering often accompanying it. All face the reality of death in the context of their *faith*, either suppressing thoughts about it, fearing it, stoically accepting it, or embracing it as a door into Christ's presence.

Genetic decay *resulting from the fall*: (b) *Birth defects, diseases, and infections*: The fall—accompanied by the deterioration or mutation of components of the genetic code—gave rise to birth defects, diseases, bacterial infections, viruses, and other alterations in the performance of body organs as they age. These changes result in the eventual death of the physical body. These maladies, a result of the fall, are accompanied by the possibility of both physical and emotional suffering. Both the righteous and the unrighteous are subjected to such "rain" in their lives, to use Christ's word in Matthew 5:45.

God acknowledged his sovereign rule over birth defects and other such maladies when he asked Moses, "Who makes [man] mute or deaf, or seeing or blind? Is it not I, the LORD?" (Ex. 4:11). The Lord does not say that he causes such defects, but that he permits them and uses them in the lives of all concerned. But birth defects today can be followed by lawsuits, finding fault with doctors who did not warn parents of a possible defect so an abortion might be considered. But those who understand God's sovereign use of such heartaches are more likely to pray for strength and wisdom to accept the physically imperfect child and love him as Christ does—seek corrective surgery after birth; seek educational help for the retarded child; help the child manage the handicap; or simply accept the challenges of the birth defect. God has purposes for suffering, and only he uses it in glorious ways.

Accidents (a) *Avoidable*: It is amazing how humans, in the free exercising of their will, can make choices that can cause *other people* to suffer injurious consequences as a result of their actions, like leaving an object on the steps. Or people have the freedom to do things that harm themselves, like driving an automobile after drinking intoxicating beverages. People injure others and themselves every year by making poor choices. Poor judgment, bad habits and carelessness lead to countless otherwise avoidable accidents.

Accidents resulting from such incidents provide opportunities for the revelation of the heart attitude of the injured. Some are quick to find fault with others—the person who left the object on the steps. Legal suits may arise from such faultfinding. Bitterness can emerge, and relationships can be permanently broken. Others stoically accept the accident as a part of life's reality. They do not see it as a part of God's providence or think that the suffering has an eternal purpose. But, by God's grace, those *in* Christ, whose world/life-view encompasses unexpected accidents, submit the final outcomes to their Lord—to conform them more fully into his likeness (Rom. 8:29). The same experience leaves one person bitter, and another trusting in the Lord's providence.

Subsequent to their fall, the tree of life was removed from the presence of our first parents, so that the physical consequences of most serious accidents are now not amenable to perfect restoration. Scars of some type are generally left. The Christian's scar is redeemable. The non-Christian withholds his scar from its possible redemption.

Accidents (b) *Unavoidable*: Some accidents are simply unavoidable in a fallen world: a misstep off the curb, tripping over our own feet, or having a tree limb fall on us and break our neck while walking through the woods. Is there a lesson to be learned from such events?

Christ used the collapse of the tower at Siloam that killed eighteen people to remind his hearers that those on whom the tower fell were not worse than all who lived in Jerusalem. The event, Christ taught, gave an opportunity for all who learned of the disaster to examine their lives before God and *repent*, for a similar thing could happen to anybody (Luke 13:4-5). Christ taught that unavoidable tragedies afford opportunities for those not directly involved to reflect on their own lives before the Lord. Such reflections should lead us to seek a right relationship with him before it is too late, for everyone will die at some future time.

Emotional Suffering Emanating from:

Worry: (a) *Worry about others' physical and spiritual condition*: The closer to us a person with a threatening physical condition is —flu, diabetes, spinal injury, cancer—the more our heart longs for a positive resolution. The more dangerous the threat, the more likely we are to *worry* about it. The chain of trust appears when the threatening condition moves away from our control or involvement in the cure. Our trust moves away from ourselves and is placed on caregivers. Those who do not know the sovereign God, who has all of our lives in his hands, have a limited array of places and people in which to place their trust.

Note Christ's admonition concerning *anxiety* in his Sermon on the Mount.
> Do not be worried about your life, as to what you will eat or what you will drink; nor for your body, as to what you will put on. Is not life more

> than food, and the body more than clothing? Look at the birds of the air, that they do not sow, nor reap nor gather into barns, and yet *your heavenly Father feeds* them. Are you not worth much more than they? And who of you by being worried can add a single hour to his life? And why are you worried about clothing? Observe how the lilies of the field grow; they do not toil nor do they spin, yet I say to you that not even Solomon in all his glory clothed himself like one of these. But if *God so clothes* the grass of the field, which is alive today and tomorrow is thrown into the furnace, will *He* not much more clothe you? *You of little faith!* Do not worry then, saying, 'What will we eat?' or 'What will we drink?' or 'What will we wear for clothing?' For the Gentiles eagerly seek all these things; for your *heavenly Father* knows that you need all these things. But seek first *His kingdom* and *His righteousness*, and all these things will be added to you. So do not worry about tomorrow; for tomorrow will care for itself. Each day has enough trouble of its own. (Matt. 6:25-34)

Christ called his hearers to put their trust in God the Father rather than in themselves or other human beings. Anxiety replaced with trust in God is anxiety converted into a *bond* between the almighty Creator and his child. God does not disappoint such childish trust; it is the heart and glory of *faith*.

Our concerns about the *spiritual condition* of those we are burdened for range from a deep concern for someone's salvation to the fear that someone is slowly drifting away from their first love (Rev. 2:4). The ungodly have no such concerns, but God's children do. Their first approach should be to acknowledge that God alone is capable of moving hearts toward himself. He alone is the giver of *saving faith*. And he alone is capable of bringing about renewal in the hearts of his people (1 Cor. 3:6; Eph. 3:16; Phil. 4:13; Col. 1:11). We are to encourage, share the Word in love, exhort, and woo our Christian brothers and sisters to walk faithfully in Christ—but the effective response is the Lord's work (1 Cor. 3:6).

Worry: *(b) Worry about our own physical and spiritual condition*: The tendency to focus on self is a mark of the fall. Genesis says, "And the man and his wife were both naked and were not ashamed" (Gen. 2:25). This is not a sexual statement. Rather it shows how unconscious they were regarding self. Neither was self-conscious or ashamed when he or she looked at the other's nakedness. But following their fall the entire picture changed—"Then the eyes of both of them were opened, and *they knew they were naked*; and they sewed fig leaves together and made themselves loin coverings" (Gen. 3:7). They immediately became self-conscious and were very concerned about self. They moved from being other-focused to being self-focused.

Some level of self-concern is prudent now that the tree of life has been removed (Gen. 3:22-24). When we get a toothache, for example, we should take care of it. Better yet, we should learn to care for our teeth so such problems can be avoided. Health is important, but the line between too much focus on one's health and an insufficient focus is a personal choice everyone faces. It is not always an easy balance to maintain.

The spiritual health God's children enjoy is ultimately guaranteed: Christ, their physician, attends to their true spiritual needs. He made us, knows us intimately, and cares for us (Rom. 8:31; 1 Peter 5:7). Those outside God's family struggle to attend to their own spiritual needs and are in jeopardy. In Christ's language, "They are blind guides of the blind" (Matt. 15:14). Those without the Spirit of Christ are without a spiritual point of reference apart from their tradition, their personal experience, or another guide instead of Christ. They may work for their salvation; they may deny there is life after death; they may do penance; they may follow a thousand rituals that promise them spiritual peace — but all such substitutes for Christ are counterfeits.

Psychological *suffering*: (a) *Emanating from broken relationships*: God's declaration that he will visit "the iniquity of fathers on the children and on the grandchildren to the third and fourth generations" (Ex. 34:7; Num. 14:18; Deut. 5:9) is observable. This does not mean that the *punishment* due the parents for their sins is placed on their children but that the way children are raised has a *great impact* on their psychological development. For example, if during the first years of life a child observes his father beating his mother, the child experiences this as normal behavior. He or she has nothing with which to compare such ungodly behavior. Therefore, what children perceive to be normal will, in all likelihood, be lived out by them when they become adults: the male believes it is all right to beat his wife; the female either expects to be beaten or avoids marriage altogether.

Those rejected in childhood tend to reject others as they grow up. Those who are physically abused as children tend to abuse their own children later. Those who are over-controlled in childhood tend to over-control their children. And on and on it goes. Bad habits—ungodly behaviors—are psychologically contagious. The Holy Spirit is, of course, able to break such patterns, but there is suffering for those subjected to the ungodly habits of their parents. And those being transformed by the loving work of the Holy Spirit experience suffering while the discipline of love takes place. Hebrews 12:4-13 is instructive in these matters. But it is the Holy Spirit's work that breaks the sinful patterns so that God can bless the redeemed children and their children after them (Acts 2:39; Ps. 103:17; Prov. 17:6).

Marriages ending in divorce create enormous emotional suffering. Broken friendships cause deep hurts. Misunderstandings dividing people often stem from poor communication, and this causes distress. The causes for such relational breakdowns are manifold—but honest confession, forgiveness, and reconciliation are their only cure. There is a greater probability of reconciliation in Christian relationships than in other kind. Why? Because forgiveness, a hallmark of the Christian faith, is *essential* to reconciliation, and without forgiveness there is no solid ground upon which to restore a relationship. Christ's purpose for becoming a man testifies to this—"Behold, the Lamb of God who takes away the sin of the world!" (John 1:29).

Psychological *suffering:* (b) *Chemically induced*: Many suffer because they experience alteration in the chemical balances within their bodies that intermittently bathe their brain, which in turn profoundly influences their emotional stability and sense of well-being. Our emotions, sense of well-being, and stability can be profoundly impacted by body chemistry. Unquestionably, the fall of our first parents, with the deterioration in the originally perfect genetic code, is the cause of the suffering that emanates from this physical problem.[96]

Spiritual *suffering*: (a) *False expectations or perceptions*: I know a man who was afraid of suffering in any form. He admits that he was psychologically unstable when Christ called him. He surrendered his life to Christ with the false expectation that he would no longer suffer. But as he walked with Christ, he gently taught him that he would be *with him* in suffering, but that he would not shield him from *all* suffering (Pss. 34:18; 46:1). He testifies that "Christ took me by my shoulders, and slowly and gently turned me around so that I could face suffering, and not attempt to run from it. Christ assured me that he would be with me as I faced the sufferings that lay ahead. He has been true to his word. I no longer live in fear of suffering." The turnaround was slow, initially accompanied by fear that gradually dissipated as Christ accompanied him in life's challenges.

False expectations can arise in almost any area of life. A husband can expect his wife to be his mother or his servant—both bad expectations. A wife can expect her husband to meet needs in her life that only Christ can meet or to be treated like a child that never has to grow up—more bad expectations. Whenever our expectations are out of conformity with God's design, emotional suffering results. Unsaved persons live with sufferings of this type too frequently.

Spiritual suffering outside of Christ takes many forms. It may be a hunger for physical pleasure while the real hunger is for true meaning and purpose that can only be realized *in* Christ. Sexual liaisons that provide erotic satisfaction require frequent re-stimulation to maintain the false hope that they can ultimately satisfy the heart's longing for a genuine relationship. Some seek pleasure through excessive travel. All these searches become stale and unrewarding. This is the meaning of the proverb "Sheol and Abaddon are never satisfied, nor are the eyes of man ever satisfied" (Prov. 27:20). If death (Sheol) and hell (Abaddon) cannot be satisfied then neither can our desires until the eyes of the heart (Eph. 1:18) are opened to see that true satisfaction only comes from a relationship with Christ (Heb. 12:1-2).

The true focus of the human soul is often masked, as the psalmist reminds us:

> Surely God is good to Israel, to those who are pure in heart! But as for me, my feet came close to stumbling, my steps had almost slipped. For I was envious of the arrogant as I saw the prosperity of the wicked. For there are no pains in their death, and their body is fat. They are not in trouble as other men, nor are they plagued like mankind. Therefore pride is their necklace; the garment of violence covers them. . . . They have set their mouth against the heavens, and their tongue parades through the earth. . . . They say, "How does God know? And is there

---

[96] It is also true that emotional problems can bring about chemical imbalances in the human body. It is often difficult to determine if the problem is triggered by a physical or an emotional condition.

knowledge with the Most High?" Behold, these are the wicked; and always at ease, they have increased in wealth. Surely in vain I have kept my heart pure and washed my hands in innocence; for I have been stricken all day long and chastened every morning. (Ps. 73:1-14)

The psalmist had taken his eyes off God. He was thinking about what his eyes saw: the prosperity, lack of suffering, good health, and seemingly worry-free life of the ungodly. At that time he was not reflecting on their final outcome. But God brought him back to reality

[Then] I came into the sanctuary of God; then I perceived their end. Surely You set them in slippery places; You cast them down to destruction. How they are destroyed in a moment! They are utterly swept away by sudden terrors! (vv. 17-19)

God, by his grace, did not let the psalmist remain in misperception. If he had continued in it he would have missed the daily chastening at the hands of his Savior who loved him enough to persevere in training him in godliness.

Spiritual suffering: (b) Guilt: Unconscious guilt is like undetected cancer; it eats away at our spiritual health without our even being aware of its destructiveness. For example, we do not know why we dislike someone. Perhaps he stirs subconscious senses regarding our own unattractive habits—he dominates a conversation; he is selfish. Our aversion to the other person becomes a substitute for dealing with our own defects. We become judgmental rather than humble. We find fault with others rather than confront our faults. Without Christ's help there is no way to alter such sin-patterns, so the spiritual cancer of sin and guilt may continue to their natural conclusion in death.

Recognized-but-suppressed guilt has the same impact as unconscious guilt. The denial and perverted ways of dealing with recognizable guilt leads to depression, broken relationships and suffering of the spirit. Unresolved guilt separates people from those they have hurt, or it eats away at their self-esteem if they are involved in a detrimental habit but refuse to quit.

A woman who borrows $500 from a friend with the promise to pay it back in thirty days, and does not meet the obligation to repay the loan will not want to be in the presence of the lending friend. The longer she delays repaying the loan, the worse the guilt becomes; and the desire to avoid the lender grows correspondingly. The relationship will continue to deteriorate unless mended—debt repaid, or debt forgiven by the lender. Guilt leads to separation!

Another example of guilt that eats away at self-esteem is a man's falling into the habit of looking at pornography. He knows God desires sexual purity, a one-flesh relationship with a wife in fidelity. The more the man looks at pornography, the worse he feels. The violation of God's prescribed norm, however, is easily rationalized as the sensuous appetite is fed through looking at pictures of naked women. The habit can become addictive and we need God's grace to break it. Christ must become more attractive to the person than the sensuous pleasure.

Immediately following the fall, God addressed the serpent (Satan), "I will put *enmity* between you and the woman, and between your seed and her seed; he

[Christ] shall bruise you on the head, and you shall bruise him on the heel" (Gen. 3:15). Enmity, bitterness, hostility, and spite would characterize the relationship between the children of the evil one and God. And those in Satan's family also dislike those individuals in God's *family*. God ordained this enmity—What have light and darkness in common; what have righteousness and unrighteousness in common? He, however, has manifested infinite grace by redeeming a bride out of the family of Satan and giving her to Christ. The weapons employed in this war are very different. The children of God are to overcome evil with good (Rom. 12:21), even loving their enemies (Matt. 5:44; Luke 6:27, 35). "The weapons of our warfare are not of the flesh, but divinely powerful" (2 Cor. 10:4). But God's weapons are effective only in the Holy Spirit's hands.

The weapons of those opposing God are not kindness and love. The first example of hostility of someone outside of the family of God toward his children was Cain's murder of his brother Abel (Gen. 4:8). What is revealing is Cain's reason for the murder—"Because his [Cain's] deeds were evil, and his brother's were righteous" (1 John 3:12). Righteousness—*light*—always makes unrighteousness—*darkness*—uncomfortable. And while it is true that light drives out darkness, it is equally clear that darkness hates light. The two are enemies.

The human conscience was dormant before the fall but was activated by it. Its becoming active was a manifestation of God's grace, for the active conscience is designed to serve to restrain our fallen nature—a nature that puts *self* ahead of all. But the conscience that is unheeded and hardened, resents righteousness—for it makes unrighteousness extremely uncomfortable. A spirit of enmity, not love, naturally inhabits the heart of the unrighteous.

And so it is. Those who do not love Christ often resent those who do, when they are "the salt of the earth" and "the light of the world" (Matt. 5:13-14). Christ continues, "Let your light shine before men *in such a way* that they may see your good works, and glorify your Father who is in heaven" (v.16). Two things are noteworthy. First, the words "in such a way" are a strong reminder that our light must be used in a Christlike manner. We are not to be holier than thou or condescending. God's light is not a weapon; it is a searchlight, calling lost souls to return to their Creator. His light must be used in love.

And second, those who encounter God's light through us may have many reactions. They may smile and think we are naive and quaint. They may simply ignore us. Or they may assault us. And some, by God's grace, are drawn to the light, and desire the Light from which our light arises. But those who reject God's light will only glorify God at the last judgment—"Keep your behavior excellent among the Gentiles, so that *in the thing in which they slander you as evildoers*, they may because of your good deeds, as they observe them, *glorify God in the day of visitation*" (1 Peter 2:12). Note, Christians are often slandered, and more. Christians can suffer—indeed, are called to suffer—at the hands of non-Christians by God's eternal decree.

Christ—the head of the church—certainly experienced enmity from many of those he came to serve. They rejected and crucified him. But he suffered *with a purpose*, in fact, multiple purposes. "He learned obedience from the things which He suffered" (Heb. 5:8). He never disobeyed but he was *tested* in his obedience and he matured by the testing—"He withdrew from them about a stone's throw, and he knelt down and began to pray, saying, 'Father, if You are willing, remove this cup from Me; *yet not My will*, but Yours be done'" (Luke 22:41-42). Jesus accepted his Father's will at every point. Jesus did not enjoy his many sufferings, but he learned and grew through them. Indeed, as the God-*man*, Jesus had to grow up in all areas of his life as all humans do (Luke 2:52).

Indeed, "it was fitting for Him [God the Father], for whom are all things, and through whom are all things, in bringing many sons to glory, to *perfect* the author [Christ] of their salvation through *sufferings*" (Heb. 2:10). If the perfect God/*man* was perfected through sufferings, how much more will God use suffering to perfect us! Suffering is a teacher in the hands of God who uses it for his good purpose. In the life of God's children it is a refiner.

As Christ experienced the enmity of his creatures, he calls his brothers and sisters to follow him into the same suffering—in which they *learn* and *mature*. More importantly by *knowingly* enduring suffering Christians bear witness to their allegiance to their holy and glorious Savior, who empowers them to suffer as he did. The suffering that comes to us from the enmity of those who reject Christ is *special*. It is an honorable suffering with a reward and a purpose, as Scripture bears witness:

> More than that, I count all things to be loss in view of the surpassing value of knowing Christ Jesus my Lord, for whom I have suffered the loss of all things, and count them but rubbish so that I may gain Christ, and may be found in Him, not having a righteousness of my own derived from the Law, but that which is through faith in Christ, the righteousness which comes from God on the basis of faith, that I may know Him, and the power of His resurrection and the fellowship of His sufferings, being conformed to His death; in order that I may attain to the resurrection from the dead. (Phil. 3:8-11)

> For to you it has been granted for Christ's sake not only to believe in Him, but also to suffer for His sake. (Phil. 1:29)

> If when you do what is right and suffer for it you patiently endure it, this finds favor with God. For you have been called for this purpose, since Christ also suffered for you, leaving you an example for you to follow in His steps. (1 Peter 2:20-21)

> [We are] always carrying about in [our] body the dying of Jesus, that the life of Jesus also may be manifested in our body. (2 Cor. 4:10)

> But even if you should suffer for the sake of righteousness, you are blessed…and keep a good conscience so that in the thing in which you are slandered, those who revile your good behavior in Christ may be put to shame. For it is better, if God should will it so, that you suffer for doing what is right rather than for doing what is wrong. (1 Peter 3:14, 16-17)

> Beloved, do not be surprised at the fiery ordeal among you, which comes upon you for your testing, as though some strange thing were happening

> to you; but to the degree that you share the sufferings of Christ, keep on rejoicing, so that also at the revelation of His glory you may rejoice with exultation. If you are reviled for the name of Christ, you are blessed, because the Spirit of glory and of God rests upon you . . . but if anyone suffers as a Christian, he is not to be ashamed, but is to glorify God in this name. (1 Peter 4:12-14, 16)
>
> For just as the sufferings of Christ are ours in abundance, so also our comfort is abundant through Christ. (2 Cor. 1:5)
>
> The Spirit Himself testifies with our spirit that we are children of God, and if children, heirs also, heirs of God and fellow heirs with Christ, if indeed we suffer with Him so that we may also be glorified with Him. (Rom. 8:16-17)
>
> Now I rejoice in my sufferings for your sake, and in my flesh I do my share on behalf of His body, which is the church, in filling up what is lacking in Christ's afflictions. (Col. 1:24)

These passages provide insight regarding our call *in* Christ. As we live as he did, according to his will: (1) we will participate "in the fellowship of his sufferings"[97]; (2) we suffer "for his sake"—for his glory; (3) we have been called to suffer as a testimony to our commitment to him; (4) we carry the dying of Jesus about in us so that his life will be seen in us; (5) our suffering may occur because righteousness stirs up enmity in unrighteous hearts; (6) we are blessed, we are to rejoice, and we are not to be ashamed when we are reviled for his sake; (7) we suffer for Christ, so we are comforted by him; (8) our suffering for righteousness is evidence of our relationship with him; and (9) we are "filling up what is lacking in his afflictions."

What does it mean that we are "filling up what is lacking in Christ's afflictions"? It means that Christ, while living in us, is still wooing the unsaved through us and that their enmity toward him, that caused him such suffering, is an ongoing reality. What is different is that now *Christians* are called upon to suffer this rejection by the ungodly. (Of course, we also share in the *joy* of those who come to Christ through the gospel!) Christians are the heirs of the ongoing sufferings Christ would experience if he were still physically among us. We are heirs of the enmity directed at Christ whenever we represent him well and are rejected. It is Christ *in* us who suffers. We are filling up what is lacking in his afflictions.

Rejection takes many forms. To be with a group when an off-color joke is told, and not to laugh along with the rest, calls attention to our different perspective as to what is appropriate. And our not laughing can be *convicting*. It presents a contrast between righteousness and unrighteousness. The unrighteous do not *like* being exposed to the contrast. They may start with a verbal attack: "What is wrong with you? Are you too good to have a bit of fun?" Or your

---

[97] Fellowship, in this context, points to the believer's grasping and entering into a deeper understanding of Christ's suffering on their behalf.

restraint may be passed over then, but you may not be invited to the next get-together. To not gossip—or worse, to be in a group that is cutting up a person concerning whom you stand up and say something nice—is a good way to become ostracized by any group.

Bill, a man who loves Christ, was in graduate school and working one summer with the university crew painting vacated student apartments. Ross, the crew's foreman, was the only non-academic employee of the six, and was much older. He had the student painters rotate assignments every time they went to a new apartment. Every fifth apartment, a student was assigned to paint the kitchen and bathroom, where enamel paint was used. In the rest of the apartment latex paint was used, so the students had four turns with latex paint and one turn with enamel paint, which was harder to use and clean up. Everyone, except the foreman, would paint for a good span of time and then the foreman would call a fifteen-minute break. During the breaks profanity prevailed; dirty jokes and perverted stories were often told. Bill developed the habit of sitting a little away from them and reading an old newspaper that was used as a drop cloth, rather than joining in the sport. Ross approached him one morning and asked, "What is wrong with you? Are you too good to sit with us and enjoy the fun?" Bill answered, "No, not at all. In fact, for many years I used to enjoy this kind of fun, but it just isn't fun for me anymore." Ross shot back, "Oh, you must be the kind of guy that likes Billy Graham!" Bill responded, "Well, as a matter of fact, I do admire Billy Graham very much." "The last guy on my crew who liked Billy Graham, I put ice picks through his tires," Ross retorted. "Well, I am certainly sorry to hear that," Bill replied. The conversation ended.

Bill painted every kitchen and bathroom with enamel paint for the rest of the summer. And seven months later, he called home one morning to hear his wife say, "Sweetheart, when I went out to go grocery shopping this morning I found both tires next to the curb flat. I called the Texaco station, and the man said that the tires had been punctured right next to the rims and could not be patched." Bill said, "Honey, don't worry about it. Ross has 'done his thing.' The Lord will take care of it."[98] Bill and his wife suffered for righteousness sake.

Persecution of Christians by other religious faiths has been rather common in history. Many who immigrated to North America from Western Europe in the seventeenth and eighteenth centuries did so because they were being persecuted for their Christian faith in England and on the Continent. Many of the earliest settlers came to America seeking religious freedom. Simply to bear Christ's name can make one a target of hatred when ethnic, tribal, or national attitudes of exclusiveness rise to bar all but their own from the community or nation. This general enmity toward those who are different is at times expressed toward any

---

[98] Three years later Bill and his wife learned that the university was firing Ross for another gross misconduct.

minority deemed to be unacceptable. And in many parts of today's world, Christians fill that bill and are persecuted! Our focus here, however, is on the enmity between righteousness and unrighteousness.

Those who hate God revealed in his Son, Jesus Christ, are at enmity with him because he is *holy, righteous,* and *sovereign.* Those who hide from God do not like his purity. It highlights their impurity that they enjoy in their fallen state. Those who resent God's righteousness reject it because the virtuous bar is so high in Christ that they know they cannot attain it, and thus resent it showing them up as sinners in need of forgiveness and Christ's righteousness. Their self-acclaimed, "I am OK," is shown to be a hollow claim of independent rightness. And the manifestation of Christ's holiness and righteousness establishes his headship as humanity's King of kings, who possesses the rightful authority over the entire creation. The fallen spirit wants to be independent, and wants to be god. When we present Christ to the world those who resent God will resent *us.* We suffer both their passive and active forms of rejection of Christ, an affliction that is "filling up what is lacking in Christ's afflictions" (Col. 1:24).

Suffering, though, has a wonderful purpose in God's economy. It bonds us to Christ. It matures us. It strengthens our faith. And the Christian can be certain of his or her union with Christ when his suffering is accompanied by joy. *Joyful suffering* is a special gift from the Lord, a gift reserved for his chosen ones. The Christian is also comforted in his suffering when he remembers that God is wholly sovereign, even over all forms of suffering.

12

God Is Love: What Does This Really Mean?

We have come to know and have believed the love which God has for us. God is love, and the one who abides in love abides in God, and God abides in him. (1 John 4:16)

The word "love" has many meanings in English. It is commonly assumed that the primary component of love is emotion. People say, "It was love at first sight" or "I fell in love." These are romantic expressions communicating that the speaker experienced exciting feelings. The person having the pleasant experience is attracted to the one who makes him or her feel good. In this sense, love is someone's emotional response to another person making them feel happy, special, or wanted. Love, is feeling good about how another person makes me feel. From this perspective, Love is all about self. Is this what the biblical message, "God is love," means?

Love is also associated with love-making in English. Here love is associated with a desire to become one flesh with someone else. Love, in "love-making," has a large component of anticipated *sensuous* pleasure. God is the author of human sexuality; it is beautiful in the context of marriage as God designed it to be; and it has several God-ordained purposes—pleasure, bonding, and procreation. But is this what the biblical declaration that God is love means?

Philadelphia, the City of Brotherly Love, derives its name from the Greek verb *phileo* (φιλεω)—"to be friendly, to love as a friend." Friends usually have activities they enjoy in common. Friends share their private thoughts with each other more than with casual acquaintances. The closer the friendship, the more likely the sharing in greater depth. Sharing exposes our inner being to others, and a component of trust must be present before we risk being vulnerable to another person.

And a nice thing about having friends is that we can have a number of them. Each friendship rests on a combination of interests. For example, common literary interests can become the basis for friendship. Those who love to read the Puritans have a common point of interest around which friendships might develop. Friendships are also often established around hobbies. Hiking, traveling, and board games offer opportunities to connect. Common interests bind people together.

A fascinating interplay between two concepts of love occurs in a conversation between Christ and Peter after Christ's resurrection. The setting was the Sea of Galilee where seven of Christ's disciples had fished through the night. Early in the morning, Christ called to them from the shore and asked if they had caught anything. They said, "No." He then told them to cast their net on the right side of the boat and they would make a catch. They obeyed and unexpectedly their net was overflowing with fish. Up until then the disciples had not known it was Christ who was speaking. John suddenly knew that it was Jesus and said, "It is the Lord" (John 21:7). Peter put on his outer clothing, jumped into the sea, and swam ashore, where he and Christ had this conversation after breakfast:

> Jesus said to Simon Peter, "Simon, son of John, do you *agapao* (love) Me more than these?" He said to Him, "Yes, Lord; You know that I *phileo* (love) You." He said to him, "Tend My lambs." He said to him again a second time, "Simon, son of John, do you *agapao* (love) Me?" He said to Him, "Yes, Lord; You know that I *phileo* (love) You." He said to him, "Shepherd My sheep." He said to him the third time, "Simon, son of John, do you *phileo* (love) Me?" Peter was grieved because He said to him the third time, "Do you *phileo* (love) Me?" And he said to Him, "Lord, You know all things; You know that I *phileo* (love) You." Jesus said to him, "Tend My sheep." (vv. 15-17)

The interplay between the two words for love, *agapao* and *phileo*, is fascinating. The Greek verb *phileo*, which is translated as "love," means "to love as a friend." It connotes liking, enjoying, approving, and identifying with another regarding certain common interests. *Phileo* has at its core love that is rooted in likes and dislikes. Emotions play a central role in its character. There are, in fact, three Greek nouns translated into English as "love," that are rooted in feelings. They are *philos* (friendship), *storge* (parental love), and *eros* (erotic love).[99] All three notions are heavily attached to feelings.

The Greek word *agape* (love), on the other hand, is not even found in Hellenistic or classical Greek. But it does occur in Koine or marketplace Greek—Greek found in writings during New Testament times and spoken in the marketplace. This word is distinctive to the understanding of the expression "God is love" (1 John 4:16). When Jesus questioned Peter regarding his love for him, Jesus asked if Peter loved *him* as he loved *Peter*. Remember that Peter had denied Jesus not many days earlier. We can surmise that Peter was now aware that, based on his own character, he could not *agapao* Christ. What, then, is the nature of *agape*? And if God commands us to *agapao* him with all of our heart, soul and mind, and to *agapao* our neighbors as ourselves (Matt. 22:37-39), just what does he command?

God commands us to do something *impossible* until we are reborn and renovated. Even *after* rebirth, it is impossible to *agapao* another by one's own effort. God's commandment is for those who truly know him, for *agape* love is his *gift* to his children. They are called to utilize the gift of love that he gives them

---

[99] We have discussed *philos* and *eros*. We will treat *storge* in chapter 23.

when they are regenerated, and which increases as they are transformed into Christ's likeness. No one completely fulfills the injunction, but the child of God is riveted by the command and continues to seek God's help to more completely fulfill its intent. The commandment is not intended for those outside of Christ—other than to point to a goal that they know is unobtainable. They are incapable of obeying it because they are dead to Christ, and cannot comprehend its true purpose and meaning. They are incapable of producing *agape* love!

Agape love is a *gift* from God to his children. It reflects a renovation in the nature and character of those who are given saving faith in Christ. *Agape* is the evidence that its possessors are true children of God. Christ told his disciples, "A *new* commandment I give to you, that you love *(agapao)* one another, even as I have loved you, that you also love one another. *By this all men will know that you are My disciples, if you have love (agape) for one another*" (John 13:34-35). God enables his children to be able to more and more *agapao* him and their neighbors.

Agape, a uniquely biblical word used to describe an aspect of God's nature, is only rightly understood in the light of God's self-revelation in Scripture and made alive in our hearts by the Holy Spirit. *Agape* is, on the one hand, an easy-to-understand orientation of God's heart shown in a complex array of out-workings that are, on the other hand, best grasped when placed on an imaginary continuum between the messages of 1 Corinthians 13:4-7 and Hebrews 12:4-11.

The easy-to-understand orientation of God's heart is discerned in the fact that God is not self-oriented or selfish. We see this in the life of Christ. He never puts himself before others. He is never self-centered or selfish. He was always other-concerned. He unselfishly served others. He gave his very *life* for them! Indeed, he gave his life to save his *enemies*! Christ, the image of the invisible God (Col. 1:15), lived a selfless life before the watching world.

The Father's eternal love for those ensnared in the consequences of Adam's fall most powerfully appears in his sending his unique Son to be the propitiation for our sins (1 John 4:9-10). And what is propitiation? It is a sacrifice that absorbs God's wrath. All sin must be punished; justice demands it. And God's holiness cannot tolerate anything unholy. So Christ became God's solution to the dilemma generated by Adam's fall. Christ is the means by which the Father "might be *just* and the *justifier* of the one who has faith in Jesus" (Rom. 3:26). As our substitute, Jesus suffered the wrath of God. The Father looked upon the travail of his Son's soul and was satisfied that the penalty due all unrighteousness had been paid (Isa. 53:1-12, especially v. 11). No greater love can anyone have than to lay down his or her life for one's friends (John 15:13). The Father's sending Jesus and his willingness to come and absorb the Father's wrath for us speak volumes about God's great *agape* love.

Agape is selfless. It is dead-to-self love. The new commandment Christ gave his disciples is to love others as he loves others, not just to love others as we love ourselves (the "old" commandment). The bar has been raised. If the old commandment was too difficult, the new one is impossible apart from the Spirit's work in those whom God *enables* to fulfill his will.

When Adam and Eve fell from grace, they went from being other-oriented to self-oriented (Gen. 2:25-3:12). Being self-centered is a primary mark of the fall. Self has dominated the human's psychological orientation since the fall. Denying one's self and taking up one's cross daily is strong evidence of God's redemptive work in a life (Matt. 16:24). Indeed, such a lifestyle is impossible apart from the work of the Holy Spirit (John 14:16-17, 26; Luke 11:13).

Agape love, compared to *philos, storge,* and *eros* loves, is rooted in something other than emotions. As beautiful as *philos, eros,* and *storge* are, they are not dependable—because they are rooted in variable feelings. The buffeting we experience in this fallen world makes our feelings unreliable. Feelings rise and fall with our experiences. It is important that God never commands *philos, eros,* or *storge*. All three are gifts made available to all. They could be called gifts of common grace. The righteous and the unrighteous are both benefactors of these three types of love. That is not true of *agape* for it is given only to God's children.

If *agape* is not rooted in feelings, then in what is it rooted? God's *agape* is rooted in his *volition*—his ability to make and follow through on an immutable decision. Specifically, this means *agape* is the manifestation of God's nature that *chooses to do what will accomplish the greatest good in the lives of those who bear his image.* God's entire being nourishes and controls *agape*, but it is God who "according to His purpose . . . works all things after the counsel of His *will*" (Eph. 1:11). *Agape* is anchored in God's *will*! This is why God commands *agape* that he imparts to our nature through the Holy Spirit, and does not command *storge, eros,* or *philos* that are rooted in emotions.

The fact that *agape* love is rooted in God's nature does not imply that his attribute of love is not closely related to his compassion, mercy, patience, and grace. But the fact that his love for us is anchored in his *will* explains why God can love his enemies and can insist that we grow to the point in our Christlikeness where we too can love our enemies. Christ's teaching is explicit:

> I say to you who hear, love your enemies, do good to those who hate you, bless those who curse you, pray for those who mistreat you . . . . If you love those who love you, what credit is that to you? For even sinners love those who love them . . . . But love your enemies . . . and your reward will be great, and you will be sons of the Most High; for He Himself is kind to ungrateful and evil men. Be merciful, just as your Father is merciful.
> (Luke 6:27-36)

To sum up the easy-to-understand orientation of God's heart as shown in his *agape* love: it is selfless and oriented toward others. We turn now to the complex array of options God uses to accomplish the greatest good for those whom he engages. We will create an imaginary continuum between 1 Corinthians 13:4-7 and Hebrews 12:4-11. The first text speaks of what we will call *tender agape*. The second text addresses what is called *tough agape*. Everyone enjoys tender love, but tough love is unpleasant. But we need both, to grow up in Christlikeness.

The way to get at the heart of *agape* love is to look at its characteristics:

> Love is patient, love is kind and is not jealous; love does not brag and is not arrogant, does not act unbecomingly; it does not seek its own, is not provoked, does not take into account a wrong suffered, does not rejoice in unrighteousness, but rejoices with the truth; bears all things, believes all things, hopes all things, endures all things. (1 Cor. 13:4-7)

Hebrews 12 presents *agape's* tough components. It addresses the *discipline* component of love. It tells of what seems not to be joyful, but sorrowful while we are *trained by it*. The biblical concept of discipline involves being trained rather than being punished. Christ bore the punishment for our sins on the cross; we are now being disciplined or *trained* by God.

> You have not yet resisted to the point of shedding blood in your striving against sin; and you have forgotten the exhortation which is addressed to you as sons, *My son, do not regard lightly the discipline of the Lord, nor faint when you are reproved by Him; for those whom the Lord loves He disciplines, and He scourges every son whom He receives.* It is for discipline that you endure; God deals with you as with sons; for what son is there whom his father does not discipline? But if you are without discipline, of which all have become partakers, then you are illegitimate children and not sons. Furthermore, we had earthly fathers to discipline us, and we respected them; shall we not much rather be subject to the Father of spirits, and live? For they disciplined us for a short time as seemed best to them, but He disciplines us for our good, *so that we may share His holiness.* All discipline for the moment seems not to be joyful, but sorrowful; yet to those who have been *trained* by it, afterwards it yields the peaceful fruit of righteousness. (Heb. 12:4-11)

Tender Qualities Found in Agape Love

1 Corinthians 13:4-7 mentions fifteen characteristics of *agape* love, each of which we will now describe briefly to provide the sweet aroma of tender *agape* love.

1. Agape Love Is Patient

We see patience: (a) God's willingness to wait; (b) his willingness to refrain from imposing his will; (c) his forbearance in the face of resistance; (d) his perseverance in wooing, admonishing, encouraging, teaching, and renovating his children; (e) his refusal to let go of us; (f) his longsuffering with those who reject him; and (g) his determination to conform us to Christ's image. God continuously manifests these characteristics of *patience*. Those to whom he gives the gift of *agape* love will become more patient over time as God renovates their lives and patiently fulfills his promise to make them over into Christ's likeness.

2. Agape Love Is Kind

We see kindness in: (a) God's willingness to make himself known to us; (b) God's grace—the giving of a vast variety of good temporal and spiritual things to the undeserving; (c) his mercy—the withholding of his wrath deserved for godless thoughts and behavior; (d) God's offering the alienated the opportunity to be reconciled to him; (e) his offering forgiveness to all who trust Christ as Savior; (f) his being a very present help in times of trouble; and (g) his sending the Spirit to teach and guide those who are Christ's. Those who acknowledge God's kindness, and are being renewed in Christ's likeness, will show kindness to others. The presence of *agape* love in one's life is manifested through expressions of kindness.

3. Agape Love Is Not Jealous or Envious

The gift of *agape* brings contentment: What more could we desire than God himself? "God . . . has blessed us with every spiritual blessing in the heavenly places in Christ" (Eph. 1:3). *Agape* love does not begrudge another's being honored. *Agape* is glad that another experiences the joy of being honored. *Agape* love is devoid of covetousness; it supersedes thirsting for another's possessions—spouse; home; job; wealth. What is lost or acquired by another is of no consequence when compared with God's *agape* love for us. The longing for what another has is voided by the realization that God's *agape* is of an infinitely higher value than anything else. *Agape* dissolves envy. Christ existed in the form of God before his incarnation but he emptied himself and became a bondservant; there was no *envy* to be found in him, and those in Christ become more and more content with Christ in their lives.

4. Agape Love Does Not Brag

"With humility of mind let each of you regard one another as more important than yourselves" (Phil. 2:3). Humility trumps self-aggrandizement. Boasting is one of the worst forms of self-love. Bragging is an attempt to elevate self and lower others. At its heart, bragging forgets the truth: "*What do you have that that you did not receive*? And if you did receive it, why do you boast as if you had not received it?" (1 Cor. 4:7). *Agape* love is far removed from bragging. It resides with humility and modesty. Those growing in Christ will brag less and less about their accomplishments, and boast more and more of the Trinity (Jer. 9:23-24; 2 Cor. 10:17-18). Only God has the right to brag—and he never does for he is *agape* love and that does not brag.

5. Agape Love Is Not Arrogant

Thesaurus reveals why arrogance is antithetical to *agape* love. The following synonyms describe arrogance: aloof, autocratic, conceited, contemptuous, egotistic, haughty, insolent, overbearing, pompous, presumptuous, scornful, self-important, and smug. None of these words is ever associated with God's character. They all bespeak of a fallen nature that elevates itself. They point to being puffed up. *Agape* does not puff itself up; it elevates others.

6. Agape Love Does Not Act Unbecomingly

It is inappropriate to identify ourselves with Christ and to live in a manner that does not reflect his character. This is taking his name in vain. Was Christ a gossip? He was not. Then Christians who gossip are unbecoming in God's eyes. Was Christ vulgar? He was not. Then it is unbecoming for a Christian to be vulgar. Would Christ have enjoyed pornography? He would not. To promote or to use pornography is unbecoming for Christians. To share information given in confidence is shameful. To laugh at a tragic event that has brought another person to tears is unbecoming. *Agape* love is faithful to Christ. It does not contradict his nature and character.

7. Agape Love Does Not Seek Its Own

It is easy to consider ourselves before others. Children can fight over who gets to choose first between two pieces of pie. Parents can find this pie-choosing behavior exasperating, but then turn right around and race another car to an open parking space at the mall. The old nature wants to win or receive the recognition. *Agape* love, a gift from God, puts self aside and seeks the good for others before it seeks the good for itself. (Rom. 12:10).

8. Agape Love Is Not Provoked

What provokes you? Being ignored? Someone's being late for an engagement? Someone's teasing you? Someone's dominating a conversation? *Agape* love does not become provoked when others act antithetically to Christ. Such people need Christ, not ridicule or anger. The gift of *agape* love enables us to love those who ignore, disappoint, or hurt us. Those in Christ gradually understand that those who hurt them are either immature in Christ or without him. Either way, Christ is not yet formed in them.

9. Agape Love Does Not Take into Account a Wrong Suffered

We suffer wrongs. And we are guilty of wrongdoing. When we wronged others, and were convicted, we confessed and our guilt was removed. We were forgiven. Tasting God's forgiveness is experiencing his *agape* love. Availing ourselves of the blessings of Christ's forgiveness teaches us to forgive those who wrong us. Christ asked the Father, from the cross, to forgive those who had crucified him, even without their asking his forgiveness (Luke 23:34). *Agape* love eventually matures those in Christ so they are more concerned about the spiritual state of those who hurt them than they are about their own hurt.

10. Agape Love Does Not Rejoice in Unrighteousness

The ungodly find pleasure in wickedness (2 Thess. 2:12). They even boast about the evil they plan to do (Ps. 52:1). But unrighteousness is antithetical to *agape* love, which finds its meaning in what is good for others. So the godly person will have no room in his or her heart for rejoicing over what is bad. Seeing people treated unjustly or observing people acting in an unbecoming manner elicits groans from the godly, which are precious in God's sight (Ezek. 9:3-6). The righteous may not be in a position to alter the behavior of the unrighteous but they are always capable of groaning—a testimony to the unrighteous ones around them. By doing so they indicate they have a heart that is in tune with God's heart.

11. Agape Love Rejoices with the Truth

Truth is having and sharing accurate perceptions of reality. Truth opens doors for the establishment and maintenance of a healthy world/life-view that fosters wholesome relationships. Truth sets us free from the bondage of false perceptions. Christ said it best: "If you continue in My word . . . you will know the truth and the truth will make you free" (John 8:31-32). But those who do not know Christ ask, as did Pontius Pilate, "What is truth?" (18:38). Those given the gift of *agape* love know Christ and grow in their grasp of truth, for he is truth. And they *rejoice* with the truth and in all who promote it even when it hurts. *Agape* love *loves* truth.

12. Agape Love Bears All Things

Such love does not give up. It keeps on supporting under circumstances that would cause self-centered persons to abandon those in need. *Agape* love does not give up on children born with Down's syndrome. Nor does *agape* love abandon an adult parent with Alzheimer's. This special love keeps on moving forward while withstanding the stresses that tempt us to think of ourselves above others. The weight of the challenge may be great but the will to stand up under the stress overcomes the thoughts of giving up. *Agape* love bears the weight that is providentially cast upon it, as did our loving Savior who bore the full weight of our sins on the cross.

13. Agape Love Believes All Things

The person with *agape* love knows Christ, trusts him, and therefore believes his promises. We know that "God causes all things to work together for good to those who love God, to those who are called according to His purpose. For whom He foreknew, He also predestined to become conformed to the image of His Son" (Rom. 8:28-29). "God is . . . a very present help in trouble" (Ps. 46:1). "'For I know the plans that I have for you,' declares the LORD, 'plans for welfare and not for calamity, to give you a future and a hope'" (Jer. 29:11). *Agape* love is nurtured in the belief that Christ faithfully keeps his word.

14. Agape Love Hopes All Things

True hope embodied in *agape* love is rooted in God's character, acts, and promises. Indeed, the child of God grows to understand that there is nothing that is holy and right that is impossible for God (Luke 1:37; Gen. 18:14; Jer. 32:17; and Matt. 19:26). God can make the spiritually dead alive. Where there is strife, he can bring peace. Where there is want, he can bring plenty. Where there is sorrow, he can bring joy. Hope is always focused on the future. And God is the absolute Ruler over everything in the future. The hope that accompanies *agape* love is hope inextricably united with Christ, and it holds to the promises he has made to his people.

15. Agape Love Endures All Things

Partaking of God's divine nature (2 Peter 1:4) requires much renovating work by the Holy Spirit. The evidence that this work is taking place is the manifestation of *agape* love in our lives. And this love is endowed with the ability to persevere. This love withstands the strain that accompanies *suffering*. It is a love that is born in the assurance that God is ultimately victorious and that our small part in his plan is to be faithful to him in everything. It is a love that submits to the wise and sovereign God who knows the end from the beginning. *Agape* love endures!

This concludes our look at the tender side of the *agape* love continuum, the end that is welcomed when others *agapao* us. The fifteen attributes of *agape* are the comforting attributes of love that bring no pain unless it is a convicted conscience for the recipient, who knows that such love is undeserved. Such tender love is useful in the hands of the Holy Spirit, for he may choose to use it to convict the ungodly of their corrupt nature. Biblically, this is called heaping burning coals on the heads of the ungodly (Rom. 12:20; Prov. 25:21-22). But typically, the characteristics of *agape* love, when brought to bear in the conflicts of life, bring peace, joy, and appreciation.

Tough Qualities Found in Agape Love

The overwhelming proportion of God's disciplinary training occurs in the normal course of our reading Scripture, attending worship services where the Word is faithfully preached, and in hearing the testimony of others about the Holy Spirit's convicting them. A light pricking of the conscience is generally sufficient to set the child of God on the path of repentance. Stronger discipline, always administered in love, is appropriate under three conditions: (1) when the besetting problem is so deeply ingrained that a prolonged situation may, in God's wisdom, be appropriate for its eradication or radical transformation; (2) when the child of God is stubbornly resisting the gentler calls to repentance; and (3) when God's child has matured to the point that his manifested perseverance in the face of suffering creates a public testimony. In that situation, God's faithfulness and love are declared to be true in the face of all contrary evidence, the person is openly transformed more and more into Christ's likeness, and God is glorified by his mercy.

When God seeks the greatest good for his children he secures them to himself and matures them through *loving discipline* as well as tender encouragement. Hebrews 12:4-11 describes this: "Do not regard lightly the discipline of the Lord, nor faint when you are reproved by Him; for those whom the Lord loves He disciplines, and He scourges every son whom He receives" (vv. 5-6). The message is clear: Take God's discipline seriously. This is especially true if the discipline is being administered to secure us to him. Many Christians identify with the psalmist's candid declarations: "Before I was afflicted I went astray, but now I keep Your word. You are good and do good; It is good for me that I was afflicted, that I may learn Your statutes; I know, O LORD, that Your judgments are righteous, and that in faithfulness You have afflicted me" (Ps. 119:67, 71, 75). Here God administers tough love, an essential component of *agape*.

Hebrews 12:1 admonishes us to "lay aside every encumbrance and the sin which so easily entangles us . . . fixing our eyes on Jesus, the author and perfecter of faith." We often need some form of discipline to mature us to be more diligent in staying close to Jesus. We need to be *trained* to stay close to him. We too often are like two-year-olds who run off without thinking about how they are endangering themselves. God's discipline may be as mild as awareness brought to our consciousness through reading a portion of his Word, or as drastic as what is implied in Psalm 119. God disciplines everyone he loves.

And we are encouraged not to faint when our Savior reproves us. *Thayer's Greek-English Lexicon of the New Testament* defines the word faint (Lexical # 1590) as meaning: "to have one's strength relaxed, to be enfeebled through exhaustion, to grow weak, grow weary, be tired out." Positively, we are called upon to persevere when we are disciplined. We must also remember that Christ bore the punishment due us for our sins. God's discipline is not to be thought of as punishment. Discipline is *corrective*, not retributive, as set before us in Hebrews 12. We are unable to pay the price justly due the Father for our sins: "No man can by any means redeem his brother or give to God a ransom for him—for the redemption of his soul is costly, and he should cease trying forever—that he should live on eternally, that he should not undergo decay" (Ps. 49:7-9). Discipline is easier to endure if we remember that its purpose is to draw us closer to Christ; to mature us; and to conform us more and more to his likeness.

Hebrews 12:6 informs us that *everyone* who is loved and brought into God's family will be *scourged*! All of God's children will experience afflictions in one form or another. It is *this* suffering (scourging, afflicting) that God uses to renovate us and makes us Christlike. But why is such painful training necessary? Why isn't tender love sufficient to remake us? The fall we all experienced in Adam separated us so far from godliness that the renovating work demands *radical* alterations in our character, necessitating a complete overhaul from the inside out. This requires a heart transplant, and an identity makeover!

Verse 10 reassures us that the discipline we experience is for *our good*. And what is this *good*? It is that we may share His holiness. What an awesome thing to reflect on: We, God's enemies, are reconciled to him through the work of his Son and Spirit, and we are gradually trained to avoid ungodly thoughts, motives, and conduct. We actually partake of God's nature and become more Christlike. The profane is renovated into holiness! Only God could have such a plan before creaton. And only he could carry it to fruition through our life's experiences.

All Christians can identify with the end of Hebrews 12:4-11—"All discipline for the moment seems not to be joyful, but sorrowful; yet to those who have been trained by it, afterwards it yields the peaceful fruit of righteousness." Discipline is a mark of God's *love* for his children! Through it he transforms us to share his holiness and manifest the fruit of righteousness. By it he gives us a new way of life that flows from the heart he circumcised when he gave us new life in Christ. The heart of *stone* is transformed into a heart of *flesh*!

Discipline is by nature corrective. Discipline applied to the heart of those who know Christ softens their hearts. Discipline applied to the hearts of those who reject Christ hardens their hearts. This is a correct understanding of Romans 9:18: "So then He has mercy on whom He desires, and He hardens whom He desires" (Also see Ex. 7:3; Deut. 2:30; John 12:40; Rom. 11:7, 25). What does Scripture mean when it says "God hardens whom He desires?" God does not harden a good heart, does he? No. He does not turn hearts of flesh into hearts of stone; he only turns hearts of stone into hearts of flesh! All hearts are hearts of stone as a result of the fall until they are, by the Holy Spirit's work, regenerated and made hearts of flesh. Hard hearts, by their very nature reject God and his loving discipline, his *agape* love. His effort to work in the lives of those who reject him gives rise to their stubborn refusal. Their reaction is negative. They either feign allegiance to him, put him off until tomorrow, renounce him silently in their hearts, or openly fight against him. They want no part of him! Their hearts become harder.

The Spirit's regenerative work, on the other hand, produces a new heart, one of flesh. It is a new creation. The old heart is done away with and a new heart is put in its place. The new heart, when immature, may complain to God about the discipline it is enduring, but a person with a regenerated heart will not leave God permanently—for God has chosen them and given them to Christ. And Christ will not lose a single person the Father has given him (John 6:37, 39, 44).

The holiness and peaceful fruit of righteousness manifested in the lives of God's children reveal the gracious disciplining work of the Holy Spirit in their hearts. The holiness and righteousness become evidence of the truth that God's children become partakers of his divine nature (2 Peter 1:4). God's divine nature is not merely imputed to his children—although these attributes *are* imputed to them through their faith in Christ's redemptive work—but the Holy Spirit actually begins a *transformation* of their character so that they become partakers of God's divine nature. *Their hearts are renovated and transformed.* How? The answer to that is the focus of our next section: *How Do People Become Partakers of the Divine Nature?* Chapters 13–20 seek to explain how God's divine nature, the subject of this opening section (*What Is the Divine Nature?*) is imparted to his children—which enables them to manifest Christlike behavior, the focus of the third section: *Manifesting Christ's Divine Nature.*

Conclusion

In eleven chapters we examined a number of God's attributes with four goals. First, it is hoped that the reader's comprehension of God's attributes has expanded and brought a greater appreciation of God's awesome nature. Second, it is hoped that the biblical teaching regarding Christ in you and you in Christ has renewed meaning for the reader. An intimate relationship with Christ is priceless! Third, it is hoped that the realization that Christ is being formed in you will motivate readers to seek a deeper relationship with Christ. The full formation of Christ in us is generally a slow process, but the rewards are immeasurable. And finally, it is hoped that the understanding that God wants his children to be partakers of His nature will make the next section, How Do People Become Partakers of the Divine Nature?, a building block to becoming more Christlike. These four goals are lofty, but they are worthy aspirations.

> All attributes of Christ, as God and man, are at our disposal.... His omnipotence, omniscience, omnipresence, immutability and infallibility, are all combined for our defense.... How vast His grace, how firm His

faithfulness, how unswerving His immutability, how infinite His power, how limitless His knowledge . . . . The fathomless love of the Saviour's heart is every drop ours . . . His wisdom our direction, His knowledge our instruction, His power our protection, His justice our surety, His love our comfort, His mercy our solace, His immutability our trust.[100]

---

[100] Charles H. Spurgeon, *Morning and Evening* (McLean, VA; Macdonald Publishing Company), 558.

Part 2

How Do People Become Partakers of the Divine Nature?

Lay aside the old self...be renewed in the spirit of your mind...and put on the new self, which in the likeness of God has been created in righteousness and holiness of the truth. (Eph. 4:22-24)

The following eight chapters have five goals. World/life-views regarding human nature are diverse. Views of human nature are generally shaped by personal experiences and observations of conduct, until the Spirit imparts God's view. First, then, we will look at how those who do not know God define human nature. Then we will look at how God defines it.

Second, we want to explore both what is involved when the Bible speaks of people being born from above and also the subsequent work involved with our putting off the old and putting on the new. Theologically, this process is called being sanctified—set apart for the work of Christ. Here we present this process as becoming partakers of the divine nature.

Third, God describes human nature in two ways: (a) as our having been made in his image, and his work of overhauling the hearts of believers. He restores *the true image of God* to them, and he does this in three areas that correspond to three of God's attributes. And (b) God speaks pointedly about the human *heart* and its components that are the inherent characteristics of human nature. We will examine human nature through these two lenses: the meaning of *bearing God's image* and exploring the human *heart*.

Fourth, biblical revelation sets before us three components of the human heart that are distinct but interactive: the *mind*, the *passions*, and the *will*. We will examine these.

Fifth, we want to review those *qualities* of God's attributes that he wants us to partake of so we can manifest a Christlike nature that is discernible through practical holiness.

13

Human Nature:
The World's Description/God's Description

*He who has found his life will lose it, and he who has lost his life
for My sake will find it. (Matt. 10:39)*

Henry David Thoreau (1817–1862), an author of considerable note, wrote numerous literary pieces, but perhaps his best remembered is *Walden; or, Life in the Woods*. In this self-reflective work he wrote things such as:

> Direct your eye right inward, and you'll find
> A thousand regions in your mind
> Yet undiscovered. Travel them, and be
> Expert in home-cosmography.[101]

> I find in myself, and still find, an instinct toward a higher, or, as it is named, spiritual life, as do most men, and another toward a primitive, rank and savage one, and I reverence them both. I love the wild not less than the good.[102]

My father (1902–1988) used to quote Thoreau's saying, "Know thyself." The world/life-view underlying these statements, when examined in the light of Christ's exhortation above, is not in harmony with his world/life-view. But the statements do reflect the world/life-view of slaves to self who reject Christ. To follow him is to die to self. To reject Christ is to wander while searching for meaning, purpose, and one's true identity—"Who am I? Why am I?"

One of the most interesting experiences in life is that of *our being frequently reintroduced to ourselves*. What does this mean? It means experiences bubble up new aspects of our nature into our consciousness, and this brings us face to face with new insights into ourselves. Some of the new discoveries may be pleasing; others disheartening. For example, I met new negative and positive qualities in myself when I left home to be on my own; when I got married; when our first child was born; as I assumed the responsibilities of parenting; when I began to write—I am a dyslexic; when our youngest son broke his neck; and on many

---

[101] Henry David Thoreau, *Walden; or, Life in the Woods* (Cambridge, MA: H. O. Houghton & Co., 1893), 494.
[102] Ibid., 327.

other occasions. Being in my seventies has not yet put an end to this type of experience.

Jesus said: "The eye is the lamp of the body; so then if your eye is clear, your whole body will be full of light. But if your eye is bad, your whole body will be full of darkness. *If then the light that is in you is darkness, how great is the darkness!*" (Matt. 6:22-23). "*If . . . the light . . . is . . . darkness*"—what a truly tragic thing to contemplate. But look at Thoreau's opening line in the first quote of his above: "Direct your eye right inward." Does he not invite us to find ourselves? Is not his light darkness? He suggests that we go and look for ourselves—as his writings indicate that he did. Christ's warning regarding this approach is clear: He who has found his life will lose it. It is not that Christ does not want us to know ourselves. He does. But he knows that if knowing ourselves is our goal, we will be self-absorbed and die in the search-mode. Only Christ can lead us to a true understanding of ourselves—to see ourselves as *God* sees us, and be humbled by his grace in the light of who we really are.

Chapter 1, "The Mind of Christ: The Essential Component of a Christian's World/Life-View," discussed the important difference between having spiritual discernment and not having it. To have spiritual discernment is to understand that an unregenerate *heart* is alienated from God and at enmity with him. Such persons want to be their own god; they want to do things their way. They do not want a Helper to *show* them the way. They want to define human nature so as to think highly of themselves. The diagram of an Eye in chapter 1 depicted how new things we observe are filtered through our experiences and human nature into our *heart*, where the new experiences are interpreted in the light of our *presuppositions*—which guide our *mind, passions,* and *will*. In our *heart* we form our view of human nature. We now look at how those separated from the God who has revealed himself in Scripture, view human nature.

The World's Description of Human Nature

Two very broad world/life-views dominate the thinking of most North Americans and are not directly influenced by the mind of Christ. They are the *deterministic* and the *good/bad* schools of thought.[103] Both schools are deeply influenced by *personal experience*, and the *deterministic* school is also greatly influenced by the fields of psychology and neuropsychology.

The Deterministic World/Life-view

Historically it was widely believed that people were born with an *inherent* understanding of good and evil, which is called *a priori* knowledge—knowledge one possesses before birth. John Locke (1632–1704), an influential English philosopher, challenged this historic presupposition regarding pre-birth knowledge and substituted in its stead the idea of *a posteriori* knowledge, knowledge acquired after birth. He did this by describing the mind at birth as a

---

[103] Those who have a non-Biblical world/life-view about good and evil generally soften the Biblical teaching that Adam and Eve ate from the tree of the knowledge of good and evil to the idea of good and bad.

tabula rasa—Latin for a blank tablet. Locke's contention was that innate *a priori* knowledge is a fiction and that only experience furnishes the mind with ideas.[104] His thoughts have gained so much ground over the years that now there are virtually no intellectual discussions on the subject of *a priori* versus *a posteriori* knowledge. Indeed, many Christians have adopted the *a posteriori* presupposition through *cultural saturation*, by being immersed in the presuppositions of their culture, so that the ideas surrounding them are absorbed without thought.

The adoption of *a posteriori* presupposition opens one up to the world/lifeview that humans are altogether determined by experiences after birth. Post-birth experiences are presumed to be responsible for how we think and act. This replaces the idea that humans possess an *innate* understanding of good and evil. It opens the door to the logical conclusion that right and wrong are simply learned social constructs. There are no eternal verities—no truths that transcend and are *inherent* in the human spirit at conception. This leads one to associate the idea—which can quickly become a belief—that the very notion of the existence of a god is learned. This in turn fosters the idea that there is nothing innate in the human *heart* to distinguish humans from other animals. Our *nature* does not bear the image of an omnipresent, holy God. This line of reasoning shows how a *secondary presupposition* can quickly descend the ladder of logic and supplant a *foundational presupposition*. An *a posteriori* belief regarding human nature can supplant a historic foundational presupposition with a new belief, "God" is learned.

How often have we heard, "Oh, look at that sweet, innocent baby." This tactful, polite, hopeful statement is in all probability undergirded by the *tabula rasa* presupposition. If the child grows up to be an outstanding citizen, it is assumed that he or she had all of the right environmental forces to support his or her accomplishments. Mom and dad did a good job. No neighborhood bent them in the direction of antisocial behavior. They were simply lucky. And the reverse is often assumed to be true too. If the child grows up to be criminal in character, he or she is a *victim* revealing the negative experiences encountered in their environment.

Another twist to the presuppositions associated with determinism is the idea that what was historically thought to be immoral conduct—sexual perversions, alcoholism, drug addictions—can really be explained by genetics. Their genes *cause* them to behave this way. Both environmental and genetic determinism have moved to the center of many esteemed publications in the fields of secular neuropsychology and psychology. It is presumed that humans are caused to do what they do by things that impact them either before birth (genetics) or after birth (the external environment). The notion that we are by *nature* repositories of innate, eternal values—who will someday give account to a

---

[104] Anthony Flew, ed., *A Dictionary of Philosophy* (New York: Macmillan, 1979), 323; see also 189.

Higher Authority—has faded so far away from most people's thinking that the very idea is unthinkable.

The lines on the continuum regarding the presupposition that all behavior can be explained by deterministic forces are being blurred regarding what should be considered aberrant behavior. It is beyond our scope to explore a movement in the fields of neuropsychology and psychology from soft determinism—mild to substantial influence is relevant to an inquiry into human behavior—toward hard determinism, where everything is held to be determined by genetics and/or external forces. Psychologists are becoming the new priests and ministers—leading the way into new understandings about human nature. The phenomenon popularly known as political correctness is very influential here too, because there is an underlying belief in intellectual circles that the human can be explained only by the presupposition that we are *a posteriori* creatures. This is the politically correct way to think. Nature has made us this way.

And Nature becomes the new god. She (Nature) only needs to be observed by autonomous humans who can draw sound conclusions from observations. And their experiences and observations only need to be passed through the presuppositional filters of their *hearts* to realize that there is no help beyond themselves—nothing that can assist them to unravel the big questions of life. Humans are on their *own*, and have determined that they are creatures determined by their environment and their genes. These *presuppositions*, and others like them, are becoming dominant in our society. Those who subscribe to these presuppositions discern another benefit: Mother Nature does not require that she be worshiped.[105]

The broader public encounters the genetic/environmental deterministic presuppositions in a variety of forums. An example is when we encounter media reports about criminal cases, and the defenses being offered to explain the conduct of those charged with crimes. Both professional and amateur psychologists analyze the criminal behavior for us via the media. They try to explain the conduct—the causes, the various triggers. The criminal, being assumed to be *amoral* (neither moral or immoral), is *presuppositionally* viewed as a person who has had unfortunate experiences in his background which *caused* him to act in a socially unacceptable way. Then countless films and television programs portray similar perceptions. Are not crime and violence major components of the news, movies and television? These continuous presentations subtly influence the thinking of the general public about *human nature*.

Those who have the ear of the public set the basic *presuppositions* that guide a society. Shifts generally begin in the *hearts* of leaders: intellectuals, theologians, parents, peer-group leaders in school, church, gangs. So d*eterminism* has a strong

---

[105] It has puzzled me for years how those who set themselves up as authorities regarding determinism seem to exclude themselves from the deterministic calculus. They think they stand apart from the reality they describe. They appear to me to be looking down on the mass of humanity and seeing everybody *else* as determined, except them!

hold on many today regarding *human nature*. Many determinists are secular humanists, agnostics and atheists, who spurn God. Others are merely non-religious evolutionists. They may be found in either the deterministic world/life-view, or the good/bad world/life-view camp. But regardless, they perceive people as disconnected from any transcendent force. The human evolved and is on his own. It makes little difference to one's psychological sense of well-being whether we are conceived of as rigidly determined or substantially free, so long as there is no deity attached to us.

We now turn to those who hold a world/life-view that in some aspects reflects the biblical view of *human nature*. People in this group integrate their presuppositions and experiences into a view of life that is also substantially different from the Bible's. Their view is incomplete; it does not take into account the contrast between what they observe about the human and the awesome character of God—his holiness, righteousness, justice. But their view of human nature is gaining ground in the public's mind. They regard human nature as a blend of *both* good and bad.

The Good/Bad World/Life-view

There are within this camp two broad groups of people who hold that *human nature* is a jumble of good and bad. Thoreau's quotation represents *one* of these groups:

> I find in myself, and still find, an instinct toward a higher, or, as it is named, spiritual life, as do most men, and another toward a primitive, rank and savage one, and I reverence them both. I love the wild not less than the good.

Thoreau's statement sets forth the inner conflict between good and bad in every human *heart*. In his case, though, it is not set forth as a struggle but a delightful reality! While this perspective is certainly not common, it clearly recognizes the existence of a *divided nature* where both good and bad reside in the human heart. Thoreau identified the good side of his nature as the higher, or spiritual life, and the bad side as a primitive, rank and savage one. And he concluded by referring to them as the wild and the good. Because Thoreau lived from 1817–1862, he was not under the sway of the foundational presupposition of either a theistic or natural evolutionist, but he was probably a deist or religious neutralist[106]—both, however, denying the presence of a personal deity. In any case, Thoreau experientially had come to believe in the divided nature that expresses itself on a continuum from good to bad.

Deists typically understand *human nature* to have always been in the divided state in which it is currently experienced and observed. That is, *human nature* is not reflective of some historic fall of humanity. The deistic Creator or

---

[106] A religious neutralist is a person who has a vague notion that there is some higher power or guiding force out there somewhere, but this power or force has no definable characteristics or understood nature or personality.

higher power is an impersonal deity who simply observes the creation and does not involve itself in earthly affairs. The deity is looking to find out how each individual manages his or her divided nature. The deity *created* the divided nature. The deity is the creator of *evil*. The deity is the creator of *good*. The character and attributes of this deity stand in contrast to those of the Trinity. The deity is not holy, nor omniscient, for the deity learns as it observes human behavior; the deity is not immutable, nor sovereign, nor love.

The religious neutralist and the deist typically consider themselves religious. They will generally acknowledge they have an intuitive sense that in the future they will be called upon to account for their life to the deity. During their earthly life they generally attach their identity to good causes and thereby maintain a sense of doing good that provides an inner sense of well-being. They acknowledge that bad exists, and that some bad plays a part in their life, but they perceive that their good more than offsets the bad. And they recognize that the bad does get the upper hand in some lives, but not their own. That is why, if you ask them what will happen when they give their eventual accounting, they will typically answer along these lines: "My good will outweigh my bad." The deity presumably employs moral scales to measure lifelong conduct.

The *second* group which has a *good/bad world/life-view* is cultural Christians. They divide into two types. First are those who are saturated in the Christian ethos and deeply influenced by common grace.[107] They *assume* they are Christians. They have absorbed parts of God's common grace that has impregnated the general culture, but they are Christians in name only. They think of themselves as Christians: they grew up in a Christian community; their parents called themselves Christians; they may have been baptized; they may have been married in the church; their friends think of themselves as Christians too; they think they live in a Christian nation. They assume that almost everybody around them is a Christian; Christianity is a cultural phenomenon. They may go to church at Easter or Christmas. They may go to an occasional church wedding or funeral. They have little to do with what they call the organized church. They generally believe you can relate as well to God as an individual outside of the church as you can by joining one. They never think of the church as the body of Christ. They are *isolated* Christians. And they, too, generally assume they will be put on the good and bad scales to be judged some day, with their good hopefully outweighing their bad.

The second variety of cultural Christians grow up in Christian homes, attend church, absorb Christian vocabulary, and think of themselves as *committed* Christians—they are actively involved in good works in and out of the church. Unknown to them they have never been born from above. Going to church

---

[107] Briefly, common grace can be described as: (a) the overflowing influence of the gospel's message on the true Christians so that there is a spillover from their lives into the thinking and behavior of the broader public and (b) there are those whose dispositions and thoughts are manifested in publicly accepted patterns of conduct that are deemed to be good even though their intentions are not related to Christ.

makes them feel good about themselves; they are not motivated by a genuine desire to worship God; church is more a social institution than a body of believers who love the Lord. They do not know that they are not trusting in Christ's righteousness *alone* for their acceptance by God. They unknowingly rely within on aspects of their own righteousness to please God and thereby get to heaven. Christ may have had this sad reality in mind when he said, "*Many* will say to Me on that day, 'Lord, Lord, did we not prophesy in Your name, and in Your name cast out demons, and in Your name perform many miracles?' And then I will declare to them, 'I never knew you; depart from Me, you who practice lawlessness'" (Matt. 7:22-23).

These cultural Christians, when asked, "Why should God accept you into heaven?" will generally respond, "Because I have lived a good life." They have either never heard the real gospel message, or have not understood it in their *heart*. They may have asked God for forgiveness for specific bad things they have done, but they have probably never grasped the reality that they have a *sin nature*, that is the wellspring of sin. Christ, the Lamb of God, came to take away the sins of the *world*—not just to atone for specific sinful acts. Christ has also come to *atone* for our *sin nature*. And this *sin nature* will be with us until we are *glorified* and transformed into Christ's likeness in heaven. So long as we are living on earth, we are *sinners* even if we are not visibly sinning at a given moment. Who has ever had a *pure motive*, or a *wholly pure thought* that preceded a personal *holy activity* (1 Cor. 4:5)? Christ *alone* is the *righteousness* of true believers, and until one understands this he cannot enter the spiritual Sabbath rest, offered in Christ—rest from any dependence on works to please God (Heb. 4:1-11).

Many cultural Christians hold to the *good/bad world/life-view* in their standing before God. They presume all is well. They rely on the belief that their good deeds outweigh their bad ones. They do not have a problem admitting that they do, on occasion, act in an ungodly way—but all people do that. God is kind; God is good; and God is love. They believe, "He will accept me even though I am not perfect." This partial truth is life-threatening; to retain it is lethal. The fall of humanity is typically not denied, but its permeating effects are underestimated! God is too benevolent, in their mind, to allow many, if any, to experience eternal separation from him.

The world's description of human nature differs greatly from God's description of it.

God's Description of Human Nature

God's description of human nature is best seen in two time-frames: (a) human nature before the fall of Adam and Eve; and (b) human nature after their fall. There are some misconceptions of the nature of human beings in both time-frames, especially regarding human nature before the fall. We will first examine the *very positive* aspects of human nature *before* the fall, and then we will look at the *very negative* aspects of human nature *following* the fall.

Human Nature before the Fall

Genesis 1 tells of God's acts of creation, and concludes . . . "and behold, it was very good" (v. 31). While Genesis teaches that God created man and woman in his image (1:27), what this means is not revealed until the New Testament speaks of the *restoration to God's image*—namely, to gain a particular type of knowledge and be renovated in righteousness and in holiness (Col. 3:10; Eph. 4:24).

Genesis 2 is a parallel revelation, focusing on a more detailed account of God's creation of the first man and woman. It does not contradict Genesis 1 but takes what is revealed in 1:27-29 and gives more detail regarding our creation in 2:7-25. Genesis 3:1-17 is also important to understanding our first parents' pre-fall *nature*. 2 Corinthians 11:3 and 1 Timothy 2:14 underline what is revealed in Genesis 1-3 about the pre-fall status of Adam and Eve.

We will let Scripture speak for itself as we seek to uncover the *nature* of Adam and Eve before their fall. We will begin with Genesis 1:27 and 31.

> And God created man in His own image, in the image of God He created him; male and female He created them.

> And God saw all that He had made, and behold, it was very good.

These two verses imply that Adam and Eve were perfect, without sin. Their *nature* was one of moral purity. How do we infer their moral purity from these two verses? It is implied by the fact that a holy and righteous God looked at them, and the rest of his creation, on the sixth day of creation and declared, "Behold, it is *very good*." God's own holiness does not allow him to look upon anything with a taint of corruption and declare it to be very good. God's own *nature* substantiates the conclusion.

Genesis 2 reveals:

> Then the LORD God formed man of dust from the ground, and breathed into his nostrils the breath of life; and man became a living being. (Gen. 2:7)

> And the LORD God took the man and put him into the Garden of Eden to cultivate it and keep it. The LORD God commanded the man, saying, "From any tree of the garden you may eat freely; but from the tree of the knowledge of good and evil you shall not eat, for in the day that you eat from it you shall surely die." (Gen. 2:15-17)

We note several things from these four verses. First, Adam comprehended God's command not to eat from the tree of the knowledge of good and evil, upon penalty of death. We know this because Adam later repeated the command to Eve. She did not subsequently tell the serpent the *exact* command. She added the idea that the fruit should not even be touched (3:1-3). We do not know if this was her alteration or Adam's. But she received a command that *was clear enough to follow without getting into trouble*.

Second, before Eve knew good and evil how would she be able to comprehend death or its consequences? We do know there was no *fear* of death to deter her behavior. Third, assuming Eve received the command from Adam, how could Eve delineate the authoritative difference between Adam's voice and the serpent's? How would she know which one to listen to? We cannot answer because we do not know all that was involved in her being pure and innocent— without the knowledge of good and evil—but we do know that she did not delineate between the voices she had encountered.

Fourth, we know that though Adam and Eve did not know about good and evil, they were able to comprehend God's command, and they were able to obey it. *But* even though they could obey God's command, they had no moral connotation connected with it because before the fall they had no knowledge of good and evil.

Next, the account describes the creation of Eve and our first parents' nakedness.

> Then the LORD God said, "It is not good for the man to be alone; I will make him a helper suitable for him." ... So the LORD God caused a deep sleep to fall upon the man, and he slept; then He took one of his ribs, and closed up the flesh at that place. And the LORD God fashioned into a woman the rib which He had taken from the man, and brought her to the man.... And the man and his wife were both naked and were not ashamed. (vv. 18, 21-22, 25)

The recording of their nakedness has nothing to do with sexuality. Rather, it is a profound declaration that they were not self-conscious. It is a clear revelation that they were other-focused in an innocent, supportive way that caused no self-concern on their partner's part. They were *innocent, without selfishness, completely other-oriented*, and incapable of feeling *shame*. They were *incapable of sinning before the fall*. Genesis 3 begins:

> And he [the serpent] said to the woman," Indeed, has God said, 'You shall not eat from any tree of the Garden'?" And the woman said to the serpent, "From the fruit of the trees of the garden we may eat; but from the fruit of the tree which is in the middle of the garden, God has said, 'You shall not eat from it or touch it, lest you die.'" The serpent said to the woman, "You surely will not die! For God knows that in the day you eat from it your eyes will be opened, and you will be like God, knowing good and evil." When the woman saw that the tree was good for food, and that it was a delight to the eyes, and that the tree was desirable to make one wise, she took from its fruit and ate ... and she gave also to her husband with her, and he ate. Then the eyes of both of them were opened, and they knew they were naked; and they sewed fig leaves together and made themselves loin coverings. (vv. 1-7)

Look at what happened *immediately* after they ate fruit from the tree of the knowledge of good and evil. *They fell*. And the result? "Then the eyes of both of them were opened, and they knew they were naked." It is critical to understand: *Adam and Eve did not sin and then fall*. They ate the forbidden fruit and instantly fell—had a *sin nature* rather than a *pure, innocent nature*.

Some argue that Eve sinned first and then Adam, and their fall followed their sinning. No, they did not sin and then fall. They had no sin nature before the fall. They fell and *then* had a sin nature. This is an important point. If the logic of their sinning before the fall were followed, it would mean that they had a sin nature before the fall. God's account of the fall contradicts this. Let's see what verse 13 says took place between God and the woman.

> They heard the sound of the LORD God walking in the garden in the cool of the day, and the man and his wife hid themselves from the presence of the LORD God among the trees of the garden. Then the LORD God called to the man, and said to him, "Where are you?" He said, "I heard the sound of You in the garden, and I was afraid because I was naked; so I hid myself." And He said, "Who told you that you were naked? Have you eaten from the tree of which I commanded you not to eat?" The man said, "The woman whom You gave to be with me, she gave me from the tree, and I ate." Then the LORD God said to the woman, "What is this you have done? And the woman said, The serpent deceived me, and I ate." (vv. 8-13)

The woman did not say, "I disobeyed you." Nor, "I yielded to temptation and sinned." She did not make a confession of sin. Nor did God tell her she had sinned, rebelled, or disobeyed. Many use these words to describe Eve's act of eating the forbidden fruit, but these words have ethical connotations *on this side of the fall only*. Sinning, rebelling, and disobeying had no place in Eve's *heart* prior to the fall. She was innocent of such negative qualities altogether. She confessed to an *act*: "The serpent deceived me, and I ate." *She was deceived*, and Scripture does not attribute this to her having sinned or to her having a sin nature. Scripture affirms this truth. 2 Corinthians 11:3 says, "But I am afraid that, as *the serpent deceived Eve* by his craftiness, your minds will be led astray from the simplicity and purity of devotion to Christ." And this is further confirmed in 1 Timothy 2:14 where we read, "And it was not Adam who was deceived, but *the woman being deceived, fell into transgression*." Eve's falling into transgression is strong support for the fact that she did not sin and fall or have a sin nature before the fall.

And the same point is true regarding Adam. He did not sin and then fall, as the following verse makes this clear.

> Then to Adam He said, "Because you have listened to the voice of your wife, and have eaten from the tree about which I commanded you, saying, 'You shall not eat from it'" (v. 17)

God charged Adam with having listened to the voice of his wife, not with having sinned. Neither Adam nor Eve was guilty of sinning, and subsequently falling. Adam was not rebelling against God when he listened to the voice of his wife and ate of the fruit. He had no sense of doing *wrong*. One has to have the knowledge of good and evil before he or she can know they are morally wrong.

The reason we discussed this in such detail is the *fact* that many Christians think Adam and Eve sinned and *then* fell. They, without thinking, presuppositionally have Adam and Eve with a *sin nature* before the fall. This further presumes that God created his image-bearers with a *sin nature*. This makes God the *Creator of evil*, for a *sin nature* is synonymous with having a *heart* alienated from God. Scripture tells us that Adam and Eve became afraid of God, and hid from him, *after the fall*—(vv. 8-11 above). God did not create Adam and Eve with a sin nature. To think that God did so calls into question his holiness, righteousness, goodness, and love.

Human nature before the fall was in the state of innocence, purity, and selflessness. And Adam and Eve possessed the capacity to freely carry out God's pre-fall creation mandates regarding work, family, and worship (Gen. 1:26, 28-29; 2:15, 24). But they did not follow God's directive; they fell; their nature was perverted; they became sinners; and their progeny was born in sin.

Human Nature after the Fall

We begin by connecting two biblical accounts and one diagram, and then building on this work, we will develop a biblical picture of human nature emanating from the fall. We will connect Genesis 3:7—"Then the eyes of both of them were opened. . . ." with Matthew 6:22-23: "The eye is the lamp of the body; so then if your eye is clear, your whole body will be full of light. But if your eye is bad, your body will be full of darkness. *If then the light that is in you is darkness, how great is the darkness!*" Then we will relate these two texts to the Eye diagram in chapter 1.

Because Adam and Eve enjoyed good physical eyesight before the fall, when Scripture says that the eyes of both of them were opened, it does not mean there was a change in their physical sight. Instead, their *perceptions, understandings,* and *interpretations* of the physical reality radically changed. Their interpretative eyesight changed. And their progeny's interpretative eyesight has been more distorted because they have not enjoyed God's fellowship as their first parents did before the fall. Indeed, it is God's coming to his children and *restoring* them to his likeness that returns true light to their understanding.

Matthew 6:22-23 says that *the light now possessed by those born in sin, but yet to be redeemed, is not light at all, but darkness.* God is the light of the world. Christ is the light of the world (John 8:12).[108] Light is a metaphor. It represents the ability to understand things as God intends. Things must be seen in the light of *God's* intentions. Psalm 36:9 puts it this way: "In Your light we see light." And Psalm119:105 states: "Your word is a lamp to my feet and a light to my path." The Holy Spirit brings illumination so regenerated people can see things as God sees them. When someone exclaims, "Oh, I see!" he means he now understands what he previously saw but did not understand.

The Eye diagram in chapter 1 depicts this concept pictorially. It is a flow diagram showing how things observed in our outer environment are taken into our consciousness through our eyes (and ears) and interpreted inside of our *heart.* When the interpretation in the heart does not conform to God's reality, the distorted *gestalt* is called darkness. Paul illustrates this well:

---

[108] See also John 1:4-9 and 3:19-21.

> And even if our gospel is veiled, it is veiled to those who are perishing, in whose case the god of this world has blinded the minds of the unbelieving so that they might not see the light of the gospel of the glory of Christ, who is the image of God. (2 Cor. 4:3-4)

Here the good news (gospel) is not being comprehended. The god of this world (Satan) has blinded the minds' of those who are unbelieving so that they are prevented from seeing the light—the reality that Christ is the image of God. They see but they do not see. They hear but they do not hear. They are *spiritually blind* and *spiritually deaf*.

> But a natural man [not yet born from above] does not accept the things of the Spirit of God, for they are foolishness to him; and he cannot understand them, because they are spiritually appraised [only understood in the light of spiritual comprehension—eyesight]. (1 Cor. 2:14)

What changed when Adam and Eve fell and their eyes were opened? They instantly became aware they were both naked. This tells us they became self-conscious. They suddenly became aware of themselves in a new way. They were no longer predisposed to be outwardly focused. They now perceived reality from a new (fallen) vantage point. Reality suddenly changed from being *out there*, with *nothing* to fear to being *in my world*, with *much* to fear. They suddenly possessed the knowledge of good and evil. They knew they had done what they ought not to have done. *They were afraid of God!* They hid themselves from him—something all lost persons have done ever since. But God in his *mercy* sought them while they were hiding.

The knowledge of good and evil also carries with it the reality that all fallen humanity has an *activated conscience*.[109] By activated we mean that the *latent* conscience that God fashioned in us at creation was awakened by the fall. The conscience was turned on to be the inner light by which people would have know *inherently*, or *intuitively*, the good and the evil. But the selfish orientation of fallen persons frequently leads them to suppress and even repress the *innate* conscience that is in them. It is the conscience that manifests the *a priori* knowledge that is in all of God's image-bearers—the knowledge of good and evil. Christians have believed throughout the ages that humans are born with an *innate* knowledge of good and evil. The *a posteriori* presupposition, which contends that *all knowledge is acquired after birth*, stands in stark contradiction to the biblical presupposition that we all are born with the *a priori* knowledge of good and evil. The historic Christian world/life-view affirms that all humans possess, from the time of conception, an *ethical/moral* compass—a conscience.

The Bible tells us that all are born in sin—with a fallen nature (Ps. 51:5). This does not imply that the conjunction of husband and wife which gave rise to the conception of the child was inappropriate in God's sight. To the contrary, God

---

[109] The *conscience* is spoken of frequently in the Scripture. See John 8:9; Rom. 2:15; 9:1; 13:5; 1 Cor. 8:7-12; 10:25-29; 1 Tim. 1:5, 19; 3:9; 4:2; 2 Tim. 1:3; Titus 1:15; Heb. 9:9, 14; 10:22; 1 Peter 3:16, 21.

commanded us to be fruitful and multiply (Gen. 1:28; 2:24; 9:1, 7). Psalm 51:5 teaches that the fallen nature is inherited through procreation. Our sin nature is inherited genetically. The sin nature is passed on to the children *genetically*. This is called traducianism.

The Christian church, over the centuries, has had two competing answers to the question, "How does the *human spirit* come to reside in the body?" One is continuous creation and the other traducianism. Continuous creation hypothesizes that God continues to create each individual human spirit and places each spirit in a fetus in the mother's womb.[110] This doctrine carries with it the presupposition that the unborn child's inherited sin nature comes from *both parents*. This led the Roman Catholic Church to hypothesize that Jesus's mother, Mary, was immaculately conceived, as was Christ. Even though there is no biblical evidence for this, her immaculate conception was postulated to guard the fact that Jesus was born of a woman, *yet without sin*. If the sin nature comes from both parents—as continuous creation holds—then logic led the Roman Catholic Church to conclude that Mary had to be born without sin *also* in order to preserve Christ's sinlessness.

There are larger issues, however, associated with continuous creation. Does God create fallen spirits? Does God put fallen spirits in fetuses? Would this not make God the Creator of our sin nature? If the answer to the first two questions is No, then does the fetus cause the incarnated spirit to fall? If the answer to this question is Yes, then is *physical matter*—the fetus without a spirit—a *corrupting* substance by nature? Can unspirited matter cause a spirit to fall? Or is the newborn child innocent at birth and capable, in theory, of living a sinless life, as did Christ? This presumption flies in the face of Scripture (Ps. 51:5; Job 15:14; Ps. 58:3; Eph. 2:3).

Traducianism avoids the enigma associated with continuous creation. However, it has its own problems. Traducianism has two presuppositions. First, it contends that the human spirit is an integral part of procreation: the human spirit is brought into existence through the process of fertilization, with no biblical revelation as to how this occurs. The second presupposition divides into two alternative but mutually exclusive thoughts: (1) the sin nature of the child is inherited from the father alone;[111] or (2) it is inherited from both parents.

Those who hold to traducianism and who believe that the father alone passes the sin nature on to his children believe this view is warranted by Romans 5:12-21. Here the account of sin entering the world is attributed repeatedly to *one man* (Adam). This text also attributes righteousness restored to the redeemed by the life of *one man* (Christ). Here Adam is represented six times as being the one person through whom sin entered the world, and Christ is described four times as

---

[110] Scriptures used to support this presupposition are: Eccles. 12:7; Isa. 42:5; 57:16; Zech. 12:1; Num. 27:16; Job 34:14; Acts 17:25. Those who reject this view believe it reflects a Platonic world/life-view.
[111] Biblical passages used to support this presupposition are: Heb. 7:9-10; Gen. 15:4; 46:26; 2 Sam. 7:12; 16:11; Ps. 51:5; Rom. 5:12-21; 1 Cor.15:22.

the one through whom righteousness is restored. The argument goes: if Christ is the *one man* through whom righteousness is restored—as Christians have always believed—it is just as appropriate to hold that Adam was the *one man* originating sin.

Regardless of whether one holds to continuous creation or traducianism, Scripture presents humanity as born with an inherent fallen nature that is self-conscious, selfish, and devoid of any saving spiritual discernment. Is it any wonder that parents have to expend so much energy to *train* their children to be good? Children are born with a predilection to be disobedient, selfish, inconsiderate, and just plain bad. This is *natural*. Children have a *heart* problem, just like their parents. It is true that children can sometimes appear to be angelic, but at a moment's notice they can be as perverse and nasty as the worst of sinners. They begin life with a fallen nature, a *divided* nature. They struggle with the pull to be bad and the inner knowledge that they should do what they inherently know is right. They struggle with this from the beginning of their lives!

Christians have difficulty communicating the idea of a fallen sin nature to those without spiritual discernment: The undiscerning think sin must involve bad physical *conduct*—crime or physical harm, and many other forms of bad *behavior*. Our fallen nature expresses itself in such forms, but also resides in those who are socially *acceptable, good* citizens, and *successful* in their jobs and social settings. The fallen nature is discerned in the *heart's* focus and attitudes as well as in conduct. Thus the Bible says: "God sees not as man sees, for man looks at the outward appearance, but the LORD looks at the heart" (1 Sam. 16:7). The world is full of good people, as it defines good. But remember Christ's question to the rich young ruler: "Why do you call Me good? No one is good except God alone" (Luke 18:19). The person lacking spiritual discernment evaluates human nature by a different standard than God does. And God teaches his children to use *his* standard when evaluating their nature.

Dimensions of the Heart

We conclude with nine dimensions of the *heart* that tell us that we are conflicted and out of harmony with God's design.

(1) Ask anyone, "Have you ever done something that you knew was wrong before you acted but you did it anyway? The answer is universal: "Of course." This shows that all possess the knowledge of good and evil, and it also shows that all humans rebel at times against what they know instinctively is good. The *a priori* knowledge of good and evil is an inherent aspect of our fallen nature. And our willful violation of our conscience testifies to our fallenness.

(2) Starting with the *presupposition* that the Bible is God's word, those who are fallen and unredeemed hold foundational beliefs out of sync with God's revelation. Christians testify that their understandings of God, human nature, and the created order have all undergone big adjustments during their post-conversion years. Their radically altered perceptions of reality, and of the meaning of life, bear witness to something new. The old fallen nature with *its*

perceptions of reality is being replaced by new perceptions of reality! Darkness is giving way to light.

(3) Our knowledge about reality changes as our beliefs about it change. We reorder, and connect data differently as we grow in seeing reality as God sees it. The unredeemed see things in a way that lets them retain the illusion that either there is no God or that the God they imagine is not to be feared. Remember, beliefs precede knowledge in all *qualitative* areas of life—including morals. The ideas about knowledge held by a person with a fallen nature are limited so that significant aspects of *spiritual reality* are excluded.

(4) The unregenerate always seek to satisfy their *God-created need* for unconditional acceptance—only found in Christ—from sources offering limited and conditional acceptance. The initial affirmation of our worth, in a fallen world, comes from our parents. And some poor souls know from their beginning that their parents do *not* love them! Subsequently friends, loved ones, and neighbors either reinforce or undermine our sense of personal worth. But the initial building blocks of acceptance require something more *substantial*. If our deep need for ultimate acceptance is not met, we seek to reinforce the need by striving for promotions; by manifesting conspicuous consumption; by getting divorced and remarried; by moving to start over; and by many other self-generated efforts. Nevertheless, the acceptance of our parents and friends cannot save us from the certainty of death. There is a *need* for acceptance that is deeper than one human can provide another. Humanity's fallen nature longs for ultimate and unconditional acceptance.

(5) The fallen nature has a whole set of criteria by which it tries to manifest itself as successful and competent—another God-created set of needs. Some people will cheat in order to demonstrate their competence—provided that they are not caught. Others will lie to avoid having their incompetence discovered. Others brag to advertise their greatness in comparison to less successful people. God created people to be successful, but sin perverts its better manifestation. God's definitions of success and competence differ markedly from the world's. The Holy Spirit makes God's definitions real and desirable in his children's *hearts*, but the unredeemed fallen nature is stuck with the world's definitions of success.

(6) Oh, how we long to belong to an important body that elevates our self-esteem! We strive to become a member of the U.S. Senate; or at least of the Country Club, the Boosters Club, Fraternity A, or Sorority B. God created us as *social* beings. And *belonging* is therefore very important. Without it we feel alone. The opportunities an unsaved person has to fulfill this God-created need—to belong to a significant group—are limited when the *spiritual* dimensions of reality are excluded from their view.

God has designed an alternative: To join his family. Become a part of the body of Christ, the church—which is God's spiritual hospital, recovery center, and place of fellowship. Despite its imperfections, the fellowship of a God-fearing, Christ-loving body of believers provides great companionship. King David expressed his heart: "As for the saints who are in the earth, they are the majestic ones in whom is all my delight" (Ps. 16:3). And later, "I am a companion of all those who fear You, and of those who keep Your precepts" (Ps. 119:63).

(7) The human will very quickly reveals our fallen nature. Humans are self-willed to the core, until somebody else supersedes us in importance. And many substitutes clamor to be more important in our mind's eye than ourselves—a boyfriend or girlfriend; a spouse; a good friend. But in time the old self generally reasserts itself. Hence divorce, diminished friendships, or other adjustments take place until self is comfortably re-enthroned. Christ's antidote to self-will is: "He must deny himself, and take up his cross, and follow Me" (Matt. 16:24; Luke 14:27).

(8) What happens when there is a conflict in us between what we know is right and what we desire? The universally experienced process of rationalizing begins. The conflict between our thoughts and feelings related to the desires demand a resolution. They are at war with each other. And which dimension of our *heart* generally wins? The fallen spirit opts for what is desired rather than what is known unless the effects of pursuing the desires are extremely negative.

(9) What motivates people? What we *love* motivates us. The unregenerate love themselves. They are self-centered. So they seek what will enhance their identity—money; power; position; automobiles; drugs; athletics, etc. But one thing is certain; it is not their love of God that motivates them. God has no place on the throne of an unredeemed *heart*.

Am I really motivated by love for God? This important question needs an answer. Do I seek him with all my heart, mind, strength, and soul? Do I long to see him glorified in all the earth? God desires us to do this. Why don't we love him perfectly? We are easily distracted. That is what hinders our spiritual progress. Hebrews expresses the difficulty of our journey:

> Let us also lay aside every encumbrance and the sin which so easily entangles us, and let us run with endurance the race that is set before us, fixing our eyes on Jesus, the author and perfecter of faith, who for the joy set before Him endured the cross, despising the shame, and has sat down at the right hand of the throne of God. (Heb. 12:1-2)

14

Being Created in the Image of God: What Does This Really Mean?

God created man in His own image, in the image of God He created him; male and female He created them. (Gen. 1:27)

One of the beliefs most accepted by Christians is that humans are created in the image of God. The assumption is simple enough: We were made like God in certain ways. Yet this teaching is misunderstood and misapplied. Why? Due to a lack of sound biblical teaching.

Our ability to do things associated[112] with creating, communicating, making choices, and thinking complex thoughts has led many to hold that these are the characteristics of God's image. This conclusion seems plausible on the surface, for God is certainly creative, a choice maker, a communicator, and a complex thinker. As true as all of this is, though, these are not the grounds upon which God declares that we bear his image.

Before we explore the Scriptures about our being made in God's image, we will cover one more thing. Christians are currently being renewed in the image of God. He is *not* doing this in the lives of unbelievers. God's renovative work is the focus of Scripture after the fall. We bore God's image before the fall and everybody bears *a distorted image of him after the fall* and prior to their being born from above. The Greek word used to describe this work of restoration is *anakainoō*. It carries with it the idea of causing to grow up. This is important for those who are not being caused to grow up remain distorted images of God. Those not in Christ distort God's image in significant ways, either in their hearts or in their actions and behavior.

Two biblical passages explicitly describe three qualities God is restoring in his children:

> Do not lie to one another, since you laid aside the old self with its evil practices, and have put on the new self who is being renovated to a true knowledge according to the image of the One who created him. (Col. 3:9-10)

> [But] in reference to your former manner of life, you lay aside the old self, which is being corrupted in accordance with the lusts of deceit, and that you be renewed in the spirit of your mind, and put on the new self, which in the likeness of God has been created in righteousness and holiness of the truth. (Eph. 4:22-24)

---

[112] Chapter 4 critiqued five flawed understandings of what it means to be created in God's image.

God is restoring *true knowledge, righteousness* and *holiness* in his children. These are the three things that God pointed to in Genesis 1 and 2 when he said he would make males and females in *his image*. No other creatures have these qualities; only humans are endowed with them. God is *omniscient*; we can possess true knowledge. God is *righteous*; we can be righteous—we can enjoy Christ's imputed righteousness and grow in righteousness. And God is *holy*; he wants his children to be holy. So Christ enables his people to separate themselves from their old ways of living and causes them to grow up in genuine holiness.

We will study each of these three renewable characteristics.

Being Restored to True Knowledge

What is this *true knowledge* Scripture refers to? Doesn't the fallen image-bearer already possess much true knowledge? From God's perspective the answer is No. Then what is the difference between the knowledge of unregenerate and regenerate human beings? To answer we will first look at the biblical concept of *true knowledge*. Two Greek words used for true knowledge appear nineteen times in the New Testament.[113] The two words are variants— *epiginosko* (a verb) and *epignosis* (a noun). *Epiginosko* means "to become thoroughly acquainted with, to know thoroughly, to know accurately"; and *epignosis* means "precise and correct knowledge."

The context in which the two words appear is critical for comprehending them. True knowledge is first and foremost *true knowledge about God* and who he really is! The fact that he loves those he regenerates; that he wants the best for them. True knowledge is God-centered and Christ-centered knowledge. It is, secondly, knowledge that integrates *temporal reality* with *spiritual reality*. It relates God's existence, nature, and work, with observations made in the temporal arena. It is knowledge that knows that God is Creator and that life has meaning and purpose. It is knowledge that can grow to understand the purpose of evil and suffering. It is knowledge that becomes holistic, unifying God, humanity, and the universe. This is awesome to contemplate! For example, a Nobel Prize astrophysicist who knows much about the physical universe but does not associate that knowledge with Christ, the Creator of the universe, does not possess *epignosis* that brings meaning to that knowledge. Persons do not possess thorough and accurate knowledge of anything in the temporal environment until they correctly associate that knowledge with the Creator. The astrophysicist has partial, incomplete knowledge because it is disconnected from its true purpose. But a young person who rightly relates the universe to God has some *epignosis* about the universe that is fuller than that of the astrophysicist.

True knowledge is evidence that a person enjoys a true relationship with God. This *true knowledge* is the new knowledge Job awakened to when God asked him the questions in Job 38–41. Job's response is memorable: "I have heard

---

[113] Matt. 14:35; Acts 4:13; 24:8; Rom. 1:28; 3:20; 10:2; Eph. 1:17; 4:13; Phil. 1:9; Col. 1:9, 10; 3:10; 1 Tim. 2:4; 2 Tim. 3:7; Heb. 10:26; 2 Peter 1:2, 3, 8; 2:20.

of You by the hearing of the ear; but now my eye sees You; therefore I retract, and I repent in dust and ashes" (42:5-6). God enabled Job to reunite his previous knowledge with God himself. This renovation created in Job a whole new *gestalt*. And Job's knowledge would never be the same again.

The person not born from above can have momentary glimpses of true knowledge as disclosed in Romans 1:28: "And just as they did not see fit *to have God in true knowledge [epignosis] any longer*, God gave them over to a depraved mind" (a literal translation). This verse teaches that unregenerate people suppress the truth. Truth makes demands on those who would hold it in their minds. Truth is light that chases out darkness. But those committed to darkness flee from the light and even hate it. True knowledge that reassociates the temporal and the spiritual is a gift from God that requires his restorative work. Without that, the true knowledge will be suppressed or reconfigured to please the self-centered God-denying *heart*.

So *epignosis*, true knowledge, is what God restores to those he adopts. He renovates his children so that they begin to associate the *temporal reality* they have lived in all their lives with the *spiritual reality* that is also a part of their experience. The two realities are deeply intertwined; they are really one integrated reality. Joseph, the Old Testament patriarch, possessed this true understanding. He revealed this to Potiphar's wife immediately after she urged him, "Lie with me." Joseph refused, "Behold, with me here, my master does not concern himself with anything in the house, and he has put all that he owns in my charge ... and he has withheld nothing from me except you, because you are his wife. *How then could I do this great evil, and sin against God?*" (Gen. 39:7-9). Joseph knew that Potiphar's wife belonged to God first. She was God's and he had given her to Potiphar. Joseph *knew* this. He had *true knowledge*.

This *true knowledge* restored to God's children when they are born from above allows them to look at a tree and see God's *glory*. It is God who designed, created, and maintains the trees all around us. The restored natural ability to relate the tree to God is the evidence of true knowledge. In the same way, an *automobile* glorifies God. Was it not God who created mankind—who was then endowed by God with the abilities necessary to reconfigure what he had already created and make an automobile? The inventor's glory pales in the presence of God's glory, but we glorify God when we do his will—for we are exercising creative dominion over the earth (Gen. 1:26; 2:8, 19-20; Ps. 8:6-8).

Epignosis is being restored in the hearts of God's children in every area. Not only do we have a new understanding of the created order—it is God's handiwork!—but God's act of redemption through his Son Jesus Christ, becomes the best of true knowledge. We have eternal life in Christ. The sting of death has been removed. Our sins are forgiven. All of life has a new meaning when properly discerned with true knowledge. And we now regard all of the providential events in our lives as instruments of God's love, for they are from the hand of the awesome Triune God. True knowledge becomes the new knowledge. Our possession of the mind of Christ takes on new meaning. Christ certainly had true knowledge. As he gives his people the ability to discern afresh true knowledge, they manifest the mind of Christ that is being renewed in them through the Holy Spirit's work.

Being Restored to Righteousness

Biblically, righteousness has several concepts associated with it. These senses are derived from two Hebrew words—*yasar*, which means being straight, and *mishpat*, which means judgment—and a Greek word, *dikaiosune*, signifying that which conforms to a norm, the very character of God.[114] Keeping these meanings in mind, we will look at the restoration of human nature as it is being renovated to the likeness of God's own character; its capacity to be a fair judge of what is right; and its being made straight once again.

Righteousness: Manifesting Christ's Character

This book is based on the premise that God desires his children to become partakers of the divine nature (2 Peter 1:4). After the fall of Adam and Eve it was impossible for unregenerate people to manifest God's righteousness. Fallen humans hide from God. They desire to establish their own standards for right and wrong. Even though some of the human-created standards may parallel God's norms, they lack the true standard by which they are to be measured: Christ. Christ is God's righteousness manifested to us in bodily form (1 Cor. 1:30). God desires that we put on Christ through faith. The Holy Spirit dwelling in the hearts of Christ's people and *actively transforming and renovating them into his likeness* reveals the possibility of their being *renovated in righteousness*—restored to the image of God.

Our section, "What Is the Divine Nature?," looked afresh at God's attributes to magnify the wonder of his majesty and to point out aspects of his nature transmittable to human character. For example, God desires to impart to us aspects of his *omniscience*. There is the general knowledge that all acquire through observations of the created order, regardless of spiritual condition. But there is the *true knowledge*, described earlier, that is only acquired by regenerated persons. This knowledge transforms its possessors' world/life-view. It reunites the temporal and the spiritual and allows the study of God's attributes to impact the way we live.

The *righteous* relationships modeled between the persons of the Trinity can impact us in our relationships in dating, marriage, family, church, business, and public arenas. How we live *righteously* in such relationships will be the focus of chapters 21–27. We often experience tensions as we express ourselves in words and actions that reveal what we *really believe* in such areas as: "What role does inequality play in our lives?" Or, "who is in charge, and what role does submission play?" And, "how do I express my individuality as I relate to the community?" "What are my rights and responsibilities?" "How can I distinguish

---

[114] *Baker's Dictionary of Theology* (Baker: Grand Rapids, 1960), 461-462.

between freedom and license, and where do self-control and external controls meet?" The relationship between the persons of the Godhead is the perfect model of a *right* relationship. Learning to navigate in a godly manner the tensions that accompany the relationships just described shows the reestablishment of Christ's character in our lives. This manifests righteousness!

Our discussion on God's *immutability* concluded that while believers cannot become immutable, they can, by the Spirit's renovative work, have their character shaped so they keep their word even at great cost (Ps. 15:1-4). Our commitments should not be broken. God's hating divorce illustrates his abhorrence of any failure to keep one's commitments and vows (Mal. 2:16). And if God's *omnipresence* is meaningful, then when is it right for *us* to be present in the lives of those we are called to love? On what occasions is our personal presence meaningful and life giving? The renewal of these traits in the lives of God's children is evidence that Christ's character is being restored in them. These manifest righteousness!

God's *wisdom*—is it not freely given to us? Then is it *not* right for us whom God has enlightened to share our insights with those who need them? Counseling one's friends, and holding one another accountable before the Lord, is love in action. Scripture and experience both tell us God is *good*. God's *goodness* and *righteousness* are virtually mirrors of one another. When we are being renovated in *righteousness*, this will be seen in expanded acts of goodness. Christ's character is manifested through his people's sharing wisdom and goodness. These manifest righteousness!

God's *omnipotence* is awesome to contemplate, and by his mercy we typically experience it in gentle forms. Shouldn't the meager power God gives us be used to accomplish *righteous* ends? Of course! And finally, if God is *love*—and he is—then the two greatest commandments urge his children to the highest possible levels of righteousness. There is no such thing as *un*righteous love. Love is the delivery of what is *right* and *good* in a godly manner. Restoring the attribute of righteousness into the character of God's children will manifest itself in a godly blending of power and love. Our ability to be *righteous* was one of the three things God meant when he said he was going to create us in his image.

Righteousness: Being Fair Judges

It is easy to confuse the warning "Do not judge lest you be judged" (Matt. 7:1) with not using appropriate forms of judgment. We are, after all, called upon to judge between right and wrong. We are to call sin "sin." We are to defend the rights of orphans, widows, and the poor. To do this we must judge rightly, and to do this is righteous! "The righteous is concerned for the *rights* of the poor, the wicked does not understand such concern. Open your mouth for the mute, for the *rights* [lit.: judgment] of all the unfortunate . . . . Open your mouth, *judge righteously*, and defend the *rights* of the afflicted and needy" (Prov. 29:7; 31:8-9). Christians do not condemn others when they uphold the rights of the disenfranchised.

"Do you not judge those who are within the church?" (1 Cor. 5:12; read 5:1–6:6). There is appropriate and inappropriate judgment. Judgment that condemns a person before God is wrong. An individual has no authority to do this.

> But you, why do you *judge* your brother? Or you again, why do you regard your brother with contempt? For we will all stand before the judgment seat of God.... So then each one of us will give an account of himself to God. Therefore let us not *judge* one another anymore (Rom. 14:10-13).

But we are to judge sin as being sin, and sin is destructive and ought to be eradicated.

> It is actually reported that there is *immorality* [sin] among you ... that someone has his father's wife.... I, on my part, though absent in body but present in spirit, have already *judged* [lit.: made a decision regarding] him who has so committed this.... I *have decided* to deliver such a one to Satan for the destruction of his flesh, so that his spirit may be saved in the day of the Lord Jesus (1 Cor. 5:1-5).

Christians are called upon daily to make decisions about right and wrong. And they are to speak out on such matters when it is appropriate. We are not to be busybodies or moral policemen in the world, but are to be especially watchful and helpful to one another in the body of Christ, as Paul taught:

> I wrote you in my letter not to associate with immoral people; I did not at all mean with the immoral people of this world, or with the covetous and swindlers, or with idolaters, for then you would have to go out of the world. But actually, I wrote to you not to associate with any so-called brother if he should be an immoral person, or covetous, or an idolater, or a reviler, or a drunkard, or a swindler—not even to eat with such a one. For what have I to do with *judging* outsiders? Do you not *judge* [approve or disapprove the conduct of] those who are within the church? But those who are outside, God *judges*. (1 Cor. 5:9-13)

Paul, alluding to Deuteronomy 13:5; 17:7, 12; 21:21; and 22:21, concludes, "Remove the wicked man from among yourselves."

Christ imparts to his brothers and sisters the understanding of what is and is not appropriate judgment. He accomplishes this by the Spirit's use of the Scripture to transform their comprehension of how to manifest non-judgmental *righteousness*. Growing in the ability to do this indicates God's renovative work in their hearts as they are renewed in the image of the One who created him.

Righteousness: Being Straight. When a person says to another, "You were not straight with me," he is complaining that the second party was in some sense not truthful; or that the individual was devious; or was hiding something that was important. The offended person was not dealt with fairly. He was misled.

But there is, of course, the opposite form of unrighteousness. There are cases where a person is very straight but is unloving in his or her use of the truth they possess. Paul told the people at Ephesus, "We are no longer to be children, tossed here and there . . . by every wind of doctrine . . . but *speaking the truth in love*, we are to grow up in *all aspects* [including righteousness] into Him who is the head, even Christ" (Eph. 4:14-15). Bludgeoning people with truth is not loving them, and if it is not loving it cannot be *righteous*. Being straight does not imply insensitivity to the thoughts and feelings of others. Love does not hide the truth, but neither does love attack with truth!

Being straight means being forthright and dependable as one who is a builder of life, not its diminisher. Straightness and trustworthiness are fair synonyms. God wishes to impart to us a quality of straightness, the attribute of *righteousness*. This requires God's restoration. Those brought into the kingdom of Christ need to be restored to his image. They need to be made *straight*. We all enter the kingdom *bent*.

Being Restored to Holiness

Early it was noted that God's holiness is his only attribute used to describe the *quality* of some of his other attributes. For example, his power is a holy power. Holiness is revealed in Scripture as having two components. First, there is the idea of absolute *purity*, derived from the biblical account of God's character. God has told us, I am holy. And he has commanded us to be holy: "Be holy, for I am holy" (Lev. 11:44; 1 Peter 1:16). There is no hint of unholiness or evil in God. Such is inconceivable! This is not the case with fallen people, of course. Since the fall, unholiness has infected all of our first parents' progeny.

A degree of purity is restored to God's children as he renews them in the likeness of Christ. This is made known as God's people begin to have thoughts that appreciate God's purity. Not only will their appreciation of God's goodness increase, but they will have a renewed appreciation for the good things they see others do. They will grow in their dislike of things that are not holy and grow in their delight of what is good and just. Values are changed. The children of God begin to delight in what God delights in.

The second component of holiness that is germane to God's children being renewed into his likeness is their restored ability to *discern* between what is godly and what is not, with the desire to be *separated* from the latter. And Christians have a cooperative part to play in this. Humans have no control over the *initial thoughts* that pop into their minds, so any idea of the Christian's old nature being completely eradicated in this life is unrealistic. The unsavory thoughts that come into our minds are reminders of our sin nature; hence, until we are glorified there is no chance of our becoming completely pure. But we can be taught by the Holy Spirit to begin "taking every thought captive to the obedience of Christ" (2 Cor. 10:5), and thereby not allow the initial thought to determine our subsequent behavior. The old thought is dealt with as Christ instructed: "Now you Pharisees clean the outside of the cup and the platter; but inside of you, you are full of robbery and wickedness. You foolish ones, did not he who made the outside make the inside also? *But give that which is within as charity* [your gift of love], and then all things are clean for you" (Luke 11:39-41). The child of God recognizes, confesses, and gives his or her bad thoughts to Christ for renovation. Then these reminders of our sin nature do not become activated sin. We are also enabled to flee from sin, to separate ourselves from the environments that stimulate what is ungodly.

For example, God's children can learn to flee pornography. Males, who are especially subject to visual stimulation, can change channels quickly when something pornographic appears on television. Or they can simply refuse to look at printed pornography. Erotic stimulation is becoming more pervasive in our culture, but is avoidable in the sense that people do not have to read magazines, or watch DVDs, movies, or TV programs that arouse them sexually. Human sexuality is a beautiful aspect of God's creation. God intends it for pleasure, bonding, and procreation. But sexuality becomes debilitating when it is stimulated and misappropriated.

Those who desire to please Christ should avoid auditory and visual stimulation that promotes the devaluation of godly character. God is life-giving and life-elevating. He does not diminish human worth or undermine human character. This does not mean that Christians are to withdraw from the world and be unaware of what is going on around them. The question becomes one of diet. What are we to feed the *heart*? God is aware of evil. But he does not take it into himself so that it becomes a part of his nature. The Christian must be careful even in his or her learning. Are we learning, or are we secretly enjoying the perverse things we are exposing ourselves to? There are no secrets before God: he is omniscient. We are to be wise and discerning. God promotes and desires holiness. He wants his children to separate their thoughts, motives, and behavior from what is ungodly. "Be holy, for I am holy."

We must carefully consider ingested physical stimulants also. Food and drink are good when enjoyed as God intended. But food was created for the body; the body was not created for food. If food rules us, and becomes a substitute for something else that is needed, food has usurped a role in our lives contrary to God's purpose. The same for drink. Is what is in the drink good for us? Does it nourish us? Or does it break down our self-control? The Spirit of God brings self-control to God's children. Does our drink undermine self-control? Being holy encompasses being in charge of our bodies so that they serve Christ. We are to enjoy food and drink but we are not to be ruled by them.

Mind-altering drugs are another area subject to the standards of holiness. There is a biblical warrant for a doctor prescribing a drug following surgery to help us deal with pain. "Give strong drink to him who is perishing" (Prov. 31:6). But even here, we must be careful that the drug does not become habit-forming. Addictions are real, and are often very difficult to confront. They can become masters irrationally followed. Seeking mind-altering drugs for pleasure is akin to seeking a lobotomy from what is God-intended. It distorts reality. It is transportation into a false world. It is unholy to distort and pervert what God intended for good. The so-called pleasures to be derived from drugs are like the sirens of Greek mythology that lured mariners to their sure destruction by their singing. The finale of their song was death!

Holiness, as *absolute* purity, transcends God's intentions for us before glorification. All in Christ shall be made perfect in *heaven*, but not *before* then (Heb. 11:40; 12:23). But those born from above are reunited to a *delight* in what is good and righteous. What is obviously unholy is an abomination to them. They no longer love what is unholy, but a love for what is wholesome, merciful and life-giving is renewed. The love of sin and sinning is dismantled.

Holiness, separation from what is unholy, is restored degree by degree in the lives of God's children. The Lord's renovating work is, however, under the Spirit's direction and not ours. This is important to remember when we observe others in Christ. It is easy for one Christian to find fault with another's conduct, even to doubting their salvation. For example, a person might find himself thinking about a professing brother, "If he were really a Christian he wouldn't curse like that!" But God may well be working on another important aspect of that Christian's heart. Christ may plan to address his language later. This does not mean that his language is unimportant, for bad language is a perverting of something fundamentally true. Perversions are certainly not good; but God may be cleansing the same believer of another inappropriate appetite that he wants dealt with first.

The professing Christian, especially in the early years of adoption into God's family, may not assume the characteristics of true knowledge, righteousness, or holiness as soon as we might desire, but they belong to Christ, not to us. And Christ alone has the wisdom regarding just what aspects of their character need renovating first, and in what order. Paul wrote the church in Rome the following regarding Christian liberty:

> Who are you to judge the servant of another? To his own master he stands or falls; and he will stand, for the Lord is able to make him stand.... But you, why do you judge your brother? Or you again, why do you regard your brother with contempt? For we will all stand before the judgment seat of God. For it is written, As I live, says the Lord, every knee shall bow to Me, and every tongue shall give praise to God. So then each one of us will give account of himself to God. (Rom. 14:4, 10-12)

Conclusion

Though it is popular to hold that being made in God's image includes human creativity, the ability to communicate, to make intelligent choices, and to think complex thoughts, this is not scriptural. Furthermore, the fallen image-bearer is badly distorted. This is especially true when one realizes that the original image was to be manifested in the *heart* of our *spirit*. The image was first and foremost to be the innermost character of our *heart*. The heart was originally designed to possess *true knowledge*; to be *righteous* in all thoughts, intentions, and actions; and to be pure, separated from evil. We were created to be *holy*, as our Lord is holy.

God renews true knowledge, righteousness, and holiness in believers' hearts. As these qualities are being restored, we are being refitted with God's image. The old is being put off and the new is being put on. This is the glorious work of the Holy Spirit.

15

The Biblical Concept of the Heart: A Compressed Depiction

And I will give them a heart to know Me, for I am the LORD; and they will be My people. (Jer. 24:7)

And I will take the heart of stone out of their flesh and give them a heart of flesh. (Ezek. 11:19)

The Father sent his Son into the world to be the Christ, the Savior of those the Father gave his Son as his eternal inheritance. But those to be saved needed to be *redeemed*. They had accumulated unpayable debts to God. But they could *not* pay; they were bankrupt! God knew this would be the case, before creation. Therefore the Trinity agreed that the Son would become incarnate and pay the price to free the fallen ones. So in the fullness of time, Christ came and paid the price to redeem those who had condemned themselves with debt. Isaiah predicted this: "As a result of the anguish of His soul [the coming Messiah's], He [God the Father] will see it and be satisfied" (Isa. 53:11). The debt has been paid!

But after their purchase, God needs to perform two more steps for the redeemed to meet his specifications. They need to be given *faith* in Christ's finished work. And they need to be cleaned up—*renovated* into the likeness of God. Yes, hearts needs to be transformed for the redeemed to begin to manifest Christlike characteristics. Scripture speaks of a heart of stone and also of a heart of flesh. There is a heart that remains in its fallen, unredeemed state of *stone*. There is likewise a heart born from above and renewed in Christ's likeness. It becomes *flesh*!

Twenty-five years ago I asked what the biblical concept of the *heart* encompasses. The word heart appears in the Bible repeatedly. I was arrested by the word, and enquired: "What does God mean by his continued use of the word heart?" I discovered that our English word heart represents several Hebrew and Greek words. The Hebrew words *leb* and *lebab* are both rendered heart. And *kardia* is the Greek word for heart. These words in various forms appear in Scripture 966 times. And if we add words like faint-hearted, hardhearted, brokenhearted, tenderhearted, and stiff-hearted, the count goes over 1,000. I concluded that God conveyed important meaning by the word heart. Then I asked: "What *gestalt* has God intended in his use of the word *heart*?"

Further study revealed that the word heart sometimes referred to the entire human personality, as in, "the secrets of his heart are disclosed," meaning that everything is revealed" (1 Cor. 14:25). But mostly the word pointed to one of the three components of our nature: our *mind* (Rom. 1:21); our *passions* (9:2); or our *volition/will* (2:5). Paul uses the word heart 52 times in his epistles, according to this distribution: 15 times *kardia* denotes the general personality; 11 times it describes the intellect; 13 times it speaks about the seat of our emotions; and 13 times is addresses the volition.[115] Thus Paul's use of the word is evenly-distributed.

Surprisingly, however, most biblical references to the heart point to some aspect of the *mind*, though not in Paul. Indeed, people commonly treat the words heart and mind as separate entities and it was hard for me to learn to think of the *heart* as a biblical concept that routinely includes the mind — the *mind* is a component of the *heart*. The words are usually synonyms. The mind is a *subset* of the heart. The word heart encompasses a larger concept than the word mind, but the two are not to be considered as opposing elements — as they often erroneously are.

Moreover, the fact that the word *kardia* is often used to refer to the *mind* or *intellect* is significant. This does not mean that the *mind* is more important than the *passions* or the *volition/will*, but that the *mind/intellect* is God's primary avenue for engaging and shaping the entire *heart*. For example, if our *passions* or *will* are to be altered, how is this to be done? If God wants to bring someone's passions into conformity with his will, he engages the person's *mind* to have him or her realize that their desires are not in conformity with his. Surely the person needs to *realize* — a mental process — that his passions and will were leading him in a direction not pleasing to God for him to want to change his passions and will. Didn't Paul say as much: "Do not be conformed to this world, but *be transformed by the renewing of your mind, that you may prove what the will of God is*, that which is good and acceptable and perfect" (Rom. 12:2)?

This is illustrated in the command, "You shall love the LORD your God with all your *heart*, and with all your soul, and with all your strength, and with all your *mind*." Here the word mind is used as a reminder that it is an aspect of the heart. The double expression is being used as a reinforcer: "Don't forget your mind when you love God or you will not *really* love him." You cannot love God without the mind being engaged. *Agape* love can be defined as God's commitment of his will to seek the best for us. *Agape* love is not feeling-based. It requires engagement of the *mind*. We can have a *philos* love, primarily a feeling of love for God, but that is not what is commanded in Luke 10:27. To *agapao* God is to bring our wills into conformity with his, and this requires the use of our mind. To recap: We are to love the Lord our God with all of our *heart*, which includes our *mind, passions, will, strength, soul, might* — or *everything* we possess. The *heart* is the whole inner man.

---

[115] *Baker's Dictionary of Theology* (Baker Book House, Grand Rapids:1960), p. 262.

We will begin to draw a series of diagrams to build a picture of *what* the Bible includes in the heart. The diagrams will help organize what God reveals about us when he speaks of the heart. The expanding diagrams will extend beyond the use of the words *mind, passions,* and *will*. Each section of the heart has subparts of these three major categories, including, for example, "conscience," "knowledge," and "reason." In fact, the biblical concept of the *heart* seems to grow larger and larger as it is examined and contemplated.

Figure 15.1 is a simple diagram with three corners labeled with the three major biblical components of the *heart*. The *mind* is placed at the top because it is the most frequently referred-to aspect of the heart, and is the major avenue into the other two components.

We will employ these abbreviations: Mind is **M**; Passions **P**; and Volition/Will **W**.

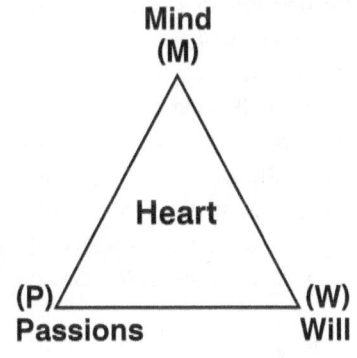

Figure 15.1 *Major Components of the heart*

Figure 15.2 shows that our *mind, passions,* and *will* are not three separate entities but three *facets* of a single *complex* entity. The original fallen nature is not eradicated when we are born from above. Even though we receive a new nature, this struggles with the residual of the old nature as long as we live. But believers do not have two hearts. There is a new heart of flesh cooperating with the Holy Spirit as he restores Godlikeness over time. This involves the shedding of what is ungodly but not the eradication of either the memory or residual consequences of the old nature. Paul describes God's work in his people: "It is God who is at work in you, both to will and to work for His good pleasure" and "I am confident of this very thing, that He who began a good work in you will perfect it until the day of Jesus Christ" (Phil. 2:13; 1:6). God works in us, abating the influence of the old nature and building up our self-control faculties.

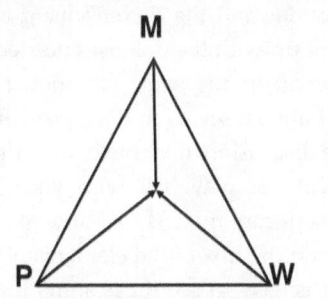

Figure 15.2 *Three facets of the heart*

This diagram depicts the unity that exists between the three facets of the heart and their subcomponents. Though we discuss the three facets as though they are separate entities, they are *not*. They are three in one.

The confluence of the three arrows reinforces that the three dimensions of the heart are three ways to talk about distinctive components of a unified entity. Genuine benefit is derived from the Aristotelian tendency to break down things into subparts for analysis, but much can also be lost through this. The botanist may dissect a rose and describe the many parts that make it up. But the dissected parts are no longer a rose. The rose, to be enjoyed for the reasons it was created, must be intact. The same is true of the heart. We dissect it to understand it, but it can only glorify God in its restored and holistic state.

There is another complexity as God describes the heart. While every heart has a *mind, passions,* and *volition/will,* the distribution of these elements varies in individuals. We use different screening systems to observe the world and integrate observations into our world/life-views. We described the screens of *empiricism, rationalism, existentialism,* and presuppositions from *ontological beliefs*. A rationalist will usually exhibit more of his *mind* in action than his *passions*. But an existentialist will generally exhibit more of his *passions* than of his *mind*. His feelings tend to override other aspects of his heart. In addition, the same individual will also have, over time and in different situations, diverse mixes of the three components in his heart. The heart is not static but dynamic, ever revealing the unique personality of each person. These three examples depict alternating mixes of the heart's components:

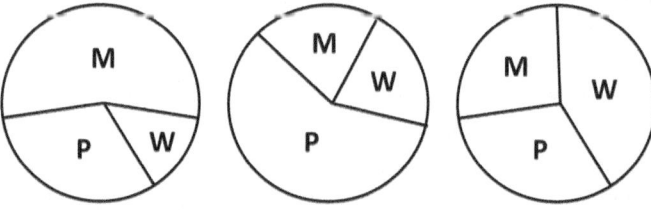

Figure 15.3 *Distribution of the elements*

The mix of the *Mind* (**M**), *Passions* (**P**), and the *Will/Volition* (**W**) is always changing. Something strikes one person's emotions and the **P** component may shut down out of fear, and the **M** component fill up with the defenses needed to ward off the emotions. Or someone else present in the same situation may expand his or her **P** in the situation, and the **M** almost seems to disappear. And in some **W** appears to dominate. No matter the discussion, they have to be right. Or you must do what they want or they will not play ball with you. The possibilities of the degrees by which a person can mix **M**, **P**, and **W** are innumerable. The intensity of the fluctuations and the mix of the elements of the heart vary, even from situation to situation. It is easy to see these shifts in the lives of other people, but harder to see them in ourselves.

We expand the model in Figure 15.4 through 15.8 by setting forth the subcomponents of the *three primary facets* of the heart. We focus on each of the individual primary facets, one at a time.

The Mind's Subcomponents

There are three primary subcomponents of the mind: innate knowledge, ontological beliefs, and epistemological knowledge. The mind, of course, is not *static*. It is always active and dynamic, even when we are asleep. The mind is ever reasoning, reviewing, and contemplating. These mental activities are engaging the *content* of the mind: innate knowledge, ontological beliefs, and epistemological knowledge are all contained therein.

Innate Knowledge

Those who presuppose that humans are not endowed with any inherent or innate knowledge believe that we only possess *a posteriori* knowledge, acquired after birth. Their world/life-view regarding human nature differs radically from those who believe we are born with *a priori* knowledge of *good* and *evil*. But believing that the *conscience* and *a priori* knowledge are not only inseparable but are foundational elements of *innate knowledge* puts *this* aspect of the mind in the lead-off position. It precedes *a posteriori* knowledge.

Ontological Beliefs

How did life originate? Does its genesis give it meaning and purpose? The answers to these questions rest on the presuppositions that underpin our *beliefs* about our true genesis. By that we mean the genesis that goes back to Adam and Eve. The answer provides the key to the second set of questions pertaining to life's meaning and purpose. If the foundational presuppositions are wrong, the conclusions about life and its meaning must also be wrong. One cannot start with incorrect presuppositions about life's genesis and end up with correct conclusions. Indeed, incorrect conclusions regarding life's foundational presuppositions will misdirect subsequent understandings regarding life's purpose and meaning.

Epistemological Knowledge

How do you *know* that you have *accurate* knowledge? The knowledge component in our lives is very important. *Reality, truth,* or *true knowledge,* whatever we call it, is essential to a holistic world/life-view. In Isaiah 11:2, the Spirit of God is called "the spirit of *wisdom* and *understanding,* the spirit of *counsel* and *strength,* the spirit of *knowledge* and the fear of the LORD." He is the only One who transforms general knowledge into *true knowledge,* and true knowledge into genuine *understanding,* and ultimately expands it into godly *wisdom*. True knowledge is a key ingredient in the Spirit's work in recreating a *transformed mind* (Rom. 12:2) in us.

Figure 15.4 is an expanded representation of the mind and its subcomponents, both dynamic (thinking, reasoning) and static (innate

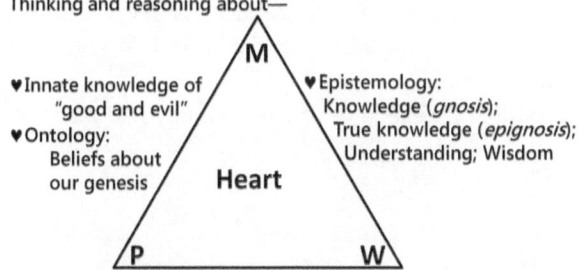

Figure 15.4 *Expanded Representation of the Mind*

knowledge, ontological beliefs, and epistemological knowledge).

We will now consider the divisions within the passions subcomponent of the heart.

The Passions' Subcomponents

The second major component of the heart in Scripture is broad and diverse, but can be described as the *passions* dimension. Those who consider the heart and mind as separate entities are really noting the division that can arise between the **P** and the **M**. The split between them is often real. Here we note that many Christians believe the **P** is the heart within the heart. They thereby reveal an unarticulated presupposition: The **P** is the most important part of the heart. Without denigrating the **P**, we recall that God who designed the heart placed the **M**, **P**, and **W** within it. And furthermore, we recall that most heart references in the Bible point to the **M**.

Desires

We have all *felt* an involuntary attraction or revulsion toward certain things and people. It is a *feeling* phenomenon, not a rational event. We often simply desire something without knowing why. Having desires is part of life's experience. They are part of the **P** element in our heart.

Affections

Compassion, empathy, pity, fondness, and love (parental, sexual, friendship) are *feelings* associated with *positive* affections. Anger, hate, resentment, disliking, and rejection are *emotionally felt* and are *negative* affections that produce disaffections. Affections are as involuntary in character as desires. They emerge from the depths of the heart and reveal much about its character. The heart of flesh grows in its manifestation of positive affections.

Identity Needs

There are three core needs in the **P** critical in the shaping of personal identity. These are universal needs inherent in every human's psychological make-up. The big question is "How will these needs be satisfied?" The three core identity needs are: (1) the need for *unconditional acceptance*; (2) the need to be *competent* or *successful*; and (3) the need to *belong to a significant family*. These are God-created needs, not just wants. The means by which they are satisfied is critical for our *emotional well-being*.

Figure 15.5, continues the development of the heart diagram that began with Figure 15.1 and was expanded in Figure 15.4. We now add the P elements to the diagram.

Next we outline the elements of the volition/will dimension of the heart.

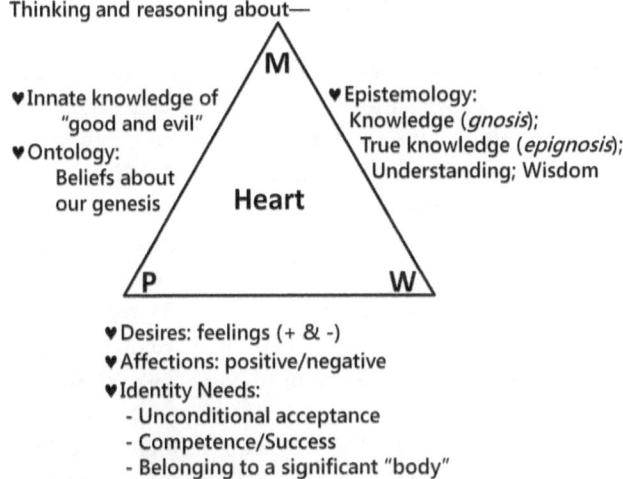

Figure 15.5 *Passions' Subcomponents*

The Volition's/Will's Subcomponents

The third and final component of the heart is the human volition or will. It is best described as the mental capacity to make a choice and to pursue its fulfillment. The will is also described as making a choice *not* to pursue a course of action. It has both an active and a passive potential. It may be deliberative or habitual in its manifestations. It may be exercised following much thought, or it may act spontaneously without thought—perhaps revealing the deepest recesses

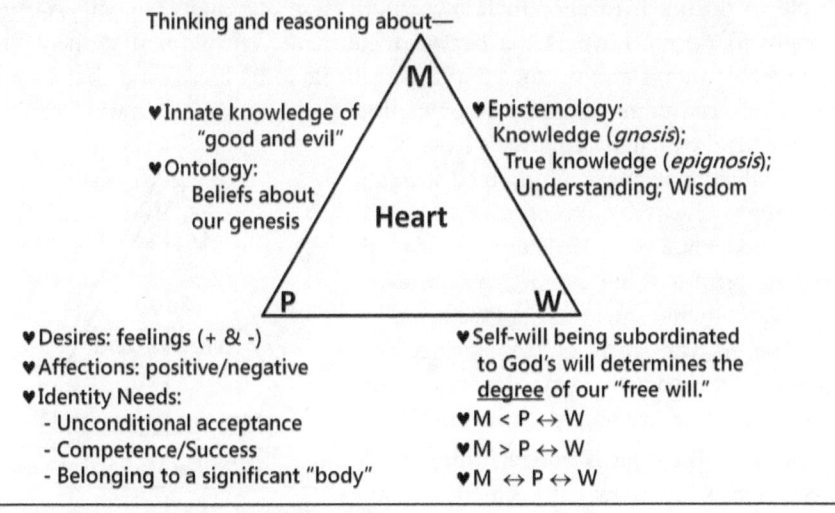

Figure 15.6 *Volition's/Will's Subcomponents*

of the **M** and **P**. It always reflects a mix of the heart's **M** and **P** components. The will may be manifested with varying degrees of intentionality and force. The management of the will is perplexing to contemplate. No two people exercise control over their will in the same way.

What are the will's subcomponents? The **W** divides into two subcomponents: (a) the sought-after will; and (b) the component relationships of the will. The sought-after will concerns itself with the bonding of one's will to God's will, or the manifestations of self-will. The relationship between these two subcomponents determines the *degree* to which one has a *free will*.

The interaction between the **M** and **P** components of the heart constitutes the second subcomponent. By this we mean there are times when the **P** component takes an improper precedent over the **M** component—(**M** < **P** ↔ **W**)—and the **W** reflects this imbalance. Then there are times when the **M** and **P** components are in their proper relationship—(**M** ↔ **P** ↔ **W**)—and the **W** mirrors this harmony. And there are times when the **M** component dominates the **P** component—(**M** > **P** ↔ **W**)—and the **W** acts accordingly. And finally, there are times when the strong motivation of the **W** seemingly overrides all else. This arises from an unconscious strong commitment to another subcomponent of the heart that the person exercising his or her will is not in touch with then. Figure 15.6 frames all this.

We now conclude depictions of the building of the heart by adding a *motivation* factor.

The Motivation Factor

The subject of motivation is somewhat elusive. Its presence or absence is easily observed, but the ability to stimulate or suppress it is subtle and difficult to achieve—in a godly manner or God-honoring environment. Indeed, people are unable to do much to alter their own motivation although they may desire strongly to do so. Love is the central focus here. We recall that there are innumerable things and persons that are available to be loved, and that all but one—God—can unintentionally become an idol and thus a false motivator that God will deal with in his children's lives.

Motivational love is intertwined with all of the heart's components and subcomponents. Figure 15.7 helps to develop a mental picture of the interaction that takes place between the many pieces of the heart.

The **M** can latch on to an idea, or perceive that something is important or dangerous, and seemingly override the **P** components. The same is true regarding the **P** forces. One's passions and emotions can

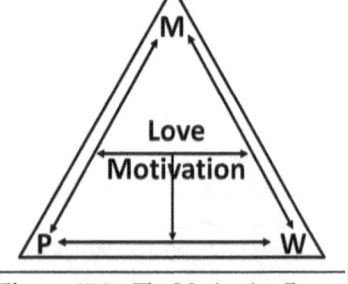

Figure 15.7 *The Motivation Factor*

simply obliterate any rational thoughts about what might be appropriate or inappropriate. The love for the idea or the feeling blots out other considerations. How the **M**, **P**, and **W** interact is beyond full comprehension, but what we love determines the final outcome for what we do or refuse to do—the volitional response.

We will develop one last depiction to indicate the forces and potential conflicts that can arise between the **M** and the **P** components. When there is a failure to reach a **M** = **P** agreement between the two components a *rationalization* process will take place. This is particularly true when **P** > **M** (see Figure 15.6; the **W** corner; and the last three subcomponents.) And on the other side of the depiction, we must recognize that there is *no necessary correlation between what one knows and what one will do*. This means that knowledge alone does not always determine what is done. Figure 15.8 highlights these two realities.

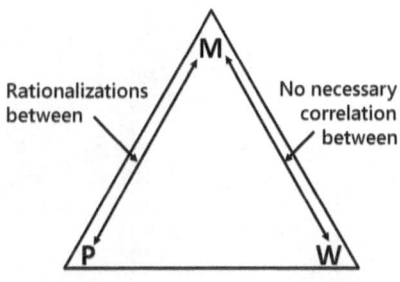

Figure 15.8 *Correlation*

Now combining Figures 15.6, 15.7, and 15.8 yields the complete model to be unpacked in chapters 16-19. See Figure 15.9. The key to comprehending our full thrust is to understand that the Holy Spirit brings about the osmotic permeation (i.e., leaven-like pervasion) of the heart with true knowledge, which transforms someone's world/life-view as Christ's mind is being gradually formed in him. A God-centered reality emerges and dominates the renovated person's comprehension of all that exists and happens—so that he or she is enabled to become a partaker of the divine nature. His or her heart is transformed. Christ, I believe, described this very process when he spoke the parable: "The kingdom of heaven is like leaven, which a woman took, and hid in three pecks of flour until it was all leavened" (Matt. 13:33; Luke 13:21).

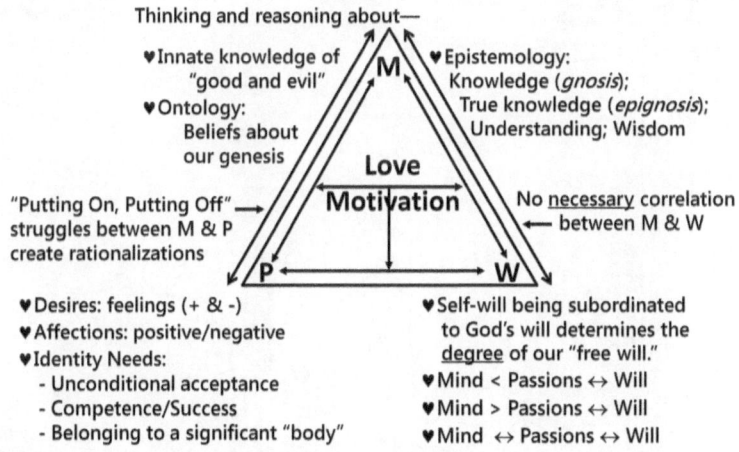

Figure 15.9 *Combined Depictions of the Heart*

The broad conceptual picture of the *heart* has now been set before us, but *how* the *osmotic permeation of the heart with true knowledge* takes place is the work of chapters 16–20.

16

The Heart: The Location of Our Mind—Our Ability to Believe, Truly Know, and Reason

Be transformed by the renewing of your mind. (Rom. 12:2)

God, in creating the *mental* component of the heart, designed it so that it is a repository, receiver, thinker, and discharger—all operating simultaneously and interdependently. As a repository, the mind not only receives and stores data from external stimuli, it begins life with a deposit of *a priori* knowledge of good and evil.[116] People have an inherent moral sense inside from conception. Perhaps the biggest nonsense perpetrated by postmodernists is that there is no way for human beings to know right or wrong, and that all we have is our personal opinions. Common sense and our experiences tell us that this understanding is bogus. The postmodernist who says right and wrong are unknowable lives in a world of denial that contradicts his own life's testimony to the absurdity of such a notion. They play word games to assert their *presumed autonomous lives*. They ignore their own *involuntary reactive moral nature*.

Human Beings Are People with a Conscience

Who enjoys having his personal property stolen? Who likes to be lied to? Who believes it is okay if someone wants to kill him for the fun of it? No one wants these things to happen to him or her. When faced with such things, we *react with a sense of moral offense*. We are morally violated when we are treated in any of these ways. It is an inborn and natural reaction to avoid what threatens our well-being. We are moral beings with an inherent sense of right and wrong. We are people with a conscience. The intellectual postmodernists may talk about moral relativism, but in truth they avoid God, pervert the evidence of the knowledge of good and evil within themselves and try to redefine reality so as to be autonomous.

The statement, "We are people with a conscience," is something with which all can identify, even if some question its validity. Is there anyone who has not experienced the prompting of conscience? The word conscience is used thirty-two times in the New Testament. *Thayer's Greek-English Lexicon of the New Testament* (# 4893) defines the Greek word *suneidesis* as: "the soul [spirit] as

---

[116] *A priori* and *a posteriori* knowledge have been discussed or mentioned in chapters 1, 5, 7, 13, and 15.

distinguishing between what is morally good and bad, prompting to do the former and shun the latter, commending the one, condemning the other; conscience." The *conscience* is an inherent part of the human spirit as are the *knowledge of good and evil* and being a *moral agent*. These three designations express that humans are created in God's image and as a mental repository possess these moral attributes from conception.

We need say little more about the mind's subcomponent ♥ **Innate Knowledge of 'good and evil,'** shown below in Figure 16.1, except to note that, at the last judgment, those who have not heard God's Word will find "their conscience bearing witness and their thoughts alternately accusing or else defending them, on the day when, according to my gospel, God will judge the secrets of men through Christ Jesus" (Rom. 2:15-16). This says an accounting is going to be made of how well the innate knowledge of good and evil was obeyed (Rom. 14:12). Those in whom the Spirit of Christ dwells need not fear this accounting for they have been promised that Christ's righteousness has been credited to them, even as he helps them grow in Christlikeness. Christ is their righteousness (1 Cor. 1:30).

Placing the Mind at the top of the depiction was deemed appropriate in the preceding chapter because most biblical references to the heart point to some aspect of the *mind*. We pointed out that the *mind/intellect* is God's primary pathway for reshaping the major areas of the *heart*. The mind seems to be the portal through which God enters the heart. Fortifying these observations is that Scripture says we are to "be transformed by the renewing of your mind" (Rom. 12:2). I could not discover in God's Word any statement that focuses so intentionally on either the *passions* or the *will*. These latter two areas of the heart are important to God—and they will be transformed in his children, just as the mind—but this is accomplished through the *mind*, for it is the basic conduit through which the other two elements are transformed.

The Holy Spirit Applies the Word

A biblical truth in Figure 16.1 was added to the original depiction of the Mind component (Figure 15.4, in chapter 15). It depicts the presence of the Holy Spirit in the heart of all the regenerate. It is the Holy Spirit who writes God's Word on people's hearts when they read or hear the Word of God. The Holy Spirit illumines the Word so its true meaning is understood and incorporated into believers' lives. (Col. 1:25-27 is noted in Figure 16.1):

Figure 16.1 *Addition of Biblical Truth*

> I was made a minister according to the stewardship from God bestowed on me for your benefit, so that I might fully carry out the preaching of the word of God, that is, the *mystery* which has been hidden from the past ages and generations, but has now been manifested to His saints, to whom God willed to make known what is the riches of the glory of this *mystery* among the Gentiles, which is *Christ in you*, the hope of glory.

"Christ in you" is the mystery God made known to Paul and to which he refers. Christ's presence in the heart of his saints is what makes them different from all other people. Christ's parable of the sower who went out to sow (Matt. 13:3-9) speaks of this reality from a different perspective. Christ makes it abundantly clear that only those with a heart of good soil (v. 8) will *retain* the Word in a fruitful manner. And what is good soil? Good soil is a good heart prepared in the one regenerated by the Holy Spirit (James 1:18; 1 Peter 1: 23). God does not leave the Christian's mind alone to reason on its own. Christians have the Spirit of Christ in their hearts; and he is depositing God's Word there; and he is tutoring them in proper applications of the Word.

The area of the mind we want to turn to now is ♥ **Ontology: beliefs about our genesis**. In philosophy the word ontology indicates the study of existence itself.[117] In theology one early focus is on the genesis of everything—How did what exists come to be? Philosophy attempts to resolve the questions regarding existence through reason and logic alone. Philosophers deliberately attempt to keep consideration of God out of their contemplations. After several thousand years, they are still unable to prove by logic alone their metaphysical conjectures.

Christians have learned through the Spirit's guidance that they must *accept* some things by *faith* rather than seeking to prove them through reason. What God did before creation is one of those things. The record of God's activities in the ongoing history of his people is the basis for our *faith* in God's account of creation. The author believes the *ex niliho* doctrine because of Jesus Christ's resurrection. God has given us *evidential faith* rooted in his activities in the time/space history of humanity. He does not want his people to live by blind faith.

We will now investigate that subcomponent of the Mind treating ♥ **Epistemology: knowledge;** *true knowledge;* **understanding; wisdom** set out in Figure 16.1. Epistemology is the study of the theory of knowledge: How do we know that we can really know anything, especially in the *qualitative* area of life—morals, values, virtues, and the spiritual?

We will not get bogged down in epistemological debates. It is sufficient to acknowledge that we cannot have *exhaustive* knowledge. We do acknowledge that *sufficient* knowledge is available in many areas of the physical/temporal realm so that most are able to agree on many basic things in that realm. There are, to be sure, some real battles going on within and between certain intellectual fields of

---

[117] Anthony Flew, *A Dictionary of Philosophy* (London, England: Pan Books in association with The Macmillan Press, 2nd printing, 1980), 238.

study. This is true of the interchange between psychology, neuropsychology, genetics, and theology—to mention one battleground.

Knowledge and True Knowledge

But we want to focus our attention on the biblical distinction between *knowledge* and *true knowledge*. Romans 12:2 says: "be transformed by the renewing of your mind." This suggests a key question, "What does Paul mean when he says we are to be transformed?" He means we are going to experience a metamorphosis—be changed into new persons. But we cannot metamorphose ourselves. This can only happen through a process of renovation in which God radically changes our minds. The mind is going to undergo a metamorphosis. Does God give us additional information that will help us comprehend Romans 12:2? Yes, he does!

God tells us there are *three things* he renovates and metamorphoses in those he adopts. But he only does so *centuries after* he revealed that he *had* made us in his image.[118] God created people in his image, but did not say what this meant until after Christ's resurrection and after the coming of the Spirit to build up the church. The two New Testament passages which give the *three* aspects of the heart to be transformed are:

> Lay aside the old self, which is being corrupted in accordance with the lusts of deceit, and . . . be renewed in the spirit of your mind, and put on the new self, which in the likeness [image] of God has been created in righteousness and holiness of the truth. (Eph. 4:22-24)

> Put on the new self who *is being renewed* [anakainoō[119]] to a true knowledge [epignosis[120]] according to the image of the One who created him. (Col. 3:10)

We will study Colossians 3:10. What does it mean to possess the mind of Christ? And what is the *key* to understanding the process God uses to impart the mind of Christ to his people?

Anakainoō (a verb), the first word italicized in the Colossians passage above, is merely a grammatical variant of the word *anakainosis* (a noun) which was highlighted earlier in Romans 12:2. It means to be thoroughly renovated—*to be made over completely*. God says he will renovate, transform, or metamorphose his people so that they will possess *epignosis*. And what is *epignosis*?

Epignosis is a key word. The word *gnosis* in Greek means knowledge. The word *epignosis* means true knowledge. What is the distinction between them? Does Paul use *epignosis* for emphasis only, or is there another reason? Do not all people possess some true knowledge? Why would God's Word make a distinction between knowledge and true knowledge? There is a *profound* difference in God's use of the two words.

---

[118] Early revelation: Gen. 1:26-27; 5:1-2. Subsequent revelation: Eph. 4:24 and Col. 3:10.
[119] *Thayer's Greek-English Lexicon of the New Testament*, Lexical reference # 341.
[120] Ibid., Lexical reference # 1922.

Epignosis appears nineteen times in the New Testament.[121] And it has a special meaning in certain *contexts*. It is not the literal translation of *epignosis* that makes it so important. It means: *to become thoroughly acquainted with; know thoroughly; know accurately; know precisely;* and *hold correct knowledge.*[122] This is all straightforward, but it is its *distinctive contextual usage* that is illuminating.

Six of the nineteen times *epignosis* occurs in Scripture, it describes persons who possessed true knowledge and subsequently rejected it, with tragic consequences—their eternal separation from God. Five of these six negative examples are:

> And just as they did not see fit to have God in *epignosis* any longer, God gave them over to a depraved *nous* [mind]. (Rom. 1:28)

> For if we go on sinning willfully after receiving the *epignosis* [true knowledge] of the truth, there no longer remains a sacrifice for sins. (Heb. 10:26)

> For if, after they have escaped the defilements of the world by the *epignosis* [true knowledge] of the Lord and Savior Jesus Christ, they are again entangled in them and are overcome, the last state has become worse for them than the first. (2 Peter 2:20)

> For I testify about them that they have a zeal for God, but not in accordance with *epignosis* [true knowledge]. (Rom. 10:2)

> ... always learning and never able to come to the *epignosis* of the truth. (2 Tim. 3:7)

We therefore conclude that those *not* born from above may sometimes have in their minds, temporarily, true knowledge (*epignosis*), but that they cannot retain it, love it, or obey it. Or they may know certain things about God but pervert what they know. In either case, they do not retain *true knowledge of the truth*. (See Heb. 10:26 and 2 Tim. 3:7 above.) *True knowledge* brings with it certain consequences that are either unwelcome or misunderstood in the hearts of unbelievers.

What, then, is true knowledge, and what are its positive consequences? The negative illustration contained in 2 Peter 2:20 gives us a strong hint of what this *true knowledge* is: "... escaped the defilements of the world by the *true knowledge of the Lord and Savior Jesus Christ.*" It is first and foremost *true knowledge about God*.

These five passages contain five of the thirteen positive uses of the word *epignosis*. They bear the same understanding: true knowledge is God-imparted and leavens the heart with the true knowledge of the character of the Trinity.

---

[121] Matt. 14:35; Acts 4:13; Acts 24:8; Rom. 1:28; 3:20; 10:2; Eph. 1:17; 4:13; Phil. 1:9; Col. 1:9; 1:10; 3:10; 1 Tim. 2:4; 2 Tim. 3:7; Heb. 10:26; 2 Peter 1:2; 1:3; 1:8; 2:20. The two variations on the one word are listed in Thayer's Lexical as # 1921 and # 1922.

[122] Thayer, *Lexicon*, Lexical # 1922. *Gnosis*, the Greek word for knowledge, as contrasted with *epignosis*, can be found in *Thayer's Lexicon* as # 1108.

> ... that the God of our Lord Jesus Christ, the Father of glory, may give you a spirit of wisdom and of revelation in the *epignosis* [true knowledge] of Him. (Eph. 1:17)
>
> ... until we all attain to the unity of the faith, and of the *epignosis* of the Son of God, to a mature man, to the measure of the stature which belongs to the fullness of Christ. (Eph. 4:13)
>
> ... so that you will walk in a manner worthy of the Lord, to please Him in all respects, bearing fruit in every good work and increasing in the *epignosis* of God. (Col. 1:10)
>
> Grace and peace be multiplied to you in the *epignosis* [true knowledge] of God and of Jesus our Lord; seeing that His divine power has granted to us everything pertaining to life and godliness, through the *epignosis* of him who called us by His own glory and excellence. For by these He has granted to us His precious and magnificent promises, in order that by them you may become partakers of the divine nature. (2 Peter 1:2-4)
>
> For if these qualities are yours and are increasing, they render you neither useless nor unfruitful in the *epignosis* of our Lord Jesus Christ. (2 Peter 1:8)

True knowledge is a thorough, precise, and accurate *knowledge of God*—first, of his nature and character; and second, of how he has manifested his nature and character through creation, redemption, and providence. It is *true knowledge* that acts as *leaven* in the hearts of God's people.

The Holy Spirit *transforms* (*metamorphoō*) believers through the *renovation* (*anakainosis*) of their *mind* (*nous*). The Spirit imparts the *mind of Christ* into their *heart* in *true knowledge* (*epignosis*) drawn from the *Word* that is chiefly *true knowledge of God*. This true knowledge then acts like *leaven*, permeating the entire heart. The *leaven of true knowledge* enlightens and transforms the person's understanding of and relationship to God. This transformed understanding of God then permeates one's understanding of God's desires, affections, and behavior. In turn, all of this impacts the person's relationships.

Several important points warrant further elaboration. The statement "The Holy Spirit transforms the persons 'born from above' through the renovation of their mind" merely applies Romans 12:2. This highlights that Paul's exhortation, "Do not be conformed to this world, but be transformed by the renovation of your mind," can only occur by the Holy Spirit's power. We cannot transform our own minds. If we could, wouldn't we all do so *immediately* so that we could love the Lord our God with all our heart, strength, soul and *mind*? Of course we would, but we cannot. *God* is the transformer and renovator of the *mind*.

The statement "The Spirit imparts the mind of Christ into their heart in the form of *true knowledge* drawn from the Word" is based on Colossians 3:10, that says God thoroughly renovates his adopted children so they possess *true knowledge*—precise and accurate knowledge regarding him and his conduct. And Christ possessed *true knowledge* in his pre-incarnate and incarnate states. Indeed, Christ never possessed anything but *true knowledge*. If this is true, then Paul's statement that we have the mind of Christ must mean that those given *true knowledge* have the mind of Christ (1 Cor. 2:16). And where else is *true knowledge* to be found than in the Bible? God tells us of no other place where *true knowledge* of him can be found.

The question was also asked, "Do not all people, regardless of their relationship to God, possess some *true knowledge*?" The biblical answer is No! Only the regenerate *possess* and *retain* such knowledge. There were five negative biblical illustrations given where people did, for a time, possess *true knowledge*— but their subsequent rejection of it proved disastrous. People are better off never having had it than to have had it and later reject it (Luke 9:62).

Why Does Scripture Distinguish between Knowledge and True Knowledge?

Our most important question, however, is "Why would God's Word make a distinction between *knowledge* and *true knowledge*?" There are several good reasons. First, because any knowledge not *leavened* with the *true knowledge* of its rightful relationship to God is imperfect, incomplete, and maybe even *pseudo* knowledge. A Nobel Prize-winning astrophysicist who does not connect his knowledge of the universe with its Creator has *unleavened* or incomplete knowledge. *True knowledge leavens* one's entire world/life-view.

A second reason for this important distinction is so *true knowledge*, *knowledge that leavens*, will be *held in humility*. The *leavening process* is ongoing. Paul gave *true knowledge*, "For we *know* in part . . . but when the perfect comes [at the time of glorification] the partial will be done away . . . for now we see in a mirror dimly [lit.: *in a riddle*], but then face to face; now I *know* in part, but then I will *know fully* just as I also have been *fully known*" (1 Cor. 13:9, 10, 12). Paul wrote this when he possessed much *true knowledge*. But the more we truly know God, the grander he becomes, and the more we realize our finitude. We also grow in awareness of our own imperfections. We become smaller in our own eyes as God becomes greater in them.

A third reason for the distinction between *knowledge* and *true knowledge* is the contrast between what is often called *biblical integration* and what is here called *the leaven of true knowledge*. The difference between the two is grasped when we see the distinctive *processes* of the two terms at work. The acquirement of *true knowledge* is an *internal*, God-initiated, God-directed phenomenon *inside* the *heart*. The gift of true knowledge *leavens* all that it encounters. *True knowledge* is under God's administration, and it works from *inside* of the believer and can subsequently be transmitted to the *outside*. It is an inside-to-the-outside process. *Biblical integration*, on the other hand, is the human's endeavor to rightly associate what he or she observes in their *external* environment with what they have retained in their *internal reservoir* of knowledge. This external-to-internal process may or may not be aided by the Holy Spirit, but is an outside-to-the-inside process. *It is the inside-to-the-outside event, however, that determines the correctness of the outside-to-the-inside effort.*

An illustration will help. Two Christians are asked to share their thoughts on capital punishment. The first says she believes capital punishment has its rightful place, when rightly administered, in God's economy in the modern world. She believes capital punishment reflects a true dimension of God's nature. The second says he believes that capital punishment should be completely done away today; it is incompatible with God's nature. Both have integrated their observations of the external world regarding capital punishment with their internal beliefs. But both sets of internal beliefs cannot be correct. One of the two manifests *pseudo-knowledge* and the other reflects *true knowledge* about God's true nature.

This difference between *true knowledge* and *biblical integration* illustrates the importance of the Holy Spirit's work in imparting *true knowledge* into the *hearts* of believers. With *true knowledge* we have a meaningful component of Christ's mind. Without *true knowledge* we do not, for Christ had only *true knowledge* in his mind. This should make us yearn all the more to truly know God, and not simply to know about him. We depend upon the Holy Spirit to help us develop our relationship with God. This is an incredible incentive to prayerfully read the Word of God, asking Christ to *leaven* us with the *true knowledge* so we may grow in true understanding of God.

True Knowledge Acts Like Leaven

The next assertion is "This *true knowledge* acts like *leaven*, osmotically permeating the entire heart." Osmotic permeation is an analogy to depict an *entering, permeating, transforming, totally-making-over course* followed by the Holy Spirit as he *forms Christ in the hearts of believers* (Gal. 4:19; Eph. 1:18). The *true knowledge* is not simply *integrated* into the heart, although integration is often used to describe our growth in the application of God's Word in our lives. Integration implies bringing together diverse things or people and joining them. Simply joining old knowledge and new knowledge is not what God is doing. Something more profound is going on. God is *transforming* what was there prior to the *permeation* and *leavening* that takes place when the *true knowledge* saturates the *heart*.

As *true knowledge* begins to *leaven* our previously presumed knowledge of God, he becomes one to be feared. Proverbs 1:7 puts it this way: "The *fear* of the LORD is the beginning of *knowledge*." The Hebrew word used for fear throughout the Old Testament is *yirah*. It carries the connotation of a continuum of emotions from absolute terror to exhilarating awe. The idea can be portrayed as follows:

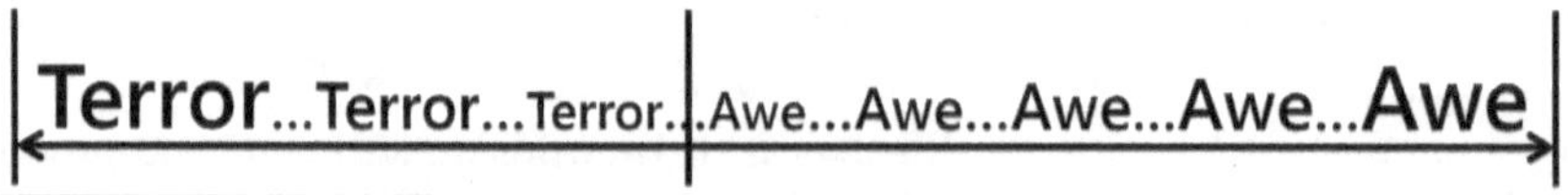

|◄── Terror...Terror...Terror...│...Awe...Awe...Awe...Awe...Awe ──►|

Figure 16.2 *Fear Continuum*

Note that the fear of the Lord is the beginning of *knowledge*. The blessing, however, is that the Lord begins at once to address the fear raised by God's Spirit. The life of Isaiah shows this. God began his transforming work when he *leavened* Isaiah with the *true knowledge* of his holiness (Isa. 6:1-13). Isaiah saw God's holiness and cried, "Woe is me, for I am ruined!" (v. 5). But God immediately had a seraphim touch Isaiah's lips with a burning coal from the altar, and said, "Your iniquity is taken away and your sin is forgiven" (vv. 6-7).

The fear of God, rightly understood, leads its possessor along the path of an increasing *awe of God*. He becomes to believers more and more as he actually is—as revealed in Scripture. This transformation of our understanding of God *leavens*, over time, all we know. For some, like Peter, the *leavening* takes place over much time in a series of small transformations (Luke 5:4-11; Matt. 16:13-20; John 21:3-7, 15-22).

The Holy Spirit Imparts God's Characteristics into Believer's Minds (Hearts)

The Spirit of God may select any one of God's characteristics to begin imparting *true knowledge* into the *mind* (heart) of a believer. When someone has *true knowledge* imparted to him about an aspect of God's nature, that aspect becomes elevated in his mind. That attribute takes on a significance which was not there before. This elevated attribute begins to *leaven* his thinking about God. It changes how he wants to live with his family, friends, neighbors, and even his enemies! This reflects Christ's statement: "The kingdom of heaven is like *leaven*, which a woman took and hid in three pecks of flour *until it was all leavened*" (Matt. 13:33).

The patriarch Joseph showed his *leavened knowledge* of God when he said to Potiphar's wife, following her request for sex, "How could I do this great evil and sin against God?" (Gen. 39:7-9). Joseph knew that all belonged to God. He knew God was the absolute Sovereign. He knew that God had appointed proper relationships between people, including spouses. And he knew that a sexual union with Potiphar's wife would contradict God's holy will. He knew God was holy, because he knew such an act would be a great evil against God.

Another transformation of the *mind* is Job's sudden possession of *true knowledge* regarding God's omnipotent nature revealing his glory. This occurred as a result of God's conversation with Job (Job 38–41). Job's transformed mind appears in his response to having received the *true knowledge*: "I *know* that You can do all things, and that no purpose of Yours can be thwarted. Who is this that hides counsel without *knowledge*? Therefore I have declared that which I did not *understand*, things too wonderful for me, which I did not *know* . . . . I have heard of You by the hearing of the ear; but now my eye sees You; therefore I retract, and I repent in dust and ashes" (Job 42:2-6). Job's *mind* was transformed as God opened the eyes of his heart to see as never before. God's opening the eyes of the heart is found in many texts (see Eph. 1:18, Acts 26:18; 2 Cor. 4:6). Scripture is full of examples of the *leavening effect of true knowledge* on our understanding of him and its implications for all of life.

Holiness and True Knowledge

God uses his *holiness* to transform our minds with *true knowledge*, as he did Isaiah's, but in a different way. He elevates this attribute to a new place of prominence in our minds. For example, he can convict us of a sin that suddenly stands out in stark contrast to his absolute purity. Or reading about Christ's life, we could suddenly become aware of his consecration of all that is divine, sacred, and pure. It might be Christ's selfless life, lived day after day, that breaks through our old perception and replaces it with a sense of his holiness. He has willed to redeem an impure people and transform them into a people who will become purer and purer. Oh, what love! He can use anything to bring *true knowledge* to our minds.

The Spirit's imparting *true knowledge* into the fertile ground of a Christian's *mind* opens the door for God to begin making us partakers of the divine nature (2 Peter 1:4). But how are we to partake of God's *holy* nature? This prompts another question: What is God's standard by which we are to understand what a *holy* human is? The answer is found in Jesus's life, death and resurrection.

Jesus fully embodied the divine nature: "For it was the Father's good pleasure for all the fullness to dwell in Him." Paul explains: "For in Him all the fullness of Deity dwells in bodily form" (Col. 1:19; 2:9). Jesus is the personification of a *holy* person. How did he manifest holiness? He was always committed to his Father's will. He was never vulgar or profane. His behavior was always constructive. He spoke only the truth, was helpful, kind, patient and gentle. He sought the best for others, was pure in his selflessness toward others. He never made excuses or needed to apologize for any misconduct—omission or commission. He was perfectly *holy*.

But how are we to become *holy*? As the Holy Spirit imparts *true knowledge* to our minds, it is self-evident that we are not like Jesus in many ways—even though there is an accompanying desire to be like him. The Spirit introduces us to the process of putting off and putting on whereby we begin to embrace the idea of dying to self. God's gift of true knowledge is thus deposited in an old nature that is replaced piece by piece over time, so that the new nature is set free to become more and more like Christ.

Putting off the old and putting on the new can be as simple as fleeing from what we know tempts us to dishonor Christ. For example, flee *pornography* wherever it appears. It can be found with a press of the button; it can be avoided with a press of the button! There is nothing *holy* associated with pornography. Nor is there anything holy associated with the worship of our *stomach*—so we will flee *gluttony*, if that is our temptation. Putting off the old and putting on the new is illustrated in Figure 16.3.

The Bible describes the process of laying aside the old and taking up the new as taking time. The old is put aside; the new is put on. Paul, for example, exhorts, "Clean out the old leaven so that you may be a new lump.... Therefore let us celebrate the feast, not with old leaven, nor with the leaven of malice and wickedness, but with the unleavened bread of sincerity and truth" (1 Cor. 5:7-8). Paul uses malice and wickedness as examples of what is unholy and must be put off, and sincerity and

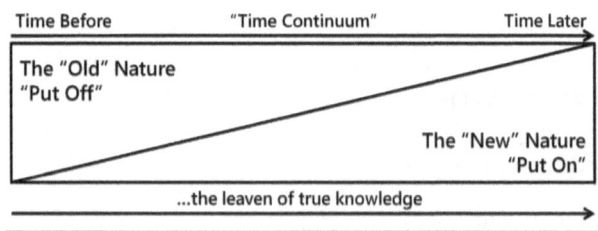

Figure 16.3 *Putting Off and Putting On*

truth as what is holy and must be put on. He frequently uses the ideas of putting off and putting on in his letters to churches.[123]

Christ asks his followers, for example, to put off the inappropriate use of their tongues. Stop: gossiping, slandering, saying untrue things, and things that hurt others' feelings when it is not helpful. And he asks his people to put on a Christlike tongue. Say things that are instructive, encouraging, kind, supportive, and that help others to grow spiritually. We are to ask Christ's Spirit who resides in us for help, for "apart from Me you can do nothing" (John 15:5). He may convict us when these things are not done, and remind us the need to do them when we have an opportunity to be salt and light. And this process of putting off and putting on is extended to our eyes, hands, ears, feet, stomach, sexual organs, and other areas where our desires tend to lead us into excesses or inappropriate expressions of good things. This is a lifelong endeavor to which Christ calls us as we take up our cross daily and follow Him (Luke 9:23).[124]

Other Divine Attributes and True Knowledge

God uses his *immutability* to transform us. He uses his unfailing faithfulness to us, in the face of our faithlessness, to awaken us to his unchanging nature. He makes us aware that we are as distractible as a child with too many Christmas presents, and that he is ever attentive to our needs. He is never distracted, but is steady and unwavering. His promises are certain to be kept. He is truly "the same yesterday, today, and forever" (Heb. 13:8). We must realize that "He who began a good work in you will perfect it until the day of Christ Jesus" (Phil. 1:6).

His being immutable strengthens us as *we partake of his divine nature*. His immutability encourages our steadfast loyalty to him. The *true knowledge* we receive about his immutability transforms us. For example, if I have the habit of beginning projects with great enthusiasm and of quitting them before they are finished, God's grace may change my resolve to finish what I start. Or perhaps I realize I have not taken my word seriously enough, and that I am not always faithful in doing what I promised. Christ is not like this. By his grace, I can learn to put off the old and put on the new.

God imparts *true knowledge* to us by making us aware of the significance of his being an *omnipresent* Spirit. He can, if he chooses, transform our minds by bringing this truth to our hearts during a particular time of need, when a close friend or spouse abandons us. We could believe the void in our spirit was unfillable, but the Holy Spirit, just as we are sinking into despair, may fill us with the assurance of God's unfailing presence and fidelity. He can fill a heart to overflowing with the realization that his promise is certain: "I will never desert you, nor will I ever forsake you" (Heb. 13:5). That he never leaves us in whom he takes up residence *leavens* a wilting spirit. This truth brings profound hope, courage, comfort, joy, and contentment.

This kind of *true knowledge* about God can also lead us to the cross where we long, by God's grace, to *partake of his divine nature* and show it by attentiveness to

---

[123] See: Rom. 6:2-14; 2 Cor. 5:17; Eph. 4:20-24; Col. 3:9-10.
[124] See also: Matt. 10:38; 16:24; Mark 8:34; 10:21; and Luke 14:27.

others' needs when they are all alone. We grow in our desire to put on a new concern for the lonely!

God can use his being absolutely *wise* to bring *true knowledge* to our minds. He can bring to flower the realization that life's worst hurts have been under his watchful eye and that he has redeemed them by using them to conform us to Christ's likeness (Rom. 8:29). God, in his mercy, can place in our hearts the realization that what others intended for evil, he allowed to occur to bring about a greater good. Understanding that everything works for our good is a sweet balm to a weary spirit. Perhaps in our old age, when looking back on the terrible hurts that occurred years ago, we will realize that God has used them to bind us to Christ and transform us into his likeness. Such *true knowledge leavens* the rest of our world/life-view.

Receiving such *true knowledge* can build within the recipients a reservoir of *wisdom* that they praise the Lord for when, in his merciful providence, they have opportunity to share a word of encouragement with someone hurting. For example, if an older person who has taught Sunday school for years, has been appropriately *transparent* about the trials God faithfully led him or her through, then those experiences can be an encouragement—for the person being tested knows the teacher too has been tested, and delivered.

The presence of elders in a church is God's provision—for a number of his older children have acquired wisdom over the years. They have become *partakers* of *God's wisdom* by simply being old and having been shepherded by the Holy Spirit. Life's experiences, as we walk with Christ, will generally lead us to an understanding of what to put on and what to put off regarding the common sense concerns of life.

Awakening to the reality of just how *good* God is can also transport our spirit into songs of joy. God uses our seeing the created beauty that surrounds us and cause us to become conscious of the endless bounty of the benefits flowing from its wellspring. This can cause us to marvel at the display of his goodness that is all around us! He can use simple things like these to make us thankful. He can refresh our memories of prior forgiveness for grievous sins of our youth and give us a heart of gratitude. God's washing us with the Word and removing our sense of guilt can humble us to the core so we will never be the same (Eph. 5:26; Titus 3:5). *True knowledge* can free us to enjoy God and the many things he gives us.

As God awakens us to how good he is through the gift of *true knowledge* regarding the *goodness* of his nature, it is natural for us to be good even as he is good. (Only God is *truly* good.) Scripture offers us many examples of ways we too can be good—the giving of a cup of water to a thirsty person; clothing those in need; feeding the poor; caring for widows and orphans; visiting those who are in jail; helping the sick. The *partaking of the divine nature* of Christ requires the putting off of apathy, neglect, bad attitudes, and other inhibiters, and the putting on of self-sacrifice, care, and commitment of time, money and self. There is little or no putting on without the struggle of putting off.

The Spirit uses our reading of Christ's calling Lazarus from the tomb to awaken us to God's *omnipotence*. Or Christ's resurrection takes on a new place in our understanding of God's commitment to us. The *true knowledge* of either event may become a pillar in a Christian's faith-structure as God's power over death becomes a reality. We learn to *pray* for those things that only God has the power to do, and to seek the Spirit's help in putting off, for example, a bad temper, and his aid in putting on a patient, kindly ability to deal with exasperating situations.

Not only is God *omniscient* regarding everything past, present, future, and suppositional, he is also omniscient regarding *himself*. He knows that his attributes bring glory to his name when impressed on his people's hearts in *true knowledge*. Each attribute of God is transforming when discerned as *true knowledge*. And this in turn leavens not only the *mind* but the *rest* of the heart too. God's gift of *true knowledge* to believers is an act of *grace*, for it is never deserved!

And God's gift of true knowledge of himself has a leavening effect far beyond the renovation of our understanding of him. The *leaven of true knowledge* shows itself throughout our lives. This is what Christ referring to, "The kingdom of heaven is like *leaven*, which a woman took and hid in three pecks of flour *until it was all leavened*" (Matt. 13:33)? One of the earliest indications of God's leaven in our lives is a growing interest in the Word. Our love, comprehension, and application of the Word is elevated to new heights. The Word, in the hands of the Spirit, draws us to Christ. We see him and hear him in the Word. His *testimonies, precepts, and judgments* are all embodied in the Word, and these become Christ's guiding help for us as he dwells in us. We are motivated to put off the old and put on the new in attitudes, thoughts, desires and behavior that bring glory to Christ *in* us.

We turn our attention now to the element of the *mind* that concerns *understanding*. With *true knowledge*, our understanding of people and life is transformed. Joseph's life offers a good illustration. His brothers' resentment of him grew so intense that they sold him to some Midianite traders who resold him in Egypt to Potiphar, an officer of Pharaoh. Potiphar noted God's blessing on Joseph, and put him in charge of everything except his wife, who later framed Joseph and had him thrown in prison. However, Pharaoh removed Joseph from prison and elevated him to the second-highest position in Egypt. After seven fruitful years a life-threatening famine came that extended beyond Egypt, even into Canaan where Joseph's family lived. The famine forced Jacob to send Joseph's brothers to Egypt to buy grain. The same brothers who sold Joseph into slavery stood before him, requesting to buy grain. Upon discovering that the Egyptian lord was their brother Joseph, they feared for their lives. They thought he would seek revenge. Joseph's response reveals a deep *understanding* on his part of God's purposes:

> And now do not be grieved or angry with yourselves, because you sold me here, for God sent me before you to preserve life . . . . It was not you who sent me here, but God. (Gen. 45:5, 8)

> But Joseph said to them, Do not be afraid, for am I in God's place? As for you, you meant evil against me, but God meant it for good . . . . (Gen. 50:20)

Joseph's *understanding* had been *leavened* with the *true knowledge* regarding God. Joseph had been given *true knowledge* of God's *sovereign* rule over all events.

How else could he have said to his brothers, "God sent me . . . it was not you who sent me." And in his statement to his brothers, "God meant it for good," Joseph also shows his true knowledge that God is *good*.

God warns us not to boast of our natural power or worldly wisdom, . . . "but let him who boasts boast of this, that he *understands* and *knows Me*, that I am the LORD" (Jer. 9:23-24). When God instructed Moses regarding the tabernacle's construction, he said that he prepared specific people to work on it. He told Moses, "See, I have called by name Bezalel . . . and I have filled him with the Spirit of God in *wisdom*, in *understanding*, in *knowledge*, and in all kinds of craftsmanship" (Ex. 31:2-3). Bezalel had Spirit-given wisdom, understanding, and knowledge.

Understanding that is the fruit of the *leaven of true knowledge* regarding God is *true* understanding. It manifests the mind of Christ. It is generated by the develpmental work of the Holy Spirit. It adjusts and transforms its possessors' world/life-views. It reflects the impact of all that transpires in the person's renovated mind. It is a gift from the Spirit of the Lord, who is referred to in Isaiah as the spirit of *wisdom* and *understanding* (11:2). It manifests his work.

Wisdom is another aspect of the nature of the Spirit of the Lord. Wisdom is the path that leads to godly ends. Wisdom is God's way of proceeding; it employs God's methods; it is the path God would have us take. Wisdom in its fullness belongs only to God, but we have access to his wisdom through his Word and the leading of the Holy Spirit. We are to walk in the light of his Word. We are to follow his prescribed paths. To do so is itself a manifestation of wisdom.

Things we thought were wise before salvation we now consider unwise, and what we deemed unwise earlier we now consider wise. After rebirth the beliefs we had of God and the universe are transformed. Our foundational presuppositions regarding the origin of the universe and of God's purpose for it are changed. Stewardship, as a lifestyle-calling, begins to take hold. Caring for our neighbors takes on new meaning. Every corner of our thinking is affected by the *leaven of true knowledge*. Our minds are renovated by it! It transforms our *understanding* of God, ourselves, and everything else! It brings *wisdom*, the light to be sought and walked in.

Conclusion

Our ontological beliefs, knowledge, understanding, and wisdom are all transformed in our mind by the gift of true knowledge that leavens everything else. Our world/life-view, biblical integration, and understanding of self are leavened. The one given true knowledge becomes a new person in Christ who slowly partakes of the divine nature.

We now look at how a transformed *mind* is united with the *passions* and how the two interact. The *leavening* process that begins in the *mind* osmotically permeates the *entire* heart of the Christian. The putting on and putting off process, while rooted in the *mind*, and aided or resisted in the *will*, is primarily manifested by the renovated *passions*. We will consider this next.

17

The Heart: The Location of Our Passions—Desires, Affections, and Core Identity Needs

Rejoice with those who rejoice, and weep with those who weep.
(Rom. 12:15)

The exhortation to weep with those who weep was a primary reason why I did not enter the pastorate as a young man. I could laugh, but I could not weep when others wept. The tendency to avoid my emotions was so deeply entrenched that, when a substantial array of emotions would begin to rise and threaten my emotional comfort zone, my mind would grab hold of my emotions and overwhelm them with rational thoughts which alleviated the discomfort. I was in my thirties before God began to transform this defensive mechanism in my make-up. And four decades later, there are still occasions when my former tendency to avoid feelings reappears—but the Spirit has helped me much in putting off this old habit.

Many Christians are confused about the relationship between their mind and their passions, the heart's component encompassing desires, affections, and identity needs. And our passions are always clothed in feelings and emotions. They are the positive and negative barometer indicating the intensity of our affections or aversions. It is either people who distrust their feelings, or people uncomfortable with their minds, who foster the confusion. The biblical view of the relationship between our mind and our passions is important, because God works to renovate both in believers. What, then, is the relationship between the mind, passions and heart?

Many consider the *heart* and the *mind* as two different things. The *heart* is the location of sympathy, kindness, and empathy, where tenderness and compassion reside. It is the location of all of the good (and bad) personality. They believe these qualities reside in the *heart*. In fact, they *do*—in the *passions* component of the heart. On the other hand, these same people often believe the mind is *separate* from the heart rather than understanding that the mind is a *component* of the heart. The mind is suspect; it is to be distrusted. As many distrust the *mind* as distrust emotions. They believe that the mind is where people think and generate confusing theological theories that create divisions in the church. And they believe that thinkers rarely do anything with their thoughts to help people with genuine needs. They view the mind as the cold, logical, analytical component of the human personality, which is more likely to rationalize why a poor beggar should *not* be given a handout on the street than it is to feel compassion. To them, the heart is warm; the mind is cold. The heart is tender; the mind is suspicious and hard.

Those uncomfortable with feelings and those uncomfortable with the mind both need God's renovating grace. These unbiblical views of the *heart* and *mind* are found throughout the Christian community. God's revelation, however, is very clear. The mind is a *component* of the heart and not an entity separate from it.

Some of our foremost Christian writers, like C. S. Lewis, have attempted to correct some of the worst fallout coming from this false dichotomy, but even they have left the *heart* separated from the *mind*. For example, Lewis said, "The heart never takes the place of the head: but it can, and should, obey it."[125] The *heart* and *head* are seen as different things in this statement rather than it viewing the head (mind) as a component of the heart. Lewis uses the word heart to connote the seat of our *feelings* and head to refer to our *minds*—which gives the impression that the mind is *not* part of the heart. He is correct that our *felt desires* should be in sync with our *head* (mind), but he nonetheless separates the two inappropriately. The *heart* is the overarching repository of the *mind, passions* and *will*.

Usually the inappropriate distinction between *mind* and *heart* expresses an unarticulated belief that the heart's *passions* are more important than its *mind*. And this belief often comes with another assumption: the mind's thoughts will not result in godly actions. It is believed that the thoughts will either be the end of it (the object is only thought about), or the thoughts will lead to a subverted, rationalized action. The belief that the *desires* and *affections* are more important than the *mind* is often an unconscious and mistaken belief that *desires* and *affections* are the *heart of the heart*. Advocates often assume that these qualities should override the *mind*. C. S. Lewis offered his antidote: "the heart . . . can, and should, obey it [the head—*mind*]." He is biblically correct with these qualifications: (1) the *heart*, as he uses it, refers to the *passions*; and (2) the *mind* accurately reflects the *mind of Christ*. But Scripture envisions our growing to understand that the heart is the *seat* of our *mind, passions* and *will*, and that all three are to be, by God's *grace*, transformed so that they are in harmony, displaying Christlike qualities.

Why did we choose the word "passions" to represent the component of the heart encompassing *desires, affections,* and *identity needs*? *Strong's Concordance* is keyed to the Authorized and Revised translations of the Bible, and it lists "passion"—singular—only one time, in Acts 1:3. The *NASB Interlinear Greek-English New Testament*[126] translates the Greek word *pascho*, found in Acts 1:3, "he suffered," referring to Christ's suffering—his passion. Similarly, *Strong's Concordance* only lists the word "passions"—plural—two times, in Acts 14:15 and James 5:17. In Acts 14:15 the Greek word *homoiopathes* is rendered in the *NASB Interlinear Greek-English New Testament* "of like nature," and in James 5:17 it is translated "of like feeling." These are the only three references to "passion" in *Strong's Concordance*, so the word "passions" is not commonly used in the Bible. But we use the word because it connotes a disposition or inclination of the *heart* which incorporates God-created emotions and zeal that accompany the *desires*,

---

[125] C. S. Lewis, *The Abolition of Man* (HarperSanFrancisco: HarperCollins Edition, 2001), 19.
[126] *The NASB Interlinear Greek-English New Testament* (Grand Rapids: Zondervan, 1984), p. 462.

affections, and *identity needs* that are so central to the human character. "Passions" covers the *entirety* of a person's *desires, affections,* and *identity needs* that are clothed in moods, tendencies, and temperament—that are all related to, but different from, their thought processes and volition. As we used "mind" to encompass innate knowledge, beliefs, knowledge, true knowledge, understanding, and wisdom, we use "passions" as embracing the sum of our *desires, affections,* and *identity needs.*

We will now begin unpacking the Passions component of our Heart illustration. The heart's *Mind* and *Passions* portions, along with their subcomponents, are shown below. We start by discussing the subcomponents of the Passions, and the interrelationship between them and the Mind.

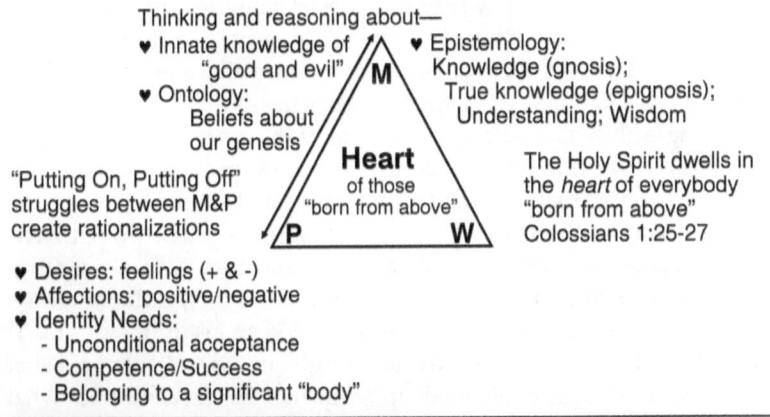

Figure 17.1 *Subcomponents of the Passions*

The first ♥ under the Passions component of the Heart—♥ Desires: feelings (+ & −)—introduces us to the first broad subcomponent of our *passions* that is laid before us in Scripture. There are, in fact, numerous desires described and discussed in the Bible. It is also interesting to note that there are times when the biblical context and the specific word chosen to describe a particular desire reveals that the desire being portrayed is almost entirely related to an emotional feeling. On other occasions, however, desires are more closely tied to the mind and its logical functions. This wide array of possible interconnections—thought of as representing a continuum of possible relationships between one's emotions/feelings associated with their desires and their intellectual faculties—can confuse people about the relationship that exists between their desires ↔ feelings/emotions ↔ mind. The closer the desire is to the purely emotional end of the desires continuum, and the stronger it is, and when there is an accompanying conflict between the *desire* and what is known deep in the *mind* to be the appropriate thing to do, the more likely we are to be confronted with a temptation to *rationalize* our way out of the conflict—to justify seeking what we *desire*. (See the 'Putting On, Putting Off' struggles between M & P line in Figure 17.1 above.) The intensity of the emotion that accompanies a desire can be graphically depicted as follows:

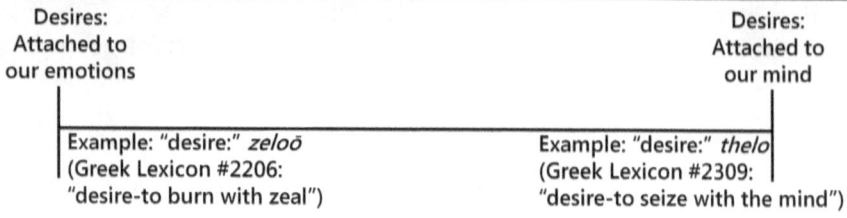

Figure 17.2 *Desires Attachment Continuum*

Both Hebrew and Greek have a diverse array of words translated into English as *desires*, and these fall on a desires attachment continuum of emotional and mental intensity. There are twenty different Hebrew words[127] and fourteen Greek words[128] translated as "desire" (noun) or "to desire" (verb).The two New Testament words placed on the ends of the continuum above illustrate this. The Greek word *zeloō* is emotional, connoting emotions raised to the boiling point: the desire is burning with zeal. And at the other end of the continuum the word *thelo* is used, because it connotes that the desire has the deepest involvement of the mind. This word implies that the desire is under the mind's control.

The Bible expresses our fallen propensity to *desire* what we do not have in various ways, that grow in their intensity as they move from *desires* → *longing* → *lusting* → *coveting* → to a sinful thought-pattern or action. As the intensity of longing grows, so does rationalizing what is wanted to justify the desire. This occurs so that what is *desired* is accepted as all right, or even elevated to what is deserved.[129] The effort is generally made to reconcile what is *desired* with what is *thought*. To do otherwise is to do what we know is wrong and to do it anyway. Such acts are called sins of presumption. King David asked God to "keep back Your servant from presumptuous sins; let them not rule over me; then I will be blameless, and I shall be acquitted of great transgression" (Ps. 19:13). Peter wrote with this in mind, "The Lord knows how to rescue the godly from temptation, and keep the unrighteous under punishment for the Day of Judgment, and especially those who indulge the flesh in its corrupt desires and despise authority. Daring, self-willed, they do not tremble when they revile angelic majesties" (2 Peter 2:9-10).

The various Hebrew and Greek words translated "desire" carry a range of meanings: the longing to win souls to Christ; to desire empty glory; to desire pardon; to desire information; to think it is right for me to have it; demanding for one's self; to lust after; to covet; to pine after; making a simple request. The

---

[127] Twenty Old Testament Hebrew words translated as desire: *abeh* (Lexical # 15); *abiyownah* (# 35); *avah* (# 183); *amar* (# 559); *bah* (# 1156); *baqash* (# 1245); *chamad* (# 2530); *chephets* (# 2656); *chashaq* (# 2836); *kacaph* (# 3700); *maavay* (# 3970); *machmad* (# 4261); *mishalah* (# 4862); *nephesh* (# 5315); *ratson* (# 7522); *shael* (# 7592); *shaaph* (# 7602); *taavah* (# 8378); *tav* (# 8420); *tshuwqah* (# 8669).
[128] Fourteen New Testament Greek words translated as desire: *aiteo* (# 154); *axioō* (# 515); *exaiteomai* (# 1809); *eperotao* (# 1905); *epithumeo* (# 1937); *epipothia* (# 1974); *erotao* (# 2065); *eudokia* (# 2107); *zeloō* (# 2206); *thelo* (# 2309); *himeiromai* (# 2442); *kenodoxos* (# 2755); *oregomai* (# 3713); *parakaleo* (# 3870).
[129] Read: Rom. 7:21–8:2 and James 4:1-4.

emotional intensity associated with these words is as far ranging as their meanings. Some are hot or heavy desires and others are simple likes and wants. Some are strong desires and others are weak ones. These all carry either positive or negative *feelings*.

Humans were created to *desire*. Adam and Eve possessed this inherent quality before they fell. This is plain: "When the woman saw that the tree was good for food, and that it was a delight to the eyes, and that the tree was *desirable* to make one wise, she took from its fruit and ate" (Gen. 3:6). Eve saw these things regarding the tree before she fell but after she was deceived by the Serpent (Gen. 3:13; 2 Cor. 11:3). But after the fall the desires component of human nature became distorted and deformed, so that now our eye is not satisfied with seeing, nor the ear filled with hearing (Eccl. 1:8).

The fall perverted the heart's *desires* component as well as its *mind* component. When people are not closely related to God, they do not desire what he desires. They replace him in their hearts with created things. They worship the creation, not the Creator. They desire their own glory more than God's glory. They desire things that serve their own self-interest and not things that serve God's interest.

Only the Spirit harnesses our insatiable desires for what we do not have. Paul says that contentment is a state of *mind* that needs to be *learned* over time, with the Spirit's help. The Spirit helps our *minds* to bring our *desires* under control and into conformity with what God desires. The *desires* and *mind* are unified only by God's transforming grace.

> I have learned to be content in whatever circumstances I am. I know how to get along with humble means, and I also know how to live in prosperity; in any and every circumstance I have learned the secret of being filled and going hungry, both of having abundance and suffering need. I can do all things through Him who strengthens me. (Phil. 4:11-13)

The Holy Spirit in us makes the heart changes needed regarding our perverted desires. He renews our hearts. Like Paul we can learn to be content and to accept diverse circumstances. How? By asking God to give us the true knowledge that whatever befalls us is under his rule rooted in his loving intention to conform us to Christ. He trains us to *trust* him.

God promised to renovate two more areas of the heart as he restores us in Christ's image:

> Lay aside the old self, which is being corrupted in accordance with the *lusts of deceit*, and that you be *renewed* in the spirit of your *mind*, and put on the new self, which in the *likeness* [image] of God has been created in *righteousness* and *holiness* of the *truth*. (Eph. 4:22-24)

As our partaking of God's nature depends on being *leavened with true knowledge of God*, it also depends on our being restored to Christ's likeness in *righteousness* and *holiness* by the Spirit. What does this mean? It means our *passions* need renovation so we *desire* what God desires. And what is that? He desires us to be *righteous*—to be straight, right, fair, and just. These are *qualities* that govern mature Christians' *passions*. And God wants us to be *holy*, so *holiness* also must be restored. The Holy Spirit must renovate us so that we are set apart to manifest what is good and pure. Both of these qualities must be rebuilt into our character. The old nature is not dedicated to them. We are, by God's hand, to become people who *desire* what is straight, right, and fair, as God is straight, right, and fair. And we are to remain dedicated to becoming *holy*—consecrated, set apart, and pure—like *Christ*, in our focus and commitments.

It is only the *mind* that possesses the *true knowledge* of God, and thereby *knows* wholesome, God-honoring *desires*. It is the *mind* that informs us if the desire is *godly* or not. It is the *mind alone*, that engages a desire by evaluating it and deciding if it is worthy of pursuing. A battle between the *desires* and the *mind* is not uncommon in maturing Christians' lives. But as C. S. Lewis said, the desires, with their accompanying feelings, must obey the mind. There is always a residual of our old nature in us warring with our new nature, and we thus frequently are tempted to rationalize to satisfy wayward desires. But Christ *in* us helps us overcome the ungodly desires. Figure 17.1 illustrates the struggle we face by the arrow that runs between the *Mind* and the *Passions* components in the Heart, and is labeled "the 'Putting On, Putting Off' struggles between M & P create rationalizations." We are tempted to rationalize when there is a disconnect between what we know and what we desire.

As the Holy Spirit must renovate us by giving us true knowledge of God, he must also renovate us in righteousness and holiness if we are to partake of God's nature. The Bible reveals these three areas require renovation for us to be restored to the image of the Triune God. And this must take place if the *mind* and *desires* are to become united and mutually supportive.

• • • • •

The second ♥ label under the Passions component of the Heart (in Figure 17.1) draws attention to the presence of positive and negative *affections* found there. We note that Jonathan Edwards employs the word "affections" in his *The Religious Affections* in a slightly different *relational* thrust from that used here.[130] Edwards understood the *religious affections* to be the more vigorous and sensible exercise of the *inclination* and *will* of the soul[131] in its manifestation of the soul's love to Christ and joy in Christ.[132] Edwards' use of the word affections is clear and consistent throughout his work. We will treat the *inclination* to love Christ separately and not include it with the *will* component of the heart as Edwards did. And we treat our *affections* as a subcomponent of our Passions, which also includes our *identity needs* and *desires*. We do this not because there is anything wrong with what Edwards did—for the heart is composed of the *mind, passions, and will*—but he did not focus on the biblical revelation regarding the *entire heart*. He focused on what he called true religion, and the religious affections that must

---

[130] Jonathan Edwards, *The Religious Affections* (Carlisle, PA: The Banner of Truth, 1961; first published 1746).
[131] Ibid., 24.
[132] Ibid., 22-23.

be manifested if one is to believe he or she demonstrates true religion.[133] Edwards was concerned that many who thought they were Christians were self-deceived. True Christians grow in and manifest religious affections, and do not simply attend church. Our focus is different from Edwards'. We develop a holistic model of the heart that lets us comprehend how God imparts aspects of his nature to restore his children to Christ's image, which is manifested in Christlikeness.

The *affections* are associated with what a person either loves or hates. And Christ says what he *desires* regarding the temperature of our affections. God takes no delight in apathy, or lukewarm commitments:

> And to the angel of the church in Laodicea write: the Amen, the faithful and true Witness, the Beginning of the creation of God, says this: 'I know your deeds, that you are neither cold nor hot; I wish that you were cold or hot. So because you are lukewarm, and neither hot nor cold, I will spit you out of My mouth.... Those whom I love, I reprove and discipline; therefore *be zealous* ['hot'] and repent.' (Rev. 3:14-16, 19)

Christ desires us to love passionately all that is godly, and to hate all that is ungodly. Righteousness and unrighteousness have nothing in common. What is unholy does not belong with what is holy. God notes and remembers his people's groans when they encounter what is ungodly. The groans are accounted to them as righteousness (Ezek. 9:4-10). The repetitiveness of some evils in society make it easy to become accustomed to them and to overlook them. We can easily cease to be grieved by ungodly conduct. We can end up taking for granted the perversions of righteousness. But this should not be. Apathy, losing interest in changing destructive lifestyles, or becoming callous to any sin reflect a lukewarm heart and grieve Christ. We are called to repent if we are lukewarm concerning persistent sins. Sin results in death. And God takes no delight in death, not even the death of the wicked (Ezek. 18:23, 32).

There are holy and unholy *affections*. And for what does God desire us to have holy affections? Jonathan Edwards listed what he considered to be at the center of God's heart for which he wants us to have *holy* affections: fear, hope, love, hatred, desire, joy, sorrow, gratitude, compassion, and zeal.[134] We will elaborate on what it means to have *affection* for each of these ten potential heart-qualities.

Ten Potential Heart-qualities

1. *Fear*

The idea of loving fear is incredulous to those who have not been *taught by God* to love it. But it is not a general idea of fear that we are to learn to love; it is a specific fear. It is the fear of the Lord that we are to be taught. God *desires* to teach his children to fear him: "Come, you children, listen to me; I will *teach* you the fear of the LORD" (Ps. 34:11).

---

[133] Ibid., 21-48.
[134] Ibid., 31.

The fear of the LORD is a theme repeated throughout Scripture. And *learning to fear the Lord* is a point repeatedly made in Deuteronomy (4:10; 14:23; 17:19; and 31:12-13). Joseph even used his fear of God as *the* primary reason why his brothers ought to believe him: "Do this [go home and bring your younger brother back] and live, for I fear God" (Gen. 42:18). Joseph told his brothers he feared God too much to lie. And Jethro, Moses' father-in-law, counseled him to select judges from among the people to help him cope with the overload of complaints, and his recommended criteria for selection was: ". . . able men *who fear God*, men of truth, those who hate dishonest gain" (Ex. 18:21). But those who reject *true knowledge*—accurate, Spirit-imparted knowledge of God—choose to remain separated from the fear of the LORD to their own destruction (Prov. 1:29).

The *wrath* of God always appears in any list of his attributes because of its prominence in Scripture. God is a God of wrath! And Christ became incarnate to be a propitiation for us by absorbing God's wrath in our stead. Christ took our punishment. Peter illustrates well the wrath of God:

> For if God did not spare angels when they sinned, but cast them into hell and committed them to pits of darkness, reserved for judgment; and did not spare the ancient world, but preserved Noah, a preacher of righteousness, with seven others, when He brought a flood upon the world of the ungodly, and if He condemned the cities of Sodom and Gomorrah to destruction by reducing them to ashes, having made them an example to those who live ungodly thereafter . . . then the Lord knows how . . . to keep the unrighteous under punishment for the day of judgment. (2 Peter 2:4-6, 9)

We must remember God is to be feared—both in *terror* and *awe*. Isaiah tasted the terror of God (Isa. 6:5). Daniel was terrorized by his vision of the pre-incarnate Christ (Dan. 10:1-12). John fell to the ground as dead when Christ, years after his resurrection, appeared to him on Patmos (Rev. 1:9-20). Persons Christ draws to himself, when convicted by the Spirit that they deserve God's eternal punishment, may experience genuine terror. But this fear is replaced through the administration of God's grace in assured forgiveness showered upon new believers by the Holy Spirit. The Christian is not to live in terror but is to learn that God is to be greatly feared when he is rejected. Any thought of turning away from God should strike terror in our hearts.

The other end of the fear continuum is the *goal* of fear—to be filled with *awe* regarding God. He wants his people to *truly know* him, not merely know about him. And the *true knowledge* of him is accompanied by a sense of awe when this special, God-imparted knowledge is uppermost in our minds. Who but God could plan and speak into existence so awesome a universe out of what was not even visible (Heb. 11:3)? Who else can maintain all that has been created (Col. 1:17; Heb. 1:3)? Who else is omnipresent, holy, good, omnipotent, immutable, infinitely wise, and sovereign? Who else holds so majestic a position of Headship in the universe and beyond? Who else elicits from his image-bearers gratitude, adoration, and heartfelt worship? Time devoted to contemplating God, in light of his revealed *true knowledge* of himself, will necessarily generate an inner feeling of *awe* in the person blessed by his gift of *true knowledge*.

2. Hope

Hope in Scripture looks forward to the certainty of the fulfillment of those things God has either revealed about his future activities, or his promises to his children of resurrection and eternal life. Hope cannot be separated from God or his promises. Biblical hope is waiting and believing God will accomplish his announced intentions at his time. Hope is akin to trust. It is accompanied by a sense of security because it is rooted in *true knowledge* of God and his revealed will. As Jonathan Edwards pointed out, hope is one of the three great things of which [true] religion consists[135] — faith, *hope,* love (1 Cor. 13:13). Hope is not a vaporous concept in the Bible but a future promise made certain by God's other performances. God said he would do, thus-and-so and then did; therefore, when he tells me he will do this-and-that, I believe him, and wait with *hope* for its fulfillment. The *affections* of our *heart* should be attached to God and all his promises. We love him and hope in him!

3. Love

Christians should long to grow in their capacity to love as Christ has loved. Love is a mark of their relationship to Christ — "By this all men will know that you are My disciples, if you have love for one another" (John 13:35). To love as Christ has loved certifies our authenticity (1 John 4:11-13). *Agape* love is selfless. It is God's gift to his children, enabling them to die to self and live for Christ. It is the ability to do all for Christ. It reveals the genuine transformation of the *heart's passions* that finds the individual lovingly putting others before him or herself. It considers the interests of others before its own interests. It is Christ-centeredness that spills over into other-centeredness and displaces self-centeredness. Of all the *passions* the *heart* could desire to manifest, the ability to *love* is the most important.[136]

4. Hatred

Like fear, many Christians would not consider hatred something believers should desire. This misperception, however, rests in the false belief that to hate is ungodly. This may be our first thought but it is not true. To hate what God hates is to be like God:

> He no longer regards the offering or accepts it with favor from your hand. Yet you say, "For what reason?" Because the LORD has been a witness between you and the wife of your youth, against whom you have dealt treacherously, though she is your companion and your wife by covenant. But *not one has done so who has a remnant of the Spirit.* . . . Take heed then to your spirit, and let no one deal treacherously against the wife of your youth. For *I hate* divorce, says the LORD, the God of Israel, and *him who covers his garment with wrong,* says the LORD of hosts. So take heed to your spirit, that you *do not deal treacherously.* (Mal. 2:13-16)

---

[135] Ibid., 31.
[136] Chapter 14, "God Is Love: What Does This Really Mean?" might be profitably reviewed again at this juncture.

There are things the Lord hates, and his children are to hate those things. The passage above speaks of divorce, what is wrong, and things treacherous. Divorce is easily defined, but things that are wrong cast a broad shadow. What is meant by wrong? What is wrong is anything not in conformity with God's Word. God hates all things that break his commandments, ways, or judgments—because he is *holy*. And he hates all that is ungodly, for such things lead to an eternal separation between him and those who practice them. We are to be holy as he is holy, consecrated in the pursuit of righteousness. These are what we are being transformed into as we are remade in his image. Christians should find abhorrent anything God finds unholy, untruthful, or unloving. We are to hate all such things with a passion. We are not, however, to hate the individuals who fall into such ungodly practices. They need our prayers, patience and witness.

5. Desire

Believers should yearn for God to build in their heart the desires that are in his heart. For example, "God *desires* all men to be saved and to come to the *epignosis* [true knowledge] of the truth" (1Tim. 2:4). That is, a true knowledge of Christ, for Christ is *truth* (John 14:6). God desires this. The Christian should have *affection* for such passions. Peter affirms the same desire of God: "The Lord is not slow about His promise . . . but is patient . . . not wishing for any to perish but for all to come to repentance" (2 Peter 3:9). God desired that the Jewish leaders who opposed Jesus would be saved, but they rejected God's purpose [their salvation] for themselves (Luke 7:30).[137]

All of God's commands involve showing love—one of his basic desires. Those being renovated in *true knowledge, righteousness,* and *holiness* love God's desires being done in their lives. God's desires become theirs. Christians' affections grow for all that God desires.

6. Joy

By God's common grace all humans experience a general joy under certain conditions. Examples include: someone having a sense of *satisfaction* at the completion of a job; having a good laugh at something funny. Being *merry* and *cheerful* are forms of general joy. These, however, are not the kinds of joy Christians are to set their hearts on.

That joy is Christ-related. The fall of our first parents created enmity between God and all their descendants. The regenerated are reconciled to God through Christ, and the old enmity is done away with.

> But now in Christ Jesus you who formerly were far off have been brought near by the blood of Christ. For He Himself is our *peace,* who . . . broke down the barrier of the dividing wall, by abolishing in His flesh the enmity, which is the Law of commandments contained in ordinances . . . thus establishing *peace,* and might reconcile [both Jews and Gentiles] to God through the cross, by it having put to death the enmity. (Eph. 2:13-16)

---

[137] The Greek word used in Luke 7:30 for "purpose" is *boule*, which means purpose or will, but *Thayer's Greek-English Lexicon of the New Testament* emphasizes that in the context of Luke 7:30 the word means especially of the purpose of God respecting the salvation of men through Christ—Lexical #1012.

The peace Christ established between the Father and those reconciled to him through Christ's finished work brings true *joy*. Jesus put it this way: "Peace I leave with you; My peace I give to you; not as the world gives do I give to you" (John 14:27). There is joy when war ceases. There is lasting joy put in place when the enmity between God and a new believer is eliminated. This is a Christ-related joy that accompanies salvation.

There is a joy that accompanies the *hope* associated with Christ's resurrection; with God's promises to his children in Christ; and with assurance of eternal life with Christ. These joys are all Christ-related. Indeed, all of God's special gifts bring joy to his children's hearts.

The gift of faith brings joy to believers even in the midst of great suffering. How much can one suffer and still retain joy in Christ? Joy is a fruit (a gift) of the Holy Spirit, and there is no known limit to its endurance (Gal. 5:22). The Bible even tells us that the joy set before him enabled Jesus to endure the cross (Heb. 12:2). We should long for Christ-related joys.

7. Sorrow

Like *fear* and *hatred*, sorrow seems at first blush a strange experience on which to set our affections. But sorrow is strong evidence of forthcoming humility. A common saying is, "A person cannot have a whole heart until they have first had a broken heart." This is similar to the axiom, "If one wants wine, he must first crush the grapes." I agree with those who believe the beatitudes in Matthew 5 have *first* an ever-increasing humbling direction, and then an increasingly encouraging thrust. They say the first three beatitudes point to the Spirit's work in preparing the *heart* to receive Christ's righteousness:

> Blessed are the poor in spirit, for theirs is the kingdom of heaven. (v. 3) [How poor in spirit is one to become?]
>
> Blessed are those who mourn, for they shall be comforted. (v. 4) [Become poor in spirit to the point of mourning.]
>
> Blessed are the meek [KJV], for they shall inherit the earth. (v. 5) [Poverty of spirit, and mourning, lead to acknowledging one's moral bankruptcy.]
>
> Blessed are those who hunger and thirst for righteousness, for they shall be satisfied. (v. 6) [It is God's will that his children will come to realize that Christ alone is their righteousness.]

This progression through the beatitudes is the humbling sense of direction they take before they turn upward in encouragement—the fourth beatitude, v. 6, is the foundational beatitude and grounds for the final outcome of the beatitudes (v. 12). The encouraging thrust proceeds as follows:

> Blessed are the *merciful*, for they shall receive *mercy*. (v. 7) [The Christian is merciful because he or she has received God's mercy—been given Christ's righteousness.]
>
> Blessed are the *pure in heart* [single focus on Christ], for they shall see God. (v. 8) [Those humbled by *sorrow*, and who accept Christ, will be blessed to see God.] etc.

James reveals this same truth when he wrote, "Be *miserable* and *mourn* and *weep*; let your laughter be turned into mourning, and your joy [general joy] to gloom. *Humble yourselves* in the presence of the Lord, and He will exalt you" (James 4:9-10). And how do people humble themselves? By remembering their unrighteousness compared to the infinitely righteous God, and their deserving God's wrath apart from Christ's righteousness imputed to them by God.

There is a *godly sorrow* that the Christian's affections should be set upon, for "the LORD is near to the brokenhearted, and saves those who are crushed in spirit" (Ps. 34:18). In fact, Christ was set apart by the Father "to bind up the brokenhearted . . . and . . . to comfort all who mourn" (Isa. 61:1-2). God designed godly sorrow produced by the internal work of the Holy Spirit to draw his children near to him in the full realization of his *glory* and their unworthiness.

8. Gratitude

Grateful passions manifest themselves in expressions of *thanksgiving*. Thanksgiving is a mark of real gratitude for assurance that God is in charge of everything. Paul admonishes, "Be anxious for nothing, but in *everything* by prayer and supplication with *thanksgiving* let your requests be made known to God. And the *peace* of God, which surpasses all comprehension, will guard your *hearts* and your *minds* in Christ Jesus" (Phil. 4:6-7). What does *everything with* thanksgiving include? Everything: food (John 6:11, 23); answered prayer (John 11:41); healing (Luke 17:16); deliverance from dangers (Acts 27:34-35); fruit from gospel proclamation (Col. 1:3-4); grace bestowed (1 Cor. 1:4); acceptance of God's Word (1 Thess. 2:13); participation of others in the gospel (Phil. 1:3-5); growth in faith (2 Thess. 1:3); election (2 Thess. 2:13); spiritual blessings (Col. 1:12); liberty in giving (2 Cor. 9:6-15); brothers and sisters in Christ (1 Thess. 3:9); deliverance from bondage to sin (Rom. 7:25); sacrificial service of others (Rom. 16:4); things we might have done but did not do (1 Cor. 1:14); gifts of the Spirit (1 Cor. 14:18).[138] Literally, we are to thank God for *everything*.

Passions distinguished by their *gratitude in everything* are united in love with Christ. They trust Christ with everything. They value his will over all other wills. They reside in humility. They are godly. They are passions to be highly sought in prayer.

9. Compassion

"And seeing the multitude, He [Christ] *felt compassion* for them, *because* they were distressed and dispirited like sheep without a shepherd" (Matt. 9:36). Compassion is a deeply felt emotion that wants to see relief brought to the hurting. *Racham* frequently speaks of compassion in the Old Testament (Lexical # 7356). It conveys tenderness, pity, and love that reside deep in the womb, as does a fetus being harbored and protected. *Splagchnizomai*, its New Testament corollary, (Lexical # 4697), points to deep feeling in the bowels of sympathy. Compassion is a feeling crying out to bring relief to others' hurt.

---

[138] I relied heavily on Wick Broomall, "Thanksgiving," *Baker's Dictionary of Theology* (Grand Rapids: Baker Book House, 1960), 516.

Compassion is the *feeling* that moves one to act graciously or mercifully: to pray; provide food, clothing, or shelter; to take time to listen; to offer good counsel; to bind up a wound; to give or lend money; to come alongside the hurting—and endless other ways of aiding others. Compassion is associated with grace and mercy—grace being the gift of something *undeserved*, and mercy being the setting aside of *deserved* punishment. God has shown compassion to us, a disposition of the *heart* that, when present in the life of professing Christians, offers evidence of their being renewed into the Savior's likeness.

10. Zeal

The zeal with which we pursue an objective says a great deal about what we value most. In Revelation 3:14-16, 19 Christ loathes a lukewarm spirit and calls for a *zeal* for his will. Christ would spit from his mouth those who are lukewarm. They are called to repent and by God's grace to rekindle a zeal for those things Christ desires. Those who love Christ are expected to walk in his ways. The redeemed are called to become like Christ! They are called to *love*, to *hate* that which God hates, to *desire* what he desires, to be *grateful* for Christ's benefits, to know godly *sorrow* and spiritual *joy*. They are given *hope* in God's many promises after they have learned to *fear* the Almighty. And they are to be *compassionate* as Christ is compassionate. And all these affections are to be manifested with a godly *zeal*.

• • • • •

The last ♥ symbol displayed under the Passions component of the Heart diagram (Figure 17.1) is the subcomponent "humans' Identity Needs."[139] There are three such needs common to all humans:
- Unconditional acceptance
- Competence/Success
- Belonging to a significant body

They are *needs* because God created us with these needs. And these needs are ultimately satisfied only in those who are regenerated and reunited with the Trinity. Those separated from God are consigned to the self-condemning effort of seeking their identity in the world apart from God. But we were created to identify with the Creator—not his creation. Separation from God distorts our world/life-view. We examine the biblical warrant for this hypothesis: Our true identity can only be found in the Triune God who created us in his image.

Identity Needs
Unconditional Acceptance

Earned acceptance is the plight of all who remain distanced from Christ. There are innumerable ways of earning acceptance. Children quickly learn that good behavior brings acceptance, and bad behavior brings negative responses from their parents. They do not think of it as *conditional* acceptance, but it often is.

---

[139] Chapter 1, footnote 8, recognized the work of Dr. William T. Kirwan as the source of the thoughts expressed in this portion of the chapter.

Good athletic performance earns the coach's attention and recognition in teammates' and fans' eyes. Good grades gain approval of teachers and parents. But some parents say, "You got a *B* in math. That's fair, but you could earn an *A* if you put your mind to it." They may think this encourages their child to do his or her best, but the child may well interpret it as "I love you *more* as you do better." It suggests that conditions must be met to earn *full* acceptance.

Many go through life only experiencing conditional acceptance—acceptance based on performance. A promotion at work signifies one is doing well and that his superiors approve of his performance. Gaining a position of power means that others have to respect your power or suffer the consequences—minimally, they need to feign acceptance or go elsewhere.

Acceptance earned by meeting some condition is acceptance without *rest*—the condition must be continually met. The Lord wants his people to enter his rest. Hebrews 3-4 speak of those who hold firm to their belief in Christ as those who will enter Christ's rest—rest from <u>earning</u> God's acceptance, an impossibility. The condition to be met to gain God's acceptance has been eternally established by him. Fallen humanity cannot meet God's acceptance requirement by anything they do. God enables those born from above to understand what Christ has done for them. Christ became the propitiation [the bearer of God's wrath] for our sins (1 John 4:10). He paid for our acceptance by the Father. By *faith* the Father's children receive his *unconditional acceptance through Christ's finished work*. Those in Christ rest from working to earn God's acceptance. They rest in Christ. He is their perfection and they find their rest in him.

God offers unconditional acceptance *in* Christ. Our being in him appears ten times in Ephesians 1:3-14. Being *in* Christ is the requirement for receiving God's unconditional acceptance in his *grace* and *mercy*. It is appropriated through faith—believing that Christ was the Son of God who died to redeem a people given him by the Father. It is a belief that the suffering and death of the Son on the cross satisfies God's just demands (Isaiah 53). The Father sent his Son to be our righteousness "that He might be *just* and the *justifier* of the one who has faith in Jesus" (Rom. 3:26). And *all of this was done for us.*

It is heartbreaking to see people wanting their fellow human beings' acceptance more than God's. This tragic *disposition* is seen in the life of King Saul. The Lord sent the prophet Samuel to Saul with instructions for him: "Go and strike Amalek [a foreign, wicked king] and utterly destroy all that he has, and do not spare him; but put to death both man and woman, child and infant, ox and sheep, camel and donkey." Saul defeated Amalek, but did not follow God's instructions. When Samuel confronted Saul regarding his disobedience, he insisted that he had obeyed. The prophet countered, "What then is this bleating of the sheep in my ears, and the lowing of the oxen which I hear?" Saul gave a lame explanation, but later confessed, "I have sinned; I have indeed transgressed the command of the LORD and your words, *because I feared the people and listened to their voice.*" God then rejected Saul from being king over Israel (1 Sam. 15:1-26). Saul wanted the acceptance of the people more than he feared God and wanted his acceptance. But the fear of the Lord is the beginning of wisdom.

John records another such account. Jesus had been in public ministry for about three years, and his crucifixion loomed, when this condemning account was written: "Nevertheless many even of the rulers believed in Him, but because of the Pharisees they were not confessing Him, for fear that they would be put out of the synagogue; for they *loved [agapao] the approval of men rather than the approval of God*" (John 12:42-43).

God made us with a *need for unconditional acceptance*. The world offers only *conditional acceptance*. A spouse or one's children may give real unconditional acceptance as they walk with Christ, but even their best love cannot bestow *eternal* acceptance. Until we know God's unconditional love in Christ, there will always remain a void in our hearts that is unfillable by any other person or thing. The conclusion is clear: God created us with an *identity need* to be unconditionally accepted, and he graciously provides us eternal, immutable, unconditional acceptance in *Christ*. It is not found elsewhere.

Competence/Success

The second identity need God made all humans with is the need to be *competent* and *successful*. He did not intend for us to be failures. All face the same question, "What is success?" Apart from God's design, being reconciled to him through Christ's work, and God's sending his Spirit, we must define success ourselves. And then we must attempt to convince others that our definition is correct. On this basis owning a good home, driving a quality car, earning a college degree, getting a high paying job, becoming wealthy, and a zillion other things represent success in the world's eyes. But this is the world/life-view of those alienated from Christ. People from disadvantaged backgrounds who achieve worldly success are often referred to as self-made people. Those without *true knowledge* of God do not realize that it is the Lord God Almighty who provides *everyone* with skill, strength and opportunities for success, even as the world defines it (Hos. 2:8; Deut. 8:18; Prov. 10:22).

We are not to "compare ourselves with . . . those who commend themselves; but when they measure themselves by themselves and compare themselves with themselves, they are without understanding . . . . For it is not he who commends himself that is approved, but he whom the Lord commends" (2 Cor. 10:12, 18). Those who define success for themselves must compare themselves against the so-called successes of others. If a low achiever is chosen as the standard of measurement, then success is easily achieved. However, if a high standard is chosen, then someone wanting success may work hard, yet may fall into an ungodly pattern of conduct to try to realize the high goal. But regardless of effort, it is at its heart a form of self-effort.

God defines success differently. Although the things mentioned are forms of worldly success, none of them will be accounted as success on the day of judgment, for no earthly treasures can be brought into heaven. Christ admonishes those who would be wise to "lay up for yourselves treasures in heaven" (Matt. 6:20). What are treasures in heaven and how do they relate to success?

The best way to address this question is to rehearse our thrust: God wants all of his children to become partakers of the divine nature (2 Peter 1:4). And it is the Holy Spirit who develops in believers' *hearts* the *fruit of the Spirit*—"love, joy, peace, patience, kindness, goodness, faithfulness, gentleness, self-control"—and who imparts *gifts of ministry*—"prophecy, service, teaching, exhortation, liberality, evangelism, wisdom, knowledge, faith, healing, miracles, distinguishing spirits, administration, tongues"—for the edification of the church (Rom. 12:3-9; 1 Cor. 12:7-12, 28-30; Gal. 5:22-23; Eph. 4:8-13). Success is: (a) the manifestation of the fruit of the Spirit, and (b) the Spirit's application of spiritual gifts to edify others *in* Christ. Treasures in heaven are God's record of his loving accomplishments through his children. Even those treasures are gifts from God accomplished through the Holy Spirit's work.

Once more, the conclusion is clear. As our identity need for unconditional acceptance is mercifully given to those *in* Christ, the desire to be *competent* and *successful* is satisfied for those regenerated and tutored by the Holy Spirit. Humans' deepest identity needs can only be satisfied *by* the transforming work of the Trinity. God wants his children to identify with him, not with those things created by him.

Belonging to a Significant Body or Family

The third and final *identity need* is our created, natural hunger for relationships. We were created as social creatures. We earnestly desire to belong to a spirit-satisfying group who have the same *heart* as we do. The family, as God designed it, is his most basic common grace social-construct in which children are to be nurtured and loved. The family is the most basic building block of society. Societies stand or fall depending upon the health of the families that constitute them. But even families that have given their children a sense of their basic worth can be torn asunder if a foundational belief which threatens some members of the family takes hold of others in the family. So Christ has brought about a rift in many a family, for his very *person* generates an allegiance to him in those who come to know him.

> I have come to cast fire upon the earth; and how I wish it were already kindled!
>
> . . . Do you suppose that I came to grant peace on earth? I tell you, no, but rather division; for from now on five members in one household will be divided, three against two and two against three. They will be divided, father against son and son against father; mother against daughter and daughter against mother, mother-in-law against daughter-in-law and daughter-in-law against mother-in-law. (Luke 12:49-53)

People outside of God's family often seek to satisfy their hunger for membership by joining a socially-recognized group that appeals to their self-identity. These groups can be as diverse as country clubs are from criminal gangs; as groups that espouse collectivism are from those that foster a libertarian philosophy. Belonging to groups that hold similar values or world/life-views is widely accepted normal conduct.

People like to identify with winners. For example, when an athletic team is in first place many people begin to wear apparel that identifies them with the winner. You rarely see people wearing identity apparel that identifies them with a consistent loser. There are exceptions to this, but winning promotes people's desire to be recognized as supporters. There is generally nothing wrong with such behavior, but none of these worldly group-relationships assuage the deep hunger to belong to a meaningful body of spirit-satisfying people.

But there are tragic examples of people not listening to the sound advice they receive. For example, the Israelites had been warned by God not to make any alliances with the people who occupied the Promised Land where he was leading them:

> Be sure to observe what I am commanding you this day: behold, I am going to drive out the Amorite before you, and the Canaanite, the Hittite, the Perizzite, the Hivite and the Jebusite. Watch yourself that you make no covenant with the inhabitants of the land into which you are going, or it will become a snare in your midst. But rather, you are to tear down their altars and smash their sacred pillars and cut down their Asherim—for you shall not worship any other god, for the LORD, whose name is Jealous, is a jealous God—otherwise you might make a covenant with the inhabitants of the land and they would play the harlot with their gods and sacrifice to their gods, and someone might invite you to eat of his sacrifice, and you might take some of his daughters for your sons, and his daughters might play the harlot with their gods and cause your sons also to play the harlot with their gods. (Ex. 34:11-16)

The people did not retain in their hearts God's words but chose to align themselves with people in the surrounding country. They fraternized with those who did not know God. They wanted to be accepted by them and become part of their society. They seemed, in Israel's collective mind, to be a significant group with which to align. They wanted to belong:

> While Israel remained at Shittim, the people began to play the harlot with the daughters of Moab. For they invited the people to the sacrifices of their gods, and the people ate and bowed down to their gods. So Israel joined themselves to Baal of Peor, and the LORD was angry against Israel. (Num. 25:1-3)

The Israelites joined the Moabites in order to secure their approval and have access to their daughters. The Israelites joined themselves to this society in order to gain what they thought would be beneficial. God's commitment to all of Israel was so immutable, however, that he sent a plague upon the people and destroyed 24,000 Israelites in order to turn the rest away from the folly that would have resulted in the eternal self-condemnation of the whole nation (Num. 25:9).

God's remedy for the deep longing we all have for a spirit-satisfying relationship with a community of like-minded people is to adopt believers into his family. This transfer of loyalties from the father of lies to an eternal commitment to God the Father is the consequence of being born from above. The new birth produces a change that eradicates rebellion against God, and results in people truly addressing God as Father. Christ referred to God as Father over 100 times in the Gospel of John. This change in the believer's relationship with God is very significant.

> For all who are being led by the Spirit of God, these are sons of God. For you have not received a spirit of slavery leading to fear again, but you have received a spirit of adoption as sons by which we cry out, Abba! Father! The Spirit himself testifies with our spirit that we are children of God, and if children, heirs also, heirs of God and fellow heirs with Christ, if indeed we suffer with Him so that we may also be glorified with Him. (Rom. 8:14-17)

Once more the conclusion is plain: God meets our identity need to belong to a significant family in himself, in the person of God the Father. The world cannot satisfy this need. The Trinity brings full identity-satisfaction to God's children. Our need for *unconditional acceptance* is met *in* Christ; our need to be *competent* and *successful* is met by the regenerating and transforming work of the Holy Spirit; and our need to be *members of a significant family* is met by our adoption by the Father. This makes us members of Christ's body, the church. The search for an identity in the world, apart from God, is doomed to failure. God transforms his children and transfers their identity from the world into himself—God the Father, God the Son, and God the Holy Spirit.

Summary

The *passions* component of the heart, consisting of our *desires, affections*, and *identity needs*, makes up the second major area in the heart identified in the Bible (the *mind* and *will* are the other two components). The *mind* component is the most often referred-to aspect of the human *heart* in the Bible. But the *passions* realm is the aspect of the heart that brings life front and forward. That life, however, must be *righteous* and *holy* if it is to manifest God's character; and it also must be nurtured and governed by the *true knowledge* of God that he imparts to the *mind* of his children—and with which he subsequently *leavens* the *rest* of their heart. If the *passions* component of the heart can be called the life element in the heart, the *mind* component could be called the command center of the heart.

We turn next to the heart's final component, the *will*.

18

The Heart: The Location of Our Volition— Our Will to Act

Why do you call Me "Lord, Lord," and do not do what I say? (Luke 6:46)

Ephesians says God's children are adopted "according to the kind intention of His will." In doing so, he graciously "made known to us the mystery of His will and has given us "an inheritance ... according to His purpose who works all things after the counsel of His will" (Eph. 1:5, 9, 11). God has a purpose he is working out through his sovereign will[140]—and he has made this known in his Word! Those willing to seek it there can know God's will (Matt. 7:7).

All human beings have a will, but the unregenerate have little interest in God's will. If they express such an interest, it is generally to justify their thoughts and behavior. Even if they speak of his will, they usually ignore it in their lives. This is common with cultural Christians—those raised to know the gospel but who don't really know Christ. They believe, but do not live out their belief. But biblically, to believe is *truly to know*—to *desire* to live in conformity with one's beliefs. The Bible calls those who profess a *belief* but whose lives belie it *hypocrites*.

Those surrendering their lives to Christ have difficulty fully manifesting God's will they have come to *desire*. They want to love the Trinity with all their heart, soul, strength, and mind; and they want to love their neighbors as themselves. But they cannot! What is wrong with their *will*? Do human beings have a free will or not? This key question deserves a careful answer. What is the *nature* of our will? Is it *free* or *determined*? Is it a *self-focused will*, a *sometimes-influenced free will*, or a *partially-constricted/partially-restored free will*?

The term "free will" does not occur in the Greek New Testament. And the word translated "free will" from Hebrew into English appears fifteen times in the Old Testament, always of a free-will offering to God (Lexical # 5071: *nedabah*). But it is plain that both redeemed and unredeemed people are morally accountable for their decisions. We know this from passages such as: (a) "But I say to you that Elijah already came, and they did not recognize him, but *did to him* whatever they *wished*" ["willed": Lexical # 2309] (Matt. 17:12); (b) "But each one is tempted when he is carried away [acts] and enticed by *his own lust*" (James 1:14); and (c) "I have

---

[140] In chapter 8, "God Is Wise: His Wisdom Is Ours Upon Request," under the section heading, "Wisdom is revealed in the 'right end' nurtured by the right reasons, God's will was discussed as having both an active or creative dimension and a permissive or decretive dimension." A review of this section might be helpful if the reader does not recall the distinctive of each. God's decretive will is also mentioned in chapters 9 and 11.

set before you life and death, the blessing and the curse. So *choose life* in order that you may live, you and your descendants" (Deut. 30:19). To make choices and act on them is basic to human life. And each choice and act carries a moral responsibility for which all are held accountable (Rom. 14:12).

Does God Have Free Will?

Before addressing the *type of will* humans have, we ask, "Does *God* have a free will?" We begin thus to set a benchmark for defining free will. We must because the word "free" needs qualification. Neither God nor humans can be simply *free*. One is either *free to*, *free from*, or free in some other qualified form. Freedom is always qualified by a context.

How shall we describe God's will? Do God's active will and decretive will both flow from the same *base* will? Is God free to do anything? No, he is not! God is not free to violate his *nature*. God is not free to be *unholy*, *unjust*, to stop being all-knowing or all-powerful, to set aside his immutability and become *mutable*. God is not free *not to be God*! But God is free to *choose*, to *do*, and to *permit* anything that agrees with his holy and wise purpose *which always conforms to his divine nature*. God is free to be all that he is! He is free *from* all that would contradict his nature. He is eternally and infinitely free *to be* all that he is within his *godly nature*. But he is not free to alter his nature. God is the awesome I AM WHO I AM (Ex. 3:14).

If God's will must be conceived in a qualified way, then how should we qualify the will that is a component of every *human* heart? How should will and its *freedom* be defined? The *will* interrelates with the *mind* and the *passions*, but is essentially the inherent ability to *pursue* a course of *action*. The *will* is the ability to act or not act on the heart's *mental* and *passions* components. This is true of the will of saved and unsaved. They both *freely act in accordance with their nature*. But the two do not have the same kind of nature, because believers receive a new nature. Therefore, both groups have a different understanding of the freedom of their will.

But even many Christians argue that they can do whatever they choose. They are free to decide what they will or will not do. In essence, they believe they can decide anything and everything for themselves. However, this sort of definition of free will merely reveals that the speaker has a strong self-will. He is not speaking about *true* free will; for even God is not free to violate his nature. Such a perspective substitutes self-will for free will and subordinates God's will to human will. Because God's will establishes the standard for a will it makes more sense to think of free will in this way: A human free will is a will that can be voluntarily brought into a perpetual and perfect conformity with God's revealed will—the only benchmark by which a person can ascertain whether or not his will is truly free rather than being merely an ill-defined self-focused will, or a partially-constricted/partially-restored free will.

Do Fallen Human Beings Have Free Will?

Adam and Eve had free will. They were created with the ability to keep their will in perpetual conformity with God's will. They were not created sinners. They were free to do whatever they chose to do, except to eat from the tree of the knowledge of good and evil—being warned that "in the day that you eat from it you will surely die" (Gen. 2:17). They both ate from that tree and *fell*—became fearful of God; hid from him; were alienated from him; became knowledgeable regarding good and evil; and became slaves of their new self-focused will. They *lost* what they possessed—a *free will*: the ability to conform their will to God's. This is depicted:

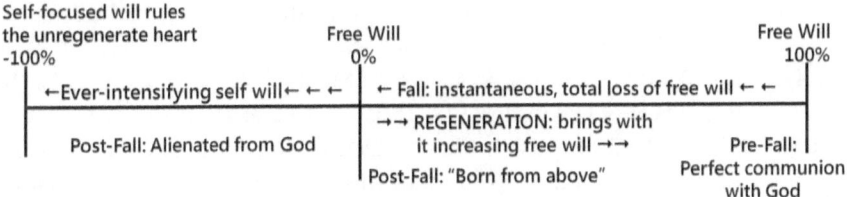

Figure 18.1 *The Will Continuum Model*

Figure 18.1 reflects the biblical account. After Adam and Eve ate of the fruit from the tree of the knowledge of good and evil "the eyes of both of them were opened, and they knew that they were naked" (Gen. 3:7).

The fall was instantaneous. They immediately became afraid of God. Not only were they transformed into self-conscious individuals, they became self-protective and fled from God in fear. They could no longer bring their will into conformity with his. God quickly regenerated them. How do we know? Because he immediately made a distinction between the children of the serpent and the children of Adam and Eve: "And I will put enmity between you [the serpent] and the woman, between your seed [children] and her seed; he shall bruise you on the head, and you shall bruise him on the heel" (Gen. 3:15). And at Cain's birth, Eve believed he fulfilled God's promise, "I have gotten a manchild *with the help of the* LORD" (Gen. 4:1). But Cain was not the fulfillment of God's promise of a future Savior, but the first murderer (Gen. 4:8).

Do Regenerate Human Beings Have Free Will?

The model reveals several important truths. First, Adam and Eve had free will when God created them. Second, when they fell they lost their free will and became slaves to their self-will. Third, those who remain separated from God remain captives of their self-will—without hope, apart from God, of ever having a free will again. And finally, those who are regenerated gradually have a free will restored, which continues to increase as long as they partake of the divine nature and are being *leavened* by the *true knowledge* of God.

Some reject the *Will Continuum* model above. They don't believe that anyone is destined to be a slave of unrighteousness and is confined to the necessity of exercising free choices within the bounds of their self-will. One's nature is *not* enslaved to self-will. They believe people can will themselves to become slaves of Christ and gain an even larger degree of free will than previously, after an *independent* choice to receive Christ.[141] In essence, they hold that unbelievers are free to choose to associate themselves with God apart from *God's first initiating a change in their heart* that enables them to become united to Christ.

Debates over the two views regarding the state of the human will before salvation—it is a slave to self-will; it is free to will an association with Christ— rarely resolve differences between the two views. The view set forth here, represented in the *Will Continuum* diagram, is consistent with the biblical references set forth in this paragraph. We invite those unsure how to resolve issues concerning free will to study it in light of the following biblical topics: *Born*—John 3:3-8; Romans 9:11-24; Galatians 4:29; 1 John 2:29; 3:9; 4:7; 5:1, 4, 18 (NT: Lexical # 1080). *Elect*—Isaiah 45:4; 65:9, 22; Matthew 24:24, 31; Mark 13:22, 27; Luke 18:7; Romans 8:33; Colossians 3:12; Titus 1:1; 1 Peter 1:1-2; 2 John 1, 13 (OT: Lexical # 972; NT: Lexical # 1588). *Chosen*—Deuteronomy 7:6; 14:2, Psalm 33:12; Matthew 20:16; 22:14; Mark 13:20; John 13:18; 15:16-19; Ephesians 1:4; 2 Thessalonians 2:13 (OT: Lexical # 977 & 970; NT: Lexical # 1586, 1588, 138). *Predestined*—Romans 8:29, 30; Ephesians 1:5, 11 (NT: Lexical # 4309).

In addition, there are other passages such as Acts 13:48: "And when the Gentiles heard this [the gospel], they began rejoicing and glorifying the word of the Lord; and as many as had been *appointed* to eternal life believed" (*appointed*: Lexical # 5021; sometimes translated ordained). Those who reject the view that the Holy Spirit must *first* bring new life to the *heart*, before the *will* is free, must interpret all of the above passages in a way other than: *the Bible simply means what it says*.

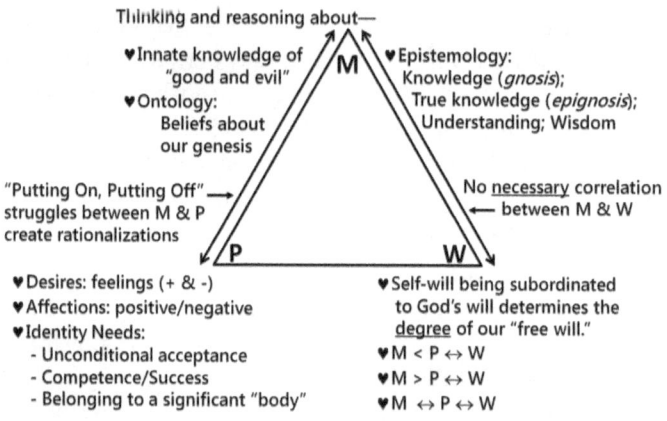

Figure 18.2 *The Volition's Will Component of the Heart Model*

---

[141] Paul uses the language "slaves of unrighteousness" and "slaves of righteousness" in Rom. 6:12-23. The Greek word, and its variations, that is used by Paul to describe the idea of being slaves is the word *doulos* (Lexical #1401) which means "one who gives himself up totally to another's will" (*Thayer's Greek-English Lexicon of the New Testament*, 158).

Now we incorporate the *will* component of the heart into the Heart Model. The expanded model, encompassing the three components, the *mind, passions,* and *will* look like Figure 18.2.

Self-will's Subordination to God's Will Determines Our Degree of Free Will

The first ♥ under the Will component of the heart is: "Self-will being subordinated to God's will determines the *degree* of our 'free will.'" The truthfulness of this rests upon two presuppositions. First, a human can only continually, from the heart, desire to do God's will after regeneration—because prior to rebirth people are *dead to God*. It is true that they cry, "Oh Lord, get me through this operation and I will follow you," and think they are sincere. But, as in the parable of the sown seed (Matt. 13:3-9), their hearts are unable to bear the fruit of believers. Indeed, Matthew says next: "And in their case the prophecy of Isaiah is being fulfilled, which says, 'You will keep on hearing, but will not understand; and you will keep on seeing, but will not perceive; for the heart of this people has become dull'" (vv. 14-15; Isa. 6:9-10).

And some genuinely appreciate the gospel's *logic* and intend to obey it, but there is no Spirit-wrought *heart* renovation that transforms their *mind* so they can prove what the will of God is (Rom. 12:1-2). They are still under the grip of self-effort and are slaves of their self-will.

Here is the second presupposition: People must not only be regenerated by the Spirit to regain a degree of free will, they must also be trained, chastened, guided, and helped by the Spirit throughout the course of life to put off the old nature and put on the qualities of Christ's divine nature. God alone gets the credit for any advancement in Christlikeness in our lives. The two biblical statements that best illustrate this are: "For I am confident of this very thing, that He who began a good work in you will perfect it until the day of Christ," and "for it is God who is at work in you, both to will and to work for His good pleasure" (Phil. 1:6; 2:13).

The more we genuinely subscribe to God's will, and the more enabled we are to bring our will into conformity with God's, the higher our degree of free will. This varies from person to person, but regardless there are struggles along the way between the old nature, embodying self-will, and the new nature, embodying a growing free will. This struggle is illustrated in the dynamics outlined in the next two ♥s in the Will section of Figure 18.2.

When the Passions Dominate the Will

The second ♥ is M < P ↔ W. This means that the *passions* component of the heart has great influence on the *mind* and thereby dominates the *will*. For example, a person finds him or herself in a situation with someone they really want to be accepted by, but that person wants them to participate in something displeasing to God. And down deep they *know* it is not in their best interest. But their desire to be accepted is so overwhelming that they rationalize: "I will do it only this one time;" or, "It doesn't bother John when he does it, so why should it bother me?" Rationalizations take many forms.

Some begin their Christian life with their previous belief that their feelings should determine right and wrong. If you feel all right about something, it must be all right to do. Feelings are not, however, the best guide. That is why medical doctors do not operate on their family members—their emotions can easily cloud their judgment.

Another example of feelings leading to ungodly behavior is the many younger adult Christians whose parents divorced and who themselves get married and divorce. Parents who divorce give their children permission to do the same. Is this true? Yes! The genesis of the permission lies in the psychological experiences associated with the parents' divorce. Children generally love both parents; but even if they love only one, the permission is *experiential* and *self-justifying*—thus powerful. Why? Because what people experience typically becomes *their truth*, and is easier for them to believe than a *propositional truth* that may only seem *theoretically true* to them, in a particular situation, but not in their circumstance. For example, God says, "I hate divorce and . . . not one has done so who has a remnant of the Spirit" (Mal. 2:14-16). But those who watch their parents go through a divorce, and who love them, are likely to *rationalize*, "That may be true, but God loves my parents." And let's accept that God loves their parents. Nevertheless, the seed of permission has been sown—"God loved my parents and 'He knew it was best for them to get divorced,' so it will be OK if I divorce my spouse." The difficulty is in the fact that *philos* love has overruled *agape* love. The feelings for their parents govern their heart, not God's character or their commitment to his *will*.

Agape love is a commitment of the *will* to do what is holy and righteous in seeking the godly end of a matter. It is a love rooted in God's character. It dies to self and lives for Christ. The root of divorce is always a perverted self-love. When self-love becomes self-centered and self-justifying, it finds rationalizations that give permission to do what we would otherwise frown upon. It allows us to make exceptions to God's standards for those we *phileo*, or for ourselves. In this case the *passions*, as they are oriented to divorce, simply govern the *mind* so that the negotiations and feedback that go on between the three components of the heart rule the *will*—it follows the bent of the *passions*. In other words: M < P ↔ W.

When M and P struggle, we generally become engaged in rationalization. We see this on the left side of Figure 18.2. On the right-hand side is the statement, "No necessary correlation between M & W." Indeed, when M < P there is *no* correlation between *mind* and *will*. The *passions* prevail and the *will* follows. In such cases, the emotions dominate the situation.

When the Mind Governs the Will

The third ♥ under the Will component is: **M > P ↔ W**. This is the opposite reality from the one just described. Here, the *mind* prevails over the *passions* so the *will* follows the *mind*. Examples of this are common. Those who keep a Christian laundry list of dos and don'ts can become legalistic without being aware, and can slip into behavior that reveals a M > P pattern.

Christ confronted this in the Pharisees' traditions. They concocted an arrangement of giving to God what was called "Corban." A wealthy person would take an oath and vow that his wealth, at that time, was given to God; but it was to be physically relinquished to the religious ministry at the time of the donor's death. By practicing Corban, the committed wealth was unavailable for other uses to which the Spirit might have directed it. Christ gave his evaluation:

> You are experts at setting aside the commandment of God in order to keep your tradition. For Moses said, "Honor your father and your mother"; and "He who speaks evil of father or mother is to be put to death"; but you say, "If a man says to his father or his mother, whatever I have that would help you is Corban," you no longer permit him to do anything for his father or his mother; thus invalidating the word of God by your tradition which you have handed down; and you do many things such as that. (Mark 7:9-13)

Opportunities like Corban exist for Christians today too. Many charitable organizations offer opportunities for supporters to establish Charitable Remainder Trusts. People are asked to give the organization a gift, and in exchange receive a fixed percentage return on the balance in the account at the beginning of each year. This can be a godly thing to do as a part of estate planning—all estates worth more than a governmentally-predetermined amount will pay a designated proportion of the estate to the government. Options available to the wealthy before death are: Give what is allowed by law to your family; give it to your favorite charities; or give it to those who govern, in estate taxes. So, charitable trusts can be a wise option. *But* they can also be used to guard money so it serves me and does not meet others' needs!

Family and charitable trusts can be like the rich man in Christ's parable who reasoned, "I will tear down my barns and build larger ones . . . and say to my soul, 'Soul, you have many goods laid up for many years to come; take your ease, eat, drink and be merry.' But God said to him, 'You fool! This very night your soul is required of you; and now who will own what you have prepared?' *So is the man who stores up treasure for himself, and is not rich toward God*" (Luke 12:18-21).

Christ also met many forms of legalism that indicate M > P. The religious leaders particularly objected to Christ's activities on the Sabbath.

> Jesus went through the grain-fields on the Sabbath, and His disciples became hungry and began to pick the heads of grain and eat. But when the Pharisees saw this, they said to Him, "Look, Your disciples do what is not lawful to do on a Sabbath." But He said to them, "Have you not read what David did when he became hungry, he and his companions; how he entered the house of God, and they ate the consecrated bread, which is not lawful for him to eat nor for those with him, but for the priests alone? Or have you not read in the Law, that on the Sabbath the priests in the temple break the Sabbath, and are innocent? But I say to you that something greater than the temple is here. But if you had known what this means, "I desire compassion [mercy], and not a sacrifice," you would not have condemned the innocent. For the Son of Man is Lord of the Sabbath."

> Departing from there, He went into their synagogue. And a man was there whose hand was withered. And they questioned Jesus, asking, "Is it lawful to heal on the Sabbath?"—so that they might accuse Him. And He said to them, "What man is there among you who has a sheep, and if it falls into a pit on the Sabbath, will he not take hold of it and lift it out? How much more valuable then is a man than a sheep! So then, it is lawful to do good on the Sabbath." Then He said to the man, "Stretch out your hand! He stretched it out, and it was restored to normal, like the other." But the Pharisees went out and conspired against Him, as to how they might destroy Him. (Matt. 12:1-14)

Christians are not immune, in parts of their old nature waiting to be put off, from having a rigid attitude in a corner of their heart that the Holy Spirit wants to correct by building the new nature—through putting on compassion and mercy. The *letter of the law*, before this happens, can take precedence over the *spirit of the law*. M > P is a possibility when the letter supersedes the spirit. The *mind* can, in inappropriate ways, rule over the *passions* component of the heart.

A Holistic and Integrated Heart

The fourth and final ♥ in the Heart Model (Figure 18.2) is: **M ↔ P ↔ W**. This represents a holistic and integrated heart where the *mind* and *passions* are not in conflict and a struggle for supremacy. The *mind* and *passions* agree. They are at peace with each other.

A lawyer, who probably fit into the M > P pattern, tested Jesus, and asked, "Who is my neighbor?" He was trying to test Christ and to justify himself, as he deemed himself worthy of eternal life. In the face of this effort at self-justification, Jesus told the story of the good Samaritan and concluded by telling the lawyer, "Go and do the same" (Luke 10:25-37). The lawyer left. And that is the tragedy! The lawyer needed to confess that he could not go and do the same. He needed Christ to begin a work of transformation in his *heart*. The good Samaritan had a *whole heart*. He was unconsciously revealing the M ↔ P ↔ W holistic heart pattern. His *mind* embraced his *passions*, *desires*, and *affections*. He *felt* compassion. He *showed* mercy. And he willingly shared his wealth with a stranger in deep need. He modeled love for his neighbor while simultaneously defining who his neighbor was. But the lawyer had a *mental defense* against being neighborly with certain classes of people. God, however, is no respecter of humanly derived concepts of classes or types (Acts 10:34; Rom. 2:11; Gal. 2:6; Eph. 6:9).

But in some situations we need wisdom to maintain harmony between the *mind* and the *passions*. An example of this is facing the question, "Should I *give* money to Henry; or, should I *loan* Henry money?" Scripture speaks of both, lending and giving, as reflecting God's desire: "If there is a poor man with you, one of your brothers . . . you shall not harden your *heart*, nor close your hand from your poor brother; but you shall freely open your hand to him, and shall generously *lend* him sufficient for his *need* in whatever he lacks (Deut. 15:7-8). And also: "But whoever has the world's goods, and sees his brother in *need* and closes his *heart* against him, how does the love of God abide in him?" (1 John 3:17). And

James exhorts us to show love by *giving* clothing and food to those in need (2:15-16). When do we lend and when do we give?

Answering this question requires discernment. If people are hungry, we are to *give* them food. If people are naked, we are to *give* them clothing. These are *acute* needs that ought to be addressed as quickly as possible. *Giving* is always appropriate when we encounter such needs. *Lending*, however, is another matter. To whom, when, and with what expectations do we lend? Deuteronomy 15 teaches we are to lend to fellow Christians and not just anybody or everybody. This is based on the premise that there is an order of priorities that we face when we assume adult responsibilities, in accord with God's revealed expectations. After acknowledging and thanking Christ, our priorities are: first, our family; then our brothers and sisters in Christ; and then others. Our lending to those in need does not imply that Christians are to become free-floating bankers serving everyone.

Chronic needs cry out for helping hands that do not cause shame or destroy the recipient's self-respect. Christ transforms Christians' hearts so they will, if able, *lend* to their brothers or sisters with chronic needs. Those meeting those needs should not continue to *give* repeatedly. And expecting someone with a chronic need to repeatedly *ask* for help puts him in a very embarrassing position. Lending resources—money, materials, means of transportation—makes several non-verbal statements: We are confident that you, the recipient, are going to be able to take care of your own needs in the not-too-distant future; you will be able to honorably return what has been loaned to you; and you are part of the family and we care for you. All of these unspoken hopes are uplifting. Lending indicates *trust*. Lending assumes the person will be responsible and repay what has been loaned. Lending allows the person to assume his rightful responsibility for the future.

The burden of repayment is great for the poor, and therefore the Lord has told us to lend to poor Christians without charging interest (Ex. 22:25; Deut. 23:19-20; Ps. 15:5). But interest itself is not inappropriate when money is loaned to a financially-stable borrower who borrows the money to use in creating more wealth. Interest, in that case, is like rent: the people renting (borrowing) the money are expected to pay for the use of the money while it is being rented (loaned) to them (see Matt. 25:27; Luke 19:23). But loans to the *poor* are to be interest free.

Lending to a poor brother or sister in Christ also carries one other God-revealed provision: lend without expecting to be repaid. Christ said:

> If you lend to those from whom you expect to receive, what credit is that to you? Even sinners lend to sinners in order to receive back the same amount. But love your enemies, and do good, and lend, expecting nothing in return; and your reward will be great, and you will be sons of the Most High; for He Himself is kind to ungrateful and evil men. (Luke 6:34-35)

But this too carries the need to realize that the Lord does not ask us to lend irresponsibly. To illustrate, if potential lenders are so financially strapped that their lending money to a needy neighbor would leave them unable to meet their own existing financial obligations, they will not act in a godly or wise manner. Common sense must be used. God does not expect his children to lend what they do not have available to responsibly lend. We lend from our available surplus, not from an essential supply for our own basic needs. We can *give* from our basic supply, but *lending* generally involves a larger sum which comes from savings. There is, to be sure, room to discuss what is *essential* and what is a *surplus*, but that is not our purpose.

We periodically learn of acute and chronic needs. These are, hopefully, dealt with in the context of an M ↔ P ↔ W heart, an integrated one. But life is made up of a great variety of situations that expose the heart. And, thankfully, most of these opportunities to think, feel, and act are met without any internal conflict between the *mind* and the *compassions*—which makes the expression of the *will* psychologically satisfying. Indeed, most of life is lived with a balanced heart. Most decisions requiring action are routine and are simple reflections of our value preferences. They are actions that express our *will* as it is related to our patterns of life.

We are generally not in internal conflict over what route to follow to work. Nor do we generally struggle in selecting items at the grocery store, or over what grade of gas to buy. We make freely the overwhelming majority of decisions in the context of our nature, without moral conflict. M ↔ P ↔ W is a relatively normal state of affairs in our daily lives. It is when we are called upon by the Holy Spirit to consider others before ourselves that the internal tension between the M and P challenges us. The more Christ's divine nature is imparted to believers, however, the more likely their growing free will will be demonstrated, and their renovated attitudes and behavior that reveal *Christ in them* will be exhibited. But there is a continuing struggle between the old nature and the renovated new nature that goes on until death ushers God's children into the state of glorification where *all* of the old is done away with. Hallelujah!

The question remains: What *motivates* people to act, or not act, as they do? Why are we turned on by some things and are apathetic toward others? What motivates us?

19

The Heart: Love Is the Motivator

To what then will I compare the men of this generation, and what are they like? They are like children who sit in the market place and call to one another; and they say, "We played the flute for you, and you did not dance; we sang a dirge, and you did not weep." (Luke 7:31-32)

The question implicit in the quote above is "What will please you? What *motivates* you?" What makes the question impossible to answer is its *direction* and depth. The question takes a we-to-you direction—"We played the flute for you and you did not dance; we sang a dirge, and you did not weep." And it asks something that transcends mere physically related motivations. When most show an interest in *motivation* they look for the *key* to unlock ways to motivate their children, friends, neighbors, customers, voters, and others, *not themselves*.

At a superficial level there are things that motivate people regarding their basic physical needs—food, sex, shelter, security. So people in business, for example, appeal to certain quality-quantity-price relationships attractive to those who look to satisfy a specific desire at a point in time. They can appeal to these physical desires and needs in a general sense, and customers in the broader population will respond positively to the variety of offered satisfactions.

The context of Luke 7:31-32 focuses on the *type* of motivation that we are concerned about. Two of John the Baptist's disciples were sent to Jesus while John was in prison. They went to ask Jesus, "Are you the Expected One, or do we look for someone else?" (v. 19). Jesus responded, "Go and report to John what you have seen and heard: the blind receive sight, the lame walk, the lepers are cleansed, the deaf hear, the dead are raised up, the poor have the gospel preached to them. Blessed is he who does not take offense at Me" (7:22-23). Next, Christ asked the people present why they had gone out to see John when he was preaching and baptizing in the wilderness. Jesus answered his own question by stating they had gone out to see and hear a *great prophet*, and the people agreed. And Luke gives this illuminating word, just prior to the original quote:

> But the Pharisees and the lawyers rejected God's *purpose* for themselves, not having been baptized by John. (v. 30)

The word *purpose* here is *boulē*, which means deliberate and thoughtful intention. The Jewish leaders ignored God's deliberate intentions regarding *his plan for their salvation.*[142] The playing of the flute and singing of the dirge quoted at the chapter's beginning follows right after the rejecting God's purpose passage. Christ made a point by asking the Pharisees, "What will motivate you to seek, listen to, and obey God?" Christ referred to dance music and funeral music, which ordinarily move hearers to action. He asked, "What will it take to permanently attract you to God?" This is the great motivational question! When people are motivated to seek and listen to God, all other motivations are gradually brought into proper relationship with the greatest motivation—*true knowledge* of God's infinite, holy, and eternal *agape love* for us.

We will consider two things. First, it is our love of self, things, people, and/or God that motivates us. *Love* is the primary motivating force underlying all human actions. There are four kinds of love: *storge*, the love of a parent for a child; *eros*, sexual desire for another person; *philos*, friendship; and *agape*, the commitment to seek the highest good for another. Love can, of course, become perverted. It can become hidden behind emotions such as fear, anger, or hatred, that take prominence. But it is still love, though buried underneath an alternative motivator.

Second, the *object* of our love moves. What we love changes with circumstances and over time, for we are mutable. This is wonderful because it allows God to transform our hearts so we transfer love from things of the world, which previously captured us, to the persons of the Godhead. The hope for such change reassures believers' hearts.

Figure 19.1 facilitates discussion of the above two points and assists in picturing the abstract concept involved.

Love of Self Is the Primary Motivating Force of Unbelievers

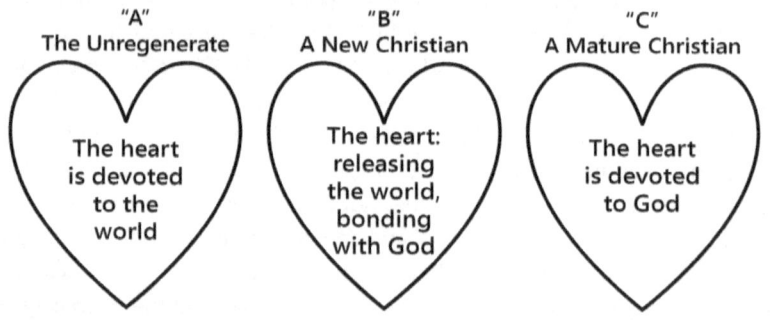

Figure 19.1 *Love and Its Devotion*

Before a person is born from above, his or her only option is to be a self-oriented slave-of-self, and lover of the things offered in the world by its ruler

---

[142] See *Thayer's Greek-English Lexicon of the New Testament*, 104, Lexical # 1012: the word *purpose* is a word meaning God's purpose regarding salvation.

(John 12:31; 14:30; 16:11). This is a direct result of the fall of Adam and Eve. Indeed, our self-consciousness, self-centeredness, and self-concern are *marks* of the fall. Self-love dominates until one is delivered from bondage to self. While in this bondage, the heart always scans the world in search of things—physical objects; activities; worldly philosophies; false gods—that will satisfy the heart's hunger for significance. This is represented in the **A** segment of Figure 19.1—The Heart Is Devoted to the World. The unregenerate are captives of the world. Those in Christ are in the world physically, but their spirits are separated from the world so that its tempting qualities are supplanted by a higher quest—to *truly know Christ, to partake of his divine nature, and to become more like him.*

Some may reason, "Isn't the second greatest commandment, 'You shall love your neighbor as yourself'?" Then isn't self-love the norm? This commandment recognizes the fall, and the fact that we do love ourselves. But it is preceded by the first commandment, "You shall love the Lord your God with all your heart, and with all your soul, and with all your mind" (Matt. 22:37-39). We should acknowledge that we cannot fulfill either commandment. The commandments are *light* to us, showing us our need for Christ's righteousness and his help. He fulfilled the requirements of all God-given laws, for us. We are as incapable of fulfilling the law of God as are the unsaved. But the saved receive two special gifts: (1) the righteousness of Christ is imputed to them; and (2) the Holy Spirit begins to transform them so they are gradually renovated into Christ's likeness, a process only to be completed at their glorification.

The saints seek Christ's righteousness by faith, and ask the Spirit to renovate them so they grow to love God and neighbor as Christ did. This was why Christ said to his disciples at the last supper, "A *new commandment* I give to you, that you *love one another, even as I have loved you*, that you also love one another" (John 13:34). This requires the Spirit's renovating work and is a part of the putting off and putting on process. The shedding of self-love, and the manifesting of *agape love*, is God's transforming work (Phil. 2:13).

Apart from God, the human cannot find his or her purpose in life. They lack purpose for they are separated from God. When the Pharisees rejected *God's* purpose for them, they lacked purpose. They floundered in their search for significance. There are millions of alternatives for people to seek in search for meaning. The *natural result* of all this searching for self-worth leads people to compare themselves with one another. In this way people can feel that they are at least equal to and maybe better than others, if they select a self-serving comparative group.

But equal to or better than others in what sense? The answer depends upon what the heart seeks. If someone believes living in a 3,500-square-foot house is better than living in a 1,600-square-foot one, then his identity will be *temporarily* elevated when he buys the larger house. The problem, of course, with this kind of search for personal significance is that every effort offers only short-term happiness. We could illustrate with attitudes toward cars, boats, clothes, jewelry, tattoos, job titles, prestigious schools attended, IQ, and how much we have published. But these identity boosters are shallow, temporary, and in the final analysis, counterfeits.

Scripture is replete with warnings concerning dangers for those not united to Christ. Paul warns Timothy that some suppose that *piety towards God*[143] is a means of gain (1 Tim. 6:5). Some today believe in prosperity theology—If we tithe, God will open the windows of heaven and pour great wealth on us. But nowhere does God promise *individuals* such a material outpouring. The promise that is often misapplied was God's pledge to the *nation of Israel* when it was backsliding and in distress (see Micah.) But Paul tells Timothy, and us:

> But godliness actually is a means of great gain when accompanied by contentment. For we have brought nothing into the world, so we cannot take anything out of it either. If we have food and covering, with these we shall be content. But those who want to get rich fall into temptation and a snare and many foolish and harmful desires which plunge men into ruin and destruction. For the *love* of money is a root of all sorts of evil, and some by longing for it have wandered away from the faith, and pierced themselves with many griefs. (1 Tim. 6:6-10)

Paul also says: "In the last days . . . men will be lovers of self, lovers of money, boastful, arrogant . . . ungrateful, unholy, unloving . . . without self-control . . . lovers of pleasure rather than lovers of God" (2 Tim. 3:1-4). Loving the things of the world is also referred to as loving "the passing pleasures of sin" (Heb. 11:25). Seeking physical possessions is one way unbelievers assert their self-worth and personal identity. The underlying belief is, the more possessions we have the better persons we are, or the more secure we are, or the more important we are. Self-love motivates them to seek the things of the world.

Those separated from Christ assert their personal worth in other ways also. One way is to attach identity or significance to a commitment to a specific cause that promotes, for instance, saving the whales; saving the earth; conquering cancer or Alzheimer's; defending abortion rights; promoting socialism or capitalism. This does not mean that Christians may not be committed to the principles underlying some of these causes, but they will not have their identity absorbed by them. Their identity will be gradually transferred from the world's causes to the Trinity. The causes God's children associate with are means to serve Christ, not self.

It is in *this* world, full of those separated from Christ, that Christians live. They are to share the good news of his propitiatory death for all who believe in him. They are to make it known that he desires *all* people to come to him. And they are to show a Christlike presence in their midst. In so doing, they will see Christ's parable of the sower lived out (Matt. 13:1-23). Some simply ignore the good news (vv. 4, 19). Others hear it and quickly rejoice. This creates excitement, but the rejoicing proves premature when the hearer faces affliction because of the

---

[143] *Thayer's Greek-English Lexicon of The New Testament*, # 2150, *eusebeia*: piety toward God, godliness.

gospel and ceases to follow Christ (vv. 5-6, 20-21). And then there are some who hear of Christ's love, respond with a seeming commitment, but eventually are deceived by the world's riches or are distracted by worries and are fruitless (vv. 7, 22). But happily some *do* hear, and prove to be *good soil*. These bear fruit, some a hundredfold, some sixty, and some thirty (vv. 8, 23). This latter group initially makes up the **B** segment of Figure 19.1: "A New Christian—The Heart: Releasing the World, Bonding With God." Believers typically enter their new life in Christ with great joy and zeal. Christ has become their *first love*.[144]

Love of Christ Is the Primary Motivating Force of Believers

The **B** segment of Figure 19.1 informs us that believers undergo an identity transplant when Christ becomes resident *in* their *hearts*. The transplant may be painful, long, and full of personal resistance. A child born to Christian parents and raised in a Christ-centered home, who is born from above at an early age, may have little to adjust to regarding their personal identity when they are joined to Christ. But someone born to parents with no regard for God, who lived deeply attracted to the world, if converted late, will face significant spiritual surgery as he or she is transformed into Christ's image.

Those regenerated in their late teens or twenties have significant psychological pillars undergirding their old world/life-view that need to be either replaced or substantially adjusted. This can be emotionally challenging. Old securities are disrupted and removed; old thought-patterns are turned upside down and replaced by new ones; and the Spirit gradually puts new presuppositions deep in the *mind*. The first months of new life will typically be full of *mental* adjustments that are followed by some minor and some substantial changes in the *heart's passions*, all of which are accompanied by changes in the *will*. Typically, the older someone is, the further they have been from wholesome common-grace influences. The more they have experienced the pleasures of sin, the greater the transformation they will need—and the more challenging the putting off of their old nature and the putting on of the new one. We thank God that the *paracletos*, the Holy Spirit whom God gives to all his children, helps those who face such enormous psychological adjustments.[145]

It is new believers' *love of Christ* that motivates them. There are some beautiful biblical examples of people coming to recognize who Christ is for the first time. Zaccheus' conversion account reveals *true knowledge* of Jesus established in his *heart* and his early transformation:

---

[144] "First love" (Rev. 2:4) points to the reality that Christ has become the most important One, the One to be given highest honor, respect and devotion. There is to be no one, or anything, that supplants God's rightful position of being first in a believer's *heart*. Those in the church at Ephesus were being warned here that they had left their *first love*, and were being admonished to repent and put Christ first in their lives again. Their good works had supplanted Christ. Their identity was at risk of being attached to their work, and not Christ.

[145] John 14:13-17, 23, 26; 15:26; 16:7-10, 13-15.

266 *Becoming Partakers of the Divine Nature*

> [Jesus] entered Jericho and was passing through. And there was a man called by the name of Zaccheus; he was a chief tax collector and he was rich. Zaccheus was trying to see who Jesus was, and was unable because of the crowd, for he was small in stature. And he ran on ahead and climbed up into a sycamore tree in order to see Him, for He was about to pass through that way. When Jesus came to the place, He looked up and said to him, "Zaccheus, hurry and come down, for today I must stay at your house." And he hurried and came down and received Him gladly. When they saw it, they all began to grumble, saying, "He has gone to be the guest of a man who is a sinner." Zaccheus stopped and said to the Lord, "Behold, Lord, half of my possessions I will give to the poor, and if I have defrauded anyone of anything, I will give back four times as much." And Jesus said to him, "Today salvation has come to this house, because he, too, is a son of Abraham. For the Son of Man has come to seek and to save that which was lost." (Luke 19:1-10)

Zaccheus' birth from above was *not* the result of his having promised to give half of his wealth to the poor, or to restore fourfold to anyone he had defrauded. Rather, his *salvation* was a gift from God who gave Zaccheus to Christ before times eternal. God "has saved us and called us with a holy calling, not according to our works, but according to his own purpose and grace which was granted us in Christ Jesus *from all eternity*" (2 Tim. 1:8-9).

Here is another biblical example of someone being overwhelmed by being shown *true knowledge* regarding Jesus, and his immediate desire to travel with him.

> They came to the other side of the sea, into the country of the Gerasenes. When He got out of the boat, immediately a man from the tombs with an unclean spirit met Him, and he had his dwelling among the tombs. And no one was able to bind him anymore, even with a chain; because he had often been bound with shackles and chains, and the chains had been torn apart by him and the shackles broken in pieces, and no one was strong enough to subdue him.... [Jesus said,] "Come out of the man, you unclean spirit!" And He was asking him, "What is your name?" And he said to Him, "My name is Legion; for we are many." [Jesus sent the demons into a herd of swine.] And [the people of Gerasene country] began to implore Him to leave their region. As He was getting into the boat, the man who had been demon-possessed was imploring Him that he might accompany Him. And He did not let him, but He said to him, "Go home to your people and report to them what great things the Lord has done for you, and how He had mercy on you." And he went away and began to proclaim in Decapolis what great things Jesus had done for him; and everyone was amazed. (Mark 5:1-20)

Scripture has numerous accounts of conversions that are the culmination of the Holy Spirit's preparatory and regenerating work. The two accounts just given reveal the great joy that accompanies the early phase of a relationship with Christ. But given the fact that all of the old nature is not immediately put off, often during a Christians' maturing years the Holy Spirit must call them back to their *first love*. For example, King David pleads with God to "restore to me the joy of Your salvation" after God sent Nathan the prophet to confront David about his adultery with Bathsheba (Ps. 51:12).

The Antidote to Backsliding Is Fixing Our Eyes on Jesus

Charles Spurgeon, in his devotional *Morning and Evening*, points out: "Some Christians are for living *on* Christ, but are not so anxious to live *for* Christ."[146] Spurgeon means that such Christians are not yet mature. Christ is their friend, but they have not yet become a *doulos*—a fully committed bond-slave of Christ's.

Backsliding is not an uncommon experience in a Christian's life. God warns his children about it. For example, Jeremiah 3 condemns Israel's faithless behavior or backsliding (vv. 6, 8, 11, 12, 14, 22). "Return, O faithless sons, I will heal your faithlessness" (v. 22). And it continues: "Behold, we come to You; for You are the LORD our God." And Hebrews warns: "Take care, brethren, that there not be in any one of you an evil, unbelieving heart that falls away from the living God. But encourage one another day after day, as long as it is still called 'Today,' so that none of you will be hardened by the deceitfulness of sin. For *we have become partakers of Christ*, if we hold fast the beginning of our assurance firm until the end" (3:12-14). The author continues to warn believers of apostasy and concludes with encouragement: "But, beloved, we are convinced of better things concerning you, and things that accompany salvation, though we are speaking in this way" (6:9).

The author, after recounting how Abel, Enoch, Noah, Abraham, Sarah, and many others triumphed in life by believing God, continues:

> Therefore, since we have so great a cloud of witnesses surrounding us, let us also *lay aside* every encumbrance and the sin which so easily entangles us, and let us *run with endurance* the race that is set before us, *fixing our eyes on Jesus*, the author and perfecter of faith, who for the joy set before Him endured the cross, despising the shame, and has sat down at the right hand of the throne of God. (Heb. 12:1-2)

This is further acknowledgment of our struggle with the old nature. Believers are easily distracted and entangled in sin. And we commit sins of omission because we are so busy with the tyranny of the urgent. We are easily drawn away from Christ's concerns by the demands placed on us by those around us. The sins of commission suddenly pop up because we are tired and do not think before we speak, or we are frustrated by problems.

But the author also provides the *antidote* for backsliding and leaving our *first love*: We can overcome sin and distractions by fixing our eyes on Jesus. Indeed, doing so is the way to *maintain the motivation that will keep Christ in position as our first love* (Heb. 12:1-2). But how do we fix our eyes on Jesus?

---

[146] Charles H. Spurgeon, *Morning and Evening* (McLean, VA: Macdonald Publishing Company), 558.

The eyes referred to are clearly the eyes of the *heart* that were earlier discussed[147] along with Matthew 6:22-23: "The eye is the lamp of the body; so then if your eye is clear, your whole body will be full of light. But if your eye is bad, your whole body will be full of darkness. *If then the light that is in you is darkness, how great is the darkness!*" The Holy Spirit, however, provides a believer with the necessary *true knowledge of God's nature* so that this precious understanding of God *leavens* his *heart*, transforms his world/life-view, and provides him with the necessary *spiritual memory* to *fix his eyes on Jesus.*

Fixing our eyes on Jesus is individual and personal. A person with some *true knowledge of God* can *meditate* on the nature of God: The Lord is beautiful in his holiness; he is good, as is seen in the splendor of creation, the wonder of redemption, and his merciful daily providence; he is patient; he is *love*, as supremely understood in his gift of his Son as Savior. The Holy Spirit uses such meditation to humble us by establishing God as the One with whom we should compare ourselves—not fellow humans. This creates in us a *true love for him*, both *for who he is and for what he has done*, which enables us to retain Christ as our *first love*. The greatest *motivator* in the universe is what springs from a heart that recognizes the *love of God* and is thereby transformed and enabled to love him *in return*. Lovers of God discover that their works are not efforts to impress God or others, but are responses that reveal an interest in the well-being of those ministered to—*agape* love. Being loved by God sets us free to love God and others.

All warnings against backsliding—removing Christ from preeminence—are important and right, for some who appear to be walking well with Christ suddenly turn their back on him. They do not heed the warnings about backsliding. John speaks about such people: "They went out from us, but they were not really of us; for if they had been of us, they would have remained with us; but they went out, so that it *would be shown* that they all are not of us" (1 John 2:19). Such occurrences, although relatively rare, occur, and remind us that humans are limited in their evaluation of faith, while only God looks upon the *heart* (1 Sam. 16:7).

The journey of the new Christian through the early maturing stages of his or her life in Christ—the **B** segment of Figure 19.1—is made possible by the Holy Spirit's work. The Spirit trains immature believers to help them slowly mature and detach their identity from the things of this world. This is simultaneously accompanied by the believer's growing desire to be satisfied only by his union with his heavenly Father, his divine Brother, and the Holy Comforter (Pss. 16:2, 5, 8-9, 11; 25:4-5; 73:25-28). The journey of the identity-transplant in every Christian's life is a personal journey that usually occurs by *the means of grace*: (a) time spent in the Word; (b) fellowship in the body of Christ; (c) prayer; (d) discipline; and (e) the sacraments.

---

[147] This was first treated in chapter 1, with a diagram entitled The Eye; the Heart; and World/Life-Views.

Maturity Motivated by Christ's Love Leads to Love for Christ

Those with whom God has walked and is pleased to keep near himself gradually realize a level of maturity in Christ. This maturity does not mean they are without temptations or struggles or will not sin anymore. The **C** segment of Figure 19.1 represents this new plateau in the Christian's life. It recognizes that a Mature Christian is one whom the Holy Spirit has remolded to such a degree that he has a heart that is *truly* devoted to God and no longer seeks the things of the world.

Mature Christians are *motivated* by Christ's love to love Christ—to trust him in all life's circumstances. Job is such a model. In the midst of all of his distress—the loss of children and wealth—he said, "Naked I came from my mother's womb, and naked I shall return there. The LORD gave and the LORD has taken away. Blessed be the name of the LORD" (Job 1:21). And Christ, when speaking to a woman by a well in Samaria, told her that if she drank from that well she would thirst again. Then he added, "but whoever drinks of the water that I will give him shall never thirst; [for] the water that I will give him will become in him a well of water springing up to eternal life" (John 4:14). Spurgeon elaborated:

> He who is a believer in Jesus finds enough in his Lord to satisfy him now, and to content him for evermore. The believer is not the man whose days are weary for want of comfort, and whose nights are long from absence of heart-cheering thought, for he finds in religion such a spring of joy, such a fountain of consolation, that he is content and happy. Put him in a dungeon and he will find good company; place him in a barren wilderness, he will eat the bread of heaven; drive him away from friendship, he will meet the friend that sticketh closer than a brother. Blast all his gourds, and he will find shadow beneath the Rock of Ages; sap the foundation of his earthly hopes, but his heart will still be fixed, trusting in the Lord. The heart is as insatiable as the grave till Jesus enters it, and then it is a cup full to overflowing. There is such a fullness in Christ that He alone is the believer's all. The true saint is so completely satisfied with the all-sufficiency of Jesus that he thirsts no more—except it be for deeper draughts of the living fountain. In that sweet manner, believer, shalt thou thirst; it will not be a thirst of pain, but of loving desire; thou wilt find it a sweet thing to be panting after a fuller enjoyment of Jesus's love.[148]

But it is an error to say that maturity in Christ ends the struggle between the old man and the new. It is also wrong to say that mature Christians are done sinning. The sin nature will always seek to trip the believer. And mature believers will be tripped by their own distractions and weaknesses. But mature Christians eagerly confess their sins to Christ and say with David, "When I kept silent about my sin, my body wasted away through my groaning all day long. For day and night Your hand was heavy upon me; my vitality was drained away as with the fever heat of summer. I acknowledged my sin to You, and my

---

[148] Spurgeon, *Morning and Evening*, 560.

iniquity I did not hide; I said, 'I will confess my transgressions to the LORD'; and You forgave the guilt of my sin" (Ps. 32:3-5).

Experiencing the forgiveness of sin and remembering the cost God paid to secure this blessing for us; living at peace with the Triune God; knowing that God is committed to us; knowing that we are members of his family; and knowing that we will enjoy eternal life in his presence is to *truly know* that we are loved. And being loved in this way frees us and motivates us to *agapao* God and *agapao* our neighbor. God's love produces in his image-bearers their ability to love. Yes, *what a person truly loves, motivates him.*

20

God Imparts Aspects of His Divine Nature to Renovated Hearts— Christlikeness Made Possible

For those whom He foreknew, He also predestined to become conformed to the image of His Son, so that He would be the firstborn among many brethren. (Rom. 8:29)

For by these [divine power and true knowledge] He has granted to us His precious and magnificent promises, so that by them you may become partakers of the divine nature. (2 Peter 1:4)

These verses capture our purpose—God intends to conform his children to his Son's image, and he does this by the Spirit's developing aspects of God's nature in their hearts. We have three goals: (1) to draw together the preceding chapters; (2) to explore what aspects of the divine nature his children can partake of; and (3) to discuss how the Spirit imparts these aspects into their renovated hearts. This is a summary and defining chapter—intended to set the stage for the next section, *"Manifesting Christ's Divine Nature."*

Christ made it clear that his sheep are to live *in* the world but are neither to be *of* the world, nor to live for the *things* of the world. His prayer, in John 17, discloses his mind:

> I do not ask You to take them out of the world, but to keep them from the evil one. They are not of the world, even as I am not of the world. Sanctify them in the truth; Your word is truth. As You sent Me into the world, I also have sent them into the world. For their sakes I sanctify Myself, that they themselves also may be sanctified in truth. I do not ask on behalf of these alone, but for those also who believe in Me through their word; that they may all be one; even as You, Father, are in Me and I in You, that they also may be in Us, so that the world may believe that You sent Me. (vv. 15-21)

Being separated from the world's ways and from seeking our identity in the things of the world does not imply we are to disassociate from slaves to sin who find their meaning in the world's trappings. Christ gave us a *mission* in the world. We are to be the salt of the earth and the light of the world so that men may see our good works, and glorify our heavenly Father (Matt. 5:13, 14, 16). We are to be Christ's ambassadors in the world (2 Cor. 5:18-20).

We began discoursing on the spiritually-dead, and thus perverted, intellectual condition of those ensnared in the world/life-view of modernism and postmodernism. They put the *human* at the center of reality. God has been removed from their thinking, except to exist on the same plane as humans. God is *small*, and humanity is *large*. God is merely a crutch who is needed only by those who are weak and not intellectual. God has become an afterthought.

God calls Christians to live in the midst of those who ignore and renounce him. Those regenerated are called to the task of being salt and light to others. We are given a sufficient amount of the mind of Christ to carry out God's work and are being transformed by the renovation of our nature. By imparting a true knowledge of God's attributes to our minds, the Holy Spirit subsequently leavens our entire heart—mind, passions, and will. The first chapter explored this reality, which led to the question, "What Is the Divine Nature?"

In chapters 2–12 we examined the biblical revelation of God's divine nature, his self-revealing statements and activities. We considered the relationship of the persons of the Trinity to provide insight in such troublesome areas of *human* tension as: (a) equality/inequality; (b) authority/submission; (c) individual/community; (d) rights/responsibilities; and (e) freedom/control (chapter 3).

Also examined were the following attributes of God: aseity, eternality, infinitude, omniscience, patience, spirituality, holiness, immutability, omnipresence, wisdom, goodness, omnipotence, sovereignty, and love. Six other attributes were not looked at in depth: God's invisibility, life, justice, wrath, righteousness, and mercy. We now ask, "What aspect of each attribute does God impart to his children, by giving them true knowledge of it?"

God Is Trinitarian

The mystery of one God in three Persons is worthy of contemplation though it transcends our comprehension. God revealed himself to us so we would understand in part the relational roles within the Godhead. Perfect unity exists between the divine persons in their roles. We speak of positive co-working tensions—not because there is any tension between the Trinitarian persons, but because these relations create tensions in human relationships. The five relations are: (1) equality/inequality; (2) authority/submission; (3) individual/community; (4) rights/responsibilities; and (5) freedom/control. It is good for us to consider these relations because (a) they are God-created; (b) all humans experience them; (c) our fallenness perverts our ability to balance the tension between these roles or to accept them as God intended; and (d) God has modeled how we are to manage these tensions.

What do believers partake of God's Trinitarianism? (1) Regarding *equality/inequality*: believers are to appreciate that all persons are *authentic*. All deserve the respect God affords them. Christ died for all (1 John 2:2; 4:14; John 3:16; 4:42). Before God, all humans are equal. *But* God also authored human *inequality*. There are the strong and the weak, the wise and the foolish, the rich and the poor, and the healthy and the unhealthy. God ordained both *role* and *ability* differentiations and we must recognize, honor, and reward them. But, *"from everyone who has been given much, much will be required*" (Luke 12:48). The Spirit of God works in his children's hearts, creating godly attitudes and contentment, so "an *attitude of the righteous*" (Luke 1:17) is formed in them through the *true knowledge* of God.

(2) Regarding *authority/submission*: God instituted human relationships that place some people in positions of authority—parents, governors, school teachers, owners—and others in positions of submission—children, taxpayers, students, employees. Everyone is to be in subjection to the governing authorities. "For *there is no authority except from God*, and those which exist are established by God" (Rom. 13:1). Such authority/submission exists within the Godhead, and has been revealed to edify us. We are to learn how to live with appreciation and contentment in God-ordained authority/submission roles.

(3) With regard to *individual/community* relations, persons are each due his or her privacy, but all have community obligations. God created us as social creatures. And the *body of Christ*—the true and invisible *church*—is a positive example of this. First Corinthians 12 best reveals God's mind about his children's connectedness. He speaks of giving spiritual gifts to the members of Christ's body for the common good (v. 7). Everyone is given a spiritual gift "for the equipping of the saints for the work of service, to the building up of the body of Christ; until we all attain to the unity of the faith, and of the *true knowledge* of the Son of God, to a mature man, to the measure of the stature which belongs to the fullness of Christ" (Eph. 4:12-13).

(4) Concerning *rights/responsibilities*, Scripture reminds us of our personal need to be concerned for the *rights of others* and also to be cognizant of *our responsibilities*. Because of our fallen nature our tendency is to reverse this: we are concerned for *our* rights and *others'* responsibilities. The greatest right God has given people is *the right to ask him to save them from their bondage to their fallenness and to restore them to a right relationship with himself*. And their greatest *responsibility* is for them to *love the Lord God with all their heart, and with all their soul, and with all their mind, and to love their neighbor as themselves*.

(5) And concerning *freedom/control*, God has granted to everyone the freedom to exercise free choice *within the bounds of our nature*—whether we are alienated from God or reconciled to him. For those alienated from God, the choices tend to be self-serving. But those in union with Christ serve him and seek to make choices according to his Word. The discussion of control, then, heads in two directions. For those serving self, the discussion tends toward the control of the environment or control of others. For those serving Christ, the discussion focusses on self-control. Self-control is a *"fruit of the Spirit"* (Gal. 5:23). Scripture says, "He who rules his spirit [is mightier] than he who captures a city" (Prov. 16:32).

The persons of the Trinity have revealed how they live in harmony with these five positive co-working tensions. The Holy Spirit tutors those in Christ so they too learn how to live in harmony with these tensions. As earth is held in its place in the universe through the counterbalancing forces of gravity and centrifugal force, so the five tensions bring balance and unity to the lives of those who bear God's image. Balance, however, is rarely achieved between the competing five sets of tensions until a reasonable level of *maturity in Christ* is produced by the patient work of the Holy Spirit in the hearts of God's own.

What Aspects of the Divine Nature Are Imparted to Those Born From Above?

1. God's Aseity [Latin: indicating absolute independence]

God is independent of everything external to him. His *aseity* declares his wholeness, his completeness, his absolute sufficiency in his eternal, Trinitarian existence. He has needed nothing throughout eternity and he will *never* experience a need. In his aseity, he stands in absolute contrast to his creation. His creation is *dependent* upon him for its existence and continuance. Every breath we draw is dependent upon God's continuing grace. He, on the other hand, is *independent*, sufficient in himself. He had no need to create. And he does not need what he created. He stands alone in his eternal, Trinitarian fellowship. This is an essential reality to *truly know*.

Every attribute of God is fixed in its unity with every other attribute. This means that if God did not possess the attribute of aseity, he would have needs. And what would a needy God be like? He would work to satisfy his needs. And that means he would *change*; he would be *mutable*. And imagine a God whose holiness, righteousness, power, wisdom, etc. were subject to alterations! He could be as prone to error as we are! Thank God we do not face such horrible possibilities because God is independent of his creation.

God's aseity undergirds his exalted position of glory which sets him apart from all creation. His aseity draws our attention to his exalted worth. Contemplating God's aseity moves us toward the *mystery* associated with each of God's attributes. Mystery stimulates *awe* and breeds respect for his majestic character. And we ascribe great worth to him, which means we *worship* him. We are drawn to the beauty of his transcendence and of his *grace* poured upon us.

What do believers partake of God's aseity? Humility! *Each* of God's attributes give rise to *humility* when that attribute is discerned with *true knowledge*. And humility is a wonderful attitude to have formed in our hearts. What is it? It is a *submissive spirit* wrought in our hearts through the Spirit's administration of *true knowledge* that illuminates the superiority of I AM WHO I AM. This typically takes place degree by degree. But there are exceptions to this—such as Moses meeting God at the burning bush (Ex. 3:4-6), Isaiah seeing God on his throne (Isa. 6:1), or Paul being blinded by the Lord on the Damascus road (Acts 9:3-9). They were overwhelmed with the instant, powerful, and direct revelation of God's character. But most recognition of his character occurs through a series of biblical illuminations and experiences over time.

As one breaks a wild horse not by breaking its spirit, but by persisting in doing what is necessary to bring the horse to surrender to the touch of the trainer, so it is with the Holy Spirit and those he is breaking for Christ. He is the Master Trainer.

At its heart, humility is *surrendering to God's will*. Biblical theology helps us to understand that he is absolutely sovereign over every event. But surrendering to this magnificent truth often requires specific events that expose our unrecognized self-will. The struggle between what I want and what God wants is tempered over time as I learn to surrender increasingly to the will of God, realizing that his will is what is truly good for me. This is the perfecting of humility!

Jesus exhibited the perfect surrender of his will to the Father's will when, in Gethsemane, he said, "Father, if You are willing, remove this cup from Me; yet not My will, but Yours be done" (Luke 22:42). The Holy Spirit blesses us with the next verse: "Now an angel from heaven appeared to Him, strengthening Him" (v. 43). It comforts us to know that Christ needed to be strengthened in his humanity as he submitted to the perfect will of his and our Father.

Awe for the superiority of the King of kings produces humility. He is great! We are unimportant. He is perfection! We are imperfect. He is worthy! True knowledge regarding God's *aseity* breeds humility in believers' hearts. To contemplate that God has been ignored, rejected, and grieved by his creatures—when he had no need to create or to put up with the rebels—magnifies his character. He is a God without need, giving sustenance to those who need him for everything. We say with John the Baptist, "He must increase, but I must decrease" (John 3:30).

Other attitudes besides *humility* are stimulated in the Christian heart when God's aseity is truly known. *Respect* or *fear* might also be the heart's response to grasping the significance of God's aseity. Variations in response occur—because, as we examine the remaining attributes, we will describe specific qualities as *examples* of what the Spirit may impart to us; but the examples are not exhaustive. The Holy Spirit's work cannot be boxed. He accomplishes what he wills.

2. God Is Eternal

To be *eternal* is to be outside of time, separated from time. The old earth theory holds the universe is older than 13 billion years. And we have trouble getting our little minds around such a number! But 13 billion years is nothing compared to the *eternal* God who called the universe into being. But it matters not if the universe is 10,000 years old (young universe belief – my belief) or 100 billion years old (old universe belief). God is the Creator of time and transcends time. He is I AM WHO I AM. He never had a beginning. This entire consideration—eternity—transcends our ability to comprehend, but reminds us that God is awesome! He is eternal!

What do believers partake of God's eternity? God's gift to those who think about his eternal nature is hope. What is hope? Biblically, it is an expectation of fulfillment. And the hope that God gives his children is often tied to *eternal life*: "Paul, a bond-servant of God and an apostle of Jesus Christ, for the faith of those chosen of God and the *true knowledge* of the truth . . . in the *hope* of eternal life, which God, who cannot lie, promised *before times eternal* [Lit.]" (Titus 1:1-2). Scripture often ties God's promise of eternal life to hope.[149]

Believers are given hope in an eternal future. And an eternal future is a reasonable expectation in the light of God's eternal past. Since God has no beginning, it is logical to believe that he will have no end. And in that light it is reasonable to attach one's hope to the belief that those in Christ will receive the gift of eternal life in the presence of the Trinity. God's *eternity* gives birth to a *hope of eternal life* in those united to Christ in this life.

3. God Is Infinite

Infinity exceeds the parameters of measurement. It is the *unity of continuous continuity that describes God's boundless character*. God's every quality is infinite. And every quality is infinite in *perfection* as well as in *dimension*. Psalm 147:5 states: "Great is our Lord . . . His understanding is infinite [lit.: *innumerable; beyond numbering*]." Every attribute is infinite—beyond measurement. The perfections of God's attributes exceed our comprehension in their length, depth, breadth, and excellence. God is unquantifiable, measureless, inestimable!

What do believers partake of God's infinity? Confidence! King Nebuchadnezzar threatened Shadrach, Meshach, and Abed-nego with a fiery furnace for failing to bow down and worship a golden image. And how did these three men respond to his threat?

> O Nebuchadnezzar, we do not need to give you an answer concerning this matter. If it be so, our God whom we serve is able to deliver us from the furnace of blazing fire; and *He will deliver us out of your hand*, O king. *But even if He does not*, let it be known to you, O king, that we are not going to serve your gods or worship the golden image that you have set up. (Dan. 3.16-18)

The three were thrown alive into the fire clothed (v. 21), but neither their clothing nor hair were so much as singed or smelled of fire (v. 27). Indeed, while the three men were in the furnace, the king saw a fourth person with them whom he described as someone "like a son of the gods" (v. 25). He saw the preincarnate Christ, but had no idea of that. But he did call the three men "servants of the Most High God" (v. 26).

From where did these three get such courage? Courage that is willing to die must be attributed to *confidence* in the only *true God*. They told the king, God "will deliver us out of your hand. . . . But even if He does not . . . we are not going to serve your gods or worship the golden image." Their confidence was in God's person, not in the outcome of rescue from death. God enabled them to understand his infinite character so their resolve to be faithful was unshakeable.

Abraham exhibited this same confidence in God when he offered his son Isaac as a sacrifice to God. He placed in Abraham's heart confidence that God

---

[149] See John 3:15; 6:54; 10:28; 12:25; 17:2-3; Acts 13:48; Rom. 2:7; 5:21; 6:23; 1 Tim. 6:12; Titus 3:7; Heb. 9:15; 1 John 2:25; 5:11, 13.

would raise Isaac from the dead. Scripture says: "And Abraham said to his young men, 'Stay here with the donkey, and I and the lad will go yonder; and *we will worship and return to you,'*" and that Abraham "considered that God is able to raise people even from the dead" (Gen. 22:5; Heb. 11:19). Job had this same confidence in God's resurrection intentions and ability, for Job said, "Even after my skin is destroyed, yet from my flesh I will see God; whom I myself will behold, and whom my eyes will see and not another" (Job 19:25-27).

Some will protest that God's *aseity, eternity,* and *infinity* cannot be imparted to wholly dependent, time-defined, and finite people. And moreover, the *attitudes* of *humility, hope,* and *confidence* described as the benefits imparted to Christians are not *attributes,* but are temperaments or traits of the *heart.* That is correct, but the Holy Spirit renovates and *metamorphoses* the *mind, passions,* and *will*—the *heart.* Thus it is vital to have *true knowledge* of as many of God's attributes as he imparts to us. God wants to change our hearts as he transforms us increasingly into Christ's likeness, because he wants us to mirror Christ's heart. To have his heart is to be Christlike.

4. God Is Omniscient

We repeat this paragraph from chapter 2.

> God's knowledge is infinite.... He has known everything—past, present, future and possible—throughout eternity. Knowledge is inherent to God's independent, eternal and infinite nature.... He is knowledge; and humans grow in knowledge.... God knows all things distinctly—absolutely and fully (1 Cor. 13:12).... God knows all things infallibly (Isa. 14:24; 46:10). We know sufficiently, but never perfectly or exhaustively. God knows all things immutably (Ps. 139:1-6, 16; Isa. 46:9-10). Our knowledge is ever changing. God knows all things perpetually. He is always in the act of knowing all things, for all things are present eternally before him.... And God did not come upon his knowledge sequentially.... His omniscient nature is an attribute of his personality.[150]

Such an attribute is incomprehensible to finite minds. It transcends our ability to imagine how God can know the future choices of his creatures (perfect foreknowledge). This depends upon his perfect knowledge of our fallenness so he knows our choices before we know a choice is in the offing. And God's suppositional knowledge, knowledge of what would have happened if choices were made other that the ones that were made, is still more baffling.[151] Such knowledge transcends our capacity to fathom, but nevertheless, belongs to God's omniscience.

A marvelous benefit of his being *omniscient* is that God also *is* and *possesses* all *truth*—"The Word became flesh ... full of grace and *truth;* I am the way, and the *truth,* and the life" (John 1:14; 14:6). Postmodernists argue that truth is

---

[150] See page 35.
[151] Illustrations of God's suppositional knowledge include Matt. 11:21, 1 Sam. 23:10-13, and Luke 7:30.

unknowable, but this is not true, for God is truth and has communicated truth to those who will believe it in his Word, the Bible.

What do believers partake of God's omniscience? God gives his children *true knowledge* of himself, as Paul explains: Each believer is "being renewed to a *true knowledge* in the image of the One who created him" (Col. 3:9-10). God gives this *true knowledge* of himself to his children: "that the God of our Lord Jesus Christ, the Father of glory, may give you a spirit of wisdom and of revelation in the *true knowledge* [*epignosis*] of Him" (Eph. 1:17).[152]

And our *true knowledge* of God gradually transforms all our knowledge—of ourselves, of things spiritual, of human nature, and of all created things. Indeed, over time God transforms our entire *heart* by *true knowledge* in our minds. And the Holy Spirit gives every Christian sufficient *true knowledge* of God to be saved.

And believers can also know and retain *truth*—knowledge in Scripture that is, of course, accurate and dependable about spiritual matters, moral issues, and values. For example, God reveals the *truth* that it is wrong to engage in sexual relationships outside of marriage between one man and one woman. Those who reject it do not thereby make it untrue. But they stumble over it and hurt themselves, along with all who either join them in such sinful activities or who follow their example. God is *truth*, and to *truly know* him is to know *truth*. All that he has communicated is *truth* and to know God's communication is to know what is *true*.

5. God Is Patient

God is slow to anger (Nah. 1:3; see also Ex. 34:6-7; Neh. 9:17; Ps. 103:8). God's wrath will be justly manifested at the Last Judgment against those who rejected his only Son, the Lord Jesus Christ. And he displayed his wrath in history when he destroyed Sodom and Gomorrah, providing an example of his certain wrath for all who reject his gift of imputed righteousness, offered to sinners through faith in Jesus (2 Peter 2:6). In the meantime, even *now*, God is *patient*. God restrains his judgment, anger, and wrath.

We are to "regard the patience of our Lord as salvation" (2 Peter 3:15). Without his *patience* there would be no time for his *mercy*. And if that were true, there would be no time for *repentance, forgiveness,* and *salvation*. God's patience is why he spared Adam and Eve after their fall. Without his patience he would have destroyed them immediately. But God exhibits his patience when he causes his sun "to rise on the evil and the good, and sends rain on the righteous and the unrighteous (Matt. 5:45). He does not deal with us according to what we deserve. Instead, he patiently sends his heralds to tell all of his redemptive love offered in his Son.

What do believers partake of God's patience? "I therefore . . . implore you to walk in a manner worthy of the calling with which you have been called, with all humility and gentleness, with *patience*, showing tolerance for one another in

---

[152] Eph. 4:13; Col. 1:10; and 2 Peter 1:2-4, 8 make this same point.

love" (Eph. 4:1-2). "So, as those who have been chosen of God, holy and beloved, put on a heart of compassion, kindness, humility, gentleness, and *patience*, bearing with one another, and forgiving each other" (Col. 3:12-13). *How* do we put on *patience*? Patience is a gift given by the Spirit—"But the fruit of the Spirit is . . . *patience*" (Gal. 5:22). So how is the fruit given and how does it become a part of our character?

Christ says, "I am the vine, you are the branches; he who abides in Me, and I in him, he bears much fruit; for apart from Me you can do nothing" (John 15:5). And Christ in us, the Holy Spirit, helps us to recall God's patience with us and empowers us to show patience. Patience does not belong to the old nature; it is learned. It is wrought through loving discipline and through waiting upon God's providence (Heb. 12:10-11). By accepting the imperfections in us and in others, we learn patience from the Spirit.

Those trained by the Spirit learn of God's patience toward them. They could not enjoy salvation apart from it, nor would they persevere in the faith apart from God's continued grace, mercy, and patience. They remember God's patience with them when their patience is tried by circumstances or people. This encourages them to emulate Christ's patience toward others. And they ask Christ to strengthen them within so they can be patient in all situations.

Another fruit of the Spirit that accompanies patience is *self-control* (Gal. 5:23). Patience and self-control are like the heads and tails of a coin. They are different but are companions. There can be no patience without self-control. And self-control always involves our making choices. So patience also involves the will. The development of patience, then, is evidence of growth in free will—choosing to bring our will into conformity with God's will.

6. God Is Spirit

It is easier to say what a spirit is *not* than to say what it is. Negation is clearer than affirmation: God has no bodily form; he is invisible; he is of a spiritual essence unlike any corporeal matter; he is a simple, uncompounded being—he is undetectable by any sensory organs; and God is the Father of all created spirits which differ vastly from his own non-corporeal essence. His quality is infinitely higher and finer than that of the created spirits. God's essence and our spiritual essence are both spiritual, but the essences are very different.

The mystery in the very notion of God being a spirit is best understood in Christ's incarnation. Contemplating the incarnation is the best way to affirm what God as spirit embraces. Christ is "the image of the invisible God" (Col. 1:15). Indeed, "No man has seen God at any time; [but] the only begotten God . . . has *exegeted* Him" (John 1:18). To exegete is to interpret the object being examined. The Son of God incarnate has shown both what God as spirit is and what he desires *us* to partake of, by the Holy Spirit's power.

What do believers partake of God's spirituality? We identify with the incarnate Christ in two ways. First, we believe that humans are living *souls*—"Then the LORD God formed man of dust from the ground, and breathed into his nostrils the breath of life; and man became a living *soul*" (Gen. 2:7). The *soul* thus is the union of body and spirit and humans are incarnate spirits. And second, we realize that Christ's spirit is perfect while our spirits are in dire need of perfection. And this realization moves us to ask Christ for his spirit to transform us more into his likeness.

The *true knowledge* of God's spiritual nature is the doorway to understand that we only relate to God on a spirit-to-spirit basis. God created the human spirit so that there could be communication and fellowship between his spirit and ours. The Spirit of God communicates the truths of God to the believer's spirit when the Word is written on our *heart*, as Paul explained:

> For who among men knows the thoughts of a man except the spirit of the man, which is in him? Even so the thoughts of God no one knows except the Spirit of God. Now we have received, not the spirit of the world, but the Spirit who is from God, so that we may know the things freely given to us by God, which things we also speak, not in words taught by human wisdom, but in those taught by the Spirit ... [by which] we have the mind of Christ. (1 Cor. 2:11-13, 16)

Rather than our partaking of God's spirit, God created us with a spirit[153] incarnate in a physical body. There is a mystery regarding our make-up: Where does the spirit reside in the body? What is the relationship between the brain—the physical organ associated with the humans' mind, passions and will—and the *spiritual heart*, the home of our nature, character, and personality? We can only answer in the sense that God created us whole and undivided with a union of body and spirit. But the fall destroyed this perfect union. Death became a reality. Not only was the relationship between God and humans broken in spiritual death, but physical death also became a reality. Spiritual death resulted in everybody thereafter being born alienated from God. Everybody's spirit is conceived and enters life with a perverted interest in self and a blindness toward God (Ps. 51:1-5).

In God's eternal purposes the period of abnormality is the time between our first death[154] and the resurrection of our body from the grave, when our body and spirit are separated as the spirit awaits its new, imperishable body. Here is a scene of the *spirits* of those slain while doing God's will, and who wait for his judgment and the redemption of their *physical bodies*:

> I saw underneath the altar the *spirits* of those who had been slain because of the word of God, and because of the testimony which they had maintained; and they cried out with a loud voice, saying, How long, O Lord, holy and true, will You refrain from judging and avenging our blood on those who dwell on earth? And there was given to each of them a white robe; and they were told that they should rest for a little

---

[153] See Num. 27:16; Job 34:14; Eccles. 12:7; Isa. 42:5; 57:16; Zech. 12:1; Acts 17:25.
[154] Scripture not only speaks of a first death but also of a second death awaiting those who have rejected Christ and who will live thereafter separated from God. Eternal separation from God and placement in the lake that burns with fire and brimstone is called the second death (Rev. 2:11; 20:6, 14; 21:8).

while longer, until the number of their fellow servants and their brethren who were to be killed even as they had been, would be completed also. (Rev. 6:9-11)

God created a *spirit* for his image-bearers so they could communicate and fellowship with him, the eternal God who exists as the perfect spirit. The human spirit partakes of the divine nature of the Creator.

7. God Is Holy

God is absolutely holy.[155] Just what is this *quality* of God's nature? The word holy signifies God's *moral perfection* and *purity*. It also represents his inviolate commitment to see that all who bear his name manifest the moral perfections and purity of the eternal and infinite I AM WHO I AM—"You shall be holy, for I am holy" (1 Peter 1:16).

God's holiness is his attribute most often referred to. This has clear implications. His holiness is the most significant attribute for us to contemplate and ask him to impart to our character! Holiness is also used more often in Scripture than any other attribute to describe other attributes. For example, "O sing to the LORD a new song, for He has done wonderful things, His right hand and His *holy arm* [holy *omnipotence*] have gained the victory for Him" (Ps. 98:1). God delights to tell us that his holiness is a permeating and governing quality of his nature.

His holiness is also the only quality that appears as a trilogy—"Holy, Holy, Holy" (Isa. 6:3; Rev. 4:8). And it is the primary name in Scripture for the third person of the Trinity—the Holy Spirit. No other word is so often associated with the Spirit of God. He is the *Holy Spirit*!

What do believers partake of God's holiness? It is God's intent to transform all of his children into his likeness in holiness:

> Lay aside the old self, which is being corrupted in accordance with the lusts of deceit, and . . . be renewed in the spirit of your mind, and put on the new self, which in the likeness of God [His image] has been has been created in . . . *holiness* of the truth. (Eph. 4:22-24)

"Truth," the last word quoted, is the Greek *aletheia* (Lexical # 225) that literally means the unveiled reality or the veritable essence of a matter. God renovates his children into holiness like his. It is not a false or imperfect humanly-defined holiness. It is holiness like God's and a holiness that only he can recreate.

Hebrews 12:10 describes God's tough love, his discipline of his children: "But He disciplines us for our good so that we may share his *holiness.*" Remember that God's discipline is not punishment but is training that creates conformity to his likeness.

---

[155] Scripture is filled with the declaration that God is holy: see Lev. 11:44; 19:2; Isa. 6:3; Josh. 24:19; 1 Sam. 6:20; Job 6:10; Ps. 22:3; 71:22; 78:41; 89:18; 1 Peter 1:16; Rev. 4:8.

While the Spirit leads God's child to put off the impure and to put on the pure, he simultaneously transforms the *heart* to produce an increasing desire to be *single-minded*. What does that mean? To give undivided attention to the interests of God. It means putting aside our interests and seeking God's interests. Our desire grows to put aside unkindness and put on kindness, to put aside impatience and put on patience. We long for more self-control. We desire to be the people God wants us to be. By the Spirit's power, this single-mindedness produces a holy mind, passions, and will. Single-mindedness is the path along which holiness is recreated.

8. God Is Immutable

Objections to God's immutability need answers. It is wrong to hold that God is immutable with regard to essentials but not with regard to nonessentials. Such a position undermines God's other attributes. For example, those who reject God's being *omniscient* with regard to his foreknowledge undercut his *immutability*. God would be forever learning if he lacked foreknowledge. He is thus reduced to a god who is no different from human beings. Without his immutable character, God is made small—open to making mistakes. He would be an inept god if he were not *immutable*. But God *is* immutable (Mal. 3:6; Ps. 102:25-27; James 1:17).

What do believers partake of God's immutability? Believers will never become immutable, for they are infected by the fall; but they can grow in manifesting many of the *fruits* associated with God's immutability. For example, God cannot lie (1 Sam. 15:29). God's children can stop lying, with the Spirit's aid. Indeed, Christ's follower can swear to his own hurt rather than stoop to a falsehood (Ps. 15:4). Christians should manifest a character of dependability.

This means that believers become more and more reflective of Christ's immutable character. We will fail, but our improvement in keeping God's commands should become evident. We are new people. The Spirit enables us to put off the old self and put on the new *character of Christ*. Having a single-minded devotion to follow Christ faithfully according to his Word, under the Spirit, is to go a substantial distance to show an immutable Christlikeness.

9. God Is Omnipresent

Scripture speaks often of God's being everywhere (Ps. 139:7-12; Jer. 23:24; Prov. 15:3; 2 Chron. 2:6). God has always been everywhere there is a place to be. There is no space beyond God. The great news here is that *all of God* is present where he is. He has a *repletive* presence; he fills everywhere with every attribute. As a spirit God has no parts or pieces. The essential simplicity of his spirit nature is everywhere present.

God is so thoroughly *everywhere* that the Bible says, "In Him we live and move and exist" (Acts 17:28). We live *in* him; we move *in* him; and we exist *in* him. We must distinguish this from *pantheism*, where nature and mankind are not independent of God but are all-inclusive, so that humans and nature are *elements of God's very being.* Nothing that God created shares his essence, his very being. Though everywhere present, God is independent of his creation.

What do believers partake of God's omnipresence? God is everywhere present, but his Holy Spirit does not *actively renovate* every *heart* so that everyone is being restored to Christ's likeness. The unregenerate are unaware of God's presence. They do not know that they live, move, and exist in him. God may be an idea they think about on occasions, but they have no genuine intimacy with him.

The regenerate have the Holy Spirit living in them. In that key aspect, God's children *partake* of him directly. He becomes their eternal companion, Savior, and God. They become his subjects, disciples, and worshipers. And this relationship grows in intimacy over time. God knows his own perfectly before their adoption, but they grow in their absorption of his revealed *heart*. The intimacy grows as the *true knowledge of God leavens their hearts* through the Holy Spirit's patient, tender, and persistent work.

A great mystery of our relationship with God is that he never forces his way into our hearts. The Holy Spirit first gives life to previously dead hearts (John 3:5-8). Thereafter the human spirit made alive by the Spirit learns truth regarding the Trinity in many ways—hearing the Word preached; reading it; friends sharing their experiences in Christ. The quickened spirit asks a member of the Godhead to give the identified grace to it. Every gift of grace is freely given and freely received. Christ comes to those spiritually alive, who invite him into their *hearts* by *faith*: "Behold, I stand at the door and knock; if anyone hears My voice and opens the door [of their *heart*], I will come in to him and will dine with him, and he with Me" (Rev. 3:20).

Every *quality* and *quantity* of the divine nature of which believers *partake* is *imparted* by the *omnipresent* Holy Spirit while he resides in their *hearts*.

10. God Is Wise

God alone is truly wise (Rom. 16:27). This is an obvious conclusion if one accepts the truth that God is omniscient, which includes his foreknowledge. As stated previously:

> Wisdom is part of God's essence.... His knowledge and understanding are infinite and perfect.... His absolute foreknowledge of... all second causes is such that God ordains the accomplishment of the right end for all of his creation! Indeed, he has declared the end from the beginning (Isa. 46:10)....[156]

Such all-inclusive wisdom belongs to God alone. Only he knows the right ends, means, and circumstances within which to accomplish what he reasons is the perfect conclusion to a situation in his creatures' lives. His wisdom is absolute in every regard.

---

[156] Phrases are drawn from Chapters 2 and 8.

What do believers partake of God's wisdom? God has shared much of his wisdom in his Word. Important wisdom to guide us is available to all who will avail themselves of it. The Proverbs are full of wisdom and are even appreciated by many unsaved people. Many of their sayings are substantiated by common sense in the course of everyday life. Consider these words: "Poor is he who works with a negligent hand, but the hand of the diligent makes rich" (10:4) and "The naive believes everything, but the sensible man considers his steps" (14:15).

Some complexities in life, however, require more than common sense. For example, should a new job opportunity be pursued or avoided? What standard do we use to decide if the opportunity is genuine or merely a change of location that temporarily scratches an itch? Many factors need to be considered. Discerning God's will in such cases calls for our prayer and his guidance. We should see if the Word sheds any light on the decision. Our spouse should be intricately involved. The counsel of respected godly friends can be sought. And an assessment of gifts and heartfelt desire to undertake the new challenge should be considered.

The wisdom most often needed pertains to wholesome daily living with family, those at work, at church, and with whom we rub shoulders in the general public. It is wisdom not unlike the fruit of the Spirit: "The wisdom from above is first pure, then peaceable, gentle, reasonable, full of mercy and good fruits, unwavering [and] without hypocrisy" (James 3:17). The point is plain; it is *wise* to live a godly life. And the Spirit enables us to *partake* of God's wisdom.

11. God Is Good

"No one is good except God alone" (Luke 18:19). The truth of this statement escapes all but those who are regenerate and who understand their fallen nature which causes them so much trouble. And what is embodied in the truth that God is good? It means that God displays his benevolence and bounty to us through creation, redemption, and providence.

What do believers partake of God's goodness? The Holy Spirit begins a transforming work on our motives[157] and actions so we become benevolent toward those around us. We notice those shut in with illness, or offer an opportunity to one without work. It is benevolent to share the good news regarding Christ with neighbors. It is a mark of caring to support those whose lot in life has put them in difficulty. There are innumerable ways to be benevolent.

Self-centeredness is gradually replaced by concern for others. The practice of taking up our cross daily and following Christ becomes a way of life. By this transformation persons so affected become free from self and free to be Christlike.

---

[157] "But wait until the Lord comes who will both bring to light the things hidden in the darkness and disclose the *motives* of men's hearts; and then each man's praise will come to him from God." (1 Cor. 4:5)

12. God Is Omnipotent

"For nothing will be impossible with God." Scripture is full of such statements (Gen. 18:14; Jer. 32:17; Zech. 8:6; Matt. 19:26; Luke 1:37). Christ answered the Pharisees who demanded he silence those declaring, "Blessed is the King who comes in the name of the Lord; peace in heaven and glory in the highest!" during his triumphal entry: "I tell you, if these become silent, the stones will cry out!" (Luke 19:40). The stones will cry out? Yes, God is powerful enough to cause stones to cry out. He demonstrated his power in many ways. He gave Abraham and Sarah a child when they were long past childbearing (Gen. 21:1-2). Through Elisha, God raised a sunken axe head from the water (2 Kings 6:4-6). Jesus raised Lazarus who had been dead four days (John 11:17-44). Christ's miracles show God's infinite power.

What do believers partake of God's omnipotence? Jesus made an astounding statement to his disciples on the eve of his crucifixion: "Truly, truly, I say to you, he who believes in Me, *the works that I do, he will do also; and greater works than these he will do*; because I go to the Father" (John 14:12). How can this be? Because the same Holy Spirit who lived in the Lord Jesus is given to God's children. Christ as God incarnate (John 1:1-2, 14) was fully human (Matt. 1:18-25), and he was given the Holy Spirit (Mark 1:9-13). And the miracles the Father performed through him were performed by the Spirit (Matt. 12:28). Therefore, Jesus said: "The works that I do, he will do also; and greater works than these he will do." The Holy Spirit given to believers is the same Spirit who descended upon the Christ. We, therefore, have access to God's *omnipotence* through *faith* and *prayer*. God's power is not under our *control*, but it is *available* to us if we "ask anything according to His will" (1 John 5:14). This is why God's people have observed miracles through the centuries since Jesus's ascension to God's right hand.

Some profess to be God's children and have a form of godliness, but deny its *power* (2 Tim. 3:5). They are "always learning and never able to come to the *true knowledge* of the *truth*" (3:7). But when the Holy Spirit lives in a person, he or she is the child of the *omnipotent* God who can do whatever he pleases. The significance of this is incalculable. The child of God has *access* to his heavenly Father's *infinite power* and need not concern himself with how weak he is. God uses people with little power to do his will. And surely no Christian lacks the power to *pray* to the *omnipotent* God who delights to give good things to us.

Sixty-eight people in my family, not counting myself, are in various stages of relationship with Christ—hot, lukewarm, and cold. The most important thing is to have an intimate relationship with Christ, with all its wonderful benefits. But I cannot regenerate them—the necessary prerequisite for fellowship with Christ. But as powerless as I am, I am in relationship with the *omnipotent* One who can do all things! So I pray. I ask God to order their lives through providence so that other people, events, or even *I* might be used by the Spirit to guide them to a place where they too will come to know Christ.

God's children do not have to pretend to have power or to desire it. They are related by adoption to the *omnipotent* God. His power is sufficient to meet all their needs. They need but ask in faith, according to his will, and await his wise answers to their prayers.

13. God Is Invisible

Christ is "the image of the invisible God" (Col. 1:15). For "in Him [Christ] all the fullness of Deity dwells in bodily form" (Col. 2:9). God is an invisible spirit. But God the Son, who from eternity past was "the only begotten God . . . has *explained* Him" (John 1:18). Christ, before his incarnation, was an *invisible spirit*. Jesus made eight I AM statements in the Gospel of John, which many trace back to the I AM who instructed Moses to lead the Israelites out of Egyptian bondage.[158] Furthermore, Christ's statement to the Jews, "Truly, truly, I say to you, before Abraham was born, I am," means that he was preexistent (John 8:58).

The incarnation sends strong messages: (1) God wills to identify himself with humanity. (2) He displays infinite love for us. (3) He left his exalted position in heaven to become the second Adam to reverse the consequences of Adam's fall. (4) He willed to suffer death to rescue us. (5) He revealed the standard of life which God, the *invisible spirit*, expects of those created in his image. (6) He revealed to us the Godlike character he wants to impart. And (7) His grace was made tangible when he sent the eternal King to give a foretaste of the eternal blessings to come. In a word, *the invisible God became visible through the incarnation*.

What do believers partake of God's invisibility? God's being both *invisible* and a *spirit* necessitates his giving us the *gift of faith*.[159] Many Christians do not know that even the *saving faith* they possess is a gift from God: "God has allotted to each [of his children] a measure of *faith*" (Rom. 12:3). There are three kinds of *faith*: blind faith attached to skewed presuppositions that do not mirror spiritual reality; a leap-of-faith attached to emotions that guide one's understanding of spiritual reality, but not necessarily in the light of God's Word; evidential faith, nurtured by the Spirit as he persuades us of God's involvement in the events in Scripture. The allotted . . . measure of faith God gives is rooted in his real involvement in our lives. Peter pens his second epistle to "those who have *received a faith of the same kind as ours*" (2 Peter 1:1).

Peter's faith was rooted in the time/space/history of his time with Jesus. It was an evidential faith, a gift from God. But remember that Judas Iscariot was also with Jesus for his three years of ministry, and Judas did not have saving faith though he saw the same evidence as the eleven (John 17:12). Why not? And, Satan was allowed to test Peter in hopes of destroying his faith; but Christ prayed for him, that his *"faith* may not fail" (Luke 22:31-32). And finally, does not the question, "What do you have that you did not receive?" (1 Cor. 4: 7) lead us to conclude that *saving faith* is a gift given to God's children by the Holy Spirit?

Scripture repeats: *saving faith is a gift that God gives to his adopted children*. Let us praise him for this!

---

[158] I AM—Greek: *ego eimi* – John 6:35; 8:12, 24, 58; 10:7, 11; 11:25; 14:6.
[159] Chapter 2 was filled with material about the Christians' dependency upon *faith*, its source, and its types.

14. God Is Life

The Gospel of John is filled with *life*. "In Him was *life*, and the *life* was the Light of men" (1:4). "Just as the Father has *life* in Himself, even so He gave to the Son also to have *life* in Himself" (5:26). "I am the resurrection and the *life*; he who believes in Me will live even if he dies, and everyone who lives and believes in Me will never die" (11:25-26). "I am the way, and the truth, and the *life*" (14:6). Each person of the Trinity is *life*. It is an attribute inherent to God. And he is the *genesis* of all life external to himself.

What do believers partake of God's life? All human life is sacred, a gift of God. God alone is life and he alone gives life. Therefore *life* is to be guarded, respected, and nurtured in accordance with his revealed will.

God desires that all human life begin within a loving family. He gives to each person talents to be used to serve humanity. And those who heed his call to follow Christ are promised *eternal* life, life that continues forever in God's glorious presence.

15. God Is Just

"The Rock . . . all His ways are *just* . . . and without injustice" (Deut. 32:4). God's being *just* brings great joy to those who live in the faith of being *justified* by the *just* Judge (Rom. 3:26). And God's being *just* brings great fear for those who reject Christ's sacrifice for sinners, the sacrifice that satisfied God's *justice*. The unsaved will give an accounting (Rom. 14:12) of their sins to Christ on Judgment Day when his *justice* is revealed.

What do believers partake of God's justice? To be *just* is to do justice—"He has told you, O man, what is good; and what does the LORD require of you but to *do justice*, to love kindness, and to walk humbly with your God?" (Mic. 6:8).

What does it mean to do justice? The *true knowledge* of God's righteousness, as shown in Jesus's life, *leavens* our *hearts* to change us more and more into his likeness. There is a sensitivity to see that the poor and the afflicted are not taken advantage of by uncaring souls in power (Prov. 31:8-9). An internal heart-interest is formed in serving family members and neighbors with integrity. The Holy Spirit begins to transform a Christian's heart so Christ is formed in him over time (Gal. 4:19). Godly thoughts and behavior drive out the old self-serving ones. Doing what is just, fair, and right replaces self-serving behavior. Justice replaces injustice!

16. God Is Wrathful

Paul warns sinners:

> The Lord Jesus will be revealed from heaven with His mighty angels in flaming fire, dealing out retribution to those who do not know God and to those who do not obey the gospel of our Lord Jesus. These will pay the penalty of eternal destruction, away from the presence of the Lord and from the glory of His power, when He comes to be glorified in His saints on that day. (2 Thess. 1:7-10)

God's *holy* wrath reveals the opposition of his holy character to all that is unholy—impure and twisted. God cannot love what contradicts his own nature. God is *perfection*, and that which is imperfect must eventually be either restored to his likeness or be banished from his presence forever. The holy cannot abide the unholy! But God's patience and mercy come to the sinners' rescue. The Father, in his patience and mercy, sent his Son, Jesus Christ, to deliver helpless sinners.

> God demonstrates His own love toward us, in that while we were yet sinners, Christ died for us. Much more then, having now been justified by His blood, we will be saved from the wrath of God through Him. For if while we were enemies we were reconciled to God through the death of His Son, much more, having been reconciled, we will be saved by His life. (Rom. 5:8-10)

The wrath of God is holy and fierce. It is being restrained at this moment. But God's wrath is real and eternal.

What do believers partake of God's wrath? The believer must learn to hate sin, for it is destructive and condemns those who reject God's remedy, his only Son. Sin kills and separates people from God and from one another. It needs to be covered by the righteousness and blood of Christ. Anything which prevents that from taking place is to be defeated whenever possible. But offenses and wrongdoings are to be overcome by *agape* love not by human anger. We are to be angry about sin because of the death it causes, but we are not to handle our anger sinfully (Eph. 4:26-27) for "the anger of a man does not achieve the righteousness of God" (James 1:20). Evil must be overcome with good, not wrath (Rom. 12:21).

We believe in the certainty of his wrath. We know he will mete it out justly on those who deserve it on Judgment Day. The knowledge of God's judgment should move believers to share the good news that God has provided a way for sinners to escape his coming wrath—God the Father "loved us and sent His Son to be the propitiation for our sins" (1 John 4:10).

17. God Is Righteous

"The LORD is righteous; He loves righteousness" (Ps. 11:7). What is righteousness? It is performing deeds that are right, equitable, and proper. Most often the Old Testament uses the Hebrew word *yashar* to convey the idea of doing right. Its literal translation is *being straight*. The New Testament Greek word translated "righteous" is *dikaios*, meaning equal—conveying the idea of *equity* and *fairness*. *Salvation* and *righteousness* are closely associated (Isa. 45:8; 46:13; 51:5-6). God's righteousness is closely tied to his rescuing his people from their sins through Christ's finished work on the cross.

What do believers partake of God's righteousness? The regenerate are given the *true knowledge* of God's righteousness and God's imputation of Christ's righteousness to their account by faith—"the righteous man will live by faith" (Rom. 1:17; Gal. 3:11; Heb. 10:38). In conjunction with this, the Holy Spirit implants in each believer's heart the sense of what is *right*. He makes the crooked *straight*. Believers have renewed interest in what is right, equitable, and honorable! Our salvation gives us a desire to see those who have rejected Christ saved. The implanted heart's desire to be right lends credibility to our testimony of Christ's love for the lost—"By this all men will know that you are My disciples, if you have love for one another" (John 13:35).

18. God Is Merciful

Mercy was symbolically represented as covering the Law's demands in the design of the Ark of the Covenant that God gave Moses. The ark had a Mercy Seat placed atop it, above the testimony of the Law (Ex. 25:21). Mercy is God's undeserved compassion to evil human *hearts*. We deserve death; he offers the free gift of eternal life. Christ's death shows the depth of God's mercy. The Hebrew word for mercy, *hesed*, is often translated "lovingkindness." The idea embodied in mercy is one of compassion, forbearance, and gentleness. Psalm 136 speaks of God's mercy, or lovingkindness, twenty-six times in twenty-six verses. It declares, "His lovingkindness is everlasting"—it is endless.

There is a general mercy extended to all, believers and unbelievers alike. And there is a special mercy poured out only on the redeemed. God's general mercy is seen in his goodness in providing multitudinous physical benefits to all, who are undeserving. God's special mercy is seen in the gift of his Son, Jesus Christ, who died to save a people from their sins. Mercy is thus withholding deserved punishment and replacing it with life in Christ.

What do believers partake of God's mercy? Peter asked Jesus how often to forgive someone who sinned against him: "Up to seven times?" Jesus replied, "Up to seventy times seven" (Matt. 18:21-22). Jesus then told a parable of a slave who owed his king $10,000,000 but could not pay. The debtor asked for patience of the king, who *felt compassion* for him. The king did more than asked; he forgave the debt. But later the slave was unforgiving to a person who owed him a small sum, and the king heard of it and summoned him: "You wicked slave, I forgave you all that debt because you pleaded with me. *Should you not also have had mercy on your fellow slave, even as I had mercy on you?*" (vv. 32-33).

Christ paid an incalculable price to redeem those the Father gave him. His *mercy is infinite*. To *truly know* this opens the spiritual glands of compassion in the heart of those blessed by God's mercy. Experiencing the mercy of God *with a comprehending heart*—made possible by the Holy Spirit—will circumcise the old, hard heart and transform it into a new heart of compassion. Such a heart freely extends mercy as it was freely given mercy.

19. God Is Love

First John 4:7-21 says more about what it means that God is love than any other fifteen verses. Here God's love is described as manifested in sending "His only begotten Son into the world so that we might live through Him. In this is love . . . that He loved us and sent His Son to be the propitiation for our sins" (vv. 9-10). God's *agape* love is not emotionally based but a commitment of his will to do the highest good for his people. *Agape* love is the willingness to give one's life—figuratively and literally—to impart life-giving benefits to others.

What do believers partake of God's love? The person who *truly knows* God will love God *and* his or her fellow humans. John describes this in multiple ways: "Let us love one another, for love is from God; and everyone who loves is born of God and knows God. The one who does not love does not know God, for God is love. If we love one another, God abides in us. The one who abides in love abides in God, and God abides in him. We love, because He first loved us" (1 John 4:7-8, 12, 16, 19). Those who *truly know* God will love God and their neighbors.

Believers will *truly know* God and will be taught by the Holy Spirit to love— follow Christ; impart life-giving benefits to those around them; share Christ with them through words and deeds; and administer their physical resources in ways that serve God's ends. People who walk with Christ in their *hearts* will, by the Spirit's renewing work, put on the character of Christ and behave in keeping with his life.

20. God Is Sovereign

His sovereignty rules over all (Ps. 103:19). All history is foreknown by God. There is nothing outside of his rule and oversight—even his permission of *evil*! Many have difficulty grasping God's *decretive* (permissive) *will*, but God *permits* many things to take place that contradict his nature. And *all* that takes place proclaims his *infinite wisdom* and resounds to his *eternal glory*. His patience with the ungodly; his perfect redemption of the nasty, hurtful things that befall his children; and his final judgment that will set all things right—all these must not be overlooked by those troubled by the truth that God is sovereign over *all*.

What do believers partake of God's sovereignty? Confidence in God's authority over all that transpires in the created order; *faith* in his perfect purposes to wrap up all things that come to pass; *hope* fixed on God's promises tied to his attributes; and *awe* that naturally wells up in the hearts of those who comprehend even a modicum of God's rule, are fruit of the *true knowledge* of God's sovereignty over *all*.

Many an earthly king, governor, business executive, sports hero, and ordinary citizen has mistakenly believed *they* were sovereign over their realms— but they have been myopic regarding Christ's kingdom. Note his response to Pontius Pilate, when he said, "You do not speak to me? Do You not know that I have authority to release You, and I have authority to crucify You?" Christ replied, "You would have no authority over Me, unless it had been given you from above" (John 19:10-11). Only God is truly sovereign. Our true role is to be faithful with the little that he entrusted to us, not to perceive ourselves as being great over much. Christ gave his Parable of the Talents to teach this lesson. The master says to his slave, "Well done, good and faithful slave. You were faithful with a few things, I will put you in charge of many things; enter into the joy of your master" (Matt. 25:14-30; especially vv. 21 and 23).

Summary of Imparted Aspects of the Divine Nature

This is a list of the *aspects* of the divine nature—*the attitudinal shifts in the heart*—imparted to those in Christ: humility, emulation of God's will, a deep respect for, a wholesome fear of God, the hope of eternal life, confidence in God, true knowledge—of God, truth, ourselves, things spiritual and things created, patience, self-control, mercy, kindness, a spirit of forgiveness, an understanding that we as spirits incarnate relate to God on a spirit-to-spirit basis, holiness, gentleness, and becoming faithful to righteousness. Amazingly, believers become partakers of God, for he dwells in them. God grants them his wisdom, a benevolent spirit, his power available through prayer, faith as a gift, a comprehension of the sacredness of life, a concern for the rights of others, a hatred of sin, *agape* love as real and shown, a sense of responsibility for things entrusted to them, joy, and the peace of Christ. There is a *banquet* of divine attributes to be enjoyed!

This concludes "What Aspects of the Divine Nature Are Imparted to Those Born From Above?" We next treat how such attributes are communicated to the lives of believers.

How Is the Divine Nature Imparted to Those Born from Above?

The Holy Spirit is given to all who are regenerated. As a result, they have died to sin—that is, no longer *practice* those things that are displeasing to Christ. Indeed, they are baptized into his death. They are buried with him in their baptism. But Scripture also says that those buried with him—united with Christ in the likeness of his death—are then enabled to "walk in newness of life" (Rom. 6:4): live as Christ lived while upon the earth (vv. 3-5).

Christ told those given to him, "Apart from Me you can do nothing" (John 15:5). We can do nothing pleasing to God without abiding in Christ and having his Holy Spirit transform the old nature into the new one. So *how* does the Spirit impart God's nature to those in Christ?

A number of mysteries surround this question. Scripture never sets forth the proportion of effort used by the Holy Spirit versus that used by the person who is being renovated. One hundred percent of the *increase* or actual growth in Christlikeness is always attributed to the Spirit (1 Cor. 3:6). But those in Christ are told to put off the old and put on the new. So how much of the effort to do this is to be credited to them and how much to the Holy Spirit? The child of God does *participate* earnestly in receiving God's imparted attributes, but his or her efforts are only a medium that God gives beforehand and uses to accomplish his purposes. "For I am confident of this very thing, that He who began a good work in you will perfect it until the day of Christ Jesus. . . . For it is God who is at work in you, both to will and to work for His good pleasure" (Phil. 1:6; 2:13).

A better question might be, "*What* does the Holy Spirit *use* to impart the divine nature to believers?" This is not a new question. For centuries theologians have spoken of the means of *grace* whereby Christ is revealed to and built up in the *hearts* of those whom God saves. These means are typically given as: the Word, prayer, and the sacraments. But in answering this question we will treat the following five (5) elements: the Word of God; the human *mind (heart)*; *true knowledge*; providence; and the infinite skills of the Holy Spirit.

First, the Holy Spirit Employs the Word

There is nothing magical about the words of the Bible. But Holy Spirit *uniquely* uses the words he has assembled in Scripture to accomplish God's purposes. There are no other words ordained for his use to bring people to Christ, to transform their hearts, and to keep them safe in the body of Christ.

God has testified, regarding his Word, that it is *special* because it is *his* Word, and he will use it as he deems appropriate. So, he said, "So will My word be which goes forth from My mouth; it will not return to Me empty, without accomplishing what I desire, and without succeeding in the matter for which I sent it" (Isa. 55:11). And his Word will be kept for his explicit purposes, as Jesus testified—"Heaven and earth will pass away, but My words will not pass away," and "For truly I say to you, until heaven and earth pass away, not the smallest letter or stroke will pass from the Law until all is accomplished" (Matt. 24:35; 5:18).

And he wants his children to use his words as they communicate their experiences and understanding of God and his purposes. God described his covenant with his chosen people, "As for Me, this is My covenant with them, says the LORD: 'My Spirit which is upon you, and My words which I have put in your mouth shall not depart from your mouth, nor from the mouth of your offspring, nor from the mouth of your offspring's offspring,' says the LORD, 'from now and forever'" (Isa. 59:21). Paul expressed it in this way: "For since in the wisdom of God the world through its wisdom did not come to know God, God was well-pleased through the foolishness of the message preached [the Word] to save those who believe" (1 Cor. 1:21).

God uses his Word to cleanse and purify his people (Eph. 5:26; 2 Peter 1:9). At the Last Supper, Christ told his disciples that they had already been made clean by the words he had told them (John 15:3). And in his high priestly prayer he asked the Father to "Sanctify them [his followers] in the truth; Your word is truth" (John 17:17). His Word is also the sword of the Spirit—the instrument the Holy Spirit uses to pierce the hearts of those who reject Christ (Eph. 6:17; Acts 7:54-60; 5:29-33). The Word is the Spirit's primary tool used to convert souls, transform *hearts*, sanctify believers, and keep them walking with Christ throughout their lives.

Second, the Holy Spirit Opens Believers' Minds

"Then He opened their mind to understand the Scriptures" (Luke 24:45). John wrote, under the Holy Spirit's influence: "We know that the Son of God has come, and has *given us understanding,* so that we may know Him who is true; and we are in Him who is true, in His Son Jesus Christ" (1 John 5:20).

The Word of God tells believers that they have been taught, not by mankind, but directly by the Lord: "All your sons will be taught of the LORD" (Isa. 54:13). And Christ quoted this passage: "It is written in the prophets, 'And they shall all be taught of God.' Everyone who has heard and learned from the Father, comes to Me" (John 6:45). The Holy Spirit is designated the Paraclete by Christ, signifying that he is our Helper, Teacher and Advocate. He is sent to all who are born from above to teach, train, transform, and mature them.

Spiros Zodhiates, executive editor of the *Hebrew-Greek Key Word Study Bible*,[160] provides a helpful explanation of the Greek word *parakletos* (# 3875). It reads in part:

> Christ designates the Holy Spirit as Paraclete (John 14:16), and He calls Him *allos* (243), another [referring to Christ's statement: He will give you *another* Helper . . .], which means another of equal quality and not *heteros* (2087), another of a different quality. Therefore, the Holy Spirit is designated by Jesus Christ as equal with himself, God (1 John 2:1). This new Paraclete, the Holy Spirit, was to witness concerning Jesus Christ (John 14:26; 16:7, 14) and to glorify Him. The Holy Spirit is called a Paraclete because He undertakes Christ's office in the world while Christ is away from the world as the God-Man. He is also called the Paraclete because He acts as Christ's substitute on Earth.

To think that someone can learn the Scripture and effectively apply it to his life apart from the transforming unction of the Holy Spirit is to totally misunderstand the processes of sanctification, purification, edification, consecration, and glorification. All require the indefinable work or hand of the Holy Spirit. The Holy Spirit opens the mind of the believer. The Holy Spirit writes the Word in the *heart* of the believer. The Holy Spirit is the One who actively cleanses, chastens, trains, disciplines, encourages and matures the child given to Christ by the Father.

It is also the Holy Spirit's work to recall to believers' *minds* the Word of God as it might serve his purposes: "But the Helper, the Holy Spirit, whom the Father will send in My name, He will teach you all things, and *bring to your remembrance all that I said to you*" (John 14:26). This truth is helpful to recall when the question is raised, "How did the writers of the four Gospels recall all that they recorded of Christ's many statements and teachings?" John answers in John 2:22: "So when He was raised from the dead, His disciples *remembered* that He said this; and they believed the Scripture and the word which Jesus had spoken." And the word Jesus had spoken was recorded under the Holy Spirit's supervision and became the New Testament accounts of Christ's life, death and resurrection.

Third, the Holy Spirit Imparts the True Knowledge of God into Christians' Minds
The Spirit does this so to transform us more and more into the likeness of Christ. The true knowledge leavens our mind, passions, and will so that we possess, over time, more of the mind and world/life-view of Christ. He is formed in us so that our intentions, motives, and conduct mirror God's character and will.

---

[160] Spiros Zodhiates, editor, *Hebrew-Greek Key Word Study Bible*, New American Standard Bible (Chattanooga, TN: AMG Publishers, 1984 & 1990), 1864.

The *true knowledge* of God, contrasted with the believer's growing understanding of just how unlike God he or she is, stimulates the believer to repent of their *un*Christlike attitudes and behavior; creates within them a longing to be more like Christ; and motivates them to surrender *self* and cooperate with the Spirit as he does his renovating work.

The Spirit, by opening Christians' minds to the true knowledge contained in the Word of God, begins to transform the believer's entire *epistemology*—his way of thinking about reality. These mental shifts are accompanied by alterations in one's *ontological* perceptions regarding the genesis of the entire universe—including that of God's image-bearers and the realignment of the innate knowledge that has been badly warped by our self-centeredness. As a result, their perceptions of good and evil are made to conform to what God revealed in his Word about good and evil. In short, the entire *mind* is gradually renewed.

Simultaneously, the believer's *passions* are being osmotically permeated by the leavening influence of *true knowledge*. His *desires, affections,* and *identity needs* are all brought more and more into conformity with the revealed *passions* Christ manifested. The Holy Spirit does this as he renovates the lives of those who belong to Christ.

And concurrently, the Holy Spirit transforms the *will* of God's children to bring it into conformity with his expressed will. The expression in the Lord's Prayer, "Your will be done," becomes a *heartfelt* desire of the follower of Christ. He or she is growing to understand God's will and to genuinely want the same things done as God does. They become ambassadors for God—"We are ambassadors for Christ" (2 Cor. 5:20).

It is accurate to say, then, that those in Christ are having a transformational spiritual experience under the Spirit's guidance. He reconditions their entire *hearts* as the *true knowledge* of God is being imparted to their *hearts* and is permeating them.

Fourth, Providence

The Holy Spirit employs God's immutable guidance of *all matters* through the exercise of both his *decretive* (permissive) *will* and *causative* (active) *will* to promote the work he is doing in believers' lives, teaching them God's Word.

The Spirit alone has the knowledge and ability to use our circumstances to accomplish God's ends—to conform us into Christ's likeness (Rom. 8:28-29). The relationship between a person's life and his or her growth in Christlikeness is a very personal and individual matter—no two people's growth in Christ is exactly alike. And this is also a strong reason to examine experiences in the light of God's Word. That in part lies behind John's admonition, "Beloved, do not believe every spirit, but test the spirits to see whether they are from God" (1 John 4:1). One person cannot deny the reality of an existential experience in the life of another, but the person who has had such an experience would be wise to ask, "Does my experience lead me to do, or not do, something that I know is in keeping with God's revealed will?" The Holy Spirit will never alter, contradict, or eliminate any of God's Word that the Spirit superintended in the first place. The Spirit is as unchanging (immutable) as are the Father and the Son.

But the Holy Spirit who indwells every Christian makes himself known to each one. He does this in the providential experiences that make up our lives. The Spirit communes with the spirit of God's children (Rom. 8:16; Acts 5:32). We live every moment in the context of our larger providential experiences. Remember, God is sovereign over every event in our lives.

Fifth, the Holy Spirit's Infinite Skills

The Spirit has limitless skills with which to work out his will and good pleasure in our lives. He has all of God's attributes in his own make-up. He has all wisdom, power, knowledge, love, etc. at his disposal. As God he knows the end from the beginning.

At times God has manifested his *patience* and *gentleness*. And at times he has manifested his wrath—the great flood, and the destruction of Sodom and Gomorrah. God can whisper in a still, small voice (1 Kings 19:11-13) and he can speak loudly so that those who hear, but do not understand, believe they heard thunder (Job 40:9; John 12:28-29). The Holy Spirit has the ability to do whatever is in keeping with his holy nature and suits his perfect purposes.

Part 3

Manifesting Christ's Divine Nature

You will know them by their fruits. (Matt. 7:20)

The two preceding sections each had a simple goal. Part 1 described God's attributes in an abbreviated way to draw attention to those aspects of his nature he imparts, in varying degrees, to his adopted children. Part 2 described the three major components that make up the human heart into which the Holy Spirit comes to dwell and transform into the likeness of Christ by renovating the old fallen nature into a new regenerated nature manifesting characteristics of God's divine nature—an ongoing, living process.

The third section looks at the "proof in the pudding"—the manifestation of receiving Christ's divine nature. If what has been said up to now is correct, then there has to be a demonstrable proof of its veracity. There are many cultural Christians who profess a relationship with Christ but who merely hold to a form of godliness, but deny its power (2 Tim. 3:5). There is little evidence of the Holy Spirit's transforming work in their lives. They offer intellectual assent to Christ, but are content to simply hold to their knowledge *about* Christ and are unwilling to "come to [Him] so that [they] may [truly] have life" (John 5:40). They are spiritually immature.

Chapters 21–27 show what a transformed, Christlike life looks like in seven areas: dating, marriage, rearing a family, singleness, the business community, government, and the public arena. Christ calls upon all who profess him to "love one another; even as I have loved you, that you also love one another. *By this all men will know that you are My disciples, if you have love for one another*" (John 13:34-35). And Paul exhorted those in Corinth: "Be imitators of me" (1 Cor. 4:16). And he told the Ephesians: "Be imitators of God, as beloved children, and walk in love, just as Christ also loved you and gave himself up for us, an offering and a sacrifice to God as a fragrant aroma"(Eph. 5:1-2). And we are called upon to examine ourselves to make certain that Christ dwells in us. "Test yourselves to see if you are in the faith; examine yourselves!" (2 Cor. 13:5).

21

Christ's Divine Nature Manifested in Dating Relationships

Mary had been betrothed to Joseph. (Matt. 1:18)

Those dating, those who remain single, those married, and those with families— are *all* under stresses not present fifty years ago. We are bombarded—almost daily—with examples of relationships antithetical to God's revealed will for us. The tragedy is that the conduct of those who reject God's lordship has an increasing influence on those who profess a desire to follow Christ. Premarital sex and divorce, for example, have spread almost like a pandemic virus.

The first four chapters relate God's wisdom to interpersonal relationships and problems encountered in the four arenas. This chapter, however, addresses *thoughtful* but largely *ignored* aspects of dating, not the more popular aspects. The one exception to this, however, is that we will look at human sexuality in the context of dating, hopefully in a fresh way.

Marriages have been consummated historically as the outcome of one of several processes: arranged marriages, marriages of convenience, authoritative marriages, and selective dating. Dating, as it is experienced in the West, is the newest of these processes.

- *Arranged* marriages are an old and honored tradition. The parents and community leaders determined the match by assessing what each person would bring to the union. Motivating factors were family and community interests, along with what was good for the couple.

- Marriages of *convenience* were entered into to meet a specific need—a helper was needed on the frontier; companionship was desired; sons and daughters were needed to assist in carrying on the work.

- *Authoritative* marriages were established where those who held leadership roles were allowed to personally choose their mate, and the woman selected generally had little or no recourse but to become the spouse of the nobleman making the selection.

- *Dating*, as it generally occurs in North America today, is a relatively new way of developing relationships. A number of *laissez-faire* and *permissive* characteristics have become associated with dating. By laissez-faire we mean, there are fewer perceived necessities for the parents or guardians to oversee in regard to the dating process. By permissive we mean that many young people now determine what the *parents* used to assume was their responsibility. This *laissez-faire/permissive* shift has occurred for many reasons. In many families, both parents are employed outside of the home. This creates less time for the parents to focus on their children growing-up. Children must make more and earlier choices than previous generations—creating a *perceived* greater maturity on the part of teenagers. But this condition often reflects neglected values, leaving the young adult without genuine wisdom or true maturity.

And the number of young adults raised in single-parent homes has increased enormously over the past decades. This creates the same types of problems as dual-career families, but to a greater extent in most cases. Indeed, one half of the God-intended parental model is absent. Single parents can be fraught with extreme fatigue and guilt, neither of which promotes in training responsible adults. Adolescents need wholesome relational values and positive family models. Many times children are left to find their own way in the world.

Then there is the relentless bombardment from a myriad of invasive electronically-transmitted entertainment sources. This repeated stimulus inhabits the *mind*, permeates the *passions*, and brings new directions to the *will*. The entire *heart* is impacted. That might be good if the *quality* of the stimulus were godly, but such is seldom the case. Rather, permissiveness is suggested, especially in the area of sex. There is ongoing pressure on young adults to conform to their peers' standards to accept the inevitability of premarital sexual activity at an earlier age. Also, pressure to exhibit anti-authority attitudes. And a growing segment of the populace holds it is acceptable to use mind-altering stimulants. *Relativistic tolerance* dominates the broader culture. So it has come to be generally accepted that to do your own thing is your birthright.

Within this cultural melee dating takes place. And even parents who work hard to seek positive influences for their children know that they are not inoculated against the surrounding forces, inviting them to try what the world has to offer. What follows is offered for those who desire to know God's mind about premarital relationships, who desire to marry in the Lord, or who want to counsel *others* on the subject of dating.

God's Word does not explicitly talk about dating. But it sets forth *principles* that bear on the subject. Biblical principles that apply to dating are examined in six areas: developing healthy male/female relationships; dating in the Lord; discerning *agape* love; discerning *philos* love; controlling *eros* love; and deciding to become engaged.

Developing Healthy Male/Female Relationships

God intends for children to grow up in families where the relationships between the parents serve as positive models for their children. Children's observations of how their parents treat each other greatly influence the formation of their presuppositions about intimate male/female relationships. Of equal impact is the early childhood relationships formed between each parent and child in the family. These relationships have a profound influence on children's expectations about the specific relationships they are subsequently to form in life.

To illustrate: some years ago, when my wife and I visited our son Jeff and his wife and their two children, we were all together in a large kitchen/eating room. Sue was standing at the stove, preparing supper. Their three-year-old son Samuel was standing behind her, making some loud attention-getting demands. Our son spoke to Sam, in a firm but moderate tone of voice: "Samuel, that is my wife you are speaking to, and you are not to treat her that way." Sam turned, looked at his dad, looked back at his mom, and repeated this zigzag looking procedure for a few seconds. You could almost read his mind by his facial expressions and body language: "What is this, 'his wife' stuff? I thought she was my mom. I don't understand. Oh, it must mean she is *his*. And if she is his, oh my gosh! I had better treat her differently than if she were *my* personal possession." Sam finally smiled at his dad and turned and walked away from his mom. At three years old he had learned an important lesson about how he should view and treat his mother.

When a husband affirms his wife's contributions within and without the family, listens attentively to her, and respects her as a person of great worth, the children absorb his respect and love for their mother. And while the child's relationship to parents differs from the one that exists between the parents, he or she grows to believe that the relationship modeled by his or her parents is the appropriate one to seek and form in marriage later in life.

Bad modeling of parental relationships has the same impact as good modeling, only of the opposite sort. If the mother demeans the father openly before the children, girls in the home *learn* that this is what wives do. And boys grow up expecting their future wives to do the same to them, and may choose a mate accordingly. Such modeling makes it difficult later for the grown children to practice the Lord's will regarding a wife's proper relationship with her husband: "The wife must see to it that she respects her husband" (Eph. 5:33).

The same problem, of course, exists if the father treats the mother in an ungodly manner and disobeys God's Word: "Husbands, love your wives, just as *Christ also loved the church and gave Himself up for her*" (Eph. 5:25). Children learn that wives can be ignored, mistreated, and demeaned so as to diminish their God-given worth, dignity, and role in the family.

This discussion is important because everybody has been raised in a family that, to varying degrees, coincided with or violated God's will regarding family relationships. We learn how to relate. And most of the learning takes place in the family at an early age. We will treat dating as a preliminary step to marriage. And many begin dating with inappropriate early-life experiences that foster unhealthy male/female relationships.

The difficulties we have in forming and sustaining wholesome relationships are brought into the arena of dating, but are often hidden or disguised. This occurs because most know that negative conduct is unattractive, so they are on their good behavior while dating. This is a good reason to get to know someone over a period of time, to observe them in a variety of settings. That is, has the person you are dating been tested in your presence, and if so, how did he/she measure up to expectations? Settling into a relationship with someone willing to accept our imperfect relational skills and who will be faithful as we grow in life is a key goal of dating.

Dating in the Lord

Young adults who know Christ should date only other young adults who are believers. Why? Because one never knows when an incredibly strong *emotional* attraction will develop in a relationship. And the *passions* component of the heart can rattle one's better judgment and justify making an exception to a serious biblical principle: "Do not be bound together with unbelievers; for what partnership have righteousness and lawlessness, or what fellowship has light with darkness?" (2 Cor. 6:14). An unmarried person is free to marry whomever he or she wishes, so long as it is "only in the Lord" (1 Cor. 7:39).

Life's road is full of unequally-yoked partners. The troubles that accompany such unions are many. Some may object to this and think, "But I am not dating at this time to find a lifelong mate. I am simply dating to have fun with my friends." True, but attractions are not altogether rational experiences. When there is a conflict between the *mind* (what we *know*), and the *passions* (what we *desire*), many *rationalizations* tend to drag us toward what we *desire*. The stronger the attraction between two people, the harder it is to focus on the foundational components necessary for the lifelong commitments Christ desires for his people in marriage.

Having two people in a dating relationship in the Lord is so important. It is difficult to overemphasize its importance. Why? Because we all *need the Holy Spirit's help* in establishing and sustaining wholesome, godly relationships in marriage—the logical outcome of dating.

The Holy Spirit produces the fruit of "love, joy, peace, patience, kindness, goodness, faithfulness, gentleness and self-control" in our lives. God desires these qualities in marriages. The Spirit imparts aspects of God's nature to Christians' *hearts*. The Spirit teaches us to practice the Scriptural principles that undergird life-fulfilling relationships. The Spirit breaks down false pride that easily asserts itself in relationships. Christ's *grace* and *mercy*, administered by the Spirit, enable a man and a woman to be faithful to their marriage covenant until the death of one of them. The Holy Spirit teaches God's children forgiveness in Christ, and also teaches them to forgive one another. A good marriage cannot exist apart from ongoing forgiveness. Indeed, the Spirit enables two who have joined together in matrimony to manifest true, godly, *agape love*.

Discerning Agape Love

Agape love is the first of three types of love essential to a wholesome Christian marriage. And because dating is a preliminary to marriage, the right understanding of each is important in maturing a relationship while dating. We will look at *philos* and *eros* love later.

Agape love is the only one of the three types of love unavailable to the lost. It is *will*-based and not rooted in the *passions*. And *agape* love flows out of death to *self*. It demonstrates a positive response to Christ's admonition: "If anyone wishes to come after Me, he must deny himself, and take up his cross daily, and follow Me. For whoever loses his life [surrenders 'self'] for My sake, he is the one who will save it" (Luke 9:23-24; Matt. 10:38-39). And no one can die and *remain* dead to self apart from the Spirit's working in the heart. *Agape* love is imparted to his children who *partake of his divine nature.*

Dying to self is a kingdom identifier. There are only two kingdoms: the kingdom of God and the kingdom of the prince of this world, Satan. Those not in Christ's kingdom are, due to the fall, members of the kingdom of the one who instigated the fall. They do not discern spiritual truth (1 Cor. 2:14). Although blind, they believe they see and accuse those *in Christ* of blindness!

We point this out because a God-honoring relationship rests on the foundation of *agape* love. And this means that young adults engaged in dating relationships should answer the question, "Does Bill/Mary evidence real *agape* love?" The answer might be discerned by observing how your date speaks about his or her family, friends, and those whom they dislike. If someone treats you well but shows little concern for those outside of a friendship circle, they probably cannot express true *agape* love for anyone who does not stroke their ego.

Ask the question, "Does my date consistently put *others* (not you) before him or herself?" If not, the time will probably come when that person will put *you* behind himself or herself too. When that happens, they will exhibit self-love that controls their heart, not *agape* love that comes from the Spirit.

Agape love that puts Christ and others first reveals the *character* of the one being dated. Honest communications cannot be sustained without *agape* love. Faithfulness will not be maintained without it. Compassion for those who become sick or are born with a birth defect is not sustainable in a godly manner without *agape* love. It is the backbone of lasting relationships.

People do not *feel agape* love; they *will* it. They are committed to putting others before self. They have, by God's grace, resolved to take up their cross daily, die to themselves, follow Christ, and serve others. Of course this self-sacrificing is not done perfectly. But when the mark is missed he or she confesses failure, seeks forgiveness, and prayerfully moves on in the Spirit.

Agape love is most commonly overlooked by those dating. This is tragic, because it is the glue that sustains the marriage bond and allows it to grow lovelier and lovelier over time. When two sinful yet forgiven people unite in marriage, they need forgiveness along the way. Much energy must be expended to keep the relationship growing. And much attention is required to meet each other's needs. Those who give of themselves to their spouses must also reveal their own needs and hurts *to* their spouses. This is essential for both partners to mature.

This becomes a reality when *agape* love is at the heart of the relationship. Without it, the best that might occur is two people living together without much conflict—but there is little bonding. They are two individuals with little oneness. A good marriage is led by the Spirit so that the union is really a trinity—

comprised of Christ, the husband, and the wife—in which a bond nurtures the holistic well-being of the couple; they become one.

The person who does not try to discern the presence of *agape* love in the friend they date fails to seek the best God offers in marriage. It is far better to start a dating relationship with a fellow-Christian—where two want Christ to grow them into his likeness over the years.

Discerning Philos Love

Far too many who begin a dating relationship base it upon their *philos* interests, or, even worse yet, their *eros* interests, without knowing that *agape* love is essential for a healthy relationship. But even the right kind of *philos* interests are often overlooked.

Philos love is connected to our likes and dislikes, our interests, and our feelings and passions. And there is often a so-called chemistry associated with good *philos*. It takes forms, such as, "I like him"—often a feeling without much content. Or "She is fun to be with." These are wonderful feelings, and are to be enjoyed. God is the *author* of such positive emotions.

Such feelings generally arise when the other person expresses an interest in our interests. Or they compliment us when we are mutually engaged in an activity. But what is to be guarded against is the untalked about fact that much dating occurs in environments not sustainable *every day*—going to the museum, to the races, to the movies, going shopping, playing board games. Everyday life is not made up of such events.

A good building block in *philos* relationships is compatible *world/life-views*. Similar world/life views are fundamental to a good relationship. They help us formulate our convictions on many matters such as: marriage; having and raising children; money management; how parents are to be respected through the years ahead; and even such philosophical topics as war and peace; capitalism and socialism; sex and pornography rest upon our world/life-views and are built on our presuppositions about life—its genesis, purpose and meaning.

Philos love requires respect for the differences present in others. The ability to talk about the full array of life brings substantive meaning to *philos* love. This does not mean there must be agreement on every topic. Indeed, our differences in perspective help both partners develop a fuller-orbed understanding of matters discussed. But the basic values and premises of good and bad and yes and no need to be in tune if a relationship is to be healthy and enjoyed over the years. And remember, dating is a first step to finding a partner with whom to *share life*.

When a couple's world/life-views differ substantially, the turf that each partner occupies may subconsciously bring about a peaceful division of the couple's interests, but the mutually supportive union of the whole persons that is God's design is forfeited. If discussions about the news that is received, and hopefully talked about by a couple, is to be enjoyed, their world/life-views must rest on compatible presuppositions that give understanding to life's experiences.

Dating that is going somewhere is, hopefully, a relationship-maturing process. At the beginning, it is enough to know that one's date professes belief in

Christ. But discerning true commitment to Christ—shown by actual *behavior*—then becomes the priority—followed by a growing understanding of compatibility between the two persons' world/life-views. Other areas of common interest are great to enjoy, but they are *not* the glue that bonds a couple together! It is fun to share activities—they are a cherry on top of a sundae—but they do not go to the heart of a good, long-term relationship. Good communications undergirding agreed upon goals, and activities that foster their accomplishment, are the ingredients of a good relationship.

A common, strong commitment to Christ, shared world/life-views, and the many moral values that flow from shared presuppositions, are the right ingredients in a *philos* relationship. These are the things that last. Feelings and emotions come and go. We get upset with those closest to us because we become self-focused, or perhaps they sin against us. When that happens, forgiveness is necessary, and things deeper than fun are needed to restore the relationship to health. Fidelity that resides in *agape* love, and compatible world/life-views that allow people to enjoy one another's company—*philos* love—are what makes for a strong and lasting relationship.

The positive feelings that accompany early dating relationships, and are considered signs of compatibility, are not trustworthy indicators of long-term supportive qualities that foster harmony and fulfillment. Positive emotions are indicators of how the other person *makes me feel*, and that is pleasant, but such an orientation indicates a self-focus that evaporates when the other person is not focused on *me*. The person focused on feeling good may be unconsciously seeking a codependency relationship—one unconsciously dependent upon another to keep them going. The level of self-need can be so great that it is very difficult for the person so enslaved to self to coexist with another person in a mutually beneficial relationship.

Every person in a healthy dating relationship has needs—to be listened to and understood, to be respected and valued. But when healthy relationships are not developed early in life, in a loving family, unreasonable demands are placed on relationship partners. Sometimes people with poor relationship skills are attracted to one another, and, by God's grace, work their way through their early relationship deficiencies, but the journey can be very hard and painful.

Another thing must be considered. An appropriate amount of *time* is needed in a dating relationship to discern if *agape* and *philos* love are genuine, healthy components of the relationship. How much time? That varies with the experience and maturity of those in the relationship. But neither partner can obtain *certainty* regarding the final outcome of a relationship. *Faith* and *trust* must eventually be factored into the decision to let it continue.

Controlling Eros Love

God is the author of everything sexual in males and females. God created people with a visual ability to discern if those they see are males or females. It is natural to unconsciously seek to identify the gender of a person who comes into view. Indeed, sexual identification begins with the first imaging of a child in the womb or at birth. The things of first importance, concerning the child, are the child's *health* and *sex*. But often we speak of the gender first—"You have a girl!" or "You are expecting a boy!" And this announcement means their sex has been identified. It is an important determinant of who we are. Our personal identity is closely tied to our sexual identity. And the time of transition from being a boy or girl into a man or woman is of extreme importance. We attempt to identify the gender of a child before us by his or her clothes, or the color of the clothing if they are infants. But as people mature, the *shape* of their body is the common means of ascertaining their gender.

Some want us to believe that the *only* difference between men and woman is the configuration of their bodies—external and internal parts that constitute sexual identity. Such an approach defies simple, common observations and experiences. In addition to the obvious physical differences, there are hormonal differences that impact how the genders feel and act. This does not mean that all women experience periods of menstruation identically, but women do have a significant, recurring experience that impacts their identity which men neither experience nor completely understand. And there are emotional and psychological differences that are identifiable in general between the sexes. God created male and female to complement and fulfill one another in marital union, not to be identical (Gen. 2:18; 1 Cor. 11:8-9).

Sex itself has been trivialized in today's society. We are constantly taught to think about it through visual and linguistic invitations. The visual appetite of the male to see the female form is exploited at every turn. Television more and more displays more and more nudity. James Bond portrays fornication as a merry game to be emulated. Pornography has been declared protected by the First Amendment right to free speech. And millions of males are addicted to the pornographic display of naked women. Young Christian males are growing up in this environment, where sex is portrayed almost as commonplace as asking someone to go with you to eat. And this spills over into males believing that women are mere objects, not bearers of God's image who should be treated as God's own possession.

And because sex is so terribly misunderstood, it is now being experienced in many ways God never intended. One of the saddest publicly-talked-about examples is the case of a well-known female TV star who had her own show and is a practicing lesbian. She has said publicly that she tried sex when she was thirteen and it was no fun. So she decided to experiment with sexuality. The result? She decided that a female/female relations was the way to enjoy sexuality. This is not new, for Paul spoke of it: "For this reason God gave them over to degrading passions; for their women exchanged the *natural* function for that which is *unnatural*" (Rom. 1:26).

In God's plan, sexual union between one man and one woman was intended to be a *sanctified* experience—a oneness, set aside for God's purposes, where two people use their bodies for pleasure *and* to give themselves to the other person to communicate that he or she is loved—trusted, wanted, respected, valued. This does not occur when each focuses on his or her own pleasure. *Godly sex is selfless*, concerned for the *completeness of one's partner*—physically, emotionally, and spiritually. It can be experienced to this depth only in marriage.

There is true oneness in the Trinity: God has revealed that three Persons, each truly God, constitute one Godhead. As unfathomable as this is, it represents reality. And God intends the union between man and woman in marriage to replicate the oneness/threeness in the Trinity. Paul described the *mystery* of marriage (in Eph. 5:22-32) and likened it to Christ's relationship with the church—his body. A godly marriage takes the form of a trinity of its own—Christ, a husband, and a wife—all under God the Father (1 Cor. 11:3). And dating, ultimately, is an exploration of the possibility of two people forming a marriage union in the future.

This is important as we discuss *eros* love because God intended it to have three purposes. If we disregard any one of these, we end up with less than God wants us to understand and enjoy. God had a beautiful end in mind when he created the sexual union between a man and a woman, intending that it be experienced *exclusively in marriage*. To misplace God's intent is to make sex sterile, unfruitful, and harmful. And to experiment with sex outside of marriage robs sex of its beautiful meaning, and creates thereafter regret, guilt, and diminished self-esteem.

What were God purposes when he designed us as sexual beings? He intends sexual union to foster three things: *pleasure, expansive oneness,* and *the creation of children*. Two of these three purposes *cannot be realized*—as *God* intends—*outside of marriage*: pleasure and expansive oneness. And the third, the creation of *children*, harms many when it occurs outside a loving and stable family environment.

Pleasure

We ask of the *pleasure* dimension of *eros*: "To whom does the person you are dating *belong*?" A humanist would never ask this. But the answer provides a critical guide regarding premarital sex. The humanist's perspective generally is: Sex is a bodily function available to anybody who desires to engage in it. There is nothing wrong with it; it is a personal choice. There are no moral implications attached to the decision to have sex. Besides, it is fun—and who will know? Young adults hear this message day in and day out in media and from close friends.

Numerous biblical passages connected with the *true knowledge* of God say the persons we date *belong to God*. And God has said a lot about sex, in and outside of marriage.[161] But the many biblical references to the sin of fornication,

---

[161] See: Acts 15:20, 29; 21:25; 1 Cor. 6:13, 18; 7:2; 10:8; 2 Cor. 12:21; Gal. 5:19; Eph. 5:3; Col. 3:5; 1 Thess. 4:3; Jude 7. The Creator of all things is also the Owner of all things. The account of Joseph and Potiphar's wife, who attempted to pull him into an affair with her, illustrates well the point being made (Gen. 39:7-9), as does Ps. 51:4 where the account of King David's repentance regarding his adultery with Bathsheba, and the killing of Uriah the Hittite, are recorded. In David's confession to God he said, "Against You, You only, I have sinned."

premarital sex, seem far away to many young Christians facing sexual temptation, because the *feelings* associated with sex are powerful and appealing. These feelings cloud attempts to think clearly. Clear thinking must precede engaging in sexual conduct while dating. We can avoid the burning urge to let ourselves go if specific behavior is avoided before it can ignite stronger feelings—namely, staying away from stimulating sexual urges by touching. Females are tactually stimulated; males are visually stimulated. Females should therefore dress modestly and be careful with their body language. And males need to be careful about touching their dates. It is not wise to see how far you can go before the sexual urge is turned up high. It is better to see that the sexual urge is not turned on. Our goal is to show why God has *lovingly* made premarital sex off limits for the unmarried.

Sexual pleasure, as God intended it, must: (1) be physically pleasant; (2) be psychologically uplifting; and (3) remain a pleasant memory over the years. The *male* always realizes the first of these criteria whether it is experienced outside or within marriage. This is often not true for the female. In fact, the female partner when experiencing her first sexual union may be excited, but that by itself does not produce pleasure. There is typically a difference in the male's and female's pleasure in a sexual union for the first time, *especially outside of marriage.*

(1) The description that follows is intended to develop a basic understanding of human sexuality, not to be stimulating. Think for a moment about the physical *structure* of the male and female sexual organs. And then ask, "Who is the one that enters the other? Who is the receiver? Which partner is guaranteed sexual pleasure? And which partner is dependent upon the other partner to provide sexual pleasure?" Our anatomy and bodily functions answer these questions, and the *pleasure outcome* for the partners is therefore realized differently. The male and female do different things in their sexual union. The male *enters the female*. The female *receives the male*. The male *is guaranteed physical pleasure in the sexual union*—his body's motion brings him a physical climax. The female has *no guarantee of physical pleasure*. The male is *not dependent upon* any *specific action by his female partner* to guarantee his physical pleasure. The female is *totally dependent upon her male partner's performance to provide her physical pleasure*. The male partner must *learn* how to provide pleasure to his partner.

The Bible, when speaking about sexual unions outside of marriage, describes them as: the male "went into" the female. It is described as a mechanical process, devoid of any positive value. Examples include: "Judah saw a daughter of a certain Canaanite whose name was Shua; and he took her and *went in to her*" (Gen. 38:2). Judah had such an experience with Tamar, and ". . . and [he] went in to her" (Gen. 38:18). This expressive pattern is *repeated* in Scripture.

(2) The next test sexual pleasure must meet, if it is to qualify as God-intended pleasure, is to answer the question, "Is the pleasure accompanied by genuine psychological pleasure?" A sexually inexperienced male today is typically so naive about sexuality that he is probably only aware of the personal, physical pleasure he expects from his first union. He probably does not know

there *is* a psychological component associated with sexual union, other than to falsely think of himself as a man. If his self-focus has brought him to have sexual union with his girlfriend, true love would have kept him from expressing his love for her in this way. He is more likely trying to reassure her—assuming it is their first sexual experience—that it was OK for her to have the experience with him. She is more likely to be in doubt because somewhere inside she knows she has been *used*, even if she was a willing partner. A female inherently knows that in sexual intercourse she has two possibilities: (1) being *loved* or (2) being *used*!

It is nearly impossible for a young female to feel psychologically fulfilled by sexual union with a boyfriend on a date. She has given something away that she cannot regain. The physical pleasure, to the degree that some was present, was probably not brought through to its God-intended conclusion. Sexual fulfillment is learned by experience. But a truly *completed* sexual act is experienced by males and females differently. The male's and female's rising and falling erotic patterns differ. And what completes the sexual union differs for each gender. Sex, as God designed it, is not just an automatic physical experience, that is easy to understand, because it has both physical and psychological dimensions.

(3) The final test sexual pleasure must pass is to answer positively the question, "Will the premarital sexual union create an experience that will remain pleasant, and without regret or guilt, in our long-term memory?" The answer will be "no" for a Christian. Premarital sex cannot create a long-term pleasant memory because it violates God's infinite wisdom, revealed in his creation of our physical, psychological, and spiritual qualities that accompany sexual union. God designed sexual pleasure to be an integral part of marriage, intended to provide for an *expansive oneness* to be formed—and this oneness cannot occur outside of the covenant of marriage.

Expansive Oneness

The expansive oneness of marriage is the greatest blessing of two people becoming one. How we express our sexuality in marriage plays an important role in its realization. Experiencing sexual unions while dating cannot contribute to the creation of an expansive oneness later in marriage. In fact, living together before marriage reduces the probability of achieving a wholesome *expansive oneness* in marriage because the conduct reveals a self-centeredness that blots out any evidence of *agape* love.

In over four decades as a ruling elder in the church, I failed only twice to bring about reconciliation between marriage partners who professed faith in Christ. Both occurred when a deep conflict emerged late in marriage and children were involved. In both cases, the major offense, from the wives' perspective, lay in premarital sexual activity with the man who was now her husband. Both wives repeated, "If you had loved me, you would not have treated me that way." The husbands were dumbfounded, "Yes, but you were a willing participant." And the wives retorted, "That doesn't matter; if you had loved me, you would not have done it!" Reason was absent at premarital unions and postmarital explosions.

Raw emotions were the driving force both times, and on this offense hung all their other problems.

An *expansive oneness* embodies many of the same mysteries associated with the Trinity—one God in three persons. Remember, marriage is also a kind of trinity: Christ, husband, and wife, all under God the Father. A godly marriage becomes a cause for *worship* when its beauty is realized and God is glorified through it, for the couple praises and honors God in public *worship* for his presence in their marriage. Their marriage is a sacred union and is not to be defiled. And observers recognize the couple as manifesting a God-honoring relationship.

Creation of Children

Every young adult understands that God intended human beings to populate the earth through their enjoyment of a sexual union. Contraceptives and fertilization in a dish have not altered God's design for couples. But it is also understood—certainly by Christians—that God intends children to be conceived and born in *families*. Humans have the longest dependency-period for the formation of their physical, mental, psychological, social, and spiritual health of any creatures. The normative model is for children to be nurtured in a family.

Deciding to Become Engaged

Making a decision to become engaged is very important, and while the engagement is entered into with the intention of marriage, it provides time to continue to grow in preliminary oneness—without physical union. It is a time to reassess the ability of your loved one to participate in the establishment of a deep interpersonal trinity. Is he or she more in love with Christ than with me? Remember, the *biblical model* is one of loving God first and foremost. Is he (or she) willing to be guided by the biblical model for marriage? While I have dated her (him), is there strong evidence of her (his) affections for Christ, and a desire to grow in Christlikeness? A union in the Lord is essential for a healthy, happy fifty- or-more years together.

Think carefully about your partner's formative family relationships. They will impact his or her ability, and thus yours, to form deep bonds. You and your children will be impacted by the past. This is the outworking of the biblical statement that God "...visits the iniquity of fathers on the children and on the grandchildren to the third and fourth generations" (Ex. 34:7; Num. 14:18; Deut. 5:9). This does not say children are found guilty for their parents' sins, but that they are impacted by their parents' failures. It can take several generations to rebuild what has been lost in a previous one. Needing to grow in building relationships is not necessarily a reason to refrain from marriage, but you should do it knowing you will surely need Christ's help. These realities *reinforce* the biblical standard that God's people should marry only in the Lord. With God's help, all things are possible; without it, nothing that is pleasing to him is possible.

Before answering, "Will you marry me?" a girl needs insight into the character of her potential spouse. Integrity is not glamorous but is the foundation of a wholesome marriage. It is also the character-wellspring in which the Holy Spirit forms *agape* love that in turn is the source from which the spouses will draw and manifest *agape* love toward those with whom they live and work. Without *agape* love, *philos* love and *eros* love are put under such an inordinate strain that they typically disintegrate. Even if the marriage were to last, it would be very stressful.

Philos love is best nurtured with compatible world/life-views. Young people sometimes wonder what couples talk about after five, ten, twenty, forty, fifty, or sixty years of marriage. A compatible world/life-view provides a basis for enjoying external stimuli that *will* bombard you throughout your life. Expressions like, "You know, I was thinking about what so and so said and…" or "What do you think about such and such?" provide continuous opportunities for *intimacy*. People *hunger* for an intimate relationship. The immature male often thinks of intimacy as a sexual relationship, but the female intuitively knows better. A sexual relationship is an intimate aspect of marriage, but the expression of oneself through sexual union falls far short of what God considers genuine intimacy.

Sharing your deepest, most private thoughts with another is a mark of true intimacy. Proverbs 3:32 provides insight: "For the devious are an abomination to the LORD; but He is *intimate* with the upright." The word "intimate" translates the Hebrew *cowd* (Lexical # 5475), which initially means "a couch or cushion upon which one sits and shares his or her mind with another." The NASB marginal note says the literal rendering of "He is intimate with," as found here, is "His private counsel is." So the translation could be "…but His private counsel is with the upright." We might paraphrase "…but He will sit on a couch with the upright and share His private counsel with them." The most significant and deepest form of intimacy is one's willingness to share deep, private thoughts with another. This can be frightening. But it is an important component of *philos* love.

A word of personal testimony. During our engagement, I listed twenty-six things I liked about Shirley and four things I did not like about her. (I remember only one of those four things, and it was utterly unimportant, but, in my immaturity, it was on my list.) After considerable time reviewing my list, I asked myself, "Am I willing to live with the four things I do not like, *and keep my mouth forever shut about them*?" I answered "Yes," and the next time we were together I asked Shirley to marry me. That was over fifty-five years ago.

The controlling of *eros* love should continue throughout the engagement. It is perfectly acceptable for those developing a serious relationship to express to their loved one, in a non-erotic way, that they are looking forward to physical union. Such a union is part of God's design, and fulfilling that design is something to anticipate with joy. The union is best enjoyed throughout the years if the urge to consummate it is controlled until marriage.

These thoughts reflect the ideals set forth in God's Word. And few people fulfill all the Scriptural ideals. But if they have been ignored and their importance is only subsequently recognized the appropriate response is one of confession and repentance. If the guilt-producing aspect is still ongoing, confess your specific mistake to the person affected by your conduct. And *stop* whatever it is that causes the problem. Repentance is a part of our salvation. Repentance, the ceasing of an ungodly habit or event, is evidence that the old nature has been put off and the new nature—*in* Christ—has been put on. That is something to rejoice over!

22

Christ's Divine Nature Manifested in Marriage

For this reason a man shall leave his father and his mother,
and be joined to his wife; and they shall become one flesh. (Gen. 2:24)

God had a *purpose* in mind when he established marriage between a man and a woman. God formed man's body from the dust of the earth and breathed life into him so that he became a living *nephesh*—Hebrew for soul: a *body* and *spirit*, united to form a breathing human[162] (Gen. 2:7). After his creation God placed the man (Adam) in a garden and commanded him not to eat from the tree of the knowledge of good and evil (Gen. 2:8, 17). God declared, "It is not good for the man to be alone; I will make him a *helper suitable* for him"—Hebrew: *ezer* (Lexicon # 5828)—"one who helps or a helper corresponding to him" (v. 18). So God made a woman (Eve) *from the body* of the man (Adam)—she was bone of his bone and flesh of his flesh (vv. 21-23).

From the beginning, the words used to describe the *man* and wo*man* were intentionally selected. The Hebrew word for man is *ish*, meaning "to be." The Hebrew word for woman is *ishshah*, meaning "out of 'to be.'" God the Creator is the eternal I AM. Man was created to be by I AM, and he was created to bear the image of I AM.[163] And the woman was taken out of the man and formed into a person who also bore God's image. But she was not a he.

She was a different kind of human. She was to complement, correspond to, or harmonize with the man while being his *helper*, yet differentiated from him. Her differentiation is apparent in her physical differences. But there are significant differences not seen in the outward or inward form of the woman, but associated with hormones that impact her both *physically* and *psychologically* differently from the male. She is like the man—she bears the image of God; she is a human. She is not like the man—physically or psychologically. The differences are God-intended and significant. And a proper understanding of God's *design* in Scripture aids a godly marriage.

Marriages that ignore God's will regarding the *purpose* or *roles* in marriage are unions that cannot realize God's best intentions. God has best purposes for everyone in all areas of life, but those who reject his counsel also reject his purposes for them (Luke 7:30). To grasp God's best purposes for us in marriage, we will treat five areas: The Marriage Trinity; Leaving and Cleaving; One Flesh;

---

[162] *Nephesh*: see the Brown-Driver-Briggs, *Hebrew and English Lexicon*, reference # 5315.
[163] To be created in God's image incorporates the following: the human has the capacity to possess true knowledge of God, to truly know him (Col. 3:10), and to be righteous and holy (Eph. 4:24).

Expansive Oneness; and Marriage: A Primary Relationship in Which Godly Transformation Takes Place.

The Marriage Trinity

The mystery of the Trinity is impenetrable by reason—there is but one God, one Eternal Spirit, who exists eternally in three Persons: the Father, the Son, and the Holy Spirit. While unfathomable, this is nevertheless made plausible by spiritual discernment.[164] Our own spirit stirs us to look for a God who is in charge of everything—God the Father. Our spirit seeks a God with whom we can identify and through whom we can understand in part what the invisible, transcendent God wants us to know about him and ourselves in relation to him—God the Son. And our spirit wants a God who will be forever with us and help us become whom he purposed—God the Holy Spirit.

In chapter 3, "The Trinity: Our Model and Mentor," we discussed five paradoxes that exist in personal relationships. And living with these seeming paradoxes, in our fallen state, is often fraught with tensions. These tensions arise for us between *equality* and *inequality*; *authority* and *submission*; *individual* and *community*; *rights* and *responsibilities*; and *freedom* and *control*. These paradoxes are never *negative*; nor are they experienced as tensions by the persons of the Trinity as they manifest the godly harmony that they want to exist in our lives. But we must strive to reconcile these five juxtapositioned but dissimilar components of life.

Our *struggles* with these five paradoxes occasion specific tensions in our fallen *hearts*. Marriage is the most intimate human-to-human relationship that God designed. It is, therefore, where these paradoxes are most likely manifested in ungodly ways. But God—who knows the end from the beginning (Isa. 46:10)—designed marriage to mirror the relationship between the persons of the Trinity: "Christ is the head of every man, and the man is the head of a woman, and God is the head of Christ" (1 Cor. 11:3; Eph. 5:23). Christ's *indwelling* presence in a couple's life is the hope for their marriage: that the relationship will become a union in which *two, indwelt by Christ, become one* in a manner that emulates that between the Trinitarian persons.

Christ—the Head of the Man

Christ is, of course, the head of both husband and wife. The expression "Christ is the head of every man, and the man is the head of a woman" does not imply that Christ is not the head of the wife. It, however, denotes the line of authority and accountability God established to bless those who marry in the Lord. It is spoken to those who seek his guidance in establishing a union that reflects his design. To only give lip service to the marriage trinity design is to condemn the marriage to a distorted shadow of its God-intended fullness. If Christ is not the head of the marriage, one of several perversions will emerge. (1) The husband will lead and promote means and ends that serve his ideas of what is right and best but will miss God's intentions. (2) Or the wife will emerge as the

---

[164] Spiritual discernment can be best understood by reading 1 Cor. 2:11-16.

leader and usurp the husband's God-given role. In this reversed arrangement, the wife will lose respect for her husband, and he will lose his self-respect. Or (3) they will struggle for headship and either divorce or work out separate turfs on which each can express his/her individuality, as he/she chooses—but there will be little of the two becoming one.

Both the man and the woman must sincerely want Christ to be the *head* of their union. Such a true desire will be shown in several ways. First, both will seek to learn what Christ has revealed in his Word regarding God's design for marriage. The man must understand what is involved in loving his wife as Christ loved the church (Eph. 5:25). He must grow to learn to live with her in an understanding way (1 Peter 3:7). She must grow to understand what is involved in her being subject to her husband (Eph. 5:22-24). And she must comprehend what God's Word means when it says that she respect her husband (Eph. 5:33).

Second, husband and wife will recognize their dependence upon the Holy Spirit to keep God's wholesome standard for their relationship. They will be sensitive to the Spirit's guiding by both the written and spoken Word, and his providence by which they become aware of their nonconformity with his will. This awareness gives an opportunity for them to reassess their attitude and/or behavior, seek the Spirit's help, and begin afresh to follow him.

And finally, their acknowledgment that they need the Holy Spirit will lead them to seek his grace as they *take up their cross every day*, die unto their old self-will, and follow Christ in seeking the best for their spouse. Dying to self daily is *essential* to maintain a godly marriage. The killer in every dying or wilting marriage is self-centeredness. Living for Christ embodies fostering Christ's love for my spouse, through me—seeking my spouse's highest good.

The Word reveals this prescription for marriage, and only God the Holy Spirit can build a marriage into its God-intended *oneness*. This can only be realized when Christ is truly the head of the man.

Man—the Head of the Woman

Biblically, man's *headship* in marriage must be understood in light of Christ's headship in the church. Paul taught this clearly:

> For the husband is the head of the wife, as Christ also is the head of the church, He Himself being the Savior of the body . . . . Husbands, love your wives, just as Christ also loved the church and gave Himself up for her; that He might sanctify her, having cleansed her by the washing of water with the word, that He might present to Himself the church in all her glory, having no spot or wrinkle or any such thing; but that she would be holy and blameless. (Eph. 5:23, 25-27)

Christ died for the church! A husband must die to himself and put his wife's interests first. This *assumes* the male understands his *purpose* as a husband and what God intended when he made the wife his *helper*. Male and female role reversals occur when couples either fail to comprehend God's design for marriage or choose to follow their own design.

The husband's *headship* is a call to *serve* his wife. Remember that Christ said, "The Son of Man did not come to be served, but to serve . . ." (Matt. 20:28). But it is not a call for him to inappropriately serve his wife: (a) encourage her to be the head of their oneness—God has assigned *primary accountability* for the constitution of a biblically-patterned marriage to the husband; or (b) passively consent to her pursuit of a lifestyle contrary to her becoming Christlike.

Ephesians 5:23, 25-27 says: "sanctify her," cleansing her "with the word," helping her to be "holy" and "blameless." What do these point to about a husband's headship? That he is accountable to Christ for the couple's spiritual diet—family prayer and devotions; public worship; the literature in the home. Does their daily lifestyle foster Christlikeness? The answer to this question is a husband's basic responsibility. He serves his wife when he desires what is Christlike for her. This does not mean that he dictates the ingredients that make up their spiritual diet. Indeed, a husband who does not understand his wife's *heart* in all such matters is not living with his wife in an understanding way. But this description of the couple's spiritual diet underscores the husband's accountability to God for their spiritual well-being.

1 Peter 3:7 is another foundational Scripture for husbands:

> You husbands in the same way, live with your wives in an understanding way, as with someone weaker, since she is a woman; and show her honor as a fellow heir of the grace of life, so that your prayers will not be hindered.

God instructs the husband to live with his wife in an understanding way. This is so for two reasons. First, a man cannot love his wife without *understanding* her. Second, it is difficult for a man to *understand* a woman to the depth that God calls him to, without much effort. This is due to the way God has made men and women. Women generally understand men. They know what makes them tick. But the Bible describes women thus, "A garden *locked* is my sister, my bride, a rock garden *locked*, a spring *sealed up*." The bride's song follows, "Awake, O north wind, and come, wind of the south; *make my garden breathe out fragrance*, let its spices be wafted abroad. May my *beloved come into his garden* and *eat its choice fruits!*" (Song 4:12, 16).

Young husbands often believe that if they can repeat their wives' words, this qualifies as understanding them. That may be so, if the wife has asked the husband to pick up the dry cleaning. But if the wife has said that they should stick with the cleaners they have dealt with for years while the husband believes that a new cleaners needs to be patronized, the *emotional, relational,* and *rational thoughts* underlying their perceptions are probably miles apart.

Reflecting on the heart model—*heart* = *mind* (knowledge), *passions* (desires, affections, and identity needs), and *will* (volition)—will help us understand what a woman requires to perceive that she has been understood. A man, when expressing himself, is usually only conscious of what is going on in his *mind*. He thinks; he speaks. But a woman usually incorporates her *passions* with her *mind*. Both inform and shape her verbal expression. Thus for a husband *to understand* his wife he must do more than listen to her words. He must encourage her to express both her *passions* and *thinking*. And he must make every effort to grasp *how* the two components of the heart relate in her *mind*. This is the "rock garden locked, a spring sealed up" that he is invited into to "eat its choice fruits." Some men are wired so that their *passions* and *mind* are united but most are not so equipped. Obtaining unity with the *passions* and *mind* is typically a component of the man's transformation into Christlikeness by the Holy Spirit. And a wife is a frequent instrument used by the Spirit to bring this about. Doubtless, marriage is a relationship God employs to sanctify us.

Husbands must appreciate the *differences* between them and their wives. Doing so will impact several things. First, he will discover that his wife's *passions* are often important to God, and thus to final decisions. God's desires and affections are in harmony with his thoughts and actions. Our passions must become a godly part of our decision-making. Second, he will discover that most decisions that affect the spousal relationship will be more harmonious when the wife *knows* she is understood. Third, she will find it much easier to submit to her husband's role as head when she knows that she is understood. And finally, the *motives* of every decision made in marriage will be altered by the inclusion of the *passions* component with the *mind* element of the heart. And God is in our motives as well as our actions (1 Cor. 4:5; Prov. 16:2).

1 Peter 3:7, "live with your wives . . . as with someone weaker," directs the husband to be *gentle, kind,* and *considerate*. He is to love her as his own body (Eph. 5:28-29). He is to protect her, as one might protect a delicate piece of crystal. She is not to be treated coarsely. She is not to be the iron sharpening iron described in Proverbs 27:17. It is appropriate for men to sharpen and be sharpened in governmental assemblies, boardrooms, or even classrooms, but it is rarely appropriate for spouses to hone one another. Such conduct will typically dull a marriage, not sharpen it. Debate is oriented toward proving a point or winning an argument, neither of which is conducive to fostering marital harmony. God did not design a marriage as a competition; it is a union built on care and support.

And the instruction, ". . . show her honor," means to recognize the contributions she makes to the union. To illustrate, God gave my wife a gift of hospitality. I do not have that gift, but I encourage her to use hers, which she joyfully does. Because of this, many think I too am hospitable. In truth, I am an *a-social* person, not *anti-social*, but *a-social*. I tell her privately that I appreciate her gift and the good reputation it fosters for our family. In addition, when we have guests, and I thank God for the meal, I include my wife and her gift of hospitality. I do this to *honor her*. It is a small way to express my love for her and to honor her before friends.

1 Peter 3:7 concludes by saying that if the husband does not live with his wife in an understanding way, or does not live with her as with a weaker vessel (KJV), or does not honor her, *his prayers will be hindered*. God has clearly taught how he expects regenerated men to live with their wives. Husbands who profess to love God but disobey his instructions will experience the consequences until they repent and walk again in the ways of the Lord. Husbands cannot worship God and enjoy the benefits of his fellowship—answered prayers—when their relationship with their wives is not in keeping with his will. God will not bless what is ungodly.

Woman—Being Subject to and Respecting Her Husband

A woman who does not love Christ more than she loves her husband and herself will not receive the blessing God has for one who *subjects* herself to and *respects* her husband. This is because she does not understand that God has, analogously, placed her in the third position in the marriage trinity, with a role drawn from and following the example of the third person of the Trinity, the Holy Spirit.

A woman of the world is more concerned with *her equality* (if not superiority), *her rights,* and *her liberation* than she is with her God-designed purpose. The woman separated from Christ does not think of herself as designed by God to be her husband's helper, to complete him, to be suitable for him. Her role does not imply that the husband is more important than the wife, "for those who have clothed [themselves] with Christ . . . there is neither male nor female; for you are all one in Christ Jesus" (Gal. 3:27-28).

Some in the church upset the biblical teaching regarding the wife's role of subjection. They do this by quoting, ". . . and be *subject* to one another in the fear of Christ" (Eph. 5:21), and using it to modify the following teaching: "Wives, be subject to your own husbands, as to the Lord . . . as the church is *subject* to Christ, so also the wives ought to be to their husbands in everything" (vv. 22 and 24). The erroneous reasoning is: "Ephesians 5:21 is the controlling teaching—it teaches that everyone in the body of Christ is to be subject to everyone else in the body of Christ. The New Testament teaches universal subjection; there is equal subjection; the husband is to be as much in subjection to his wife as his wife is to be in subjection to him—the focus of verses 22 and 24."

This is not good exegesis. The error is used to reinforce a presupposition that supports the *equality* aspect of the *equality/inequality* tension modeled in the Trinity. The Son became incarnate and always did the Father's will (John 5:26; 6:57; 8:16-18; 14:28). Scripture portrays the Holy Spirit as subservient to the Father and the Son (John 14:26; 15:26; 16:13-14). There is *role* differentiation in the Trinity and God intends there to be *role* differentiation in marriage.

Many Christians have been taught that the message conveyed by the Greek verb *hupotasso* ("be subject"—Lexical # 5293), that appears in Ephesians 5:21 and 5:24, is that the wife is not under her husband's headship but is on an *equal* plane with him. Not so! Husbands and wives are clearly equal (without distinction) in their worth in God's eyes. But God has distinguished and ordered their roles in marriage. Peter makes the same point in 1 Peter 3:1-7. Colossians 3:18-19 does the same. The husband's *headship* role means he is responsible before God *to love and serve his wife as Christ serves and loves the church.* And as Christ is the *head of the church,* he has appointed husbands to be *heads of their families.*

Being *subject* to one's husband is also promoted by understanding that certain attitudes and behavior *are not* included in the biblical injunction. A wife's subjection to her husband does not mean that she is to be thought of as being under his thumb or feet—to be used, dominated, or thought of as a lesser person. She becomes *part of him* when they are married; he is to love her as he loves his own body (Eph. 5:28-31). She is not to be silent, but is to express herself. God has given her a *mind* too. The Holy Spirit also indwells her. Her *passions* are frequently needed to shape the intentions of her husband. The two are one.

Then what is *subjection*? It embodies: (a) the wife's full participation in the aspects of decision making that affect them both; (b) her recognition that her husband is accountable to God for the decisions that flow from their discussions; (c) her acceptance of the decision that is forthcoming; and (d) her support of the decision and subsequent action. In good marriages, this subjection process is unconscious in that the conversations that lead up to decisions and actions are most often agreed-upon experiences without thought about who participates, who is accountable, or if the decision be accepted and supported.

If the husband and wife have married in Christ, and share world/life-views, the number of times a wife might be called upon to reflect upon her need to submit to her husband will be few and far between. Significant differences will occasionally arise, however, and these occasions will surface the need to reflect upon marriage roles. For example, when our oldest son was twelve years old he expressed the desire to go hunting. In high school my wife had a classmate killed in a hunting accident, and was not in favor of letting our son go hunting. A lengthy discussion ensued. I listened carefully to her objections and fears. I understood them, for I knew a boy in high school who had four fingers blown off in a hunting accident. But I concluded that our high school experiences should not prevent our son from learning how to hunt under the training and watch care of a good friend.

Following this decision, my wife said, "I am glad you are accountable for this because I do not agree with you." And *my* decisions, as distinct from *our* decisions, have been wrong as well as right; but to my wife's blessed credit, she has never reminded me of my mistakes. The point to remember is: most decisions made by a couple are *consensus decisions*; both agree with each other. But on occasions without a consensus, a wife's commitment to her calling in Christ to submit to her husband is tested.

Submission, to be effective, i.e., to carry with it a blessing, must be accompanied by *respect*—". . . the wife must see to it that she respects her husband" (Eph. 5:33). The Greek word for "respects" is *phobeo*. It has three possible meanings: (1) "to be put to flight"; (2) "to be seized with alarm"; and (3) "to respond with reverential obedience." The context of Ephesians 5:33 indicates that the third meaning is correct.[165] The biblical injunction is: the wife's *submission* to her husband's decisions, when a difference in opinion arises, is to be shown in a spirit of *reverential obedience*—without complaining; without putting him in the emotional doghouse; and without a subsequent rejoinder such as "I told you so," or "See, you were wrong!"

A wife's submission, with reverential obedience, provides room for the Holy Spirit to work in her life and her husband's. Her submissive spirit gives the Spirit an opportunity to enlarge her trust in his presence and work in her

---

[165] See Joseph H Thayer, *Thayer's Greek-English Lexicon of the New Testament*, Lexical # 5399—*phobeo*; pages 655-656.

husband's life. Her acceptance of his leadership will do more to encourage him to seek God's guidance than ten thousand critical words. Her godly attitude will encourage him to be thoughtful and wise. Remember, this entire discussion takes place in the context of the marriage trinity. The Spirit will work in her husband's life if she married in the Lord. She can trust God to do what he promised—"He who began a good work in you [and your husband] will perfect it until the day of Christ Jesus" (Phil. 1:6).

Leaving and Cleaving

"For this reason a man shall leave his father and his mother, and be joined [shall cleave, KJV] to his wife; and they shall become one flesh" (Gen. 2:24). God reveals three of his intentions related to a man becoming a husband. He is to leave his parents; to cleave to his wife; and they are to become one flesh. We will examine God's purposes for the man's leaving and cleaving.

The separation of a son from his parents at marriage is both *symbolic* and *substantive*. It is symbolic in that it points to the establishment of a new union—a husband and wife. They are not a subset or appendage of the families in which they were raised. They are an entity unto themselves. This is symbolic of their independence. The couple is to *leave* the old *parent/child* relationship and enter into a new *parental/coequal* relationship.

But the separation is more than just symbolic; it is *substantive* as well. The parenting role has ended. New lines of authority and submission are established. The husband's and wife's obedience to the 5th commandment, "Honor your father and your mother," assumes a new shape. It no longer carries the idea of obeying one's parents. The parents are no longer in a position of authority over the new couple. Parents have the authority to instruct, counsel, deny, and require things of their children so long as they remain in their homes and are dependent upon them. But such parental obligations, authority, and rights cease when their children get married.

Problems arise when God's command, ". . . a man shall leave his father and his mother," is ignored by parents or the husband. He is responsible for the solidarity of the marriage, and for following this directive. Parents who fail to recognize their obligation to relinquish all authority they had over their children prior to marriage sow seeds of alienation between themselves and the married couple, or inject debilitating influences into the union. The afflicted marriage will either break down or become deformed. It is the husband's responsibility to guard the marriage and prevent outside influences from hindering its godly development.

Tensions between parents and their married children most often arise when parents seek to maintain control over them. Such predispositions spill over into the new couple's life in the form of *ideas* from the parents which can subtly lead the couple to make decisions that they would not otherwise make. Parents and in-laws both interfere in a marriage in this way. The couple does things the parents want them to do that they would not do otherwise. It is the husband's responsibility to tactfully—graciously—guard against this kind of parental influence.

An illustration may help. My wife and I were married ten years when one of her aunts approached at a social event and said, "Oh Shirley, I am so glad to see how Dick protects you from your mother" [their sister]. Tears began to stream down my wife's cheeks. I did not comprehend the substance of the aunt's statement. Gradually the light went on. My mother-in-law, with whom I had a wonderful relationship as long as she lived, had a predisposition to try to control those close to her. Not having been raised by her, and therefore not having lived under her influence, I had listened to her *ideas* over the years and had felt free to respond in light of what was best for Shirley and me. This does not mean we never did what my mother-in-law suggested; it means we never did things *because* she suggested them. I had always been able politely to tell her that we would consider such an idea on another occasion, but that at this point we were going to do something else. This is *establishing appropriate boundaries*.

What did God mean when he said, "For this reason a man . . . shall cleave to his wife"? What is God's conception of *cleaving*? The Hebrew word for cleave is *dabaq* [Lexical # 1692]. It calls for a husband to demonstrate an *unwavering commitment* to his wife. He is to let nothing separate them. He is to "catch the foxes . . . the little foxes that are ruining the vineyards, while our vineyards are in blossom" (Song 2:15). The husband is responsible to keep anything from coming between him and his wife. The little foxes, the circumstances and people that wiggle their way in between a couple when insufficient attention is being paid to the marriage, are to be removed, for they can destroy the contentment and commitment (the blossom) of a good marriage. It is the first commandment prohibiting divorce, and it is repeated throughout Scripture. The New Testament corollary is Jesus's words, "What therefore God has joined together, let no man separate" (Matt. 19:4-6). The husband is the person primarily responsible before God for the nurture and preservation of the marriage.

A husband demonstrates an *unwavering commitment* to his wife in numerous ways. He will respect her thoughts, support her creative expressions, encourage her to use her God-given *gifts*, compliment her, affirm her God-given worth, and be sensitive to her feelings. The wife must know that she is thoroughly loved—*philos, eros*, and *agape*.

One Flesh

There are at least five aspects of a husband and wife becoming *one flesh* important for both spouses to understand. It is easy to presume that something is known when no such awareness exists. The sexual union is as much a psychological phenomenon as it is a physical one. Women are particularly conscious of this. Men are frequently unaware of this important truth. We will discuss five significant areas: preparing to know her; knowing her; pleasure; periods of abstinence; and communications.

Preparing to Know Her

The sexual union of spouses is the confirmation and consummation of their *ever-growing* awareness of who they are. We grow together imperceptibly, degree by degree. Over time we realize that God's design and plan are bearing fruit. And we forever meet ourselves in life's circumstances. We become increasingly aware of who our partner is, and who we are. A godly relationship is never stagnant. Relationships are either progressing or diminishing. Our old sin nature prevents them from being on an uninterrupted ascent. The advancement of a marriage requires nurturing—work. Godly marriages do not just happen.

A time of preparation precedes the physical union a couple anticipates enjoying. Indeed, the anticipation should be part of their pleasure. The preparation differs markedly for men and women. The male, having been given a visual nature by God, can see his wife step from the shower and BAM, he is turned on and ready to be joined with her. On the other hand, most women look at their husband's naked body and are not moved. What is going on here? It is the playing out of the sexual differences between men and women. Men are much more visually stimulated than women. This is why almost all pornography is the pictorial exposure of women, not men. And it is men that are addicted to XXX-rated films, not women.

Husbands must realize that all that transpires between them and their wives a day or two prior to physical union prepares their wives for a fulfilling union. A husband can hurt his wife at 8:00 p.m., recognize the hurt, ask her to forgive him (which she does), and be excited about enjoying a wonderful physical union with her at 9:00 p.m., only to discover that she is not interested. Now the husband is disappointed, and perhaps hurt. He has either forgotten, or never understood, that God sexually constituted females differently.

The psychological dynamics that play a large role in a woman's preparation, anticipation, and participation in sex are generally not at the forefront of a man's thoughts as he anticipates sex. Men need to *learn* this. Their learning partially fulfills God's exhortation, "You husbands . . . live with your wives in an understanding way" (1 Peter 3:7). Husbands must understand that being good listeners, encouragers, and expressive of their love and appreciation for their wives is the best preparation for a responsive and wholesome one flesh enjoyment of the rich benefits God grants in marriage.

Knowing Her

The one flesh experience of a husband and wife transcends articulation. There is giving and receiving. And a bonding occurs in the physical union of a spiritually healthy couple—one being guided by Christ in the bonds of the marriage trinity. The flavor of this giving, receiving, and bonding is beautifully articulated in The Song of Songs, or as it is more popularly known, The Song of Solomon. The biblical text is comprised of a bride, a bridegroom, and a chorus. Noting which of the three speaks at particular places in the text, produces a sense of a physical, emotional, psychological, and expanding awareness for one another.

The bride and bridegroom are tied up in one another. The bride delights that he is like a pouch that "lies all night between my breasts" (1:13). Their "couch is luxuriant!" (1:16). She wants "his left hand [to] be under [her] head and his right hand [to] embrace her" (2:6). And the groom cautions, "Do not arouse or awaken my love until [it] pleases you to receive me" (2:7). The bride rejoices, "My beloved is mine, and I am his" (2:16). The song continues and he realizes, "A garden locked is my sister, my bride, a rock garden locked, a spring sealed up.... You are a garden spring, a well of fresh water, and streams flowing from Lebanon" (4:12, 15). And she responds, "Awake, O north [winter] wind, and come, wind of the south [summer]; make my garden breathe out fragrance, let its spices be wafted abroad. *May my beloved come into his garden and eat its choice fruits!*" (4:16).

They share an expressive relationship. She asks him about his work (1:7) and he invites her to come and discover firsthand what his daily life is like (1:8). Their life together is more than just a physical union, but the Song is predominately about their romantic, affectionate, and loving (*eros*) relationship. They take delight in one another's body (1:9-10; 1:15-16; 4:1-5, 7; 5:10-16; 6:4-7; 7:1-9). The contrast between the Song's heralding of this one flesh enjoyment in marriage, and Adam's and Eve's startled realization that they were naked, when their eyes were first opened after the fall, is stark (contrast Gen. 2:25 with 3:7). Why? Because becoming comfortable with exposing one's nakedness to another is a barometer of psychological and spiritual oneness. How so?

Two illustrations may help us understand. Years ago a young couple sought my counsel. The wife thought her feet were too large. She was very sensitive about this and had shared her sensitivity with her husband. But, whenever he became upset with her he would tell her she had big feet. As expected, she lost all amorous feelings for him for a period of time. It turns out on such occasions she had said something first to upset him and he retaliated by referring to her feet. In fact, he did not think they were big at all. Over time, thankfully, he learned how to respond constructively to his wife's occasional hurtful comments, and she to his. So they both learned to honestly share their hurt feelings, and thereby prevented their accumulation and the erosion of their relationship—"Catch the foxes for us, the little foxes that are ruining the vineyards, while our vineyards are in blossom" (Song of Songs 2:15).

Almost all have some aspect of their anatomy that they would like to change. In the case just cited, it was the young woman's feet. And what of breasts, hips, muscles, broad shoulders, and abdomens? Are not most conscious of their form and shape? The bridegroom comments lovingly on his bride's beauty:

> How beautiful are your feet in sandals... the curves of your hips are like jewels... your navel is like a round goblet... your belly is like a heap of wheat... your two breasts are like two fawns... your neck like a tower of ivory, your eyes like the pools in Heshbon... your nose... your head... how beautiful... how delightful... your stature is like a palm tree, and your breasts are like its clusters.... I will climb the palm tree... and your mouth [is] like the best wine! (Song 7:1-9)

She was beautiful to her husband. That is what matters! People are incredibly conscious of their anatomy as well as that of others. And the *full* exploration and admiration of another's body is reserved for husbands and wives as they enjoy each other.

The second illustration involves my wife. Her mother in the 1930's and 1940's insisted that she wear a girdle to keep her from jiggling when she walked. The result was that my wife grew up with an unfavorable view of her body. But I have always found her very attractive in every way, though I have been aware for years of her humble self-perception. A truly happy memory occurred five decades into our marriage, when she might have thought of herself as a bit jiggly, but said to me in a tender moment, "I have never in all my life felt so at home in my body as I do now." What a joy to hear! Those words were priceless. I thank God that his presence in our marriage could bear such fruit.

Each person's nakedness belongs to himself or herself, to the spouse, and to no one else, as Leviticus 18 and 20 teach. Intentionally exposing one's nakedness to someone other than one's spouse perverts God's best intentions for us. It turns the naked body into an object to be lusted after and used. Such thoughts and conduct reveal that sex is thought of as an *end in itself*, or as a means of getting what I want. But sex is neither of those. These are selfish objectives.

Sex is intended to be an *integrating element* in a growing awareness of an intimate relationship that fosters *expansive oneness*. Godly sex flows out of a wholesome, loving relationship that *treats* one's spouse as *his or her own body*—we are one! Sex is the giving of oneself and the receiving of another's self that creates an inseparable bond. God knew that it was not good for Adam to be alone. In general, God does not intend for us to live alone. Getting to know one another is a lifelong task, and the more you grow to know the one you love the deeper the relationship becomes. And the deeper the relationship, the richer the sexual unions.

Pleasure

God incorporated three purposes in his creation of *eros* love. He intends the sexual union to be pleasurable, to promote expansive oneness, and to create children to continue his purposes generation after generation. The Bible makes it clear that the "one flesh" facet of marriage is intended for *pleasure*. (It is sad how little is taught in the church regarding sex.)

When Christ appeared to Abraham,[166] who was 99, and after Sarah had passed the age of childbearing (she was 90!), the Lord promised, "I will surely return to you at this time next year; and behold, Sarah your wife will have a son. Now Sarah was listening at the tent door . . . and Sarah laughed to herself, saying, 'After I have become old, *shall I have pleasure*, my lord being old also?'" (Gen. 18:10-12). It is wonderful to peek into Sarah's heart and see that her sexual relationship with her husband recalled memories of *pleasure*. This is what Christ wants; he created sex to be pleasurable.

Scripture speaks in other ways of sexual delights that God created for us to enjoy. The Song of Songs tells of the bride's and groom's delight in one another. The law uses different words to instruct newlyweds: "When a man takes a new wife, he shall not go out with the army nor be charged with any duty; he shall be free at home one year and shall give *happiness* to his wife whom he has taken" (Deut. 24:5). "Happiness" and "pleasure" are euphemisms for sex.

---

[166] Read John 8:56-58. The Genesis 17 and 18 accounts of God's speaking to Abraham are referred to as theophanies—a visible manifestation of the preincarnate Christ.

Proverbs 5:15-20 in yet another way describes this God-intended union in marriage.

> Drink water from your own cistern, and fresh water from your own well. Should your springs be dispersed abroad, streams of water in the streets? Let them be yours alone and not for strangers with you. Let your fountain be blessed, and rejoice in the wife of your youth. As a loving hind and a graceful doe, let her breasts satisfy you at all times; be exhilarated always with her love. For why should you, my son, be exhilarated with an adulteress, and embrace the bosom of a foreigner?

Many figures of speech appear here. In biblical times water was something to be shared with thirsty strangers. The water, the cistern, the springs, the streams of water, and the fountain used in this passage are all euphemisms. These words are poetic ways to describe a very private, intimate, and beautiful phenomenon called *intercourse*.

The *pleasure* associated with being one flesh is never the same/always the same. The pleasure is never the same psychologically, or physically, as it is experienced. Every time a union is experienced, it is unique in the sense that it is, in subtle ways, different from any past union. This is, in part, what keeps one flesh experiences fresh over many decades. There has never been another union *just like this union*.

The *thoughts* that accompany sex also vary, but are tied to the particular experience at the time. The *thoughts* that accompany the physical sensations and psychological sense of well-being, or the desire to *give one's self* to one's partner, differ with every union. And the physical pleasure also varies with every union. Tenderness, excitement or vigor, and the physical motions are never exactly the same from union to union. Nothing is static.

Although sexual experiences are never the same, in another sense they are always the same. They always include many thoughts connected to the experience, and hopes that our companion is as pleased as we. There is always mental activity associated with being one flesh.

Hopefully the husband realizes that his wife's *psychological* pleasure is *deeply* dependent upon his hours of caring for her before the union. And hopefully he understands that her *physical* pleasure during sex is *completely* dependent upon his *words and touch* leading up to and during it. His *physical performance*—clitoral and vaginal stimulation causing fulfillment—completes the entire experience. The husband is *responsible* for his wife's pleasure. When a man goes into a woman who is not his wife, he thinks only of his physical pleasure. But when a husband knows his wife, he thinks about her and trying to please her. He knows *his* physical pleasure is guaranteed, not hers. She will receive him with joy, pleased that he has experienced once again the wonderful physical pleasure that only God could have designed.

A husband's *psychological pleasure* is tied to his having learned, with his wife's help, how to fulfill her. He can be satisfied only when he knows that their union has provided her a corresponding psychological and physical pleasure. If she is not fulfilled, he has *failed her*. It is the husband's *pleasant duty* to prepare his wife for the anticipated joys of their union and to complete her physically so she knows that she has been cared for with satisfaction and fulfillment. Her pleasure is his responsibility. He is the giver; she is the receiver.

And there is another dimension to sex of which many men are ignorant: the importance of the ten or fifteen minutes immediately following the physical union. This time is very important to the pair's bonding. It is a time to hold one another, to express appreciation and love, to show that *the union meant more than just pleasure*. It also represents an abiding commitment and fulfillment. It is a time when the glue of the bond is gently applied and seals their oneness.

Periods of Abstinence

Here we focus on a single *inappropriate* but all-too-common form of abstinence. There are appropriate times to abstain—during menstruation; just before and just after a baby is born; while coping with health problems; and *agreed upon times* for special reasons. Such legitimate periods of abstinence must be recognized and respected.

The abstinences that are relationally destructive are those born out of unresolved hurts, unreconciled differences, or uncontrolled diversions. Of course, two people deeply in love will occasionally disappoint and hurt each other. The old sin nature within, while no longer dominant, still occasionally causes trouble even in good marriages. For example, it is easy to think, "That comment hurt. I know it was unintended. I will just keep quiet about it. Why interrupt a pleasant time by bringing it up?" Scripture addresses this: "Catch the foxes for us, the little foxes that are *ruining the vineyards*, while *our vineyards are in blossom*" (Song 2:15).

The "little foxes" are the comments, disappointments, and jealousies that, if not dealt with, run around in a marriage and knock off the blossom—joy and contentment—from otherwise good times. The foxes undermine the life in a relationship. They knock off the blossoms and thwart the *relational* fruit. If hurts are not handled constructively, the foxes will diminish the couple's cleaving. Sex will lose its appeal. Alternative partners may even enter our thoughts. Unattended foxes give rise to a gradual and ever-increasing emotional separation between those Christ wants to be united. *The foxes must be caught and eliminated!*

Rebuke is better than concealed love (Prov. 27:5)—for *arguing is better than silence*—then *learning* to share one's hurts that arise in marriage is godly. The consequences of failing to do so can be the greatest form of *inappropriate abstinence*—"I am emotionally shut down and do not want to have sex with my husband." Since husbands are primarily responsible for the *pleasure* associated with sex, wives are primarily responsible for avoiding *inappropriate abstinences*, for they are the primary proponents of abstinence. Their desire for sex is shut down more easily by emotional upsets than a man's.

Denying a spouse sex is analogous to denying him/her food and drink. Once the one flesh experience has become part of someone's normal life, adjustments to its pattern generally are psychologically and physically difficult. Past pleasant experiences and memories fuel present desires. Denying a partner sex is close to inviting them to become adulterers.

Paul speaks to this:

> The husband must fulfill his duty to his wife, and likewise also the wife to her husband. The wife does not have authority over her own body, but the husband does; and likewise also the husband does not have authority over his own body, but the wife does. Stop depriving one another, except by agreement for a time, so that you may devote yourselves to prayer, and come together again so that Satan will not tempt you because of your lack of self-control. (1 Cor. 7:3-5)

The apostle is unambiguous. Responsibility accompanies the wonder and pleasure of the one flesh experience. In the end, the union is a *duty*. And each partner has *authority* over the other's body. Paul uses obligatory language to highlight the importance of sex and to underline a specific problem that arises from *inappropriate abstinence*—the temptation to commit adultery.

The first line of defense against this is to work together to maintain a healthy and mutually supportive relationship—to keep "the foxes" out of the marriage. Be kind, gentle, and understanding, but *quick* to disclose hurts, disappointments, and failures of understanding to each other before they undermine marriage harmony.

The second line of defense takes practice. When a wife does not feel open to her husband's sexual advances, she needs to be simultaneously *honest* and *providing* (self-sacrificing). Let us suppose that a husband hurt his wife's feelings. She quickly explained her hurt. He realized that he had sinned against her, acknowledged his sin to her, asked her to forgive him. She believed his repentance was sincere and forgave him. But she finds herself emotionally flat. The original hurt, the rehashing of it, and the energy expended has left her drained. She is emotionally down and needs time to recover. How is she to handle his amorous advances? He has fully recovered from the evening's up-down-up emotional event. She has not.

First, she needs to be *honest*. "Sweetheart, I am emotionally empty. I am not able to respond to your desires with enthusiasm." But she needs to follow this honest expression of emotion with a *providing* addition: "But if you have an intense need, I will not refuse you. I am afraid I will not be responsive, but I am yours and will never deny you." This will accomplish several things. The husband will become aware that his wife has not fully recovered and recall that her preparation occurs over one to two days. He will need to evaluate the urgency of his need. And he will surely have a deeper appreciation of her commitment to him—"She is willing to give herself to me even when she has no desire to do so." That is *agape* love in full view. It speaks volumes about her character and commitment to him. Probably, he will thank her for her loving willingness of support, express his deep appreciation for her thoughtfulness, and state his understanding of her feelings and his willingness to wait for a better time for physical union.

What is the probable outcome of this type of *abstinence*? The couple has exhibited positive traits that build healthy marriages. The emotional hurt was expressed when it occurred. The hurt was acknowledged; forgiveness was asked for and received; the problem was resolved, even though time is needed for a full emotional recovery; and the preparation time for the next union has begun positively. Indeed, if the husband concludes that his need can wait rather than accept his wife's self-sacrificing offer, she too will appreciate his understanding and the *preparation for the next physical union will already be in progress.*

Many causes can lead to a *desire* for abstinence. Fatigue and emotional stress are two common ones. Open discussion of feelings and thoughts is necessary so that understanding and accommodation are reached in a mutually agreeable way. Abstinence without understanding and not finding a loving way to agree is a recipe for trouble. Dozens of variations of the illustration above work when a couple seeks to live by 1 Corinthians 7:3-5. Communication is the key to good solutions.

Communication

Couples often find it hard to talk about sex. This is reflected in the poor job parents usually do in talking with their children about sex. Married couples are reticent to discuss sex for several reasons. Most couples find the textbook vocabulary uninviting. The words we learned to describe our anatomy and the sex act from childhood friends, anatomy courses, and sex education classes are not appealing when expressing one's tender and amorous thoughts and desires to a spouse. We need a better way to express our thoughts.

In a western novel titled *Lonesome Dove*, published years ago, whenever the cowboys went to town to see prostitutes they spoke of going to enjoy "a poke." That was a euphemism that said a lot. The point is simple: couples will feel more comfortable communicating with each other regarding sex if they creatively construct their own euphemisms with which they are comfortable.

Good communication also helps a husband fulfill his responsibility to provide for his wife's pleasure in sex. Men are often puzzled when they discover that their wives are variable in their wants—what was enjoyable yesterday seems to produce little pleasure today. This is puzzling, but it is keeps sex fresh and exciting. The methods used in approaching, engaging in, and consummating the union are best when they are tailored for the particular occasion. And how is that accomplished? *Signals* are required.

Signals are creatively produced by words and actions during preparation, intercourse, and follow-up. Perhaps the couple's favorite euphemism is spoken and is responded to verbally or tactically, during preparation. Gentle tactical turns, pulls, and pushes with the hands, arms, torso, legs, and feet all communicate volumes. The wife is not to be a frozen cadaver. They cannot read each other's minds. They must communicate. Simple verbal encouragements are precious. Spouses must help one another enrich their times of physical union by developing a meaningful *personalized* form of communication that helps them let each other know what they are thinking, experiencing, and desiring. Godly unions are enriched by helpful communication.

Expansive Oneness

The marriage trinity is analogous to the Trinity. In the Trinity's *oneness* there is perfect harmony in the midst of a relationship of *equality/inequality; authority/submission; individual/community*. God the Father is no *less* or any *more* who he is because he enjoys a perfect union with God the Son and God the Holy Spirit. This is true of the other two persons of the Godhead as well. They are one; they are three.

Christ, the head of the marriage trinity, teaches the couple the significance of his perfect wisdom: "And he who does not take his cross and follow after Me is not worthy of Me. He who has found his life shall lose it, and he who has lost his life for My sake will find it" (Matt. 10:38-39; 16:24-25). One of the challenges we all have growing up is answering, "Who am I?" and "What am I supposed to do with my life?" We can take one of two paths when answering these questions. Those outside of Christ are *forced* by their alienation from God and their fallen nature to seek their own answer. They are on their own in their search for meaning and significance. They will find their life by defining their own likes and dislikes. They will work to discover what serves them best. And in doing so, they will "lose their life"—they will follow their own self-centered choices and remain alienated from God forever.

The one in whom Christ dwells who marries another in whom he dwells, will establish a marriage trinity under his headship. The two will be led by Christ to take up their separate crosses daily to follow him. He helps his brothers and sisters die to their self-centeredness. He teaches them his way and enables them to live for him. In giving their life to him, they forfeit the deadly opportunity to self-define their lives, and thereby receive from him the purposeful life God had planned for them in eternity. In this mysterious way they find their God-intended life as they exchange their self-will for God's.

In a godly marriage the three are one—Christ, the husband, and the wife. Both partners have the same Lord, are committed to Christ and his teaching, have compatible *world/life-views* and common *values*. Both are committed to seeking the best for their spouse, are one in *purpose*, are one *flesh*, and share the same goals—to please the Lord.

But they also remain individuals. In their oneness they do not lose their individuality. An extrovert does not become an introvert. One inclined to view things rationally does not give this up when married. The spontaneous person does not forfeit spontaneity. Their *talents* do not evaporate. In fact, their individual abilities need to be recognized, appreciated, and used. It is the flourishing of each one's individuality that underlies a marriage becoming an expansive oneness.

"What do you have that you did not receive [from the Lord]?" (1 Cor. 4:7). The context of this verse is one of admonishing God's people not to boast of their God-given abilities. And we should appreciate the talents and abilities which each partner brings to the union. The couple must learn how their individual abilities can best promote the fruitfulness of the union.

Culture and traditions guide many gender decisions, but the Bible has only a few gender-designated roles.[167] When Christ has not made distinctions, then we should ask who is best qualified, by temperament and ability, to perform the task at hand? Who should pay the bills? Do the tax return? Do the grocery shopping? Mow the lawn? Cook the evening meal? Thousands of such questions are legitimate to ask and answer. The couple needs to answer them in a spirit of sharing, mutual support, recognition of God's special gifts, and their desires.

The more bonding that takes place in a marriage—the more the couple become one—the greater their desire will be to see their loved one develop his or her God-given abilities so as to support their union. That is expansive oneness!

Marriage: A Primary Relationship in Which Godly Transformation Takes Place

No marriage can flourish in godliness without much carrying of one's cross (Luke 9:23-24). Decades ago, when I was a young lieutenant at Fort Benning, Georgia, the infantry officers' motto was "Follow Me." This symbolized the expectation that the young lieutenant would be the first to risk his life in battle. He was to set the example. His men were to follow him; he was not to follow them. If this were true in the U. S. Army, how much more should it be true in Christ's Army? He has borne his cross. He has told us that we are to follow him and emulate his life. *There is no other way to have a godly marriage.*

The death of a marriage originates in selfishness and self-centeredness. The life of a marriage is found in following Christ—applying his instructions regarding it. In doing this there is *pain* (dying to self) and much hard *work*—doing what Christ has called us to do. There is the putting off of the old and the putting on of the new. There is pruning, sacrifice, and fatigue. And there is failure that calls for rectification, forgiveness, and reworking.

There are corresponding successes and rewards. There are a partner's love and encouragement. There is someone with whom we can share the pressures and responsibilities. There is the joy and bonding that takes place in the one flesh experiences. There is maturing in Christlikeness. There is God's promise: "He who began a good work in you will perfect it until the day of Christ Jesus" (Phil. 1:6). It is Christ himself who does this. It is the Holy Spirit who *sanctifies* us—sets us apart to accomplish God's will as he acts "both to will and to work for His good pleasure" (Phil. 2:13). Marriage is God's crucible where the dross of the old nature is removed and Christ is formed in its place (Rom. 8:28-29).

---

[167] The Bible specifies a few gender-designated roles. The *elders* that constitute the church leadership are to be males (1 Tim. 3:1-7; Titus 1:5-9). Men are accountable before God for the way they carry out their headship roles in marriage (Eph. 5:23; 1 Cor. 11:3; Gen. 3:16). God holds the husband primarily responsible for the physical provisions for his wife and family (Gen. 3:17-19; Eccl. 2:18-23; 2 Thess. 3:10; 1 Tim. 5:8). The wife, in agricultural societies, worked beside her husband doing those tasks that suited her muscular strength and skills. The husband typically did the heavy work. Work is one of three pre and post-fall creation mandates—families, work, and worship—thus women were also created to work; but their work ordinarily was specialized—being mothers, and the hard work associated with this role. The woman was created for the man (Gen. 2:18; 1 Cor. 11:9) and God gave her the responsibility of bearing children and *loving* (nurturing) them. The *loving* and *nurturing* are to be carried out *by keeping their children in the natural environment of the family* (Titus 2:3-5; 1 Tim. 5:14).

23

Christ's Divine Nature Manifested in the Family

How blessed is everyone who fears the LORD, who walks in His ways. . . . Your wife shall be like a fruitful vine . . . your children like olive plants around your table. . . . Indeed, may you see your children's children. (Ps. 128:1, 3, 6)

"How blessed is everyone who fears the LORD, who walks in His ways. . . ." The two phrases *"fears* the LORD" and *"walks* in His ways" deserve much attention. This psalm teaches that fearing the LORD accompanies walking with him—the fruit of which is a *blessed family*. The fear of the LORD precedes a family's receiving God's blessings. But fear is not something we usually think of *positively.* How are we to understand God's blessing of *fear*?

> It is my belief that much, if not most, of what undermines the modern-day American family is *ungodly* and weak *husbands*—husbands who are not Christlike. God gave husbands roles of leadership and responsibility in the family and far too many husbands have ignored, abandoned, or never understood what their God-given responsibilities are. This is especially true regarding their role as *fathers.* A father who does not teach his children a godly fear (Hebrew, *yare*) of him that *emerges from his love for his children* fails his children profoundly. The delicate, hard-to-balance relationship between *fear* and *true love* is something we will examine in this chapter. Has God not said, "He will restore the hearts of the fathers to their children and the hearts of the children to their fathers, so that I will not come and smite the land with a curse?" (Mal. 4:6; repeated in Luke 1:17). Fathers must learn that godly love involves godly discipline—tough love (Heb. 12:4-13).

The word "fear" in Psalm 128 is the Hebrew word *yare* (Lexical # 3373). It belongs on a continuum—spanning the absolute *terror* of God to an inexpressible *awe* for him! Implied is that the one who *fears* the Lord: (a) has been made aware of his perverse nature by the Holy Spirit; (b) has realized that he is unholy and deserves God's wrath; (c) was at the moment of realization filled with an absolute *terror* of the Lord God; (d) was soon thereafter blessed with the grace of forgiveness *in Christ*; (e) experienced reconciliation and peace with God; and (f) is now *being taught* by the Holy Spirit the exalted *fear* (respect, awe, and wonder) of the Lord—"Come, you children, listen to me; *I will teach you the fear of the* LORD" (Ps. 34:11).

Here we focus on the nurturing of children, the fruit of marriage. The word "family" can refer to a childless couple, but we focus on the special changes that occur when *children* are present. The husband is now also a father. The wife is now also a mother. And the children must learn that they not only relate to their mother as a mother, but also as their father's wife. The corollary is also true: their father is also their mother's husband. Complexities multiply greatly when children enter a family. And the more children, the more complex the relationships become, for siblings are powerful sources of influence.

We will treat these subjects: (1) children are born with a sin nature; (2) their hearts need transformation along with the training of their behavior; (3) having God at the center of the family's values; (4) the need to discipline, not punish; (5) appropriate fear; (6) the need to learn appropriate self-restraint; (7) triangulation: a *no-no*; (8) children of the *covenant* belong to God; and (9) parents greatly impact their children's perceptions of the Trinity.

Children Are Born with a Sin Nature

"Behold, I was brought forth in iniquity, and in sin my mother conceived me" (Ps. 51:5). David here describes his nature in a way expressed throughout Scripture. He was born (brought forth) with a sin nature (in iniquity). From his conception he had the nature of a sinner—"in sin my mother conceived me." Paul made an equally clear statement to the Ephesian church:

> And you were dead in your trespasses and sins, in which you formerly walked according to the course of this world, according to the prince of the power of the air, of the spirit that is now working in the sons of disobedience. Among them we too all formerly lived in the lusts of our flesh, indulging the desires of the flesh and of the mind, and were by nature children of wrath, even as the rest. (Eph. 2:1-3)

Scripture teaches that only Christ is sinless. There are three views in our culture regarding human nature. First, humans are conceived and born in innocence: there are no innate perversions in the human personality at life's beginning. The *environment* corrupts people following birth. Second, some believe that humans are evolving creatures and that evolution has not finished its course. Many who hold this view also think that those they deem more intelligent are more highly developed morally, and are thus a better stock of people. Much of the arrogance in the agnostic intellectual community is rooted here. Third, we are all, from conception, depraved—have a fallen (twisted, warped,) nature that permeates all aspects of our personality.

Why is it important to have a proper understanding of a child's nature at birth? Because it impacts our understanding of what we face as parents. We need the Holy Spirit's help in raising children, who need their *hearts transformed*— which we cannot *control*. But as parents we are responsible to learn proper ways to generate the appropriate *behavior* in children's lives.

Children Need Their *Hearts Transformed* and to Be Taught *Appropriate Behavior*

Children come from their mother's womb with predilections. They are wired in ways that shape their entire personality. For example, parents may speak of their children as having a strong or a compliant will; as being sensitive or insensitive; as being open-minded or closed-minded. These characteristics are personality traits or penchants.

The Word of God speaks often of child-discipline[168]—an essential aspect of "train[ing] up a child in the way he should go, [so that] even when he is old he will not depart from it" (Prov. 22:6). Training is seeking a revision in the child's *behavior*. This is so important if our fallen, self-centered nature is to learn to include in our lives other family members and the broader community. But even nurturing positive behavior-changes does not accomplish *transformation* of the child's *heart*. Because parents have no control over their children's hearts—motives, attitudes, and *allegiances*—how can they guide them to know what their parents so earnestly want them to understand?

Parents experience no greater blessing, apart from salvation, than seeing their children walk with the Lord (3 John 4). Indeed, how far will parents' love go to see their child walking with Christ? Paul wrote to the church in Corinth and his friend Timothy: "I have decided to deliver such a one [who rejects Christ] to Satan for the destruction of his flesh, that his spirit may be saved in the day of the Lord Jesus" (1 Cor. 5:5; cf. 1Tim. 1:20). Uppermost in godly parents' hearts, as they raise the children God entrusted to them, is the children's eternal life. How can parents encourage their child's understanding of his or her need for a transformed *heart*?

Opportunities to plant the seed of understanding arise every time the child needs to be disciplined. A parent needs only to say things such as:

> John, your heart needs a "Helper." You know better than to _____. You did what you knew was wrong. Daddy loves you so much that he is giving you a "time out" in your chair so that you can think about what you did. When I come back to get you a little later, I want you to tell me why you need a "Helper"; why doing _____ was wrong; and why your "time out" is a good thing for you.

This might be the four-hundredth time out John has experienced in his four-and-a-half years of training. And by now he knows the Helper is Jesus, whom he needs to come and live in his heart. It does not matter at this point in time if John has any deep understanding of who Jesus is or how this Jesus can live in him ("Where will my food go if Jesus is in there?"), or what this new heart is like. John is absorbing some fundamental truths: "I know I am misbehaving when I punch my sister—I need help"; "Dad and Mom love me"; "Mom and

---

[168] See: Gen. 18:19; Deut. 6:7; 11:19; 2 Sam. 7:14; Prov. 3:12; 10:1; 13:24; 17:25; 19:18; 22:6, 15; 23:13-14; 29:15, 17; Eph. 6:4; Colossians 3:21; Heb. 12:4-11; Rev. 3:19.

Dad are trying to help me"; "There is always a consequence to my bad behavior."

Little John undoubtedly has other incorrect thoughts at the same time he is learning that he needs help. He probably thinks his correction is harsher than his sister's. He wonders why he always seems to get caught. And he gets mad at his parents, his siblings, and the whole world, including the cat. At times, life just seems confusing. He probably thinks, "I don't want to be bad, but sometimes I just can't help it." And therein is the truth of our fallen condition. That is why a heart transplant is so important. And a child needs to learn this fundamental truth early.

Establishing God at the Center of the Family's Values

Children are discerning. They learn quickly what is most important in their parents' *world/life-view*. They know early on if Christ is important to their parents, or if they only pay him lip service. Throughout their rearing children must hear from godly parents that Christ's will is the reference point they follow wholeheartedly. Fathers are told: "bring [your children] up in the discipline and instruction of the Lord" (Eph. 6:4), an abridgement of Deuteronomy 6:5-7:

> And you shall love the LORD your God with all your heart and with all your soul and with all your might. These words, which I am commanding you today, shall be on your heart. You shall teach them diligently to your sons and shall talk of them when you sit in your house and when you walk by the way and when you lie down and when you rise up.

It is essential that the children of godly parents know that Christ is their parents' Lord, Guide, Comforter, Priest, and ever-present King.

Charles H. Spurgeon encouraged parents to teach their children of the Lord:[169]

> *Tell ye your children of it, and let your children tell their children, and their children another generation.* Joel 1:3
>
> In this simple way, by God's grace, a living testimony for truth is always to be kept alive in the land—the beloved of the Lord are to hand down their witness for the gospel, and the covenant to their heirs, and these again to their next descendants. This is our *first* duty, we are to begin at the family hearth: he is a bad preacher who does not commence his ministry at home. The heathen are to be sought by all means, and the highways and hedges are to be searched, but home has a prior claim, and woe unto those who reverse the order of the Lord's arrangements. To teach our children is a *personal* duty; we cannot delegate it to Sunday School Teachers, or other friendly aids; these can assist us, but cannot deliver us from the sacred obligation; proxies and sponsors are wicked devices in this case: mothers and fathers must, like Abraham, command

---

[169] Charles H. Spurgeon, *Morning and Evening: Daily Readings* (McLean, VA: MacDonald Publishing Company), evening reading for July 11.

their households in the fear of God, and talk with their offspring concerning the wondrous works of the Most High. Parental teaching is a *natural* duty—who is so fit to look to the child's well-being as those who are the authors of his actual being? To neglect the instruction of our offspring is worse than brutish. Family religion is *necessary* for the nation, for the family itself, and for the church of God.... Would that parents would awaken to a sense of the importance of this matter. It is a *pleasant* duty to talk of Jesus to our sons and daughters, and the more so because it has often proved to be an *accepted* work, for God has saved the children through their parents' prayers and admonitions.

Parents too often worry about how to keep their young children focused during family worship, or how to bridge the age range between children. Such worries are unfounded. The parents' pleasure should be in *reading the Scripture, their* discussion of it, and *their* time of prayer. The littlest children are to learn to *be still* and to *be quiet*—they first observe their parents doing something *important together*. In time their curiosity will lead them to listen and take in more than their parents imagine. As the years go by, the children can be invited to read Scripture and to join in the prayer time. As they grow older, they can be encouraged to ask questions. Do not worry about the children's *understanding* of the content of family worship when they are very young. Their interest in the content will follow naturally as the years pass.

Children Need to Be Disciplined, Not Punished

Evildoers are punished;[170] those *in Christ* are disciplined.[171] The child of a parent in Christ is a *covenant child*, one who is accounted by God as *holy* (1 Cor. 7:14). In God's *grace* he includes believers' children in his family. We do not know when this period of grace ends, for Scripture does not say when a child of the covenant becomes personally accountable. And there are Esaus among the multitudes of those born to Christian parents. In the meantime, though, all children of believers are to be treated as *covenant children*.

Why make a sharp distinction between *punishment* and *discipline*? Because *Christ bore the punishment for his people's sins*. God *disciplines* his adopted children; he does not *punish* them. Christ paid the redemption price. He is the propitiation for our sins—the absorber of God's wrath (1 John 4:10). God's discipline is training; God's punishment is never-ending reprobation.

Discipline comes in many forms. Requiring a child to make up his or her bed is one. Such discipline contributes to the ordering of the family according to parental values. Emptying the trash; cutting the grass; playing the piano; sticking with the team until the end of the season—no quitting allowed; weeding the garden; washing the car; doing homework; and many other tasks are all opportunities to "train up a child in the way he should go" (Prov. 22:6).

---

[170] See: Matt. 25:46; 2 Thess. 1:9; 2 Peter 2:9.
[171] See footnote 1.

Children need training to help them learn how to sit through a worship service that seems eternally long to a four-year-old. Self-control—discipline—is needed when learning to wait one's turn, in a variety of situations. Self-discipline is the behavioral goal parents are laboring to help their children obtain. Having a godly attitude and spirit about doing something is the fruit of a transformed heart. Children need to be told by their parents, repeatedly, what the purpose of their training is. It helps them *eventually* to grasp their parents' *agape* love.

God has a larger goal in mind *that he will accomplish—conforming his children to Christ's likeness*—which he accomplishes through the *providential* occurrences in our lives that test our Christlikeness.

> You have not yet resisted to the point of shedding blood in your striving against sin; and you have forgotten the exhortation which is addressed to you as sons, "My son, do not regard lightly the discipline of the Lord, nor faint when you are reproved by Him; for those whom the Lord loves He disciplines, and He scourges every son whom He receives." It is for discipline that you endure; God deals with you as with sons; for what son is there whom his father does not discipline? But if you are without discipline, of which all have become partakers, then you are illegitimate children and not sons. Furthermore, we had earthly fathers to discipline us, and we respected them; shall we not much rather be subject to the Father of spirits, and live? For they disciplined us for a short time as seemed best to them, but He disciplines us for our good, so that we may share His holiness. All discipline for the moment seems not to be joyful, but sorrowful; yet to those who have been trained by it, afterwards it yields the peaceful fruit of righteousness. (Heb. 12:4-11)

This passage is God's discourse on *tough love*. It acknowledges, "all discipline for the moment seems not to be joyful, but sorrowful, but its fruit is *holiness* and *righteousness*"—traits of Christ. It is tough love that is wise enough to know that even our new, transformed heart needs to be built up into the likeness of Christ. God uses life's trying events as providential opportunities to continue the good work he began in us when he gave us life in Christ (Phil. 1:6).

The word "scourges" (Lexical # 3146: *mastigoō*; used in Heb. 12:6) is a metaphor to describe God's merciful intentions to use even the *afflictions* in our lives to make us like Christ (Rom. 8:29). Only God, in his sovereign wisdom and power, uses devastations brought about by natural disasters, tragic consequences of accidents, suffering that accompanies an illness, the trauma of rejection, the premature loss of someone we dearly love, and a host of other afflictions to *prune, strengthen,* and *form* in us the very likeness of his Son.

We must leave afflictions in the hands of a sovereign God; no godly parent would ever intentionally afflict their child. God is to be loved for his ability to transform the very worst a fallen creation can produce into benefits for us. He did this in the crucifixion of Christ. He does this in the lives of his children. Testimonies can be found in any group of Christians of God's transforming power in affliction.

Parents must select the modes of discipline they use in the intentional training of their children. But the same forms of discipline do not fit all children. What works in the life of one child may fail in the life of another. We need wisdom in administering discipline. For example, our youngest son David had a high threshold for pain as a child that led me to find other ways to discipline him than spankings. Spankings were not a good disciplinary option for David for he felt no pain. Restrictions, reduced allowances, and extra chores worked wonderfully, however.

Children Need an Appropriate Fear of Their Father

The concept of the fear of the LORD runs the gamut from *terror* to *awe*. Recall God's expression of *agape* love: "Come, you children, listen to me; I will teach you the fear of the LORD" (Ps. 34:11). Parents who love (*agape*) their children ought to teach them *appropriately* to fear their daddy.

Corrective discipline must carry with it consequences that *fit the offense*. A three-and-a-half year old who fails to do what she is told—"Put the toys back on the toy shelf. It is time for lunch"—might profitably experience the loss of the privilege of playing with her messy toys after lunch. The more the child can relate the unpleasant result to specific inadequate behavior the sooner he will learn to guard against unwanted consequences. This must be reinforced by ensuring that the consequence serves as a sufficient deterrent against a casual repetition of the undesired behavior.

Here is the rationale: when a consequence for specifically defined inadequate behavior has been sufficiently communicated to the person accountable, should he fail to meet those standards, he must know that the consequence will come in full measure. To preannounce a consequence and then fail to administer it when the infraction is perpetrated undermines the parent's credibility in the child's mind.

My dad generated an appropriate fear in me when he administered a just consequence following a disobedient act that surprised him—I was considered compliant. I had turned sixteen and got my driver's license. I was going on my first solo date, and was instructed to be home by midnight. When I arrived home a little after 1:00 A.M., my mom was waiting in the front hall and informed me, "Your *father* [a word rarely used] is in the kitchen waiting for you." The expected questions, for which I had no good answers, were forthcoming. My father became prosecuting attorney, jury, and judge. I was sentenced to no driving of the car, except when dispatched on a specific errand, for the next six months. The sentence stuck to the last day of the six months. It was a fair, though bitter, price to pay for my disobedience, and an appropriate fear of my dad's authority was kindled. *I only wish it had been kindled years earlier.*

Fear attached to the *certainty* that serious and unwanted consequences will accompany one's inadequate behavior is *appropriate fear*.

Children Need to Learn Appropriate Self-Restraint

"He who rules his spirit [is better/mightier] than he who captures a city" (Prov. 16:32b). "But the fruit of the Spirit is . . . self-control" (Gal. 5:22-23). Apart from the Spirit's control, self-control is the most important kind available to the human spirit. People all too frequently try to control those with whom they live, work, and play—to direct; be in charge of; dominate; rule. There are many reasons why this is so, but the Holy Spirit promotes *self-control* in our lives.

Parents have a special God-given opportunity to help their children learn appropriate self-control that will serve them throughout their lives. For example, children need to learn to take turns; to not interrupt others who are talking; to sit still and be quiet at public events; to wait patiently for others to finish what they are doing before starting what the child wants to do; and many other practices that show respect for and accommodation to others.

Life is filled with various stimuli that require responses, first within our *hearts* and then in our behavior. The responses either serve personal self-interests or take into account the interests of others. At the juncture of self-interests and the interests of others self-control becomes an indicator of whom or what we *worship*—hold to be of highest value. If we love Christ we will obey him. We will do battle with the old nature that tempts us to follow its ways and instead do what honors Christ. The Holy Spirit helps us do this. He forms the Christlike character of *self-control* in us by providing many tests whereby we *learn* to exercise self-control.

As parents become impatient with their children, they experience a test of their own self-control. And if they recognize their need for self-control and that it is a fruit of the Spirit in their lives, such times remind them of their duty to instruct their children in the benefits of self-control and the consequences of its absence. These occasions are also opportunities for parents to teach their children the need for a new heart and Christ's help to build in them self-control.

Peter includes self-control in a list of godly qualities that evidence our relationship with Christ:

> For by these [God's divine power, and true knowledge of Him] He has granted to us His precious and magnificent promises, so that by them you may become partakers of the divine nature, having escaped the corruption that is in the world by lust. Now for this very reason also, applying all diligence, in your faith supply moral excellence, and in your moral excellence, knowledge, and in your knowledge, *self-control*, and in your *self-control*, perseverance, and in your perseverance, godliness, and in your godliness, brotherly kindness, and in your brotherly kindness, love. For if these qualities are yours and are increasing, they render you neither useless nor unfruitful in the true knowledge of our Lord Jesus Christ. . . . Therefore, brethren, be all the more diligent to make certain about His calling and choosing you; for as long as you practice these things, you will never stumble. (2 Peter 1:4-8, 10)

Self-restraint is necessary if one is to be an effective member of any community. Only the Holy Spirit in our *hearts* makes self-control possible in the battle of putting off the old nature and putting on the new Christlike one. Godly parents find this one of the most challenging aspects of childrearing, for it highlights the conflict between the child's self-will and the parents' will and ultimately God's will—"Our Father who art in heaven, hallowed be Thy name, Thy kingdom come. *Thy will be done* . . . ." (Matt. 6:9-10).

Triangulation: A No-no

After Adam and Eve fell and covered their nakedness with leaves, "they heard the sound of the LORD God walking in the garden in the cool of the day, and the man and his wife *hid themselves* from the presence of the LORD God among the trees of the garden" (Gen. 3:8). Hiding, in its multitudinous forms—from those we fear and from those we separate ourselves from because we disagree with their *world/life-view*—is a mark of the fall. Children will lie to their parents to avoid accountability. They will complain to their parents about a sibling displeasing them. Most children either want a parent to solve the problem or they will solve it in an inappropriate manner. Children do not like to confront those with whom they differ, especially if the offending person is bigger or stronger than they. Children need to be taught to appropriately solve *problems* and *negotiate differences that are preferences but not true problems*.

But either there was little constructive teaching in many homes, or the teaching was ignored concerning dealing appropriately with conflict. The world is filled with folk complaining to people other than those with whom they have the problem, but few solve problems constructively. This bad habit begins at home, and is a life-diminishing problem—a sin. Children complain to their parents about their siblings, playmates, and schoolmates. How to constructively confront *slights*, *hurts*, and *disappointments* is a *learned* ability that requires much practice.

Parents need to give special attention to the warning: "The first to plead his case seems right, until another comes and examines him" (Prov.18:17). When children criticize others in their absence, parents need to remember that the person charged with the offense has another perspective on the matter. Yes, Tommy is telling the truth when he reports that Mary threw the block and hit him, but he left out the part that he knocked down Mary's block castle just before she threw a block at him. How can they learn constructively to resolve their conflicts?

Let's assume that Tommy was overcome by an *inner urge* to destroy Mary's castle. He needs his parent's reminder that he has a *heart* problem and that his behavior is unacceptable. He might be *disciplined* by requiring him to rebuild the castle *under Mary's supervision*. This will require the parent's time to oversee the rebuilding—Mary may abuse her authority—but training our children is a primary responsibility of being parents, and is time consuming.

Now Tommy may learn to avoid the kind of problem he created for himself, but even that learning does not bring about a heart transformation.

Further, Tommy needs to be guided over the years to practice Jesus's admonition for Christians:

> If your brother sins [many mss. add: "against you"], go and show him his faults in private; if he listens to you, you have won your brother. But if he does not listen to you, take one or two more with you, so that by the mouth of two or three witnesses every fact may be confirmed. If he refuses to listen to them, tell it to the church. (Matt. 18:15-17)

Learning to face up to *our responsibility* to be reconciled to those from whom we feel estranged, and to live in peace with them, *insofar as it is within our power to do so* (Rom. 12:18), is a lesson that is hard for most people to learn.

God commands us to "be angry."[172] This is immediately followed, with the admonition ". . . and yet do not sin; do not let the sun go down on your anger, and do not give the devil an opportunity" (Eph. 4:26-27). Anger is a God-created emotion that needs to be controlled and attached to that which justifies it. Sometimes we get angry and discover later that we were either at fault or had no reason to be angry. Facing the person we are angry with affords us the opportunity to sort out the misunderstandings and restore the relationship—insofar as we can.

Godly parents need to take seriously their responsibility to teach and model for their children how to engage, in godly ways, people who hurt, disappoint, or anger them, and thereby damage their relationships. Children must be taught that their parents cannot solve all the relationship challenges in their lives. They must learn to do this hard work themselves.

Children of the Covenant Belong to God

God is a covenant-making God. But his covenant—a formal relationship between him and his people—differs in two significant ways from human covenants. First, God's covenant is established by God. The terms of the covenant are not negotiated, but are set by him alone. Those adopted into God's family learn of the terms long after they were established and accept them gratefully. The covenant is a gift that promises eternal life. Second, the fulfillment of the terms of the covenant depends upon the Spirit's gracious transformation of believers' hearts. No one can believe and keep the terms that God places on them in the covenant. Two passages from Deuteronomy show this well. First is the following *command*:

> Hear, O Israel! The LORD is our God, the LORD is one! You shall love the LORD your God with all your heart and with all your soul and with all your might. These words, which I am commanding you today, shall be on your heart. You shall teach them diligently to your sons . . . . (6:4-7)

---

[172] The phrase "Be angry. . . ." appears in the *present imperative* form in Greek. This means that it is a command; we are to *be* angry when we are angry.

This familiar biblical command is repeated in 30:6, but in a different framework: God will enable those born from above to fulfill his will that they should truly love him. And how will God accomplish this?

> Moreover the LORD your *God will circumcise your heart* and the heart of your descendants [lit.: *seed* or children] to love the LORD your God with all your heart and with all your soul, so that you may live.

God circumcises the heart of believers. He turns hearts of stone into hearts of flesh (Ezek. 11:19). Only God enables his chosen ones to fulfill the terms of his covenant—to be spotless, blameless, and holy before him: made possible through faith in Christ, the sacrifice for our sins. *It is Christ's perfect fulfillment of the terms of the covenant that is imputed to those who believe that he came as God incarnate to live and die for sinners.*

The wonder is that God extends his priceless covenant to the *children* of parents *in Christ*. What a profound comfort and hope this is to those who know Christ and have infants in the womb or children who have not trusted Christ. Scripture affirms that God loves the children of his chosen people:

> Peter said to them, Repent, and each of you be baptized in the name of Jesus Christ for the forgiveness of your sins; and you will receive the gift of the Holy Spirit. For the promise is for you and your children and for all who are far off, as many as the Lord our God will call to Himself. (Acts 2:38-39)

> For I will pour out water on the thirsty land and streams on the dry ground; I will pour out My Spirit on your offspring and My blessing on your descendants. (Isa. 44:3)

God calls the children of even one believing parent *holy* (1 Cor. 7:14). His promises are for believers and for their children. God loves children and wants them to come to him. Jesus showed this throughout his earthly ministry. He would not let his disciples prevent people from bringing their *babies* and *children* to him. He told them, "Permit the children to come to Me, and do not hinder them, for the kingdom of God belongs to such as these" (Luke 18:15-16; see also Matt. 19:13-15; Mark 10:13-16).

This should encourage Christian parents to stand strong in the knowledge that the Trinity will be with them as they raise their children according to his instructions and with his help. Apart from Christ, we can do nothing (John 15:5), but with him, all things are possible (Matt. 19:26; Luke 1:37). No parent can know when God will seal their children into Christ—in their old age (Prov. 22:6) or from the womb (Luke 1:41). And no godly parent is assured that there will not be an Esau or Jezebel in their family. But Christian parents can be certain that Christ is with them as they nurture their children with the nutrients of his Word.

Parents Greatly Impact Their Children's Perceptions of the Trinity

Untold adults think of Christians as *hypocrites*. What is a hypocrite, and why this terrible perception of professing Christians? Christ said, "By this all men will know that you are My disciples, *if you have love for one another*" (John 13:35). The visible church has always had tares mixed in with the wheat—they look alike (Matt. 13:24-30). Christ permits the tares to grow up alongside the wheat. He even instructs that the tares are not to be removed until the harvest—the Day of Judgment. The visible church has always had in its midst some who talk the talk but do not walk the walk. They are *social Christians* who are attracted to the body because of what they receive, but do not have a *heart of flesh* that manifests the *fruit of the Spirit*—love, joy, peace, patience, kindness, goodness, faithfulness, gentleness, and self-control.

Children discern the true *heart* and *passion* of their parents early in life. If their parents give lip service to Christ on Sunday but contradict that profession the rest of the week, children learn that their parents are hypocrites. Children can easily come to believe that people like their parents make up the church.

Similarly, believing parents have a profound impact on their children's perception of God. Christians do not all have the same disposition for the Holy Spirit to work on, the same habits to alter, the same thought-patterns to refocus, nor the same experiences. But they are all alike in this: they are sinners in need of Christ's redemption. And Christians are all unique: we have our individual personalities and experiences. Every child growing up in a Christian family will have a different perception of what mom and dad are like as parents. This being so, it should come as no surprise to anyone that each child will be impacted separately by his or her parents' understanding of God.

If a dad is stern and distant, as his children develop they will likely perceive God the Father as stern and distant. If a dad is affectionate and caring, then his children will probably think of God the Father as affectionate and caring. If a mom is critical and judgmental, her children will likely perceive God similarly. If she is sensitive and empathetic, her children will probably find it easy to project these same qualities onto God.

Because of this transference of identity—God is like my dad and/or mom—parents need to be transparent in their children's presence. So, during family devotions it would benefit children to hear dad acknowledge to the Lord that he is in need of his help as he struggles with a situation at work. If the parents tell their children that *they* need Christ's help, it is good for the children to know that the parents also need Christ's help in *their* lives.

It is also appropriate for parents, when they have erred in the administration of discipline, to ask their children for forgiveness. It is not unlikely that a parent on occasion might overreact to a child's transgression. Reflecting on this, it would be proper for the parent to tell the child they overreacted and to ask him or her to forgive them. Such practice of forgiveness in a family teaches the legitimacy of the doctrine of forgiveness that is an integral part of the gospel—Christ forgives us of our sins if we will *repent* and *confess* them to him.

Some children hear their parents seeking Christ's help with their hearts' struggles; asking Christ to forgive them of their sins of omission and commission; and even asking their children for forgiveness. Children blessed with such family experiences will learn that their parents *genuinely believe* in Christ's presence, and that God is greater than their parents. Both are important lessons to internalize.

Summary

"Therefore be imitators of God, as beloved children; and walk in love [*agape*], just as Christ also loved you ...." (Eph. 5:1-2). Christian parents have an enormous challenge raising children in a post-Christian culture that opposes their biblical world/life-view and values. Parents can expect no help from such a society. But the absence of the culture's support should stimulate godly parents all the more to seek Christ's help in home and church in rearing their children.

While children are conceived in sin and born with a nature that is a prisoner of self, God has put an inherent knowledge of good and evil in each child's heart (Point 1). This is an ally that godly parents have in rearing their children. When a parent tells a child that he or she has a heart problem and that they need Christ's help to control its impulses, the child knows that is true (Point 2). They know when they have done wrong—and they know they need help if their behavior is to change. Children are far more in tune with their own thought patterns and disposition than most parents realize.

Placing God at the center of the family's values is so important because it establishes God as the standard against which all is interpreted (Point 3). It brings continuity to the conversations about heart and behavior. God is established as the standard—the point of reference. It then behooves everyone in the family to get to know God well; to grow in their comprehension of him; to understand his character; and to grasp better what he expects of us.

Part of our children's nurture is accomplished through discipline (Point 4). It is important that they learn that God does not punish them for their sins, and therefore neither do their parents—Christ bore the punishment due sin on the cross. It is also important for children to know that God *disciplines all* his children, *parents and children alike*, so they may become more Christlike in their attitudes and behavior (Rom. 8:28-29; Heb. 12:10-11). It is appropriate for children to be aware when their parents are being disciplined. Children should not believe that only *they* are disciplined.

Parents should also share stories with their children of how they were blessed to have an appropriate fear of their fathers, and of how this helped them develop a healthy fear of the LORD (Point 5). Testimonies of the parents' struggles with their fallen nature, and their surrender to Christ, can be very meaningful to their children. These can serve as an incentive for the children to ask Christ to help them gain self-control over their self-centeredness (Point 6).

Learning to deal constructively with conflicts, injustices, and other affronts is a neglected area in our lives. There are unintended and intended hurts, but hurts are inevitable in this fallen world. So children need to learn how to face such things *constructively*; and teaching them to do this is hard and time consuming. Gossip, backbiting, and talking with *other* people about our enemies will not mend the relationships. Nor does hoping to find someone else to solve our relationship problems (Point 7). The job of repairing wounded relationships is effectively tackled only by those directly involved, and *pride* must not be allowed to thwart an honest effort at reconciliation. Broken relationships point to *sin*.

Above all else, parents must remember that God is with them and will help them raise their children if they *ask, seek, and knock* (Matt. 7:7). The children of God's children are *children of God's covenant* with his people (Point 8). God has *promised* his adopted children that he will be an advocate for their children. Believers have this precious assurance! Parents have the best Tutor in the universe to help them as they raise their children: the Holy Spirit. Parents need always to remember that apart from him they can do nothing that will result in their child's gaining eternal life. They must not neglect their part of the covenant: keep a close relationship with Christ (John 15:4-5). May the Lord help every godly parent remember just how dependent he or she is upon Christ for any true success in child-rearing.

Finally (Point 9), dads and moms need to remember that their children gain their first impressions about God from the way their parents treat them and each other. We represent God to our children in their earliest years. May Christ help us manifest his demeanor and character to our children and grandchildren so we are not a stumbling block to them, even as we confess our need for Christ's forgiveness. Children *do* know that their parents are sinners too, even as the children come to understand that they *themselves* have a heart that needs transforming.

24

Christ's Divine Nature Manifested in Singleness

One who is unmarried is concerned about the things of the Lord, how he may please the Lord. (1 Cor. 7:32)

The woman who is unmarried, and the virgin, is concerned about the things of the Lord, that she may be holy both in body and spirit. (1 Cor. 7:34)

These passages speak of a *voluntary* choice to remain unmarried to more fully serve the Lord. God designed marriage so that the couple would minister to one another, to their children, and to those beyond their family. Marriage is a relationship that absorbs time and energy that might otherwise be devoted to God's call—a call that requires the focus and time that only unmarried persons have. Singleness is a *special* status, offering *special* opportunities. Marriage in the Bible is the *more expected* state in which to live, but marriage is *not a higher* state.

We will address singleness from two perspectives. First, observations will be made concerning "three circumstances giving rise to singleness": (1) *those voluntarily electing singleness*; (2) *those providentially experiencing singleness but desiring marriage*; and (3) *those conflicted regarding marriage*. The second section, "the freedom that accompanies singleness," will explore: (1) *the freedom from particular concerns*; and (2) *the freedom to be single-minded*.

Three Circumstances Giving Rise to Singleness

Being single is a status that may prove to be either a phase in one's life or a permanent experience. Regardless, a person experiences singleness in the context of a set of prevailing conditions. And those conditions, described below, are integral to one's *heart* and external *environment*. The combination of the heart and external factors gives rise to real choices.

(1) Those Voluntarily Electing Singleness

A number of men and women elect to remain single because of a *call* God placed on their hearts. But others elect singleness because they have had *providential experiences* that have been greatly influential. In both cases the choice is a conscious one. The distinction is between God's *active will* working in someone's heart—his call—and God's *permissive will*, whereby he allows circumstances to influence decisions without direct involvement—his *decretive will*. In the case of God's call, singleness is an accepted state in which to remain. But the case of influential circumstances is based on personal reasons that are independent of any specific calling from God. Nonetheless, God uses it to fulfill his purpose in the person deciding to remain single.

(a) Singleness: A response to God's personal call to a task. There are times when God calls individuals to specific ministries, irrespective of their state of singleness or marriage. Here is an example:

> Now there were at Antioch, in the church that was there, prophets and teachers: Barnabas, and Simeon who was called Niger, and Lucius of Cyrene, and Manaen who had been brought up with Herod the tetrarch, and Saul. And while they were ministering to the Lord and fasting, the Holy Spirit said, "Set apart for Me Barnabas and Saul for the work to which I have called them." Then, when they had fasted and prayed and laid their hands on them, they sent them away. So being sent out by the Holy Spirit, they went.... (Acts 13:1-4a)

Barnabus and Saul (later named Paul) were set apart and called by the Holy Spirit. Of course, Christ had initially called Saul years earlier, while traveling on the road to Damascus (Acts 9:1-9). Eighty-year-old Moses was called by God at a burning bush (Ex. 3:1-22). And the prophet Samuel was called by the Lord as a small boy (1 Sam. 3:1-14).

Every Christian has a *general call* to Christlikeness. This is what the doctrine of sanctification speaks about—every child of God is set apart to become more like Christ through the transforming work of the Holy Spirit. In addition, each Christian has a *specific calling*—to serve Christ as a plumber, salesperson, mother, lawyer, teacher, mechanic, or secretary.

In some, however, God forms a deep *passion to serve him* in a particular ministry setting—in cancer research; in ministering to the poor in India; in Bible translation. And some called to these particular challenges believe they can *better* serve Christ in their calling without the distractions of marriage. They choose to remain single, and hence free to devote all of their passionate energy to serve Christ in their calling, *at this time*.

"At this time" is an important qualification. The choice to be single today does not preclude marriage in the future. For example, a man might be called to Bible translation in a remote area and know of no godly woman with a similar passion to serve Christ there. He could answer Christ's call as a single man. But he might return home on a future furlough, meet a godly single lady who, in God's providence, has a burden to assist someone in linguistic work for Christ, and marry her—and return with her to *their* call to translation work.

The *initial* commitment to singleness for Christ is complicated, if it is accompanied by a *vow* to remain single for life. Nothing in Scripture teaches that God wants us to make such vows, yet some believe that a *vow of celibacy* is analogous to the *covenant vows* of marriage. When conscience leads someone to this conclusion, and he takes a *vow of celibacy* in the name of the Trinity, the commitment has a binding quality that hinders thoughts of altering it. The vow has been made to God in the belief that his specific call necessitates permanent celibacy.

It is one thing to believe that a particular call is better met by remaining single, but it is far different to think God requires that one remain single when responding to his call. I believe that, if God desires celibacy, he providentially *builds* that desire into his child's heart and does not set him up to *struggle*. The *struggle* typically occurs in the area of sexual urges. The poor man who has made a *vow of celibacy* and is *struggling* with his sexual drive might think on Christ's words: ". . . and there are also eunuchs who made themselves eunuchs *for the sake of the kingdom of heaven*" (Matt. 19:12).[173]

(b) *Singleness: A choice influenced by previous providential experiences*. When someone's choice is not motivated by a strong sense of God's call to serve him while remaining single, this is usually due to negative and hurtful providential experiences. It is appropriate again consider to Romans 8:28-29:

> And we know that God causes all things to work together for good to those who love God, to those who are called according to His purpose. For those whom He foreknew, He also predestined to become conformed to the image of His Son . . . .

Providence describes *God's immutable guidance* of *all* that occurs—the good and the bad. God accomplishes this through either his *active will* or *permissive will*. Without his ability to *redeem* the horrible consequences of evil, we would lose sight of the great truth that *God is love*.

This profound truth regarding the *active* and *permissive* aspects of God's will is well illustrated in Acts 2:23: "This Man [Jesus Christ], delivered over by the predetermined plan and foreknowledge of God, you nailed to a cross by the hands of godless men and put Him to death." God, in his infinite goodness, actively delivered Christ over—his active will—to be crucified and put to death by godless men—his permissive will. God *willed* this to redeem those he had given to Christ before the foundation of the world (Eph. 1:4-5), and he utilized both his *active will* and *decretive will* to accomplish it. God the Son took upon himself the full wrath of God the Father to pay the redemption price required to forgive us of our sins. Oh, what love, *agape* love!

Negative and hurtful providential experiences can run the gamut from childhood sexual abuse, to observing a hateful relationship between parents. Such experiences can lead to the conclusion that marriage is not an attractive option. The many facets of an interpersonal relationship provide many possibilities for negative thinking: "this relationship may not work well"; "something is missing"; "it is sure to break down." Such thoughts undermine willingness to commit and expend the energy needed to create and maintain a God-centered relationship. Remaining unmarried becomes the acceptable default option. Marriage is viewed as too risky.

---

[173] The *eunuch* Christ refers to is one who voluntarily submitted himself to castration—the removal of his testes. The passage implies that such a commitment is laudable when it is *for the sake of the kingdom of heaven*.

(2) Those Providentially Experiencing Singleness but Desiring Marriage

Every person who is single, but who would like to be married, needs to be cautious, and reflective. All who desire marriage should resolve to keep the *mind* component of their heart actively engaged in the *looking* process and not allow the heart's *passions* to race ahead and propel their *volition* into a decision they may later regret. As the exploring goes on, *waiting for the right person* can produce its own temptation toward impatience which can arouse tendencies to be impulsive or to rationalize.

The search for a partner is largely shaped by three things: the *expectations* held regarding a partner; the *zing* and *vibes* expected when looking for marriage; and the *availability* of a partner who satisfactorily has these two qualities.

(a) Expectations regarding a marriage partner. Today, it is the *zing* and the *vibes* that chiefly determine if a couple will eventually decide to get married. And while this is understandable in our post-Christian culture, where hedonism—a belief that pleasure and happiness are the chief ends—dominates people's values, it is tragic that many professing Christians are swayed by the hedonistic world/lifeview. God calls his children to *righteousness*, not happiness, and certainly not pleasure. Happiness is a byproduct of righteousness. And pleasure is enjoying God's created order according to his design. Neither happiness nor pleasure is a God-ordained end to be sought by his people. *The chief end of our lives is to glorify God and to enjoy Him forever* (Rom. 11:36; 1 Peter 4:11; Ps. 73:24-28).

But too many single Christians, if they thought about it, would discover their expectations are so high that the availability of finding a mate is remote. Marriage is almost out of the question. Such persons should consider themselves members of a third group: *Those conflicted regarding marriage.* Now we are considering singleness providentially thrust upon someone who *desires* marriage. Is he or she willing to be realistic about the qualities a fallen and redeemed human being could *reasonably* be expected to bring to a relationship? Otherwise the too high requirements are an *inhibitor* to marriage.

God's Word establishes *only* one qualification for marriage. It states this singular requirement in both positive and negative forms. Christians are free to be married as long as they marry "in the Lord" (1 Cor. 7:39). Paul gives the negative form of this injunction:

> Do not be bound together with unbelievers; for what partnership have righteousness and lawlessness, or what fellowship has light with darkness? Or what harmony has Christ with Belial, or what has a believer in common with an unbeliever? Or what agreement has the temple of God with idols? For we are the temple of the living God. (2 Cor. 6:14-16)

Apart from this standard—Christians are to marry only *Christians*—they are free to unite with anyone of the other gender they choose. Marrying a person in whom Christ dwells assures both partners that the Holy Spirit is present as their Helper.

Marrying a Christian brings with it the *expectation* that the *fruit of the Spirit*—love, joy, peace, patience, kindness, goodness, faithfulness, gentleness, and self-control—is developing in the prospective mate's life. The Spirit builds Christlike character into those abiding in Christ. They are putting off the old nature—lying, stealing, sexual immorality, excessive drinking, and difficulties with anger, envying, and other ungodly propensities. They are being taught to persevere and to be diligent as they live for Christ. It is appropriate to expect that the basic qualities of godly character be present in anyone a Christian considers marrying. These are at the heart of *agape* love which is at the core of every good marriage.

One must be aware that expectations can also be closely tied to *preferences*. And it is unfair to *expect* someone else to embody our personal preferences. When preferences are shared, friendships are more easily formed. And when a friendship deepens, *phileo* love is its normal companion. Marriage is enhanced when friendship is an integral part. Companionship and harmony are more easily achieved when *preferences* and *expectations* coincide. But some differences in the couple's *preferences* are wholesome. They provide opportunities for new experiences, discoveries, and growth.

Lifestyle expectations, too, are critical considerations for those desiring marriage. These generally flow out of the unconscious portion of a world/lifeview. Does marriage involve a working husband and a stay-at-home wife? Do I want one child or as many as the Lord provides? What are my material expectations? Is my automobile's style important? The answers are significant, both to my relationship with Christ and with my spouse. In short, what do I expect from marriage?

(b) The zing and vibes expected when looking for a marriage relationship. Feelings! Personal feelings top most people's list of qualifications for marriage. Today many issues regarding *right* and *wrong* are evaluated on the basis of *feelings*. Indeed, right and wrong as categories for making moral judgments are becoming irrelevant to most younger people today. Feelings play the dominant role, particularly for those under forty-five. And this is tragic. The contemporary divorce rate is chilling: Marriages rooted in feelings are in serious danger of unraveling when tested by the recurring stresses and strains of life.

Letting feelings guide us when we ask or answer the question "Will you marry me?" is a big mistake for two reasons. First, if marriage is entered into under the sway of impassioned feelings, then those led by feelings must realize that even a godly marriage will not, indeed *can*not, continue to be enveloped in unwavering, positive feelings. Feelings *vary* with time; they are *not sustainable*. They are neither the *glue* nor the *substance* of marriage. Feelings can be likened to a barometer in that they rise and fall. They reveal an emotional reaction to a stimulus; they are not in themselves substantive.

The second reason feelings are a poor guide for marriage is that they are initially stirred by the *external qualities* in the one to whom we are emotionally attracted—their face pleases our aesthetic taste; their voice resonates with us;

their physique/shape is pleasing; they present themselves in an alluring way; their laugh is music to our ears—or many other external qualities. These qualities, however, are only superficially connected to character, temperament, habits, and more substantive aspects of the inner being, which take time to get to know.

We do not mean that feelings are connected only to superficial aspects of physical characteristics, or that affections are without value. We do mean that feelings diminish substantive, thoughtful reflection in persons influenced by postmodern presuppositions—everything is relative; values reflect personal beliefs, not verifiable truths; all beliefs are to be tolerated; you cannot know truth; pleasure and happiness are chief ends. Such postmodern views move people away from thoughtful consideration of marriage and toward feeling-led assessment.

In postmodern culture the *vibes* we feel have gained importance in determining the rightness of a relationship. The synchronization of positive feelings between the *yang* (masculine) and the *yin* (feminine) are *signs* that the relationship *ought to be*. *Chemistry* becomes a significant determining factor. *Zingy* stirs of joy and excitement are considered to be good omens of compatibility. More and more marriages are consummated with little more than good feelings at their core. This is clearly far away from the biblical standard—men having the character so they love their wives as Christ loved the church when he gave himself up for it (Eph. 5:25); and women marrying men they *respect* (Eph. 5:33). Both requirements rest squarely on *hearts* that are Christ-centered and Christ-led.

(c) *The availability of possible partners who meet the qualities "I would like."* Matching Christian men and women is diverse and complex. Some matches occur serendipitously: one discovers a mate when not looking for one. Predictably, many mates are found while fellowshipping at church; at a Christian school; while attending campus meetings of parachurch groups; when attending Christian conferences or camps; or while working for a Christian organization. These are natural places, because there is a higher concentration of committed Christians in them. Christian organizations plan functions to help Christian singles to mix and find partners.

Those who go where Christians gather to find a mate also need godly discernment. Wolves in sheep's clothing are sometimes among the true sheep. Cultural Christians are attracted to these groups. The tares look like the wheat. Prayer and discernment are needed, and counsel is appropriate. Counsel can be important because a discerning friend may pick up insights about someone to whom you are attracted, whom you misread. It is easy to overlook character components or habits that should be considered.

While few Christians today in North American would consider an arranged marriage, some of the components found in that procedure appear in modern dating services, where *compatibility tests* are given before dates occur. These tests are a substitute for the judgment of parents and community leaders (tribe, clan, elders), that was so important to arranged marriages.

(3) Those Conflicted Regarding Marriage

Many singles must first *honestly face themselves* before they can sensibly contemplate marriage. They need to resolve inner conflicts that sabotage their desire to be married. The thought of matrimony is attractive. They want to be married; they long for it. But simultaneously, they find that they are never in a psychological frame of mind to move forward to consummate a relationship. Apathy or disinterest seems always to overtake a good beginning.

Pride and *shame* are two hidden umbrellas under which many marriage inhibiters hide. Pride is the more subtle of the two. It often disguises itself, appearing as, say, standards and requirements. For example, a woman sets her dad on a high pedestal and uses him as a shield to measure all other men, making it impossible for others to attain her standard. All women would be blessed if they had dads who treated them as Christ would—but sometimes we can hide behind or misinterpret the "good." Maybe the dad who never harmed her physically also never supported her emotionally. Maybe her mom repeatedly told her what a great father he was while he was too busy to pay her attention. His passive rejection left her with a high intellectual view of the perfect dad, and a dwarfed ability to relate to men emotionally. The woman is proud of her dad—with a false pride—and hides her unconscious fear of men behind her unfulfilled relationship with her "perfect dad."

The fallen human mind is capable of misinterpreting anything, good or bad. And false pride is a universal mark of the fall. Sometimes it is used, in God's providence, to allow people to accomplish things that they would otherwise never have achieved. But false pride can also become a deterrent, as in the scenario above.

Shame is on the other end of the emotional continuum, but it too plays heavily in the lives of many conflicted about marriage. Shame is a painful emotion with more than one genesis. It is generally rooted in a sense of guilt. But guilt itself may be either a justified reaction to ungodly conduct, or may be false in both its genesis and application. For example, a mother drums into her daughter's mind: "You will never be fit to marry as long as you keep stuttering." Mother is unaware that her insistence upon a standard of perfection in her daughter's speech creates the tension that manifests itself in the daughter's stuttering. And the whole problem is exacerbated through the teasing she endured throughout her schooling. Now, she is simply too ashamed to believe that she would have any value as a wife. She has been shaped by shame.

Inner conflicts are at the heart of why many remain single. Most often such conflicts are born in the midst of circumstances beyond the control of the person weighed down by them. Those who are so encumbered will eventually do one of two things. They will either acknowledge the conflict, or they will continue not to recognize the conflict, and remain single. Those in the first category have several options. They may prayerfully wrestle with the conflict and discuss it with a helper—Christ, a friend, or a counselor—and devise a strategy to overcome the barrier to marriage.

A good listener is a friend indeed! Sometimes friends can help us resolve conflicts by asking questions whose answers bring clarification to our problem and possible ways to resolve it. There are times, of course, when problems are so deep and convoluted that someone *trained* may be more helpful than a good friend. Or the conflicted person may determine that he or she does not wish to address the underlying issues and elect to remain unmarried and serve Christ with the gifts he has given.

We noted three preceding circumstances that give rise to singleness—those voluntarily electing singleness; those providentially experiencing singleness but desiring matrimony; and those who are conflicted regarding marriage. There is neither a simple description of singleness nor a simple resolution for those who experience either the second or third circumstances described. But regardless of which category the single person is in, there is a *blessing* waiting for those who will wait upon the Lord. They can realize the *freedom* God has for them.

The Freedom that Accompanies Singleness

The level of *contentment* someone experiences with singleness will probably determine their heartfelt receptivity or irritation with the *freedoms* discussed here. The discontented heart will say, "I don't want that kind of freedom!" But the contented heart will find purpose in accepting God's will *at this particular time*. Singleness is not necessarily *permanent*.

Paul acknowledged, "I have *learned* to be content in *whatever circumstances* I am" (Phil. 4:11). We can learn to be content in circumstances that seem to say we have a right to be *dis*contented! This in turn raises the question, "*How*, then, are we to learn contentment?" And, we add, "*How are we to judge the circumstances in which we find ourselves?*" The answers transcend the issue of singleness and apply to any area of life in which we become discontented.

Contentment is learned by *practicing the nearness of God*. God is waiting for us to approach him whenever we want, because he initiated a growing relationship with us. That is why we are encouraged, "Draw near to God and He will draw near to you" (Zech. 1:3; James 4:8). Christ invites us to draw near to him in prayer. He invites us to ask him to give us *all* things that are in keeping with his infinite wisdom and perfect will (1 John 5:14).

God does not want his child to have a lifelong partner he or she loves more than God. The first commandment is still the most important: "You shall love the Lord your God with all your heart, and with all your soul, and with all your mind" (Matt. 22:37). Contentment is learned by loving God; being near to God; trusting God; being satisfied with God; and knowing—by faith—that God is sovereign and has our best interests foremost in his heart. These *heart* qualities are to be sought first. They are the fruit of practicing the nearness of God.

(1) Singles Can Enjoy Freedom from Particular Concerns

The concerns a single person is free from are the obligations associated with marriage. Scripture draws attention to the *distraction* of such things: "how [a man] may please his wife, and how she may please her husband" (1 Cor. 7:33-

34). Scripture is clear, however, that the distractions that accompany marriage are not sinful—they are simply things that take attention away from more focused ministries like prayer, attending to the needs of those beyond our family, or soliciting others' commitment to serve and minister (1 Tim. 5:5).

In a godly marriage the husband devotes time to live with his wife in an understanding way (1 Peter 3:7). If a man is to fulfill this requirement he must spend considerable time with his wife, listening attentively to her. A good husband wants to please his wife. He loves her. But this requires time and energy. And he needs to respond to what he has discerned are her needs—and this can take thought, energy, time, and money. This may all be important to the couple's well-being, but it is less focused on ministering to others.

The wife's situation is similar to her husband's, in that she too wants to please her spouse. What would they both enjoy eating; what has occurred in his life today that he needs to talk about; will he like me in this outfit? The mutual concerns and interests that are such an integral part of a couple's life together are beautiful, but a single person does not have to devote time and energy to them. The single person is *free from* these specific concerns.

If children join the family, the couple's commitments of time and energy increase greatly. Children are a blessing from the Lord, but children are a serious responsibility from the Lord. The demands a child puts on a couple in their early years is amazing. The single person has been given freedom to do other things that the Lord knows are *better*—things that serve him and that he will use to conform that person more and more into his own image.

(2) Singles Can Enjoy Freedom to Be Single-Minded

Children of God who accept their single status from the hand of providence can please the Lord in a way unavailable to those married; they can devote their full attention to "the things of the Lord" (1 Cor. 7:32). Verse 34 states that those who remain single also have a better opportunity to remain *holy*, in physical and spiritual endeavors, than those married. Paul ends his discourse on singleness, "This I say for your own benefit; not to put a restraint upon you, but to promote what is appropriate and to secure undistracted devotion to the Lord" (v. 35).

What do these phrases mean: (a) to "please the Lord"; (b) to devote full attention to "the things of the Lord"; (c) to experience a better opportunity to remain *holy*, both in physical and spiritual matters; (d) "to promote what is appropriate"; and (e) "to secure undistracted devotion to the Lord"? We will briefly examine each of these phrases, but point out that none of them suggest "super-spirituality" when practiced or experienced. They all address matters of *degree*, for the person who remains single has an *opportunity* to live her or his life in a more focused and engaged manner that is congruent with the perfection called for in Scripture.

To clarify: Christ said, "You are to be *perfect*, as your heavenly Father is perfect" (Matt. 5:48). The Greek word for perfect is *teleios*, a directional word—calling Christians to devote themselves to the goal of complete maturity or

Christlikeness. The single person has an opportunity, under Christ, to become more mature in areas of *true piety* than if married.

(a) *The freedom to please the Lord.* An ear attuned to hedonism hears the word "please" and thinks of physical pleasure or pleasing sensations. And Christians too can try to please God by *their actions*. But the motivation for such intentions is typically polluted with self-righteousness not pleasing to God. Yet his Word tells that he does takes pleasure in his children.

In what, then, does God take pleasure? The sacrifices that please God are "a broken spirit; a broken and a contrite heart . . . . " (Ps. 51:17). "But I am afflicted and in pain; may Your salvation, O God, set me securely on high. I will praise the name of God with song and magnify Him with thanksgiving. And *it will please the* LORD *better than an ox* . . ." (Ps. 69:29-31). "Blessed are the poor in spirit. . . . Blessed are those who mourn. . . . Blessed are the gentle. . . . Blessed are those who hunger and thirst for righteousness . . .": these attitudes of spirit please God (Matt. 5:3-6). Sound faith pleases him (Heb. 11:5). "And do not neglect doing good and sharing, for with such sacrifices God is *pleased*" (Heb. 13:16).

We please God when we are: (1) in a state of complete dependence upon him; (2) suffering and yet praise him for who he is even while we are afflicted; (3) truly humbled by our sin nature; (4) hungry for Christ's righteousness; (5) using the *saving faith* God placed in our *hearts*; (6) doing things for others that show God's heart; and (7) sharing with others what was entrusted to us. God is pleased with these, for they reveal the transforming work of the Spirit.

(b) *The freedom to devote full attention to the things of the Lord.* We must contemplate what constitutes "the things of the Lord" with care. This does not deny that married people do "the things of the Lord," nor that what single persons do is more acceptable to the Lord. But the married and unmarried are dissimilar. We distinguish between the natural (and obligatory) actions that accompany marriage and the time-permitting actions that we perform for those to whom we are not married—neighbors, friends, strangers, and even enemies.

Single persons have more time to devote to others. This is especially true compared to married couples with dependent children. Single persons have more discretionary time than married people. And it is the single person's opportunity to devote this time to "the things of the Lord" that allows them to be used in ways a married person could not be.

Thus under normal circumstances single people have more time to devote to "the things of the Lord." What, then, is the content of "the things"? A big asset of single persons is *discretionary time*. Without spouse and children, the single person has time to visit the sick and elderly; counsel and encourage others; hold a neighborhood Bible Study; or many other services.

Paul identifies the single's opportunity to persevere in *entreaties* and *prayers* that emulate Christ's work for us (1Tim. 5:5). "Christ Jesus is He who died . . . who was raised . . . [and] who also intercedes for us" (Rom. 8:34). Christ lives to make intersession for those who draw near to God the Father through him (Heb. 7:25). Do any Christians pray enough on behalf of others? Single persons generally have more opportunity to undertake this ministry than married persons. Singles simply have chances to do "the things of the Lord" to a greater extent than the married when those "things" are comprehended in the light of singles' *freedom*.

(c) The freedom for a better opportunity to remain holy in physical and spiritual endeavors. Human holiness means first and foremost the dedication of one's life to serve Christ. And it secondarily signifies being pure and righteous in conduct. We refer to the first of these when we speak of the positive aspect of remaining single. So, the freedom to remain holy parallels the discussion of the freedom to devote one's full attention to "the things of the Lord." But one's consecration to the Lord's will significantly amplifies an important sense-of-self.

The single person can become the Lord's *doulos*. Paul referred to himself as a *doulos* of Christ several times (Rom. 1:1; Phil. 1:1; Titus 1:1). What is a *doulos*? The Greek word indicates persons who voluntarily surrender themselves *completely* to a master's lordship. Christ's *doulos* has been led by God to want his or her will completely submitted to his will, for the *doulos* loves Christ above all else. Having been bought with a price, the blood of Christ, their *hearts* yearn to serve him (1 Cor. 7:23). They do not belong to themselves; they belong to him. And they become burdened to manifest this with their *whole hearts*!

Christ has multitudes of *douloi* in his service—every child of God should become a *doulos*—but these servants do not all serve at the same level of dedication. The intensity of commitment varies. Some *douloi* are more easily distracted than others. And marriage multiplies distractions. The husband wants to "please his wife" and she wants to "please her husband" (1 Cor. 7:33-34). This is not wrong or ungodly, but is a reality. Single persons have an opportunity to remain *holy* to a greater degree than married persons do.

(d) The freedom to promote what is appropriate. Once more, the distinctions between the married and unmarried are those of *degree*. As Paul distinguishes between greater and lesser gifts given to the church by the Holy Spirit,[174] it is also appropriate to distinguish between: (a) those who can give their money, and (b) those who can give their time, attention, and money.

For example, those with family responsibilities may be willing to give money to support a God-honoring project such as opening a shelter for the homeless, but would be unable to devote much time to such an undertaking. Their discretionary time is devoted to their family. Of course parents can involve children in mercy ministries and other projects that allow them to experience blessings that flow from "regard[ing] one another as more important than himself" (Phil. 2:3). A single person, however, may have more time for such ministries.

Also, singles are often freer to reject opportunities given them by society than are their married counterparts. For example, Christian parents with a child

---

[174] See 1 Cor. 12:28-31; 14:1.

in public school may be involved in a number of time-consuming commitments that are part of the public school routine—chaperoning class tours; participating in promotions; going to school plays. All Christian parents must decide how to educate their children. Are they to be home-schooled, sent to a Christian school, or to a public one? Such decisions are time consuming, especially if home-schooling is selected. Adults who remain single are exempt from such life-challenging decisions.

Married couples also face the challenge of what kind of reading material, TV programs, radio stations, and other educational/entertainment materials the family will consume. What is harmless for one family member may challenge another one. What a particular movie will stir up in one person's mind might never surface in another's mind. A single person does not have to be concerned with these issues. He/she needs only guard his/her own heart. Each one can, as Christ's *doulos*, select what is befitting as they live for him.

(e) *The freedom to secure undistracted devotion to the Lord.* "Let us lay aside every encumbrance, and the sin which so easily entangles us, and let us run with endurance the race that is set before us, *fixing our eyes on Jesus*, the author and perfecter of faith" (Heb. 12:1-2). All believers are like sheep: we are easily distracted, prone to wander from the One we love, and easily entangled in sin—in our thoughts, actions, and failures to do what we should do.

What advantage does a single person have over a married person when it comes to undistracted devotion to the Lord? The answer is not because the single is a better person or more deserving or less distractible inherently. Rather, there are two answers. First, the Christian is single providentially. God has decreed it for his good—to transform him more and more into Christ's likeness. This part of their sanctification may last only a season, with marriage ahead. Or, should God will, their sanctification may continue to be blessed by remaining single.

But second, the single Christian has opportunity to spend time with God in prayer, meditation, and Bible study not commonly available to the married who are occupied with spouse and children. Singles thus have the *freedom* to serve the Lord without distraction.

Summary and Conclusion

The chapter was designed to help singles grow while wrestling with their singleness. We saw that those voluntarily electing singleness enjoy a peace that accompanies the decision to remain single: (a) God has called me to a specific task or ministry that can be better carried out by remaining single, or (b) God has allowed me to have *providential experiences* that have led me to conclude that I am suited for singleness. Resolution and peace accompany both cases.

The most difficult position for a single person is to be providentially experiencing singleness but desiring marriage. This demands patience, a fruit of the Spirit, but a difficult character-trait to have formed in us—for we are by nature impatient. There are temptations associated with this circumstance like not taking time to discern if the *zing* and *vibes* we enjoy now are leading to long-term regrettable rationalizations. Being single can be trying, when the nearness of the Lord is much needed and precious. So, hopefully, those experiencing this have learned that *Christ's presence* is more important than anything a spouse could ever add.

The third circumstance giving rise to singleness involves intense *inner conflict*. Here the abstract *idea* of being married is emotionally appealing but the *reality* of facing a living partner is so emotionally threatening that relational paralysis sets in. So no real movement toward marriage is possible. The person in this situation needs to pursue one of two courses. He/she must either recognize his condition and accept singleness as providentially ordained by the Lord who will employ it to further his or her sanctification (Rom. 8:28-29), or seek help from a godly friend or professional to conquer the underlying condition that overwhelms the desire to marry.

Those brothers and sisters in Christ who do come to accept singleness can, by God's grace, rejoice in the *freedom* singleness provides *to be single-minded* and *fully devoted* to "the things of the Lord" (1 Cor. 7:32), and also to enjoy their *freedom from the distractions* that accompany marriage.

And there are typically more temptations regarding the things of the world if one is married than if one is single. For example: one's place of residence is likely to be more important to a married person than it is to one who remains single. This type of benefit must be *learned* if it is to be enjoyed, however, for it is different from the sanctifying lessons learned through *marriage*. There is a simplicity in singleness; there are not two people to please and make decisions around.

Being single and being married are both *blessed* circumstances when they are accepted as being providentially decreed by God! God *calls* most of his children to marriage, but he calls some to singleness. We must seek and follow his guidance. God cannot make a mistake!

25

Christ's Divine Nature Manifested in Business

He has told you, O man, what is good; and what does the LORD require of you but to do justice, to love kindness, and to walk humbly with your God? (Mic. 6:8)

Thus says the LORD, Let not . . . a rich man boast of his riches; but let him who boasts boast of this, that he understands and knows Me, that I am the LORD who exercises lovingkindness, justice, and righteousness on earth; for I delight in these things declares the LORD. (Jer. 9:23-24)

Micah and Jeremiah were God's messengers centuries ago, but they are as much his messengers to us today as they were to their contemporaries. Micah tells us, in context, that God will not overlook *ethical sins in the business activities* of his children—then or now. Micah was speaking to those who lived in Judah in the last third of the 8th century B.C., but the message is applicable today. We whom the Father gave to Christ are being transformed into *Christlikeness*!

In short, Micah emphasizes God's intention that his people *do justice* and Jeremiah emphasizes his intention that his people *become* more just and *do* what is righteous.

Micah expresses God's call for *justice* with the Hebrew word *mishpat* (Lexical # 4941), which carries the idea of a judge's judgment and also the need to obey God's law by rendering *what is due* to those with whom you do business. There is also a Hebrew word *tsadaq* (Lexical # 6663), which means "to be or to do what is right and just." This is significant because the word for *righteousness* in Jeremiah 9:23-24 is the noun *tsedaqah* (Lexical # 6666), meaning "what is right or just." And "righteousness" is revealed to us clearly in the biblical accounts that declare God's character and record his behavior.

So what does God tell businessmen of the 8th century B.C. that still pertains to us today? He expects us to *do what is just and right* in all their dealings in the marketplace. But God, upon observing the commercial transactions in Israel, was grieved:

> Woe to those who scheme iniquity, who work out evil on their beds! When morning comes, they do it, for it is in the power of their hands. They covet fields and then seize them, and houses, and take them away. They rob a man and his house, a man and his inheritance. (Mic. 2:1-2)
>
> Can I justify wicked scales and a bag of deceptive weights? (6:11)

> Woe is me! For I am like the fruit pickers, the grape gatherers. There is not a cluster of grapes [for the grape pickers] to eat, or a first-ripe fig which I crave. (7:1)

The prophet Malachi likewise cries out in God's name against those who oppress the wage earner in his wages (Mal. 3:5). This refers to those who are laboring and being paid a competitive wage. What troubles God? The workers are still experiencing poverty—after receiving payment determined by the market—while the business owners are getting richer and richer. God sees an injustice in this marketplace experience.

And the prophet Amos expresses similar concerns in the mid-750's B.C.:

> Thus says the LORD, "For three transgressions of Israel and for four I will not revoke its punishment, because they sell the righteous for money and the needy for a pair of sandals. These who pant after the very dust of the earth on the heads of the helpless.... Who oppress the poor, who crush the needy, ... who turn justice into wormwood and cast righteousness down to the earth, ... impose heavy rent on the poor and exact a tribute of grain from them,...trample the needy, ... saying, 'When will the new moon be over, so that we may sell grain, and the Sabbath, that we may open the wheat market, to make the bushel smaller and the shekel bigger, and to cheat with dishonest scales, so as to buy the helpless for money and the needy for a pair of sandals, and that we may sell the refuse of the wheat?'" (Amos 2:6-7; 4:1; 5:7, 11; 8:4-6)

It is possible to react to the quotes above with an attitude of, "Well, I have certainly never done anything criminal like that in my business practices." That is probably true, but surely the reader does not consider him or herself without sin in the work environment. Sin is ubiquitous—around us and in us. And it is easier to see ungodly conduct and attitudes in others than it is to see them in ourselves. Jesus spoke of this difficulty when he told a parable that pointed out the human tendency to observe "the speck that is in [our] brother's eye," and of our being slow to notice "the log that is in [our] own eye" (Luke 6:41-42).

There are gross sins and there are subtle sins. Here we will focus on the subtle sins we so easily fall into rather than the grosser sins which even the blind can see.

Preliminary Reflections

We remember that the child of God is not under the *Law*, for so many of the Scriptures in Figure 25.1 are Old Testament references. But we also remind ourselves that "the Law is good, if one uses it lawfully" (1Tim. 1:8). The individual laws are a guiding light on life's journey. But we are not saved by keeping the Law, for whoever breaks one part of the Law is guilty of breaking it all (James 2:10). Rather, the perfect righteousness of Christ is imputed to our credit through faith in his atonement. But God does not simply leave his children to try their best. Instead, he begins a remodeling work in each heart when he adopts them, and gives them the Holy Spirit to dwell in them. The Spirit begins the task of rebuilding them into a clearer *image* of God.

Believers have their *minds, passions* and *wills* gradually renovated by the Holy Spirit's use of the Word (Eph. 5:26; Heb. 4:12). God's image begins to take shape in them by degree. They thus become partakers of the "divine nature" (2 Peter 1:4). This transformation benefits them in three ways: they are (a) being "renewed to a *true knowledge* [of God] according to the image of the One who created him"; (b) being "renewed in the spirit of [their] mind, and put[ting] on the new self, which in the likeness of God has been created in *righteousness*"; and (c) being renewed in the "*holiness* of the truth" (Col. 3:10; Eph. 4:23-24).

God forms the *true knowledge* of himself in his children's *hearts* by having an *intimate* relationship with them.[175] This relationship is formed *propositionally* and *experientially*. The Holy Spirit takes the *propositional* (written) truth recorded in Scripture and writes it in the believer's heart, and this truth, like leaven, saturates and osmotically permeates the believer's mind, passions and will. And this propositional truth is, in turn, solidified through the believer's life *experiences*. For example, not only is the statement that God is a "very present help in [times of] trouble" (Ps. 46:1) a propositional truth to be written on his children's hearts, but his presence and comfort become a memorable experience for his children when they need it in a crisis.

We will treat the subtle habits of the mind that guide our thoughts—and occasionally leak out by way of our tongue or behavior—in the business environment. Christ once told a Pharisee:

> You Pharisees clean the outside of the cup and of the platter; but inside of you, you are full of robbery and wickedness. You foolish ones, did not He who made the outside make the inside also? But give that which is within as charity [your gift of love], and then all things are clean for you. (Luke 11:39-41)

Christ points out that it is much easier for us to appear *ethical* in our outward behavior than it is to be truly *godly* in our hearts. He gives an important instruction: "But give that which is within as charity [a gift of love to God], and then all things are clean for you." We are told to give our unholy, unclean, impure inner thoughts, motives and intentions to God as a gift of love. How can such filth and poison be seen as a gift of love? Perhaps an illustration will help clarify this blessed truth. Suppose your two-year-old child comes to you holding a box of deadly rat poison, and saying, "Look what I found!" Would you scold the child for giving you the box of poison that might have killed him? Would you not, rather, react with joy that your child had brought you the poison instead of keeping it, playing with it, and perhaps eating it? God wants us to give him

---

[175] God's intimacy with His children is wonderfully expressed in Prov. 3:32: "For the devious are an abomination to the LORD; but He is *intimate* with the upright." The word "intimate" here is the Hebrew *cowd* (Lexical # 5475) which literally means couch or cushion. So the translators give the verse the following marginal translation: ". . . but His *private counsel* is with the upright," i.e., "I will sit on the couch with you and share My thoughts with you". We do not have to give God a penny for his thoughts; He freely gives his thoughts to his children.

that which poisons our minds. But the conclusion is better yet: "... and then all things are clean for you" — covered by Christ's blood.

What Does the Lord Require of Us in the Marketplace?

Employers Doing Justice (what is right) Toward Employees
1. Paying a fair wage – Malachi 3:5
2. Employees' Health and Safety – Deuteronomy 22:8; Exodus 21:28-29, 33-36
3. Avoiding Unfair Discrimination – Acts 10:34; Romans 2:11; Galatians 2:6
4. Stewardship of Employee Ideas – Proverbs 12:15; 19:20; 20:18

Employees Doing Justice (what is right) Toward Employers
1. Working hard for employers – Colossians 3:23; 1 Corinthians 10:31; Romans 14:6-9
2. Being good stewards of employers' resources – 1 Corinthians 4:2; Luke 12:41-48; 16:1-2
3. Obeying superiors – Ephesians 6:5-7; Colossians 3:22; 1 Timothy 6:1-2
4. Avoiding gossip – Proverbs 11:13; 20:19; Romans 16:17-18; James 1:26; 3:2-12

Business People Doing Justice (what is right) Toward Customers
1. Telling the truth always – Psalm 15:1-4; Zechariah 8:16; Ephesians 4:25
2. Avoiding all forms of deception – Psalm 32:2; Proverbs 12:20; Jeremiah 9:5-8

Business People Doing Justice (what is right) Toward Competitors
1. Never "pirate" products or ideas – Ephesians 4:28; Exodus 20:15, 17
2. Never spread false information about a competitor – Exodus 20:16; Deuteronomy 19:18-19; Psalm 58:1-3
3. Never act with the intent to harm – Matthew 10:16; Romans 16:19; 1 Corinthians 14:20

Managers Doing Justice (what is right) Toward Owners
1. Owners should earn a fair return on their investment – Matthew 25:14-30; Luke 16:1-13; 19:11-26
2. Managers should not engage in "leveraged buy-outs" of the business they manage but should seek to maximize the value of the business for the stockholders or those they work for, not themselves – Titus 2:9-10; Matthew 5:16; Exodus 20:15; Leviticus 19:11

Business People Doing Justice (what is right) Toward Government
1. Never bribe officials – Exodus 23:8; Psalm 26:9-10; Isaiah 33:14-15
2. Obey the laws – Romans 13:1-7; 1 Peter 2:13-15

Business Leaders Doing Justice (what is right) Toward Society
1. Be good stewards of the environment – Genesis 9:8-12; Deuteronomy 20:19-20; 23:13
2. Support justice in the larger community – Proverbs 29:7; 31:8-9; Jeremiah 5:28

Figure 25.1 *Biblical Principles in Business*

There are three premises underlying what follows: (1) if our thoughts, intentions and motives are right, our decisions and conduct will follow in a *righteous* and *holy* way — a part of having the *image of God* restored; (2) if our thoughts, intentions and motives are ungodly, a moment's reflection and/or notification from the Holy Spirit will tell us that they are ungodly; and (3) those in Christ will quietly seek to "die to their old self" and "put on the new," which is being renovated into Christ's likeness, and do what is right. It is in relationship to premise 2 that we are to give to God our gift of charity, i.e., that which is within and is ungodly. With the Holy Spirit's help, this process becomes a means of sanctification, without which no one will see the Lord (Heb. 12:7-14). Character is built and *integrity* is formed in this way.

Even the ungodly admire integrity. Integrity is one of the first attributes mentioned when people discuss business ethics or those admired for their business leadership. What is integrity? It is something difficult to describe in words, but is readily recognized when habitual. Integrity is important to God and to those who serve God in the business arena, as we shall see.

Integrity

A definition of integrity: Integrity is a difficult word to capture because it represents a *gestalt*—a configuration of intangible physical and psychological phenomena that are so integrated as to constitute a unit with properties not derivable from a simple summation of its parts. Integrity in business is the solidarity between what one professes to be proper and his behavior; it uniformly models inner beliefs and outward confession of what is right. People of integrity are known to be *believable, stable, consistent, knowable, reliable*, and *trustworthy*. These attributes are deeply respected, and they encourage similar conduct in one's associates.

The significance of integrity: Integrity is the bonding component between people that generates cohesion between positive past-experiences and anticipated good future-experiences. Only time and experience can affirm the presence of authentic integrity. Once discerned, *trust* is its fruit. Trust is the most powerful motivator in the establishment of long-term, successful relationships, between individuals or organizations. Trust cannot be bought or be counterfeited for long. It emanates from a unified personality. Its value is incalculable; its benefits discernible.

The benefits of integrity: The confidence, respect, and trust that integrity engenders translate into open, honest relationships that provide an environment in which people can seek long-term mutually beneficial associations. Integrity is not presumptuous. A person possessing it does not attempt to trade on his or her integrity or take advantage of its presence. In fact, he or she is typically unconscious of possessing it.

However, a person doing business must also be *adept and proficient*, not simply have outstanding character. One steeped in integrity knows that the products and/or services he offers must be of the quality and quantity they are purported to be. Prices must be competitive. Supportive consultative counsel, if needed, must be available. The supporting expectations—delivery dates, time of completion, prompt support when needed—will be dependably and adequately met. The union of *proficiency* and *integrity* creates a powerful environment for the accomplishment of mutually beneficial goals.

The person possessing godly integrity is guided by *truth*. Truth is not *situational* per se, as postmodernists claim and as, sadly, many Christians believe. Truth reflects what is *real*, not what is *wished, wanted,* or *felt*. And truth is *knowable*, for God has entered into history and revealed in his Word the *moral, honorable, just,* and *principled* way of doing business. The Word is made alive in the hearts of Christians who seek God's guidance to glorify him through their right living. The fact that integrity has a *spiritual* foundation is practically expressed by C. William Pollard, the retired CEO and Chairman of ServiceMaster, in *Serving Two Masters?*:[176]

> Several weeks ago, I had the opportunity to give a lecture at the Wharton School of Business. I talked about the soul of our firm and reviewed how our objectives to honor God in all we do, to help people develop, to pursue excellence, and to grow profitably provides a source and standard for seeking to do what is right and to avoid what is wrong.
>
> Most of the questions at the conclusion of the lecture related to how one determines what's right or wrong. A number of students felt God is too religious to be an appropriate source for a standard of ethics in business. Most agreed, however, that a moral compass is needed and that one litmus test of whether something is right or wrong is whether there is benefit or harm to the people affected.
>
> I have often asked the question of how one determines right and wrong when interviewing people for leadership positions. The responses lead me to conclude that many business leaders have not thought deeply about the source of their ethics or integrity.
>
> The story of Joseph, son of Jacob and great-grandson of Abraham, is the story of a man of integrity. Because he was favored by his father, he was sold into slavery by his jealous brothers. He became a faithful and incorruptible servant and manager for his Egyptian master and then was unjustly accused. Sent to prison, he was a patient inmate and effective leader and manager for the warden. He was true to his faith in God when called before Pharaoh and proved to be an honest and prudent ruler of the land of Egypt. From his privileged position, he became a forgiving and generous provider for his brothers and family in their time of need.
>
> No matter the circumstances, Joseph could be trusted. The God he loved was the source of his righteousness and his faith was reflected in his leadership. He knew what was right and did it.
>
> It was Socrates who said that an unexamined life is not worth living. As we have examined the question of integrity and the development of character within ServiceMaster, we have concluded that a person's humanity cannot be defined solely by his physical or rational nature. It is unique in that it also has a spiritual side. It is this spiritual side of our humanity that influences our integrity, our ability to determine right and wrong, to recognize good and evil, to make moral judgments, to love or to hate, to develop a philosophy of life that provides an ultimate framework for doing the right thing even when there are no prescribed rules or when no one is looking.

Integrity, while it may be difficult to define, is not hard to recognize when it is operative. Joseph, described above as a man of integrity, was a Christ-type—

---

[176] C. William Pollard, *Serving Two Masters?* (New York: HarperCollins Publishers, 2006), pp. 94-95.

he manifested the attributes of a godly man. Manifesting Christ's divine nature in our business calling requires the active work of the Holy Spirit in our lives. It is *he* who forms integrity in the life of believers.

We now reflect on everyday situations that those in business face frequently and we ask: What should a person of integrity do in each circumstance? Is what I would do *Christlike*?

Nineteen Situations to Reflect on

(1) You are an employer. You employ a person—maybe to clean your house; to clean the office; to make home deliveries; to be a sales clerk; to operate machinery—and you pay what others pay in the open market for the same labor. Why do you believe that the going rate is a just wage? History has shown that sometimes the market overpays—and that those so paid eventually either face a downward wage adjustment or are laid off. But more often the market underpays—and workers are thereby unjustly treated. Those in business, however, generally assume that the market itself establishes a fair wage. Such an assumption keeps us from thinking: Are we employing an *average* worker? Would it be wise to employ an above-average worker? Or can I achieve my ends while at the same time helping a below-average worker? What is a fair wage?

There is no publicly prescribed right answer to such questions. If you were a private entrepreneur, would the answer to them necessarily be the same as it might be if you were a professional manager leading a public corporation? Life is complex. *If . . . you lack wisdom . . . ask of God . . . and it will be given* (James 1:5; Matt. 7:7; meditate on Mal. 3:5; Isa. 58:3).

(2) You are an employer. You require your employees to work in intense and stressful environments; or in a toxic environment; or up high on construction projects; or with power tools and machines that can easily cause bodily harm or death. There are standard precautions that may have been mandated by law. (If precautions have been mandated, they are probably in place because those before you were deemed to have done too little on a voluntary basis to protect their employees' welfare.) Protection and care cost money! And costs in a competitive market are to be minimized if one is to be *successful*. Do you think of your employees, first and foremost, as a factor of production—costs—or as *authentic persons* deserving your respect and consideration as image-bearers of God?

A reflective answer to this question may impact the priority and balance of concerns and protections. How are the *risks* associated with your employment environment shared by you and your employees? Would you be willing to personally work in their work environment? Does God care about the health and safety of your employees? *If . . . you lack wisdom . . . ask of God . . . and it will be given* (James 1:5; Matt. 7:7; meditate on Ex. 21:28-29, 33-36; Deut. 22:8).

(3) You are an employer: the CEO of a public corporation. You are wise enough to know that discrimination, in appropriate and inappropriate forms, is ever present in the work environment—in you and in those you employ. And

you are well informed of the laws that forbid discrimination in matters of employment and promotion. But, let us say, you are personally turned off by people who bite their fingernails. It represents wasted energy. You see the habit as signaling nervousness, insecurity, and unresolved tensions. You have these thoughts, but you know that the habit does not predetermine how well the nail-biter will carry out his responsibilities. Nevertheless, the practice bothers you to the point of conscious prejudice. It is now at the forefront of your awareness. The Chairman of the Board's son (an outside director) has risen to a position that reports directly to the Senior Vice President of Operations—and that son is one of three logical replacements for the Senior VP, who will retire in five months. Yes, he bites his fingernails to the quick. You fear your judgment will be affected by your prejudice: "Will I try so hard to overlook the habit that I will be 'too soft' in my assessment of him; or will I be so determined to avoid that mistake that I will be too hard on him?"[177] *My help comes from the* LORD (Ps.121:2; meditate on Acts 10:34; Rom. 2:11; Gal. 2:6).

(4) *You are the floor manager in a machine shop.* The company that owns the shop has twelve such operations in major metropolitan areas around the country where a wide variety of industrial corporations are located. The company has a consulting engineering arm, a fabricating division, and a flexible and diverse machine shop at each location where special machining jobs are carried out. You have six years of experience overseeing this type of work, and eight of the twenty-three people working under your supervision on the floor have fifteen or more years of experience. You have learned by experience that there are many, many ways to configure the layout of the machines on the shop floor (sixty-percent of the machines can have their steel platforms moved from one area of the shop to another and still remain stable enough to perform precision work). You also have over two-hundred feet of movable conveyor track, thirty inches wide, with ball-bearing rollers for moving heavy items from machine to machine. No two contract jobs are the same, but most jobs allow you from three to five working days to plan for the next layout arrangement. It takes approximately five hours to complete a layout shift, but those who will be working on the tail end of a job can help put the things in their order (prescribed by you). And there are typically five to seven different jobs in various stages of completion underway at any one time on the floor.

The other day a senior machinist asked you if you had thought about a different arrangement of the machines for the job he was working on. You told him you had not, listened to him, and thanked him for his suggestion. This started you thinking, "Am I being a good steward of the ideas that many of the men working on the floor must have? They are good machinists with years of experience. They must have some useful ideas about how to best do things. Should I solicit their thoughts? If I do, should it be done informally? Or should I

---

[177] Every time I had a student whose parents were close friends of my parents or whose parent was a colleague of mine, I struggled with this very issue—how to be fair.

set up a formal structure of brainstorming?" *If . . . you lack wisdom . . . ask of God . . . and it will be given* (James 1:5; Matt. 7:7; meditate on Prov. 12:15; 19:20; 20:18).

(5) *You are an employee.* You have been doing your job for seven years. You have the freedom to work at your own pace. The work is continuous, flowing from a never-ending stream of requests, and there are seven others besides you in the office doing things similar to you. You work for the state in the Department of Motor Vehicles. You have never been given a *standard* by your supervisor regarding just how much output you should reach in a given period of time. And you have asked, "Am I doing all that I should be doing?" Last night, during Bible reading you read: "Whatever you do, do your work heartily, as for the Lord rather than for men" (Col. 3:23). This made you wonder about what doing your work *heartily* might look like in the context of what you do every day. And this stimulated you to further wonder what it meant to do your work "for the Lord rather than for men." *If . . . you lack wisdom . . . ask of God . . . and it will be given* (James 1:5; Matt. 7:7; meditate on 1 Cor. 10:31; Rom. 14:6-9).

(6) *You are an employee.* You work in the sales department as Director of Special Product Promotions. You are not directly involved in sales but are a part of a team of staff personnel involved in things like deciding when price incentives should be used as a sales stimulator; what trade shows to participate in; and what kinds of promotional kits should be included in the bag of tools incorporated in the field sales presentations. You know there is a tendency to operate on the assumption that more is better. But you also know that this is *not* true. Both a *quality* and a *quantity* of promotion are involved. It is a challenge to get those involved to think in terms of a return on investment in promotions. You wonder, "How am I to demonstrate I am a good steward of my employer's resources?" *If . . . you lack wisdom . . . ask of God . . . and it will be given* (James 1:5; Matt. 7:7; meditate on 1 Cor. 4:2; Luke 12:41-48; 16:1-2).

(7) *You are an employee.* In college you were immersed in the pervasive cultural phenomenon later labeled the anti-authority *modus operandi*. Authority existed but it was ignored whenever possible. Authority represented *restraints*, and freedom was the *in* thing. You never discussed the distinction between *freedom* and *license*. And you would probably have ignored such a discussion before you became a Christian. But two years ago you surrendered your life to Christ—soon after the girl you wanted to marry rejected you. She declared you the most self-centered person she had ever known, and walked out of your life. You were crushed. But the Holy Spirit *once again* called. You had been raised in a Christian home. You had wrestled with the Lord before, but had always resisted him. Finally, you acknowledged your rebellion and need of help—first to yourself, and then to the Lord. You now know that you are forgiven, that Christ is the supreme authority, and that *authority* is part of God's wise plan. You also believe that God is sovereign over all in authority; and you currently have a supervisor you do not respect. Your circumstances have caused you to think about the whole authority issue and how God would have you interact with your boss. *My help comes from the* LORD (Ps. 121:2; meditate on: Eph. 6:5-7; Col. 3:22; 1 Tim. 6:1-2).

(8) *You are an employee.* Six of you work together as a team. You help each other on assigned projects, eat lunch and take breaks together, and know much about each other professionally and personally. You have become aware recently that two people in the group keep inserting tidbits of gossip about other mutual acquaintances. Also, they find fault with a member of the leadership team above your group. Lately you have been reacting negatively to this gossip and criticism. It is not right; but you find yourself both enjoying it and sometimes even participating in it! What should you do? Remain silent and not add to the input? Withdraw from the group? Speak positively about the subject of the gossip? Or search for a way to tell the group that what it is doing is wrong. (Half of the group does not profess faith in Christ; one gossip does, one does not.) *If . . . you lack wisdom . . . ask of God . . . and it will be given* (James 1:5; Matt. 7:7; meditate on Prov. 11:13; 18:8; 20:19; Rom. 16:17-18; James 1:26; 3:2-12).

(9) *You are the owner of a carpet company.* You have met with the developer of an office complex who is about ready to order 4,000 square yards of high quality carpet for the complex. You represent a mill that has been supplying you with a carpet that meets the developer's quality and decorative standards. For the past two years you have been buying the material from the mill for $20 a square yard. Today you and the developer had lunch and he said he was ready then and there to work out an agreement to purchase the carpet you had shown him. You were very excited, because he has done a lot of development work in the area—and you believed this was an opportunity to establish a favorable relationship with him. You negotiated to deliver the carpet for $22 a square yard. This was a couple dollars below your regular price, but seemed appropriate to you to establish the relationship. The price did not include the cost of installing the carpet. He told you that charge could be discussed later to be negotiated separately. You agreed, knowing that the installation might or might not be done by your firm. So you verbally agreed to deliver 4,000 square yards at $22 a square yard. Back at your office after lunch you called the manufacturer to order the 4,000 square yards, and were knocked off your feet when you learned the price of the carpet had risen to $25 a square yard twenty-four hours earlier. You explained your need, but were told that the $25 is firm! What are you going to do? There was no signed agreement. *If . . . you lack wisdom . . . ask of God . . . and it will be given* (James 1:5; Matt. 7:7; meditate on Ps. 15:1-4; Prov. 6:2-5; Zech. 8:16; Eph. 4:25).

(10) *You are an entrepreneur.* You enjoy the freedom of decision-making that accompanies being your own boss, but deep down you know that you really want Christ to be the Boss. And this reality causes you to reflect often on the question, "Just how much of the 'whole truth' should I share with my sales force?" This question arises whenever you begin planning the introduction of product changes that will be made available soon, while your sales force is busy selling the *current* best available product line. When should you let them know about your plans for an upcoming 20% price reduction in the current line to move the present inventory out and make room for the new, upgraded line that will offer the customer a 15% increase in efficiency? How do you handle these kinds of things and retain the integrity you demand of yourself and others? You

know that God hates deception, and so do you. *If . . . you lack wisdom . . . ask of God . . . and it will be given* (James 1:5; Matt. 7:7; meditate on Ps. 32:2; Prov. 12:20; Jer. 9:5-8).

(11) *You are a corporate CEO.* You know that stealing, pirating, and lifting of other's ideas is rampart in the electronics, drug, and music industries. And in your own industry as well—the food processing/canning industry. Two corporate chefs were hired away from you by competitors who perceived that you had better baked beans, chilies, soups and stews than they did. You believe your competitors stole proprietary property from you. The two chefs had been with your organization for over ten years; they had been trained by others in your company's kitchens. (As does everyone in your industry, you buy your competitors products, test them, and see if you can learn things about their recipes and ingredients, but you never intentionally hired a chef away from a competitor to pirate their formulas and recipes.) The question arises in your mind, just what is proprietary property? Does not everyone who has worked for someone else in a sensitive area have the potential to become a carrier of proprietary assets that belong to the original employer? What kind of obligation does this put on me in my hiring practices, if any? *If . . . you lack wisdom . . . ask of God . . . and it will be given* (James 1:5; Matt. 7:7; meditate on Eph. 4:28; Ex. 20:15, 17).

(12) *You are the owner of a small home-building corporation.* Your organization builds about one-hundred homes a year in small developments and on individual lots in established neighborhoods. You do most of your building in a three-county area, in new subdivisions where the infrastructure—streets, curbs—has been put in place by those who contract with you to build the homes on designated lots. The only speculative home-building you do is on individual lots you purchase occasionally in developed neighborhoods. There is one other builder about your size that you compete with and dozens of small speculative builders—some of whom do very good work. Over the years, the building codes have become more stringent, but you considered this a good thing with only a few exceptions, where you believed the new requirements were unnecessary. You believe yours is quality work because you do work that considerably exceeds the building code's requirements.

You are asked by a developer to look over the fourteen house plans he wants you to bid on, as he chooses a builder to work with him in a new ninety-home development. You ask the developer who else had been asked to submit bids. His answer is that only the other builder about your size. The rumor is that he fudges on the code and cuts corners to enhance his profit margin. You wonder if you should allude to this when you submit your bids. *My help comes from the LORD* (Ps. 121:2; meditate on: Ex. 20:16; Deut. 19:18-19; Ps. 58:1-3).

(13) *You are the owner* of a wholesale/retail appliance business that buys refrigerators, freezers, stoves, washers, dryers, and other smaller appliances from seven of the largest manufacturers. You concentrate on selling to motel chains; to large subdivision home contractors; to public laundromats; to hotels; to apartment complexes and other small retailers. You maintain an efficient maintenance department and sell maintenance contracts to many of your

corporate customers. Your business is located in a population area of about three million people in a geographic area of about four hundred square miles. You have one major competitor in the area, and the two of you have about 75% of the defined market that you both serve—with that being divided about 60% to 40% in your favor. Your competitor just had a huge warehouse fire that destroyed 95% of his stock. He has come to you with a request for immediate help: he had a shipment of 200 bar/lock refrigerators promised for delivery in a few days to a large resort hotel opening next week, and the manufacturer of the refrigerators cannot replace his lost stock in the next sixty days. You have 250 of the particular refrigerators in stock—and no deliveries committed to for the next ninety days. The competitor has been a tough opponent—sometimes a bit rough around the *ethical edges*. You wonder: "Do I help him or hurt him? He doesn't know that I have the full inventory. If I don't help him, I could suck all of the potential profit on the deal out of his hands into mine." *If . . . you lack wisdom . . . ask of God . . . and it will be given* (James 1:5; Matt. 7:7; meditate on 10:16; Rom. 16:19; 1 Cor. 14:20).

(14) *You are a professional manager*, not the owner of the corporation you lead. The market capitalization of the corporation is $250,000,000, with 5,000 shareholders. The price of the stock has averaged a 6% annual growth over the past decade, with a 2.8% dividend payout on the average annual share price—for an 8.8% average annual return on the stockholder's investment. That is not a roaring success, but is 2.4% better than the average return of those in that industry. The corporation has 3,750 employees in seven states and one foreign country. You are the industry's top wage-payer, and consider that to be to your advantage because of the quality of your employees. And the management team is being compensated at a level that places you all in the top 5% of the industry. You are also pleased that your equipment and technology are all on the cutting edge of what is available. The Board of Directors established a separate foundation six years ago when profits were unusually good and set up a policy of putting 2% of the gross profits into the foundation for distribution back into the communities and institutions that the foundation board deems appropriate. Another good year financially seems to be in the offing, and you begin to think about what you should recommend to the board regarding the distribution of the expected plenteous profits. You know that such a decision is a values judgment-call. What should be at the top of the *priority list* and get the biggest share of the growing benefits?—continued modernization of the facilities and technology; social responsibility commitments; management salaries; employee benefits; or stockholders? *If . . . you lack wisdom . . . ask of God . . . and it will be given* (James 1:5; Matt. 7:7; meditate on Matt. 25:14-30; Luke 16:1-13; 19:11-26).

(15) *You are the CEO of a large public corporation*. The Chairman of the Board and three other external board members approached you with the idea of you five forming a team and working with a large investment bank to devise a plan to orchestrate a leveraged buy-out of the company. The others argue that the company is undervalued. They believe that by selling off some of the less profitable divisions of the company (coupled with the use of highly-levered financing committed to the recapitalization of the company, and the updating of its six technology-based divisions) they could create a handsome profit for those

who undertook the risk. They believe they can attract a handful of other wealthy investors, and could end up with no more than ten or twelve individuals buying the company and taking it private. They have brought you the pro-forma financial projections of their plan, and it forecasts enormous financial benefits for those who would undertake the venture. You know that the four men who have approached you respect you greatly, and that they believe you are the person capable of managing the takeover. So you listened carefully and asked for a week to think it over. You are to meet the Board Chairman next Wednesday at the Country Club in a private dining room. You know that *If . . . you lack wisdom . . . ask of God . . . and it will be given.* You have been praying on the matter while studying Scripture (Titus 2:9-10; Matt. 5:16; Ex. 20:15; and Lev.19:11). You know that you could rationalize either a positive or negative response to the offer. Which decision embodies godly integrity?

(16) *You went to a college* that had a required ethics class in the business school, and in there you learned that extortion and bribery were, in many ways, simply two sides of the same ethical coin: those who extort hold a controlling position of power; those who bribe are trying to move those with that power. You live in a political jurisdiction where, although there is no overt extortion, there always seems to be very long waiting period when you need public approval to move forward with a privately-funded construction project. Yet there are a few companies with whom you compete that seem to never have *any* delays in their requests. This has got you wondering if some hanky-panky is going on. You think, "Is it appropriate to invite a public official to a big sports event with me?" Is attempting to smooth the way a bribe? Is there a clear line between influencing and bribing? Is there an ethical continuum regarding such matters? *My help comes from the* LORD (Ps. 121:2; meditate on: Ex. 23:8: Ps. 26:9-10; Isa. 33:14-15).

(17) *You are an entrepreneur and operate a small construction firm.* You live and work in a geopolitical area with many layers of laws that govern your business activities. There are sensible laws: they serve a purpose in everybody's interest. But there are also restrictions that make no sense to you. They represent nonsense—a bureaucrat not familiar with real world operations dreamed up a theoretical problem and solved it with a bureaucratic rule. Now they expect you to honor their nonsense. You are fed up with this and wonder if it would be smart to ignore the silly laws and risk the possible fines for noncompliance! They are smaller than the benefits gained from ignoring them. Is it okay to break such laws? *If . . . you lack wisdom . . . ask of God . . . and it will be given* (James 1:5; Matt. 7:7; meditate on Rom. 13:1-7; 1 Peter 2:13-15).

(18) *You are the CEO of a large land-development corporation.* You are aware of the cultural struggle between those who intentionally employ environmental regulations as stop-all-change weapons and those who believe that the environment belongs to whoever holds legal title to a portion of it. Should not owners be free to do what they want with their own property? There is constant pressure, from all sides of the debate, to have those who govern either add to or reduce the number of regulations. And you are certain that what occurs on one piece of property can have a collateral impact on other pieces of property. You

wonder, "Does God really care about the details of our working out something between competing viewpoints?" *My help comes from the* LORD (Ps.121:2; meditate on Gen. 9:8-12; Deut. 20:19-20; 23:13).

(19) You are the president of a locally-owned federally-insured bank in a community of 25,000 households. You also own about 20% of the bank's outstanding shares of stock. You were raised to believe that businesses should not become publicly involved in civic matters such as public education, zoning issues, and condemnation proceedings. But as you grow in Christ you question this. It is right for you not to involve the *bank* you represent in such public matters—for it is a legal entity with many owners, and some of them might not appreciate your representing their financial interests in a publicly debated matter divorced from the bank's direct interest. But you are *more* than the president of the bank. You are a citizen, a husband, a father, and a Christian. There is an issue now that involves the condemnation of a group of houses belonging to about one hundred blue-collar families. The purchase and destruction of these homes is being considered to make room for a new highway extension into the heart of the city. The families affected are upset, but lack resources to hire representation in the discussions underway. There are also one hundred and twenty-five slum properties a quarter of a mile away, which are owned by a prominent local family, that are being ignored in the discussion of alternative routes. You suspect behind-the-scenes conversations are occurring to protect the income stream of the owner. Should you speak up on behalf of the blue-collar families? *If . . . you lack wisdom . . . ask of God . . . and it will be given* (James 1:5; Matt. 7:7; meditate on Prov. 29:7; 31:8-9; Jer. 5:28).

Further Reflections

Business people face other spiritual challenges along with their need for God's *wisdom* in decision-making. The Devil is subtle and uses many means to derail those who desire to follow Christ in business vocations. Three big challenges arise from: (a) relentless daily pressures that distract people from a Christ-centered focus—sometimes called "the tyranny of the urgent"; (b) the enjoyment of success that propels people to seek the symbols of success—riches; and (c) being overwhelmed by success. We will look briefly at each of these.

The Loss of Focus

The writer to the Hebrews follows his recounting of those who triumphed over life's challenges through *faith* in God's preeminence with an exhortation:

> Therefore, since we have so great a cloud of witnesses surrounding us, let us also lay aside *every encumbrance* and *the sin which so easily entangles us*, and let us *run with endurance* the race that is set before us, *fixing our eyes on Jesus*, the author and perfecter of faith. (Heb. 12:1-2)

John Bunyan portrays Christian's struggles with distractions and temptations throughout his journey in *The Pilgrim's Progress*. Those in Christ are easily distracted. Satan tries hard to distract them, and he has a lot of material to work with: the natural attractiveness of much that surrounds us in God's created order and our fallen nature. We need the assistance of the Holy Spirit to remain focused on Christ and grow in spiritual maturity.

The Love of Money

The Word is full of warnings about wealth's lure. Christ states plainly, "No one can serve two masters. . . . You cannot serve God and wealth" (Matt. 6:24). Paul says we should be content with God's provision of our food and covering and then says:

> But those who want to get rich fall into temptation and a snare and many foolish and harmful desires which plunge men into ruin and destruction. For the *love* of money is a root of all sorts of evil, and some by longing for it have wandered away from the faith and pierced themselves with many griefs. (1Tim. 6:8-11)

The putting of anything ahead of Christ is idolatry (Col. 3:5). We are to "have no other gods before Me," the first of the Ten Commandments (Ex. 20:3). The Holy Trinity constitutes the *absolute highest worth* and is therefore the only One worthy of worship.

The Overwhelming Effect of Success

Max Weber's The Protestant Ethic and the Spirit of Capitalism quotes John Wesley (1703-1791):

> I fear, wherever riches have increased, the essence of religion has decreased in the same proportion. Therefore I do not see how it is possible, in the nature of things, for any revival of true religion to continue long. For religion must necessarily produce both industry and frugality and these cannot but produce riches. But as riches increase, so will pride, anger, and love of the world in all its branches. How then is it possible for Methodism, that is a religion of the heart, though it flourishes now as a green bay tree, should continue in this state? For the Methodists in every place grow diligent and frugal; consequently they increase in goods. Hence they proportionately increase in pride, in anger, in the desire of the flesh, the desire of the eyes, and the pride of life. So, although the form of religion remains, the spirit is swiftly vanishing away. Is there no way to prevent this—this continual decay of pure religion? We ought not to prevent people from being diligent and frugal; we must exhort all Christians to gain all they can, and to save all they can; that is in effect, to grow rich.[178]

Wesley notes when abundant blessings overshadow the daily dependency upon God for food, covering, and life itself, this dulls our appreciation for God's goodness in providing the blessings that we took for granted. This parallels Christ's parable of the sower who cast his seed so that some fell beside the road, some on rocky soil, some among thorns, and some on good ground. Success is similar to the seed sown among thorns where it was "choked with . . . riches and pleasures of this life [and thus did not] bring . . . fruit to maturity" (Luke 8:5-15). Success brings many challenges just as suffering does. We must heed Peter: "Be

---

[178] Max Weber, *The Protestant Ethic and the Spirit of Capitalism* (New York: Charles Scribner's Sons, 1958), 175.

on the alert. Your adversary, the devil, prowls around like a roaring lion, seeking someone to devour" (1 Peter 5:8).

Conclusion

Christians should never presume that by just reading the Bible—for example, the references listed at the conclusion of each of the nineteen reflective situations offered above—that God's Word will easily yield its applicable truth or tell us exactly how to act in every situation. His Word may or may not provide us with an immediately clear and specified direction. God has given us the opportunity to seek his face in prayer and *if we lack wisdom to ask him for it*. And God has given us minds to use, and choices to make in complex circumstances that do not always exactly mirror the biblical illustrations. Most of the situations set forth above had three or more biblical references noted at the conclusion of each illustration. This format was intentional. A good habit to form is one of looking for *multiple* Scriptures that speak to issues, problems, or questions before us. This provides the searcher with a broader base of biblical input upon which to reflect as he or she looks for *guiding principles* to assist in reasoning. This serves everyone affected by the final decision better than looking for a particular law or rule. Rules tend to be rigid and narrow; principles tend to be broader and more widely applicable, when seeking help to deal with the *spirit* of an issue. And using multiple references tends to help prevent the misinterpretation and inappropriate application of God's Word.

The *spirit* of God's commands, laws, testimonies, precepts, ordinances and judgments embodied in Scripture are more easily discerned as one draws nearer to God by the Holy Spirit. The person who lives in the presence of God—in prayer, meditation and reflection—is blessed with a greater *true knowledge* of him.[179] God uses his Word to sanctify his children; sanctification equals transformation, which equals becoming more like Christ, and that enables Christians to do justice, to love kindness, and to walk humbly with God (Mic. 6:8) in the field of business. This whole process becomes an aspect of partaking of God's divine nature when the Holy Spirit is involved in the decision-making process.

---

[179] For more discussion of the significance of having *true knowledge of God*, see Richard C. Chewning, "*Gnosis* to *Epignosis*: God's Transforming Work," *The Journal of Biblical Integration in Business* (Fall 2005), 190-203.

26

Christ's Divine Nature Manifested in Government

*Know that the Most High is ruler over the realm of mankind,
and bestows it on whom He wishes, and sets over it
the lowliest [basest] of men. (Dan. 4:17)*

*Every person is to be in subjection to the governing authorities.
For there is no authority except from God, and those which exist
are established by God. (Rom. 13:1)*

*Submit yourselves for the Lord's sake to every human institution,
whether to a king as the one in authority, or to governors
as sent by Him. (1 Peter 2:13-14)*

    Daniel's words are intriguing. The Holy Spirit through the prophet says that God often puts the *lowliest* or *basest* of men over mankind to govern us.[180] The Hebrew word *shephal* translated "lowliest" is rooted in the idea of someone being humbled or humiliated. But the fruit of abasement is not necessarily a humble spirit. And a humble spirit can be generated by things other than humiliation. In fact, the person blessed with humility and the person troubled by a humiliation usually harbor entirely different self-perceptions and psychological self-concepts. The humble are unpretentious and accept their personal imperfections and inadequacies; they also accept those same imperfections in others. They are not proud or arrogant. And they are typically submissive to those in authority over them, especially if they are maturing Christians.
    People affected by a humiliation can easily set into motion a psychological process of denial, suppression, or even revenge. They often feel a need to show they are superior to those who oppose or challenge them. The unconscious desire for *power*—to prove to themselves that they are better than their rivals—can become a driving force. Arrogance and haughtiness, in their many disguises, typically serve as their defenses, even if masked by layers of sophisticated social or political skills. Persons humiliated, but not genuinely humbled, become the *lowliest* of all people in their facade of superiority! And their false pride is an abomination to the Lord.[181]

---

[180] The Hebrew word used in Dan. 4:17 is *shephal* (Lexical # 8215).
[181] Prov. 16:5.

It is, then, not unfair to conclude that the Most High—who rules over all who govern on earth (whether they know him or not)—places *humble* leaders over those peoples he wishes to bless and puts *base* leaders over those he chooses to discipline or diminish. He does this in the eyes of all to testify to his awesome authority. This being the case, how are God's children to show Christ's divine nature in the political and governing arenas?

Christians interested in running for public office must remember whose kingdom they are entering to do battle. Although God is sovereign over all kingdoms, he exercises his sovereign rule through both what he *causes* to take place and what he *permits*. And in the kingdom on earth God has *permitted* Satan to rule over much of what transpires. For example, the Holy Spirit led Jesus into the wilderness at the beginning of his public ministry to be tested by Satan:

> The devil took Him to a very high mountain and showed Him all the kingdoms of the world and their glory; and he said to Him, "All these things I will give You, if You fall down and worship me." (Matt. 4:8-9)

To a large degree our omnipotent God has given jurisdiction over this world's kingdoms to the devil. He sovereignly limits the devil's authority as he deems appropriate,[182] but Christ's kingdom is not of this world. His kingdom is in the *hearts* of his people and in the heavens. Jesus called the devil "the ruler of this world" more than once (John 12:31; 14:30; 16:11). And Paul calls our great enemy "the god of this world" and "the prince of the power of the air" (2 Cor. 4:4; Eph. 2:2). John tells us that "the whole world lies in the power of the evil one" (1 John 5:19). These are authoritative reminders that those who enter the realm of politics in the hope of governing and serving their peers embark on a path fraught with *inhuman* challenges.

> For our struggle is not against flesh and blood, but against the rulers, against the powers, against the world forces of this darkness, against the spiritual forces of wickedness in the heavenly places. Therefore take up the full armor of God. (Eph. 6:12-13)

Within the first three generations of human life—Adam, Seth, and Enosh—"men began to call upon the name of the LORD" (Gen. 4:26). Yet no mention is made of how people governed themselves prior to the days of Noah and the great Flood. Presumably they organized themselves into clans, tribes, and other pre-nation groupings. Generations after Noah his descendants gathered at Babel to make a name for themselves, but God scattered them over the face of the earth (Gen. 11:4-9). We can surmise that this was the beginning of early nation building.

---

[182] We are given a ringside seat to observe God's *absolute restrictions* on the devil's authority and power in the book of Job, when God limits the pain the devil can inflict on Job. Satan argues with God, but God limits him initially by stating, "Behold, all that he has is in your power [Lit.: *hand*], only do not put forth your hand on him" (Job 1:12). Satan then touches Job's property and children, but not his physical body. Satan later seeks permission to destroy Job's health. He is again restricted: "Behold, he is in your power, only spare his life" (2:6). God is sovereign, but the devil is ever seeking opportunities within the restrictions placed on him to destroy the kingdom of God.

God's first intention of building for himself a *great nation* was his call of Abram, after his father Terah had left Ur of the Chaldeans and settled and later died at Haran (Gen. 11:31-12:2). God then told Abram, "I will make you a great nation." For over five hundred years God formed his *nation of people* through Abraham, Isaac, Jacob, and the subsequent gathering of his twelve sons and their families in Egypt. They lived in Egypt for over four hundred years, where they became a multitude. God then sent Moses to lead them out of Egypt as a *nation* and *to* but *not into* the Promised Land. Joshua had the privilege of leading them *into* the Promised Land.

Moses was a *type of Christ*; he was God's direct representative. God spoke to him and he spoke to the people for God. He was God's prophet but was not a king. And neither was Joshua—God was the King of Israel. Joshua was a transition leader, God's godly and authoritative representative, between Moses's life and the emergence of the judges (God's heroes) who for about 350 years periodically rescued the backsliding Israelites who lacked an earthly unifying leader.

Samuel was the next great prophet God raised up to guide his people. During the later years of his ministry he appointed his sons Joel and Abijah to be judges over Israel, but the people rejected them and asked him to "appoint a king for us to judge us like all the nations" (1 Sam. 8:1-5). Samuel was very displeased, but "the LORD said to him, 'Listen to the voice of the people . . . for they have not rejected you, but they have rejected Me from being king over them'" (v. 7). For centuries thereafter, the nation of Israel had kings who ruled them like the other nations. But after Solomon's death the nation was divided into two, and the two portions had their own dynasties. Some of the kings walked in the ways of the Lord and the people they governed were blessed. Other kings displeased the Lord and were disciplined by him, even being captured by their enemies and taken into exile. But the Jews retained a national identity from the time they left Egypt under the leadership of Moses until Christ's death and resurrection.

During this expanse of time the nation of Israel was a synonym for the people of God. The two concepts, the nation of Israel and the people of God, were inseparable. But following the resurrection of Jesus, God entered into a new covenant with those he chose to *inhabit*: a remnant taken from the Jews, and others taken from among the Gentiles. Christ spoke of this as "new wine" being put into a "new wineskin" (Luke 5:36-39). The nation of Israel was spiritually decommissioned, and a new *life form* was commissioned: the *church*—a people in whom Christ's Spirit would dwell (Col. 1:25-27; Rom. 8:9; John 14:17). Paul refers to those in whom the Spirit dwells as "the temple of God" and "the temple of the Holy Spirit" (1 Cor. 3:16; 6:19). In both texts the Greek word for temple is *naos*, which means "the habitation of God." And in the Old Testament temple worship this word referred to the "Holy of Holies." How amazing! Sinners are regenerated, hidden in Christ's righteousness through faith, forgiven, and become God's own residence: his "Holy of Holies."

In the days before Christ's resurrection, the nation of Israel lived under an arrangement that embodied *civil*, *criminal*, and *moral* laws. And many of the moral laws were ceremonial in form. They looked forward to Christ's life, death, and resurrection. These ceremonial/sacrificial components of the moral law have now been fulfilled. The sacrament of Communion, for example, Christians now observe as a sign of their faith in and remembrance of Christ's sacrifice for their sins (1 Cor. 11:23-32). And the sacrament of Baptism has replaced the law of circumcision (Col. 2:10-14).

But the new "wineskin" is the church, not a nation. It is the body of Christ (Col. 1:18, 24; 2:19). And this body is scattered throughout the world and obeys Christ in every nation where it is planted.

This *true* church is *invisible*. It is comprised of those who have been given to Christ and who have been born from above. Sadly, there are members in the *visible* church who are not part of the *true* church. They are *tares* (Matt. 13:24-30). They outwardly look like Christians; they are *cultural* Christians. But their hearts have not been regenerated. They are simply copycats, not the genuine children of God.

The *true* and *invisible* church, however, has no *civil* or *criminal* laws under its purview. And the *moral* law it professes is revealed in the Word of God and written on the hearts of those who constitute the true church. The God-revealed *moral* law becomes their *spiritual* law. It transcends the bounds, rules, and regulations of those who live under the law. The old law, however, becomes their prefiguring *light*; the letter of the law is transformed into the *spirit* of the law. The civil law, criminal law, and moral law—when mirroring the revealed biblical law—all become *one in spirit*. These laws become *the way of the Spirit, by which their spirits will live*.

The first-century church, the "new wineskin," was born in an environment of persecution. The Jewish nation that subsisted under the civil rule of the Romans *rejected* Christ's followers, who were first called "Christians" in Antioch of Syria (Acts 11:26). Subsequently, the Roman authorities persecuted the early Christians because they refused to acknowledge the Caesars of Rome as divine in character—worthy of ultimate allegiance. But Christians did recognize the Caesars' and every other governing authority, in all matters of *civil* and *criminal* law. Paul and Peter had, by the Spirit, taught the early Christians that all governing authorities exist under the sovereign oversight of God (Rom. 13:1-7; 1 Peter 2:13-17). And Christians believed, then as now, that they should obey the governing authorities' directions unless they demanded violation of God's revealed will (Acts 4:18-20; 5:27-29; Dan. 3:15-18).

The separation of the church from the governing authorities in the United States is best understood in the light of the English Magna Carta, first issued in 1215 and subsequently amended. It was a document of freedoms that wrestled with the relationship between the English monarchy (King John), the Roman Catholic Church (Pope Innocent III), and the English barons. It was a document that had significant influence on the United States Constitution and Bill of Rights many years later, which led to the prohibition of the federal and state governments establishing a religion of preference or barring the practice of a specific religion.

This brief review brings us to the two central foci of this chapter: (1) *the spiritual qualifications a Christian needs to possess in order to be a godly public servant;* and (2) *the primary responsibility a Christian assumes when he or she is providentially elected to a position of public service*—e.g., school board, city council, state representative, U.S. Congress; or is *appointed* to a judiciary position, where appointment rather than election determines who is to be a judge. This eliminates from our discussion those who are employed in non-elected positions, such as government agencies and other supporting-staff positions of responsibility.

The Spiritual Qualifications Needed in Elected Officials

Although it is possible to make different lists of spiritual qualifications for those seeking elective office, six qualities will be highlighted: (1) a right fear of the Lord; (2) wisdom; (3) discernment; (4) perseverance; (5) hatred of evil; and (6) a spirit of meekness shown through gentleness and humility. A seventh qualification—a commitment to being just—is so critical that it will be the focus of the last segment of the chapter.

A Right Fear of the Lord

The "fear of the Lord" was treated in chapters 16, 17, and 23. The Hebrew word for "fear" (*yirah*) is a word that describes a spectrum of emotions that extends from terror to awe. God gives his children a *true knowledge* of himself, a godsend so that knowledge gradually takes on a new meaning. Understanding and wisdom are now comprehended in a whole new paradigm.

In the context of ten passions (holy affections) of the heart, we discussed (in chapter 17) the passion of *fear*. The Lord deems the fear of him to be so needful that he teaches his children to fear him, a common biblical theme.[183] The fear of the Lord is indispensable for living righteously. It tempers our perspective on life.

Chapter 23 treated a child's proper fear of his or her loving parents as analogous to an adult's God-generated fear of the I AM. A healthy fear of the Lord generates a longing to please the Lord, and an abhorrence of displeasing him. As children mature they slowly grow to realize that their parents have lovingly taught them to fear disobedience. The discipline was unpleasant, but they learned that following their parents' instructions resulted in a healthy, peaceful, and rewarding relationship. And we know that God disciplines every child he adopts, while loving them for their own good and for the good of the church (Heb. 12:6-8).

Surely those who believe that they are answering God's call when seeking a position of public trust would be better equipped to honor God if they first possessed a genuine *fear of the Lord*. Such persons would seek the Lord's mind in their times of Bible study, prayer, corporate worship, and counsel to apply it when carrying out their public duties. Their public life, prior to seeking office, should reveal a pattern of righteousness. Their public discourse while seeking office should reveal a commitment to principles compatible with God's revealed

---

[183] See Deut. 4:10; 14:23; 17:19; 31:12-13.

will. And if genuine, their fear of the Lord will deeply influence all they do while in office.

Wisdom

As noted in chapter 8, God imparts wisdom to believers in the hierarchy of Isaiah 11:2—"the spirit of knowledge", "the spirit of understanding," and "the spirit of wisdom." *Wisdom* rests upon *knowledge* (both the static facts and the dynamic systems in which those facts are used) and upon *understanding* (which reflects a comprehension of the consequences of the use of the knowledge). But absolute wisdom requires foreknowledge, which only God possesses. So a skeptic might argue, "If wisdom requires foreknowledge, then wisdom is not available to human beings." For persons in whom the Spirit of Christ does not dwell, that is generally true. But Christians have the Word of God, God's revealed wisdom, and the Spirit of God who illumines the wisdom in the Word. Hopefully, the Christian seeking elective office has the maturity and experience necessary to make wise judgments while in office.

What about the need for wisdom in matters not explicitly addressed in Scripture? For example, if you are on the City Planning Commission and the city has just annexed thirty square miles west of its former boundary, and you work with a team of six others to provide a long-range plan for the development of the newly annexed area: What is the wisest possible use of the annexed land? The Bible will not provide you with an explicit answer. Will prayer?

Prayer is our only hope in such cases. And for what should a Planning Commissioner ask? A prayer asking for a *godly spiritual gestalt* (unified plan) would be a good place to start. And what might that look like? The "godly spiritual" aspect of the phrase means the commissioner is *motivated* to develop a long-range plan that will *best serve the welfare of the people* in the area, *without regard for who might gain the most monetarily* by the resulting zoning laws. Every decision has an economic impact, and a commissioner needs a godly character to withstand pressures that are sure to manifest themselves. Be forewarned: "Like a trampled spring and a polluted well is a righteous man who gives way before the wicked" (Prov. 25:26).

The "gestalt" component of the phrase, *a godly spiritual gestalt*, refers to the best use of the land physically after considering a myriad of factors: topography; the prevailing wind; existing rivers and streams; the current use of the annexed area; what is currently taking place in the surrounding area; the pressures from within the existing precinct which motivated undertaking the annexing initiative; the promises made to those in the annexed area that solicited their willingness to be annexed; the anticipated needs for parks, recreational facilities and open space. Likewise, the future need for churches, mosques and synagogues; the probable psychological impact of strategic decisions on those who will oppose various aspects of whatever is decided; aesthetic considerations—there are hundreds—such as the design of bridges, tree-planting requirements, allowed height of recognition signs for commercial establishments And on and on it goes! The *gestalt* is enormous, and there are as many opinions on every aspect of any proposed plan as there are people impacted by it.

Wisdom is needed. Wisdom rests atop understanding, knowledge and facts. And the best a person involved in the planning can do is first to absorb as many *facts* as possible and then ask God for help to arrange them into a unit that constitutes his *knowledge* of the task. Then he needs an *understanding* of how the components of the larger mosaic of the interrelated elements fit together. And finally, he needs *wisdom* to decide how this complex picture should be directed if the optimal outcome is to be realized. In short, what plan will serve the best long-term interests of the majority of the people represented and affected. Such a process follows this prescription: Wisdom seeks to foster right ends nurtured by right reasons pursued through appropriate means—supported by historic observations (lessons) reflected upon in the light of God's wisdom in Scripture, and have been bathed in prayer that has sincerely sought his wisdom.

Discernment

Discernment is the ability to distinguish between *right* and *wrong*; the *straight* and the *crooked*; the *genuine* and the *false*; the *honest* and the *dishonest*; what is *truthful* and what is a *lie*. It is the ability to separate what will *build up* from what will *tear down*. It is the gift of God to tell the difference between what is *just for all* and what favors only a *few*.

A public official is often confronted with requests that benefit those making the request. Requests that are beneficial for all are rare. Those making requests are generally concerned with their own interests; even their interest in *others* is usually self-serving. Thus an early matter to discern is who will benefit if I represent the interests of the people making the request? Scripture tells us that the righteous are concerned for the *rights of others* but that the wicked do not understand such concerns—they are self-absorbed and self-willed (Prov. 29:7).

Discernment is a *gift* from the Lord,[184] and is typically accompanied by patient listening. A corresponding gift is the ability to ask substantive questions whose answers, when coupled with other information, reveal more than the information gained in the latest response. This type of developed discernment is highlighted in 1 John 4:1: "Beloved, *do not believe every spirit*, but *test* the spirits to see whether they are from God; because many false prophets have gone out into the world." Testing a *spirit* involves matching the *spirit* of a comment with God's revealed standards and thereby ascertaining the speaker's fidelity to those standards.

This means that a *godly* elected official needs to recognize the character of those seeking his or her help to accomplish the ends being sought. This is because right ends must be nurtured by right reasons that must, in turn, be worked out through appropriate means and circumstances. A repeated tragedy in the public arena is that of *beginning* things that seem right and good but that result in unanticipated consequences that are hurtful. Godly *discernment* is badly needed.

---

[184] 1 Cor. 12:10 contains a continuation of a list of the Holy Spirit's gifts to the church and includes this: "...and to another the *distinguishing* of spirits." The Greek noun for "distinguishing" is *diakrisis* (Lexical # 1253). Its verbal cognate, *diakrino* (# 1252) means: "to separate one from another; to divide; to part; to *discern*; to distinguish; to be able to tell the difference between things."

Perseverance

Ecclesiastes tells us "There is an appointed time for everything. A time to tear down and a time to build up. A time to search and a time to give up as lost; a time to keep and a time to throw away" (3:1, 3, 6). Those are temporal truths for those who live "under the sun,"[185] but for those who live "under the Son" perseverance has a deeper meaning. For the person living under the sun perseverance may mean stubbornness or a strong will—"I will do what *I* deem best." For those under the Son perseverance may also involve a strong will, but its wellspring is different. It is a *grace* the Holy Spirit gives to the *spirits* of God's children, moving them to hold firmly to the illumined will of Christ. As a public official, I will consciously, graciously, and persistently hold onto "Christ's mind"[186] as it relates to all matters in question, and will continue to pursue them without regard for my own good. It is *Christ's* will shown through me, his servant.

Perseverance in this context involves the pursuit of righteousness, fairness, helpfulness, and all things God loves. Perseverance is the unyielding commitment to listen to Christ and to follow him, no matter the cost. There is a great temptation to rationalize conflicts that arise in our heart between *what we know* and *our passions*. Chapter 17 dealt with this potential conflict where we developed a continuum of desires, and then examined the connection between our desires and our identity needs. When someone's identity becomes attached to his position, it is easy to rationalize actions that will aid in his reelection rather than taking a righteous stand for an unpopular decision. "If I don't do what is popular now, I will not have opportunity to do what is 'good' in the future: I will not be reelected." This is why we so need *perseverance* under the Son, a *grace*; we need the Spirit's prompting to hold onto Christ and his will above all else. An *identity* not rooted in Christ will easily deviate from his revealed *heart*.

Hatred of Evil

The unregenerate person cannot hate evil, but the regenerate one cannot *help* but hate it! Their hearts are irreconcilable. And so are their world/life-views: the one hates righteousness; the other *loves* it! God loves righteousness and hates evil. It is said of Christ in Hebrews 1:9, quoting the Psalms: "You have loved righteousness and hated lawlessness; therefore God, Your God, has anointed You with the oil of gladness above Your companions." Holiness can have no companionship with unholiness. "What partnership have righteousness and lawlessness, or what fellowship has light with darkness?" (2 Cor. 6:14).

God's children are called upon to *hate* evil everywhere it is found. Hear God's Word:

> Hate evil, you who love the LORD, who preserves the souls of His godly ones. (Ps. 97:10)
>
> From Your precepts I get understanding; therefore I hate every false way. (Ps. 119:104)

---

[185] Under the sun is a frequent reference in Eccl.: 1:3, 9, 14; 2:11, 17-20, 22; 3:16; 4:1, 3, 7, 15; 5:18; 6:1, 12; 8:15; 9:3, 11, 13; 10:5.
[186] 1 Cor. 2:16; John 15:15; Jer. 31:33.

> Therefore I esteem right all Your precepts concerning everything; I hate every false way. (Ps. 119:128)
>
> I hate and despise falsehood, but I love Your law. (Ps. 119:163)
>
> The fear of the LORD is to hate evil; pride and arrogance and the evil way, and the perverted mouth, I hate. (Prov. 8:13)
>
> A righteous man hates falsehood. (Prov. 13:5)
>
> Hate evil, love good, and establish justice in the gate [the place court was held]. (Amos 5:15)

If an elected official does not hate evil, he or she will soon make accommodations with its ways—or worse yet, adopt them. Evil is generally subtle and disguised in forms such as: "This will gain the support of . . ."; "If you vote for my bill, I will vote for yours"; or "Just this once, I will do this." It takes godly character to avoid sliding into compromise with those who pervert righteousness in the public domain, because to be elected requires the acceptance of those who *vote*. And we all *need* to be accepted. The difficulty arises when we want acceptance so badly that we will exchange the acceptance of Christ for the acceptance of men. This is tragically illustrated in John 12:42-43:

> Nevertheless many even of the rulers believed in Him [Christ], but because of the Pharisees they were not confessing Him, for fear that they would be put out of the synagogue; for they loved the approval of men rather than the approval of God.

I had a great awakening when I realized that, to be accepted by my college peers, I was doing ungodly things. I remember the thought flooding my mind: "Yes, I want badly to be accepted; but from now on, I will not compromise God's revealed will to gain others' acceptance." That was enormously freeing! I would no longer be a slave to any human acceptance that might jeopardize my relationship with God. From then on, I would say: "But as for me, the nearness of God is my good" (Ps. 73:28). The love of God's nearness taught me to *hate* that which is unlike him—*evil*.

A Spirit of Meekness Shown through Gentleness and Humility

Meekness is a *trait* not an action; it rests *behind* actions and gives them tone. Meekness (Hebrew: *anav*—Lexical # 6035; Greek: *praotes*—Lexical # 4236) is a word without an exact English corollary. In Hebrew and Greek it points to an *outward humble and gentle demeanor* that seems to deny the strong will that lives beneath—requiring *full submission to the sovereign God*. To illustrate: Scripture describes Moses (Num. 12:3) as "very meek" (literally). Moses was certainly no patsy or milquetoast. He was strong, and hated every form of evil. But he manifested strength through perseverance and longsuffering, not by pushing and shouting or displays of temper. His outward demeanor was one of *humility*.

In terms of qualifications for elected officials—Psalm 25:9 is instructive: "[God] leads the meek in justice, and he teaches the meek his way."[187] Christians

---

[187] The word meek is the literal Hebrew word used twice in this passage: Lexical #6035—*anav*. Other translations render the word humble or even afflicted.

seeking good candidates for public office should pray that God will raise up *meek* officials, for he has promised to lead and teach such. The truly meek will stand strong for righteousness in a winsome and kind spirit.

The cause of Christ is set back by those who profess him but who do not present their arguments in a spirit of meekness. Christ was *meek*. We find him saying, "Take My yoke upon you and learn from Me, for I am meek [*praos*— Lexical # 4235] and humble in heart" (Matt. 11:29). But Christ had a strong will. He confronted evil whenever he met it. But he was gentle *and* firm; he was unyielding, while giving others the freedom to reject him and his teaching; he was silent and secure when others railed against him with false accusations. Christ was *meek*.

This concludes the discussion on the spiritual qualifications for elected officials. The six qualities, if discernible in the life of someone seeking public office, provide credible evidence of his or her character. Christians will want to see people with these qualities elected. A right fear of God, wisdom, discernment, perseverance, a hatred of evil, and a spirit of meekness shown in gentleness and humility add up to *godliness*—the highest quality to be sought in public officials.

The Primary Responsibility of Christians Elected to Positions of Public Service

Those in elected positions represent the entire body politic, not just those who voted for them. And their first responsibility is to strive to be *just* in all decisions and orders. The greatest negative transformation in the public political arena over the past one-hundred years has been the blurring of the distinction between *justice* and *love*. Those in elected positions of authority are not called upon by God to *love* those they affect; they *are* called upon to do what is *just* for them. And determining what is just is very often difficult because of the diverse and conflicting interests in the broader community.

Failure to distinguish between doing what is *just* for the populace and manifesting *love* for a particular subgroup within it is the incubating grounds of a social cancer—unjust discrimination or artificial inequities. God is the author of both human equality and inequality.[188] When his image-bearers fail to discern the beauty of both and attempt to override this, favoring a particular God-ordained differentiation, the end result is the creation of a public injustice.

Neighbors are to *love* their neighbors. But those who govern are to seek to establish a system of governance that does not favor certain individuals or collective interest groups over those with different interests. *Equity* and *equality* are two very different objectives. *Equity* is *striving for a freedom from bias or favoritism—a commitment to give everyone the same* treatment under the law. Equity is a search for *fairness* and *justice*.

Equality, on the other hand, is the search for *sameness*; it presumes that things should be *equal*. This particular ideal has been a source of social indigestion for centuries in nations that have enjoyed democratic/representative

---

[188] The tension and unresolved disputes between those who differ in their understanding regarding human equality and inequality is what gave rise to chapter 3, "The Trinity: Our Model and Mentor," where it was pointed out that there is equality and inequality in the *perfect relationship* between the members of the Godhead: the Father, Son, and Holy Spirit.

forms of government. All such nations began wrestling with this human rights tension (people are equal and unequal) in the context of Christianity's biblically-grounded values—such as freedom, personal initiative, personal responsibility, creativity, stewardship, personal accountability before God, and charity.

Conversation on the subject of *equality* can focus on many topics—civil rights; voting rights; gender roles; judicial privileges—but it will be limited here to a look at distributive *justice*, and at the role of those who are elected to lead and represent us in our nation's capital or are appointed to our highest judicial court. There is an intensifying struggle going on there between the world/life-view that favors democratic socialism—reflecting an egalitarian set of values—and the historic world/life-view that subscribes to a utilitarian/libertarian set of values. These two competing understandings of what it means to be *just* are outlined in Figure 26.1 on the following page.

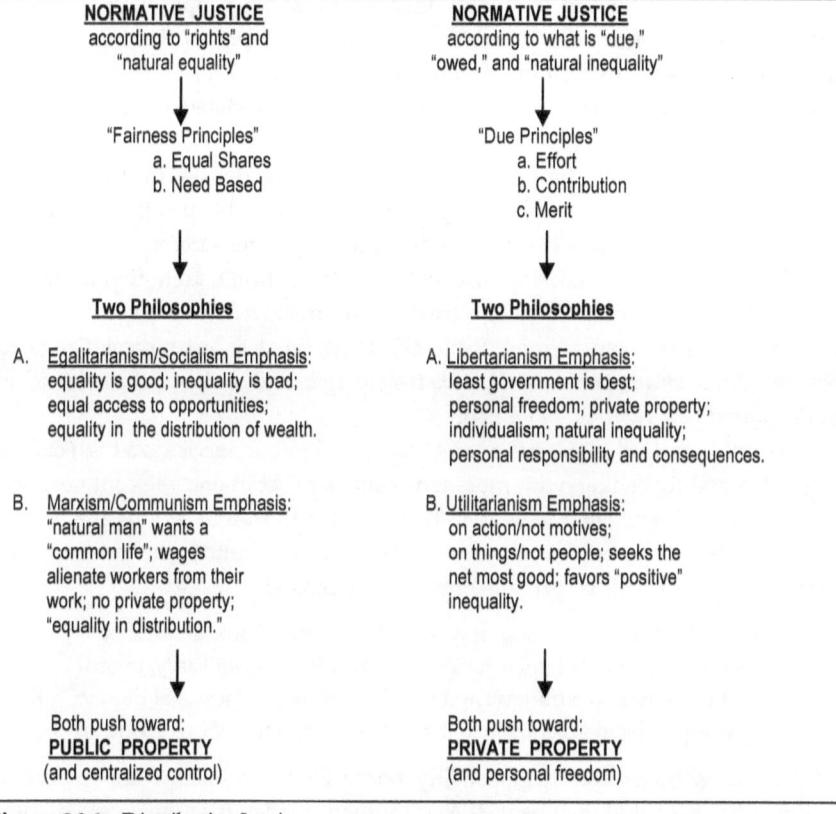

Figure 26.1 *Distributive Justice*

It is fascinating to note that both sides involved in the call for *distributive justice* refer to their position as representing normative justice. The position taken by those represented by the left side of the diagram purports that natural equality is the fair or just grounds upon which to distribute wealth. Inequality, in a *de facto* sense, is simply a bad basis upon which to allow scarce resources to be distributed. A higher authority (government) should redistribute wealth in keeping with the needs of those who are the constituents; or in a more radical form, they should be distributed equally. The disadvantaged have a right to a share of what the advantaged enjoy.

Persons represented by the position shown on the right side of the diagram argue that natural inequality is the fair or just basis upon which to base the distribution of scarce economic resources. They generally have a dim view of the government's ability to make the multitude of judgments regarding the creation and sustaining of the marketplace. They believe that what those who enjoy an advantage may do with it does not *physically* diminish or deny those less-productively/creatively endowed a share of the available resources. In their mind, *availability* is a function of demand and supply and is not related to any inherent scarcity. The size of the economic pie is not fixed; it is very elastic. One's having does not equal another's not having.

The fruits of natural inequality enjoyed by some people, however, may stimulate other people to *envy, covet,* or *resent* their differences. But this reveals a *heart* problem, not a distribution-of-resources problem *per se*. And godly attitudes and Christlike hearts are not created by anything associated with distributive *justice*.

There has been a struggle, an ebb and flow, in the debates for the past one-hundred years between those holding the two irreconcilable positions regarding what is the normative and best way to distribute scarce resources.

The purpose of discussing distributive *justice* is to illustrate two things: (1) those *elected* to positions of public trust are ultimately accountable to God for their *just* decisions and actions;[189] and (2) doing what is *just* typically requires *wisdom, discernment, perseverance, a hatred of evil,* and *a spirit of meekness,* all undergirded by *a right fear of the Lord*.

A call from God to pursue a career in elected public service is a high calling. It is a demanding calling, with more temptations to act in one's self-interest than many other callings. The roadway to honoring God through serving the general public is hard work, requiring a close walk with Christ under the guiding hand of the Holy Spirit. This is certainly one reason that God

> urge[s] that entreaties and prayers, petitions and thanksgivings, be
> made on behalf of all men, *for kings and all who are in authority,* in order
> that we may lead a tranquil and quiet life in all godliness and dignity.
> This is good and acceptable in the sight of God our Savior. (1 Tim. 2:1-3)

There is no greater responsibility borne by those elected and placed in public office than that they be *just*. And those in public office who seek, discern, and foster what is *just* in the sight of God while serving in their positions of trust manifest Christ's divine nature in their calling.

---

[189] See 1 Cor. 4:5; Rom. 14:10-12; Prov. 16:2; 1 Sam. 16:7; 1 Chron. 28:9.

27

Christ's Divine Nature Manifested before the Watching World

Let your light shine before men in such a way that they may see your good works and glorify your Father who is in heaven (Matt. 5:16)

The life believers live in various public arenas is an essential part of the evidence of who they really are. Christ exhorts each of his children, in the verse above, to live his or her daily life before the watching world "in such a way" that those watching them "will glorify [our heavenly] Father." Five significant aspects related to Christ's instruction merit reflection: (1) our lives are light; (2) our lives are part of our message; (3) our good works cause observers to glorify God; (4) sanctification without boasting; and (5) biblical illustrations of good works.

Our Lives Are Light

The use of light as representing the lives of those in whom Christ dwells, and darkness as representing those who remain separated from him, is a common biblical metaphor. For example, John 1:4-5; 3:19-21; 8:12; 12:35-36, 46 all use the metaphor of light and darkness. And when Christ says, "Let your light *shine*," he points to the fact that how we walk, talk, dress, pay attention or ignore, stare, how we do hundreds of things—all send messages to observers.

Our bodies have their own languages. Our tongue does not have a monopoly on the art of communicating. The body also speaks. A common aphorism says: "Your actions speak so loud, I cannot hear a word you are saying." This implies there is a contradiction between one's behavioral message and one's verbal one. Such contradictions, when they persist, create yet another message—hypocrisy!

And we have all heard someone say, "The church is full of hypocrites." To a *degree* this is true, for we all fall short of consistent living. But the statement usually reveals one of two things: the person making the statement was disillusioned by experiencing hypocrisy in his formative years; or, the person is using the statement to mask his personal unwillingness to admit that he needs a Savior. Either case, however, substantiates the point: Everybody's life is a testimony regarding the family to which he belongs, the family of light or the family of darkness. Christ calls upon his children to "Let your light shine before men...."

Our Lives Are Part of Our Message

The second aspect of Christ's statement arrests us: "Let your light shine before men *in such a way* that...." The words "in such a way" are vital to the *character* of the message. For example, Paul told the Ephesians that they were not to be fooled by tricks or craftily constructed arguments made by those holding a perverted world/life-view. They were to counter such twisted perceptions by "speaking the truth in love" (Eph. 4:15). And the apostle ends this sentence: "... we are to grow up in all aspects into Him who is the head, even Christ." Paul calls for Christian maturity! And the mature Christian will *speak the truth* about Christ, his headship, his righteousness, our lostness, his forgiveness, his presence, his love, his guidance, his chastening, and his comfort *in love*! Truth without love can be as destructive as a hammer.

Truth without love is typically judgmental. It can become a club. It can also present itself as an enslaving legalism. Truth separated from love is likely to become distorted. Remember, it is the Holy Spirit who empowers truth to accomplish God's purposes. For example, only the Holy Spirit can convict hearers of their need to *repent*—change their thinking and subsequent actions. God's children have no such power. We should not try to assume the Spirit's work. Truth cannot be forced into the heart of a listener.

Then how is truth delivered in love? When truth is delivered with a spirit of grace, love *accompanies* it. Truth in love is surrounded with *mercy*. It is accompanied by *humility*. A self-righteous attitude in the speaker of truth is spotted easily by those outside Christ's Kingdom. Love will show a genuine *concern* for the well-being of those who need *truth*. Love is *patient* and not hurried to see the effects of truth. Truth accompanied by love has a face of *meekness*—it is under the control of Christ. Truth accompanied by the fruits of the Spirit is truth accompanied by *love* (Gal. 5:22-23)!

Our Good Works Cause Observers to Glorify God

The third component of Christ's statement above regards the fact that people who observe the lives of God's children in the public arenas and how they go about their tasks will form opinions about the *quality* of their works. They are to be good works, works in keeping with God's character and purposes. Spirit-guided work is uplifting, not demeaning; it is work that encourages, not discourages; it is work that adds value, it does not devalue; it is work that benefits others. Christ does not say that one's work must be good consistently for it to be useful, but he implies as much. Fluctuations back and forth from good work to mediocre work will not create the results that he desires—". . . that they may see your good works and *glorify your Father who is in heaven*"—the conclusion in Christ's instruction.

This points directly to the *greatest end of man*: "Man's chief and highest end is to *glorify God*, and fully to enjoy him forever" (1 Cor. 10:31; 1 Peter 4:11).[190] Christ encourages us to carry out our God-honoring efforts before the observing world to bring glory to our heavenly Father. But God's Word reveals that those who observe our God-honoring worship and works do not always react positively. For example, we read in 1 John 3:12 that Cain murdered his brother Abel "because his [Cain's] deeds were evil, and his brother's were righteous." Cain resented his Abel's righteous acts; they made him angry. His heart turned against his brother because his brother's works were good, and his were not. Abel's good deeds cast a revealing light on Cain's evil deeds.

We also read in 1 Peter 2:12, "Keep your behavior excellent among the Gentiles, so that in the thing in which they slander you as evildoers, they may because of your good deeds, as they observe them, glorify God *in the day of visitation*" [final judgment]. It is thus apparent that when Christ said his people's good works should "glorify [their] Father who is in heaven," he did not mean that

---

[190] Quoted from The Larger Catechism, put together and approved in 1648 by the General Assembly of the Church of Scotland. The Larger Catechism and The Shorter Catechism are typically found along with The Westminster Confession of Faith which was written and presented to the Parliament of England by the same Assembly of Divines at Westminster.

the unregenerate people in the world would immediately recognize the glorifying quality of the works. Indeed, much of that recognition will only occur on the Day of Judgment, when "at the name of Jesus *every knee* will bow, of those who are in heaven and on earth and under the earth, and that *every tongue* will confess that Jesus Christ is Lord, *to the glory of God the Father*" (Phil. 2:10-11).

Christ also speaks of the idea of his followers being "in the world but not of the world" (John 17:14, 16). He said, "If you were of the world, the world would love its own, but because you are not of the world, but I chose you out of the world, because of this *the world hates you*" (15:19). That is strong language—"the world hates you." James also weighed in on this subject: "Do you not know that friendship with the world is hostility toward God? Therefore whoever wishes to be a friend of the world makes himself an enemy of God" (James 4:4). So, we ask: How does being Christ's followers in daily life distinguish us from our neighbors who have no desire to follow him? Can those who are children of darkness distinguish those who profess to be children of light from their own kind? *And if they cannot, why not?*

Sanctification without Boasting

The biblical doctrine that speaks directly to Christians being separated or different from the world is *sanctification*.[191] To be sanctified is to be separated and set apart for a holy use—to be transformed into the likeness of Christ; to become a partaker of God's nature; and to act as he would act. God is interested in how we act in our *families*, in the *church*, and in the *world at large*. He wants us to serve Christ wherever we are, and in so doing we glorify God. Being sanctified is a lifelong process. It is good, however, to take inventory of our spiritual health every once in a while. We are called to be God's *salt* and *light* in the world. We are not to hide our light or lose our cauterizing/purifying effect (saltiness) on those with whom we come in contact.

Furthermore, Scripture rejects the notion that Christians have some grounds for boasting about their positive spiritual state or good works. It is explicit: "We are His workmanship, created in Christ Jesus for good works, *which God prepared beforehand* so that we would walk in them" (Eph. 2:10). Paul asked the Corinthians, "What do you have that you did not receive? And if you did receive it, why do you boast as if you had not received it?" (1 Cor. 4:7). The "good works" Christ referred to are born of the Holy Spirit's work in believers' hearts. Good works are a public evidence of our regeneration and faith in Christ (James 2:14-26) but they do not enhance one's relationship with any member of the Trinity. When a person is born physically, he or she begins to breathe; when one is born from above, he or she will respond to God's love by seeking to do his will—to do the works "which God prepared beforehand so that [he or she] would walk in them."

Christians are called to be "zealous for good deeds," "careful to engage in good deeds," to "show yourself to be an example of good deeds," and to be "zealous for what is good" (Titus 2:14; 3:8; 2:7; 1 Peter 3:13). This is all a part of being light in the world that has rejected Christ, the true light. This is not a call to be holier-than-thou or self-righteous or judgmental in spirit. Rather, good works are to reflect a joyful spirit of thanksgiving for God's free gift of eternal life. Christ

---

[191] In the Old Testament the Hebrew word used for sanctification is *kawdash* (Lexical # 6942). It means to be set apart and cleaned up, refurbished, or sanctified. The Greek New Testament word for sanctification is *hagiazo* (Lexical # 37). It too means to be set apart for cleansing. God accomplishes this through the use of his Word—See Eph. 5:26; Titus 3:5; 1 Cor. 6:11; John 15:3; 17:17.

died for my sins; I will gladly do his bidding. That is what good works are to communicate. This is what Peter encouraged in his readers:

> Sanctify Christ as Lord in your hearts, always being ready to make a defense to everyone who asks you to give an account for the hope that is in you, yet with gentleness and reverence; and keep a good conscience so that in the thing in which you are slandered, those who revile your good behavior in Christ will be put to shame. (1 Peter 3:15-16)

Even those not united to Christ notice selfless acts of kindness, sincere words of encouragement, patience, uncomplaining suffering, cheerful generosity, and other marks of a Christlike life. Such a life typically stimulates one of several responses from observers. Some are sincerely attracted to it, but make no comparison between it and their own lifestyle. Others perceive it as unreal, and are either amused by it or attempt to take advantage of it. But some are convicted by it. And those convicted typically have one of two reactions: Either they hate it—*you*—and become angry because your Christlike behavior reveals their own self-centeredness; or they are moved to want to become like the person—*you*—who exhibits the Christlike quality. This is an opportunity to tell observers our story and introduce them to Christ through Scripture.

Earnest Christians face the challenge of falling into the default mode of the Christian life. And what is that? In computer language it means the computer will return to its *original settings* when it is turned off and turned back on. The Christian, analogously, will return to a behavior pattern that relies on his or her personal strength and forgets Christ who strengthens us. That is unconsciously returning to works righteousness. Works righteousness is the *default mode* of all humans. Christ had to remind the church at Ephesus of this. He commended them for their "deeds," "toil," "perseverance," "testing of false apostles," and "endurance." But he had one thing against them that hurt their relationship with him: "You have left your first love"—Christ. They were told to *repent* (Rev. 2:2-4).

This discussion of the Christian's default mode is important for three reasons. First, we all assume it at times, and need to be on guard against it. Second, we need reminding that showing Christlike conduct before the public is not keeping a Christian laundry list of do's and don'ts. And finally, we must remember that the antidote to such default behavior is to maintain a close conversational (prayer) relationship with Christ. This last point is vital because our circumstances change constantly and call for new forms of good works—Christlike responses.

Paul encouraged the church at Philippi always to relate their current experiences to the person of Christ:

> Just as you have always obeyed, not as in my presence only, but now much more in my absence, work out your salvation with fear and trembling; for it is God who is at work in you, both to will and to work for His good pleasure. Do all things without grumbling or disputing; so that you will prove yourselves to be blameless and innocent, children of God above reproach in the midst of a crooked and perverse generation, among whom you appear as lights in the world. (Phil. 2:12-15)

The clause "work out your salvation with fear and trembling; for it is God who is at work in you" sometimes confuses immature Christians—who rightly associate their salvation with Christ's imputed righteousness *alone*, not their good works. The confusion arises from their not realizing that salvation is a *past, present*, and *future* reality; and that it encompasses a dimension of physical/temporal deliverance as well as (the more typical) one of spiritual/eternal deliverance. But salvation includes, "Lord, please *save* me from this physical threat to my life," as well as "Lord, please teach me to *repent*, and *save* me from my sins." We are to *work out our salvation* in the ever-changing contexts of life with the assurance (faith) that God is present and works in and through us to accomplish his will and his good pleasure.

Biblical Illustrations of Good Works

Scripture contains a host of *illustrations* of good works—not to be thought of as self-righteous work but as mirrors with which to compare our attitudes and reactions to the situations we encounter. These illustrations tell us what God wants to form in us. Our actual responses—works—afford us opportunities to reflect on our good works and converse with Christ about their *quality*: "O Lord, my act may have looked good, but my motive was mixed. Please change my attitude in such situations." Or, "Lord, I was not kind when you wanted me to be kind."

We will look at some biblical illustrations of good works that God wants to build into his children's character. "Good deeds" are called "excellent behavior" in 1 Peter 2:12. They could be anything from taking a neighbor shopping to stopping to help a stranger pick up a bunch of scattered papers she dropped on the street. A good deed is giving of yourself or your resources to someone who can benefit from your help. It is a deed done without an expected payback. It is as spontaneously done for someone you do not know as it is for a friend. And it is even done, by God's grace, for an enemy.

Another good work is protecting what is innocent from appearing to be ungodly. For example, Paul was given the responsibility of transporting to Jerusalem a monetary collection raised by the people of Corinth: "[This gift] which is being administered by us for the glory of the Lord Himself . . . [we are] . . . *taking precaution that no one should discredit us in our administration of this generous gift*; for we have regard for what is honorable, not only in the sight of the Lord, but also in the sight of men" (2 Cor. 8:19-21). Given humanity's fallen nature and people's tendency to think the worst of other people's behavior, propriety is important. For example, a teacher ought to have an unspoken rule that he or she will never have an unaccompanied student of the opposite sex in their office with the door closed. This is to avoid the appearance of indiscretion. An old saying goes: "An ounce of prevention is worth a pound of cure." It is a good work to prevent a bad appearance.

Christ described the heavenly accounting of his brothers' and sisters' good works, of which they were *unaware*, when he spoke to a crowd following him when he left the temple:

> But when the Son of Man comes in His glory . . . He will sit on His glorious throne. All the nations will be gathered before Him; and He will separate them from one another, as the shepherd separates the sheep from the goats . . . . Then the King will say to those on His right, "Come, you who are blessed of My Father, inherit the kingdom prepared for you . . . . For I was *hungry*, and you gave Me something to eat; I was *thirsty*, and you gave Me something to drink; I was a *stranger*, and you invited Me in; *naked*, and you clothed Me; I was *sick*, and you visited Me; I was *in prison*, and you came to Me." [And they will not know when they had done all those things for Christ.] And the King will answer and say to them, "Truly I say to you, to the extent that you did it to one of these brothers of Mine, even the least of them, you did it to Me." (Matt. 25:31-40)

The good deeds Christ mentions are the ordinary things of life: being hungry, thirsty, etc. There is nothing unusual or dramatic in his enumeration. Elsewhere he instructs:

> But I say to you, love your enemies and pray for those who persecute you, so that you may be sons of your Father who is in heaven; for He causes His sun to rise on the evil and the good, and sends rain on the righteous and the unrighteous. For if you love those who love you, what reward do you have? Do not even the tax collectors do the same? If you greet only your brothers, what more are you doing than others? Do not even the Gentiles do the same? Therefore you are to be perfect, as your heavenly Father is perfect. (Matt. 5:44-48)

The attitudes and acts listed here are more radical than those in Matthew 25, but they also reflect the character of God. And we, his children, are being transformed by the Holy Spirit so we follow Christ's example in the world. The Spirit is building a Christlike *heart* in us so we will do the works of Christ. Luke's account of this same sermon carries an even *higher* expectation of God's children: "Do good to those who hate you; Bless those who curse you; Pray for those who mistreat you; Offer the other cheek when you have already been hit; Do not withhold your shirt though they have previously taken your coat; and Whoever takes away what is yours, do not demand it back" (Luke 6:27-30). Such godly conduct is beyond the reach of fallen humanity apart from the Spirit's regeneration, transformation, and empowerment.

James is also full of instructions regarding the public display of godliness. In 2:1-13 he describes the ungodly problem of *showing partiality* by our making judgments regarding the importance of certain people. In 3:1-12 he discourses on the *tongue* and its ability to do great harm. He calls it "a fire." In chapter 5 he describes the sin of withholding a day's wage from those who ought to be paid the same day they do the work. Such wages should be paid when the work is done.

And John writes, "But whoever has the world's goods, and sees his brother in need and closes his heart against him, how does the love of God abide in him? Little children, let us not love with word or with tongue, but in deed and truth" (1 John 3:17-18).

Scripture is replete with examples of what being "light" in the world looks like. And yet none of this *doing* earns a child of God more salvation. But rather, it is a sober reminder of what kind of *being* the Trinity want us to be. But praise be to God, by knowing this we can be certain that God intends to transform us into *children of light*—people who bear the evidence of having become *partakers of the nature of God*, whereby we will *manifest Christ's divine nature* in the world, even though we are no longer of the world.

28

Conclusion

*He who began a good work in you will perfect it until
the day of Christ Jesus. (Phil. 1:6)*

Though God is so awesome that we cannot exhaustively know him, it is nevertheless possible for his image-bearers to possess *true knowledge* of him and to become—by his work alone—more like him. To promote this understanding, we have examined the following four topics: (1) the popular postmodern world/life-view that promotes a divergent understanding of reality and causes many to wonder, "Is reality knowable?"; (2) God's gracious revelation of his incomparable but knowable nature; (3) fallen mankind's ungodly nature, and the Holy Spirit's observable restorative work in the sinful hearts of God's children—gradual renovation into God's image; and (4) the manifestation to the world *of Christ's divine nature* through the redeemed intentions and conduct of those regenerated.

Most people either do not acknowledge the spiritual reality within which they exist—"[The Creator] is not far from each one of us; for *in Him we live and move and exist. . .*" (Acts 17:27-28)—or they have a humanly derived explanation for their thoughts about spiritual reality. Their well-meaning ideas arise from their logic and creative imagination, both of which are distorted by the *nature* they inherited at conception. Everyone inherits a severely warped *heart*. Modernity that got underway in the 1600's put humanity at the center of reality. Modernity called upon humanity to *determine* reality. Those who accepted this impossible challenge eventually became postmodernists. They represent the culmination and logical climax to this distorting requirement—you must think and act as if you are the center of reality. They turned their backs on the benchmark of reality: God and his special revelation. The postmodernists privatize truth and thereby misinterpret it.

The privatization of truth heightens the importance of understanding that the things we *presuppose* shape our *beliefs* about everything. And without a belief in the personal involvement of God in creation and the history of humankind, postmodernists have created a set of presuppositions that give rise to what could be called "irrational rationality"—the logical ordering of observed phenomena that rest atop faulty underlying beliefs. The false premise upon which the logic is applied creates a false conclusion, although it appears to those employing it to be logical because it supports their incorrect presuppositions. Postmodernists' presuppositions regarding *spiritual reality* have led them far away from *reality*. They are *spiritually blind*.

The defining distinctive of true Christians is the presence of the Holy Spirit *in* their *hearts*. The Holy Spirit blesses those adopted into the family of God by giving them a sufficient—not exhaustive—portion of Christ's mind (1 Cor. 2:16), which he accomplishes through his use of the Word. He puts the Word in their *hearts*. The Word believed—written on the heart—transforms our presuppositions. All of life looks different. It is the mind of Christ in the Christian that shapes his or her world/life-view.

At the foundation of what has just been described is the *relationship* that exists between the Father, Son and Holy Spirit and his adopted children. They are given the privileges associated with being *called, regenerated, converted, justified, sanctified,* and promised eternal *perfection* (glorification).

As salvation is biblically understood to be an ongoing past, present, and future process, so is the Christian's *sanctification*. It is continuous throughout one's life. It is God's impartation of an ever-increasing *true knowledge* of him that causes his children to hunger and thirst for Christlikeness, and leads them to plead with God for that realization.

The Attributes of God Revisited

In chapters 2–12 we examined the biblical revelation of God's divine nature, his self-revealing statements and activities. We considered the relationship of the persons of the Trinity to provide insight in such troublesome areas of *human* tension as: (a) equality/inequality; (b) authority/submission; (c) individual/community; (d) rights/responsibilities; and (e) freedom/control (chapter 3). These polarities do not, however, create any tension in the Godhead. They are complementary realities. This is not the case in the fallen world. But God works to materially reduce the tensions and conflicts in these areas when they arise in his children's lives. God is our Mentor. And the Holy Spirit renovates us so we become more Christlike and thereby more comfortable with the godly intentions that surround our natural manifestations of equality/inequality; authority/submission; rights/responsibilities.

We identified twenty of God's attributes. We examined nine of them in a chapter of their own, five others in a single chapter, and interspersed the remaining six in the ensuing discussions. None of the attributes was described as being fully incorporable into the character of his image-bearers, but to some degree *aspects* of all of them are either formable in us or the *understanding* of them is beneficial to the nurturing of our character.

- We first discussed God's *aseity*, his absolute independence from his creation. Its contemplation compels us to realize that God did not create us because he needed us. God needs nothing! He created us to reveal his *awesome glory*! It is beyond our ability to adequately pay tribute. But we worship him in an effort to acknowledge his greatness to the watching world. It was from a heart of pure *love* that the I AM created a people and provided them with the opportunity to have *true knowledge* of him. We mortals are the antithesis of God's aseity; we are dependent upon God for everything related to our existence. To grasp this contrast that exists between God and us is vital because believing it *imparts humility* to our hearts.

- The *eternal* nature of God is mind-bending when we attempt to encompass its implications. This is because the word" eternal" communicates that God exists *outside of time*. God has never existed in a time-continuum. Our life experience, on the other hand, has been inside of such a continuum. By its nature the created order exists within a process of *sequencing*. God has never existed in a *sequential* progression. He was not formed or developed. He did not grow up. He has simply always existed in his eternal and infinite glory. But all that he planned and placed in the created order exists *inside* of an order of sequential progression.

- This sequential order is closely tied to God's *omniscience*, his all-knowing nature. He built the sequence! He put all creation in the sequence! And he knows everything that has occurred, occurs, and will or can occur within the sequence! This is true despite the fact that he has given men and women the freedom to make choices. Yes, God knows everything that will occur within the sequencing process, even though he has given humans the ability to make free choices. But our *freedom of choice* is exercised in the context of our personal *nature*, and God knows our nature so exhaustively that he knows what our free choices will be even before we act! This kind of knowledge exceeds our ability to fully comprehend—but believing it builds our faith in his complete and perfect nature. And we *should* believe this revealed truth, for God has both declared it and demonstrated it in history. We see this in Isaiah 41:21-23; 44:7; 45:21; 46:10. God has clearly exhibited his foreknowledge through numerous prophecies the Holy Spirit made through the writers of Scripture that were fulfilled hundreds of years later.

As God's children we will ultimately transition into *eternal life* and out of the time-continuum—when our mortality ends at death and we inherit *immortality*. In the meantime, we have the privilege of possessing limited but sufficient knowledge. Moreover, we have access to *aspects* of God's infinite knowledge. But most importantly, we have been given the incalculable privilege of possessing some *true knowledge* of God.

Following the examination of God's four attributes—his aseity, eternity, omniscience and infinity—we treated his *patience*. We noted at the end of chapter 2: "if there were no divine patience, there would be no time for divine mercy. [And] if there were no time for divine mercy, there would be no time for repentance, forgiveness and salvation." Peter wrote "we are to regard the patience of our Lord as salvation" (2 Peter 3:15). Patience is an attribute of God that he intends to build into believers' character as a "fruit of the Spirit" (Gal. 5:22).

- In chapter 4 we contemplated that God is a *spirit*, and this truth is foundational to all that is known about God. Apart from the thirty-three years of God the Son's incarnation, and his earlier appearances in the form of a theophany, the persons of the Godhead have throughout eternity been purely spirit. This truth underlies the reasonableness of God's creational requirement that a relationship between him and us would be carried on only through *faith*. He created Adam, his first image-bearer, with a physical body and breathed a spirit into his body, and the man became "a living being"—a body with an incarnate spirit. It thus follows that those in communion with God live in a "spirit-to-spirit" relationship with him. God bears witness with our spirit that we are his children (Rom. 8:16). And those "being led by the Spirit of God . . . are sons of God" (Rom. 8:14). Those prior to Christ's incarnation lived by faith too, and those of us who have lived since his ascension have of necessity lived by faith. Christ's incarnation, while it provided irrefutable evidence of God's character, did not alter the principle of faith. From the beginning God has tied his people to himself by faith. The fact that "God is spirit" (John 4:24) undergirds the truth that "the righteous man shall live *by faith*" (Rom. 1:17; Gal. 3:11; Heb. 10:38).

- God's *holiness*, his most often referred-to attribute in Scripture, was discussed in chapter 5. God's holiness is the hallmark of his purity and perfection. It connotes his eternal and absolute separation from all that is evil, perverted, unclean, and impure. It refers to his spotless character. It tells us that God is single-minded, focused, and unfailingly committed to the perfection of holiness in his children: he calls us to be holy too! In order to accomplish this, the Father sent the Holy Spirit to dwell in us to wash us with the Word. The Word, in the Spirit's hands, transforms our *hearts* (Eph. 5:26). This is his work! It is a work of renovation and leads to the restoration of the image of God in his children's character (4:23-24), for we are called to be holy as he is holy. Without this *sanctifying* work "no one will see the Lord" (Heb. 12:14).

- Chapter 6 explored the unfathomable reality of God's *immutability*. The questions that surface regarding this topic are, in many cases, unanswerable until addressed in the context of other attributes. For example, every time we humans learn something we grow and change. Then how can God not change or grow when he observes the free choices we make? Doesn't God learn something when this takes place? The answer is "No," for God already knew what would happen. This truth rests in our accepting the reality that God has perfect foreknowledge—an aspect of his *omniscience*—and knows everything *past, present, suppositional,* and *future*.

Christians who accept God's immutability also accept his *omniscience*. And this belief brings with it no lessening of our belief in freedom to make true choices with real consequences. It simply transports us into the mystery of God's full knowledge of what a person's free choices will be before they are made. The key question to be answered is: "Does God know the character and nature of his creatures so as to know how they will exercise their free will?" The Bible answers "Yes!" This is important, because God's immutability can motivate believers to hold to God's revealed, perfect, and unchanging Truth—Christ—and to plead with the Father to renovate them more and more into Christ's likeness. Then one's life begins to reflect stability and unwavering commitment to God's revealed truth. This, in turn, creates over time less and less deviation from God's standard of righteousness: we become more like "Jesus Christ [who] is the same yesterday and today and forever" (Heb. 13:8). Believers thus partake of benefits flowing from God's *immutability*.

• Chapter 7: All Christians, always, can truthfully say "in Him [God] we live and move and exist," because God is *omnipresent* (Acts 17:28). God is everywhere and has eternally been everywhere. Doesn't this mean that this is one attribute of God of which we are *unable* to partake? In one sense, of course it does: I am here and you are there. But in a larger and more important sense, such a conclusion robs us from a wonderful truth than is best approached through analogy. In our technologically sophisticated society we can contact a friend two-thousand miles away. All we have to do is call on a cell phone and chat. Were we *with them* while speaking on the phone? In a sense, yes, but in another sense, no. But we can expand the illustration to include telecommunications where our images also are transmitted, along with our voices. Extending this idea, Christians are blessed to know that they have an open line of communication with the Father, through the Son, by the power and eternal presence of the Holy Spirit. This being true, our concerns for anyone or any group, anywhere in the universe can be expressed to God at any time with the certainty that the *omnipresent* God will hear and answer our prayers in keeping with his perfect will. There is a sense in which all of God's children are connectable with each other through the Holy Spirit's omnipresence. In this larger sense, Christians are privileged to *participate in the benefits* that accompany God's *omnipresence*.

• *Wisdom*, discussed in chapter 8, is made available to all in and through "Christ Jesus, who became to us wisdom from God" (1 Cor. 1:30). Christ, the incarnate God, is also the incarnation of wisdom—for God alone is wise (Rom. 16:27). Anyone who seeks to discover his or her purpose in life apart from Christ will miss God's best intentions. But he who gives up his life to follow Christ will be led in the realization of true life (Matt. 10:39). The *big* questions in life are all answered *in Christ*: "Who am I?" I am God's child. "Why do I exist?" I exist to fulfill God's purpose for me. "What is my purpose?" My purpose is to do what God has ordained for me to do in my family, work, and worship—in a Christlike manner—and thereby to glorify God. "Can any sense be made out of unjust suffering?" Yes, but only when seen in the light of the cross, knowing that God alone can bring eternal good out of unjust suffering. "Does anyone care?" Yes, God cares infinitely and eternally. "What is to be experienced at the end of this physical life?" First, a temporary separation from this physical body, but later we will be given a resurrected and glorified body. On and on, the seemingly imponderable questions flow—but they are all answerable in Christ.

> In the beginning was the Word, and the Word was with God, and the Word was God.... All things came into being through Him, and apart from Him nothing came into being that has come into being.... And the Word became flesh, and dwelt among us, and we saw His glory, glory as of the only begotten from the Father, full of grace and truth.... No one has seen God at any time; the only begotten God who is in the bosom of the Father, He has *explained* [exegeted] Him. (John 1:1, 3, 14, 18)

And all who "keep on asking," "keep on seeking," and "keep on knocking"[192] have God's promise that they will receive the wisdom they thirst for (Matt. 7:7). The only requirements are that it be *God* who is asked, and that we *believe* he will provide the answers: "If any of you lacks wisdom, let him ask God, who gives to all generously . . . but he must ask in faith without any doubting" (James 1:5-6). In his Word God describes his *wisdom* as an attribute he delights to impart to his children! We need only *ask* him for it.

• When we examined the truth that God is *good* (in chapter 9), we noted that Scripture speaks about God displaying his *goodness* in three ways: (a) through his creation of all that exists; (b) in his redemption of the lost; and (c) through his sovereign rule, called providence. Scripture also reveals that one of the fruits of the Spirit brought forth in the life of those who are born again is *goodness* (Gal. 5:22). The Greek word for "goodness" used here (Lexical # 19: *agathosune*) carries with it the idea of *actively displaying a zeal for truth and goodness* by all means; including not only service and care, but also rebuking, correcting, and chastising. The fruit of "goodness," which flows out of being "constitutionally good" (Lexical # 18: *agathos*), is generated by God. These Greek words denote an active effort to advance the well-being of others, not a passive, self-contained quality of character. Those adopted by God are transformed and empowered by the Holy Spirit to display *active goodness* toward others.

• God's *omnipotence* (chapter 10) is unmistakenly displayed in his creation. Psalm 19:1 reminds us that "the heavens are telling of the glory of God, and their expanse is declaring the work of His hands." The fact "that the worlds were prepared by the word of God, so that what is seen was not made out of things which are visible" testifies to the awesome power of God who was and is able to "call into being that which does not exist" (Heb. 11:3; Rom. 4:17). Who, other than God, can "give life to the dead" (Rom. 4:17)? But giving life to the dead means two things in Scripture. It means raising the physically dead to life again. (For example, see 1 Kings 17:17-24; 2 Kings 4:32-37; Luke 7:12-15; John 11:38-44; and Acts 20:7-12.) But it also includes giving spiritual life to the spiritually dead (John 3:3-8, 15-16; 11:25-26). This is the blessed work of salvation. And God, in his infinite mercy and grace, uses his children in his work of spiritual rebirthing, and also in the transformational work of sanctification. The Holy Spirit uses the spiritual gifts of pastoring, teaching, evangelizing, administration, and serving in his work of regeneration and maturing. To paraphrase Paul, we are part of God's planting and watering team—while simultaneously we credit the actual increases in growth to God alone (1 Cor. 3:5-9). Christians become instruments

---

[192] Matt. 7:7 is translated, "Ask, and it will be given to you; seek . . . knock. . . ." The words "ask," "seek," and "knock" are, however, in the *present imperative* form. That carries with it the instruction to do it both now and in the future, in a repeated and continuous manner—*keep on asking; keep on seeking; keep on knocking.*

through whom God displays his power, thereby giving incredible significance to their endeavors.

- God's absolute *sovereign* rule over every aspect of his creation—great and small, static and dynamic, as well as all free choices of his creatures—is mind-boggling (chapter 11). The best we can do in attempting to understand it is to relate this truth to God's *omniscience,* and specifically his perfect *foreknowledge.* This allows us to at least glimpse how such an attribute can be understood. And when these two attributes are, in turn, united in our minds with his *holiness, goodness, wisdom* and *love,* the whole idea of God's *sovereignty* brings comfort and rejoicing to our hearts. God is in charge; he is in control. And he will "cause all things to work together for good to those who love God, to those who are called according to His purpose. For those whom He foreknew, He also predestined to *become conformed to the image of His Son*" (Rom. 8:28-29). Such an ability to govern is, of course, impossible for us. Satan, who was created with the seal of perfection on him, attempted to usurp God's sovereign reign after he beheld his own beauty, and the resultant pride "corrupted his wisdom by reason of his splendor" (Ezek. 28:12-17; Isa. 14:12-17). And while Satan failed miserably in his attempt to usurp God's role, he managed to bring about the fall of humanity through his deceitful efforts. This all occurred, however, under the *sovereign watchcare* of God, who in his *infinite wisdom* knew this *too* would lead to his greater glory.

Sovereignty is imparted to God's redeemed people, as a vice-regent is a regent's deputy. Those in Christ are his ambassadors. We represent Christ when we are identified with his name—we are Christians. That is why we are not to take his name in vain—misrepresent it. We are, by God's grace, given the gift of self-control. Self-control is formed in us by the Holy Spirit to help us carry out the responsibilities we have in our families, at work, and in Christ's church. "He ... is better ... who rules his spirit, than he who captures a city" (Prov. 16:32).

- Finally, the greatest attribute of God that is imparted to his children is his *love* (chapter 12). Love can rightfully be called the sign or true mark of Christians. It is the premium fruit of the Spirit. Some theologians even believe that love is *the fruit* and that the other eight fruits—joy, peace, patience, kindness, goodness, faithfulness, gentleness, and self-control—are simply *aspects of love* (Gal. 5:22-23). We must remember that the love *God* commands, and imparts to the circumcised heart of believers, is not an emotion. It is the strength to commit our will to seek the best for those we are brought into contact with, even enemies. This is *agape* love. This does not mean that feelings, such as empathy, may not accompany *agape* love. But it does mean that when we do not feel like doing what is reflective of God's perfect character we are, with his help, to make every effort to extend *love* to those in need of it. God plants, nurtures, and matures *agape* love in the *hearts* of believers.

How the Holy Spirit Imparts God's Nature into the Character of His Children

This review of God's attributes logically leads us to the next question, *How* does the Holy Spirit impart aspects of the divine nature into our character? Eight chapters (13–20) were devoted to this question. God created his image-bearers with what he described in the Bible as a *heart*. Our search of Scripture revealed that the heart is the seat of human beings' *mind, passions,* and *will*. These are each further described in the Word as being the seat of many complex sub-components. For example, the *mind* is the repository of our *innate knowledge of good and evil;* our *beliefs* about our existence, purpose, and meaning; our ability to *know* things about ourselves and our environment; and the ability to have *understanding,* even *wisdom,* derived from the natural laws that are observable around us. But the mind's greatest ability is its capacity to possess *relational knowledge* or *true knowledge* of God. We have the capacity not just to know *about* God but to possess *true knowledge of God, coming from the intimate involvement of the Holy Spirit in our lives.*

The second component of the heart, constantly interactive with the mind, is *the passions of the heart*. The *passions* were also subdivided into three areas: our *desires, affections,* and *identity needs*. These passions are in every human heart! But these characteristics of the human spirit were all badly distorted at the fall of our first parents. It requires the loving work of the Holy Spirit to restore them to anything like their originally intended state.

The *desires* component of our passions carries with it all of our *emotions,* and the fervor with which we respond to stimuli. The desires of the unregenerate are typically oriented toward serving their self-centered appetites—their hunger for attention, security, and significance. The desires of Christians, through the Spirit's transforming work, become more and more focused on the things God has a first interest in. For example, we hunger for Christ and want to be like him; we cease wanting to be the center of attention; and our security and peace are found in Christ.

The *affections* of the heart were described as the *fear of the Lord* (a gift of the Spirit associated with *regeneration*); *hope* in God's promises; *love,* as Christ loved us; *hatred* of all that is unholy; *joy* found in Christ; *sorrow* for all that is ungodly in us; *gratitude* to God for his goodness and blessings; *compassion* that moves us to act graciously and mercifully to meet others' needs; and *zeal,* the motivation born of love that strengthens one to follow Christ in everything. These are not the affections discovered in the unregenerate, but they become the affections of those who are grafted into Christ and renovated by the Holy Spirit.

The third and final segment of the passions component in the heart was the *identity needs* that are inherent in every human being, the redeemed and the unredeemed. And those were identified as the need to be *unconditionally accepted,* the need to be *competent and successful,* and the need to *belong to a significant family*. Believers come to realize that only God *unconditionally loves* us. We also learn that being competent and successful, at its deepest level, is being Christlike! And we grow to realize that the family of God is the most significant family of all. God has placed these inherent needs in every human's heart and he then offers us the means of satisfying them. The Lord Jesus Christ is the *only* source of satisfaction!

Whenever there is a conflict between the *mind* and the *passions* our hearts engage in an internal struggle: we begin rationalizing. We will either try to find a way whereby our passions may prevail over what we know in our mind is best, or our mind may persuade the *will* to stand strong and not capitulate to the particular desire—the misconstrued *identity need* out of sync with Christ's higher calling.

The *will* or *volition* part of the heart—discussed last—was described as the part of the heart that reveals the true love that motivates the heart. The will has either been *converted*, thereby enabled to follow God's revealed will displayed in the life of Christ, or it remains *unconverted* and reveals a self-will still living in rebellion against its Creator. But even in the hearts of those in whom the Holy Spirit dwells, a struggle remains. There are skirmishes between the old self-centered nature and the new Christ-centered nature.

The Holy Spirit enables God's child, over time, to gain victory over his old nature. Anyone remaining outside of God's family has no such help, and remains a slave to his or her self-will. All people, those in Christ and those who reject him, are motivated by what they love most! We all assign the highest value to whatever we truly fancy. And what we love, and thus want, moves our will to either decisive *action* or entrenched resistance.

The Holy Spirit renovates, trains, and leads our *hearts*. He accomplishes this by *abiding in* and *loving* us, transforming our hearts into Christ's likeness. He may use a gentle wooing through the application of the Word. He may use a slow form of persuasion combining the Word, loving family members and friends—and a sense that it just makes sense as nothing else does. Or he may use a traumatic experience that sends us racing back to receive his comfort and truth. He uses what he knows is best suited to alter our distorted image so that we again assume his likeness. But in the final analysis, it is his *Word* that is central in his work. The Word provides the compass, the benchmark, and the standard. It is how we test the spirits (1 John 4:1). The Word contains the truth needed to keep our experiences in right perspective. The Word provides the evidence that we are spiritually mature children of God.

The renovation of the believer's *heart*, by which he or she becomes a *partaker of the divine nature*, will appear in one's daily life. The person born from above is provided *true knowledge* of the Trinity. A personal relationship is formed between believers and God. The two become intimate with one another—they share with each other what is on their minds. God encourages them to read his Word. His Word reveals what is on his mind. Believers' prayers tell God what is on their minds. God encourages them to see his hand at work all around them. God's enlightened children come to see with the eyes of the heart their Father's goodness toward them in his creation, salvation, and providence (Eph. 1:18).

Believers' Growth in Christlikeness Manifested in Every Phase of Life

In chapters 21–27 we saw that the believer's growth in Christlikeness will be shown in every phase of life. If one is single, then Christlikeness will be shown in the state of singleness. By God's grace, those who remain single are led to the understanding that "your husband is the LORD of hosts; and your Redeemer is the holy One of Israel" (Isa. 54:5). And those dating; and those married; and parents; and those who work outside the home; or who are traveling on a plane; or playing at the beach; or driving the car; or attending a party; or visiting someone in the hospital—*all* display the changes taking place in their hearts as the Holy Spirit, degree by degree, *renovates* them so that Christ's likeness becomes more apparent over time.

Manifesting a Christlike attitude or reflecting his winsome behavior through an interest and care for others becomes a habit in the life of those in union with Christ. And when his likeness is *not* being revealed in their lives, he calls them to *repentance*. Indeed, repentance in the life of the child of God occurs daily—for no one can go through an entire day without having some un-Christlike attitude, thought, conduct, or unfulfilled duty manifested in his life.

> If we say that we have no sin, we are *deceiving ourselves* and the truth is not in us. If we confess our sins, He is faithful and righteous to forgive us our sins and to cleanse us from all unrighteousness. If we say that we have not sinned, we make Him a liar and His word is not in us.
> (1 John 1:8-10)

The question before us now is: "What is the 'end' of all that has been discussed?" Is being transformed into Christlikeness our goal? It is abundantly clear that God the Father wants us to have an image that more closely resembles that of his Son. Yes, this is very important.

But ultimately, this book is not about you and me undergoing a marvelous process of restoration and experiencing godly maturity. Significant as that may be, our goal is to draw our attention to *God*, to direct our thoughts to the self-revealing God of creation and his awesome character, grace, and mercy. It is intended, above all else, to proclaim his *glory*!

To further promote that end, the final chapter, "To God Be the Glory," follows as a brief *epilogue*—a concluding statement which celebrates God's supreme *glory*!

The Epilogue:

"We were created for His glory" (Isa. 43:7)

To God Be the Glory

I am the LORD, that is My name; I will not give My glory to another. (Isa. 42:8)

The first attribute of God we discussed was his *aseity*—his absolute independence from all external to him. God has never had a *need*. But God, because of who he is, knew it would be eternally and infinitely beneficent to call into being a creation that would include image-bearers—who would have the capability of having *true knowledge* of their Creator, and in whom he would dwell. And those in whom he dwells have, throughout the centuries, sung his glory.

Gloria Patri
Glory be to the Father, and to the Son, and to the Holy Ghost;
As it was in the beginning, is now, and ever shall be, world without end. Amen, amen.   (Anonymous, second century)

Doxology
Praise God from whom all blessings flow; praise Him, all creatures here below; praise Him above, ye heavenly host: praise Father, Son, and Holy Ghost. Amen. (Thomas Kent, 1709)

Ascribe to the LORD, O families of the peoples, ascribe to the LORD glory and strength. Ascribe to the LORD the glory of His name. (Ps. 96:7-8)

It is amazing how our sin nature hides God's glory from the eyes of our hearts. I include myself in the shame implicit in this statement. We live in the midst of a glorious miracle: God has created all reality out of what did not exist. Theologians call this the *ex nihilo* doctrine—God's creating all that exists out of nothing. And within this creation God has established certain physical laws of reproduction that manifest repetitive marvelous works of God's providence that we simply take for granted, and should not. For example, a grain of corn is planted; it produces, in turn, two or three ears on a stalk, each of which has two hundred or more succulent grains on it—so the original seed becomes perhaps six-hundred new grains. And we just accept this without wonder or amazement, because it goes on around us so routinely!

Another example: When a broken bone is set and the two parts ultimately become a whole bone again, is this not an amazing work of providence? The doctor who set the bone did not heal the fracture. *God* established the process of healing! In fact, is not every conception and subsequent birth a great work of providence? Truly, *the glory of God is all around us!*

Job, who was the standard of human righteousness in his day, did not at first perceive the *glory of God* which was all around him, either. God called Job his servant, and said there was no one like him on earth—he was blameless, upright, feared God and turned away from evil (Job 1:1). Even so, Job did not discern the *glory of God* that was all around him until after the LORD permitted Satan to strike him. Yes, to Job's credit, during his long period of suffering the puzzled man did not "sin with his lips" (2:10) or falsely accuse God; but he did express his frustration at being in an unequal relationship with God. He voiced his regretted inequality:

> For He is not a man as I am that I may answer Him, that we may go to court together. There is no umpire between us, who may lay his hand upon us both. Let Him remove His rod from me, and let not dread of Him terrify me. Then I would speak and not fear Him; *but I am not like that in myself.* (Job 9:32-35)

Job accepted his unequal position in his relationship with God, and he accepted God's prerogative to do as he deemed appropriate with his life. But Job did not like it, and let his feelings be known. What followed is amazing! After a certain period of time—we know not how long Job suffered—the LORD asked Job a series of questions:

> Where were you when I laid the foundation of the earth? (38:4)
>
> Who enclosed the sea . . . and . . . placed boundaries on it? (vv. 8, 10)
>
> Have you ever . . . commanded the morning and caused the dawn to know its place? (v. 12)
>
> Have you entered into the springs of the sea? (v. 16)
>
> Have the gates of death been revealed to you? (v. 17)
>
> Where is the way to the dwelling of light? (v. 19)
>
> Have you entered the storehouses of the snow? (v. 22)
>
> Has the rain a father? (v. 28a)
>
> Who has begotten the drops of dew? (v. 28b)
>
> From whose womb has come the ice? (v. 29)
>
> Can you lead forth a constellation in its season? (v. 32)
>
> Do you know the ordinances of the heavens, or fix their rule over the earth? (v. 33)
>
> Can you lift up your voice to the clouds, so that an abundance of water will cover you? (v. 34)
>
> Can you send forth lightning? (v. 35)
>
> Who has put wisdom in the innermost being, or has given understanding to the mind? (v. 36)
>
> Can you hunt the prey for the lion? (v. 39)
>
> Who prepares for the raven its nourishment? (v. 41)
>
> Do you know the time the mountain goats give birth? (39:1)
>
> Who sent out the wild donkey free? (v. 5)

> Do you give the horse his might? (v. 19)
> Is it by your understanding that the hawk soars? (v. 26)
> Is it at your command that the eagle ... makes his nest on high? (v. 27)

"Then the LORD said to Job, 'Will the faultfinder contend with the Almighty?'" (40:1-2). After asking this question, God continued to ask Job a series of other questions about the hippopotamus (40:15-24) and the crocodile (41:1-34). And this was followed by Job's confession: "I have heard of You by the hearing of the ear; *but now my eye sees You*; therefore I retract, and I repent in dust and ashes" (42:5-6). The eye Job was referring to is the eye of his *heart*—the spiritual enlightenment of the heart that is mentioned in Ephesians 1:18 and Acts 26:18. By asking simple but obvious questions, God, by the power of the Holy Spirit, created in Job the ability to see his awesome *glory*.

Christ's telling Simon Peter, "Put out into the deep water and let down your nets *for a catch*," after Simon and the other disciples had fished all night without success, led to Peter's glimpsing the awesome *glory* of Christ. For Peter obeyed Jesus's instruction, and the result was a catch of fish so large that the boat was almost swamped—whereupon Peter fell to his knees at Jesus's feet and exclaimed, "Go away from me Lord, for I am a sinful man!" (Luke 5:1-8). Peter suddenly discerned Christ's bewildering knowledge, power, and divinity. He saw, through new eyes of faith, the *glory* of Jesus who was God's Messiah, the Christ. The result was that James, John, and Peter, all three, "left everything and followed Him" (v.11).

God's glory, *through eyes of faith*, can be seen and comprehended to be present everywhere. God's glory is to be seen in every blade of grass, every leaf, every fish, every bird, and every person! His glory is to be comprehended in his holiness, wisdom, omnipotence, omniscience, patience, goodness, love, wrath, mercy, sovereign rule over all, and redemption of a people for Christ's inheritance!

It is my prayer that God—the Father, the Son, and the Holy Spirit—will be pleased to use this book as a means of elevating the truth that his relationship with his people declares, so that all may see his awesome *glory*; for he is the ...

One Who Changes Our Hearts and

Makes Us Partakers of His Divine Nature,

whereby his children reveal to the world that they have been given to Christ by God the Father through the patient and tender work of the Holy Spirit!

To God be the glory! Amen!

About the Author

Richard (Dick) C. Chewning graduated from Virginia Tech, the University of Virginia, and the University of Washington and did post doctoral study at the University of St. Andrews in Scotland. He taught at the University of Richmond for twenty-five years, and held the *Harry and Hazel Chavanne Chair of Christian Ethics in Business* at Baylor University for fifteen years.

During his academic career Dick also served on seven different Boards of Directors/Trustees for a total of 93 years of service and served as Chairman of the Board for four of those organizations for a total of 31 years. He was also honored to serve twice as the Moderator of the Reformed Presbyterian Church, Evangelical Synod and once as the Moderator of the Presbyterian Church in America.

Dick's academic passion is reading God's Word and seeking to discern how it speaks to God's children who are called to the field of "business". In doing this he has over one hundred articles, essays, and reviews published, along with writing and editing seven books. The majority of his writing is done with members of the Christian Business Faculty Association in mind. He wants Christian business faculty to understand, as thoroughly as possible, Christ's mind as His revelation addresses the moral challenges that confront all who are called to work in business.

He loves Shirley, his wife of more than 60 years, and their children and their children's children deeply, but Dick's greatest love is for the Triune God who revealed Himself most clearly through the incarnation, life, death, and resurrection of His only Son, the Messiah, and who sends His Spirit to dwell with those who are given to Christ as His inheritance. To this end Dick considers it a high calling to serve as an elder in Christ's church and to be granted the privilege of teaching in the church for many years. He wants everyone to know that God the Creator is a Savior offering grace and mercy to all who truly love Him.

Scripture Index

Genesis
1 .... 8, 190, 200
1-3 190
1:1 28
1:2 43
1:4 124
1:10 124
1:12 124
1:18 124
1:19-20 201
1:21 124
1:26 .... 127, 193, 201
1:26-27 .... 63, 222n118
1:27 .... 44, 123, 190, 199
1:27-29 190
1:28 .... 127, 152, 195
1:28-29 193
1:28-30 21
1:31 .... 29, 78, 79, 124, 190
2 .... 190, 200
2:7 .... 60, 62, 67, 190, 280, 313
2:7-25 190
2:8 .... 201, 313
2:15-17 .... 79, 190
2:16-17 21
2:17 .... 2n4, 56, 68, 253, 313
2:18 .... 52, 306, 330n167
2:21-23 52
2:24 .... 195, 313, 320
2:25 .... 160, 323
2:25-3:12 172
3 191
3:1-3 190
3:1-17 190
3:6 237
3:7 .... 160, 193, 253
3:8 .... 98, 99, 339
3:9-13 21
3:10 98
3:12 69
3:13 237
3:14-15 137
3:15 .... 164, 253
3:16 .... 17, 49, 330n167
3:17-19 .... 79, 330n167
3:22-24 .... 80, 160
4:1 .... 100, 253
4:5 153
4:8 .... 165, 253
4:8-12 150
4:26 376
5 158
5:1 123
5:1-2 .... 44, 222n118
6:3 .... 79n61, 158
6-7 29
6-9 92
6:5-7 29
6:6 91
6:17 62
7:22 62
8:22 .... 132, 136
9:1 195
9:6 .... 44, 123
9:7 195
9:8-11 54
9:8-12 .... 362, 372
11:4-9 376
11:31-12:2 377
15 53
15:2-4 143
15:4 .... 195n111
15:5 143
16-19 21
17 .... 53, 324n166
17:18-21 143
17:19, 21 143
18 .... 324n166
18:10-12 324
18:14 .... 142, 176, 285
18:16-33 .... 21, 56
18:19 .... 333n168
19:23-25 80
21:1-2 285
22:1-5 95
22:1-8 143
22:5 277
29:30 .... 100n76
38:2 309
38:15-19 100
38:18 309
39:7-9 .... 201, 227, 308n161
42:18 240
45:5, 8 231
45:7 .... 132, 134
46:26 .... 195n111
50:20 .... 132, 136, 231

Exodus
3:1-22 346
3:13-14 33
3:13-15 86
3:14 .... 21, 23, 121, 125, 252
4:10-11 .... 132, 135
4:11 .... 131, 119, 131, 158
7:3 179
14:21 145
18:21 240
20:3 373
20:3-6 55
20:4 61
20:8-11 55
20:12 49
20:13 55
20:15 .... 14n19, 55, 362, 369, 371
20:17 .... 55, 362, 369
20:16 .... 362, 369
21:16 .... 14n19
21:28-29 .... 362, 365
21:33 .... 32n26
21:33-36 362
22:3 13
22:25 259
23:3 13
23:8 .... 362, 371
25:21 290
31:2-3 232
32:1-14 91
32:11 146
32:14 91
32:9-11 90
33:19 116
34:6-7 278
34:7 .... 161, 311
34:11-16 249

Leviticus
11:44 .... 205, 281n155
11:44-45 82
11:45 138
18 324

18:6-18 82
19:2 .... 73, 82, 281n155
19:4 61
19:11 .... 14n19, 55, 362, 371
19:13 .... 14n19
19:15 13
20 324
20:3 .... 76n59
20:7 82
22:2, 32 .... 76n59
26:2 55

Numbers
11:31 .... 80, 144
12:3 183
13:17-24 144
14:18 .... 161, 311
16:1-35 56
23:19 .... 53, 91
25:1-3 249
25:9 250
27:16 .... 195n110, 280n153

Deuteronomy
1:17 .... 13, 44n33
2:30 179
3:24 146
4:2 26
4:10 .... 240, 379n183
4:15-16 .... 49, 61
4:34 146
4:35, 39 78
5:9 .... 161, 311
5:15 146
6:1-5 55
6:4 .... 49, 51
6:4-7 340
6:5 .... 51, 54
6:5-7 334
6:7 .... 333n168
6:13-15 55
6:21 146
7:6 254
8:3 .... 6, 102
8:17-18 14
8:18 247
10:17 .... 44n33
11:19 .... 333n168
12:32 26
13:5 204
14:2 254
14:23 .... 240, 379n183
15 259
15:7, 8 258
15:7-11 14
17:7, 12 204
17:19 .... 240, 379n183
19:18, 19 .... 362, 369
20:19, 20 .... 362, 372
21:21 204
22:8 .... 362, 365
22:21 204
23:13 .... 362, 372
23:19, 20 259
24:5 324
27:15 61
29:29 .... 22, 24, 77
30:6 .... 54, 341
30:19 252
31:12-13 .... 240, 379n183
32:4 287
32:15, 18, 30 94
32:39 78

Joshua
3:1-17 144
3:8 144
24:19 .... 73, 281n155

Judges

Ruth
4:13 .... 100n76

1 Samuel
2:7-25 14
3:1-4 346
6:20 .... 73, 281n155
8:1-5 377
15:1-26 247
15:29 .... 90, 282
16:7 .... 56, 196, 268, 386n189
23:10-13 .... 36, 277n151

2 Samuel
7:12 .... 195n111
7:14 .... 43n32, 333n168
12:1-14 148
12:24 .... 100n76
16:11 .... 195n111
19:32 158
23:2 47

1 Kings
17.9 143
17:17-24 .... 145, 400
18:1-40 99
19:11-13 295

2 Kings
2:1, 11 145
4: 32-37 400
6:4-6 285
6:5-7 145
6:6 .... 132, 136
6:8-23 .... 104n81

1 Chronicles
16:35 .... 76n59
28:9 .... 386n189
29:16 .... 76n59

2 Chronicles
7:6 .... 60, 97, 282
7:14 140
19:7 .... 44n33
34:27 140

Ezra

Nehemiah
8:10 107
9:17 278

Esther

Job
1:1 406
1:7-12 133
1:12 .... 376n182
1:13-19 80
1:21 .... 157, 269
1:21, 22 .... 133, 158
2:6 .... 376n182
2:10 .... 401, 406
6:10 .... 281n155
7:17, 18 57
9:32-35 40
14:5 .... 36, 120, 134
15:14 195
19:25-27 277
21:7-19 117
22:2, 3 29
25:4 150
34:10 .... 132, 136
34:14 .... 195n110, 280n153
35:7 29

38-41 .... 132, 133, 201, 227
38:2 126
38:4 .... 113, 126, 406
38:8-10 406
38:8-11 126
38:12 406
38:12, 16, 22 126
38:16, 17 406
38:19 406
38:22 406
38:28, 29 406
38:32-36 406
38:32, 36, 41 126
38:39, 41 406
39:1, 5 406
39:19, 26, 27 407
40:1, 2 407
40:4 126
40:9 295
40:15-24 407
41:1-34 407
42:2-6 .... 126, 227
42:3, 5 .... 113n86
42:5, 6 .... 21, 69, 74, 201, 407

Psalms
1:2 68
2:7 .... 46, 50
8:5 66
8:6-8 .... 127, 201
9:7 .... 32n26
10:11 99
11:7 288
14:1-3 57
14:3 138
15:1, 2 95
15:1-4 .... 203, 362, 368
15:4 .... 95, 282
15:5 259
16:2 268
16:3 198
16:5 268
16:8, 9 268
16:11 .... 101, 107, 268
17:14 117
18:1 124
18:6 124
18:16, 17 124
18:19 124
18:31 94
18:46 94
19:1 400
19:13 236
22:18 36
23:3 .... 37, 281n155
25:4, 5 268
25:9 383
25:11 87
26:9, 10 .... 362, 371
27:4 76
27:5 104
27:8 .... 11, 101
27:10 33
29:1, 2 76
32:2 .... 362, 369
32:3-5 270
33:12 .... 116, 254
33:21 .... 76n59
34:11 .... 240, 332, 337
34:18 .... 162, 244
36:9 193
38:17 .... 88n68
40:8 .... 72, 108
41:1 14
41:13 .... 32n26
42:1-6 .... 124n89
46:1 .... 162, 176, 361

46:1-3 104
46:10 72
49:7, 8 178
51 148
51:4 .... 308n161
51:5 .... 29, 127, 195, 195n111, 280, 332
51:12 267
51:17 354
52:1 175
58:1-3 .... 362, 369
58:3 195
62:11 34
64:1-6 .... 99n74
65:4 .... 22, 101, 147n94
69:29-31 354
71:22 .... 73, 281n155
73:1-14 163
73:3-7 117
73:11 99
73:24-28 248
73:25-28 268
73:28 .... 22, 101, 384
76:7 76
76:10 111
78:39 113
78:40 30
78:41 .... 281n155
79:9 87
82:3, 4 14
89:18 .... 281n155
89:26 .... 43n32
90.2 32
90:10 .... 79n61, 158
93:2 .... 32n26
94:7 99
96:7, 8 405
97:10 382
98:1 .... 76, 282
102:25 28
102:25-27 .... 85, 86, 282
102:26, 27 33
102:27 .... 32n26
103:1 76
103:8 278
103:12 .... 88n68
103:14 113
103:17 161
103:19 .... 155, 290
104:30 43
104:31 107
105:3 .... 76n59
105:4 .... 11, 101
105:42 76
106:47 .... 76n59
110:3 76
111:7, 8 .... 34, 60
115:3 56
116:1, 2 123
116:12, 13 123
119 178
119:1-24 83
119:63 198
119:67, 71, 75 178
119:104 382
119:105 193
119:128 382
119:163 382
121:2 .... 366, 368, 369, 371, 372
128:1, 3, 6 331
135:6 .... 56, 132, 133
136 289
139:1-6 .... 35, 88, 277
139:4 .... 68, 102n77
139:7, 8 34
139:7-12 .... 97, 282

Scripture Index 411

139:15, 16............ 31n24, 120	9:3, 11, 13............. 382n185	42:1-3 146
139:16 .... 36, 88, 133, 134, 277	10:5 .... 382n185	42:5 .... 62, 195n110, 280n153
143:2 116	12:7 .... 195n110, 280n153	42:8 .... 9, 154, 405
145:7 .... 132, 134	**Song of Solomon**	42:9 121
145:8, 9 38	1:7 323	43:1-5, 7................ 30
145:21 .... 76n59	1:8 323	43:1-7 30
147:5 .... 34, 35, 113, 135, 276	1:9-10 323	43:4 151
Proverbs	1:13 322	43:7 .... 9, 38, 81, 118, 405
1:7 226	1:15, 16.................. 323	43:10-11................. 78
1:29 240	1:16 322	43:25...................... 88
3:11, 12 14	2:6, 7 322	44:3 341
3:12........................ 333n168	2:15 .... 321, 323, 326	44:6-8 78
3:32........................ 22, 100, 311, 361n175	2:16 322	44:7 397
5:15-20 324	4:1-5, 7 323	44:7, 8.................... 120, 132, 134
6:1-5...................... 96	4:12 101	44:23...................... 9, 81
6:2-5...................... 368	4:12, 15.................. 322	45:4 .... 147n94, 254
6:20 49	4:12, 16.................. 316	45:5, 6.................... 78
6:30, 31 .... 13, 16	4:16 322	45:8 289
8:13 .... 14, 383	5:10-16 323	45:21...................... 132, 134, 397
9:10 27	6:4-7 323	45:25...................... 150
10:1 .... 333n168	7:1-9 323	46:5 .... 133, 135
10:4 284	**Isaiah**	46:9 .... 35, 36, 88, 120, 277
10:22 247	1:4 73	46:10...................... 35, 36, 88, 114, 120, 277, 283, 314, 397
11:13 .... 362, 368	1:7 323	
12:15 .... 362, 367	1:8 323	
12:20 .... 362, 369	1:9, 10 323	46:10, 11................. 132, 135
13:5 383	1:13 322	46:13...................... 289
13:24 .... 333n168	1:15, 16.................. 323	48:9 .... 38, 56
14:12 .... 56, 98n73	1:16 322	48:9-11................... 87
14:15 284	2:6 322	48:9, 11.................. 13, 29
15:3 283	2:7 322	48:11...................... 154
16:2 .... 51, 56, 317, 386n189	2:10, 11................. 14	49:9, 10.................. 134
16:5 .... 375n181	2:16 322	51:5, 6.................... 289
16:9 .... 132, 134	2:22 62	52:10...................... 22
16:18 14	3:14, 15.................. 55	53 246
16:32 .... 57, 58, 153, 273, 338, 401	4:1-5 323	53:1-12................... 171
17:6 161	4:12, 15.................. 322	53:3-11................... 129
17:25 .... 333n168	4:7 323	53:11...................... 89, 150, 155, 209
18:8 368	4:16 323	54:5 404
18:17 339	5:10-16 323	54:13...................... 293
19:18 .... 333n168	6:1 274	55:10...................... 132, 136
19:20 .... 362, 367	6:1-7 21	55:11...................... 292
20:18 .... 362, 367	6:1-13 227	57:15...................... 31, 73
20:19 .... 82, 362, 368	6:3 .... 73, 76, 281, 281n155	57:16...................... 195n110, 280n153
20:24 .... 132, 134	6:3-5 74	58:1-7 55
22:6 .... 333, 336, 341	6:3-7 .... 124n89	58:3 365
22:6, 15 .... 333n168	6:4-7 323	59:7, 8.................... 57
23:7 3	6:5 240	59:21...................... 292
23:13, 14................ 333n168	6:9, 10 255	61:1, 2.................... 244
25:21, 22............... 177	7:1-9 323	63:10...................... 30
25:26 380	9:6 33	63:14...................... 132, 134
26 111	10:5-7 .... 132, 136	63:16...................... 43n32
27:5 326	11:2 .... 35, 111, 213, 232, 380	64:6 .... 56, 116
27:17 317	11:3 48	64:8 .... 43n32
27:20 162	13:11 14	66:2 31
29:7 .... 14, 55, 204, 362, 372, 381	14:4-21 78	**Jeremiah**
29:15-17 .... 333n168	14:12-17................. 401	3:6, 8, 11, 12, 14 ... 267
30:6 26	14:24 .... 35, 88, 277	3:19 .... 43n32
30:7-9 14	16:32 .... 10n13	3:22 267
31:6 206	25:28 .... 10n13	5:21-31................... 116
31:8, 9 .... 14, 55, 204, 288, 362, 372	33:14, 15................ 362, 371	5:28 .... 362, 372
	34:4 31	6:9 267
Ecclesiastes	40 .... 88n67	9:5-8 .... 362, 369
1:3, 9, 14 .... 382n185	40:6, 7, 10, 15, 17 . 28	9:23-24................... 174, 232, 359
2:11, 17-20, 22...... 382n185	40:18 120	10:10...................... 32n26
2:18-23 .... 330n167	40:21 28	17:9 15
3:1, 3, 6 381	40:25 120	17:10...................... 48
3:16 .... 382n185	40:28 .... 31n24, 34, 35, 88, 114, 120, 121, 134, 135	23:24...................... 97, 282
4:1, 3, 7, 15 .... 382n185	41:21-23................. 397	24:7 .... 41, 209
5:18 .... 382n185	41:22, 23................ 120, 134	29:11...................... 176
6:1, 12 .... 382n185	41:23 .... 132, 134	31:29-30................. 51
8:15 .... 382n185	42:1 50	31:31-34................. 72, 108
		31:33...................... 6, 102, 382n186

31:34 ....88, 102
32:17 ....141, 145, 151,
                      176, 285
51:15 111

Lamentations

Ezekiel
3:8-30 ....104n81
3:12 50
8:3 50
8:12 99
9:3-6 175
9:4-10 239
9:9 99
11:19 ....209, 341
11:19-20 6
18:20 51
18:23, 32 239
28:11-19 78
28:12-17 401
36:26-27 6

Daniel
3:4 44
3:15-18 378
3:16-18 276
3:27 ....132, 136
4:17 ....375n180, 375
4:34, 35 ....132, 133
4:35 56
5:19 44
5:22, 23 ....99n74
7:9-15 21
8:15-27 21
10:1-12 240

Hosea
1:7 ....132, 136
2:8 247
14:8 108

Joel
1:3 334

Amos
2:6, 7 360
4:1 360
5:7, 11 360
5:15 383
8:4-6 360

Obadiah

Jonah
1:3-5 106
1:6-12 106

Micah
7:19 ....88n68

Nahum
1:3 ....38, 278
1:6 76

Habakkuk
1:12 ....32n26

Zephaniah

Haggai

Zechariah
1:3 352
8:6 ....145, 285
8:16 ....362, 368
12:1 ....195n110,
                          280n153

Malachi
2:13-16 242
2:14-16 256
2:16 203
3:2 ....22, 76
3:5 ....360, 362, 365
3:6 ....33, 86, 91, 282

Matthew
1:18 299
1:18-25 285
3:13-17 107
3:16 .... 43n30, 61
3:17 .... 43n30, 50
4:1 75
4:1-4 .... 6n7
4:4 102
4:8, 9 376
5:3-6 .... 73, 243, 354
5:6 .... 82, 139
5:13-14 .... 164, 271
5:13-16 .... 52, 271
5:16 .... v, 118, 164, 362,
                            371, 387
5:17-19 82
5:18 292
5:21-26 55
5:29, 30 115
5:44 164
5:44-48 .... 44, 392
5:45 .... 156, 158, 279
5:48 .... 83, 354
6:7 102
6:8 .... 68, 102
6:9, 10 339
6:14, 15 87
6:20 248
6:22, 23 .... 5, 184, 193, 268
6:24 373
6:25-34 160
7:1 203
7:7 .... 122, 251, 344,
                            365, 367, 368,
                            369, 370, 371,
                            372, 400n192,
                            400
7:13-23 108
7:15-23 10
7:20 297
7:21 47
7:21-23 29
7:22, 23 189
8:12 115
8:21-35 87
8:23-27 80
9:36 245
10:16 362
10:16-20 108
10:28 104
10:29, 30 130
10:38 .... 229n124
10:38, 39 .... 41, 303, 329
10:39 .... 183, 399
11:4-6 .... 132, 135
11:21 .... 36, 277n151
11:27 43
11:29 384
12:1-14 258
12:27 50
12:28 285
13:1-23 265
13:3-9 .... 221, 255
13:11 117
13:14, 15 255
13:24-30 .... 342, 378
13:33 .... 217, 227, 231
13:40-42 115
14:13-21 144
14:25-27 145
14:35 .... 200n113,
                            223n121
15:3-9 45
15:14 .... 70, 161
16:13-20 227
16:24 .... 172, 198,
                            229n124
16:24, 25 329

17:5 50
17:12 251
18:4 140
18:15-17 340
18:21, 22 289
18:32, 33 289
18:35 87
19:4-6 321
19:5, 6 52
19:12 347
19:13-15 341
19:18 .... 14n19
19:26 .... 145, 176, 285,
                            341
20:16 254
20:25-28 48
20:28 315
21:12, 13 146
22:14 .... 147n94
22:37 353
22:37-39 .... 170, 263
22:41-16 .... 43n30
23:11 48
23:37 27
24:24 254
24:35 292
25:14-30 .... 291, 362, 370
25:21, 23 107
25:27 259
25:31-40 392
25:41 29
25:46 .... 115, 335n170
26:11 14
26:28 54
26:34 .... 132, 135
26:39, 42 .... 47, 93
26:75 135
27:46 145
28:19 .... 43, 49

Mark
1:9-13 285
1:10 61
1:10, 11 .... 43n30
1:13 47
4:35-41 80
5:1-20 266
5:18, 19 139
7:9-13 257
8:34 .... 229n124
9:24 103
9:35 48
9:42-49 115
10:13-16 341
10:21 .... 229n124
10:21, 22 26
10:42-45 152
11:25, 26 87
12:32 78
13:20 .... 147n94
13:20, 22, 27 254
14:36 93
14:34-36 47
15:34 145

Luke
1:17 .... 46, 273
1:20, 64 .... 132, 135
1:37 .... 145, 285, 341
1:41 341
2:10 107
2:52 165
3:21 107
3:22 .... 61, 107
5:4-11 227
5:1-8 407
5:8 74
5:11 407
5:12, 13 145

Scripture Index 413

5:36-39 377	1:4 .... 33, 287, 387	8:12 .... 193, 387, 286n158
6:27-30 392	1:4-9 .... 193n108	8:16-18 .... 43, 318
6:27, 35 164	1:5 387	8:24 .... 121, 286n158
6:27-36 172	1:12 57	8:28 .... 43, 121
6:27-38 44	1:12, 13 .... 25, 105n82	8:29 43
6:34, 35 260	1:13 .... 103n79, 115	8:31, 32 176
6:41, 42 360	1:14 .... 43, 43n30, 106, 278, 285, 400	8:31-36 57
6:46 .... 47, 251	1:14-18 42	8:34 56
7:12-15 400	1:18 .... 43n30, 61, 280, 286, 400	8:56-58 .... 21, 324n166
7:19 261	1:29 .... 147, 162	8:58 .... 121, 286, 286n158
7:22, 23 261	1:32 61	9:1-3 .... 132, 135
7:23-32 9	2:1-11 145	9:2, 3 119
7:30 .... 10, 36, 82, 242, 242n137, 261, 277n151, 313	2:6-10 137	9:3-7 145
7:30-35 115	2:12 30	10:7, 11 .... 286n158
7:31, 32 261	2:14-16 146	10:9 103
7:47 88	2:16 49	10:17, 18 .... 145, 145n93
8:5-15 374	2:19-22 145	10:28 .... 29, 105, 115, 276n149
9:23 .... 152, 229, 303, 330	2:22 .... 68, 294	10:29 46
9:24 .... 303, 330	3:1-11 .... 103n79	11:17 145
9:62 225	3:1-12 .... 25n20	11:17-44 285
10:22 46	3:3 .... 146, 147	11:25 .... 286n158
10:25-37 258	3:3-8 .... 68, 89, 115, 254, 400	11:25, 26 .... 33, 67, 287, 400
10:27 210	3:5, 6 147	11:38-44 .... 145, 400
11:13 .... 47, 108, 146, 172	3:5-8 .... 146, 283	11:41 244
11:37-41 57	3:7, 8 147	12:25 .... 276n149
11:39-41 .... 206, 361	3:8 50	12:28, 29 295
12:1, 2 108	3:15 .... 276n149, 400	12:31 .... xi, 263, 376
12:2, 3 96	3:16 .... 27, 46, 115, 272, 400	12:35, 36 387
12:15-34 46	3:18 46	12:40 179
12:18-21 257	3:19-21 .... 193n108, 387	12:42, 43 .... 247, 383
12:41 367	3:30 .... 39, 108, 275	12:46 387
12:41-48 362	3:35 46	13:8-10 108
12:48 .... 46, 273	4:7, 8, 11, 13 109	13:18 254
12:49-53 249	4:10 76	13:34 .... 93, 171, 263, 297
13:4, 5 159	4:12 21	13:35 .... 93, 171, 241, 289, 297, 342
13:21 217	4:14 .... 76, 269	14:6 .... 33, 46, 106, 125, 242, 278, 286n158, 287
14:27 .... 198, 229n124	4:16 169	
16:1 362	4:23 .... 22, 49, 68	14:7-11 42
16:1-13 .... 362, 370	4:24 .... 49, 59, 60, 72, 147, 398	14:9-11 51
16:19-31 29	4:34 .... 46, 47, 93	14:12, 14 .... 10n12, 285
16:22-26 115	4:42 272	14:13, 14 .... 92, 93
16:25, 26 117	5:3 108	14:13-17, 23, 26 .... 265n145
17:5-8 103	5:14 93	14:15 .... 93, 108
17:5-10 .... 71n56, 93, 148, 149	5:17 49	14:16 .... 44, 46, 47, 108, 109, 293
17:16 244	5:19 43	14:16, 17 .... 21, 68, 98, 103n79, 107, 172
18:7 .... 147n94, 254	5:20-23 49	14:16-18 .... viii, 42, 148
18:15, 16 341	5:26 .... 33, 43, 125, 287, 318	14:17 .... 7, 60, 108
18:19 .... 123, 138, 196, 284	5:30 .... 43, 47	14:21, 23 .... viii, 10, 93, 108
19:1-10 266	5:36 47	14:23 42
19:11-26 .... 362, 370	5:38 50	14:26 .... 10n12, 11, 43, 44, 46, 68, 72, 103n79, 108, 172, 293, 318
19:23 259	5:39 72	
19:40 285	5:40 .... 72, 297	
21:12-15 108	6:11, 23 244	14:27 .... 106, 109, 243
21:36 76	6:33 125	14:28 .... 43, 46, 318
22:29 43	6:35 .... 76, 286n158	14:30 .... xi, 263, 376
22:31, 32 .... 103, 133, 287	6:37 .... 43, 46, 115, 137, 155, 179	15:3 .... 108, 292, 389n191
22:32 105	6:27, 29 50	15:4 138
22:41, 42 165	6:38 .... 43, 47, 50	15:4, 5 .... 10n12, 344
22:42 .... 93, 275	6:39 .... 50, 51, 137, 155, 179	15:5 .... 18, 138, 229, 279, 291, 341
22:42-44 47	6:44 .... 26, 46, 108, 115, 155, 179	15:10 108
23:34 175	6:45 .... 46, 293	15:11 107
23:39-43 .... 7, 9	6:51 76	15:13 171
23:43 .... 59, 67	6:54 .... 276n149	15:15 .... 6, 382n186
23:46 67	6:57 .... 43, 318	15:16, 19 .... 147n94
24:37-39 60	6:65 .... 26, 46, 115	15:16-19 254
24:39 49	7:37 .... 76, 105	15:26 .... 42, 43, 44, 46, 47, 103n79, 108, 265n145, 318
24:45 293	7:39 .... 47, 105	
John	8:8 33	
1:1 400	8:9 .... 194n109	
1:1, 2 .... 28, 43n30, 285		
1:1-4 50		
1:3 .... 43, 400		

15:27 108
16:7 .... 148, 293
16:8 148
16:7-10, 13-15 .... 265n145
16:7-14 .... 103n79
16:7-15 .... 43n30, 44
16:8 .... 50, 108
16:11 .... xi, 263, 376
16:13 .... 10n12, 11, 44, 46, 108, 318
16:14 .... 44, 47, 108, 293, 318
16:26 50
16:33 109
17:1-6 43
17:2 .... 29, 46, 115
17:2, 3 .... 276n149
17:3 .... 31, 41, 46, 115
17:4 46
17:5 .... 33, 43n30
17:6 46
17:8 46
17:9 46
17:12 287
17:13 107
17:14 389
17:15-21 271
17:16 389
17:17 .... 146, 292, 389n191
17:22, 23 12
17:22-26 87
18:36 155
18:38 176
19:10, 11 291
21:3-7 227
21:7 170
21:15-17 170
21:15-22 227

Acts
1:1 49
1:3 234
1:16 47
2:1-4 107
2:3 61
2:4 50
2:22 .... 132, 136
2:23 .... 131, 132, 135, 136, 347
2:27 74
2:38 341
2:39 .... 161, 341
3:14 .... 74, 76
3:16 71
3:18 .... 132, 135
4:13 .... 200n113, 223n121
4:18-20 378
4:28 .... 132, 135
5 156
5:1-11 56
5:20 .... ix, 14n18, 15, 72, 86, 156
5:27-29 378
5:29-33 292
5:32 295
5:41 107
6:3 76
7:34 129
7:54-60 292
7:59 59
8:29 50
8:39 50
9:1-9 346
9:3-9 274
10:34 .... 44n33, 258, 362, 366
10:43 13
11:12 50
11:26 378
13:1-4a 346
13:2 50
13:36 115
13:48 .... 115, 254, 276n149
14:15 234
15:13-18 12
15:20, 29 .... 308n161
16:6, 7 50
17:10-12 18
17:24-31 .... 132, 133
17:25 .... 195n110, 280n153
17:27 395
17:28 .... 97, 283, 395, 399
20:7-12 400
20:20 .... 14n18, 15, 72, 86
20:21 146
20:27 .... ix, 14n18, 15, 72, 86
20:28 50
24:8 .... 200n113, 223n121
26:15-18 74
26:18 .... 9, 227, 407
27:31 .... 132, 136
27:34, 35 244
27:44 136

Romans
1:1 355
1:1-20 116
1:17 .... 289, 398
1:18-21 .... 68, 79
1:18-23 .... 98n72
1:24-32 .... 98n72
1:18-31 .... 2n4
1:18-32 .... 26n21, 118
1:20 124
1:21 .... 124, 210
1:26 307
1:28 .... 200n113, 201, 223, 223n121
2:4 146
2:5 210
2:7 .... 115, 276n149
2:11 .... 13, 44n33, 258, 362, 366
2:15 .... 194n109
2:15, 16 220
3:10 138
3:10-13 29
3:10-18 57
3:20 .... 200n113, 223n121
3:21-28 150
3:26 .... 76n58, 129, 171, 247, 287
3:27, 28 16
4:5 150
4:17 400
4:19-21 .... 132, 136
4:21 145
4:25 150
5:1 .... 146, 150
5:5 50
5:8 150
5:8-10 288
5:9 .... 146, 150
5:10 .... 41, 129
5:11 129
5:12-21 .... 29, 44, 195n111
5:16-19 150
5:21 .... 29, 276n149
6:1-14 56
6:2-14 .... 229n123
6:4 .... 116, 291
6:11-19 41
6:12-23 .... 254n141
6:16-23 56
6:17-23 55
6:19-22 26
6:21 .... 98n73
6:22 130
6:23 .... 29, 115, 276n149
7:14-8:17 56
7:15-25 41
7:21-8:2 .... 236n129
7:25 244
8:2 57
8:6, 13 29
8:9 .... 6, 7, 146, 377
8:11 .... 145n93
8:12-17 43
8:14 398
8:14-16 108
8:14-17 .... 68, 146, 151, 250
8:16 .... 60, 68, 108, 166, 295, 398
8:17 .... 29, 52, 166
8:18 134
8:19-22 79
8:23 146
8:26 .... 50, 91, 93
8:27 .... 91, 93
8:28 .... 134, 156
8:28, 29 .... 22, 33, 80, 115, 117, 119, 124n89, 131, 151, 176, 295, 330, 343, 347, 357, 401
8:29 .... 159, 230, 254, 271, 336,
8:30 .... 29, 52, 254
8:31 161
8:30-33 150
8:33 .... 147n94, 254
8:34 .... 91, 355
8:35-39 105
8:38, 39 29
9:1 .... 194n109
9:2 210
9:11 .... 147n94
9:11-24 254
9:15, 16 116
9:17 .... 132, 134
9:18 .... 53, 116, 179
9:19-21 52
9:19-23 116
9:19-24 .... 26n21
9:23 29
10:2 .... 200n113, 223, 223n121
10:13-15 89
10:17 .... 71n56
11:5, 7 .... 147n94
11: 7, 25 179
11:33 .... 13, 34, 60, 111, 135
11:36 348
12:1 .... 83, 255
12:2 .... 6, 83, 210, 213, 219, 220, 222, 224, 255
12:3 .... viii, 54, 71, 92, 148, 149, 287
12:3-9 248
12:4-13 52
12:6 71
12:6-8 10
12:10 175

Scripture Index 415

12:15 233	8:6 .... 43, 51	2:15, 16 150
12:18 .... 52, 340	8:7-12 .... 194n109	3:11 .... 289, 398
12:20 177	10:1-12 108	3:23-25 .... 71n56
12:21 .... 164, 288	10:4 94	3:24 150
13:1 .... 273, 375	10:8 .... 308n161	3:27 .... 57, 318
13:1-7 .... 49, 362, 371, 378	10:25-29 .... 194n109	3:28 .... 44, 318
13:5 .... 194n109	10:31 .... 362, 367, 388	4:6 42
13:7 45	11:3 .... 17, 52, 307, 314,	4:19 .... viii, xi, 5, 9, 226,
13:9 .... 14n19	330n167	287
14:4 107	11:8 306	4:29 254
14:6 31	11:9 .... 52, 306, 330n167	5:19 .... 308n161
14:6-9 .... 362, 367	11:11, 12 52	5:22 .... 39, 44, 57, 107,
14:10-12 .... 207, 386n189	11:23-32 378	108, 156, 243,
14:10-13 204	12 .... 52, 273	248, 279, 338,
14:12 .... 51, 220, 252, 287	12:7 .... 52, 273	388, 387, 397,
14:15 15:19 50	12:10 .... 381n184	400, 401
15:2 52	12:12-27 52	5:23 .... 44, 57, 108, 153,
1:4 .... 12n17	14:20 .... 362, 370	248, 273, 279,
15:30 .... 13, 50	14:25 210	338, 388, 401
16:4 244	12:7-11 137	5:22-26 10
16:17, 18 .... 362, 368	12:7-12 248	6:8 29
16:19 .... 362, 370	12:11 .... 50, 51	6:15 .... 57, 116
16:27 .... 111, 114, 121,	12:28-30 248	
283, 399	12:28-31 .... 355n174	**Ephesians**
17:22 29	13:4-7 .... 171, 172, 173	1:3 174
	13:9, 10, 12 225	1:3-14 246
1 Corinthians	13:12 .... 11n14, 12, 18, 36,	1:4 .... 26, 155, 254, 347
2:11-13 280	88	1:5 .... 26, 155, 347
2:16 .... 225, 280,	13:13 .... 24, 271	1:4-14 87
382n186	14:1 .... 355n174	1:5 .... 251, 254
1:4 .... 119, 244	14:18 245	1:7 155
1:5 119	15:3 145	1:9 251
1:14 245	15:3-8 72	1:10, 11 26
1:21 292	15:22 .... 195n111	1:11 .... 53, 132, 134, 155,
1:24 114	15:25 104	172, 251, 254
1:30 .... 55, 114, 122, 202,	15:26 .... 104, 145	1:17 .... 200n113,
220, 399	15:27, 28 154	223n121, 224,
2:11, 12 101	15:32 145	278
2:11-13 6	15:54, 55 145	1:18 .... 9, 69, 74, 127,
2:11-16 .... viii, 1, 314n164		155, 162, 226,
2:14 .... 7, 8, 9, 69, 107,	**2 Corinthians**	227, 404, 407
141, 194	1:3-11 130	1:19 .... 69, 74
2:16 .... xi, 1, 5, 101, 396	1:5 166	1:22 .... 52, 154
3:5-9 401	2:10-11 50	1:23 154
3:6 .... 160, 291	2:14 303	2:1 147
3:10-15 108	3:17 57	2:1-3 332
3:16 .... 68, 130, 146, 377	3:18 58	2:1-10 56
4:2 .... 362, 367	4:3-6 74	2:2 .... xi, 376
4:5 .... 51, 56, 102n77,	4:3 194	2:3 195
189, 317,	4:4 .... xi, 194, 376	2:4 68
284n157,	4:6 .... 9, 227	2:5 .... 68, 147
386n189	4:10 166	2:8 .... viii, 54, 71n56, 93,
4:7 .... 174, 287, 329,	4:16, 17 134	146, 149
389	5:17 .... 57, 89, 103n79,	2:9 .... viii, 149
4:16 297	116, 146,	2:10 389
5:1-6:6 204	229n123	2:13-16 243
5:1-5 204	5:18-20 271	2:18 31
5:5 333	5:21 74	2:19-22 6
5:7, 8 229	6:14 302	3:10 .... 132, 134
5:9-13 204	6:14-16 348	3:14-17 104
5:12 204	6:10 107	3:16 .... 153, 160
5:20 294	7:39 302	4:1, 2 279
6:11 .... 389n191	8:19-21 391	4:1-16 52
6:13, 18 .... 308n161	9:6-15 244	4:7 .... 54, 71
6:14 382	10:4 164	4:8-13 248
6:19 .... 6, 68, 130, 146,	10:5 205	4:11-13 10
377	10:12, 18 248	4:12, 13 273
6:20 129	10:17, 18 174	4:13 .... v, ix, 19,
7:2 .... 308n161	11:3 .... 190, 192, 237	200n113, 205,
7:3-5 .... 327, 328	12:9, 10 154	278n152
7:14 .... 335, 341	12:21 .... 308n161	4:15 .... 12, 205, 388
7:23 355	13:5 297	4:16 12
7:32 .... 345, 353, 357	12:20 82	4:20-24 .... 229n123
7:33 353	13:5 108	4:22-24 .... 10n12, 57, 96,
7:34 .... 345, 353	13:14 49	151, 181, 200,
7:35 353		222, 237, 281
7:39 .... 136, 348	**Galatians**	4:23 .... viii, 17, 30, 361
8:4 .... 49, 51	1:1 .... 145n93	
	2:6 .... 44, 258, 362, 366	

4:24 ...... v, viii, ix, 17, 57, 63, 66, 83, 190, 222n118, 313n163, 361	1:19 228	6:8-11 373
4:25 ...... 362, 368	1:24 ...... 166, 168, 378	6:11 57
4:26, 27 ...... 288, 340	1:25-27 ...... 220, 377	6:12 ...... 276n149
4:28 369	1:26, 27 ...... viii, 68, 109	6:16 ...... 32n26, 61
4:30 30	2:6, 7 31	**2 Timothy**
4:32 87	2:9 ...... 21, 228, 286	1:3 ...... 194n109
5:1, 2 ...... 297, 343	2:10-14 378	1:8 ...... 127, 266
5:3 ...... 308n161	2:13 147	1:9 ...... 32n26, 43, 46n37, 127, 266
5:3-6 79	2:19 378	2:9, 10 371
5:15-24 49	3:5 ...... 308n161, 373	2:10 ...... 147n94
5:21 318	3:8-10 57	2:22 57
5:22 ...... 49n38	3:9 ...... 96, 199, 278	2:25, 26 129
5:22-24 ...... 315, 318	3:9, 10 ...... 229n123	3:1-4 264
5:22-32 307	3:10 ...... viii, 5, 7, 10n12, 57, 64, 66, 96, 123, 151, 190, 199, 200n113, 222, 222n118, 223n121, 224, 278, 313n163, 361	3:5 ...... 285, 297
5:23 ...... 52, 314, 315, 316, 330n167		3:7 ...... 200n113, 223, 223n121, 285
5:25 ...... 108, 301, 315, 350		3:16 ...... 12n17
5:25-27 ...... 315, 316		**Titus**
5:26 ...... viii, 6, 48, 83, 230, 292, 361, 398, 389n191		1:1 ...... 43, 49, 51, 127, 147n94, 254, 276, 355
	3:12 ...... 147n94, 254, 279	1:2 ...... 43, 46n37, 51, 53, 127, 276
5:28, 29 317	3:13 279	1:5-9 ...... 330n167
5:28-31 318	3:15 109	1:15 ...... 194n109
5:33 ...... 301, 315, 319, 350	3:18 ...... 49, 49n38, 318	2:3-5 ...... 330n167
	3:19 318	2:7 390
6:1 ...... 49n38	3:20, 21 49	2:9, 10 ...... 49, 362
6:1-4 49	3:21 ...... 333n168	2:10 ...... 49n38
6:4 ...... 333n168, 334	3:22 ...... 362, 368	2:14 390
6:5-7 ...... 49, 362, 368	3:22-24 49	3:1, 2 49
6:5-9 49	3:22-25 49	3:5 ...... viii, 6, 47, 130, 230, 389n191
6:9 ...... 44, 49, 258	3:23 ...... 362, 367	3:5-7 150
6:12 ...... xi, 137, 376	3:23, 24 ...... 49n38	3:7 ...... 276n149
6:13 ...... xi, 376	**1 Thessalonians**	3:8 390
6:16 103	1:6 156	**Philemon**
6:17 292	2:13 244	**Hebrews**
6:18 93	3:9 244	1:3 ...... 31, 52, 132, 133, 240
Philippians	4:1-12 108	1:5-14 50
1:1 ...... 49, 355	4:2-7 ...... 103n79	1:9 382
1:3-5 244	4:3 ...... 308n161	1:10 28
1:6 ...... 105, 137, 140, 211, 220, 255, 292, 320, 330, 336, 395	5:23 146	1:10-12 ...... 32n26
	2 Thessalonians	2:4 60
	1:3 244	2:10 165
1:9 ...... 200n113, 223n121	1:7-10 288	2:18 75
	1:9 ...... 335n170	3-4 246
1:29 165	2:8 63	4:1-11 189
2:3 ...... 174, 356	2:12 175	4:12 ...... viii, 361
2:5-8 ...... 43, 129	2:13 ...... 52, 147n94, 244, 254	4:13 ...... 68, 102n77
2:5-16 48	3:10 ...... 330n167	4:15 75
2:5-17 46	**1 Timothy**	5:8 ...... 75, 165
2:7 145	1:5, 19 ...... 194n109	6:9 267
2:10, 11 389	1:8 ...... 55, 360	6:18 53
2:13 ...... 18, 53, 90, 137, 140, 211, 255, 263, 292, 330	1:17 61	7:9, 10 ...... 195n111
	1:20 333	7:25 355
	2:1, 2 26	8:12 89
2:12-15 391	2:1-3 386	9:9, 14 ...... 194n109
3:8-11 165	2:3 26	9:15 ...... 276n149
4:6, 7 ...... 109, 244	2:4 ...... 26, 200n113, 223n121, 242	9:20 54
4:11 352	2:14 ...... 190, 192	10:17 89
4:11-13 ...... 46, 237	3:1-7 ...... 330n167	10:22 ...... 194n109
4:13 ...... 153, 160	3:9 ...... 194n109	10:26 ...... 200n113, 223, 223n121
Colossians	4:1 50	10:36-39 130
1:3, 4 244	4:2 ...... 194n109	10:38 ...... 289, 398
1:9 ...... 223n121	4:4 31	11:1 ...... viii, 71
1:9, 10 ...... 200n113	5:3 45	11:3 ...... 8, 9n11, 28, 34, 125, 141, 240, 400
1:10 ...... 153, 223n121, 224, 278n152	5:5 ...... 353, 355	
	5:8 ...... 330n167	
1:11 ...... 153, 160	5:14 ...... 330n167	
1:12 ...... 7, 244	5:17 45	11:5 154
1:15 ...... 61, 171, 279, 286	6:1, 2 ...... 362, 368	11:17-19 ...... 95, 143
1:16 ...... 30, 33, 39, 43	6:1-3 49	11:19 277
1:17 ...... 31, 33, 52, 240	6:1-5 49	11:25 264
1:18 378	6:5 264	
	6:6-10 264	
	6:6-11 46	

Scripture Index

11:40 .... 82, 207	2:12 .... 118, 165, 389, 391	2:29 .... 115, 254
12 .... 173, 178	2:13 .... 49n38	3:2 151
12:1 .... 2, 162, 178, 198, 267, 268, 356, 372	2:13-15 362	3:9 254
	2:13-17 .... 49, 378	3:12 .... 150, 153, 164, 388
12:1-3 31	2:15, 16 .... 49n38	3:17 .... 14, 259, 392
12:2 .... 2, 71n56, 156, 162, 198, 243, 267, 268, 356, 372	2:16 57	3:18 .... 14, 392
	2:20, 21 166	3:19 14
	2:22 74	4:1 .... 295, 381, 403
	3:1-6 49	4:7 .... 254, 290
12:4-11 .... 171, 172, 173, 177, 178, 333n168, 336	3:1-7 318	4:7-21 290
	3:7 .... 101, 315, 316, 317, 322, 353	4:8 .... 26, 28, 56, 290
		4:9 171
12:4-13 .... 14, 130, 161	3:14, 16, 17 166	4:10 .... 171, 246, 288, 335
12:5-11 14	3:15 .... 390, 398	
12:6 .... 178, 336	3:16 390	4:11-13 241
12:6-8 379	3:16, 21 .... 194n109	4:12 290
12:7-14 363	3:18 155	4:14 272
12:9 62	4:5 51	4:15 56
12:10 .... v, ix, 10, 19, 58, 83, 151, 279, 282, 343	4:11 .... 348, 388	4:16 .... 170, 290
	4:12-14, 16 166	4:17 .... 26, 377
	4:13 .... 107, 134	4:19 .... 123, 290
12:11 .... v, 10, 155, 279, 343	4:18 48	5:1, 4, 18 254
	5:5, 6 140	5:11, 13 .... 276n149
12:14 .... 83, 398	5:7 161	5:12-21 196
12:23 .... 82, 207	5:8 374	5:14 .... 92, 285, 352
12:28 31	**2 Peter**	5:19 376
13:5 .... 33, 46, 104, 229	1:1 .... 149, 286	5:20 293
13:6 .... 46, 104, 354	1:2 .... 223n121	**2 John**
13:8 .... 33, 86, 229, 399	1:2, 3, 8 .... 200n113	1 254
13:16 354	1:2-4 .... 224, 278n152	6 108
James	1:2-10 108	13 254
1:5 .... 121, 365, 367, 368, 369, 370, 371, 372, 400	1:3 .... 19, 223n121	**3 John**
	1:4 .... v, vii, ix, xi, 5, 19, 58, 83, 137, 140, 151, 177, 179, 202, 228, 248, 271, 361	4 333
		Jude
1:6 400		7 .... 308, 308n161
1:5-8 92		20 93
1:13 78	1:4-8 339	**Revelation**
1:14 252	1:6, 7 58	1:8 50
1:17 .... 31, 54, 86, 282	1:8 .... 223n121, 224, 278n152	1:8-20 21
1:18 .... 103n79, 221		1:9-20 240
1:20 288	1:9 292	1:17 .... 50, 74
1:26 .... 362, 368	1:10 .... 108, 147n94, 339	1:18 50
2:1-7 44	1:20 .... 12, 47	2:2-4 390
2:1-13 .... 13, 392	1:21 .... 12, 47, 50	2:4 .... 160, 265n144
2:5 .... 71n56, 147n94	2:4 115	2:11 .... 56, 280n154
2:10 360	2:4-6, 9 240	2:17 51
2:14-20 108	2:6 .... 80, 278	3:14-16, 19 .... 239, 245
2:14-26 389	2:9 .... 335n170	3:19 .... 333n168
2:15, 16 259	2:9, 10 237	3:20 283
3:2-12 .... 362, 368	2:13, 14 375	4:8 .... 73, 76, 281, 281n155
3:8-12 82	2:13-15 371	
3:17 284	2:19 56	4:9-11 .... 32n26
4:1-4 .... 236n129	2:20 .... 200n113, 223, 223n121	4:11 34
4:3 .... 92, 93		5:9 44
4:4 389	3:5 8	6:9-11 .... 82, 281
4:8 352	3:7 45	6:10 76
4:9 244	3:9 242	6:14 31
4:10 .... 140, 244	3:10 31	6:17 76
4:15 37	3:15 .... 38, 278	7:9 44
5:15, 16 92	3:16 117	13:8 .... 31n25, 127
5:17 234	**1 John**	19:1 34
1 Peter	1:2 33	19:19 115
1:1, 2 .... 25n20, 254	1:8-10 .... 147, 404	19:20 .... 79, 115
1:3 .... 89, 103n79	2:1 293	20:6 .... 280n154
1:5 .... 71n56	2:2 272	20:10 63
1:6, 8 107	2:4-6 108	20:11, 12 29
1:14-16 73	2:12 .... 13, 87	20:13, 14 79
1:16 .... 82, 138, 205, 280, 281n155	2:15, 16 259	20:14 .... 280n154
	2:19 268	20:14, 15 .... 56, 115
1:23 .... 89, 103n79, 115, 146, 221	2:21 82	21:8 .... 280n154
	2:25 .... 276n149	22:18 26
2:1-3 31	2:27 108	

www.ingramcontent.com/pod-product-compliance
Lightning Source LLC
Chambersburg PA
CBHW030132170426
43199CB00008B/42